Not Without a Fight

Not Without a Fight

THE AUTOBIOGRAPHY

HELEN ZILLE

PENGUIN BOOKS

Published by Penguin Books
an imprint of Penguin Random House South Africa (Pty) Ltd
Reg. No. 1953/000441/07
The Estuaries No. 4, Oxbow Crescent, Century Avenue, Century City, 7441
PO Box 1144, Cape Town, 8000, South Africa
www.penguinrandomhouse.co.za

Penguin Random House South Africa

First published 2016

1 3 5 7 9 10 8 6 4 2

Publication © Penguin Random House 2016
Text © Helen Zille 2016

Cover photographs © Eric Miller (front), Tyrone Arthur (back right)

All rights reserved. No part of this publication may be reproduced, stored in a retrieval system or transmitted, in any form or by any means, electronic, mechanical, photocopying, recording or otherwise, without the prior written permission of the copyright owners.

Publisher: Marlene Fryer
Managing editor: Robert Plummer
Editor: Alison Lowry
Proofreader: Ronel Richter-Herbert
Cover and text designer: Ryan Africa
Typesetter: Monique van den Berg
Indexer: Sanet le Roux

Set in 10.5 pt on 14 pt Minion

Printed by **novus print**, a Novus Holdings company

MIX
Paper from responsible sources
FSC® C022948

This book is printed on FSC® certified and controlled sources. FSC (Forest Stewardship Council®) is an independent, international, non-governmental organization. Its aim is to support environmentally sustainable, socially and economically responsible global forest management.

ISBN 978 1 77609 042 6 (print)
ISBN 978 1 77609 043 3 (ePub)

Politics is about power: how it is won, used, manipulated, subverted, held to account, lost and regained.

Unsurprisingly, it attracts extremes – from idealists who want to make the world a better place, to the unprincipled who are in it for their own selfish ends.

A country's prospects depend on how it is governed. In a democracy, 'the people' make that choice.

This book is dedicated to the new generation of politicians who have the guts, the integrity, and staying power for South Africa to succeed.

You need to know: it won't happen without a fight.

Contents

Preface	ix
1. Roots	1
2. It Takes a Village	21
3. Hunger Strikes	35
4. Matters of the Heart	59
5. 'The Maree Affair'	73
6. Birth Pains and Death Throes	85
7. A Political Education	105
8. Yes, Minister	141
9. The Battle for the Soul of the DA	153
10. 'Hamba Kwa Langa'	189
11. An Unlikely Coalition	221
12. 'We Can, We Must, and We Will'	249
13. Of Crosstitutes and Criminals	263
14. Zillegate	283
15. Moral Equivalence	311
16. Damned If You Do	333
17. Varying Shades of Bad	341
18. The Plane Crash	377
19. A Deluded Agenda	403
20. Setting the Record Straight	433
21. The End of Two Eras	465
22. The Problem with Race Politics	477
23. The Struggle for Economic Freedom	497
Acknowledgements	511
Abbreviations	515
Index	517

Preface

THIS BOOK IS the story of two main strands of my life: my personal and political journey. There is a third strand required to complete the picture, which I hope will provide the content of another book. The third strand is the story of how I, together with many others, addressed the challenge of building capable state institutions at local and provincial level, to address our country's major challenges.

When South Africans elect a new national government, hopefully sooner rather than later, committed to building a capable and professional state, based on the rule of law and a culture of accountability, I hope the new cabinet's efforts will be informed and supported by our experience of trying to do the same, from the bottom up.

Cape Town and the Western Cape Province were initially the only places where we could win enough voter support to begin our quest to strengthen South Africa's democracy. And that support is growing, countrywide, making it possible to do so in more and more places.

The process has been fraught with personal and political challenges, which is what this book is about. In the process of writing it, I could sometimes hardly believe the story myself – but it is all true as I recall it. And I have loved every minute of it.

I hope it gives readers an insight into the complex, often Machiavellian (and sometimes noble) world of politics that lies behind the media statements and newspaper headlines.

HELEN ZILLE
AUGUST 2016

1

Roots

It is what it is;
You are where you are;
Your baggage will find you later
– Jewish Buddha

WHEN YOU START your memoirs, you think you are going to write your story, but you only begin to discover your story.

In the process of writing mine, I found relatives I did not know existed and read memoirs I did not know had been written. I have excavated history's hidden chains and come to terms with life's unpredictability.

My voyage of discovery started on a chilly autumn morning, 5 May 2015, in the Jewish cemetery in Pinelands, where I had been invited, as premier of the Western Cape Province, to attend the annual Yom Hashoah Holocaust memorial service.

There I heard Ella Blumenthal, a ninety-three-year-old woman, make a short speech. I did not know her. I had never even met her. But as she spoke, she peeled away layers of my own life, releasing snippets of memory I am only now, in my mid-sixties, beginning to piece together.

In a matter-of-fact tone, Ella recalled losing twenty-three members of her immediate family: her parents, her brothers, her sisters, their spouses, and eight nieces and nephews – 'the only other survivor being my eldest niece, Roma'.

Her struggles and heartbreak remained untold. So private are these that when she moved to Johannesburg after marrying a South African she had known for just thirteen days, she had the tattooed concentration-camp number on her arm surgically removed. She told her children that the scar was the result of 'an accident'.

Actually, I do know Ella Blumenthal. Almost everything about her is intimately familiar to me, from her strong accent, to her lack of sentimentality, to her determination to bury the past and keep moving forward. She propelled me back to my grandmother's tiny flat in Hillbrow, Johannesburg, in the late 1950s.

Every second weekend my father, Wolfgang Zille, took me and my younger sister, Carla, to see her. As soon as she opened the door, we could smell the over-ripe Camembert she kept on a tray under a damp cloth next to the porcelain milk jug and butter dish, because she had no fridge. The highlight of each visit was sharing the Kit Kat she always produced, as a 'surprise'.

I now regret that I did not ask her more about her life. Back then I was far more interested in when the Kit Kat would appear (we were not allowed to ask for it). In any event, it was difficult to communicate with Granny, because she had lost most of her hearing. She never learnt to 'listen with her eyes', as my sister Carla did from her earliest years, after sustaining hearing loss as an infant.

Granny had become deaf in old age, and her other senses could not adapt. She spoke halting, broken English. I understood German, but Carla, because of her hearing loss, did not, and so we developed the multilayered communication methods that are part of life in families that incorporate deafness.

Carla and I were fascinated by the large amplifier on Granny's hearing-aid, which she carried in the small breast-pockets sewn onto her blouses and dresses. If we moved it in a certain way, it squealed like our dachshund puppy.

Apart from that, the only items of interest in her flat were two photos on the wall. One showed her parents, Ernestine and Hermann Marcus, with their thirteen children (of which my grandmother was the ninth, and the fifth daughter).

I would climb on the bed (which was covered with a fraying kilim), take the photo off the wall, and ask Granny to go through their names. I was fascinated that she could remember them all, in order, starting with Fedor and ending with Fritz. The only other name I remember from the rest of the incantation was Bruno, because I felt sorry for him having a dog's name. Fritz lived in London. I recall her saying that two sisters had gone to South America. Most of them, Granny said, had died.

They died. From a child's perspective, that is what old people do. I did not give it a second thought.

Granny's chance to escape Nazi Germany came when her sons, Heinrich and Wolfgang, emigrated to South Africa. Once they had settled and found employment – as manual labourers at the Modderfontein dynamite factory – she could follow. 'A steady job was a precondition to get a relative into the country,' Dad wrote in his memoirs.

Granny came over on the *Windhuk*, one of the last boats to leave Germany, in July 1939, six weeks before war broke out. She managed to bring with her an old *armoire*, a small suitcase, some photos, an eternity ring from her husband and a brooch with five small diamonds, of which Carla and I inherited two each.

It was only after she was gone that I learnt more about her life.

Helene Marcus was widowed in 1922, when her husband, Walter Zille, died of kidney failure in the year their younger son, Wolfgang – my father – turned ten. What I know about them I learnt mostly from five pages of reminiscences written by the grandfather I never met, and whom my own father hardly remembered. Dad was two when Walter Zille was called up to active duty in the First World War.

He died after the war ended, his failing kidneys withered by the privations of army life.

His five-page 'memoir', the writing of which, Walter admits, was helped by a 'bottle of a good Johannisberger', reveals him as a romantic agnostic who took his family responsibilities seriously, showed a keen interest in politics, and loved a glass of wine.

My favourite paragraph in the brief account of his life story deals with his first 'encounter' with the grandmother after whom I was named. 'On the 31st July 1905, shortly after my return from Berlin after writing the State [law] exams, during a boat trip in glorious moonlight on the Mulde, we realised our affection for one another, but did not yet engage ourselves formally.'

The Marcus family disapproved of their relationship because Walter was not Jewish, but he persisted. 'Any differences between religious doctrines could never influence me,' he wrote. 'Such matters are not of importance to me (I myself do not practise my religion), and any differences of this kind are not important, as, in my opinion, they do not exist.'

Their wedding on 7 March 1907 was attended only by Helene's younger sister, Klaere, and her husband, Paul Homberger. The rest of their families stayed away. 'Needless to say, we dispensed with an ecclesiastical ceremony,' Walter wrote.

As soon as Helene was pregnant, Walter tried to buy a life insurance policy. The medical examination discovered his kidney condition, and he was turned down. His widow would be left virtually penniless.

What I know about my grandmother's life I have learnt from her husband's notes, and the memoirs of her elder son, my father's elder brother, Uncle Heinrich. As a single parent in Rosslau, a hamlet of 11 000 souls in what would later become East Germany, Helene supported her boys by designing children's knitwear and other garments. She turned her modest home into a small factory, employing local women to make up her designs, which she also marketed in neighbouring towns. Heinrich recalled: 'there were several sewing machines in place and my memory has the impression of a house full of female beings'.

Her business flourished, until the hyperinflation of the mid-1920s destroyed almost all small enterprises, including her own. The German currency plummeted to 4 200 000 000 000 marks to the US dollar. Her savings were worthless.

Food became very scarce. 'We lived on beets and turnips,' Heinrich wrote. 'Turnips as "coffee", as vegetables, as marmalade, as syrup – turnips everywhere. But even all this did not oppress us very much. Mother always had everything organised and under control.'

But, after the Nazis came to power in 1933, her fate, and that of her family, was no longer in her control.

* * *

As a child, I did not give much thought to the family members in the photograph above Granny's bed. There was no reason to. Today, there is.

As I listened to Ella Blumenthal in the chilly cemetery that day in Pinelands, I was seized with the need to find out what had happened to Granny's siblings who were unaccounted for. Perhaps the instinct to prevent our forebears passing into oblivion is some kind of hedge against the same fate.

It was too late to ask anyone who knew, so I followed up all the leads I had.

With the help of a Cape Town–born genealogist, Paul Cheifitz, I managed to establish the confirmed Holocaust murders in the Marcus family.

His research concluded that Paul Marcus, one of Granny's brothers and a restaurateur, was the first of the Marcus siblings to be murdered. He was attacked and shot during the murderous forty-eight-hour rampage that became known as Kristallnacht, on 9 and 10 November 1938, when thousands of Jewish homes and businesses were destroyed, leaving pavements in every hamlet, town and city across the country covered in shattered glass that looked like crushed crystal.

Antonia Marcus, one of Granny's sisters, died in the Theresienstadt concentration camp in Czechoslovakia after being transported there at the end of August 1942. Her son-in-law Herman Braunsberg died in the same camp on 19 September 1942, and her grandson Heinz Peter was murdered in Auschwitz early in September 1942. There are no records of her daughter Erna.

The deaths are recorded in the Yad Vashem archive, and I was fascinated to learn that the entry had been made by a second cousin of whose existence I was unaware. Her name is Margaret Grant, and she lives in Harrow, England. She entered the records of the murder of her grandmother (my Granny's sister), her father and her brother in the archive without recording the date of entry.

According to the genealogist, there are records that Klaere Marcus (Granny's younger sister, who had broken ranks with the rest of the family to attend her wedding) and her son Herbert Homberger suffered the same fate, although I could not pinpoint the exact location. I learnt from a letter written by my father to another family member that Klaere's other son, Erich, also died in a concentration camp, but not which one or when. Klaere's daughter Lotte was recorded as having escaped to Buenos Aires, Argentina. It seems that Granny's brother Max also managed to get to Argentina, with his wife, Else Schlesinger. They were the lucky ones.

So were the three Marcus sisters who had lost their husbands before Hitler came to power: Else, widowed since 1907, managed to get a passage to Buenos Aires; her younger sister Mimi to Asunción, Paraguay; and Helene, my grandmother, to Cape Town, South Africa, before she moved to Johannesburg and settled there.

Then there are those who remained in Germany. Fedor, the eldest Marcus brother, died long before the Holocaust.

The rest, who cannot be accounted for, were in all likelihood also murdered.

They are Karl, Bruno, Gertrude and Walter Marcus, their spouses and children. Like millions of others, they probably battled to the very end to find a way out of Germany, seeking refuge in any country that would accept them. Ironically, as the war dragged on and more Jews were murdered, it became harder to escape, either because the refugee quotas in receiving countries had been reached, or because it was so difficult to find people who were prepared to sign surety for destitute new arrivals.

It was also interesting to track down other living relatives I did not know I had, such as Renato Sternberg, in Santiago, Chile (the grandson of Else Marcus in Argentina), and his sister Susanna in the United States; Max Fraenkel (the grandson of Mimi Marcus of Asunción), and Doron Avivi in Israel (the great-grandson of Fedor Marcus, the eldest of the thirteen Marcus siblings). I have sought to make contact with them all, with differing levels of success.

I still wonder about many things, but most of all how my Granny could wake up every morning and look at that photograph hanging next to her bed, not knowing what had happened to so many of her siblings, their spouses, and her nephews and nieces. She must often have thought of their last days and their likely despair at the closed doors they found at every turn.

Yet, half a world away, Granny got up early each day, cleaned her room and watered the African violets she kept in pots on the balcony to anchor herself in the soil of a new continent. She loved their colours, the cobalt and navy blues, the deep purples and pale amethysts. When we visited her, she allowed us to water her violets. She showed us how to avoid dripping water on the fleshy, fluffy leaves, and convinced us that just a few drops would suffice. Over-watering, she warned, was as bad as under-watering. My memory of her meticulous care for her plants has given me a sense of how deeply she must have felt the human losses in her life.

She was pleased that we loved her violets. What Granny didn't know was that the real attraction of watering them was the opportunity it offered of being able to tip some water from the long-spouted yellow indoor watering can over the balcony railing and onto the street below, to 'water bomb' pedestrians. Every now and again a shout emanating from below (which Granny couldn't hear) would tell us we had hit a target.

As if her past was not enough, Granny lost every penny she had so diligently saved since her arrival in South Africa to a Ponzi scam in the late 1950s, long before the fraudulent nature of these schemes had been established. Dad only told me about the loss of her money after Granny died in 1969, which was the year after I wrote matric. There was no space for self-indulgence, let alone self-pity, in her life.

If Dad had told us about her material loss, why hadn't he said anything about the human loss? Since I started trying to uncover the Marcus family story, I have often discussed this question with Carla and our younger brother Paul. Dad certainly knew his uncles and aunts before he left Germany. Compassionate humanist that he was, he must surely have tried to find out what happened to them. Yet he did not mention a word about this in his memoirs, and nor did his elder brother Heinrich.

However, rereading Dad's letters, I can see he was trying to piece together aspects of his mother's family's lives by contacting the few surviving relatives that he knew of, such as Michael and Gabrielle in New York. But he never once discussed these issues with us, his immediate family. Today, information technology and quick access to archival records have made the search for personal histories so much easier.

I often wonder why Jews who escaped the Holocaust seemed so determined to bury their experience. Perhaps it was just too painful to confront the inevitable questions about the fate of those who remained behind in Germany. In the absence of alternatives, denial offers the only form of closure. Perhaps they wanted to avoid another barrier of prejudice as they tried to make a new start in a strange land. Perhaps they did not want to pass their baggage on to the next generation. Forging a new identity in a foreign country is hard enough without inheriting the burden of 'victimhood'. In Granny's case, was her silence reinforced by her family's rejection of her decision to marry outside their faith?

Perhaps it was what psychologists call 'survivor's guilt'. In the face of genocide, each person instinctively seizes whatever opportunity they can to save their own life. Imagine the trauma of knowing this chance never came to your kith and kin? Perhaps it was a combination of all of these things.

Helene Marcus's determination to escape her past manifested itself in many ways, big and small. She wanted us to call her Granny, not the German equivalent, Oma. Perhaps this was a way of covering the tattoos of memory that could not be surgically removed.

When Dad and Heinrich came to South Africa before the war, they dug trenches and maintained infrastructure at the Modderfontein dynamite factory by day, and at night they studied English. Dad carried a small dictionary around with him in his overalls to look up any word he did not understand. On Sundays they went to lunch with an Irish couple, the Kennys, ostensibly to practise conversational English, although the fact that there were four Kenny daughters might also have played a role. Dad would solicit Mr Kenny's help in mastering the intricacies of the English language, especially to explain the meaning of words he could not locate in the dictionary, because of the unphonetic spelling of some of them.

One day, Dad raised a problem. There was a word that was regularly used in the workplace that he could not find in the dictionary, despite looking for it under both 'f' and 'ph'. It was used in many contexts, Dad explained, such as 'Pass the fokken hammer' and 'Where's the fokken spade?'

Mrs Kenny, with impeccable manners, kept a straight face and got up to make the tea, her daughters in tow, so that Mr Kenny could explain to my father the intricacies of workplace adjectives in South African English. (Although the 'f' word has a Germanic ring to it, there is no equivalent used in the same way in German, despite a rich vocabulary of curses, which tend to be anal rather than genital.)

When war broke out, Dad and Heinrich lost their jobs because Germans were not allowed to work at strategic installations such as dynamite factories. Dad found a new position, for £5 a week, delivering bread and milk for Quinn's bakery in Troyeville, but he and Heinrich soon enlisted in the South African army. Both men served with the Allied forces in North Africa and Italy for the full duration of the war – to 'liberate our country', as my father later told us.

Dad was always politically engaged, and while he was in the army he joined the Springbok Legion, which he described in his memoirs as 'a rather leftish organization without colourbar'.

Heinrich and Wolfgang sent their stipends back to Johannesburg to support Granny, but she did not spend their money. Already adept at caring for herself, she baked and sold bread, and saved her sons' remittances in anticipation of their need for some capital to restart their lives when they returned.

My father inherited her self-reliance and silent stoicism.

But silence does not always draw a line under the past. It can deny you the tools you need to understand the present. And, anyway, your genes cannot keep your forebears' secrets. They are your biological memory, far more persistent and reliable than any other kind. They mingle indiscernibly with experience to shape who you become.

Every now and then, my genes have a habit of bursting in on my life, to let me know where I come from. When I suffered severe post-partum depression after the birth of both my sons, it helped to learn that Granny had suffered the same affliction, to the point where her boys were removed from her care for a while. Her husband, Walter, obliquely alludes to it in his 'memoirs' when he writes: 'Lene began a Carlsbader cure treatment, hopefully with satisfactory results.'

When Dad shared the story with me, my own condition became less opaque. I knew there would be an end to the tunnel, even if I could not discern a pinprick of light at the time. If Granny had come out of it, I thought, so could I.

Learning about your forebears' struggles can turn you into a fighter, rather than a victim.

As I write, I am also typing up my mother's memoirs, written in her round symmetrical script and her achingly familiar combination of English words with

German syntax. I recognise the many factors that underpinned the bond she shared with my father – not least because both their mothers faced their families' rejection over their choice of marriage partner – Dad's mom because she married a Protestant; Mom's mom because she married a Jew.

Both my grandmothers and my mom were fighters with a stubborn streak. And fighters often fight with each other.

I had a complex and rich relationship with my passionate, sensitive, beautiful mother, with highs and lows of equal intensity, just as she had with her own mother, and her mother-in-law.

T.S. Eliot, writing of the young French philosopher Simone Weil, said: 'The statement that [her] soul was incomparably superior to her genius will be misconstrued if it gives the impression of deprecating her intellect.' When Weil 'committed some astonishing aberrations and exaggerations', they sprang, said Eliot, 'not from any flaw in her intellect but from an excess of temperament'.[*] He could have been describing my mother, Mila. She was passionate and courageous and at the same time impulsive and extraordinarily vulnerable. She had intuitive intelligence that no education can bestow, and an instinct for justice that would often propel her into unwinnable arguments.

She met Dad during one of them, late in 1949, when they were invited separately to supper by newly acquired friends, who had arrived in South Africa a generation earlier. If there was one thing my mother despised, it was Jews who silently acquiesced in the oppression of others. She did not remain silent, even as a lonely newcomer in a strange land.

My unemotional dad recalls their first meeting in his memoirs as follows: 'Everybody present discussed politics, but only Mila and I were strongly anti-nationalist. On this strong foundation, we got married on the 9th June 1950.'

About nine months separated their first meeting and their marriage. Although Dad felt drawn to Mila from the start, he first had to write his exams at the end of 1949. He was studying economics by correspondence through the University of South Africa, and resolved to avoid any distractions, besides his day job, during his studies. He only made contact with her again when he had written his last paper.

My parents were polar opposites, held together by a magnet of shared experience and values, till death separated them.

I imagine the 'discussion' with friends at their first meeting was more like the arguments that, in later years, often punctuated my childhood when my parents invited guests for dinner. The lounge of our hotchpotch home (built and extended without the luxury of architectural guidance) was only accessible through my bedroom, and I would listen as the social banter next door turned

---

[*] T.S. Eliot's preface to Simone Weil's book *Roots* (Routledge and Kegan Paul, 1952)

into vehement arguments if someone casually dropped a racist remark, or justified the status quo.

My father could let an offensive comment wash off him. He knew how to pick his fights. My mother never learnt that skill, especially not when confronted by what she contemptuously called the 'I'm-all-right-Jack attitude' of some Jewish acquaintances who were silently relieved that black South Africans offered them a broad and deep buffer against anti-Semitism.

More friendships were broken than built at these dinner parties. I remember many 'mornings after' with Mom admonishing herself for being 'so emotional'. She regarded it as a weakness, but as I grew older I saw her 'emotional' response to any form of unfairness as one of her strongest qualities. She craved acceptance and inclusion, but was not prepared to make the ethical compromises required to 'belong'.

I have often wondered how much of my mother's passion was genetically determined, and how much was the result of life's tattoos, etched into her psyche.

Mom was the youngest of five children of a Jewish lawyer and his Protestant wife Emilie (abbreviated to Mila) in Essen, Germany. My mother was named Mila, after her mother. Throughout our lives we referred to our maternal grandparents as Apa and Ama, because one of their grandchildren had not managed to pronounce Opa and Oma properly, and the nicknames stuck.

Apa's real name was Carl Maximilian Cosmann. During my childhood he fulfilled the function of family patriarch, and wrote the most comprehensive of all my relatives' memoirs. It was his second attempt to record his life story, after his first account was destroyed, together with all his furniture and moveable assets, when he sent them to Amsterdam in 1939, the year he left Germany.

His second attempt makes fascinating, often moving, reading. It was translated into English by a nephew, Theodore Gutman, in 1991, so that my grandfather's many English-speaking descendants (now living across the globe from New Zealand to Canada) would be able to read it. Theodore's translation captures the authentic German idiom, so I have used his words, rather than my own translation into more idiomatic English.

Apa's story tells of fortunes made, but mostly lost; of a legal education at several renowned universities, culminating in a doctorate; of a rich cultural life spent reading great works of literature and visiting the theatre, art galleries and museums; playing his cello in chamber-music trios and quartets, even (or especially) in the darkest days of the Third Reich. It is a story of opportunities seized and missed, of a family's perilous passage through two world wars, the inflation of the early 1920s, the Great Depression, the rise of Nazism, the destruction of his legal practice, the confiscation of his property, his destitution and exile, and the sheer exhilaration of having survived. It is a story of epoch-changing times, and of personal tragedy, including three family suicides (his own mother, his nephew and his brother-in-law) and the death of two sisters from tuberculosis; of his grappling with religion and life's big existential questions. And the dispersal of his family across the world to escape genocide.

But when I read family memoirs, I always find the romantic bits the most interesting. It is hard to imagine one's grandparents falling in love. But they did.

According to my Apa, it was actually Ama who asked him on their first date, which was virtually unheard of in those days. He recalls that she was a formidable woman, from an exceptional family of medical doctors, academics and entrepreneurs. Her boldness was partly genetic, partly learnt; her own mother (my great-grandmother) is described in her son-in-law's memoirs as 'a very important, liberal woman' who was 'a big name in the women's movement and very active in social welfare work'.

Anyway, her daughter, our Ama, did not just ask Apa out on any old date. She invited him to go on a skiing trip with her to the Winterberg between Christmas and New Year, 1910. It turned out to be an eventful excursion. Apa was a good skier, and he wrote:

> I showed her some things ... and when we sat down at noon in a sunny, wind-protected gully to eat our lunch, I felt a mighty feeling growing within me.
>
> This feeling grew in the course of the afternoon. After dinner we met at the Inn of Brinkmann where a number of sports enthusiasts congregated and participated in the general Feuerzangenbowle [literally translated into English as fire-tongs punch], a traditional New Year's Eve game in which a rum-soaked sugar loaf, held in tongs, is set on fire and drips into an alcoholic concoction of brandy, wine, cinnamon and cloves.
>
> As the clock neared midnight we left the loud company and went into the clear, cold winter night; when the clock struck midnight, I was so overcome by a feeling of happiness that I grabbed her and kissed her.
>
> Now Mila was not a girl one could kiss without thinking. I realised at once the heavy consequences of my act and without another word, I quickly went to my quarters. I cannot say that I slept poorly. I was dead tired. When I showed up on January 1 at Brinkmann's, Mila sat already at the table. She had not closed one eye all night, she sat there silently and did not eat, while I enjoyed Westfalian sausage and ham.

Nevertheless, they met during the subsequent weeks and 'discussed the pros and cons of a marriage'.

'At night,' Apa records in his memoirs, 'I was awake a long time thinking what I should do.'

His memoirs even include his list of 'positives' and 'negatives', written as he wrangled with his decision:

Positives: A beautiful, healthy woman, domestic, modest, not a clothes-horse [i.e. not interested in fashion], an ideal housewife and mother, from a good family.

Negatives: the differences in our religion and our race.

Why had he used the word 'race' in this context, I wondered. On reading further, it became apparent that the social and political discourse in Europe at the time was premised on the notion of separate 'races', based on genealogical origins. The rise of Nazism sought to codify these races into a scientific hierarchy, with the Aryans and Nordic 'races' at the top, and the 'Untermenschen' (sub-humans) ranked below. These included Slavs, Russians, Serbs and Poles. Gypsies and Jews occupied the lowest sub-stratum, and as Nazism tightened its grip, were eventually deemed to be '*Lebensunwertes Leben*' (life unworthy of life), fit only for extermination.

It is clear from Apa's memoirs that neither of my grandparents considered 'race' differences to constitute an obstacle to their relationship. But they certainly anticipated that the public reaction would be negative. For any South African who has lived through apartheid, the social impact of interracial relationships does not need explaining.

For this reason, they initially conducted their courtship by correspondence. It took them a while to 'come out', so to speak. The manner in which their relationship surfaced was unanticipated. The housekeeper found one of Apa's unfinished letters to his beloved, and immediately showed it to his father, Leopold, who proceeded to interrogate his son, requesting to meet the focus of his affections.

'So,' wrote Apa, 'I went to the phone and told Mila to come to our house, my Father wanted to meet her and she agreed …

'I must mention that she came in a rather washed-out blouse and skirt to our house. My father said later on: "A store employee wears better clothes."

'But he had recognised her qualities immediately and was happy that she had come to present herself so naturally and unadorned.'

Apa wrote that, as anticipated, their engagement 'caused a sensation in Essen and was widely discussed. That a Jew wanted to marry the daughter of that family was unheard of. It was in fact daring for me. Even though I came from a well-to-do and well-regarded family, the societal standards were such that Jews formed, so-to-speak, a lower rank of society. They were not admitted to the clubs of the Christian community and were more or less restricted to social intercourse with their co-religionists.

'Thus Mila had to descend considerably regarding social status, when she married me and I was afraid that this might lead to conflicts', especially as some members of her family had 'taken a negative attitude towards me from the beginning'.

Four months after that first New Year's Eve kiss, they were married, at her parents' home. 'When the guests arrived, they found the bride in the kitchen peeling asparagus,' Apa recalled. Ama did the organisation and catering for her wedding.

My mother, their fifth and last child, was born on 18 January 1919. She was an amalgam of both her parents, the practical and philosophical, the pragmatic and intellectual, the confident and vulnerable.

She turned fourteen in 1933, the year Hitler came to power. She was soon classified a '*Mischling*' or 'half-breed' – 'like a mule', her teacher once explained to the whole class. Her dreams of doing the things she had seen her siblings do before her – joining the rowing and hiking clubs, and taking dancing lessons – evaporated as the cancer of anti-Semitism metastasised through Germany, even extending its malignant tentacles into the Protestant side of her own family.

The tidal wave of national socialism swept away good people too. Swimming against an ideological rip-current is too arduous for all but the bravest and strongest.

Ama never forgave those members of her family who chose to drift on the raft of least resistance as the rising tide of anti-Semitism and totalitarianism engulfed Germany.

Although none of my grandparents, Jewish or Protestant, practised their religions, the gulf between their families grew, as Hitler cunningly crafted the threat of an 'enemy within', the tried and trusted tactic of all totalitarian dictators.

But the seeds of anti-Semitism had been growing throughout Europe for centuries, long before Hitler came to power.

Living on the margins of the mainstream is part of the genetic inheritance of many Jews; its corollary is a deep solidarity with each other, a magnetic force of history, experience, culture, tradition and faith.

My grandfather's memoirs are particularly interesting on the subject.

'At school I soon became aware that I was a Jew and somewhat different from the majority of the students,' he wrote. 'The teacher, Lube, a fanatical Catholic and anti-Semite, gave a special treatment to myself and the other Jewish student, full of contempt and enmity. This did not prevent me from finding good friends among the Christian students.'

During his high-school years, he recorded, a Rabbi Samuel 'awakened an interest in the Jewish religion in me'.

> I was so interested in the discussion of religious and philosophical themes that I do not recall having missed a single lesson. I even played for a time with the thought of becoming a Rabbi.
>
> This religious involvement lasted only a short while. I became aware, early on, that it is more important to lead a decent, good life than the active par-

ticipation in one of the confessions. Reading the works of Lessing, Schiller, Goethe, and especially Tolstoy eliminated every form of religious prejudice. I must confess that if I had had the choice of selecting among the faiths I would still have selected the Jewish one. In Jesus Christ, I always recognized the great reformer who fought against the excesses of the Jewish rituals of the time, not the moral content of the belief, which he in fact called immortal.

He then quoted Matthew 5:18: 'Verily I say unto you, Till heaven and earth pass, one jot or one tittle shall in no wise pass from the law, till all be fulfilled.'

'Jesus,' wrote my grandfather, 'did not want a new religion, but only to lead the Jewish religion back to its ethical content and reduce all the "Giksen and Gaksen" (as my mother-in-law called the rituals).' But, as he observed later,

> Christianity has fallen into the same trap. Carrying out all the rituals seems to be more important to the priests than proper moral behaviour.
>
> While I decline a personal God, I recognise a Higher Power, which becomes evident in the entire creation and which cannot be denied... In contrast to my intellectual conviction, I have a feeling of dependency on a providence or a fate. After a happy survival of a danger, I would send a thankful look to the sky.

It was, however, important to his wife that their children were baptised and confirmed into the Lutheran Church, and Apa had no problem with this. My mother recalls her confirmation in 1933, as the last time the Protestant and Jewish sides of her family came together. 'It was very tense,' she wrote in her memoirs.

There was certainly no comfortable place in Hitler's Germany for a baptised and confirmed Protestant Jew like my mother, either in her school, the wider society or her extended family. If Simone Weil was known as the patron saint of outsiders, my mother was a close runner-up.

She was comforted by the strength of her indomitable mother, who was widely respected, and refused, even under the most pressured circumstances, to raise a straight-armed Hitler salute. It would have been far easier just to go, unnoticed, with the flow.

Ama's courage was fortified by a distinct tendency to be 'aspris', an Afrikaans word that is only adequately translated by the Yiddish word 'davka'. Literally, it means 'on purpose' (in Afrikaans) or 'precisely' (in Yiddish). Figuratively, both words mean doing something purposefully and precisely, to get up a bigot's nose. This gene has never skipped a generation in our family, and has been amply reinforced by example.

Such as on 11 November 1938, the morning after Kristallnacht, when the Gestapo swept through Jewish homes, including my grandparents', smashing windows and furniture and valuable items. My grandfather's precious old cello was one. They also arrested my grandfather. His outraged wife got straight to work, throughout the night, gathering the shards of glass from the many shattered windows in their multi-storey home, which was situated above the consulting rooms of an anti-Semitic orthopaedic specialist, and waited for the sun to rise.

My mother recalls the scene in her memoirs: 'Mother had collected all the glass in large baskets and threw it over the bannister. A tremendous racket. She hoped that the doctor, staff and waiting patients would get a nervous breakdown.'

Then my grandmother put on her coat and hat and set off to save her husband from the concentration camps.

As Mom's memoirs recall,

> Mother immediately left for Aachen where Franz Vogelsang, a friend of her nephew (Büchner) who had often come to us to play, was the Gauleiter (Gestapo Chief of our Province). When she arrived at his office without a previous appointment, the secretary would not let her in. She asked him to go and tell Vogelsang that Tante Mila wanted to see him. Immediately, and based on her powerful personality and personal connection, she was let in. Franz (called 'Fränsken' – a diminutive form of endearment – by mother) came to welcome her and she said: 'I do not want any words, Fränsken. What is the age limit for Jewish prisoners to be sent to the concentration camps?'
>
> 'What is Carl's age?' asked Fränsken.
>
> 'Fifty-five.'
>
> 'Then all Jews above 54 years (in this province) will not go into camps.'

That's how totalitarianism works. The Gauleiter's word was law in his province. It is also how oxymoron works – a Nazi Gauleiter with a surname that translates into English as 'Bird Song'!

When I read the story about my grandmother's interaction with Gauleiter Bird Song, I understood survivor's guilt. My grandmother used her contacts in high places to save her husband's life, and possibly hundreds of other men over the age of fifty-four from their province. But what about those inconveniently born a year later? These compromises, forged at the place where life intersects with death, are the hardest for survivors to face. That is probably why they never spoke about their grief. We only read about it in their memoirs, and even then only obliquely.

I would never have known from my grandfather's account of his mother's death that she had committed suicide. Bertha Katzenstein, whom he describes in his memoirs as 'short with a very big heart', had six children in quick succession. My grandfather was the fourth child (and second son).

'In May 1890 she was admitted to a Nervenheilanstalt [literally an institute for the healing of the nerves] in Bonn ... I still feel her hand as she blessed me one morning on my awakening. I never saw her again. She died on 21st of May, a week before her 40th birthday on the 28th of May,' was how my grandfather recalled his loss. He was seven years old.

His memoirs describe the family's debilitating grief, and the white lilies that arrived in their home with 'their sharp, stunning perfume'. For the rest of his life, the smell of lilies visibly triggered the emotions associated with the death of his beloved mother.

He wrote about the support of the Jewish community which helped the family to deal with the trauma. But, as the nineteenth century drew to a close, that too began to change. With the rise of anti-Semitism, some Jews decided to convert to Christianity. One of them was the family of his best friend, Theo Goldschmidt. A distance developed, driven by the older Goldschmidt generation.

Apa explained the trauma he experienced as a child: 'on one occasion I was not invited to his birthday party and I still remember the pain I felt when I unsuspectingly walked over to play at his house, and found the circle of invited friends from which I had been excluded'.

Apart from the death of his mother, the memory of the loss of these close early friendships remained more painful in his life than the rest of the persecution under the Third Reich, including the collapse of his once thriving legal practice and the confiscation of his property.

In the 1930s Apa started moving his children out of Germany. His elder daughter, Otta, married Julius Herzfeld, and they emigrated to Argentina; his second daughter, Agnes, studied physiotherapy in Sweden; his two sons, Felix and Ulrich, emigrated to South Africa. My mother, Mila, the youngest, remained with her parents in Germany. Shunned by former friends at her predominantly Lutheran school, and barred from all clubs and societies, she begged to be sent to boarding school outside of Germany. Her parents, unable to countenance life without any children, kept her at home.

Mom's memoirs on this period are uncharacteristically abrupt. 'Totally excluded socially. Tolerated. Atmosphere at home, serious.'

But her parents were determined to remain in Germany and stand their ground.

Apa changed his mind after the destruction of his beloved cello on Kristallnacht. 'If such a beautiful instrument can be so callously destroyed, human life is next,' he wrote.

Agnes, Mom's elder sister, interrupted her studies in Sweden, went to England and succeeded in finding English families who were prepared to offer guarantees that my grandparents would not become a burden on the state. Thus it was that my grandparents, Carl and Emilie Cosmann, and their youngest daughter Mila, left Germany three weeks before the invasion of Poland and the outbreak of the Second World War.

My mother, who understood hardly any English, found a job as a maid for the family of Maureen and Bradbury Clark. Apa became a night-watchman and studied English as the long, dark hours dragged by. His observations on the English language in his memoirs bear repeating: 'With a relatively small vocabulary, one can carry on a fair conversation in English. The conversation revolves mostly around weather and sport.'

Anyone who complained got the same response from Ama: '*Hör auf zu jammern. Du atmest freie Luft*' (Stop complaining. You are breathing free air). 'Free', of course, in this sense refers to freedom.

Apa attended lunchtime concerts at the Royal Academy of Music, where he could listen to free performances given by practising students. Before long, he had borrowed a cello from the Academy and was playing chamber music again.

In 1940 Germany invaded France and the danger loomed that Britain would be next. German refugees, including my mother and grandparents, were interned in separate camps on the Isle of Man.

Mom remembered this as one of her life's happiest chapters. Shortly before her death, I asked her why.

'I was called Mila,' she said. 'I did not have a label. I was liked for who I was. For the first time I met Germans who were not Jewish but who rejected nationalism, and wanted to associate with me and my family. We did things together, especially working in the garden. We laughed a lot, shared a lot, and I belonged.'

She was affirmed. And for the first time in her life, she told me, she felt free.

What a paradox: to be labelled an enemy alien, to be interned and deprived of your freedom because you are a potential danger to society, on the basis of your nationality. And yet to say that for the first time in your life you felt free.

Freedom, to my mother, meant a sense of belonging, a shared identity, based on values; and being able to be herself.

She took Russian lessons from a fellow internee. Many years later, when she did not want to 'swear in front of the children', she would say 'Gavnō!' in a tone that made its meaning pretty clear.

The way the British conducted the war turned her into a lifelong Anglophile. An almost stereotypically 'organised German' herself, Mom was amazed and delighted that 'German efficiency' was defeated by British pragmatism and what, to her, seemed like 'muddling through', even in the most desperate circumstances.

Many times during the war years she was frozen with fear, convinced that the German war machine, whose build-up she had witnessed, would be unstoppable. She recalls one such moment: walking along the cliffs on the Isle of Man, she came across some Boy Scouts, scouring the waters of the English Channel. She asked them what they were doing. 'Looking for German submarines,' they replied. She decided then and there which cliff she would jump off when the Germans invaded.

The 'British way' became her benchmark for how to deal with life's problems. She tried, repeatedly but always unsuccessfully, to adopt it. She loved almost everything British, except the point at which diplomacy and hypocrisy merge. She was glad when the war ended but was sad to leave the cocoon of safety on the island. Still struggling to master English, she studied nursing and failed her finals, twice, but was proud to have written the exams at the famous Guy's Hospital. (She eventually passed at her third attempt.)

With Germany crushed, Apa persuaded Ama to reconnect with the surviving members of her family back in Essen and Berlin. He even sent them some of their war rations, to prevent their starvation. Apa devoted the rest of his life to reuniting the Jewish and Protestant sides of our family, making several trips to his home town to reconnect with family in the later years of his life. Ama took a little longer to warm to the project. There is no betrayal harder to forgive than rejection by your own brothers and sisters.

Eventually, Apa persuaded Ama to visit them again. It was to be her last trip anywhere. She died of breast cancer on that visit, after using the opportunity to bid a final farewell to her family.

Between leaving Germany in 1939 and returning in 1958 lay two challenging decades, during which they worked hard to build new lives.

Apa and Ama remained in England when Mom set sail to join her brothers in South Africa on 23 December 1947, after ten years of working as a midwife in London, Yorkshire and the Lake District.

Her most vivid recollection of her new country was the abundance of fruit. She laughed out loud when a vendor first identified a paw-paw for her, and would giggle again every time she heard the word. (Poh-poh, in German, pronounced the same but with the emphasis on the second syllable, is slang for 'bum'.) She loved oranges the most. Her memoirs recall arriving in South Africa at the Durban docks and seeing a whole bag of oranges for sale 'for five bob'. 'Once, walking in the Lake District, I found an orange peel on the ground, picked it up and smelled it. I had not seen an orange all through the war. And here, a whole bag!! And then they told me they never eat them, just drank their juice! Incomprehensible at the time.'

Her next amazement was seeing three fried eggs served on one plate in a restaurant at Eskort bacon factory, a favourite place to break the journey on the drive from Durban to Johannesburg. 'I stood still and looked at this wonder, loving eggs so much. During the war we got 2 eggs a week in Summer, in Winter, 1 egg. And now this sight! I shall never forget it.'

The South African election of 1948, which took place shortly after my mother's arrival, gripped the country. Dad got involved, doing everything he could to oppose the election of the Herenigde Nasionale Party under Dr D.F. Malan. He had seen the destruction wrought by ethnic nationalism in his own country and believed it would be disastrous for South Africa. After attending an open-air political rally in Vrededorp, he 'landed in the casualty station of the hospital', his memoirs recall. 'I also landed on the front page of the Transvaler' (the leading Afrikaans daily newspaper of the time). Despite his efforts, and against expectations, the Nationalists won on 26 May.

Mom, who had been in South Africa for less than six months, was shattered. She now faced, for the second time in her young life, a government that mobilised followers on the basis of race and religion. Two years later she met the man who shared her passion for politics and her hatred of prejudice.

My parents moved to the property Dad had bought with Granny's savings of his wartime stipend. It was miles outside Johannesburg in a tiny village called Rivonia. The first Afrikaans word Mom learnt was 'pondok', which perfectly described the rough shelter made of bricks, wood and corrugated iron my parents moved into on their plot. Dad set about trying to fix it, bit by bit, and my mother turned the small, solid core into a liveable area. Dad and his friend Walter Rothgiesser started a small scrap-metal business.

Ama and Apa left Britain for South Africa when their children had jointly saved enough money to pay their passage. They joined my parents in the 'pondok'. Before long, Ama, a trained horticulturist, started developing what eventually became a magnificent garden, with every variety of fruit and vegetable imaginable, including asparagus, artichokes and kohlrabi; loganberries, pomegranates, loquats, almonds and various grape cultivars. I still miss the black catawbas that pop out of their skins, the tart centre in a spurt of syrup. And the white crystal with translucent skin. In summer, the branches of the apricot tree drooped to the ground with their rich harvest, and we tasted summer all year round in the whole-fruit jam my mother made in huge vats over the coal stove. When my parents were invited out, a jar of home-made apricot jam was the gift. They kept chickens and always had fresh eggs. The best part of every year was our purchase of 100 day-old chicks.

I was born in Hillbrow on 9 March 1951. My parents named me Otta Helene. My first name was a tribute to Apa's beloved elder sister, who had died of TB, and also my mom's elder sister (who died at the age of 104 in Buenos Aires in May 2016). Helene was a tribute to Granny, my father's mother. When teachers spelt my name 'Otter', my parents decided to switch to Helen, although I have never understood why they anglicised Helene.

Slowly, over the years, the corrugated-iron parts of the pondok were replaced with solid walls, when my dad could afford to build them.

My parents spoke German. Our surname was pronounced Tziller. The day before I went to school, in 1957, my mother told me that I should pronounce our surname 'Zilla'. The other children would battle with the German pronunciation, she said. I said 'Zilla' sounded funny. But it could have been much worse!

At that stage I did not yet know how lucky I was that the surname Pielsticker was my mother's mother's, not my father's father's. The literal translation of that name in Afrikaans (South Africa's second biggest language) is Penis Poker. It would have been impossible for me to pursue a journalistic or political career in South Africa with that surname. I realised this for the first time when we went to the airport to fetch an older cousin, Jochen Pielsticker, visiting us from Germany. We could not find him in the arrivals hall, so Mom went to the enquiries counter to ask them to make an announcement, and call him. When she handed over a piece of paper with his name written on it, the immaculately groomed lady behind the counter dissolved into a fit of giggles. Every time she tried to make the announcement, she choked up. She just could not get herself to say that name over the public address system in Calvinist South Africa. After that we routinely (but very lovingly) referred to our German cousins as 'Die Piele'.

Mom became indignant every time. 'The name comes from the German word *Pfeilstecher*,' she said. Because she did not know the English equivalent (quiver), she explained, 'It is something you put arrows into.'

'That doesn't help,' my sister Carla said dryly.

But back to Zille. On the night before my first school day, my mother told me about a great-uncle of my father called Heinrich Zille, a beloved satirist, artist, humourist and photographer of poor working-class families in Berlin of the early twentieth century.

Now and then, as I was growing up, Germans would ask me if we were related to Heinrich Zille and I would say yes, on a diagonal, not a direct line, although I never remembered exactly how. The family tree, carefully compiled by my dad's brother Heinrich, shows that I share a great-great-great-grandfather with Heinrich Zille's great-grandfather. Diagonal indeed.

Many years later, when I was mayor of Cape Town, the mayor of Radeburg, Dieter Jesse, contacted me and asked me to unveil a plaque celebrating the 150th anniversary of Heinrich Zille's birth in Radeburg. I happily accepted. The ceremony attracted a lot of publicity and I did several media interviews, in which the question of how my forebears left Germany inevitably came up. A few weeks later, I received a scathing letter from a woman claiming to be Heinrich Zille's only living female relative. In a tone one would use to deny one's family had syphilis, she rejected the notion that there had ever been a Jew in the Zille family. Her family tree showed none, she insisted, as if that settled the matter.

I was stunned. After everything Germany had been through, there were still

Germans capable of writing a letter like this. And someone I thought was a member of my family (fortunately, very distant) nogal!

I wrote in reply:

> When I read your letter, the pathos and sadness of your situation were quite clear. Here you are, in 2008, needing to find a sense of self-worth and social status in the fact that you had a famous relative, who was born 150 years ago. I am genuinely pleased that your belief that you are the only living female descendant of the late Heinrich Zille gives you a sense of worth and purpose.
>
> I would not wish to strip you of this status. I really do not need a distant relative to give my life meaning. Although I admire Heinrich Zille's courage, and deeply respect his empathy with the poor and marginalised, it has made no difference at all to my life, whether I am related to him or not.

Then I gave her a bit of gratuitous advice:

> I would not really give much credence to the family tree on which you rely. It is well known that, during the Nazi times, family trees were 'edited' to remove any reference to family members marrying Jews. My grandfather, Walter Zille, married Helene Marcus, a Jewish woman of great courage and intelligence. Many of her family members died during the Nazi years. She was lucky to escape.

And then I added the final line:

> It is apparent from the wording of your letter that the bigotry that led to my forebears leaving Germany, still continues today. I believe the great Heinrich Zille would have been ashamed of you. His work and life certainly conveyed a different brand of humanity.*

Aspris. This letter was the mild modern equivalent of my grandmother tossing buckets of broken glass onto an anti-Semite's doorstep. I hope, as Mom would have said, 'she got a nervous breakdown'.

---

* As coincidence would have it, when I had already submitted the manuscript for my book, I was contacted by a Martina Rohde, a German researcher, who asked for permission to research my family tree. I sent it to her, welcoming the opportunity to sort out this confusion. Just in time for the final proofs she wrote back to say that the wires had become crossed between two Johann Gottlob Zilles. One, born in 1795, was the famous Heinrich Zille's grandfather. But the one mentioned in our family tree as the son of our common ancestor was actually another Johann Gottlob, born in 1787. The Johann Gottlobs were two different people, but my uncle must have thought they were the same person, the researcher said. But, she added comfortingly, 'it is very possible that you do have a common ancestor, but to date, I haven't found him'. Whatever. It makes no difference. It is sad when people have to live their own lives on the legacy of their ancestors.

2

It Takes a Village

I ALWAYS KNEW THIS would be the most difficult chapter to write, and on Christmas day 2015, on holiday at our traditional spot next to the Keurbooms River, I understood why.

We were playing the 'present game', introduced to our family by my daughter-in-law Gretl. The purpose of the game, apart from having fun, is to save everyone the ridiculous expense of buying Christmas presents for everybody else.

There were eleven of us playing (ten extended family members and a friend).

The present game works like this: each participant buys one gift, to an agreed value (in our case around R200), and wraps it in newspaper in a way that its contents cannot be deduced from its look or feel. Then the gifts are numbered, from 1 to 11. Corresponding numbers are put into a hat. Everyone draws a number and keeps it secret until their number comes up, starting from 1 and ending with 11.

Number 1 starts, by taking the gift numbered 1 and opening it. Every player now knows what this gift is. Then number 2 takes her present. But before unwrapping it, number 2 must make a choice. Does she want to take a chance on her unopened gift or swap it for the opened one? Every subsequent player has the same choice – and, of course, the more open presents there are in the pool, the greater one's options become. An unopened present can be swapped twice, before the recipient must accept and open it.

The game combines the luck of the draw and the strategic choices you make. It is each one for him- or herself, trying to get the best gift from a random set of presents, irrespective of the preferences of others. It is all rather cut throat for Christmas but adds to the fun.

The player who draws number 1 has the fewest options. The player who draws 11 has the most, because they can choose to swap their unopened gift for any of the other ten.

As it happened, Carla drew number 1. I drew number 11.

Not only that, but gift number 1 turned out to be the audiobook of Stephen Fry's autobiography.

Carla, grasping the irony of having drawn the audiobook, roared with laughter. Everyone laughed with her. I joined in, but I felt as if someone had applied industrial-strength paint stripper to the thin veneer of humour I tried to bring to the situation.

As so often happens in families, a seemingly insignificant event can resonate with past experience, triggering a range of uncontainable emotions, incomprehensible to an outsider.

Whenever I am with my sister, I notice, for example, how often people cover their mouths when they speak, whether holding a glass in front of their lips, or using hand gestures across their face, or just turning away. This immediately cuts anyone who relies on lip-reading out of the conversation. It is hard enough for a deaf person to follow the thread of a conversation with a full, uninterrupted view of the speaking faces.

Of course Carla experiences these 'cut-outs' every day in countless interactions, but when my family unthinkingly subjects her to the same thing, it presses a button in me that sets off an internal eruption like molten lava that bursts through, no matter how thick the crust is. Carla senses my reaction and finds it patronising and demeaning. She tells me to let her deal with it. This is symptomatic of our complex relationship, which has had its ups and downs over six decades, and has evolved over time.

I have only recently learnt that my responses are fairly typical of people known as SODAs, or siblings of deaf adults (except that, with me, they started as a child). There is a burgeoning literature on the impact a variety of disabilities have within families, some of which is helpful and interesting. It is useful to recognise in oneself a psychological phenomenon, something akin to survivor's guilt, and common among people who have a sibling with a disability. It is particularly instructive to learn from those who have built constructive, supportive relationships in these complex circumstances. One day I will add my two cents' worth to the literature. It will, in summary, be this: accept, acknowledge and appreciate. But don't appropriate other people's struggles and pain. It has taken me sixty-five years to differentiate and link these simple concepts.

If I could depict graphically what I've learnt, it would be through a picture I found in my sister-in-law Isabel's exquisite photo collection, of an ancient Japanese ceramic bowl, threaded with gold leaf.

Kintsukuroi, a word Carla introduced to me many years ago, describes the art of mending broken pottery with gold or silver lacquer and perceiving that the piece is more beautiful for having been broken. The added dimension arises from a process of applying vision, insight, care, heat and precious metals to weld the pieces together, manifesting a new and deeper dimension to the original. Our modern throwaway culture has never developed this art form, whether in relation to things or people. Our default approach is to use, destroy, dump. But the other extreme is also commonplace: fret and obsess about the broken pieces, nurturing the sense of pain and loss, instead of making the effort to recreate something new, more valuable and enduring from its fragments.

I have viewed Carla's struggles from close quarters. I have seen her fortitude, her determination, her humour, her deep disappointments, and compared her life path with my own. With the wisdom of hindsight and a bit of proper advice and information, I might have had the tools to handle our relationship differently. I might have asked the right questions at the right times and listened to the answers rather than trying to interpret things from her vantage point through my eyes. As a family we might have acknowledged her situation, rather than merely accept it.

There is a difference. Acknowledging requires empathetic appreciation of the difficulties a person faces. In our family we all too often avoided facing these issues, masking denial as acceptance. And it is all too easy to do this with deafness, because it has no visible manifestation.

But I have also discovered it is never too late to start learning the art of kintsukuroi.

I took the opportunity of being with the family over Christmas to discuss how I would write about these things, and they said: be honest.

But, what is honest? Memory is a strange thing. When we siblings talk about a shared experience, it always amazes me how differently we recall its detail, what we took out of it, and how it affected us. What we all agree on is that the tide that ebbed and flowed throughout our childhood and adolescence was our mother's recurrent depressions. When the tide rose, we lost our footing on the ocean floor, and learnt to swim alone.

All of us remember, in different ways, her recurrent cycles of grief. Initially, it was attributed to her lack of sleep, due to my refusal or inability, ever, to sleep for more than a few hours during the night, from my earliest childhood. I remember the guilt I felt when my mother wept from what she (and our doctor) described as sheer exhaustion. I'm sure sleep deprivation fuelled her genetic predisposition to depression, covered by an additional layer of the post-natal variety, and aggravated by having two babies in twenty-two months.

Later in life, I got to understand an additional dimension. It is sometimes called post-holocaust trauma. It manifested in extreme sensitivity to daily interactions and events, things that other people would simply shrug off, but that triggered in her overwhelming primal emotional responses. We only got to learn about this dimension to her depressions a lot later in our lives.

Dad was hardly around. He worked day and night to get his small scrap-metal business going. Mom worked on the primitive structure they were trying to turn into a home. There was no money for curtains, let alone the luxury of domestic help. To complicate things further, Ama and Apa, who had arrived from England, came to live with the young couple, and required attention, which inevitably added a new dimension of stress.

And then came the diagnosis of Carla's hearing loss, when she was four.

I'm sure it would have helped my parents then to know that grief proceeds through the classic six stages: shock, denial, anger, bargaining, depression and acceptance.

My mother went through each stage with an intensity of which few human beings are capable. Through a lifetime of observing people, I have reached the conclusion that some people genuinely feel things more deeply and profoundly than others. And no one more so than my mother.

Just when she had moved through the six-phase cycle the first time, it began again when Carla, at thirteen, lost most of her remaining hearing.

We learnt that my sister's deafness was the consequence of ototoxic medication, administered first when she was six months old, and again later, as a teenager. It destroyed the cochlea hair cells that convey sound waves to the brain via the auditory nerve.

We differ on the details of when and how our mother found out about the link between the medication and Carla's deafness, but the impact was devastating.

Writing this chapter was the catalyst for me and Carla to talk about this for the very first time in our lives. It was somewhere I didn't dare go before.

Carla told me she had 'put two and two together' many years later when she went to an international conference for the deaf and hard of hearing.

'I went to a presentation where they listed drugs that were ototoxic to the cochlea. I recognised one of them from my last bout in hospital prior to my second hearing loss as a teenager. By the time I found out and after research confirmed it, I was already in my thirties and I felt such a mixture of emotions. Relief that I now knew what it was, and anger that this could have been prevented. When I shared this with Mom, she too was relieved that it was nothing she did in her pregnancy but was devastated for the same reason. We had always up to that point listed my hearing loss as "unknown".'

In those days psychotherapy was still a stigma-filled zone not widely accessible outside mental institutions. Mom tried a range of other 'cures' for her depression, from scientology to acupuncture, to no avail.

But as much as we remember her worst times, we also remember her heroic (and successful) efforts to be cheerful, to build a functional family unit, and to ensure that we had happy memories of our childhood. She would spend months preparing for our camping holidays, to the last detail. Although we did not have the best caravan, it was certainly the most *gemütlich*, an untranslatable German word which describes a combination of homely, cosy and comfortable.

Nothing could beat my mother's Christmas. During preceding months we would go for long walks to gather interesting foliage, pine cones and a variety of seed pods that we would dry and paint silver, creating our own decorations. Every Christmas we bought some new tinsel and a few baubles to add to our stock, until we had a box full, mostly home-made. We helped decorate the tree early in December. Then the garage-that-became-the-lounge would be locked up, and my mother would turn the interior space into a veritable fairyland. We were awestruck at the spectacle she managed to create with the simplest things, including scores and scores of candles that illuminated the dark room, liberally stacked with presents (also mostly home-made) in personal piles around the tree. As children we did not buy presents for our parents. We made things, and spent many happy hours planning and creating our gifts.

Easter also brings back wonderful memories of boiling eggs and painting them with a variety of stencils and edible colours. Our favourite was drawing designs in wax crayon and then dipping the egg in a tint, watching the colour retreat and the wax relief emerge. Then we would have an Easter egg hunt in the garden, followed by hard-boiled Easter eggs for breakfast.

Mom sewed our clothes, one party dress per season, but never the frilly pink chiffon frocks with stiff petticoats that were in vogue at the time; ours were traditional German dirndl dresses, often in rich, dark colours, with white aprons. We had a pair of white summer shoes and a pair of black winter shoes, bought at Clarks. My mother was a loyal Clarks customer, telling us that the original Mr Clark was a Quaker in England, and that the Quakers had been particularly welcoming of German refugees.

Every second Sunday, Dad would fetch Granny from her flat and Mom would cook a really good meal, no matter how low she was feeling. All the vegetables and fruit came from the garden, and sometimes a chicken too. Nothing went to waste. After boiling potatoes, she would preserve the potato water, and re-boil it with a chicken carcass to make stock for soup. If there were leftovers, they were always recycled in some new and tasty form.

And through the good times and bad, our stoic father soldiered on, usually in silence. I learnt, over time, that his emotional containment aggravated Mom's feeling of desolation. But his stability provided the raft we clung to at high tide.

In hindsight I sometimes reflect on how different our lives would have been had my father succumbed to the thrombosis that almost killed him after a serious accident when he walked through a glass door, severely cutting his face and legs. He retained a scar, in the shape of a question mark, on his prominent nose. It somehow seemed appropriate for Dad to have an existential question mark on his most prominent feature.

There were occasions, though, when his legendary slow burn reached the end of its fuse. I recall one incident, when we were already teenagers. It has become part of our family folklore.

Dad was trying to fix something technically complicated in the house, and Mom was hovering over him, offering advice and suggestions on a matter she clearly did not understand. Dad remained silent, but his exasperation grew until, finally, his patience snapped. Recalling an army phrase from the depths of his memory bank, he did something entirely out of character. He stopped working, looked my mother straight in the face, and asked in his thick German accent: 'Mila, who is fucking this cat?'

We kids had never heard my father use the F-word before, let alone while addressing our mother. We looked at each other in stunned silence.

But my literal-minded mother merely looked puzzled. 'Why the cat?' she asked. (She pronounced it 'Vy ze cat?' which made it much funnier.)

Her response captured her Germanic incapacity to grasp metaphors, innuendo or any other figure of speech. Even today, when anyone in the family has had enough of advice from one of the alpha-Zilles, they simply have to say, 'This is my cat.' And if someone fails to make the proper deduction or inference in a conversation, someone is bound to ask, 'Vy ze cat?'

Unlike many parents today, ours were not involved in the minutiae of our lives. We learnt most of what we know from them by osmosis, especially their abhorrence of any form of self-indulgence or prejudice.

They spent most of their weekends playing bowls, which they started at a relatively young age. Bowls gave Mom her first experience of being able to belong to a group in which she did not have to interrogate issues, but just play a game she became rather good at. For Dad, it was recreational respite from the challenges he faced at home and work. The bowls club gave them a social life as well, and they went out to various events and parties on Friday and Saturday evenings.

My first political memory was as a primary-school child, probably in Grade 1 or 2. Our classrooms at the time were corrugated iron, with bucket toilets in a shed outside. (Brick classrooms were built a short while after I started school.)

There were two grades per classroom, and lessons were taught in two languages, English and Afrikaans. The teachers I remember were formidable Afrikaans women, married to Scotsmen. Corporal punishment was routine, with a ruler across the hand, or a good old-fashioned hiding over Mrs Bryden's knees. The majority of pupils were the children of the Leeuwkop prison warders. Children of parents struggling to emerge from poverty mingled seamlessly with the children of refugees, like ours, striving to enter the middle class. This whites-only school knew no class distinction, but race barriers were taken as a given.

One day I came home and asked Mom to buy the kind of cheese we got at school. That is how she found out that we were being fed twice a week in class. I remember getting the square of cheese and a portion of fruit, and our teacher explaining that it was for protein and vitamins.

Mom was outraged. She told me the government had just ended the feeding schemes for black pupils, and was now instituting one for whites. She did her best to challenge 'the system' by writing a letter, which she spent days composing, protesting about food being given to children whose parents could afford to feed them, while others went hungry. Every time I taste mild cheddar today, I think of my mother's protest against our school feeding scheme.

There were similar issues that came up every day. We lived around the corner from the Reids, who had a newish ranch-style house on Homestead Road. As soon as Stan drove his Buick into 9th Avenue, a rutted dirt road, he would start hooting so that his gardener (referred to as 'the boy') could run and open the gate for 'the master'. My mother was outraged at this daily ritual. As soon as she heard the first hoot, she would run onto our front lawn and glower as Stan drove past. Carla recalls Mom once shaking her fist at Stan, who then hooted extra hard to aggravate her. Mom asked Stan once at a bowls-club social function why he did not just get out of the car and open the gate himself.

These kinds of conversations did not endear Mom to the rest of the neighbourhood. We were often simultaneously embarrassed and impressed by our mother.

Rivonia, like all small villages, was held together by the glue of gossip, emanating from the manual telephone exchange, where Miss van Harmelen operated the switchboard. As kids we would watch in awe as she took control of the calls, putting plugs into the switchboard jacks, and pulling them loose with a flick of her forefinger. She turned the invasion of people's privacy into an extension of the service she offered. 'Mr Berrington, you want to speak to your wife? She isn't home. She's at Bella's. Do you want me to put you through there?' Bella Lipschitz owned the general dealer, where one could buy everything from plastic potties to enamel mugs, from bicycles to Wicks bubblegum. Most families in the village kept an account there.

Looking back, this manual switchboard performed the function of a pre-cyber version of Twitter. It was the village's news dispersal centre. I remember once, when a young nun escaped from the cold, forbidding Carmelite convent that stood like an enclosed stone fort along the main road, how people called Miss van Harmelen to get the latest news or to pass on the latest clues in the search for her. It was as if an escaped convict was on the run. Mom said if the nun arrived at our house, we would hide her and save her from a life of imposed silence and human excommunication. I fervently hoped she would appear on our doorstep, but she never did. (She was eventually traced and helped to leave the convent and renounce her vows.)

Any snippet of news spread like wildfire, and was usually embellished in the retelling, until the original story was barely recognisable.

The 'scandals' I was involved in were no exception.

My parents, despite their liberalism, were Teutonic enough to believe that children should not question parental decisions, let alone answer back. I did both, which infuriated my mother. Her anger at my cheekiness was reinforced by her low self-esteem. When she said no, for reasons that I thought were irrational, I resisted. Some of our biggest battles, for example, were around her insistence that we take a nap after lunch. 'You can make two days out of one,' was how she tried to convince me to lie down on my bed. But I considered an afternoon nap an intrusion and interruption of my day, which I was not prepared to accept. Carla followed my example.

We sisters soon realised it would save a lot of time if we just agreed to lie down, with the curtains closed, and wait for five minutes until Mom was lying on her bed with her own door, curtains and eyes closed. We would then escape. We got to know every floorboard in the passage, to avoid those that creaked. If we inadvertently woke Mom, we faced her wrath through the plastic fly-swatter. I still recall several childhood thrashings.

Whatever it took, I tried to find a way around the injunctions I did not agree with.

One of those times happened when I was nine, my sister seven, and our friend Hazel Humphrey eight. Dad was away at the time, concluding a business deal somewhere, and Hazel was spending the night at our house. The Earls, who lived diagonally two acres away, had two sons, David and Geoffrey, who were also having friends over, to camp in their tent in the garden. We wanted to join them. Mom said no. I argued, to no avail.

So I made a secret plan. If we couldn't camp in the garden with them, we would just pop over for a midnight feast. We obligingly went to bed when we were told to, and followed the roster of keeping cavey (staying awake in rotation) until the witching hour, when I woke Hazel and Carla. We stuffed our beds and, in our blue-striped towelling dressing gowns, crept out of the window. By the light of the moon and a torch we climbed over our back fence into an open field, then into the Greys' property and finally into the Earls'. It is a miracle we did not waken the Greys' large dog.

We woke the boys (who had all gone to sleep by then), ate a bar of chocolate, drank some sparkling lemon, and had a merry time. At around three o'clock it was time to go home. I was all for going back the way we had come, diagonally across the acres separating our homes, but the boys said we should go by road, and they would walk with us. They did not want to take their chances with the Greys' dog. So off we set, one block down De la Rey Road, and then left, up to our front gate a block further down, opposite Mr Wilson's peach orchard in 9th Avenue.

We must have been five metres from our gate when the light of an approaching vehicle swung into our road. We froze. Six children in pyjamas at 3 a.m. was an even unlikelier sight than a vehicle on a deserted country road at that hour. We hadn't reckoned with Rivonia's single police van being on night patrol. We scattered. I dived through the barbed-wire fence into the orchard and tried to leopard-crawl away in the undergrowth. Carla chose the other side of the road, and crept behind one of the huge variegated cactus plants my grandmother had planted along our fence. It was each of us for herself in that moment. The paddy van stopped. Out got Sergeant Roux, the husband of Sophie Roux, who ran the haberdashery shop (a close second to Miss van Harmelen's switchboard as Rivonia's gossip centre). Sergeant Roux rounded us up, one by one. My dressing gown was full of sticky blackjack strip-seeds.

Sergeant Roux knew every family in the village, and as he grabbed each of us, he expressed his amazement: ''n Zille-meisie!' ''n Earl-seun!' ''n Dyer-seun!'

It was about 3:30 when Sergeant Roux marched us up to our front door and knocked. I do not recall a comparable moment of terror in my childhood. My mother looked through the 'peep window' at head height next to the front door. She immediately recognised the burly village policeman and opened the door. Then she looked down and saw her daughters (aged nine and seven), their friend Hazel (who was supposed to be spending the night in Mom's care), and the three boys. I will never forget the look on her face as she tried to construct a possible background narrative to this surreal experience.

My mom was shattered. She sent us to our room, asked Sergeant Roux in, and after getting as much information from him as she could, sent the boys back to their house in the back of the paddy wagon. Sergeant Roux delivered them to their parents in similar style.

Sophie's haberdashery was a busy place the next morning. And by the end of the day, the entire village had concluded that I was the ringleader.

That was the first time I realised the power of gossip in enforcing social norms. My mother told me solemnly that I now had a reputation to restore. She explained how a reputation could be destroyed overnight and take years to rebuild. I got the message, and my behaviour improved significantly. For a while.

Carla recalls that during primary school I was always organising something. When the school pool was built, I organised a gala. After school, I organised clubs and societies. And quizzes of all varieties. Carla distinctly recalls a 'what would you do if …?' quiz that I organised, because she couldn't answer her question to my satisfaction. The question was 'What would you do if you had to go somewhere smart and your shoes were dirty but you didn't have shoe polish?'

'Wipe them,' she answered.

That wasn't the answer I was looking for. It was 'Rub spit on your shoes. It is almost as good as shoe polish.'

Who knows where I came up with these questions, or the answers, but I spent many hours planning and executing these events.

I wrote the entrance exam to St Mary's School for Girls in Waverley and got accepted. My parents had chosen the school with my sister in mind. The fact that I had got in almost guaranteed her a place later. They wanted to keep her in the mainstream, and looked for a caring school with smallish classes where teachers would take account of her disability. It was a financial strain, but they were determined to do it.

I worried that I would not cope academically at St Mary's, even though I had passed the entrance exam. I found, to the contrary, how much we had learnt in our corrugated-iron, dual-medium, multi-grade primary school under the tutelage of strict Scottish Afrikaners. I was easily on a par with the St Mary's girls, and sometimes even ahead. Despite the easy academic transition, I experienced my new school as a serious culture shock.

It was my first encounter with the genetically ingrained sense of hierarchical entitlement that comes with old money, and the unconscious condescension towards those lower down the social scale. Being German, and part Jewish, with a slight Afrikaans accent, didn't do much for one's status in that environment either.

I really missed the camaraderie, the inclusiveness, of our primary school, which had characterised our village as a whole long before Rivonia became an upmarket suburb. The network of families and their children formed strong bonds which not only survived, but actually grew more resilient through all the minor scandals and social abrasions that punctuated village life.

So it wasn't long after my arrival at St Mary's that my rebellious spirit resurfaced.

By fourteen I had a boyfriend called Byron Price, who had an elder brother, George. We roamed around Rivonia over weekends, in groups, and started a 'den' in a shack on the Coombe-Heaths' property. And there were 'sessions' at the Rivonia hall where, inevitably, the feared 'Lebs' (as the Lebanese motorbike gang was known) would arrive in their leather jackets halfway through the evening. They seemed to do little more than rev their bikes outside, but now and again they would take girls for a spin. Miraculously, the news that I was one of those girls did not reach Miss van Harmelen or Sophie Roux, and my parents were none the wiser about how I spent those evenings.

I started to smoke, secretly at first and then more openly. My parents had always smoked and, before the health risks were understood, were relaxed and tolerant about us starting the same habit. Every car trip we had undertaken, from our earliest childhood, took place in the fog of my parents' cigarette smoke.

Despite this, I continued to do well at school academically, although not nearly as well as I could have done had I really applied myself. To show approval of a school report, my mother would say: 'One day you will be an excellent secretary to a top man.' And then to emphasise her point, she would repeat, 'A top man.'

Our parents' political liberalism, strangely, hit a barrier when it came to gender. Traditional gender roles were deeply ingrained in them, and this was something that would generate a lot of tension with me in later years. Mom did not, for example, believe it was appropriate for a woman to make a speech at a function when there were appropriate men available to perform this task. She vetoed me making a speech at my own wedding. And if ever anyone had to speak on behalf of the family at any function, it would either be my father or my brother, at our mother's insistence.

However, in my teenage years my battles with my parents centred on the length of my skirts, the amount of make-up I wore, breaking curfews and challenging the behavioural limits my parents set.

One night during school holidays, when Mom and Dad were scheduled to attend a social function at the bowls club, I had a friend, Gill, over to stay. She was 'going out' with Byron's brother George. I asked my parents whether Byron and George could come over for the evening. They said no.

So I told Byron and George to come at about nine, but not to ring the doorbell because it would wake my grandfather. They should just come and knock on the bedroom window and I would open it for them. They did.

It couldn't have been half an hour later that my dad's Valiant pulled into our drive. He had come back. Terror. I pushed the guys into the cupboard and switched off the light. Gill and I jumped into bed fully clothed, eyes thick with make-up, with only seconds to spare before Dad unlocked the front door and took the few short steps to my bedroom door. He turned the handle, took two further steps to the light switch, and then three steps to the cupboard door. My heart was beating like a kettledrum as he opened it.

'Good evening, Mr Zille,' said Byron, as if being in the cupboard in his fourteen-year-old girlfriend's dark bedroom was the most normal place in the world for her father to find him.

'Good evening,' echoed George.

Dad just pointed to the door. The two boys left without another word.

Typically, Dad did not reprimand me but returned to the bowls club to fetch my mother, who was once again devastated by my behaviour.

Years later I asked my dad why he had come back that evening after being at the function for so short a time. And how had he known to look in the cupboard? He said he knew I was planning something when I meekly accepted his refusal to allow Byron and George to come over while they were out. And, as for the cupboard, it was the obvious place to look, he said.

Not long afterwards, I was sent to boarding school. I was beyond my mother's capacity to handle. She just could not deal with the dynamics of our relationship.

My sister went too. My mother needed space. Carla tells me the reason

Mom gave for sending her to boarding school was that she 'couldn't send Helen alone'.

This was the start of long periods of separation between us and our younger sibling, Paul, who later also went to boarding school, and subsequently studied abroad. We only really got to know each other well as adults, when we developed a strong and close relationship.

After a while I got to enjoy boarding school, but at the end of the year, Mom (feeling the inevitable boomerang of guilt that followed her depressive cycles) took us out as abruptly as she had put us in. During my year at boarding school I had been confirmed in the Anglican Church. And Byron had broken up with me and started dating another girl in the village. It was an early heartbreak, second only to the unravelling of a friendship with a schoolgirl best friend.

During my remaining years at school I knew I did not fit in, without ever really understanding why. I did my best to belong, and I suppose the extent to which I succeeded, often against my instincts, was being made head day-girl in my matric year. But my real goal was to be picked for a sports team. I organised with my dad that he would take me to school forty-five minutes early every morning to give me time to practise whatever sport had team trials looming, usually tennis or hockey. Despite my efforts, I did not even make the third team in any sport! I did not know it at the time, but perseverance turned out to be a far more useful attribute in my post-school life than being in a sports team, or being head day-girl! I was very proud, though, when Carla made it into a hockey team.

I excelled at debating and current affairs, an interest sparked by our daily thirty-minute drive to school. The first newspaper vendor we encountered was on Corlett Drive, and my dad always bought a copy of the *Rand Daily Mail*. He would get me to skim the headlines and summarise the news for him before we arrived at school. I was soon hooked. He brought the paper home at night, and I often took it back into the car the next morning to finish the sections I had not yet read, before he bought the next copy. I followed Allister Sparks's brilliant columns, and was especially interested in their political content.

I remember fascinating discussions with my father, ranging from Ian Smith's unilateral declaration of independence in Southern Rhodesia to the United States' decision to delink the dollar from gold – a crucial development in the international monetary system. I brought all of these insights to our current affairs class at school, which was led (ironically) by our sports mistress, Wendy Nathan. I liked Miss Nathan. Although I understood why she couldn't, in good conscience, pick me for a sports team, she always affirmed me and my (different) opinions in the current affairs discussions.

Before long I had decided to become a journalist. I made an appointment to speak to Allister Sparks to ask him what I should study after school if I wanted a job at the *Rand Daily Mail*. He told me to get a broad liberal arts degree, and continue reading newspapers.

I had put on weight and lost my early popularity with boys, and I started feeling increasingly 'different' and insecure. The cultural and political canyon between home and school was deep, and I challenged the status quo at both ends of my spectrum.

Our younger brother, Paul, was sent to the Catholic school, St David's, more commonly known as Marist Brothers, after a short period at Rivonia Primary. My parents wanted to avoid the increasingly rigid parameters of so-called 'Christian National Education'.

After Paul had been there a few years, the private-school sector experienced a mini earthquake, with its epicentre at St Stithians College, a Methodist Church school established as an alternative to the High Anglican St John's College. The religious difference infused the schools with commensurately different styles. St Stithians was led by a liberal-minded and visionary headmaster named Marthinus Theuns Steyn Krige. The English teacher at St Stithians was David Brindley. He oversaw the production of the school plays, which were written and produced by the boys. One dealt with the subject of drugs – specifically heroin addiction – a taboo topic at the time. According to reports, members of the governing board were scandalised. They demanded a commitment from Brindley not to raise controversial issues again.

Brindley reportedly replied: 'Do you expect me to teach *Hamlet* without mentioning adultery?' And he refused to give the undertaking.

But the final straw apparently came when he published in the school magazine an account by a Grade 11 pupil of how he was battling to come to terms with the fact that he was gay.

Brindley was fired.

His headmaster, Steyn Krige, defended him. 'There is a principle here, and it is called freedom,' he was reported as saying at the time. That statement settled it for my mother. Although she had never met Steyn Krige, she became his greatest supporter. Later, when she had met and got to know him, he was one of the very few people for whom she reserved the Yiddish accolade *mensch*.

When Krige left St Stithians to establish South Africa's first educationally progressive school, Woodmead, in 1970 (and South Africa's first fully non-racial school), my parents resolved to send our younger brother Paul there. It was too late for Carla and me.

Mom went to tell Brother Anthony, the principal of St David's, of her decision.

'Now that's what I call faith,' Brother Anthony said kindly.

In fact, without knowing it, Brother Anthony's gentle irony had actually hit the bull's-eye. Steyn Krige was motivated by a similar faith to my mother's, a faith without dogma, centred on the Christian concept of grace. There was no other religion, she would say, that offered you the chance of forgiveness, redemption, and release from guilt and pain – and that is what she needed. Faith, prayer and grace helped her enormously to find calm acceptance of the things she couldn't change; to forgive herself and others.

Because Woodmead challenged the status quo, it was soon depicted as a school for 'alternative' children, for troublemakers, for those who would not fit into the mainstream. Although these children were welcomed at Woodmead, the truth about the school, as usual in apartheid South Africa, was the opposite.

Woodmead was pioneering the South African mainstream a full three decades ahead of its time. That was why my parents wanted to be part of it.

Apart from her religious faith, my mother's other great source of healing was the Black Sash. Her Black Sash membership changed her life. For the first time she was surrounded by like-minded people and spent time volunteering in the advice office, which gave her something practical to do about the injustices that so burdened her.

As Mom's troubles eased, mine were only starting. I desperately wanted to leave home and go to university elsewhere. During that period, I had two boyfriends, Rawdon Simon, the brother of a schoolfriend, Robyn, and William Bowler. Both were at Wits. Rawdon was studying computer science, and William accounting.

But I wanted to get away from the turbulence of my childhood. I wanted to start again. I applied to the University of Cape Town (UCT) and was accepted into residence at Fuller Hall.

As I walked out of St Mary's for the last time, I felt a weight lift from my shoulders. The future beckoned. Little did I know what it would hold. And how little I was prepared for it.

3

Hunger Strikes

THE DAY I left school I was determined to start a new life. Feeling isolated and insecure, I blamed it on my weight, gradually gained throughout my high-school years, with a quantum leap during my time as a boarder. My primary-school happiness had evaporated; the carefree cultural affinity I'd experienced among the children of refugees, prison warders and local working-class families (still all white in 1950s apartheid South Africa) had been replaced by a subtle sense of class exclusion at my English upper-middle-class Anglican high school. My parents were German, and half Jewish, and my views on most issues, from religion to politics, were accepted with the refined English condescension that tolerates 'deviance'.

Peer affirmation is perhaps the most important determinant of happiness during one's school years, and its absence is felt all the more when one has known and lost it. I left high school determined never to look back; to start my life again. The key to that, I believed, was losing weight. It was the era of Twiggy, of jutting collarbones, of miniskirts hovering atop reed-thin legs with knobbly knees.

I told my mom I wanted to see a dietician, but she waved my request away. 'There are people in this world with real problems,' she said. She knew what she was talking about, being by then a regular volunteer in the Black Sash advice office. Intellectually, I took her point, but not emotionally.

An inability to put one's problems into perspective is a feature of the teenage years. No intellectual understanding of collective suffering can trump your personal angst. And mine was hating my body.

I decided to solve my problem myself.

Going to UCT would be the start of a new life, I vowed. I would get thin. I looked forward to escaping my parents' mealtime rules, where 'fussy eating' was not indulged. You ate what came on your plate.

So in January 1969 I became a 'freshette' in Fuller Hall. All first-year students had to participate in initiation, which was mild by comparable university standards. I had heard it was great fun, so I was keen to get involved and make new friends.

One of the events, in the first two weeks, was the 'cattle parade'. The boys from the neighbouring men's residence, Smuts Hall, congregated in the Fuller common room, where a makeshift catwalk was constructed. The freshettes wore miniskirts and paraded in front of the freshers to the accompaniment of loud music, which only partially disguised the ribald commentary. A catcall was the ultimate compliment, reserved for the handful of girls with great legs. And then, after the parade, the auction began. The boys put in bids to date specific girls.

It is hard from today's vantage point to remember that this crass form of sexism was considered fun, even complimentary, to women. Back then it was one of many activities that symbolised the late arrival of the Swinging Sixties on the southern tip of Africa. The sexual revolution was at last beginning to loosen the grip of Calvinist repression and denial. In a few places at least, young people could break free from sexual inhibitions.

On the surface, everyone else seemed to be enjoying themselves, which exacerbated my sense of humiliation. But I doubt whether my objection was principled. It was personal. My legs were the worst feature of the body I loathed, and here I was, starting my university career having the opposite sex determine my value in monetary terms by the turn of my ankle and the diameter of my thighs.

I got through the catwalk stage but slipped out before the auction. I was not prepared to face what I feared would follow.

I have often wondered why I did not mobilise a counter-revolution to the superficial and misdirected 'sexual revolution' at that time, but feminism was in its infancy back then. Feminists were caricatured as embittered, frustrated prudes who burnt their bras and couldn't get laid. Bra burning and similar symbolic acts probably did more to distort than convey the feminist message. I was not ready to take on another battle. I had had enough of feeling marginalised. I just wanted to fit in.

The very next morning I went to the CNA bookshop on Main Road Rondebosch, next to the student pub The Pig and Whistle, to look for a diet book. I found only one. It was called *The Drinking Man's Diet*. I did not drink, but I thought that omitting the calories of alcohol would give me a head start.

The book told me that calories did not matter. It was carbohydrates that made you fat. And carbohydrates were measured in grams. The maximum you could eat was twenty-five grams per day, but you could have as much protein and fat as you liked. I did not believe the bit about fat, which did not make sense. I wanted fast results, so I cut out all carbs and only ate whatever lean protein was available on the residence menu.

I did not know it then, but the Drinking Man's Diet was the forerunner of the Atkins Diet, which later became known as the Banting or 'paleo' diet, which is in vogue again today. It allowed protein, fat, most vegetables (and whisky) and a little fruit, but no bread, sugar or potatoes. It was a low-carb diet, but wanting swift results, I turned it into a no-carb, no-fat and no-alcohol diet. I stuck to it rigorously and started losing weight. By the end of my first year I had lost twenty-three kilograms and I was thin. But I was also very ill. Looking back, I realise I became ill long before I became thin.

The problem was worsened by the fact that, in the process of losing weight, I proved my theory. I became popular. Boys started dating me, and I was asked to dances, to beach picnics and on outings. I was picked for the drum majorette squad – the pinnacle of my ambition – only to find that I hated everything to which I had aspired, not only because of its meaningless emptiness, but because hunger stalked me every step of the way. Not the pre-dinner kind of hunger when one hasn't eaten all day, but a pain that is well described by the word 'gnawing'. This is a throbbing, piercing hole that makes your fists and teeth clench, and forces the craving for food into every conscious moment; that makes sleep difficult and nullifies almost every normal bodily function. I was seriously anorexic even when I still had a 'sexy' body shape. Dieting came to dominate and then consume my life.

I became terrified of eating, not because I wasn't hungry, but because I feared that if I started I wouldn't stop until I had put on all the weight I had lost. A bit of food (fat-free protein) – which I dared now and again – only made things worse. My metabolism screamed for more to compensate for the months of denial. I understood Maslow's hierarchy of needs from first-hand experience. When a body is deprived of the physiological basics, there is no room for any other care or thought. I went from thin to skinny and then skeletal. I weighed forty-two kilograms when I took the interminable journey back to Johannesburg for the Easter vacation in 1970. It was supposed to be a short break, but as soon as my mother saw how emaciated I had become, she knew that if I returned to Cape Town I might never make it back home again.

In that condition it is impossible to relate normally to other people, because your mind is in another place. Everything you do or say is false and forced. The effort is too much. The only place you want to be is alone, where no effort is required. Escaping company also has the advantage of escaping any confrontation with food. The only effort you are prepared to put into life is to prevent yourself from eating and to prevent other people from forcing you to eat.

But the biggest problem of my anorexia was that it had no name. It was a rare condition back then, and none of the doctors my parents took me to diagnosed it. I was sane enough to know I had become irrational. I knew it was absolutely crazy to be starving to death and be terrified to eat when I was so thin. I lived in a parallel universe, dominated by its own carb-free rules, while trying to pretend I still inhabited the real world, of rational human beings who could enjoy a laugh and good company and share a meal.

My parents did not know what was wrong. They thought I had lost my appetite. They tried force-feeding me, which made things worse. They took me to a medical specialist, who diagnosed ovarian cysts (my periods had long since ceased), but surgery only revealed that this was not the problem.

Eventually, they sent me for counselling, but the therapists were puzzled. One Freudian searched for suppressed libidinal instincts, subliminal psychosexual childhood trauma and related psychobabble. When you are close to starvation, the last thing on your mind is sex – and these theories missed the mark. I had (then) never experienced any sexually related trauma that could have sparked sexual avoidance patterns, which was the reason, he surmised, I was trying to keep the body of an undeveloped little girl.

But Freudian psychology has a neat way of avoiding the disjuncture between theory and reality. If the analysis does not feel real, it is because you have suppressed it. It is there, somewhere buried in your subconscious, if only you would acknowledge it. But how is one to know? I was perplexed and confused. And, even if this diagnosis was true, what could I do about it?

Actually, I have concluded that the problem was much simpler: I had been a plump teenager, craving affirmation, who felt my insecurities would be solved by losing weight. As I got thinner, I got the affirmation I wanted, but by that time my endocrinal balance had already been so disturbed by progressive starvation that I was gripped by an irrational force I could no longer control.

I often thought of the chemistry experiments we had done at school and how a small drop of liquid in a test tube could alter an entire chemical reaction. Whatever endocrine-producing glands had stopped functioning, it profoundly affected my thinking patterns. From my own experience, and subsequent reading in the field, the science of biological psychology made the most sense to me in trying to understand my anorexia. By recognising the impact of the physiological on the psychological, I was able – slowly – to beat anorexia's vice-like grip.

My gradual recovery, with several setbacks, took almost a decade. During this time, I also found my faith. I needed something to fall back on in the biggest personal fightback of my life. I had to believe I would be okay if I found the courage to be myself; that the affirmation of other people did not matter; that I was not defined by the shape of my body.

And whether or not the biblical resurrection is literally true, it became a metaphor for my own life. Slowly, very slowly, I found the courage to start eating properly again. Crucial to my recovery was to start eating small quantities of roughage without too many calories or carbs – a few tablespoons of pure, unprocessed bran that moved straight through the system. It helped fill my shrivelled gut and once my system started working again, and the level of starvation reduced, rationality returned.

Many religions include a fasting regimen as a way to assert mind over matter. It makes you tough, capable of incredible endurance, able to tolerate extremes of deprivation that go way beyond the limits of normal. Nothing I have experienced since even closely approximates the pain, both physical and psychological, I went through during these years.

At the time, I also noticed that anorexia was becoming much more common. It received a lot of press, along with related eating disorders such as bulimia. A former school acquaintance died after becoming anorexic. Like me, she also underwent surgery, but her weakened heart could not survive the anaesthetic. I realised how lucky I was to be alive.

During my recovery I returned to university, this time at Wits, where I finished my Bachelor of Arts degree. I got involved with the Rag committee, and worked with the Rag chairman, Ian Davidson, who became an early and lifelong friend. I joined NUSAS (the National Union of South African Students) but became disillusioned at the prevailing Marxist dogma of student politics that brooked no alternative to the 'revisionist' analysis of South Africa's history. I preferred to become involved in the Academic Freedom Society, of which I became secretary, because it encouraged debate and questioning. As I stood up to challenge the view of the reigning student intellectuals on campus, such as Steven Friedman, I knew I was finding the courage to be myself.

I got my first job, on Saturday mornings, as a packer at Checkers in Benmore Gardens (I was later promoted to cashier), earning the R10 per week I needed for music lessons. During my final year at university I also took some courses towards a teaching diploma and studied shorthand and typing. I was a temporary secretary with an agency called Kelly Girl and worked for a variety of different companies. I was thrilled to get a post as a replacement secretary for Theo Rutstein, the chief executive of Teljoy. It felt grand to be working for a company at the cutting edge of technology, as the television era dawned in South Africa.

At the same time I pursued my dream of becoming a journalist. I applied to South African Associated Newspapers for a cadetship at the *Rand Daily Mail*, and was lucky to make it, the only woman on the second intake of 1974. I had six months to kill before the course started and spent the time working as the national youth co-ordinator of the Progressive Party, where Peter Soal, the director of the Southern Transvaal region, was my jovial and supportive first boss. I helped organise a public meeting for Helen Suzman, whom I revered, and met Tony Leon, the bolshy and articulate youngster who always seemed so self-confident and sure of his opinions. I was a shrinking violet in comparison. I got to know other people who have also made an impact on South Africa's development, such as Bobby Godsell, Gillian Hall and Ann Bernstein.

I worked very hard in the Progressive Party's 1974 election campaign as a volunteer canvasser for Rene de Villiers, a former editor of the *Star* (the politically cautious afternoon daily), who was the Prog candidate in the Parktown constituency. I went door to door from 5:00 to 7:30 each weekday evening, and on Saturday mornings. Back then, suburban security was not quite as impenetrable as it is today. If I made it past the dogs, I knocked on the door, introduced myself, requested permission to enter, and then tried to persuade any eligible voter in the house to support an inclusive democracy. The experience certainly helped rid me of my need for affirmation! But, in truth, I was rarely turned away; most people were ready to engage with me as I made the case for change.

During the 1970s many of my white student contemporaries had abandoned the liberal cause and boycotted whites-only elections. I regarded their position as a useful excuse to do nothing (with a few noteworthy exceptions). Door-to-door canvassing was hard work. It was much easier to sit around debating Marxist theory during encounter sessions in smoke-filled rooms, where the altered states of consciousness had nothing to do with cigarettes. I often wondered what some white lefties were smoking that caused them to radiate such a self-righteous sense of moral superiority over those of us who were actually trying to convert voters.

I had been influenced by the philosophy of the charismatic student leader Steve Biko, who had walked out of NUSAS, advising white students not to try to appropriate the struggle. Before South Africa could achieve non-racialism, he argued, black South Africans would first have to define their identity and liberate their minds after centuries of colonialism and oppression. White activists should rather work to reduce the resistance of white South Africans to democracy. His argument made sense to me. Volunteering in the Prog election campaign was the best option available to reduce the prospect of a racial civil war.

I – and the other Young Progs – rejected the party's 'qualified franchise' policy, which made the right to vote contingent on achieving a certain educational level, or the ownership of property. But this kind of policy detail rarely arose during canvassing. Behind the scenes the Young Progs worked hard to win support for universal franchise – and eventually succeeded in changing party policy in 1978.

But back then, in 1974, all our efforts were focused on attaining the breakthrough we so desperately needed. Helen Suzman had made it clear that if, once again, she was the only Progressive Party member returned to parliament, she would conclude that there was no prospect of progress, and close the curtain on her political career. This added an edge of urgency to our endeavours. In the absence of reliable polling, we lived in hope on random anecdotal 'evidence'. None of us really expected it, but on 24 April 1974 the breakthrough came. In addition to Helen Suzman's Houghton constituency, the Progs took five new seats from the United Party (UP), the staid and timid opposition that shied away from offering a clear, non-racial alternative to apartheid. The *Rand Daily Mail* ran a jubilant banner headline: 'PROGS HIT UP FOR SIX' – and one of the six seats was Rene de Villiers's Parktown constituency. I felt as if I had played a part in changing history. The Progs had polled a full 5.3 per cent of the white vote nationally! This high was better than anything one could achieve in a smoke-filled room, I thought, and I was well and truly politically hooked.

On the same day that the *Rand Daily Mail* trumpeted our success, another event rocked the world. It was the Carnation Revolution in Portugal, as the military coup of 25 April 1974 became known, signalling the imminent withdrawal of Portugal from its African colonies of Mozambique and Angola. Had the Carnation Revolution occurred the day before South Africa's election rather than the day after, I have no doubt that much of our 5.3 per cent share of the vote would have scurried back to the safety of their traditional laagers. Indeed, we would have been lucky to retain Helen Suzman's seat. The collapse of the buffer zone created by the Portuguese colonies would have brought the prospect of majority rule too close for comfort. Sometimes history happens in the right sequence, making progress possible!

When I joined the *Rand Daily Mail* I had to cancel my Prog party membership. It was editorial policy not to allow reporters to belong to political parties.

I was still thin, and often semi-starved, but at least capable of taking an interest in the world again and doing a good day's work. I had all the attention from men I might ever have wanted, but that created its own problems for a young woman in a predominantly male working environment. Sexual harassment was, like anorexia previously, still a nameless condition, but it was rife, and generally accepted as a manifestation of the sexual revolution. At that time, it was unthinkable that the phrase 'No means no' would one day become a slogan associated with the progressive feminist movement. When I was in my twenties, that kind of response was relegated to puritanical Victorian history. And the interregnum between these two points played havoc with my life.

Almost every time I covered a long-running story, some man (usually married) would try to track me down for a fling, often arriving at my flat at all hours of the night. They included prominent priests and attorneys in major political trials, as well as fellow journalists.

I allowed some relationships to happen, and there were also a few I actually wanted. I dated a man named Bernie Fanaroff, who had a doctorate in astrophysics from Cambridge University but worked as a trade union organiser in Johannesburg. Unbeknown to me, he was already internationally famous among astronomers for his classification of radio galaxies. He was as modest as he was clever, and he did not spend time on our dates explaining the Fanaroff-Riley classification (named after him and a colleague). Today he is also renowned as the scientist who headed the bid to bring the biggest global scientific project on our continent, the Square Kilometre Array (SKA), to South Africa. Having dated him all those years ago, I felt a special kind of pride when he landed that project.

I fell for a Swedish guy and lived with him in Port Elizabeth for a while, where he worked for Volvo. I had a relationship with a news photographer for about nine months (even though I discovered he was married after about ten days). He was funny and intelligent and took risks. He fell in love with me, but I always felt guilty about our relationship and did not see it as permanent. I broke his heart. When I was posted to be the *Rand Daily Mail*'s correspondent in Namibia, I met a lawyer who brought me back to Johannesburg, asked me to marry him, and then changed his mind.

The biggest nightmare of all was covering the Commonwealth Conference in Lusaka, preceded by Queen Elizabeth II's royal tour of Tanzania, Botswana and Malawi. There I learnt that politicians and their retinue on the conference circuit like a bit on the side; and the higher their rank, the less tolerant they are of a rebuff. I was an easy target. I wanted good interviews, but I did not want to pay the price, which was sometimes sought with minimal subtlety. In Lilongwe I went out and bought a ring for my finger so that I could say I was married. I could think of no other excuse.

At the time I thought of rape as something that happens when a stranger jumps out at you in a deserted car park or dark alley. There was no word to describe sex coerced by a friend, colleague or acquaintance. This happened more often than I care to remember, from Cape Town to Windhoek and Lusaka, and I never once complained to my editors. If I did, I thought, it would be the last time I would be sent on a good assignment; they would consider sending a woman reporter too much of a liability. If I wanted to pursue a career in journalism, I told myself, it was just an occupational hazard I had to learn to live with.

Strangely enough, these memories of sexual predation are more vivid to me now than most of the stories I covered. But I don't feel psychologically scarred. It happened. It was only later in the 1970s and in the early 1980s that the phrase 'No means no' became the rallying cry of a modern generation of feminists. It heralded a sea change. Suddenly it became cool to say no and mean it. Until then, saying no meant you would be depicted as a frustrated, frigid prig. Distinctly uncool. This empowerment shift has yet to benefit a significant majority of South African women. It is an essential foundation for challenging what is now called 'rape culture' – another once nameless condition that required a name in order to be confronted.

I loved my job, despite the tragedy and trauma to which it exposed me – in the pass courts, at sites of forced removals, and in the many manifestations of the imposition of apartheid in every aspect of life. I felt my work had a purpose, that my articles would deprive South Africans of the excuse, so often used by Germans after the war, that they 'did not know' what was really going on.

In our year of rigorous cadet training, the first stories we were let loose on were the magistrate's courts. Here we had to learn to take accurate notes, and hear that every story has two sides. Both had to be reflected, succinctly but accurately. We also learnt that there was rarely 'moral equivalence' between two arguments: one side is usually closer to the truth than another. We had to learn to evaluate this without letting our personal prejudices enter the picture. All these things were made explicit in the excellent training we received.

Our year in the courts also taught us how to sniff out a good story. With about five cadets scouring the court roll, competition was fierce. Sometimes I hit it lucky – and even found a few cases that warranted front-page status. My mother diligently cut out and filed every article I wrote.

But my passion was politics, so, after a day in the courts, I would type my story (with two carbon copies) on an old clonk of a manual typewriter with wobbly keys, in time to go to political meetings with Tony Holliday, the paper's political reporter. These took place at night, often in remote areas, where political luminaries of the governing party addressed packed halls, as the battle between the National Party's *verligtes* and *verkramptes* (the enlightened and the reactionaries) gathered momentum. The Transvaal was the key battleground for the soul of the party, and the hearts and minds of the volk.

Piet Koornhof's performances were particularly memorable. He was South Africa's sports minister, who sought to counter the international sports boycott by announcing that segregated sport had been replaced by 'multinational sport'. This aroused intense suspicion among the National Party's *verkramptes*, who argued that any deviation from strict racial separation, if taken to its logical conclusion, would eventually bring the whole apartheid edifice down. (They turned out to be right.)

Koornhof tied himself in knots trying to counter their arguments, and said different things to different audiences. 'Piet Promises' became the butt of many jokes. Once, when a cabinet colleague was asked what the government's sports policy was, he replied: 'I don't know, I haven't seen Piet since breakfast.' On another occasion, when a puzzled journalist said he could not understand Koornhof's explanation of the policy, Koornhof reportedly replied, 'That is exactly what I meant to convey.' The same became true of several other policies, as the apartheid government inched towards 'reforming' the system, against the vocal resistance of their *verkrampte* opponents.

Tony and I spent many evenings chasing around platteland towns to record these contradictions. We stayed till question time was over (because questions often elicited the best news angles) and then raced to the nearest telephone booth, or tickey box, to put through a reverse-charges call and dictate the story before deadline. I took verbatim shorthand. Tony had difficulty writing or driving because of a co-ordination problem. I was amazed how he remembered verbatim quotes that he needed for his story, only rarely double-checking against my notes. It wasn't long before I was sent to cover meetings on my own.

The biggest challenge was deciding when to leave a meeting. I was always worried about missing a good story by leaving too early, or missing my deadline by leaving too late. The only technology we had was the public telephone, and so I usually tried to locate one beforehand. Otherwise I would have to go out looking for one afterwards, which always upped my adrenalin levels.

One night, driving from a remote rural venue in search of a phone, I found myself on a rutted, potholed road. Looking over the camber on the side, I saw a straight new road, still under construction. I negotiated the crossing, over the grass, and set off at a real lick on the brand-new tar in the direction of the nearest town (I think it was Krugersdorp on the West Rand). There were no street lights. Suddenly, way too late, I noticed that the road was about to end a few metres ahead in a pile of gravel and rubble. I hit the brakes, the car skidded sideways, mounted the gravel pile and rolled over, coming to a standstill on its back. I managed to unbuckle the seatbelt but struggled, at an awkward angle, with the damaged door. Fortunately, a man in a bakkie on the potholed parallel road had witnessed the crash and he came to my aid. He managed to force open the door and pull me out, but I dived straight back in to look for my notebook. I scrambled around in the dark until I found it, and (before adequately thanking him) asked him to take me to the nearest telephone to make a call. I was a reporter with a deadline, I explained. He thought I must have hit my head and offered to take me to a hospital. No, I need to get to a telephone, I said. I am going to miss my deadline! He drove me into town, where we found a café that was still open and allowed me to use the phone. He stood next to me while I dictated my story from my shorthand notes, which looked like hieroglyphics to him. Once I had finished, he offered to take me the whole way back to the office in the centre of Johannesburg. He was dumbfounded, and I was grateful. Only the next day did I feel my bruises and the whiplash. It was not the last time that the urgency of a deadline would be a good antidote to the aftershock of physical trauma.

In Allister Sparks, I was very lucky to have an editor who understood the implications of the smallest development within the bigger picture. It is a truism that any journalist is only as good as her editor, and I was especially fortunate in the mentorship I received. It was not always gentle. On the contrary, it could be very tough, and I recall repeated occasions on which I was called back to the office late at night to double-check facts or amend copy. Allister made sure we had read our own – and rival newspapers – before the working day began. I learnt that there was no such thing as a weekend or public holiday if you were following a running story; that you went home when the job was properly done, not when your workday officially ended; that you pursued every avenue to get a new lead on the story; that you understood the issues you were writing about, so that you could cover both news and analysis (strictly separated); and that you did not indulge in 'stenographic' *he said/she said* journalism, but understood the significance of each development, so that you could not be 'used' for personal agendas. We were taught that it was possible to get closer to the truth and it was the job of a journalist to try to do that, even if in doing so your assumptions were contradicted. We took our stories personally, and I remember the devastating feeling whenever a rival publication managed to get the 'scoop' first.

The paper produced three editions each day – a rural edition, an early edition and the late final, which gave new meaning to the concept of a 'running story'. We updated for each edition. It was an era before pre-packaged press releases. You had to leave the office and find your story. And you had to take accurate notes, because there were no neatly edited speech excerpts, summarising the points the speaker wished to highlight.

Before long I was being sent on assignments that required high-speed note-taking and accuracy. In the prevailing authoritarian climate, before portable tape-recorders became common, it was crucial to get the facts right, because we could not afford to give our many opponents a valid reason to target us.

I covered the Cillié Commission of Inquiry into the Soweto uprisings, forced removals, pass courts, student resistance at universities across the country, and a host of stories that reflected the brutal edge of apartheid. I became increasingly radicalised politically and knew that the day would come when I would have to do something more than write about the injustices I witnessed.

I spent a lot of time on the road, staying at small-town hotels (usually either called the Grand or the Royal) with communal bathrooms at the end of long passages. On big stories, a photographer came too. Segregated facilities created logistical nightmares for my black colleagues. Apartheid might have been designed around a 'grand plan', but real people experienced it every day through an aggregation of racial indignities that defined each person's place in South Africa's pigment pyramid.

I often worked with the legendary Peter Magubane, who used his old-fashioned Nikon like a tracker drone to find and record the impact this had on people's lives.

Once, passing through a small Northern Transvaal town on our way to cover a student uprising at the University of the North, we were flagged down by a random resident, a burly man at the juncture of life when muscle starts turning to flab. He had taken it upon himself to find out what a white woman was doing as a front-seat passenger in a car driven by a black man. Peter, who had mastered the art of using his camera to invert apartheid's power relations, casually got out of the driver's seat and started clicking. The professional in him recognised the opportunity to capture the menacing stance of this self-appointed guardian of apartheid's inverted morality. After a few clicks, the bully skulked away, like a cocky Chihuahua cornered by a Rottweiler. Peter jumped back into the car and drove off, laughing uproariously at both the incident and my outrage.

He dissuaded me from writing a story about it. We had a more important issue to research and record about the student uprising, he said. Peter was not the kind of journalist who turned himself into the hero of his own stories.

Some of my black colleagues were detained, and after visiting them in prison I received an anonymous letter (posted from Lesotho) inviting me to join the ANC. I had become a fervent ANC supporter, but I was not an underground member. I was convinced that the recruitment letter had come straight from the security police. They were hoping I would join a banned organisation, by return of post, and give them the excuse they were looking for to put me away for a while. I was not that stupid.

But I was also not principled enough to take a much tougher stand against the insidious manifestation of apartheid that seeped into our own workplace in the form of segregated canteens; it is inconceivable, looking back, that we could have let this happen in our own building while we were exposing the injustices of apartheid outside its walls. Some of us commented on this anomaly from time to time, but there is no excuse for failing to take an uncompromising stand. All I can say is that it is often harder to resist the conventions of a hierarchy in which you occupy a lowly rung than it is to take a bold stand against a distant authoritarian government. I look back on this failure with deep regret.

There are a few events in the course of any journalistic career that are of seismic significance. You never forget where you were and what you were doing when the news broke. You know that something has happened that will change the course of history, although you don't know exactly how.

One such event occurred on 12 September 1977.

The dour and ironically titled minister of justice, J.T. Kruger, announced that the Black Consciousness leader Steve Biko, who had had such an impact on my own thinking, had died in detention 'after going on a hunger strike'.

The minister implied that Biko had starved himself to death. Everyone knew that the minister was lying. So did the minister himself, but his incapacity to grasp the enormity of the situation and his palpable disdain for the life of a black man were captured in one of the most callous four-word statements ever made: 'It leaves me cold.'

It is in situations like this that the quality and courage of a newspaper's editor really matter. Allister was determined that we would get to the truth. Some thirty-three years after this episode, he gave a comprehensive account of how we did so in a speech at a faculty seminar on ethics at the University of the Witwatersrand Medical School. The purpose of the seminar was to discuss how to address ethical issues in complex professional contexts – something that medical personnel do on a daily basis.

So do journalists. Allister summarised our response to Steve Biko's death by saying: 'We knew we had to get to the truth – but how?

'It was a story crying out for investigation, but there was nowhere to start. All the facts were secreted behind prison walls and impenetrable security legislation. No one had had access to Biko since his arrest 26 days before his death. The only independent person near him was his friend and fellow activist Peter Jones, who had been arrested at a roadblock with him, but Jones was still in detention and therefore inaccessible.'

On the morning of 29 September, the breakthrough came. The distinguished pathologist Dr Jonathan Gluckman called Allister, saying he needed to speak to him urgently. Allister describes Gluckman as one of the 'backroom heroes of the struggle for justice in this country' who preferred to work in 'the darkest corners of the apartheid state – its mortuaries – dissecting cadavers because "that's where the truth lies"'.

And the truth was recorded in the pathologists' report signed by both Dr Gluckman and the chief state pathologist, Professor J.D. Loubser. In black and white it said: 'Cause of Death: Brain Damage'.

Gluckman swore Allister to secrecy, but said he felt compelled to show us the report because he feared a cover-up was being planned; the story of the hunger strike was being concocted to avoid an inquest, he believed. So he had taken a decision to force the truth into the public domain. But he told us to ensure that his role in revealing it was never known.

'It was a conundrum,' wrote Allister. 'I knew the truth with absolute certainty, and it was obviously in the most profound public interest that I should publish it. But how could I do so when I was bound not to reveal the source of my information?'

This conundrum is common in journalism. 'But never before in my career had the conundrum been so tightly drawn – the need to publish so imperative, yet the difficulty of doing that so great and the implications so dangerous in the prevailing authoritarian climate.

'My first decision,' Allister wrote, 'was that I had to publish, come what may.

'My next decision was to call in Helen Zille. She was a young reporter but I already had a high regard for her level of accuracy, backed up by verbatim shorthand and Afrikaans *snelskrif*. This was before the days of portable tape-recorders and we could afford no mistakes or allegations of misquoting. We needed an accurate record of what was said. So I judged Helen to be determined and smart with a political savvy that I thought would enable her to think on her feet in what was obviously going to be a helluva tough assignment. Not long afterwards I was to appoint her political correspondent, one of the top jobs on the paper, largely because of her performance on this landmark story and her blanket coverage of the inquest that followed.'

This accolade is the highest I received as a journalist, and I treasure it, particularly in the context of the personal and professional trauma that followed Allister's decision to 'call me in' to cover the story.

He sent me to Port Elizabeth to interview anyone who might have had contact with Steve Biko in his final days, starting with the doctors.

With some detective work, I managed to track down two district surgeons, Ivor Lang and Benjamin Tucker, as well as a specialist physician, Colin Hersch, who was also called in to examine Biko when the security police suspected he might be feigning illness.

My question to the doctors was simple: Could they confirm that Steve Biko had died of a hunger strike? If not, why did he die?

I started with Lang, because he was the first doctor who had seen Biko in his cell in the Walmer police station, naked and shackled to the grille, in a semi-conscious state. I found out that Lang lived on a smallholding outside Port Elizabeth, and managed to find it in my small hired car (there was no GPS in those days). My heart was always in my throat for such crucial confrontations. I knew that the 'interview' would probably be over within seconds, but in that time I would have to get the information I needed.

As I approached the house, I noticed that the top half of a stable-style door at the side was swinging open. I came closer and saw the profile of a tall, balding, beak-nosed man making himself a cup of tea, in the company of two enormous, eerily silent dogs. Maybe they were accustomed to people coming and going on the smallholding, but I nevertheless found it strange that they did not bark as I approached.

My mission was to confirm that this man was indeed Dr Lang, and then ask my question before – as I suspected would happen – the door was closed in my face.

'Dr Lang,' I said, as I knocked on the door. He swung round, with the dogs silent sentries alongside him. 'Yes,' he said, still unaware who I was. As he approached the door, I introduced myself and asked my question in the same sentence.

His demeanour changed. 'Get off my property,' he said in a low, menacing growl. 'Get off my property.' The dogs became visibly agitated. 'Get off my property before I let the dogs out.'

I turned and walked away. I had asked my question and I had my answer. If Biko had died of a hunger strike, Dr Ivor Lang would have had no problem in confirming the minister's version of events. His panicked, aggressive defensiveness spoke volumes.

Next I had to track down Benjamin Tucker, the more experienced district surgeon called in after Lang, who could not determine for sure whether Biko was 'shamming', as the security police suspected. I tracked Tucker down to his office. My memory of this interaction is less clear, but it also took place at an open door. Once again, I did not make it over the threshold before the door was closed in my face, but I had landed my question and again received a response that spoke louder than words.

Then I moved on to Dr Colin Hersch, a specialist physician, who had also been called in to determine whether Biko was 'shamming'. I went to his suburban home, and when I introduced myself and asked my question, he responded differently. He asked me in. We sat in his lounge and he offered me tea. I told him I needed to confirm the minister's statement that Steve Biko had died of a hunger strike. The affable, white-haired physician stared ahead of him, visibly conflicted. He told me it was a dreadful case, but that he was under instructions not to talk about it. He would not go further than to confirm to me that Biko was not emaciated when he died; slightly overweight, in fact. The minute I had that, it was as good as confirmed that Steve Biko did not die of a hunger strike. I thanked Dr Hersch and left.

I also tried to interview the police who had seen Biko in his last days. They were polite but showed me the door the moment they knew who I was.

I went back to report to Allister. No doctor had said in so many words that Biko did not die of a hunger strike, and they certainly did not say that he had died of brain damage. But especially from Dr Hersch's account I could state categorically that he showed no signs of having died of a hunger strike, and that there was far more to the story that we would still have to unearth. It was essential to force an inquest.

We carefully crafted the story, which began:

'An investigation by the Rand Daily Mail – which included interviews with doctors who examined Steve Biko in detention – has revealed that the black consciousness leader showed no signs of a hunger strike or dehydration.'

We went on to say that Biko had died of brain damage, and that the facts we had unearthed contradicted Kruger's statement implying that Biko had died of a hunger strike. We published the report under a banner headline: NO SIGN OF HUNGER STRIKE – BIKO DOCTORS. We did not use quotation marks because the three Port Elizabeth doctors had not said this in so many words, although I had been left in no doubt that this was accurate after my discussion with Dr Hersch. Gluckman, of course, was also a 'Biko doctor', but we were committed not to reveal his identity.

We knew our story would reverberate, but even I was surprised by the earthquake that followed. When I arrived at the office the next morning, the place was in uproar. Kruger had become apoplectic, and was threatening to ban the paper. He protested that the report was false and demanded an immediate hearing of the Press Council that very day. The Press Council was a body set up by the Newspaper Press Union, the proprietors' organisation, to ward off Prime Minister John Vorster's threats to pass a press control law if newspapers did not discipline themselves.

Allister refused to be rushed. 'The rules of the Press Council allowed an editor seven days to prepare a response to a complaint and I didn't want to be bullied by Kruger into abandoning that right,' he wrote.

We also knew that in these kinds of situations, time is often on your side. When one opens a can of worms, more tend to emerge; new sources are prepared to come forward (often to save their own skin) when they know the game is up. But our own proprietors let us down. The National Press Union piled on the pressure to force Allister to accede to Kruger's demands, saying that if a censorship law was passed, it would be laid at our door for failing to show that the Press Council could work fast.

Allister records the incident in his lecture as follows: 'It was my first direct experience of the double whammy of Government pressure and unsympathetic proprietors which had driven my two predecessors from the editorial chair of the *Rand Daily Mail* and which was, in time, to drive me out as well, and eventually to shut down that great newspaper altogether just as its moment of vindication was at hand.'

So the Press Council hearing started that evening, before Mr Justice Oscar Galgut. Sydney Kentridge, then a distinguished senior counsel in Johannesburg, argued that the minister had not contested any of the facts in our report, simply claiming that the headline didn't accurately reflect the body of the report because we had not actually quoted a doctor as saying those exact words. Our argument, that the headline was not in quotation marks and therefore not intended to convey a direct quote, made no impact on Judge Galgut.

He rejected Kentridge's argument that this was 'syntactical trivia' that didn't warrant an urgent late-night hearing and the waiving of the Press Council's rules. It was the accuracy of the facts in the report that mattered – and Kruger had not challenged them.

Galgut found in favour of Jimmy Kruger. He found us guilty of 'tendentious and misleading reporting' but also, paradoxically, that the facts disclosed in the report did not contradict the minister's initial statement on the issue, which had been about Biko going on a hunger strike. As with many of apartheid's contradictions, these findings made no sense.

Judge Galgut delivered his verdict at one in the morning and ordered that we stop the presses to publish his statement in that day's edition of the paper. We had to publish, on the front page, Judge Galgut's finding that our exposé of the circumstances of Biko's death the previous day was 'tendentious and misleading'.

I was devastated. Kentridge was furious. He told Galgut that his judgment was 'completely unacceptable' and that no reasonable tribunal could have reached that conclusion.

Allister and I wanted to take the matter on review, but our proprietors were not prepared to back us. They seemed relieved that the Press Council had delivered our heads on a platter to mollify John Vorster and Jimmy Kruger. And so the verdict of 'misleading and tendentious reporting' still stands against us. But, as that great bumper sticker put it, *'Rather be historically correct than politically correct'*. Being vindicated by history is a reporter's ultimate victory.

However, at the time I felt gutted, and I offered Allister my resignation. To be described by a judge as being a 'misleading and tendentious' reporter would be the death of my career, I thought. How much credibility could any of my articles have after that?

Allister would have none of it. He told me I would have to learn to take more heat if I wanted to be a journalist in apartheid South Africa, and that he believed I was up to the task. Never in my professional career has a person's faith in me meant so much. I knew we had to fight on.

Our story thwarted Kruger's planned cover-up. An inquest was held and, battling to hear the proceedings in the dreadful acoustics of Pretoria's Old Synagogue, I filled notebook after notebook of verbatim shorthand notes for the *Rand Daily Mail*'s blanket coverage.

My most vivid memory of the week-long inquest was Steve Biko's mother, who sat motionless in the gallery throughout each day, dressed in black from head to toe. A regal woman of great beauty, grief etched on her face, she heard how her son had been manacled and transported, naked and unconscious, from Port Elizabeth to Pretoria in the back of a police van in urine-soaked blankets, while the police accused him of 'shamming'. I sat looking at her face, wondering how she was processing these words, and how powerless she must have felt to have been unable to help her child in his hours of greatest need. That feeling still haunts me today, perhaps because I have two sons of my own.

I was still looking at her face when Magistrate Marthinus Prins concluded the inquest with these words: 'The head injury was probably sustained on the morning of September 7 during a scuffle with security police in Port Elizabeth. The available evidence does not prove that death was brought about by an act or omission involving an offence by any person.'

My fury was magnified by her monumental grief.

* * *

Covering politics in South Africa was like clinging to a rope that swung on a wide arc between unfathomable tragedy at one extreme, and farcical pettiness on the other. The National Party was capable of shrugging off Steve Biko's death (symbolised by the justice minister's response) while tearing itself apart over the most inconsequential internal trivia. The height of this petty absurdity was the 'Bols' story, which still makes me chuckle in disbelief today.

It was the evening of 19 February 1979, and I was staying in my uncle's flat in Cape Town. I had given the telephone number there to a few of my contacts so that they could reach me if anything newsworthy happened. I felt safe talking on the phone there because my uncle was not politically active, and his phone was unlikely to have been tapped by the security police. One night the phone rang at about ten o'clock. I answered, and immediately recognised the voice. The caller explained to me that the internal party war between the *verligtes* and *verkramptes* had erupted again, this time over a joke Andries Treurnicht had told while replying to a toast at his fifty-eighth birthday party.

Treurnicht was the far-right-winger who had been elected the National Party's Transvaal leader in 1978, just two years after his insistence that black pupils be taught in Afrikaans had sparked the Soweto uprising of 1976.

My source told me that Treurnicht had quoted a conservative church leader, who, when offered a Bols (brandy) after an international seminar where the National Party's policies had been severely criticised, replied that he had had enough 'Bols' for one day. The wordplay caused an uproar, which of course made the story. That a lame joke based on a weak pun could generate such a furore said a lot about the National Party at the time, but it also says a lot about how wars are waged inside political parties generally: your opponents are ceaselessly on the lookout for anything that can possibly be used against you, seeking any opportunity to manufacture outrage. The Bols joke was a classic example of both its kind and its time.

I promised not to reveal my source, and to this day I have not. And no one has come close to guessing who it is. But I did a quick 'second source check' and was satisfied that the story was accurate. I wrote it up in a light satirical style, just in time for the final deadline. Next day the story appeared on the *Rand Daily Mail*'s front page.

All hell broke loose in the National Party and in its supportive press. The fact that the *Rand Daily Mail* (described as a 'sworn enemy of the National Party' in rival media) had broken the story the very next day caused more outrage than the incident itself. The witch-hunt to find my source began.

The next day a young rising star in the National Party, Barend du Plessis, came to my office in parliament in a state of great agitation. He was being suspected of having leaked the story to me, he said. He also had a list of other names, who he said were in the firing line. The story had been turned around by the Treurnicht camp to try to prove 'betrayal' by the *verligtes*. There was no greater treachery in the National Party than leaking a story to the *Rand Daily Mail*.

Letters flew back and forth between the party's factions, which make for hilarious (and disturbing) retrospective reading.

Louis Nel, a prominent Transvaal *verligte*, sent the first salvo to Andries Treurnicht:

> Dear Andries,
>
> In my personal opinion, you told a joke and made a reference that was both vulgar and inappropriate for a person with your particular background and position. I got the impression that you wanted to be one of the men, but unfortunately forgot that there were ladies in our presence. You made a tasteless reference to what can only be interpreted as the sex organs of men. Apart from my own embarrassment at hearing the story, an English-speaking member of the public later responded by calling it 'Afrikaner gutter wit' ... I, and I am certain every other Christian who had to listen to you, felt embarrassed and uncomfortable.
>
> If this letter can prevent a repetition of this unfortunate incident in our ranks, my taking a stand will have served the highest interests of the National Party and of us all. (My translation from the Afrikaans.)

To which Andries replied:

> Dear Louis
>
> You are the first person to have seen an indecent reference to male sex organs in the joke in question and I have told that old joke many times. I have never thought about it in those terms and I don't pretend to be more innocent than any other person. This is simply not an issue for me. My wife knows the joke and she has never yet warned me that it is indecent, for the simple reason that we do not quite make that connection.

And so it went on. The story raged for weeks. What had started as an attempt to embarrass Treurnicht backfired on Louis Nel, who was instructed to apologise and resign as an MP. He apologised for distributing the letter, but not for writing it, and refused to resign. Eventually, he was suspended from the National Party.

But these were just the side skirmishes in a bigger war raging inside the NP over the party's succession, which had burst into the open in 1977 through the Information Scandal, exposed by Kitt Katzen, Mervyn Rees and Chris Day, journalists on the *Sunday Express* and the *Rand Daily Mail*.

The long-running saga, leaked in bite-size chunks, filled the papers for months. It revealed that Prime Minister Balthazar John Vorster, the minister of information, Dr Connie Mulder, and the secretary of information, Dr Eschel Rhoodie, had used government funds to fight a secret propaganda war to defend apartheid. This involved the diversion of about R64 million from the Defence budget to a special fund for use by the Department of Information. They found people who were prepared to act as 'fronts' to make an offer to purchase the *Washington Star* newspaper, to buy off an international news agency, and to launch *The Citizen*, then an English-language National Party–supporting newspaper, in Johannesburg. As the scandal closed in on him, Vorster resigned as prime minister in October 1978, and found a soft landing in the ceremonial role of state president, only to resign again in disgrace less than a year later after a commission of inquiry concluded that he 'knew everything'.

In those days, when newspaper exposés of corruption were confirmed, politicians resigned.

But the battle inside the National Party involved the proverbial rearrangement of deckchairs on the *Titanic*, as the apartheid ship of state headed towards the submerged icebergs, which sometimes broke the surface in catalytic events that changed the course of South African history.

The uncompromising anti-apartheid stance of the *Rand Daily Mail* raised the ire of many white readers and accelerated South African Associated Newspapers' decision to close down the newspaper. The gulf between the proprietors and the editorial staff grew wider, and the pincer movement of political expedience and economic pressure closed in on us from both sides.

I experienced this in many ways. One was the growing confrontations I had with my own political editor (an intermediary between the political staff and the editor). I was accountable to him for my reporting from parliament. Over time, we agreed less and less about the significance of political developments. When this understanding breaks down, it is difficult to continue a productive working relationship. I knew that the *Rand Daily Mail* was losing its appetite for the fight.

An example that stands out in my mind was the argument we had over my coverage (or rather lack of it) of a story that I considered to be a 'non-story'.

It was one of those carefully laid traps for the opposition, a National Party speciality, which their liberal opponents never learnt to recognise. The Progs always assumed, despite ample evidence to the contrary, that people were basically rational, decent and fair-minded. Over the years I have learnt that this assumption is simultaneously the Achilles heel and the saving grace of liberalism.

At the time, 'gonzo' journalism, popularised by the legendary Hunter S. Thompson in the United States, was making a late arrival in South Africa. This is a style of journalism in which the writer becomes a character in the story and abandons any attempts at objectivity. But the National Party–supporting press went one step further – to what today would be called 'gotcha' journalism. In this genre, journalists do not merely become actors in their own stories; they become collaborators of powerful people seeking the demise of their opponents, often on the basis of manufactured outrage or uninterrogated 'evidence'.

Some reporters were happy to be 'used'. This involved a pre-briefing, where you were given the required spin on the story, which then entitled you to a ringside seat in the amphitheatre of parliament to watch the National Party's gladiators do battle with the beast – which had conveniently been slaughtered in the minds of much of the media before the contest had even begun.

I was always excluded from these intimate briefings because I could not be relied upon to play along. In fact, I was once even ejected from an official press briefing by then defence minister P.W. Botha when he objected to my line of questioning.

But I always knew something was up when reporters abandoned their parliamentary backgammon contests and filed into the press gallery instead of just keeping half an eye on the closed-circuit television in the journalists' common room over a cup of coffee (or something stronger).

On this occasion the press gallery was full. Pik Botha rose with melodramatic pomposity to accuse Colin Eglin, the leader of the Progressive Federal Party, of phoning Don McHenry, the American secretary of state.

As the scribes around me scribbled, I could not, for the life of me, understand what the outrage was about. Colin Eglin was the leader of the opposition and the shadow minister of foreign affairs. Surely it was part of his mandate to talk to counterparts in the rest of the world? And wasn't it a positive sign that the American secretary of state was prepared to take a call from a lowly opposition politician in South Africa?

After this initial warm-up, Pik Botha, fulminating in full throttle, piled on the accusations. He said Colin Eglin had betrayed South Africa by revealing to its enemies confidential information about negotiations over the future of South West Africa (now Namibia). It was a vintage Pik performance. 'There has been no previous example of such an abominable, blatant, arrogant breach of confidence against a member of the government as that of the leader of the opposition. If I were you I would crawl into a hole in the ground and stay there. I would never come out again.'

Who could take such theatrics seriously? I certainly didn't. I interpreted them as just another predictable example of the National Party conflating its interests with South Africa's interests; yet another attempt at painting an effective opponent as a traitor. Goodness knows, I had faced this often enough before. It wasn't hard to recognise others receiving the same treatment.

Colin was visibly gobsmacked. He rose to claim his right to make a brief point of personal explanation, as allowed by parliamentary rules. But by this time he was like a man with his head clamped into a guillotine's lunette, with as much time to make his case as it takes for the blade to drop. He could hardly be heard above the jeers and howls from the government benches. He sounded fumbling and defensive.

I couldn't hear his reply, so I spoke to him afterwards. Yes, he said, he had phoned McHenry – so what? But he had never conveyed any confidential information. In fact, he had called McHenry after a briefing from the diplomatic representative of the Western Contact Group involved in the negotiations. It was, he believed, his role to hear all perspectives on the matter.

This made complete sense to me, and I trusted Colin. He may have had a blunt and brusque style, but his integrity was unimpeachable. I had seen the National Party's tricks played out so often that I refused to fall for them. I was planning to write an analytical *Inside Mail* piece (as our op-ed page was called) exposing this chicanery, but I was certainly not going to write a front-page news story based on a maliciously manufactured 'scandal'.

The next morning I got a call from my immediate boss. I cannot recall the conversation verbatim, but it went something like this:

'Why did you miss the story?'

I knew what he was referring to, but my *aspris* gene kicked in.

'What story?' I asked.

'Where were you yesterday?' he continued.

'In parliament,' I answered.

'Why didn't you cover Pik Botha's statement?'

'Because it wasn't a story. There is absolutely nothing outrageous or even newsworthy about Colin Eglin phoning Don McHenry. If there is a story at all, it should be about exposing the motive for trying to create a scandal. We should also be investigating whether the security police are tapping the phone of the leader of the opposition. That would be a story.'

But he did not see it that way. We had been scooped. And he also didn't like the fact that I was giving him lip. The atmosphere in the *Rand Daily Mail* was changing to the point that when a superior gave you an instruction, only genuflection was in order. My anger was compounded by the fact that this non-story cost Colin his job. It turned out exactly as the National Party had planned (and *that* was the big story).

There was also a background narrative. Now that Prime Minister P.W. Botha had successfully used the Information Scandal to oust his predecessor, John Vorster, and neutralise his opponent, Connie Mulder, in the succession battle, he wanted to put a lid on the issue. But Colin Eglin was having none of it. He insisted that P.W. Botha and Owen Horwood were equally culpable. As ministers of defence and finance respectively, they also had to account for the unlawful diversion of R64 million from a special defence fund to fight an undercover propaganda war. So Pik, the effective attack dog, was sent out to close down the issue by putting a lid on Colin's leadership.

During my eight years as DA leader, this tactic was tried against me more often than I care to remember. The difference is that, even in the most difficult of circumstances, the majority of DA decision-makers – in our caucuses, Federal Council and Federal Executive – covered my back. I will forever be grateful to them for that.

Colin couldn't rely on the same support. A critical mass in his small caucus used the issue as an excuse to replace him with the much younger, more charismatic Frederik van Zyl Slabbert, whom the Progs believed would finally bring them the elusive 'Afrikaner vote'. Time would tell how wrong they were. If anyone had predicted then that the person who would achieve this breakthrough was a young, brash Jewish boykie who could hardly speak Afrikaans, they would have been considered certifiable. At that time Tony Leon was a student leader at the University of the Witwatersrand (considered a communist breeding ground by most Nationalists). It would have been impossible to imagine anyone less likely to win the support of the majority of Afrikaners for the principles of an open society. Yet it happened. History is, in truth, stranger than fiction.

By this time, the *Rand Daily Mail* was being slowly strangled, and with it, my passion for my job. When Allister was fired, like his predecessors before him, after refusing to back down in a confrontation with our proprietors, I knew my time was up too.

I stayed long enough to write as much as the paper would publish about the outrage following Allister's dismissal, and then handed in my own resignation. It was gratefully accepted.

Looking back, it is deeply disturbing to see the wheel turning full circle. While there are still many courageous journalists and publications out there, my predecessor newspapers, now corralled in the stable called, ironically, the Independent Group, have unashamedly succumbed to 'state capture'. And *The New Age*, democracy's equivalent of the then apartheid-supporting *Citizen*, continues to receive funding through the front of bankrupt state-owned entities and gets hours of free promotion time on state television. This blatant power abuse would not have been tolerated even under apartheid.

In this context, it is worth quoting the passage in Allister's Wits Ethics lecture, recalling the words of Benjamin Tucker, the Biko doctor, when he applied for readmission to the Medical Register after being struck off by the Medical and Dental Council. 'I came to realise,' Tucker wrote, 'that over a period of 30 years I had been employed as a district surgeon, I had gradually lost the fearless independence that is required of a medical practitioner when the interests of his patient are threatened. I had become too closely identified with the interest of the organs of the state, especially of the police force, with which I dealt practically on a daily basis.'

It is inevitable that institutions, organisations and individuals lose their fearless independence when a single political party has been in power too long, and acts to crush opposition and destroy the careers of its opponents.

The lessons for the new South Africa are so obvious, it is unnecessary to spell them out. But we have broken out of the downward spiral before, and I have no doubt we will do so again.

4

Matters of the Heart

During my time at the *Rand Daily Mail*, my personal life mirrored my turbulent professional life. I soon learnt that a looming deadline was the best way to blot out emotional diversions. But there is a fine line between diversion and denial. Over time, I fell into a pattern: if I worked hard enough, I could ignore personal issues I should have been confronting. Work became my drug of choice.

I covered a lot of news but especially enjoyed writing for *Inside Mail*. Every time there was more to a story than could be covered in twelve inches of hard news, I would analyse it in context, explaining the significance of developments.

Adding 'breadth and depth' to a story was how the *Rand Daily Mail* planned to retain its relevance in the era of television. This meant that I was often contacted by diplomats and foreign journalists who wanted a background briefing on political developments. I was happy to oblige.

It was one of these conversations in the late 1970s that started my long-term friendship with Caryle Murphy, then the *Washington Post*'s southern Africa correspondent (who later became their Cairo bureau chief before going on to win a Pulitzer Prize for her coverage of the Iraqi invasion of Kuwait in 1991). We became firm friends.

Soon after meeting Caryle, I received a phone call from a new correspondent with the Associated Press, an international wire service based in Pritchard Street in Johannesburg. I still remember the first time Matt Franjola called. I wrote down his name, thinking, fleetingly, how typically American it was. About a century ago, an indolent customs official must have mangled some immigrant's name at a port of entry.

Matt told me he had been assigned to cover a story I was working on, and he asked me some background questions. This was followed by two additional work-related calls, separated by lengthy intervals.

One day, sitting in our open-plan newsroom, close to deadline, I noticed heads swivel in the same direction, like a Wimbledon crowd tracking a serve. My eyes followed too, and alighted on a stranger in full stride through the newsroom. I also did an involuntary double-take at his traffic-stopping good looks before getting on with work (my default position).

'Are you Helen Zille?' asked an American accent.

I looked up. 'Yes, and you—?'

'I'm Matt Franjola. We've spoken on the phone. Thanks for taking the time.'

'Pleasure,' I said, my fingers poised above the keyboard to continue the sentence I was typing.

'You are much younger than I thought you were,' he said.

'You don't look like I imagined either,' I responded.

We exchanged a few pleasantries and he left with Steve Wrottesley, a friend of his in the newsroom. The next time he called, it was to ask me on a date. I declined. I thought he was too good-looking for me, and handsome men made me feel insecure. I assumed they would be dilettantish and unreliable, and I did not want to waste my time. About two weeks later he called again, and this time I said yes. He arrived at my flat in an open red vintage MG sports car with a leather belt around its bonnet. I was intrigued, but asked whether we could rather go out in my grey Volksie Beetle (which had once been light green). He asked why; I said I did not want us to make a spectacle of ourselves. He was unfazed. We went in my car, and had a good evening. Two weeks later, he asked me out again, then again, and before long we were what today would be called 'an item'.

I made up my mind not to get too attached. I knew that couples usually paired up at approximately equivalent levels of attractiveness, and I was nowhere near his league in looks. When we went to parties or functions, women were drawn to him like iron filings to a magnet. I still have a vivid recollection of a former Miss South Africa, Wendy Ballenden, demonstrating why a feather boa is so aptly named. She coiled her feathery fashion accessory around Matt in as sensuous a snare as I have ever seen.

On such occasions I would make myself scarce and find someone to talk to. I knew instinctively that Matt would react badly at any indication that I was cramping his style. He had been a war correspondent in Vietnam and Cambodia, and as he neared forty, had never been in one place long enough to put down roots. The fewer demands I made, the more attached he became. He met my parents and siblings, who liked his relaxed manner; he knew how to charm my mom – by going into the kitchen, lifting the lids off the cooking pots, making appreciative comments, and always having second helpings. For all his good looks, he was unpretentious, down-to-earth, and seemingly unaware of the impact he had on women. He certainly wasn't vain. The only possessions he treasured were his two cars and his small plane, which we occasionally used to cover stories as far away as Rhodesia (as Zimbabwe was still called).

But, as with many really good-looking, sporty people, I had a sense that perhaps life had come a bit too easily to him as a young man. We had fun together. I lived from deadline to deadline and blotted out questions about tomorrow, let alone our long-term prospects.

After we had been dating for about six months, Matt asked me to come and live in his rented cottage with him. I thought hard about it, and eventually said yes. But the day I moved in, he got cold feet, so I moved out again. I went to live with my parents as an interim measure, having given up my flat. Two weeks later, he had 'thought it over' and wanted me to come after all. This time I was hesitant. He then pursued me until I did. That was how our relationship worked.

With his cottage as my base in Johannesburg, I would leave for Cape Town to cover parliament. I knew he was seeing other women while I was away. He was quite open about it, which I appreciated. And the more independent I was, the more he was drawn into the relationship. I noticed he was settling down when he acquired two dogs and called them Gonzo (in memory of Hunter S. Thompson) and Tuk-tuk (after the favoured mode of transport in Vietnam). Mostly he just referred to them as 'the boys'.

I was planning to return to Johannesburg over the Easter weekend in 1979, but as often happens in journalists' relationships, history had other ideas. Early in April, Matt called to say he had been dispatched urgently to Uganda because Idi Amin was about to be overthrown.

I arrived at an empty cottage, where I found a note on the table. I kept his first written declaration of love, which captured our relationship perfectly.

> Bub, the boys are in the kennel. In the top left hand drawer of the chest of drawers is an envelope marked PRIVATE IMPORTANT for Helen. In it is a cheque to be given to Clifford Gundle or his wife, Sue. They live at 259 Jan Smuts on the corner of Smit St. Home telephone number 427010. I owe Clifford this money and this is to be given to him ONLY IF SOMETHING HAPPENS TO ME. If I'm delayed, I'll cable you instructions. Bub, I can't tell you how much I love and miss you and would much rather be with you over Easter than see Idi Amin fall.

That letter summed up Matt. He was a warm heart, wrapped in a riddle, inside a mystery, within an enigma, encased in a beautiful yet unpretentious exterior (apologies to Churchill). I avoided the three middle layers, and related to his warm interior and unpretentious exterior. He knew I would never ask who Clifford and Sue were and why he had borrowed money from them. He also knew I would not look inside the envelope to see how much he owed them. He felt comfortable with me because I didn't probe. We lived separately together, in that order. I could sense that was how he wanted it.

As it turned out, I never had to pass the envelope on, and I never raised it again. I lived with my contradictions: in my professional life I did deep drilling to get to the bottom of any story. In my personal life I did not allow a pebble even to skim the surface.

Matt and I went on several long trips together, one to the United States, where I met his parents, Maggie and Matt, staunch Catholics who lived in a suburban house in Franklin Square, Nassau County. There were seven Franjola siblings: four boys (Eugene, Matt, Andy and Steve), followed by three girls (Margie, Kathryn and Helen), all down-to-earth, unpretentious and good-looking. I got on well with the family.

The night before we left New York for Washington, Matt and I slept over in the apartment, near Central Park, owned by Andy and his Jewish wife, Joy, who were on vacation. We arrived to an immaculate flat, with flowers in a vase and a note in the ashtray enjoining us to 'Enjoy!' I picked up the note, delighted at their thoughtfulness, and uncovered what I assumed were two rolled cigarettes. Which brings me to my 'Yes, I inhaled' story. The cigarettes turned out to be two dagga 'zols' (as they were called in South Africa). I obviously knew what a zol was, but had never seen or touched one. At twenty-nine years of age, I thought it was an experience I should get under my belt, in the safety of a foreign country. So we lit up. As an ex-smoker, I had no problem inhaling.

Suddenly I experienced the sensation of my brain expanding. It got bigger and bigger. I started to panic, believing my head was going to burst. When my brain didn't explode, I became convinced that it would start oozing out of my ears. I kept feeling them to establish whether they were leaking yet. My level of panic rose and attached itself to every possible issue. We were going to leave for Washington the next day and I began panicking about how we would get there, about our transport schedule, about how we were going to close the suitcase. Matt started getting visibly worried about me, and suggested he get me to a hospital. That only escalated my terror, because I was convinced that they would arrest me and put me in jail for smoking dagga. I thought it would be better to die of a burst brain on the floor of Andy's flat. Matt made me drink water and kept telling me I was experiencing a 'bummer' and that the panic would pass. Eventually, in the early hours of the morning, I felt my brain shrinking back to its normal size and sanity returned.

It was a salutary lesson. I have never touched dagga or any other narcotic since.

We took several other unforgettable holidays. The most memorable was a trip to La Digue, an island in the Seychelles, where we stayed in a log cabin, ate gently spiced Creole food, swam in the lukewarm azure sea, rode bicycles and read John le Carré.

We also covered a few stories together, flying in Matt's plane. The one I remember in particular was a flight to Rhodesia, which must have been sometime between the conclusion of the Lancaster House negotiations on a new constitution for Zimbabwe in December 1979 and the first democratic election in February 1980, which brought Robert Mugabe to power.

We wanted to observe, at first hand, the process of demobilisation. What would it mean for sworn enemies to make the transition from war to a peaceful election? After decades of enmity and mistrust, could implacable foes build a new society together? Those were the kinds of questions that fascinated both of us, and we had fun discussing them as we flew just above the tree-tops to see whether we could detect any movement on the ground. Sitting in that tiny plane, I recalled the incident just a year earlier, when a surface-to-air missile fired by ZIPRA guerrillas had brought down a passenger aircraft shortly after take-off near Victoria Falls. I got used to the heightened adrenalin levels that were a feature of these flights, and understood why adrenalin addiction sometimes became a problem for seasoned war correspondents.

We were taken in an army jeep by a monitoring group to Delta camp, one of the bases where the guerrillas were expected to arrive, emerging from the bush. The atmosphere was tense and bristling with suspicion. The enmity of war cannot be eradicated by signatures on an accord. The guerrillas feared demobilisation might be a cover for a mass ambush. Journalists feared that the rutted rural roads might be land-mined as a final trump card, played by either side, as the civil war drew to a close. I experienced the exhilarated terror of not knowing whether the vehicle in which you are travelling might be ripped apart around the next corner. We made it safely to Delta camp. It was a peaceful place, and we scoured the horizon through binoculars from the grey-green military tents in the clearing, looking for the first signs of the fighters emerging from the surrounding vegetation. There was no sign of human life.

I wandered about 100 metres along a path towards a koppie in search of a better viewpoint. Suddenly there was movement in the grass beneath the dappled shade of the mopane trees. Their camouflage was so good that I did not see them until I was among them, hundreds of men, lying in the long grass, in fatigues and with AK-47 assault rifles over their shoulders. Alone with my notebook and pen, I froze with fear. A buzz of conversation began, as scores of tense eyes focused on me. My greatest worry was what would happen if they suspected I was South African. I could expect no mercy. After a few seconds a man stood up and moved slowly towards me. He must have seen the terror in my eyes, as he raised his hand, which came to rest on the end of my pen. I let go. In that moment, I realised that my pen was all he wanted, and smiled with relief. He smiled back and I knew I was safe. A pen was obviously a rare technological luxury for people who had been fighting a bush war for years; a smile was a primeval signal of goodwill across every human culture. I am glad I had both when I needed them.

With my heart still pounding in my throat, I turned and walked back to the camp, half expecting to be shot from behind at every step. My every instinct was to escape rather than capture the situation. I was no Peter Magubane.

Shortly afterwards the fighters arrived, in their hundreds. Deprived of almost every comfort, their relief was palpable that the war was coming to an end.

A few days later, I returned to South Africa, but Matt remained semi-stationed in Zimbabwe. On a rare trip home, he told me he planned to return to the United States. I hid my heartbreak, because I sensed that any show of clinginess on my part would bring our relationship to an end even quicker than his departure. I arranged to take over the lease of the cottage, and prepared for life on my own again. But early in 1981 he told me that he did not want to return to the States without me. He had fallen in love with me, he said, and wanted to marry me. I was elated and terrified simultaneously.

Could we turn our 'live-and-let-live' relationship into a marriage? What if we had children? I knew first hand how unglamorous raising children could be. Would he be able to stick with me through the boredom and tribulations of daily life, when he was accustomed to the adrenalin-fuelled challenges of covering coups and wars?

But whatever love was, I felt I had grown to love him too, and that he had much more innate value than his good looks superficially suggested. Above all, I concluded, he had imbibed enough of his parents' Catholicism to take marriage seriously, and I knew instinctively that he would never abandon his children. I said yes.

Matt bought me a beautiful sapphire and diamond ring. We were officially engaged.

On his next trip home he mentioned, in passing, that he had bought a small gold mine in a remote area of rural Zimbabwe. Before, I would have let this news wash over me, but now I wondered how to broach the subject of his having taken such a crucial decision unilaterally. If we were going to get married, I thought, he should have discussed such a major investment with me first. For days I grappled with finding the right method and moment to raise it. As a journalist, I had no qualms about tackling powerful people on any relevant issue, yet here I was trying to muster the courage to ask my fiancé why he had bought a gold mine in a foreign country without consulting me, when we were planning to get married and live in the United States. Today I just recall my confusion, not how I resolved it.

We set our wedding date for 31 October 1981, in New York. We would keep the occasion small, just his family and mine. I knew no one in the States, and we both liked to keep things low-key.

But a seed of doubt was germinating in my mind. I tried to suppress it, but my usual way of doing so – through work – wasn't working. Matt spent most of his time in Zimbabwe, and I spent mine in Cape Town. Every few weeks we'd spend a weekend together, either in Cape Town or Johannesburg.

* * *

On 10 July 1981 my friend and colleague, Barry Streek, called to ask if I was free that evening. He invited me to accompany him to the home of the Norwegian vice-consul who was hosting a function in Cape Town for representatives of the anti-apartheid organisations the Norwegians supported and funded. I knew Barry was going through a low point in his life, and so I went. It was a decision that changed the course of my life.

If I hadn't gone to that party, I would probably be living somewhere in the United States today, with US citizenship and American children.

I was chatting to Barry and his friends when the vice-consul asked me to join a conversation at the other end of the room, where they were speculating on why Allister had been fired as editor of the *Rand Daily Mail* a few weeks earlier. This was the subject matter of my first conversation with Johann Maree, although I didn't know who he was. I said Allister had been fired for refusing to dilute the paper's strong anti-apartheid brand to bolster white readership, considered the key to advertising sales. Allister was opposed to targeting racially defined categories of readers. He sought to attract all readers who wanted to understand what was really going on in South Africa, and wished to make an inclusive society work. He was way ahead of his time.

The first thing I noticed about Johann (after his ginger Afro hairstyle) was his slightly awkward, shy manner. The way he held his drink told me he lacked confidence, but as the evening wore on I noticed another side to him. Our host was wondering how to handle a guest who had imbibed too much and was embarrassing his partner by loud, slurred attempts to be the life and soul of the party. Johann defused the tension by calmly deflecting the guest's attention and getting him into the passenger seat of his car so that someone could drive him home.

'Who's that guy?' I asked Barry.

'Don't you know Johann Maree?' Barry responded.

'No. What does he do?'

'He's a lecturer at UCT and he's coming to my place for dinner tomorrow night. Do you want to come?'

'Yes,' I replied.

The next night, after supper, I went into Barry's kitchen to make coffee. Johann followed to help me, and we had our first one-on-one conversation. Inevitably, it was about politics. Before the water had boiled we were into the race/class debate, on different sides of the argument. He saw class as the major fault-line in our society; I saw race. We served the coffee and he said he would like to take the conversation further. I gave him my number – and I made sure he knew I was engaged.

About ten days later, he called. Did I want to continue the conversation on a walk in Newlands Forest? Yes, I did.

On our walk we talked about politics, but we also discovered we had the same taste in music. I asked whether he wanted to attend a chamber recital to which I and a 'partner' had been invited at the residence of the German ambassador. He said yes.

'You have to wear a suit,' I told him.

'A suit?'

In those days, wearing a suit and going to the German embassy (or any embassy for that matter) was not something a 'leftie' could do without attracting the opprobrium of the self-styled guardians of 'progressive' ideological purity. Johann looked a bit nonplussed, but then agreed. When he arrived on the appointed evening at my Woodstock cottage to fetch me in his rusted Fiat, I had to suppress a chuckle. His clothes looked as if they had been mothballed since the 1960s, complete with a shiny green paisley tie, and shoes with such wide, round toes, they looked as if they had come from a circus clown's wardrobe.

I instantly warmed to someone who was so clueless about fashion. On the way home after a good evening, inquisitiveness got the better of me. 'Tell me about your shoes,' I ventured. 'What about them?' he asked, quite oblivious of the impact his old leather lace-ups made in an era of shiny, pointed, slip-on footwear. Then, 'I inherited them from my dad. He bought them in Harley Street in London in 1967. He said they were the best.'

His reply was all the more heart-warming because he had no idea how uncool it was to talk about wearing fifteen-year-old inherited shoes. (Amazingly, today, thirty-five years since that conversation, and fifty years after they were purchased, those shoes still remain Johann's only formal footwear.)

It was late August 1981, and I went back to Johannesburg to spend a weekend with Matt and to consult the dressmaker who was to make my simple wedding dress, with the lace collar inherited from my grandmother. We had a great Saturday together. After breakfast on Sunday, Matt went off to borrow some equipment from the well-stocked garage of his friend, Brian Harris. He'd be back soon, he said. I cooked lunch. And then waited. And waited. I didn't have the Harrises' phone number, but I probably wouldn't have phoned even if I had. It was not the way our relationship worked. Lunchtime passed. I wasn't worried about Matt's safety; I just instinctively knew he was hanging around at the Harrises'. So I planned to get myself to the airport in time for my flight in his other car, and leave it in the parking lot. He arrived home just before I left.

For the first time in our relationship, I asked him where he had been for six hours. He said that when he arrived at Brian's, there were some friends who challenged him to a tennis match, and they got into the rhythm of the game, which was interrupted for a braai. Why hadn't he just called me to ask me to come over too, I demanded, in a tone I had never used before. He knew I had come up from

Cape Town to spend the weekend with him, and yet he was prepared to leave me alone while he spent the day with friends? I had found my voice in our relationship. He was embarrassed by his lapse, and drove me to the airport in silence. He apologised before I walked into the terminal.

But my doubt was sprouting new shoots. Instead of using work to stop its spread, doubt started smothering my capacity to concentrate on my job. I was about to make a life-changing move across the world. Was our relationship deep enough to compensate for my inevitable rootlessness in a new society? If Matt sensed my dependence, would he feel smothered?

I spoke to my friend Caryle, who understood my apprehension but reassured me about the opportunities that would await me in America, given my experience, and about the depth of Matt's affection for me.

Meanwhile my political involvement in Cape Town was escalating. Johann was writing his doctorate. We saw each other occasionally. Unlike Matt, Johann shared everything with me: his traumatic childhood at the mercy of an alcoholic father who was decent when sober but violent when drunk; his separation from his mother when she took his elder siblings to Britain, while he was 'kept hostage' by his father to ensure her return; his depressions during his transition from adolescence to adulthood; his experience of electric shock therapy in a psychiatric hospital in Grahamstown; his brief first marriage, and a second depression following its break-up during his studies towards a master's degree in economics at the University of Sussex; and an attempt to find a community of friends more attuned to his values and beliefs than the society that had shaped his early years.

I can't remember exactly when, but I knew I would have to deal with my doubts about my impending marriage by making a clear decision, one way or the other. As a journalist, I knew how to work with deadlines. So I set myself a deadline to make a final decision. I do not remember the exact date, but I do remember it was five in the morning. I was always an early riser, but I was hardly sleeping at the time anyway, primarily because of my anxiety about my future.

I got up early and sat in the basement of my little Woodstock cottage watching the clock approach five. As the hour struck, I stood up and said to myself: I can't do this. I have to end it.

My decision was made.

The problem was that my parents were already on their way to our wedding in New York. My mother had never been to America, and my father was taking her there via a short stop-over in Europe. They were in Italy, in a tiny village called Bagni di Lucca, which still had a manual exchange. I asked to be put through to Casa Marcus, where my parents were staying. My mother answered. I had woken her up. Wasting no time on pleasantries, I got straight to the point. Mom was stunned into silence.

I remember two things about that conversation with my mother: me asking her to accept my decision, because I was not going to change it; and her telling me I should see a psychologist to deal with my fear of commitment. I felt she was not listening to me and jumping to conclusions again, but it was no time for an argument. When I put the phone down, relief coursed through my body. Whether or not I had made the right decision, it was now irreversible, and I would have to move on.

Once I had told my mother, I had to tell Matt. He was back in Zimbabwe and even more difficult to reach. I do not recall our exact conversation. I think I blotted it out of my memory because it was so painful. I only remember how shocked and saddened he was. Somehow, I had expected him to respond with the same equanimity he had always shown in deflecting life's disappointments, but he was genuinely heartbroken, which made it even more difficult to suppress my residual doubts as to whether I had taken the right decision. To make it easier, we decided to cut contact, although his final words to me, when I moved my last possessions out of our Johannesburg cottage, were that he would be back to fetch me one day.

When I next saw Johann, I told him I had ended my engagement. His first response was one of apprehension and, with typical candour, he said he hoped I had not broken it off because I thought he might marry me! No, I said, don't flatter yourself; I ended the relationship because I had come to the conclusion that it wasn't right for me. He looked relieved.

We spent more and more time together, and eventually I plucked up the courage to introduce Johann to my parents. I was full of trepidation. They had grown to love Matt, and were still baffled by my decision to break off our engagement; and now I was going to arrive at their home to introduce them to Johannes Gerhardus Bester Maree.

My parents had raised us with an aversion to racial or ethnic profiling, and yet my mother's antipathy to nationalism had morphed into a tendency to conflate the ruling National Party's policies with all Afrikaners. I hoped she would have sufficient insight to see Johann as an individual, not the ethnic embodiment of an ideology. I need not have worried. Both my parents warmed to him during our first mealtime conversation. Before long, he could do no wrong. My mom shared his socialist instincts, which often left me having to argue on two fronts simultaneously. My dad agreed with me, but he didn't like to argue, which meant that I didn't always have reinforcements.

I never met Johann's parents, who died before we met, but I'm not sure his dad would easily have accepted me. I was just the kind of girl he had warned his son against. When Johann left school in Dealesville, he wanted to go to an English-medium university. His dad reluctantly agreed, on one condition. 'You can go to any university except Wits,' he said.

'Why not Wits?' asked Johann.

'Because there are many liberal Jews at Wits, and they are very clever. They will argue with you about politics and you will know they are wrong, but you won't know why.'

Johann said it was written in the stars that he would marry the kind of woman his dad wanted him to avoid.

From the outset my relationship with Johann was one of intellectual and emotional engagement. There were no 'no-go' areas, as there had been with Matt. But I always found myself on the back foot in any debate because I hadn't read 'the texts'. I just knew instinctively that Marxist ideology, developed in homogenous societies of nineteenth-century Europe, was incompatible with the complexity and multiplicity of cross-cutting cleavages in modern South Africa.

When we went out, I would often end up in heated arguments with his friends and colleagues. Obviously, I accepted that class was an important dimension of any political analysis, but not the only one, nor even the primary one. And to propose a solution that would forge one centre of political and economic power seemed to me a recipe for tyranny. As for the idea that only a small, enlightened 'vanguard' could see through the 'false consciousness' from which the rest of us suffered – well, it would have been ludicrous had this self-appointed elite not taken itself so seriously.

Fortunately, Johann was not one of these dogmatists. His socialism sprang primarily from his Christian convictions. He gave away most of his salary, in part to the Association for Rural Advancement, to help fight forced removals, and in part to an organisation supporting the families of political prisoners. He did not own a television. He had a strict weekly food budget which covered a box of vegetables, a bottle of peanut butter, a block of cheese, six eggs, a large tub of plain yoghurt, a litre of milk, two loaves of wholewheat bread, and some meat or fish now and again. (I remember the total weekly budget for food to be between R15 and R20.) Johann had a toaster that looked as if it had been rescued from the Ark. You had to turn the slices manually, and I incinerated so many that I not only dented his food budget, but left his house with a semi-permanent residual smell of burnt toast.

Dating Johann meant giving up a lot of things. He refused to attend anything that was segregated, which meant, for example, no movies. I remember wanting to see a film that was showing in Sea Point, a suburb gradually becoming more cosmopolitan. I suggested we go. Johann said I should phone to find out whether the cinema was open to all races. The woman at the other end hesitated a bit before replying, 'Well, it depends. How dark is the person you want to bring?'

I told her not to bother, and put the phone down. She was, no doubt, trying to be helpful, but the unconscious callousness of her question, reflecting the unstated assumption that rights could be apportioned according to a melanin hierarchy, made my desire to see the movie evaporate.

In 1982 I went back to UCT, primarily to study the revisionist texts of southern African economic history so that I could discuss issues with Johann from a position of comparable strength. Whenever we went out, I seemed to end up in an argument with some dogmatic Marxist (and to be fair, I probably seemed equally dogmatic to them). On more than one occasion, I thought Johann would never call me again, but after a 'cooling-off' period, he always did, and we resumed our relationship. 'You don't have to turn everything into a principle,' he once advised me. 'Just let some things you disagree with pass by without comment.' I still try to follow this advice, with varying degrees of success.

I found light relief in a wonderful satirical campus magazine called the *Clarion*, published by Andrew Kenny, an engineering student.

One of the *Clarion*'s columns was called 'Trotslot', a delightful send-up of the far left's attempt to force South African reality into the straitjacket of their ideology. In his weekly column, one 'Nigel Trots, General Secretary of the Bishopscourt Revolutionary Front' revealed 'the real issues the establishment media try to conceal'.

No writing, before or since, has captured the absurdity of the campus debates of the early 1980s better than the fictitious Mr Trots.

'With sickening regularity,' wrote Trots, 'the Capitalist media peddle the lie that the problem in SA is race, not class, whereas in fact objectively race is totally irrelevant in the South African scenario which can only be understood in terms of a dialectic class analysis. Comrades, for too long we members of the intelligentsia have self-indulgently contemplated our navels in the bourgeois halls of academia. It's time to take our message of scientific socialism to the people. Today, I am going out to meet the white workers of Parow, Brooklyn and Bellville, to confront the white boilermakers and railwaymen with their historical class responsibilities, to insist they unite with their black working class brothers and join the class struggle under the leadership of an enlightened vanguard of intellectuals such as myself and my friend Jeremy (Economic History). The Workers United Will Never Be Defeated!'

Then, as a codicil, this little newsflash: '*Mr N Trots of Bishopscourt was this afternoon admitted to Tygerberg hospital following an "unpleasant incident" outside Van der Merwe's Engineering Works, Bellville. Two fitters and turners have been charged with assault.*'

The *Clarion*'s 'Jargon Generator' was also invaluable for essay writing, providing an interchangeable list of nouns and adjectives that could be coupled in any combination. The nouns included paradigm, parameter, dichotomy, dialectic, contradiction and superstructure, which could be paired with adjectives such as seminal, empiricist, vanguardist, dualist, elitist and organicist. And the *Clarion*'s 'notice board' provided reminders of forthcoming seminars with titles such as 'The historical development of class attitudes in the Transkei: a non-organicist approach using dialectic techniques to resolve the contradictions in the class perspectives of Xhosa speaking chicken-sexers from 1892–1898.'

Fortunately, Johann could laugh at this too. The *Clarion* was the most popular publication on campus, and the piles of free copies were snapped up like slap chips outside the offices of the departments of sociology and economic history.

By the end of the year, I had drawn the conclusion that the Marxist emperor really had no clothes, which was a relief, and I could now hold my ground in any argument (although Johann had, by then, taught me that it was not necessary to argue on every issue).

I remember the evening he asked me to marry him, although he has no recollection of it at all. I replied that, although I admired his values, I also liked my comforts. I wanted a television and a pop-up toaster. (I didn't push my luck by adding an engagement ring to the list.) My request for a television was assisted by a visit he took to the families he was supporting. All of them had television sets, probably paid for by Johann's salary. He laughed at the irony, and agreed that we could buy one too.

The purchase of Johann's first TV set in 1982 was the start of what he described as 'the "embourgeoisement" of Johann Maree'.

We were married on 10 December 1982 at the slightly down-at-heel centre of the Emissaries of Light, which subsequently became the upmarket Cellars-Hohenort Hotel. We had planned to go on a brief honeymoon hiking in Lesotho, but Johann was refused a passport (not for the first time), so we joined friends on their annual Christmas holiday instead. We wanted to spend the first night of our honeymoon at the Houwhoek Inn, near Grabouw, but Johann had forgotten to book, so we went, instead, to a small hotel in Franschhoek, with two single beds and ablutions at the end of a corridor – this was long before the village became the trendy capital of cuisine.

Leftie weddings in those days were low-key affairs. We enjoyed a relaxed Christmas holiday together, blissfully unaware that our lives were going to change dramatically as we became parents in the era of escalating political struggle.

5

'The Maree Affair'

MORE THAN HALF my life has now been spent with Johann. I bonded with him from the start, but took a long time to really get to know him.

Our paths had almost crossed, inadvertently, a decade before we met. He had arrived at UCT shortly after I had abandoned my studies there. I dropped out after the first term of 1970, due to self-imposed starvation, to return to my parents' care in Johannesburg. Just as Johann was escaping the clutches of his childhood community, I was returning to the bosom of mine.

We had come to UCT for opposite reasons – Johann so that he could be himself, I to escape myself, with grim, almost disastrous, consequences. But when we finally met, in July 1981, we were drawn to each other by the shared experience of having been 'outsiders' in our transition to adulthood.

Johann's path had been more difficult, and more counter-intuitive than mine. Years later I read the full story, carefully documented in files in his two-drawer metal filing cabinet with its meticulous annotation system. Johann always knew exactly where his things are, unlike me. Filing has always been the most offensive f-word in my vocabulary. Gradually, throughout our marriage, Johann accumulated every important document, retrievable at a moment's notice.

Among them is a file labelled 'Johann: Personal', which contains a mound of cuttings, filed in date order, stretching over four years, interspersed with handwritten diary notes. The first clipping came from the Afrikaans-language National Party–supporting newspaper *Beeld* of 15 December 1969, headlined 'BOERSEUN BETOOG SAAM'. These three words defy idiomatic English translation. Literally translated, they mean 'farmer's son also protests'.

So what? That shouldn't warrant a report, let alone a front-page headline, but in the context of the time these words conveyed a level of betrayal equivalent to what the army's penal code once described as a 'shameful delivery of a garrison to the enemy'.

The 'Maree Affair', as it became known in the press, told of an Afrikaner boy, the son of a medical practitioner, prominent Nationalist and former mayor of the tiny Free State *dorp* called Dealesville (now part of the Tokologo municipality), who had committed the equivalent of high treason against his people. Not only had he insisted on going to an English university, he became an anti-apartheid activist, the chairman of the university branch of the anti-apartheid National

Union of South African Students, won a World Council of Churches scholarship (after the WCC publicly pronounced its support for South Africa's liberation struggle), and ended up protesting against the 'whites-only' Springbok rugby team while a student at Oxford in 1969.

A more comprehensive dossier of Afrikaner treachery would be difficult to compile in the 1960s.

The story of how Johann's protest became big news back home says a lot about South Africa at the height of apartheid. In Oxford, he had co-signed a letter to *The Times*, with twenty-one other students, explaining why they opposed the Springbok rugby tour to England in 1969/70. The letter looks positively innocuous today, compared with the new South African style of protests to which we have become accustomed:

> We, as South Africans studying at Oxford, wish publicly to associate ourselves with the peaceful protest against the match between Oxford University's Rugby club and the Springboks on November 5. We do this not on a casual whim to join a fashionable protest, but after a careful appraisal of the implications of our action, and the importance of identifying ourselves with a symbolic protest against systematic racial discrimination ...
>
> No doubt we will be accused of being unpatriotic and 'un-South African' but we reject these charges. We have all seen personally the dehumanising and callous effects of apartheid and the authoritarian measures necessary to maintain white supremacy. They are leading South Africa towards tragedy and disaster. We are concerned about the future of our country and the welfare of *all* of its 20 million inhabitants, and it is that concern which motivates this letter.

The only thing that seems amazing about this letter today is the fact that just fifty years ago there were only 20 million people living in South Africa (the figure has almost trebled since then). But when the letter was written, in 1969, its contents were positively seditious.

As if this were not betrayal enough, Johann and three other signatories set off for Twickenham on 5 November. Their 'common purpose' was to stop the match. The field resembled a barricaded battlefield, surrounded by a trench, a fence and English bobbies on benches with batons, standing shoulder to shoulder to ward off any attempted 'invasion'. Peter Hain (a former South African who is now a British Labour Party MP) managed to get past these lines of defence and onto the field, entering the annals of fame or shame (depending how you looked at it) before being dragged off and arrested.

There were hundreds of protesters, but according to the South African press, there was only one *boerseun* – a phenomenon that warranted front-page news and the label 'renegade'.

Johann had come to stop the game. But a few metres away, Tommy Bedford, the Springbok vice-captain (who was being rested for the day) ran up and down performing linesman duties. Tom and Johann had grown up together, close friends, and had played their first rugby match in the Dealesville under-100 pounders, when little boys were still allocated to teams on the basis of weight (and before South Africa switched to the metric system).

Loyalty to his buddy Tom, and the frisson of awe the rugby Springboks evoked in every white South African heart, did battle with Johann's political convictions. Having arrived in high spirits, he left with his inner fabric torn, an outsider from the tribe he had voluntarily left, but with no other port to call home in his personal storm.

The protest received blanket news coverage in South Africa. I remember the 'action pic' of Peter Hain's pitch invasion splashed all over the papers. Little did I know, as a first-year student at the University of Cape Town, that my future husband would soon overtake Peter Hain's notoriety.

South African commentators blamed the demonstrators for the Springboks' defeat by a university side. Johann wrote to his older brother Michiel (Mike), who was a science teacher in the Free State town of Harrismith, describing the protest and his reasons for joining it.

Mike never received the letter. It was intercepted by the security police, who leaked it to *Beeld*. *Beeld*'s embedded journalists arrived at Mike's home and, unsuspectingly, he invited them in. When they asked him about his younger brother's involvement in the Twickenham protest, Mike denied that his brother would get involved in such activities. The front-page article the next day (14 December 1969) wove extracts of Johann's intercepted letter into his brother's denial in a masterpiece of character assassination. The report ended by revealing that Johann's father, 'a leading nationalist', had recently suffered a major heart attack (his third): 'People in Dealesville say Johann's activities are breaking his father's heart.'

A low blow.

But Johann's father also refused to believe the allegations. Yes, he conceded in a newspaper interview, he could imagine Johann writing a letter to the editor. But 'waving placards around with long-haired protesters? Never!'

Die Volksblad, published in Bloemfontein in the Free State, interviewed one of Johann's former teachers, who also rejected the allegations out of hand, describing Johann as 'one of the most capable and intelligent pupils our school has ever produced'. Their shock and disillusionment came full circle when they found the reports were actually true.

When Johann returned home to Dealesville two years later, in his battle to emerge from the tunnel of depression, he found a hostile community, with the exception of his immediate family and a handful of friends who always remained loyal to him personally, even if they disagreed with his politics. He had no desire to be received as a prodigal son, but the extent of the rejection cut deep. He always remembers turning up for a game of tennis at the tiny Dealesville tennis club, only to see some of the other players pack up and leave. They would not play with a traitor.

Johann had returned to South Africa having studied econometrics, one of three Afrikaners with this qualification in the country. He was snapped up by the department of economics at the University of the Orange Free State, who required a lecturer to introduce the discipline of econometrics there. With the name Johannes Gerhardus Bester Maree, and his academic qualifications, Johann somehow slipped through the 'political' filter, and got the contract position for one year.

Neatly in his file, in its rightful place, is his letter of appointment, at an annual salary of R4350 (about R363 per month, or $25 at today's exchange rate).

After four weeks of lectures, a journalist working for a newspaper ironically called *The Friend* requested an interview. On the pretext of writing an article about the university's new econometrics course, the reporter arrived to interview Johann on 9 March 1972 – coincidentally, my twenty-first birthday.

After some initial innocuous questions, the journalist landed the one he had actually come to ask. Was he the Johann Maree who had protested against the Springboks?

'Yes,' Johann replied. 'But if you publish that, I will lose my job.'

The front-page article on 10 March that cost him his job opened with the sentence: 'A man who has been described as a brilliant student of economics at Oxford University and who took part in the demonstrations against the Springbok rugby tour of Great Britain in 1969 has been appointed as a lecturer in economics at the University of the Orange Free State.'

Within hours Johann was on the carpet in the office of the vice-chancellor, Professor Benedictus Kok.

It helps to know a little about Professor Kok to imagine this scene. His outlook on life was well known, because the media sought his comments on a wide variety of contemporary 'evils', from psychedelic music to males with long hair. Both of these Professor Kok denounced, the former for its 'soporific, sensual influence on young people, captured in deadly rhythms … poison converted to sound'; the latter because long hair was 'definitely not conducive to creating an impression of academic commitment, orderliness and discipline'.

A few weeks before carpeting Johann, Professor Kok had given marching orders to three male students who had indulged in some late-night carousing and serenading outside the women's residence. They had chosen to leave the university voluntarily rather than be expelled.

Now it was Johann's turn to face the set jaw and the forbidding black, square-rimmed glasses. He had no illusions about the fate that awaited him.

Wasting no time with due process, Professor Kok handed down the sentence. 'You must resign immediately,' he stated.

'Why?' asked Johann.

Professor Kok was not accustomed to having his authority challenged. 'Because your presence on this campus is incompatible with my responsibility to my students,' he declared, working backwards from the sentence to the judgment.

'In what way?' asked Johann. 'I teach econometrics. Has there been any problem with my course?'

Professor Kok realised he would have to start at the beginning.

'Did you protest?'

'Yes, Professor.'

'Do you regret it?'

'No, Professor.'

'Would you do it again?'

'Yes, Professor.'

With the case for the prosecution, defence and cross-examination concluded, Kok returned to sentencing: resign or be fired. 'Come back tomorrow and let me know which it will be,' he said.

The next day, when Johann returned, Professor Kok had brought in an 'assessor' in the person of the chairman of the University Council, Dr Fanie Naudé, who opened a gap for argument in mitigation of the sentence already imposed.

'Why did you do it?' asked Naudé, clearly hoping Johann would redeem himself by pleading an aberration induced by youthful excess. The university needed an econometrician, and they weren't easy to find.

'Because I am a Christian,' Johann replied, 'and I believe in equal human rights for all.'

Naudé looked puzzled. 'What kind of Christian are you?' he demanded.

It was Johann's turn to look puzzled.

'Are you a Beyers Naudé type of Christian?' Naudé continued, invoking his namesake, the Reverend Beyers Naudé, perhaps the most famous/notorious/revered/despised Afrikaner of the apartheid era. The two Naudés represented the two extreme poles, reverse bookends, of Afrikanerdom.

Beyers Naudé was a Dutch Reformed clergyman who was excommunicated from his church after reaching the conclusion that the biblical justification of apartheid was a heresy. The South African government, for its part, regarded Naudé's views as a heresy against party dogma. He was forced into religious and political exile from his people (although he always remained in South Africa), finding comfort in the embrace of the worldwide anti-apartheid community and millions of black South Africans.

'Yes,' said Johann. 'I agree with Beyers Naudé.' His answer turned the opportunity for argument in mitigation into an argument for aggravation. 'I am a member of the Christian Institute,' he continued, referring to the organisation Beyers Naudé had started to bring together Christians opposed to apartheid across racial barriers. 'But that is irrelevant to my job,' Johann concluded. 'I don't discuss politics or religion in my class. I teach econometrics.'

'You have brought the university into disrepute,' the other Naudé replied. 'We are giving you an opportunity to resign. This is in your own interest. If we fire you, you won't get another job anywhere.'

Johann refused. It was a Friday afternoon. He went back to his room in the slightly seedy Fort Drury boarding house, where he had lodgings, to wait out the weekend. The letter arrived on Monday 13 March 1972: 'Geliewe kennis te neem dat die Universiteit vanaf datum hiervan, nie verder gebruik sal maak van u dienste nie.' (Kindly take note that the university, from the date hereof, will not make further use of your services.)

Next day's newspaper headlines satisfied the rising bloodlust. 'MAREE NIE MEER IN UV SE DIENS', screamed the banner headline in *Die Volksblad*. But the subheading revealed another development – thirty-nine out of his forty-five econometrics students had signed a petition in protest against his axing. 'We do not, in any way, approve of his actions while he was in England, but we regard ourselves privileged to be able to take his course in econometrics,' they were quoted as saying. In the context, at the time, the students showed great courage.

And others stuck their necks out too. One was economics professor Jan Lange, who had appointed Johann, and who argued with the rector, against impossible odds, to retain his services. There was also an Advocate van Heerden, whom Johann did not know, but who took the trouble to contact him. 'I do not agree with your politics,' the advocate told him. 'But the university had no right to do what they did to you. Come to me for advice.' Advocate van Heerden formulated the legal documents that forced the university to pay Johann the balance of his contract for the rest of the year.

As the 'scandal' spread, a church minister, Jan Slabbert, who had married a Dealesville schoolfriend of Johann's, contacted him to offer moral support. And a stranger, Dr Ernle Young, a Methodist minister, wrote a letter to *The Friend* condemning the university's actions. These small gestures made an enormous difference. But they could not reverse the vortex of the tornado.

Politicians, who know how to wring maximum advantage out of any controversy, fell over themselves to claim credit for Johann's firing. The Herstigte Nasionale Party (Reconstituted National Party, known as the HNP) trumped their rivals by revealing that Johann's conduct was, in fact, far worse than had been previously thought.

According to the *Sunday Express* of 19 March 1972, Messrs Koos Terblanche and Charl Hertzog of the HNP held a public meeting in Smithfield (a neighbouring town) and 'strongly criticised the way Mr Maree smoked cigarettes and chatted to non-Whites in public at Dealesville, his home town'. Johann presumed they were referring to his friendship with Jakob Makgotsi.

Jakob and Johann had met in 1960, but not in their home village of Dealesville, where Jakob lived in the 'lokasie' (the separate area for blacks). They had met at the University of Fort Hare in the Eastern Cape (the university was reserved for black students under apartheid), where Jakob was a student and Johann had been part of a visiting delegation from the Students Christian Association at Rhodes.

During the holidays both returned to Dealesville and they met up again, outside Meeding's Handelaars, the town's general dealer. They shook hands and Johann invited Jakob home. News of 'the incident' spread like wildfire and caused a minor scandal in Dealesville at the time. Twelve years later, it had still not been forgotten, and the HNP used it as fuel to the fire of the latest 'Maree scandal'.

Refusing to be outflanked, the National Party's Mr J.J. Human of Harrismith proposed a motion in the Orange Free State Provincial Council congratulating the university on its 'firm stance' against subversive elements, but Mr Sampie Froneman, the National Party administrator of the Orange Free State (the equivalent of today's premier) unintentionally evoked the wrath of Professor Kok by warning that 'communists' were being 'planted' at the university. Professor Kok hit back, saying the university's firm action had been taken precisely to rid the campus of such people.

Johann turned to Catherine Taylor, a prominent member of parliament of the opposition United Party, and the shadow minister of education. She issued a press statement that was published under the headline 'PANIEK OOR MAREE ONNODIG SÊ CATHY' (No need to panic about Maree, says Cathy). She also wrote a polite letter to Professor Kok, asking for reasons why Johann had been fired. Then she went quiet. Johann followed up to ask her why she had dropped the case. She told him she had consulted her party leader, Sir De Villiers Graaff, about taking Johann's case further. Sir 'Div' wanted to see Johann's 'file' before responding. After reading it, Sir De Villiers had warned her: 'Don't touch him with a barge-pole.' She had obeyed.

I always told Johann he should rather have approached the PFP's Helen Suzman. She would have defended him on the principle of free speech and freedom of conscience, whatever his 'file' said.

Editorials appeared across the country. And the letter writers got going. One woman urged that attempts should be made to 'rehabilitate' Johann, otherwise another 'clever, capable Afrikaner' would be 'lost to the volk'. Another replied that he'd got what was coming to him and his case would serve as a warning to others.

In the meantime, Johann contacted Francis Wilson, a senior lecturer in economics at the University of Cape Town. Coincidentally, a junior lecturer had unexpectedly left the department, which enabled Johann to fill in for the rest of the year.

He left the University of the Orange Free State as a villain, and arrived at UCT as a minor hero. What was more, due to Advocate van Heerden's intervention, Free State University had to pay him R90 per month to bridge the difference in salary!

UCT might as well have been another planet. It was the year of major student protests against apartheid education and the detention of black student leaders, culminating in a sit-in at St George's Cathedral, in the year Geoff Budlender, who would later become one of the pioneers of public interest law in South Africa, was Student Representative Council president.

Geoff still laughs when he recalls his first encounter with Johann's case, in a conversation with UCT's vice-chancellor and principal, Sir Richard Luyt. Sir Richard mentioned that he had called Benedictus Kok to ask why he had fired Johann Maree. Sir Richard needed to hear first hand before Johann started at UCT.

'Have you met him?' Kok asked Luyt.

'No,' Luyt answered.

'Well, you'll know why when you do,' said Kok.

Luyt concluded that he was about to meet a wild, pot-smoking anarchist. It was no small surprise to meet the short-back-and-sides, shy, self-effacing, slightly awkward Afrikaner who spoke fluent English. (These were the days before the Afro.)

On his arrival in Cape Town, Johann rented a room in a private home next to the railway line in Kenilworth. He recalls attending his first meeting of the Christian Institute. He arrived early and found himself treated with intense suspicion by another early arrival, who ethnically profiled this Afrikaans stranger as a probable security police spy. This type of reaction is one of the reasons why, in deeply divided societies, people find it so difficult to get out of their box. Others do not easily let you into theirs – and it is cold outside. Group boundaries become entrenched, and those who claim to oppose ethnic stereotyping are often among the most exclusive – and excluding – in their attitude towards people who do not fit the mould. But, by this stage, Johann had learnt to disregard these slights and was soon fully accepted and active in the pursuits that gave his life purpose.

One of these was defending academic freedom, and he began a one-man campaign for an international academic boycott against the University of the Orange Free State. He wrote letters to academic associations in the United States and Britain to argue the case. 'Besides totally abrogating the principle of academic freedom, the UOFS has also set an extremely dangerous precedent. Once established that a lecturer can be dismissed for his political views, fear will gag many academicians,' he wrote.

Johann warned that the threat extended to liberal universities as well, because 'the ruling Nationalist Party and their supporting news media are increasing their hostility towards liberal universities and academics and threatening to remove the autonomy of these universities if they do not conform to the government's political precepts and suppress any dissident voices in their midst'.

He continued: 'In order to prevent this corrosion of academic freedom from progressing any further, I make an urgent appeal to you to act against the UOFS.' He then proposed that the 'non-recognition of all degrees of the UOFS would really make the University aware of the abhorrence with which the international academicians view their act and at the same time make them much more hesitant to violate academic freedom in future'.

He received one reply, from a Dr Michael Dummett of All Souls College, Oxford. Unfortunately, said Dr Dummett, it was too late to raise the issue of the non-recognition of UOFS degrees in the University Congregation before the start of the new academic year. However, 'I still hope to introduce a resolution to this effect although, after some consultation, I am very pessimistic about its chances of success.'

Johann replied to thank him and added: 'Even if the vote to withdraw recognition of the degrees of the UOFS gets relatively small support, the university will learn that its arbitrary actions are watched critically from overseas and could just inhibit them from doing so next time.'

And that is where the campaign ended. It was only eight years later that the calls for an academic boycott really took off – but it became a blunt instrument, targeting institutions that had opposed apartheid and those that had supported it alike, and often doing more harm than good to the cause it purported to support.

Looking back, Johann considers his firing from the University of the Orange Free State to have been a blessing in disguise. The month he had spent lecturing there was a minor diversion in his life. Of far greater significance to him was his involvement, between 1973 and 1977, in the effort to resurrect the black trade union movement, after the South African Congress of Trade Unions had effectively been crushed by the state during the preceding decade.

The attempt to achieve an industrial-relations framework based on equal rights and recognition for all workers was at the cutting edge of the anti-apartheid struggle during the 1970s. It was also a dangerous pursuit, because the state recognised the risk of the unions becoming proxies for banned political parties. The small group of NUSAS students, academics and worker activists had to approach matters carefully. They established the innocuous-sounding Western Cape Workers' Advice Bureau. It soon became the Western Cape General Workers' Union, and then just the General Workers' Union.

Early in 1973, the NUSAS leadership was banned, a major setback for the emerging trade union movement. But the real risk to which they were exposing themselves was best reflected in Johann's account of the death of a colleague, Storey Mazwembe. Johann's handwritten tribute to Storey was also there, in his personal cuttings file.

Storey died in detention in the early hours of 2 September 1976, at the age of thirty-three.

He had come to Cape Town as a migrant worker from Engcobo, Transkei, and lived with his wife in an officially all-male compound in Gugulethu. While working at Lupini Brothers, manufacturing flooring, Storey attended a summer-school course Johann had co-organised in February 1975, called 'Migrant Labour in the Western Cape'. It included community workshops.

It was a course designed to recruit activists. Based on the 'education for liberation' approach of Paulo Frere, it offered industrial-relations training, as well as a link to organisations through which participants could become actively involved in the struggle for change.

Storey stood out, Johann recalled, because he was so vibrant and engaged. By the end of the course, he had been recruited into the Advice Bureau. He started organising workers at Lupini Brothers, with Johann as the trainer of the workers' committee Storey chaired. In retaliation, the company did not renew his contract when it expired at the end of 1975.

As a result, Storey lost not only his job, but his space in the compound and his right to remain legally in Cape Town under the notorious pass laws.

In order to legalise his presence in Cape Town, Johann employed Storey as a field worker to assist with research on migrant workers. 'This justified Storey's presence among migrant workers,' Johann wrote. This job was a good cover for Storey's real job, as an organiser for the Workers' Advice Bureau.

When the countrywide student revolt hit Cape Town in August 1976, the bureau linked up with student leaders. Late at night on 1 September Storey was detained, together with Zora Mehlomakhulu, the Advice Bureau's organiser. Less than three hours later, Storey was dead. According to police, they found him hanging in his cell when they undertook a routine police inspection of the cells at 7:40 that morning. He had been dead several hours. At the inquest, police claimed that Storey had hanged himself with strips he had cut from a blanket, allegedly with a razor blade he had found in the cell. The inquest court ruled he had committed suicide.

'Storey died when he was only 33 years old, in the prime of his life,' Johann wrote. 'He literally gave his life in the struggle for the liberation and emancipation of his fellow black workers. He should always be remembered for his role and supreme sacrifice.'

This episode had a far greater impact on Johann's life than anything he had experienced before. His ordeal at the University of the Free State was a mere ripple in the pond compared to this tidal wave. Expecting to be detained at any time, Johann wrote a second letter home, this time to his mother, to explain (yet again) what he had been doing, and why. He gave it to a lawyer to post, in case he was detained. Fortunately, there was no need to do so. Not long afterwards he faced another brush with the law when he was charged under the Group Areas Act for bringing a black family to live in his home after the police demolished their shack in Modderdam outside Cape Town.

But the tide was turning. Three years later, in 1979, the Wiehahn Commission recommended that black workers be granted the same rights to organise as other workers. Johann wrote his doctoral thesis on this momentous transition.

Unlike Johann, I do not regard his transition from the Free State to UCT as a peripheral detour from the main current of his life. For me it symbolises a much bigger and more significant component of South Africa's transformation that has yet to be adequately understood.

The story that remains to be told is how the majority of Afrikaners (and whites in general) made the transition, within the space of a few years, from defending an exclusive and oppressive ethnic nationalism to supporting a rights-based constitution, guaranteeing individual freedoms – and then surrendering exclusive power peacefully through the ballot box.

Although historians and political analysts usually differ in their interpretations of the past and their predictions for the future, there was, at the time, a remarkable consensus about South Africa's future prospects as the 1980s drew to a close. The inescapable logic of our country's history was propelling us towards a racial civil war.

The prevailing wisdom held that one lesson of history was unambiguous: a government built on ethnic, religious or racial foundations does not give up power unless it is militarily defeated.

What South African historiography still lacks is an adequate study of why they were all wrong. Much of the credit has, with justification, been accorded to the extraordinary reconciliatory leadership of Nelson Mandela. But perhaps Arnold Toynbee also had a point, in his momentous twelve-volume *A Study of History*, when he identified the role of creative minorities, with bold and perceptive leaders, as a crucial and largely unrecognised factor in the development of civilisations throughout history.

What's more, having lost power, Afrikaners (and whites in general) did not retreat into a narrow ethnic party aimed at protecting sectarian interests. On the contrary, the far right, which sought to mobilise whites, and especially Afrikaners, continued to shrink at every election, and the inclusive alternative, symbolised by the Democratic Alliance, showed sustained growth from all population groups. Probably as a result of losing political power, a new generation of Afrikaners entered the economy and achieved spectacular success, just as the politically marginalised English had done several decades earlier.

As I was writing this chapter, the last National Party president, F.W. de Klerk and his wife Elita invited Johann and me to join a small dinner party at their home. It was an evening of interesting discussion at their beautifully appointed table. At some point, the talk turned to the growth of the Democratic Alliance. F.W. said it was not new growth. It represented the consolidation of opposition parties. I disagreed. His analysis, I argued, disguised a transition that was probably unique in history. It was a transition from a political culture, epitomised by Benedictus Kok and Fanie Naudé at the University of the Free State, to the embrace of 'an open, opportunity-driven society for all' – the antithesis of racial nationalism.

He could live with my analysis, F.W. said, as long as I was not implying that he had become a 'Prog' – a reference to the Progressive Party which for years had represented liberal white voters in the apartheid parliament, with Helen Suzman as its most famous public face. After all these decades, and the momentous transition he had ushered in, F.W.'s reflexive antipathy towards the Progs remained. I undertook not to label him a Prog, but added that I regarded it as a compliment!

Despite the ultimate recognition of the Nobel Peace Prize, F.W. de Klerk's leadership in navigating our transition has yet to be adequately acknowledged in South Africa. It has few parallels in history.

I had grown up imbibing the values of freedom, fairness and opportunity with my mother's milk. If I had been raised in a Nationalist home, would I have arrived at similar insights? Maybe not. That is what made Johann's story, and the subsequent story of several million others, so remarkable. It is an example of the many factors that make South African history so fascinating, particularly in the world of the twenty-first century, as new migration patterns destroy the comfortable insulation of established nation states.

Managing complex, plural societies is the world's future, and if we get it right, South Africa can lead the way.

6

Birth Pains and Death Throes

WHEN JOHANN AND I got married in December 1982, we were almost forty and thirty-two respectively. That was (then) unusually late to start a family, so we got going – only to discover that getting pregnant was not as easy as we had always assumed when we were trying not to. I had never taken the contraceptive pill because of my history of anorexia. The doctor did not want to destabilise my hormone balance again. As a result, I knew a lot about preventing an unwanted pregnancy but very little about how to make it happen (beyond the birds-and-bees basics). So I did some research.

I learnt that a woman's temperature fluctuates with her cycle, and rises slightly at ovulation. By taking your temperature first thing every morning, you can work out when ovulation occurs. I also read that male sperm swims faster, but that female sperm lives longer. This meant that if conception took place around the exact time of ovulation, the baby was more likely to be a boy. If the sperm had to hang around for a bit, waiting for an egg to arrive, conception was more likely to produce a girl.

This interested me, because I had always had a very strong preference for having boys. I asked myself why. I think it is because (at the time) I thought life would be easier for a boy than a girl. At least he could grow up being accepted for who he was, rather than for what he looked like, I thought.

I read more. I learnt that male sperm thrive in an alkaline environment, while female sperm can survive a longer time in a more acidic context. I started taking my temperature every morning and plotting it on a graph. The moment I noticed a temperature rise, I would take a bath with a few spoons of bicarbonate of soda (to lift my PH – alkalinity – level) and it was time for action.

'Can't we just do this the old-fashioned way?' Johann asked.

'We don't have the luxury of time,' I insisted.

After two early miscarriages, we eventually achieved a lasting result. I still have my temperature graph of February 1984 with the words 'I AM PREGNANT', which I wrote on it six weeks later, after my pregnancy was confirmed.

My main symptom was a massively intensified sense of smell. I could smell water coming out of a tap and chocolate inside its wrapper. During the last weeks of my pregnancy I became a caricature of the nesting instinct. We had just moved house, to Rosebank, near the railway line, and I proceeded to clean every square inch of our new home. One evening Johann arrived home to find me, eight and a half months pregnant, precariously balanced on the top of a ladder cleaning the ceiling with a mop. He instructed me to get down.

My gynaecologist had predicted that I was having a girl. It was the era before scans could produce anything more than a blur for the untrained eye. I hadn't told him about my preference for a boy, because I felt slightly guilty about caring what my child's sex would be. All that matters is the baby's health, I told myself.

'How do you know it's a girl?' I asked.

'I can tell by the shape, the way you are carrying, and the way she is lying,' he replied.

When Paul was born – after a twenty-hour labour and a difficult, but perfectly executed, forceps delivery – he turned out to be the only boy in the large maternity ward I shared with about ten other mothers at the Mowbray Maternity Hospital. I was elated and wasted no time in telling my doctor he had been wrong.

'No,' he insisted, 'I said it would be a boy. Look here, I wrote it on your folder.'

I looked. There, indeed, he had written: 'boy'.

When I was pregnant with Thomas, four years later, my doctor again predicted I was having a girl, and then wrote something in my folder.

'Let me see what you wrote there?' I asked him.

He burst out laughing. I had discovered his trick, he told me. He would predict one sex and write down the other. If the baby turned out as predicted, the mother would never challenge it. If the prediction was wrong and the mother queried it, he would show her what he had written in the folder!

I often wished politicians could pull the same trick, but our predictions are written down by others, plagiarised if they are right, and brought back to haunt us if they are wrong.

Paul's birth precipitated the first rough patch of our marriage. We had a perfectly healthy little boy, but it came close to turning out differently. Without going into all the details, after fourteen hours of heavy labour and minimal dilation, the medical team overruled my determination to have a natural birth. 'This is the twentieth century, you know,' the labour ward sister said archly, as the epidural was administered.

With the pain under control, Johann dashed to UCT in time to give his scheduled lecture to his first-year students. On his return, he watched the monitor tracking the baby's heartbeat. Suddenly, he got up and left the labour ward. After what seemed like an eternity, he returned with a sister, who turned me around, attempting to get the baby's heart rate to return to normal. She succeeded. Not long afterwards the doctor arrived. My memory is a blur of leg straps, bright lights, forceps, the fear on Johann's face, and the power with which the doctor pulled. I couldn't believe that any baby could survive that, but was powerless to do anything about it. The baby had gone into stress and had to be taken out, fast. Never, before or since, have I been so helplessly vulnerable and dependent on the expertise of others. I knew that the outcome of those few minutes would shape the rest of our child's life, and mine and Johann's. Paul emerged a light shade of purple, with two tiny red marks on his temple bones, where the forceps had been perfectly positioned to prevent damage to his brain. I was amazed, grateful to Dr Baillie, and furious with Johann.

I learnt later that being furious with your husband during and after a difficult labour is standard textbook stuff.

'How could you go and give a lecture to your students in the middle of my labour?' I demanded.

'Because your pain was controlled, you dozed off, your labour still had a long way to go, and my lecture was on a topic that is going to be in their exams,' he replied.

I was implacable. 'If you had come back half an hour later, our baby could have been damaged.'

'Well, I didn't and he isn't,' replied Johann. Which just got me angrier. I was in no mood for logic.

I battled to breastfeed and the baby got jaundice. I battled to follow the instructions on how to fold a nappy for a baby boy, despite the detailed diagram in Marina Petropoulos's lovely baby book. I battled with a hungry, crying baby who would not sleep. I battled with everything. I wondered if this was normal. Didn't all people come into the world this way? How could it be so hard? How could mothers raise multiple children in shacks with no running water and sanitation?

My parents came down from Johannesburg to stay with us and meet their first grandchild. We had planned their visit to coincide with a trip Johann was scheduled to take, to a conference abroad, because his application for a passport had been granted for the first time in fifteen years. I had no problem with this arrangement before the birth but became resentful afterwards.

Johann returned after a week abroad to find a huge pile of exam scripts waiting to be marked and a wife in the throes of a full post-natal depression. My parents returned to Johannesburg and we were on our own in a house that was not yet a home, with an old, fraying asbestos roof, and a baby who wouldn't sleep. I was producing hardly any milk, but was determined to breastfeed, so I combined the breast and bottle at each feed, which took an hour each time. If he drank enough I could get him to doze off, but he would wake again within an hour, usually just as I was going back to sleep. And the routine would begin again. Extreme sleep deprivation aggravated my depression. In a twenty-four-hour cycle I was lucky to find thirty minutes to shower and get out of my dressing gown.

I was on a hamster wheel, running as hard as I could and getting nowhere. The ancient washing machine that had come with the house (I think the original owner was pleased to be rid of it) couldn't cope with a load of nappies, so first thing each morning I would do hand-to-hand combat with the pile of nappies soaking in the steriliser bucket. The greatest achievement of my day was standing back and admiring the row of washed, white nappies on the line. Within thirty minutes the next nappy was back in the bucket. Sisyphus endlessly pushing the rock up the hill, only to watch it roll down again, was nothing compared to the nappy routine.

But what I fixated on was the fraying blue asbestos roof. I had discovered it on one of my cleaning expeditions during my 'nesting' phase. I became convinced that I was putting our baby at risk by living in a place where blue asbestos was flaking off the roof and, presumably, floating in the air. The more I read about the dangers of asbestos, the more concerned I became. Eventually, to survive the combination of work pressures and my depression, Johann sent me and our son to live in Johannesburg with my parents.

At this time my sister Carla, who was studying in London, experienced a serious setback with what remained of her hearing, which hit us all profoundly. We all felt helpless, and again, amazingly, she managed to deal with this crisis, in an unfamiliar environment, under the pressure of a very demanding design course. The guilt I felt about being depressed when, objectively, I had everything to be joyous about added to my bewilderment. The prescribed medication seemed to make no difference.

As I started to recover, I wrote an article on post-natal depression for *Fair Lady* magazine. Of all the hundreds of articles I had written in my life, none hit a collective nerve like this one did. I realised what a silent epidemic post-natal depression was. I started a post-natal depression support group with a few other mothers in similar situations. How did single mothers cope, I wondered.

When I returned to Cape Town, we moved into a friend's flat. I refused to move back to our house until Johann had the roof sealed and painted. But I was never really comfortable until we had saved enough money to change the roof a few years later.

Another aspect to my depression was undoubtedly the deteriorating political environment. On 7 October 1984, two days before Paul's birth, the South African Defence Force had entered Sebokeng, in the Vaal Triangle, to crush a popular uprising. I feared we were moving into a full-scale civil war. Conscription still loomed large for young men and I dreaded the prospect of my son having to face the same choice as my brother had had to do ten years earlier – being conscripted into an unjust war, going to jail or leaving the country. What had I been thinking about when I decided to bring a child into this world? And how could I have wanted a boy? It was too late to ask myself these questions, so I joined the End Conscription Campaign.

I would not have survived that period without the assistance of Eunice Voyiya, who had six children of her own. I marvelled at her. How had she managed it? The appearance of her coming around the corner at nine o'clock each morning was the highlight of my day. She took my baby, slung him onto her back, tied him on with a cloth, and calmly went about her chores while he slept contentedly. In the afternoon, when she handed him back to me, he inevitably started yelling again. And I began counting the hours till Eunice's reappearance.

Our friends were marvellous in the support they gave us, and none more so than Ingrid and Pieter le Roux, who invited us to go on holiday to Keurbooms River with them and their three young sons. They could see we needed support. That break was the start of my recovery – and the start of a holiday odyssey that continues to this day. After renting a holiday cottage in Keurbooms every year for five years, we eventually pooled resources to buy a cottage ourselves, and have spent many unforgettable family holidays there, jointly and severally.

At about one year, Paul started at UCT crèche, so that I could begin working again. We were battling to make ends meet on an academic's salary, so I started work as a freelance consultant focusing on public policy. Thus began the era of ear infections, grommets and repeated colds (through a fog of exhaustion). But there were some lighter moments, many that we still laugh about today.

One was the occasion I was due to present a research report to a client. I had worked almost through the night, before starting the morning routine to get Paul to the crèche. It always amazed me how much equipment – from nourishment to clothing – was required to get such a small person through the day. Running slightly late, I strapped him in his baby car seat and drove to La Grotta, the beautiful down-at-heel mansion that housed UCT's educare centre. On the way up the long drive, just as I slowed down to negotiate the speed hump, I realised I had forgotten the research report on my desk at home. 'Fuck,' I exclaimed in frustration.

It was the only word capable of expressing my exasperation with myself, despite Johann's anti-swearing policy, but, I reckoned, he wasn't around and my baby didn't understand what it meant. Apart from 'mama' and 'dada', the only word Paul had said so far was 'clock'.

Suddenly, out of the back seat, loud and clear, came his fourth word – 'fuck'. He said it again, and again and again. Now, apart from being late and having to return home to fetch my client's presentation, I had to deal with a baby who loved the sound of a word he should never have heard.

I unstrapped him from his car seat while he continued chanting his new word. I couldn't possibly take him to his class, so I walked around the large La Grotta garden, careful to avoid contact with any other parent arriving with their child. 'Look at the flower,' I said to Paul, desperate for an alternative 'f' word. 'Flower, flower, flower ...'

I soon realised it wasn't the 'f' that fascinated him, but the 'ck', which is probably why 'clock' had been his first, much-loved and oft-repeated word. He now had another, which he instantly preferred because he sensed it pressed a panic button in me. He was repeating his line like a rapper in the zone. I finally sat down on the stone step and put him on the breast. Somehow, whatever it took, I had to get him to stop talking.

Thirty minutes later I had delivered my son to his class and was on my way back home to fetch my presentation. I apologised to my client ('unforeseen circumstances') for being late.

That was not the end of the story, however. Every morning when we drove over the speed hump on the way up to La Grotta, Paul's Pavlovian response kicked in and he would start repeating his favourite word again. Even if I slowed down to a crawl, hoping he would not notice that we were going over the speed hump, it didn't help. For weeks afterwards I had to build an extra thirty minutes into our routine to get him focused on something else before I could take him to his class. I always expected his teachers, Robbie and Arabella, to call me aside when I fetched him to have a few stern words about his language, but it never happened. Nevertheless, I had learnt a hard lesson about not swearing in front of the children.

Of all the wonderful aspects of a young child's development, language intrigued me most. From about a year, Paul's vocabulary started expanding rapidly, and it was fascinating to notice the associations he created.

It was the era of videos, which he loved watching long before he could understand them. When they came to an end I would say, 'Let's rewind', and he quickly learnt that this meant the video would go back to the beginning and start again. He began to apply the word to other situations. I was still breastfeeding him, so before long, when he had sucked me dry on the one side, he would put back his head and say, 'Rewind, Mommy', and I would duly change sides.

Johann spoke only Afrikaans to Paul, I spoke English and Eunice spoke Xhosa. He was soon understanding and speaking in combinations of all three. My friend Judy Baron once visited me on her bike. He greeted her: 'Molo, Judy,' he said. 'Nice fiets.' Three words in three languages.

At the UCT crèche, Paul's closest friend was Malusi Magele, Mamphela Ramphele's younger son. I discovered that a key feature of a child learning to talk is their focus on the last syllable of multi-syllabic words. So instead of saying Malusi, Paul called his friend 'Lusi'. One day, as Paul arrived at crèche, he called out, 'Lusi, Lusi!' His teacher pulled him aside and said, 'Paul, he is not Lusi. He is MAlusi.' Paul thought about this for a moment. Then his brow furrowed. He looked his teacher in the eye and said firmly, 'No, he is not YOUR Lusi, he is MY Lusi.'

After eighteen months my depression started lifting, but it took me almost four years to consider the possibility of having another child. After two further miscarriages, we decided to be a one-child family, but by that time Thomas was already on the way. This time, I told myself, I would do things properly. We hired a midwife, who prepared me well. I avoided the mass maternity ward at the Mowbray, and allowed myself the luxury of a semi-private ward at the Constantiaberg. It was a totally different experience, a natural birth in early July, where I could lie in bed with a TV in the room watching Wimbledon while bonding with my baby. I felt indulged. But, despite the fact that Tom was a calm and peaceful baby, I did not escape the depression.

Johann was better prepared for what lay ahead. 'We are going to take this baby one nappy at a time,' he told me.

Tom weaned himself at three months, went to crèche at six months, started walking at nine months, but only started talking at twelve months. He wasn't bothered with communication, and certainly not with the complexity of three languages. He let the world and its words come to him, until one day he discovered a word he really needed.

We were standing in a long supermarket queue and I fell into the trap set for every parent. To help pass the time, I took a chocolate off the aisle shelf, unwrapped it, and let my baby suck on it. I will never forget his face. It lit up, overwhelmed by bliss, as if he had just tasted heaven. 'Chocolate,' I said. 'That's a chocolate.' 'Toto,' he announced. 'Toto!' It was his first word and the only one he regularly used for a long time afterwards. We dared not mention the 'ch' word, not even in its baby version of 'toto' for fear of setting him off. So on the rare occasion that we referred to a chocolate we would spell it out: 't-o-t-o'. One day in the kitchen, Thomas stood in front of the grocery cupboard, where snacks and sweets were also kept, pointed to the top shelf and spelled out the letters 't o t o'. He had cracked the code! As far as we remember, 'toto' was his first word, and its spelling was his second. He took functional language use to the limit. Tom has always used speech economically. We called him Mr Monosyllable as a child, because he had one of three answers to any question – Yes, No or Fine. Alternatively, we called him our 'self-raising child'. We just had to add water and stir.

My greatest regret is that we did not keep up the three languages with our sons. It just became too difficult, given the pressures of a two-career family and our environmental over-exposure to English. The fact that I often used TV as a babysitter didn't help either. I realised that language, like water flowing down a mountain, finds the path of least resistance. We made one final attempt to get Tom bilingual, at least, by sending him to an Afrikaans pre-primary school. After a rocky start he grew to love it, and his teacher, the wonderful Juffrou Cheryl, has retained contact with him to this day.

* * *

In between Paul's and Thomas's births, South Africa was heading in a downward spiral of increased repression under President P.W. Botha's securocrats. The countervailing force was the increasing cohesion and organisation in the resistance movement, symbolised by the growth and impact of the United Democratic Front. Its launch, in Rocklands, Mitchells Plain, on 22 August 1983, remains a highlight in my memory to this day. But the more organised the resistance movement became, the more repressive the state clampdown.

I was active in the Black Sash and regularly went to support shack dwellers (who were deemed to be in Cape Town illegally under the pass laws) to resist arrest and forced removal. On one occasion, while I was there with a film-maker, Lindy Wilson, we were both arrested and charged with being in a black area without a permit and interfering with the police in the execution of their duties. We could not afford a lawyer, so I decided to conduct my own defence. I thought it would be simple, given the fact that as a journalist I had covered so many court cases. It was harder than I thought. My cross-examination of the police officer who arrested me clearly did not make much of an impression on the magistrate. I was duly convicted as charged and received a suspended sentence. I was lucky not to be arrested again during the year of the sentence's suspension.

On the rare occasion that I worked in other cities when I was still breastfeeding Paul, I would take him with me. Once, when a client flew me to Johannesburg, I converted the cost of one plane ticket into two train tickets, so that a child-minder could accompany us. When I went to book tickets for myself and Nomawethu Voyiya (Eunice's eldest daughter), the booking clerk looked puzzled. 'Do you want to go in the white section, or the open section?' he asked. I was amazed that this was still an issue. 'The open section,' I replied. As expected, the 'open section' turned out to be the new name for the 'blacks only' carriages.

When we arrived and boarded the train, my baby and I were the focus of much attention. Throughout the trip a steady stream of curious fellow passengers visited our six-person compartment (which we shared with three others) to meet me and find out what I was doing there. I have never felt as warmly embraced by fellow travellers as I did on that trip. That night, when I went to buy takeaways at the dining car (passengers in the open section did not have access to the tables), I was spotted by a very drunk white man at the bar. He was fascinated to see me return to the open section and he weaved his way down the corridor until he located our compartment, where he made a clumsy attempt to persuade me to accompany him to his compartment. I told him I wasn't interested and asked him to leave, to no avail.

When he became persistent, almost the entire 'open section' rallied around me, and without mincing their words, sent him packing back to his 'whites-only' comfort. Those were moments when I felt great hope for South Africa's future, despite the deteriorating political situation.

From mid-1985 South Africa was placed under either a partial or full state of emergency, designed to smash the growing resistance movement.

Our home became a meeting-and-eating place for young struggle activists, one of whom was Mcebisi Skwatsha. I got to know him well when he was still a schoolboy and one of the Congress of South African Students leaders who frequented our home. Years later we sat on opposite sides of the provincial parliament, and today he is deputy minister of rural development and land reform. I have always retained a great personal fondness for the young man I got to know when he was a fiery young communist and still at school. I smiled when I heard he had sent his own sons to Bishops and Kearsney College, two of the most upmarket schools in the country. Back then, Mcebisi would arrive with his schoolfriends Nyami Booi, who later became parliamentary chief whip of the ANC, and Lizo Ngcokoto, who went into business but, tragically, died very young.

As young men tend to be, they were always hungry. I used to cook double portions of everything. And an extra pot too, so that they could take food with them when they left for their meetings.

Nyami and Lizo, particularly, spent many nights at our home, although sometimes they came with other comrades to eat and discuss politics, especially with Johann. Over thirty years later, Nyami recalls those evenings. 'We came to discuss socialism with Johann, but you always used to say, "Forget the socialism, study mathematics and get your matric."' He remembers me disagreeing with Johann about the socialism. I always remind him that I was right.

They were bright young men. I had always thought they had it in them to do well at school and take maths for matric – which would have opened many doors for them – but, like so many others, poor schooling barred their further path in life. I wanted to give them additional chances. With the generous help of Harold Idesis, who ran Rosebank House College, Johann and I put Lizo through matric and got Nyami extra mathematics lessons. Lizo made it to UCT and was actually accepted for study at Oxford, but decided to pursue his business opportunities in South Africa instead.

Nyami studied maths (to get through matric) but dropped out to join the ANC underground and become a full-time activist. He still remembers how angry I was that he did not complete his studies. He refers to it every time we see each other, to this day!

One day in July 1987, Johann said to me, 'Lizo and Mcebisi want me to rent a car for them. They need it for two weeks.'

We knew them well enough to know that the car would be used for political activity. We also knew not to dig too deeply. We agreed to help them. Johann went to Avis with his credit card. The two young men left in the car, which I recall was a yellow Toyota.

We did not think about it again, until the time came to return the car. We had not seen Mcebisi or Lizo for a while and we presumed they had gone somewhere in the car. It was the pre-cellphone era, of course, so we left messages with their family and friends, but they did not return our calls. Then Avis started calling us and we stalled, saying we needed to extend the rental period. Meanwhile we intensified our search for the young activists and were relieved to finally get a call from Avis saying the car had been returned – to their Bloemfontein branch.

However, they said, there was a problem. The car had clearly been involved in an accident; some repairs had been done, but the panel-beating was not up to scratch. We did not want to invite further investigation. We just told them to send the car to a proper panel beater, and we would pay the insurance excess.

I only learnt the full, amazing back story in February 2016 (twenty-nine years later!) when Mcebisi told it to me. A group of ANC activists had decided to skip the country and they needed a car to get to the border. Because Lizo and Mcebisi knew us well, they approached us for assistance. Lizo and Mcebisi had decided not to skip the country themselves, but they handed the car to two young men who wanted to join Umkhonto we Sizwe (MK), the ANC's military wing. The two were Lerumo Kalako (currently an ANC member of parliament) and Mike Coto, who was reportedly killed in action as a soldier.

But before they even left Cape Town, they somehow managed to have an accident in Gugulethu. So they went to a backyard panel beater who did a rough patch-up job before the car left for the Lesotho border near Ladybrand. There the two men abandoned the vehicle, crossed the border and met their ANC contact on the other side. The arrangement was that a courier would collect the car and drive it back to Cape Town. Except he didn't. The car, said Mcebisi, remained abandoned on the Lesotho border.

Eventually, somehow, he said, the car was identified and towed to the Avis office in Bloemfontein. I'm amazed, looking back, that the matter ended there, and that the police did not arrive to ask us further questions.

This little vignette was part of the normal course of our lives during those successive states of emergency during the 1980s.

I intensified my involvement in the Black Sash and the End Conscription Campaign, where I was elected vice-chair in the Western Cape. The ECC, in particular, was targeted by the regime as an ANC front organisation, which necessitated elaborate security precautions on our part. For meetings, there would be an initial contact point to which we would report, after which we would be redirected (in a whisper) to the real meeting place.

I often took Paul along with me, who had (yet again) worked out how to press my buttons. Because I refused to let him have a toy gun, he (inevitably) became obsessed with guns. The toy shop next to the underground parking lot in the

Riverside Centre in Rondebosch was the scene of numerous tantrums, as we locked horns in a battle of wills about buying him a gun. Eventually, I bought him a plastic water pistol for five rand, which was his favourite toy for years. He turned everything he could find into a gun. Once, in the middle of an ECC meeting in Bea Cornell's lounge, he managed to find a coat hanger, pretend it was a gun, and made shooting noises at everyone in the room. I was mortified!

Those meetings were also the site of some tough debates. The political discourse of resistance politics at the time was dominated by Marxist analysis. There was little room for, or tolerance of, nuance or alternative views. It was 'the system vs the struggle', 'racial capitalism vs socialism'. I would often argue against absolutist positions. One such intense debate centred on our response to an application from the Progressive Federal Party Youth to join the ECC. There was strong resistance to diluting the ideological purity of the ECC by including people whose party was represented in 'the system' (viz. in parliament).

I had a different view.

My logic went like this: we were trying to end conscription; young white men were being conscripted; if some of the young men facing conscription wanted to help us end it, so much the better. Yes, the PFP did participate in whites-only elections and was represented in parliament, but they mobilised white voters to oppose apartheid policies and expose its atrocities using parliament as a platform. Surely that was a valid role to play? Surely we should use whatever means we could to prevent state institutions being entirely captured for the purpose of authoritarian and racist rule? Some white lawyers and judges were doing the same through the legal system; so were journalists. So why couldn't we use parliament against apartheid as well?

I argued for acceptance of a range of different roles in the struggle, and I even proposed that we participate in the 1987 elections and vote for the Progressive Federal Party to strengthen the hand of the anti-apartheid voice in parliament. I feared, as eventually transpired, that the far right would take over as the main parliamentary opposition, and that this would intensify racial polarisation and the escalating civil war that now seemed inevitable. I had joined the ECC to try to prevent that.

As the 1987 election approached, and my voice on the subject grew louder, we organised a debate in the Rondebosch Congregational Church hall. (The church at the time was led by the compassionate and principled Doug Bax, who allowed us to make his hall the unofficial headquarters of various non-governmental organisations.) The topic was whether the 'white left' should vote in the election of 6 May 1987. I argued that we should. Up against me was Johnny de Lange, who was later to become deputy minister of justice in the ANC government, who argued against my proposition. I was given a fair hearing, and I think I made the argument reasonably well, but I completely failed to convince anyone present. When the vote was taken, I stood alone. For my part, I was more convinced than ever that voting against apartheid was a legitimate component of resistance. I believed that, in the transition from authoritarian rule to democracy, it would be easier to transform existing institutions than seek to destroy them and start rebuilding them from scratch. Using institutions against apartheid, or at least preventing them from becoming supine tools of the ruling party, was a valid role in its own right. Today, I still believe that was so. I am sure that if the white left had voted in the 1987 election, we could have prevented the far right from becoming the official opposition. So what, asked my colleagues. What difference would it have made? In fact, they argued, the quicker parliament was exposed as a tool of racist capitalist oppression, the better for the revolution.

Well, I was not sure a revolution was around the corner. I knew a civil war would exact a horrific cost, which would destroy the futures of all young people, and from which the country would take decades to recover.

I remained convinced that we had to do whatever possible to prevent irreversible polarisation in South African politics. This view was reinforced by a new phenomenon that emerged in some townships, with youth groups patrolling the streets to identify 'collaborators', who were brought before 'people's courts', where they were occasionally sentenced to death by necklacing – a petroleum-filled tyre set alight around the victim's neck, their hands sometimes tied in barbed-wire cuffs to prevent resistance.

Emigration escalated, and some of our family members and friends left South Africa. Johann and I never contemplated leaving, but I felt a rising sense of panic about what the future would hold in a situation of escalating civil war. I also sensed that I did not fit comfortably anywhere. Even the Black Sash was riven by debates about how to respond to the growing Marxist ideological hold on the resistance movements, increasingly characterised by intolerance for alternative views and a justification of random violence.

Desperate to be accepted as an authentic part of the struggle, many Sash members preferred to avert their gaze rather than confront the escalating occurrence of gruesome, arbitrary acts of violence justified by Winnie Madikizela-Mandela's notorious 'call to arms': 'With our boxes of matches and our necklaces we shall liberate this country.' It was interpreted as a justification for the murder of anyone suspected of being a sell-out. Anything more calculated to destroy the prospects of the rule of law arising from the ashes of struggle was hard to imagine.

Jill Wentzel, a long-time Sash member, sparked a timely and sometimes acrimonious debate when she wrote a paper criticising 'the liberal slide-away', about our collective failure of nerve to challenge acts of brutality and intolerance when they came from the liberation movements. But despite this failure of nerve, the

Sash continued to do marvellous work through its advice offices and presence on the ground in crisis situations. There was no doubt that Sash members' presence at scenes of forced removals and other sites of random systemic violence, including many political trials, managed to ameliorate and expose the brutality of the system, to which the Sash's silent sidewalk protests bore witness. I could also understand the argument that, while these actions were valuable, they were in themselves insufficient. But what else could we do? Increasingly, the avenues for non-violent resistance were closing.

One night at a Black Sash meeting, Jenny Schreiner, a young academic and activist, asked for volunteers to make their homes available for people who needed a place to stay. She cautioned us not to volunteer publicly, but to contact her later. It was clear that we were being asked to provide safe havens for people who were on the run from the security police.

I felt this was the least we could do in those times, so I went home to discuss it with Johann, who immediately agreed. I contacted Jenny and she came round to talk to us. Our house was ideal: it was situated next to the railway line, with various quick exit routes in different directions. It was centrally located and easily accessible. And we had a small bedsitter cottage in the garden. Soon we had Mama Dorothy Zihlangu (fondly known as Mama Shoes) and Mama Dorothy Mfaco staying with us; I had previously got to know them through Black Sash interactions with the United Women's Organisation, an affiliate of the UDF. They were such warm humanitarians, such quintessential 'gogos' (grannies), that I could hardly imagine they could be 'wanted' by the security police. They lived in our cottage for a while and then spoke to me about needing space for more people. So Mama Mfaco and Mama Zihlangu moved into the house with us and vacated the cottage for use by others. They never told me who, and I never asked. We trusted them enough to give them the gate key, so that they could use their discretion in letting people into the garden to spend the night in our cottage. I often saw movement outside the window and knew they were bringing people in. I never asked questions. The less I knew, the better, I thought.

Some people approached us directly and asked if they could stay with us so that they would not be at their own homes if the security police called. One was Cameron Dugmore, a prominent member of NUSAS, who was recruited into the ANC. When the wave of detentions began, he asked whether he could stay with us. We said sure. His mother Gillian was the sole Black Sash member in George, where Cameron's father was the principal of York High School. I knew Gill from Sash congresses and respected her courageous stand, in relative isolation from the rest of us.

Recalling his stay with us, Cameron said: 'I have good memories of the two weeks I spent at your house. The routine was getting back late at night from the endless meetings I was part of, going to sleep, and rising early to have breakfast and interesting conversations. The discussions were about race and class, strategy and tactics, and the practical work of building the coalition against apartheid.'

After that, Cameron and I maintained intermittent contact. Our paths crossed again, when we were both members of the provincial legislature, and, coincidentally, we both spent some time as provincial ministers (MECs) of education many years later. As public representatives from different parties, we gave each other a tough time across the floor of the provincial legislature, but as with people who shared a history of struggle, the underlying bond was never broken.

Offering people refuge during the state of emergency made Johann and me feel that at least we were doing something. I didn't quite understand the extent of it until later. Jenny was arrested in October 1987, along with Tony Yengeni. Their trial began sixteen months later, in February 1989. The state alleged that they were the leaders of Umkhonto we Sizwe's high command in the Western Cape. As the trial progressed, and as it was discussed in the organisations to which I belonged, I deduced that we had been involved in more than we had anticipated or realised at the time. Our house, I concluded, had probably been used as a hiding place for MK operatives. I knew we would face very serious consequences if this emerged.

Our son Paul had just turned four. Thomas was not yet born.

If Johann and I were arrested and charged under the Terrorism Act or related legislation, we would face a long jail term. Barbara Hogan had been sentenced to ten years in prison for high treason after being found guilty of furthering the aims of a banned organisation by supplying information on trade union and community anti-apartheid activity to the ANC in Botswana. If this 'crime' warranted a decade in jail, what fate would await the two of us if we were found guilty of hiding MK operatives in our house during a state of emergency?

I was trapped in an emotional tumble-dryer. On the one hand I believed we had done the right thing to make our house available. On the other hand, I was terrified of the consequences. What frightened me most was the prospect of our son growing up without us. At that stage no one had any idea that secret talks had already begun between 'the regime and the movement' to prepare the groundwork for a negotiated settlement. The then justice minister, Kobie Coetsee, was the intermediary between the government and the imprisoned ANC leader Nelson Mandela. Little did we know, at the height of the state of emergency, that the countdown to the unbanning of the ANC and a negotiated transition was already under way.

All indicators pointed towards the very antithesis of a negotiated settlement. The End Conscription Campaign was banned on the fifth anniversary of the launch of the UDF, and after receiving a warning from Paula Hathorn, whose partner Chris Giffard had been detained, I went into hiding with Paul. I travelled abroad to attend a conference and used the opportunity to plan a quick exit from South Africa should one be needed.

Back in South Africa, colleagues in the ECC were detained, and I moved out of our home to stay in the attic room of our close friends Ingrid and Pieter le Roux, who offered me a place of refuge so that I didn't have to stay at home.

Meanwhile, I had fallen pregnant with Tom – and although all the external circumstances should have increased my concern for the future, I felt inexplicably more 'chilled' and relaxed than I had ever felt before or since. I mentioned this paradox to my gynaecologist, who said: 'That's your baby's personality, affecting you.' I had always thought the mother's mood affected the baby, but the doctor said no, over the years he had become convinced it was the other way around. He may have been wrong about Thomas's sex, but he was right about his personality. This pregnancy was a happy interlude in an otherwise difficult time – and the harbinger of momentous changes to come.

In February 1989 P.W. Botha had a stroke, which provided the excuse many of his colleagues had been waiting for to oust him as National Party leader and state president. On 9 November the Berlin Wall fell, followed in short order by the disintegration of the Soviet Union. These events had consequences that changed the course of South Africa's history. Both the rock and the hard place, between which we had been trapped, had moved. We had enough room to manoeuvre. The challenge was to ensure movement in the right direction.

In April that year, between the two catalytic events, Johann and I were invited to a conference that, in retrospect, seems to have been one of many preparatory meetings for a negotiated settlement. Senator Dick Clarke of the Aspen Institute in the United States convened a conference in Bermuda to bring together representatives of the ANC-in-exile with leading members of internal political parties and other organisations, to analyse the country's political challenges and discuss options for the future.

By then the historic Dakar conference had already taken place, at which prominent progressive Afrikaners had met with ANC leaders in July 1987, amidst much fanfare. The Bermuda conference took these interactions to a new level by bringing together ANC leaders with prominent members of the ruling National Party, as well as far-right Conservative Party members, although their interactions were disguised by an elaborate logistical charade. This involved timing the arrival and departure of various delegations so that the National Party representatives were never publicly in the same room as the ANC at any one time. This farcical arrangement was necessitated by the fact that Conservative Party members spent much time stalking around conference venues with cameras, determined to capture prominent Nationalists interacting with representatives of the ANC. Such a photograph would have been electoral dynamite back home, enabling the Conservatives to label their rivals as sell-outs to the 'communist ANC'.

This anecdote conveys the extent to which the ANC had been demonised in South Africa (not to mention the South African Communist Party). This contextual reality made F.W. de Klerk's famous speech of 2 February 1990 (just ten months after the Bermuda conference) all the more remarkable.

While Johann gave a presentation on the state of trade unions in South Africa, my task at the Bermuda conference was to summarise and wrap up the proceedings, pulling together all the strings of various discussions and evaluating South Africa's future prospects. My outlook was upbeat. I concluded that South Africa was on the road to a negotiated settlement that could take us out of the cul-de-sac of a civil war.

During the preceding days, I took the opportunity to meet as many people as I could (especially those living in exile), including the urbane, thoughtful, pipe-smoking Thabo Mbeki. He was clearly aware of my political involvement in South Africa, and we spent more than an hour talking about the unfolding internal situation in the country. I was impressed by his understanding of contemporary developments. He was certainly on the cutting edge. He asked most of the questions, and wanted detailed answers. From the drift of the conversation, and the questions he asked, I realised that a negotiated settlement was a real prospect.

This conversation was to be the foundation of a long-term relationship of mutual understanding and respect, which culminated in our regular meetings when he was president and I was leader of the Democratic Alliance, South Africa's official opposition, almost twenty years later.

Back in 1990, despite my growing optimism about South Africa's future, F.W. de Klerk's historic speech took me entirely by surprise. Very few South Africans could have been as relieved as I was. The sword of Damocles, hovering over my head, had been removed.

Many years later, I also got to know and respect F.W. de Klerk. I asked him how he had come to the point of being able to make that speech, in the context of the time, taking so many of us by surprise, yet also keeping the vast majority of his supporters with him. It is always the biggest test of leadership to take a counter-intuitive decision that is deeply unpopular among your supporters – and inspire them enough to follow you.

F.W. replied that the groundwork had been prepared for some time. He and his closest advisers knew that an ANC leader with the stature and extraordinary moral authority of Nelson Mandela would never be repeated. The fall of the Berlin Wall had been the catalyst. The Soviet Union was no longer seen as a threat because it no longer had the capacity to drive its hegemonic agenda through proxies in southern Africa. 'If we did not use that moment to seek a negotiated transition, it would not have come again,' F.W. said.

South Africa avoided a civil war by the serendipitous confluence of two great leaders who appealed to the basic decency and common sense of most South Africans.

If this had taken enormous courage on the part of De Klerk, it was equally so for Nelson Mandela. Despite the fact that the ANC had ostensibly far more to gain, given that a negotiated transition would inevitably bring it to power, there was significant resistance within the movement against anything other than an outright military victory. People were not interested in 'reformism' to make existing institutions inclusive and functional for all South Africans. The air was thick with talk of revolution, of destroying the machinery of racial capitalism, of seizing the 'commanding heights' of the economy. Much of this rhetoric was political theatre, because no one seriously believed that Umkhonto we Sizwe was about to march on Pretoria and capture the Union Buildings. But it created a context in which it was easy to label those arguing for a negotiated settlement as sell-outs. It took a leader of Mandela's stature to do so.

But this was just the start. The complexity of the transition had to be negotiated. Traditional ways of governing and planning for the future no longer sufficed. My work as a freelance consultant grew rapidly as private companies, spheres of government and foreign aid agencies wished to chart their course in the new environment. I set up a consultancy with David Shandler, a friend many years my junior, with whom I had worked in the End Conscription Campaign.

Many of our projects involved bringing South Africans across the spectrum together in participative planning, policy-making and problem-solving. But progress in some of our projects was seriously jeopardised by the outbreak of extreme violence between rival taxi associations, which disrupted the entire transport system to such a degree that it undermined our capacity to involve community-based organisations in various programmes. We had to try to resolve this conflict first. One day I convened a meeting of influential local leaders at our home to discuss various possible interventions to resolve the taxi war. One of the participants in the discussion was Tony Yengeni. He looked around, especially at the cottage, and told me: 'I know this place. I stayed here with my comrades during the 1987 state of emergency.'

Over the years, other colleagues have also told me how they spent time in our cottage, including Max Ozinsky (who was then an MK operative and many years later became the ANC's chief whip in the Western Cape provincial legislature, where we had many a tough debate against each other) and Basil Kivedo (a former MK cadre who now sits on the DA's benches in the provincial parliament). Back then they had both been on the run from the security police. So my deductions had been correct. Our involvement ran deeper than we realised.

I often think of how differently life would have turned out for our family if it were not for F.W. de Klerk's speech. Had he not decided, at last, to cross the Rubicon to a democratic South Africa, Johann and I might well have spent two decades in jail. And Paul and Thomas may well have been raised by foster parents. History turns on a tickey. I still get shivers down my spine thinking of it, but I also believe we did the right thing.

By this time, demand for the services of my little business had grown, which meant I had to move out of the study I shared with Johann. I needed to rent and equip an office. This required capital that I did not have, so I went to the Standard Bank in Rondebosch to ask for a loan to buy computers, a fax machine and some furniture. The manager asked me for my business plan. Business plan? I had never heard of a business plan, so I went home and phoned my cousin Anne, who was an accountant at Deloitte, and asked her. She explained well enough for me to be able to draw up something overnight that passed muster the next morning. I left the bank having secured a loan of R40 000 and using our house as collateral. That really concentrated my mind, knowing that if my business failed we would lose our home. I was simultaneously filled with the exhilaration of running my own business and the terror of the consequences should it fail. Thomas was just over a year old. Thus began the most exhausting two years of my life: mothering two young children in the day and working late, sometimes right through the night.

An essay that Paul wrote at the end of Grade 1 captured our family circumstances well: 'My dad is good for fun. My mom is good for work. My mom works very very hard. She goes to bed late and doesn't like to get up in the morning.'

Any combination of work pressure I have subsequently faced was child's play compared to those years. At one stage I was involved in some twenty-two projects simultaneously, ranging from public transport to housing, and from project evaluations to gap analyses. I had to become an expert in new areas and new techniques of evaluation and problem-solving almost overnight.

Eunice's family became more and more involved with ours, especially her youngest daughter, Grace, a bright young girl who battled to pass exams. She was at her happiest in our home, playing with Paul and Tom (and especially cooking for them). I can't recall exactly how or when it happened, but at some point she stayed on, and has been with us ever since. She married Abel Mputing, one of Johann's university students, and had two wonderful children, Chulumanco and NgoweNceba, who have been part of our family from the moment they were born.

Grace was an invaluable help as I tried to juggle my many responsibilities and get my small business up and running smoothly. My network of contacts, built up during the years of struggle, stood me in good stead. I was able to engage people across the political spectrum and, together with others, David Shandler, of course, and also David Schmidt, from the End Conscription Campaign, create the interactions necessary to form a foundation of sufficient trust for the transition to democratic local government in Cape Town.

The networks we built during those years have surfaced in unexpected ways my whole life, often jumping generations as I encountered the children and grandchildren of the struggle stalwarts with whom I had worked.

One of my most memorable encounters was with Bulelani Mfaco in 2008, when I was mayor of Cape Town. I had initiated a programme to formalise neighbourhood watches and train their members to help promote community safety. During the round of introductions at the start, his surname struck me. Mfaco is not a common surname. So when the proceedings ended, we chatted briefly, and I mentioned that I had known a Mrs Mfaco during the struggle days.

Not long afterwards, I was profoundly moved by a piece Bulelani wrote about his gogo, which was published on Media24. He recalled:

> Gogo's work with the United Women's Organisation exposed her to other like-minded women. Women of all races united for a cause and that did not go down well with the apartheid government as the women were suspected of being the messengers to exiled members of the liberation movement ...
>
> One part of her stories that inspired me to write this was when Gogo was running away from the apartheid government. She told us that as activists they had to go into hiding as they were being harassed in their homes ...
>
> When the police were after them, white anti-apartheid activists provided shelter for them ... Gogo said she lived with a nice white friend but did not mention the name of that white friend as we were kids and would have probably not been able to pronounce the names.
>
> Last week I learned who that nice white friend was. In 2008, I attended a workshop at the City of Cape Town's civic. When I introduced myself to the Mayor, Helen Zille, the first thing she asked was 'How is Mama Mfaco?'
>
> I wondered how she knew my granny but could not ask as she was rushing to the airport so I could only greet and not talk to Helen.
>
> Last week on her Twitter page, Helen asked if I'm related to Dorothy Mfaco. And I said yes. Then she told me that she had stayed with her sometime in the 80s. I was like WOW! Helen Zille is the nice white woman who gave my granny shelter? Being a DA supporter I thought I knew Helen but clearly not.
>
> After receiving death threats one would think Zille would stop speaking out against apartheid but it only motivated her. [She was] actively involved by joining the Black Sash and other anti-apartheid activists. Zille was arrested

for being in the 'wrong' area because Zille believed South Africa was for all the people and people should be free to be where ever they want to be. What I find most interesting is how a system that sought to literally separate Gogo and Zille ended up bringing them under one roof...

If that relationship between Zille and Gogo existed in the 80s, why is it difficult to build such relationships now where we work hand in hand building this country? Zille was actually annoyed with the title 'Gogo's white friend'; she asked, why put the word 'white' because I was just her friend.

I reflected on what Bulelani had written. It was so true. His granny and her friend, Mama 'Shoes' Zihlangu, had lived with us under one roof. We ate together, laughed together and conversed like friends do. The only thing they did not share with me was the depth of their political engagement, and I did not go there. Whatever, we knew we were in it together.

I often reflect on how difficult it has been to maintain and build the commitment to non-racialism today, compared to the years of struggle. What happened? Back then, black South Africans with whom I interacted rejected the notion that they were victims, even when they were targeted, arrested and tortured.

Today, youngsters who were born long after the transition to democracy, and even some who have enjoyed excellent education and great opportunities, weave ongoing pain and victimhood into their narrative. Is it inevitably part of identity politics? Pain is for public display, not private processing. Perhaps people have discovered just how powerful a weapon it is in a context of restitution and compensation for past disadvantage.

Looking back, I think about my family members, murdered shortly before I was born, whom I only learnt about decades later. While I still wonder why our parents never told us what really happened, I am (on balance) grateful that they were intolerant of self-indulgence, and refused to countenance the language of victimhood. Learning to face the unfairness of life, even as we tried to change it, was genuinely empowering.

7

A Political Education

THE DECADE COULD not have started out on a better note than F.W. de Klerk's landmark speech, on 2 February 1990, which lifted a fog of fear from my mind. My euphoria intensified three months later, in early May 1990, when the South African government and the ANC met at the president's official residence in Cape Town, and adopted the Groote Schuur Minute, which committed both sides to ending violence and creating a climate conducive to negotiations. It included a pledge from the government to work towards lifting the state of emergency, a timetable for the release of political prisoners, and the granting of immunity from prosecution for politically related offences, so that the ANC's exiled leadership could return.

I soon learnt to avoid premature optimism. As the skies cleared, I discovered that the fog could descend again, in seconds, with the harsh call of the fog horn intruding right into my home.

Late in July 1990, it came in the form of a panicky phone call from my parents' housekeeper in Johannesburg. She told me that the police had arrived and taken Mom and Dad away. She did not know why, or where to. She just told me they had gone.

Without the 'luxuries' of cellphones and text messaging, back then communication was often a challenge. I phoned my parents' neighbours and the local police station, without anyone being able to shed any further light on the matter. I decided to take the next flight to Johannesburg. Just as I was starting to make arrangements, my dad phoned me. They were home.

His story was unbelievable, in the literal sense of the word. The police had arrived at their townhouse earlier in the day, and asked my parents to accompany them to my brother's house in Parkhurst. Mom and Dad didn't have an option, so I suppose they were technically under arrest. My brother Paul, who had spent fifteen years in voluntary exile in England, wanted to return to South Africa to support the transition to democracy. He paid a deposit on a house in Johannesburg, selected for him by our parents, and decided to let it while tying up his affairs in England.

I recall my father telling me the tenant was Canadian and that she lived there with some friends. That was all I knew.

When my parents arrived, accompanied by police, at the unassuming old-style house on 12th Street, they could not believe their eyes. There they saw a gaunt, bent man in leg irons and handcuffs being escorted around the premises. He turned out to be Mac Maharaj, who, according to reports, had recently returned to South Africa from exile, having been granted indemnity as one of the ANC/SACP's senior leaders, following the Groote Schuur Minute.

The police asked my parents if they knew him. They said they knew who he was, but did not know him personally. The police then told my parents that enough explosives had been found in the basement of my brother's house to 'blow up Johannesburg', and that Mac Maharaj was the mastermind behind the plan to do so.

This is the first we learnt about Operation Vula, the ANC's most successful underground operation inside South Africa. It was conceived after the ANC's 1985 Kabwe conference and ran at full tilt from 1988 until it was 'bust' in 1990.

Tim Jenkin, together with Ronnie Press in London and Zarina Maharaj in Lusaka, was the brain behind the communication network at the heart of Operation Vula. He has written a fascinating account of how the network and its communication nerve centre evolved, and how it was cracked.

At Kabwe, said Jenkin, the ANC had to come to terms with the fact that there was very little to show for the years of struggle, 'only hundreds of activists in the enemy's jails and the loss of tons of precious weaponry'. They concluded that the external armed struggle had achieved so little because there was no viable underground network inside South Africa. Even though the mass democratic movement was growing, the ANC could not claim to be leading it, and risked being outflanked by popular local leaders. According to Jenkin, the ANC's armed struggle involved 'hit-and-run' strikes, and its operatives were often captured. Jenkin describes MK forces undertaking incursions into South Africa in 1986 as a 'rudderless army with nowhere to hide, no contact with its leaders and with extremely fragile lines of supply'.

Mac did not entirely agree with Jenkin's analysis, but it was clear that preparations for a people's war necessitated the co-ordination of the ANC in exile and the emerging leadership inside South Africa.

Operation Vula was born, its existence known only to a handful of top leaders who decided that Mac Maharaj and Siphiwe Nyanda (soon to become chief of staff of Umkhonto we Sizwe and later head of the South African National Defence Force) would return undercover to South Africa to lead the internal strategy, and establish reliable communication links with the ANC in exile. At that time, the public knew nothing about Operation Vula, its genesis or development.

The day after my parents' arrest, a newspaper reporter called. My mother had the presence of mind to ask him to call back later, and she contacted me for advice. I still had the sense that she did not really understand how high the stakes were. She just kept telling me that Mac was looking so thin, and ill and drawn. I told her to let Dad handle the media.

It was an early experience of being on the receiving end of media enquiries, and it wasn't comfortable. As a journalist, I had learnt that the best way to get information out of an interviewee was never to let on how much (or how little) you knew. I also learnt that in a complex, multilayered story, more and more information tends to emerge over time, which often contradicts what was said at the outset. For example, was the link between Operation Vula and my brother's house purely coincidental, or was there more to it than that? We could not make a categorical statement until we knew.

But there was an additional factor at work here. I feared the revelation of Operation Vula would derail South Africa's transition to a negotiated settlement. It was the perfect excuse the intransigent rump of the National Party needed to 'prove' that the ANC was acting in bad faith, feigning preparations for negotiation while taking the gap to establish a Trojan-horse strategy aimed at intensifying the armed struggle from bases inside the country. F.W. de Klerk himself made a statement to that effect. The ANC, for its part, said they could not be sure that the National Party was entering negotiations in good faith, and that they had to have a fallback position if they needed one.

And our family was caught right in the middle of it! I didn't know how much my brother knew, if anything at all. He moved in circles that included South African exiles in the UK. What was the back story to all of this? I had no idea. I concluded that we had to say as little as possible until we knew more.

'Just say you have no comment at this stage,' I urged my father. 'We do not know all the facts, and it is better to wait till we do.'

Dad disagreed. 'If we say "no comment", they will think we are covering something up,' he said.

'Dad, please believe me,' I said. 'We don't know enough to start talking now. Please just wait.'

Looking back, he may have been right, because the newspaper was pretty scathing about my parents' 'no comment'. It wasn't ideal, but I thought it was better than the alternatives in the circumstances, given the many known unknowns, further complicated (I assumed) by a myriad unknown unknowns.

All I knew for sure was that, if the transition and the constitutional negotiations were derailed, it would be a disaster for South Africa generally, and for us as a family in particular. If either De Klerk or Mandela lost the support of their constituencies, the result would inevitably be an intensified state of emergency, and a descent into the vortex of civil war. Niceties like fair trials and due process are the first casualties in these circumstances. We would be in the firing line, both for providing sanctuary to Umkhonto we Sizwe operatives in Cape Town and, now, the Operation Vula weapons cache in Johannesburg.

I was back in the fog.

It was fascinating to look back on this experience when I spoke to Mac Maharaj in 2015 to record his memory of the incident. He had just retired from his job as spokesman for President Jacob Zuma. On a few occasions, prior to that, when we crossed paths in the course of our work, I had alluded to 12th Street, Parkhurst, but we had never discussed it in any detail. I called him to request an interview and he invited me to his spacious corner flat in a restored art deco apartment building in Durban.

Mac's memory was crystal clear. He was underground in South Africa at the time, having been infiltrated back behind what he described as an elaborate 'legend'. Because Operation Vula was so secret, he had to have a credible reason to disappear from his base in Lusaka. It was important that a plausible cover story should circulate in the underground, in the likelihood that it would be picked up by South African security agents, providing the necessary disinformation to take the spooks off the scent. A kidney disease was the cover. Mac became thinner and frailer, walking haltingly with a cane. He eventually left for the Soviet Union to get treatment, and to await a kidney transplant. Or so the legend went. He actually came back to South Africa via staging posts in Eastern Europe, East Africa and Swaziland, where he crossed the border with Siphiwe Nyanda, who had a separate 'legend'. He was supposedly undergoing prolonged military training in the Soviet Union.

They headed for Durban, the place Mac knew best, with a view to establishing a base and extending the network to Johannesburg.

While underground in South Africa, said Mac, 'I received word through our special communication channel from London that there was a house in Parkhurst available for rent. The owner of the house was living in the UK and it was possible to rent the place through a person in the UK and even to make the payment of the rental in the UK if we chose. This had enormous advantages, so I looked into it. I remember clearly that the communication said the house was owned by Paul Zille. I did not tell anyone else who the owner was. It is best for people not to know because then, even if the police arrest and torture them, they can't say.'

Mac said he knew about my mother's role in the Black Sash, about her volunteering as an observer at political trials, and about my journalistic and political involvement. He also concluded that my brother was in touch with others in war resisters' networks in the UK, who passed on the information about the house. 'Paul would never have known what the house was being used for, or who the tenants were; all he would know was that a British citizen had asked to rent the place.'

As it happened, Mom and Dad had received a call from a Canadian woman living in Johannesburg who said she had heard they had a house to let and that she was interested. The woman was the go-between for Mac, who by then was in hiding in her converted garage close by, in 11th Street, Parkhurst. Mac said he went, in heavy disguise, to inspect the 12th Street house himself. 'I was very excited when I saw it because it was ideal,' he recalled. 'It was on a slope which meant there must be a huge space for storage under the floor. We immediately agreed to rent the house.'

Mac explained to me how a man nicknamed 'Bricks', whose real name was Christopher Manye, converted the space under the floor into a huge cellar. Comrade Bricks was the husband of an MK operative, Tootsie Memela, who served as a guide to ANC operatives crossing the border from Swaziland on foot, including Mac and Nyanda. 'Bricks' had already had much experience building storage spaces – and even accommodation for cadres – in disused mine shafts.

Bricks cut a trapdoor in the main bedroom so skilfully that it could hardly be noticed. He converted the large space below into a usable cellar. The trapdoor was then covered by a carpet, and finally overlayed by a huge double bed.

I was fascinated to learn how the weapons made their way into the cellar.

Mac told me how the establishment of underground ANC structures in South Africa had to be complemented by sufficient arms to mount a 'people's war' at the right time. He said that Vula developed its own supply lines, primarily through Botswana and Swaziland. Some of the arms arrived at 12th Street through a 'front' tourist company called Africa Hinterland Safaris. 'Operation Safari', as it was known, offered the real bush experience to adventurous tourists who wanted to drive overland from Kenya, through Zambia and on to South Africa. The tourists would fly to Mombasa. There they would board a modified Bedford truck and be driven to Johannesburg and Cape Town via Lusaka, where the weapons were picked up during the tourists' overnight hotel stay.

What they did not know was that they were travelling on modified seats, concealing secret chambers that could carry up to one ton of hidden weaponry per trip. The trucks were driven by special recruits, who knew what they were doing and were prepared to take the risk. (One of the original Bedford trucks used in this operation was retrieved and is now on permanent display at the Lilliesleaf Farm museum.)

The most dangerous part of the journey involved offloading the weapons at the destination. This was done in small containers, at designated points across Johannesburg – after which they were conveyed to their destination at 129 12th Street, Parkhurst. That is how the basement of my brother's house ended up with enough explosives to 'blow up Johannesburg'.

So how did the police manage to bust this system, I asked Mac.

There are different versions. In history, as in journalism, different accounts often complement rather than contradict each other in the complex search for all the facts and perspectives that constitute 'truth'.

Mac told me there had been a security breach. Askaris patrolling Durban recognised one of the MK operatives who was in the country as part of Operation Vula. They tailed him and arrested him once he made contact with another Vula operative. Mac said that the two men – Charles Ndaba and Mbuso Tshabalala – were arrested and tortured. They were executed on the banks of the Tugela River and their bodies strapped to concrete poles and disposed of near the river mouth. The tailing and torture of the two led to the unearthing of some Vula hideouts and culminated in the arrest of Mac and others.

According to Tim Jenkin, who now lives in Cape Town, there was an additional security breach. As the network grew bigger, tasks were delegated, and one of Siphiwe Nyanda's assistants committed the cardinal error of walking around with disks and data cards in his possession, as well as the security program of the encrypted communication network. The police came upon him quite by accident. They had arrested two of his associates in a raid unrelated to Operation Vula, from which they learnt about a scheduled meeting that aroused their suspicion. They waited at the meeting venue and arrested those who arrived, together with all the data. They had everything they could have wanted and more, in one fell swoop. Technology's great advantage – the storage of huge amounts of data on small portable files – is also its greatest risk.

Mac's arrest and the raids on the houses, including my brother's in Johannesburg, followed in short order.

Mac recalled that when the police took him there, he was exhausted from forty-eight hours of unrelenting cross-examination. He noticed, on the crisp white duvet, the indentation of the person who had been sleeping on top of the covers, next to a clear outline of his AK-47.

Mac and others were charged with terrorism in October 1990, but the charges were dropped five months later, when the Vula operatives received a partial indemnity.

Fortunately, the revelations of Operation Vula, although a major hurdle, did not derail the multi-party negotiations. We felt we could breathe again. But every step the country took in the right direction seemed to be countered by forces pushing us back.

I experienced this frustration hands-on in a foreshadowing of the work I would be doing a few years down the road. It came about through the work I had secured through the small public-policy consultancy I had set up with David Shandler for our first major client – the Cape Town City Council.

In 1990 the Lingelethu West Town Council in Khayelitsha became the first black township to get full city council status in the Western Cape. The Nationalists considered this a progressive move, because it recognised and acknowledged the 'permanence' of Khayelitsha and its residents in what was previously a 'coloured (mixed-race) preference area'. But everyone else saw it as a retrogressive step to entrench racially separate local authorities. To counter this, we launched the One City initiative, and I served on its steering committee.

But the Nationalists' divide-and-rule strategy had an impact. The Lingelethu West councillors were part of the government's extended patronage network, and were determined to defend their positions. The National Party was extending its net further, to draw in the 'headmen' of various newly urbanised groups, in order to contain the influence of the recently unbanned ANC that was emerging in organised formations across the province, and particularly in the established Xhosa-speaking community of Cape Town.

The conflict manifested along every social fault-line, and the level of violence escalated dramatically.

By the end of 1990, the minister of police, Adriaan Vlok, had declared Khayelitsha an 'unrest area', giving the security forces considerable powers to bring the situation under control, and providing a perfect front for countering the ANC's organisational re-emergence.

The front line of this confrontation was the 'taxi wars' of the early 1990s. It was a devastating conflict. Within its first year, according to police estimates (March 1991), there had been 628 attacks, at least 37 deaths, 139 injuries, 34 burnt-out taxis, and at least 300 homes damaged or destroyed. The final report of the Truth and Reconciliation Commission describes these estimates as 'conservative', and notes that a death toll of 74 had been cited elsewhere.

'In some instances, whole areas were attacked and destroyed, particularly in Khayelitsha,' the TRC Report states. 'In one incident, the informal settlement of Black City in Nyanga was virtually obliterated.'*

The report also notes that the casualties exacted a particularly high cost on the ANC, with the killing of several key activists.

Ostensibly, the taxi war was being waged between two rival organisations. One was a long-established urban taxi association, aptly named Lagunya, whose members were licensed to operate between Langa, Gugulethu and Nyanga. The other was the Western Cape Black Taxi Association (Webta), with its base among recent urban migrants in Khayelitsha. Webta comprised mostly 'pirate' taxi operators with close links to various 'headmen' in the shack settlements across the south-east margin of the city. At great risk to themselves, Webta's pirate taxis had plied their trade along unlicensed routes from Khayelitsha to the CBD and

---

* TRC Report, Vol. 3, Chapter 5, Subsection 64, para 441

back. They had faced fines, arrest and impounding of their vehicles – until the authorities realised that Webta, which was loosely aligned to the traditional leaders, could be a useful ally against their rivals in Lagunya, with its historic links to the liberation movement.

Given the official recognition of Khayelitsha's town status, the authorities wished to legalise the taxi route to central Cape Town. Webta operators claimed first rights on a route they regarded as theirs, while Lagunya argued that, having worked within the law, they should not be excluded from an open application process, based on clear criteria.

Allegations of corruption abounded, with perceptions (supported by outcomes) that payment to a Webta middleman was the only guarantee of getting a permit. Inevitably, conflict erupted.

It wasn't long before I was (inadvertently) drawn in. The Cape Town City Council had initiated four key planning studies as the foundation for the transition to democracy. These were: (1) *Growing the Cape* – a plan for economic growth and job creation; (2) *The Metropolitan Transport Study* – to chart the way towards an integrated, inclusive transport system; (3) a *Municipal Development Strategy and Structure Plan* – to help determine the best land use across the city as a whole; and (4) the *Metropolitan South East Structure Plan* – to determine the best land use for the rapidly growing south-east sector of the city, home to the majority of new urban migrants.

The council contracted my small consultancy to undertake the public-participation component of these pioneering, inclusive planning initiatives.

In April 1991, we convened a large workshop at a spa resort in the Western Cape town of Caledon, where the leaders of all community-based organisations active in the south-east sector of the city were invited to receive a presentation of what the studies would involve, and discuss how to participate in achieving the best outcome.

There was an enormously encouraging response. But when we convened in Caledon, several key community leaders were absent. One was Michael Mapongwana, the Khayelitsha-based chairman of the Western Cape Civic Association, whose wife Nomsa had been killed six months earlier in an ambush aimed at him. He and several other key leaders had gone back into hiding. The escalating violence was making it more and more difficult to plan for a post-apartheid future, let alone involve community leaders in formulating those plans.

In July, the assassins struck again, this time hitting their target. Mapongwana was killed in circumstances that reflected the role of the police and courts in the Kafkaesque nature of the transition. Although Mapongwana had been a target of assassination for months, the police seemed unable to apprehend his would-be killers (who had already murdered his wife). Instead they had confiscated

Mapongwana's gun and charged him with being in possession of an unlicensed firearm. On 8 July 1991, just after he had appeared in court on this charge, the taxi in which he was travelling from Wynberg back to Khayelitsha was stopped. Both Mapongwana and the driver were pulled out of the vehicle and shot dead at point-blank range. His murder was a devastating blow to the fragile organisational network emerging after decades underground.

The City Council asked me to research and write a paper on the root causes of the taxi war, and to recommend possible remedies.

At the outset, I had been under the impression that it was a bona fide battle over access to routes and ranks. I then suspected it was the result of corruption in the Local Road Transportation Board, which, through a politically linked intermediary, appeared to be granting permits selectively to members of one taxi association.

As I did more research, I came to a different conclusion. The Webta side of the battle appeared to be immune from police action; more than that, I saw for myself how they were occasionally escorted by the police to occupy certain ranks, illegally keeping their rivals out. Webta seemed to have an endless supply of arms and ammunition, which were used with impunity, and on at least two occasions I narrowly avoided being shot at the Nyanga taxi rank myself. I had gone there to witness the front line of the conflict, to see whether the allegations of police bias had any substance.

My research role soon turned into a mediating role, as I met with the two sides separately to try to get to the root of the conflict and sort it out. I came to the conclusion that the conflict was not merely driven by competition and corruption, but also by political interests playing themselves out on a wider canvas in an escalating battle for future control of Cape Town and the Western Cape.

On 25 January 1992 Mr Michael Ndongeni, a Webta driver, was shot dead at the Nyanga taxi rank after making a sworn statement that he had been part of a Webta group that had planned the murder of Michael Mapongwana.

I concluded that political contestation was so deeply embedded in the taxi conflict that it would be impossible to resolve the underlying issues merely by addressing the logistics relating to routes, ranks and permits. I reported accordingly. We set up the Peace Committee under the chairmanship of the mayor of Cape Town, Frank van der Velde, with Archbishop Desmond Tutu as the patron, and several other influential leaders.

Our efforts to resolve the conflict failed, and I realised I was up against more than I had bargained for. A professionally produced pamphlet was distributed across Khayelitsha, painting me as a sinister force behind the violence (I wish I had kept that pamphlet, but I was not thinking about writing my memoirs in those days). A man whom I strongly suspected of being an informer, operating under the guise of being an SABC reporter, interviewed me for a documentary on the taxi war which painted me as driving an ANC agenda and seeking to advance the ANC's interests through the conflict. The truth was that the security forces were doing what they accused me of doing – but for the other side.

The taxi war dominated the local newspaper and radio reporting, with my role depicted as highly controversial.

My son Paul was nine. One day, while I was reading a newspaper, he looked over my shoulder and asked me: 'Mommy, why does everyone like Daddy, but not everyone likes you?'

I had never looked at it that way before, and was struck by the accuracy of his observation. The controversy surrounding me was clearly affecting him. I told him it was because his dad and I did different kinds of work. His dad taught students and his job was to help them. Everyone liked that. My job was sorting out problems, and sometimes I had to argue, even fight, with people to do so, and they didn't like that. I also took the opportunity to explain to him why it is often important in life to stand for principle rather than seek popularity.

During this time, Johann grew uncharacteristically worried whenever I went into Khayelitsha and did not return for long periods. Once, during a serious impasse in the discussions, some taxi association leaders agreed to meet me behind the Total Garage near Lookout Hill in Khayelitsha, where a back room was sometimes used as a meeting venue. Again, in the days before cellphones, it was impossible to keep in contact with my family. After negotiations continued for three hours, I heard a hammering on the door and the police burst in. Johann had phoned the Khayelitsha police in a panic about my non-return and had sent them to find me. In those fraught circumstances, the arrival of the police did not do my credibility any good, and I asked them please to leave. 'Next time we won't bother to come and find you' was their understandably angry response.

In the early hours one morning, I got a panicked call from Michael Kupiso, who had emerged as a Lagunya leader within Khayelitsha, saying he had word that he was going to be ambushed and shot dead in his home. He would be leaving his house and had to get out of the township without his whereabouts being known. I suggested calling the police, but he protested vehemently. He could not rely on the police, he said. In fact, he suspected them of backing the forces mobilising to remove him, as some of us believed had happened to Michael Mapongwana. To this day I do not know what possessed me in those circumstances, but I got into my car, drove to Khayelitsha to fetch him at a rendezvous point, and brought him back to our house. Johann knew there was no point in trying to stop me.

I had now become irrevocably identified with one side of the conflict, and my continued role as mediator was impossible. I had chosen a side because I recognised that this was not a bona fide conflict where legitimate competing interests could be resolved by mediation. When conflict is being deliberately fuelled by political agendas, exposure is sometimes a better option than compromise. Louise Asmal, of the Defence and Aid Fund, helped us organise funding to seek legal assistance to take the matter to the Goldstone Commission, which had been established to probe the background causes of the escalating levels of violence nationally. One of the arenas of conflict was Cape Town's taxi war. I submitted the paper I had written, joining the dots to expose the political motives behind what I concluded was the deliberate escalation of community-based conflict. Our lawyers argued the case based on my research. But the opposing legal team, defending the police against my allegations of complicity in the violence, merely dragged out proceedings until we had run out of money.

However, a subsequent attempt to bring the warring associations together seemed to succeed with the formation of an umbrella organisation called CODETA (Convention of Democratic Taxi Associations). It lasted a miraculous eighteen months before blowing apart, heralding a period of renewed conflict. In her study of the taxi conflict in South Africa, Jackie Dugard writes, 'this time the violence was more widespread, more random, more erratic and apparently more enduring'.* We realised it was something we would have to learn to live with. Although the transition at local level was immeasurably complicated by the low-intensity internecine war, we adapted to it and survived a potentially lethal threat to our local democratic transition.

During 1991 the National Party lost several by-elections in succession to the far-right-wing Conservative Party, which found traction in the white community by arguing that the government had no mandate to negotiate with the ANC. A by-election held on 19 February 1992 in Potchefstroom, considered a safe NP seat, was billed as a test of white voters' support for the negotiation process. The National Party lost. It had a seismic effect in the white community, and enormous implications for the rest of the country.

The next day, F.W. announced a whites-only referendum in an attempt to secure the negotiation mandate his conservative opponents alleged he lacked. He was heavily criticised for calling a racially segregated referendum, but I understood his logic. A political leader has to keep the majority of his supporters behind him, especially when he takes a counter-intuitive fork in the road. Once he loses his mandate, he has nothing to bring to the negotiating table. If a critical mass of whites had moved right to support the Conservative Party, the negotiation process would have broken down. Contrary to what some people romantically (and ahistorically) seem to imagine today, the collapse of negotiations would not

---

* Jackie Dugard, 'From Low Intensity War to Mafia War: Taxi Violence in South Africa 1987–2000', Violence and Transition Series, Vol. 4, May 2001

have paved the way for a military defeat of apartheid forces. In order to make progress, it was essential that white South Africans accepted, even embraced, the prospect of dismantling apartheid. Without this there could be no peace.

White South Africans were asked to answer this question with a simple yes or no: 'Do you support continuation of the reform process which the State President began on 2 February 1990 and which is aimed at a new Constitution through negotiation?'

De Klerk's reforms were supported by the Democratic Party (DP). The DP had grown out of the old PFP, which merged with the smaller Independent Party and National Democratic Movement in 1989. At first it had three leaders, Zach de Beer, Denis Worrall and Wynand Malan, but De Beer soon became the sole leader. It was the political heir of the old Progressive Party.

Apart from opposition from the right, 'reform' was also anathema to those who regarded themselves as revolutionaries. But there was no other realistic way out of South Africa's dead end. And we were blessed with leaders who understood that, and an international community who backed them.

It was an enormous milestone on the road to a negotiated constitution when, after an intense three-week campaign, 68.72 per cent of white voters gave a resounding yes. There was no going back. F.W. could proceed with the multi-party negotiations in the knowledge that he had the bulk of his support base behind him.

But even as the negotiations progressed, violence in the country escalated. It seemed inexplicable until a pattern started emerging, and the violence was revealed as the flip side of negotiation: political adversaries seeking to establish their dominance on the ground as the foundation of a future power base.

Between F.W.'s historic speech in 1990 and the first democratic election in 1994, 14 000 South Africans died in politically related incidents, according to the report of the Truth and Reconciliation Commission (Chapter 7). Most of the deaths occurred in Gauteng (4 756) and KwaZulu-Natal (3 653), but the Western Cape was by no means immune.

During the first few years of the decade, as national negotiations got under way in earnest, I was deeply involved in facilitating aspects of the transition to democracy in and around Cape Town, as a result of the work that came to me through our consultancy.

We were living through a bizarre interregnum, between apartheid's premature death notice and the new South Africa's overdue birth. It was a modified version of the situation described by the nineteenth-century Italian Marxist theorist Antonio Gramsci in his famous aphorism 'the old is dying but the new cannot be born'.

The national negotiations were soon in much more serious trouble as a result of two major political massacres. The first occurred on 17 June 1992, in Boipatong, near the industrial centre of Vanderbijlpark on the bank of the Vaal River in the province now known as Gauteng. Here forty-five people died in clashes between Inkatha-supporting hostel dwellers employed at the steelworks and their ANC rivals. There was a widespread perception that the police had assisted Inkatha in this attack, and the ANC withdrew from the constitutional negotiations in protest against what they regarded as police complicity in escalating community-based conflicts.

The second was outside Bisho, in the former Ciskei homeland, on 7 September. Protesters, demanding the removal of military dictator Brigadier Oupa Gqozo and the reincorporation of the Ciskei into South Africa, marched on Bisho. Gqozo's soldiers opened fire, killing 28 marchers and injuring 200. One soldier also died.

It was clear to all that the stalled negotiations were creating a climate ripe for escalating violence, and at the end of September, Mandela and De Klerk signed a memorandum of understanding, enabling the talks to resume. But even worse lay ahead.

On Easter Sunday, 10 April 1993, Chris Hani was assassinated in the driveway of his Boksburg home by a Polish immigrant and virulent anti-communist, Janusz Waluś. Hani, who was general secretary of the South African Communist Party and also commander-in-chief of MK, was an iconic figure to millions of South Africans. His assassination was the greatest crisis South Africa's negotiated transition faced, bringing the process to the edge of the abyss, which was no doubt the intention.

Its collapse was averted by an act of great leadership. Addressing the nation on television, Nelson Mandela brought South Africa back from the brink. I remember that speech even more clearly than I remember voting in our first democratic election. It was a pivotal moment.

'Tonight I am reaching out to every single South African, black and white, from the very depths of my being,' Mandela began. 'A white man, full of prejudice and hate, came to our country and committed a deed so foul that our whole nation now teeters on the brink of disaster. A white woman, of Afrikaner origin, risked her life so that we may know and bring to justice this assassin.'

Madiba was referring to Chris Hani's white neighbour in Dawn Park, who managed to write down the number plate of the getaway car. Her action led to Waluś's arrest and opened the trail which ended with Clive Derby-Lewis, a member of the Conservative Party.

I had always theoretically appreciated Madiba's leadership skills, but never were they as manifest as in that moment. He was seeking to build national unity out of an action that came close to plunging the country into civil war overnight.

'What has happened,' he said, 'is a national tragedy that has touched millions of people across the political and colour divide ... Now is the time for all South Africans to stand together against those who, from any quarter, wish to destroy what Chris Hani gave his life for – the freedom of all of us. Now is the time for our white compatriots, from whom messages of condolence continue to pour in, to reach out with an understanding of the grievous loss to our nation, to join in the memorial services and the funeral commemorations. Now is the time for the police to act with sensitivity and restraint, to be real community policemen and women who serve the population as a whole. There must be no further loss of life at this tragic time.

'This is a watershed moment for all of us.

'Our decisions and actions will determine whether we use our pain, our grief and our outrage to move forward to what is the only lasting solution for our country – an elected government of the people, by the people, and for the people.'

It was no coincidence that the short address repeated the most famous line of history's most frequently quoted speech, Abraham Lincoln's Gettysburg Address, delivered after a great battle during a civil war that brought an end to slavery. Like Lincoln, Mandela wove together the core values of freedom and equality with the sacrifices required to achieve them. Mandela urged the continuation of the constitutional negotiations as the best possible tribute to Hani's legacy.

In July, a collection of right-wing paramilitary organisations stormed the World Trade Centre in Kempton Park, where the talks were being held, determined to derail the process. Although there was no loss of life, it was a dramatic scene. The police were powerless to stop the armed occupation. Using a Viper armoured vehicle, the right-wingers crashed through the giant plate-glass windows that constituted the façade of the centre and routed the negotiators, who sought refuge in smaller meeting rooms. After spraying slogans on the walls and urinating on the furniture, the protesters held a prayer meeting in the main negotiation hall. Looking back, I think of this as the forerunner to the 'poo protests'.

In the year that followed, new threats arose. Fifty thousand trained and equipped right-wing paramilitary fighters, under the command of the military general Constand Viljoen, were itching to go to war with Umkhonto we Sizwe. Viljoen eventually demobilised his troops and persuaded them to participate peacefully in the civilian-led process that culminated in elections, after a clause was inserted in the draft constitution to make it possible for a majority government to pass an act of parliament enabling self-determination for minorities.

Equally crucially, the leader of the Inkatha Freedom Party, Mangosuthu Buthelezi, was also persuaded by representatives of the international Eminent Persons Group to modify his demands at the eleventh hour and participate in the elections, despite an earlier decision to boycott them. The result would have been catastrophic. The balance of forces in KwaZulu-Natal would have made it possible for Inkatha and the ANC, the most bitter adversaries, to extend the area's bloody conflict indefinitely.

Inside the bubbling South African cauldron, the constitutional negotiators at Kempton Park understood how high the stakes were. They knew there was no alternative to finding sufficient consensus for a legal framework that would enable South Africa's political rivals to use their newfound freedom within the law; and provide a magnet strong enough to draw them all into the joint project of building one of the most diverse nations on earth.

The constitution they drafted was described as the world's most progressive, and despite its inevitable flaws, it reflected the foresight and expertise that went into its formulation. Although no constituency was entirely happy, they were prepared to live with compromise, because everyone knew the famous South African aphorism was never more applicable to our situation than it was then: 'The Alternative Is Too Ghastly to Contemplate'.

Within the year we were ready for what the world hailed as the 'South African miracle', the first democratic election on 27 April 1994. The miracle lay in the fact that South Africa's legendary decency and common sense had overcome seemingly insurmountable obstacles.

Every South African who voted on that historic day remembers their specific circumstances, their neighbours in the snaking queues, the sense of purpose, the first stirrings of what we believed and hoped was the birth of a new nation.

My memories start with our car ride to the voting station.

'Who are you going to vote for?' I asked Johann.

He laughed.

'I'm serious,' I said. 'Who are you going to vote for?'

Johann was a paid-up member of the ANC. He thought I was asking a rhetorical question.

So I answered my own question. 'I'm going to vote for the DP,' I said.

'On this historic occasion?' Johann asked. 'Surely we need to celebrate liberation by voting for the party that led the struggle for it.'

I answered something to the effect that we should not regard this moment, as historic as it was, as the culmination of our struggle for democracy. It was perhaps the end of the beginning, but the next stage would be equally challenging. If I had known Coretta Scott King's words then, I might have used them. 'Freedom is never really won. You earn it and win it in every generation.'

The greatest risk to our future now, I said, was that the ANC would become too powerful. It would inevitably win an overwhelming victory, so today we had to start the next phase of our democratic struggle, to balance this democracy and prevent too much power being concentrated in too few hands. 'Now is the time,' I said, quoting a famous ANC phrase, 'to start building a new non-racial, democratic alternative. There is nothing approximating this at present, but we have to start somewhere.'

Johann reflected on what I was saying. Today, looking back, he believes I was right.

While the world celebrated South Africa's first democratic election, with good cause, the outcome gave me pause for thought. It set up our electoral architecture as a contest between rival race-based nationalisms: the African National Congress versus the National Party. By then, I had come to the conclusion that, rhetoric aside, the 'National' part of both organisations' names would override all other considerations. I had seen enough of both parties to know that, in essence, they were racial nationalist movements. If South African politics defaulted to a contest of competing racial nationalisms – black versus white – democracy stood no chance. Apart from all the other negatives of this line-up, it would preclude the possibility of power changing hands through the ballot box – a precondition for democratic accountability to work. While the world celebrated, I wondered how we would take forward the next phase of the struggle for democracy.

Tony Leon, newly elected leader of the tiny Democratic Party following the resignation of party leader Zach de Beer after the DP's near annihilation at the polls, felt the burden even more keenly than I did.

Shortly after the election, Mandela and De Klerk set up the government of national unity, with Mandela as president and De Klerk as his deputy. President Mandela offered Tony a cabinet post. He declined. It was more important for South Africa's long-term future, he said, to start building a strong alternative to the ANC. He seemed to be embracing a hopeless cause, as the leader of a 1.7 per cent party, but few others would have been prepared to take on the most unenviable job on the planet – building a viable opposition to the party led by the world's most revered statesman, Nelson Mandela. Perhaps more than anyone else, Mandela realised how important Tony's decision was for the future of democracy.

Apart from all his other contributions, in the constitutional negotiations and throughout his term as leader of the DP and, later, the DA, the decision to build an opposition rather than secure a cushy post in Madiba's cabinet will secure Tony Leon's place in history as one of the architects of our democracy.

By this time, I had accepted the offer of the position of director of public affairs and development at the University of Cape Town, tempted by the luxury of just one job, rather than concurrent major consulting challenges which saw me managing multiple projects simultaneously. David Shandler continued in the small business we had started together.

As head of an administrative department at UCT I was dealing with issues ranging from internal and external communication (including a weekly campus newspaper and other publications), alumni affairs, fundraising, student recruitment and university events, including graduations. I also wrote important speeches and contributed regular opinion pieces to the ongoing newspaper debates about the future of universities.

We faced stiff competition from Stellenbosch University, which was ratcheting up its recruitment of prospective students at UCT's traditional feeder schools. During those early years of our democracy many white English-speaking students (and especially their parents) were looking for alternatives to what they dubbed 'Moscow on the Hill'. Of course, describing an open, liberal university as 'Moscow' was as misleading as calling Table Mountain a 'hill', which gives some idea of the warped context in which we were working.

A growing number of white English-speaking students were making Stellenbosch their first choice, and to accommodate them, Stellenbosch was offering a growing range of courses in English. In the early 1990s the purpose was not to make the university more accessible to black students; it was to make Stellenbosch an easy sell to the many white parents and principals who wanted a calm campus that would not take children out of their comfort zone.

UCT's vice-chancellor, Stuart Saunders, had put the university on a different trajectory. Long before apartheid ended, he had desegregated the university residences and initiated pioneering work in the field of student recruitment based on tests to determine a student's inherent capacity to succeed at university, rather than merely measure their school-based knowledge (which severely compromised those students emerging from inferior apartheid education).

In September 1996, Mamphela Ramphele was appointed vice-chancellor of UCT, the first black woman university principal in South Africa. I already knew her well, as we had worked together on the Second Carnegie Inquiry into Poverty and Development in the early 1980s. Mamphela and I had become friends as we sought to balance parenthood with a demanding career. Our sons spent many a night sleeping over at each other's homes. Now she was my new boss, with a completely different leadership style from Stuart Saunders. She could be as tough and uncompromising as he was intuitive and understated.

One of the highlights of my job was the exceptional people I met, but probably none more so than Thandeka Kunene. We met in 1994, when I heard about a student fundraising initiative to help students bridge their fee shortfalls, and so avoid financial exclusion, which was a focus of student protest at the time.

Thandeka was head student of the enormous university residence, Liesbeeck Gardens, which housed 800 students. One Monday morning, walking around the residence, she was appalled to see the number of empty bottles and cans being removed from the flats by the cleaners, across the range of every alcoholic beverage imaginable. She assisted them to gather all the empties in one place, and then did a calculation. She worked out that over a single weekend, the students of Liesbeeck Gardens had spent R330 000 on alcohol.

'It seemed to me somewhat contradictory that we were protesting about our fee shortfalls and were still capable of spending this kind of money partying over one weekend,' she told me later.

Thandeka was strategic enough to realise that she would fail if she tried to divert the money from entertainment to fees, so she hit on another plan. She arranged to purchase alcohol directly from the suppliers and set up a student business that sold discounted alcohol, the entire profit of which went into financial aid. She called the organisation Ujima (Swahili for collective work and responsibility) and it became an instant success. Because most students did not understand Swahili, she changed the name to Ufundo, combining the word 'fund' with *funda* (learn!) in Xhosa.

Soon Ufundo was the biggest student organisation on campus, drawing together all the factional political student organisations. In their first year, they raised R1 million towards student financial aid, which was an enormous sum of money at the time.

As the department I headed was responsible, among other things, for fundraising, I asked to meet Thandeka when I heard about her initiative. I was taken aback when the slight, high-cheekboned beauty walked through my door. For some reason I had imagined her looking very different. During our first discussion I learnt that she was a postgraduate student in mathematics, having completed her Bachelor of Science in maths and applied maths in 1992. Born and raised in Soweto, she had attended St Matthews, a Catholic school run by Irish nuns close to the famous Regina Mundi church. 'One of the nuns was a fantastic maths teacher and that was where I developed my love for mathematics. I turned out to be very good at it,' Thandeka explained. She arrived at UCT on a scholarship.

But Thandeka arrived via a long detour – having been trained as an expert in military combat work in MK, into which she was recruited as a schoolgirl. She underwent training in Zambia, Angola and Zimbabwe, and was chosen as one of the operatives to be infiltrated back into South Africa to start building underground units internally.

Then she came to UCT, where she continued recruiting members into the organisation underground. She also excelled as a student. 'When 1994 came, I wanted to move away from politics to development. I thought the time was right. That was when I met you.'

For my part, I was totally amazed by her story. I had become accustomed to fundraising to try to meet student demands for financial support. To have a student from a very disadvantaged background walk across my threshold and offer to help with our fundraising blew me away. Thandeka soon introduced me to her friend Arthur Phaswana, who was also a postgraduate maths student and was equally passionate about fundraising for student financial aid. Arthur's father, Fred Phaswana, was a well-known businessman, and his networks helped.

Suffice to say, we reached an agreement which would see Ufundo raising millions to ensure we prevented student exclusions. If Ufundo raised money to prevent exclusions, the university would contribute the balance. In the first year of our co-operative agreement, the fees shortfall was R3 million (which seems ridiculously small today) and Ufundo had raised R1 million. The university duly contributed the balance. There were no financial exclusions.

Having become a maths tutor at UCT while working on her master's degree, Thandeka moved out of residence; she sublet a room in a flat near the university. She and Arthur continued to run Ufundo with great success, and I offered her a part-time job in my department, which she keenly accepted. We developed a great partnership. When the original tenant of her flat returned, she battled to find a place to stay, so I suggested she come to stay with us – which she did for three years, in the little cottage that had been the MK hideout during the states of emergency in the 1980s.

By this time Thandeka had become a passionate vegetarian Rastafarian with a growing interest in hemp. (I never dug too deeply.) She developed a firm friendship with Professor Frances Aimes, who was researching the use of medical cannabis oil, and she started the rather pompous-sounding Ancient Hemp Research Institute with her assistance. There, she says, she analysed the difference between hemp and dagga, and explained to me that hemp contains 1 per cent of tetrahydrocannabinol while dagga contains 20 per cent.

She was granted an Abe Bailey scholarship to the United Kingdom and stayed on there to do her MBA, determined to pioneer a hemp industry in South Africa. She returned to the country after graduating *magna cum laude*.

Thandeka started her first small business, Hooked on Hemp, from her mother's house, and found the practice of starting a business somewhat more challenging than the theory. Soon she was bankrupt. She struggled back to her feet before starting House of Hemp, which today has three factories producing hemp fibre and hemp oil.

When I met her years later, she was tickled to tell me that she had bought a farm in Midvaal from a man called Pieter Willem Botha. 'Can you imagine that? I bought P.W. Botha's farm. I thought that was poetic justice.'

And I was tickled when she told me: 'I could easily have become a racist if I hadn't met you.'

I was indeed privileged to have encountered many talented and enterprising students during my time in that busy UCT office. Thandeka Kunene was certainly one of them.

* * *

Before I accepted the job at UCT, I had been approached to stand for election to the governing body of my children's school, The Grove Primary School, by a visionary educator named Alixe Lowenherz. Alixe wanted me to apply my strategic-planning skills to the school's own transition. Trevor Gaunt, a politically sussed engineer, and his wife Eleanor nominated me and I was duly elected. Within a short while, I became the governing-body chairperson. In that position, I contributed to the formulation of the South African Schools Act, interacting regularly with renowned educationist Peter Hunter, who was leading the process.

I was determined to keep my children in a diversifying public-school system, while working hard to continuously improve its quality. I knew we had to diversify both our student and staff complement and increase our pupil/teacher ratio to ensure that we assisted the national effort to redistribute education resources equitably across the system as a whole. We introduced a bursary scheme which enabled middle-class parents to pay double fees to subsidise a child whose parents could not afford to pay any fees at all. A surprising number of parents volunteered to pay this extra amount. On the advice of educationists, we tried to introduce Xhosa mother-tongue education for Xhosa-speaking children in the foundation phase, together with what was called 'additive bilingualism', but we faced an angry backlash from their parents, alleging that we were trying to disguise our apartheid intentions by offering separate classes based on language. In any event, they argued, they had sent their children to The Grove because they wanted an English education for them. Parental choice, as guaranteed in the constitution, triumphed.

We appointed our first black teacher, Miss Busi Bout, and I ensured that my Thomas was in her class to signal to the school that the governing body had full confidence in her. We employed black graduates to do internships with our most experienced teachers to give them exposure to the best professional practice we could offer. It almost seems patronising and condescending to mention this today, but in a complex era of transition, these steps were important. I knew we had to keep the middle-class parents' support for public education, even as we moved rapidly to diversify the school. They brought the school professional skills, time and resources and I had to keep their support for the moves the board was making. It was a complex job, which I was soon doing alongside my role at UCT.

Our youngest son, Tom, loved sport, whereas Paul had been with the music crowd. I have to confess I was a better music mom than a soccer mom, which I left to Johann. I had put an enormous effort into supporting Paul's music after his recorder teacher, Fay Tagg, told me one day: 'When I can get Paul to sit still, I can see he is very musical. You need to do something about it.'

This led us to the Beau Soleil Music School, where, after a year of introduction to all the instruments, Paul chose the one I believed was least suited to his temperament, the violin. I was told to respect his choice. There was tough competition for the few vacancies for beginner violin lessons at the school, and I made it clear to him that if he was selected, he had to practise daily for at least five years before I would allow him to give up. If he did not do so, he would be filling a place that someone else could have used better. He got the point.

Nevertheless, after an initial burst of enthusiasm, getting him to practise became a daily chore. I was determined to make sure he did, and I braced myself for the daily head-on confrontations this involved.

When Tom's turn came around, I did not know whether I could go through this again. By that time Paul was playing the violin well, and really enjoying it. I felt it would be unfair not to do the same thing for my younger son, even if it meant a daily row. So in primary school, Tom, too, went to Beau Soleil. He chose the trumpet. I tried to get Tom into the same practising routine, but failed, even though he did not resist quite as vehemently as Paul had. One day, Tom simply refused to budge. He was not going to practise the trumpet. He wanted to play soccer. I made a token show of drawing the line until Tom said, with absolute clarity and accuracy, 'Mommy, Paul is musical. I'm physical.'

I couldn't fault his logic and was happy to call it quits. I also have to admit I breathed a sigh of relief that I no longer had to have a daily fight over music practice.

By happenstance, in an early stage of writing this memoir, I sat next to Koos Bekker, then chairman of Naspers, at a function. We chatted about the challenges of writing an autobiography. I said my book would be a warts-and-all account of my life. 'You'll be able to write honestly about everything,' he predicted, 'except your children.'

I spent a lot of time thinking about this. My genes are Jewish enough for me genuinely to believe my children are magnificent, and to be totally convinced that this is an objective assessment. Like all young people, our boys have had their challenges, their ups and downs, but I think they learnt the right lessons from them, and maybe they will one day write their own stories. Whatever they decide, it is not for me to do so for them, so I'll confine myself to some of the episodes they were too young to remember but remain indelibly imprinted in my mind.

Now, as young adults, our sons are on life's road, working on things that give them purpose. No parent could ask for a greater blessing. If I had known things would turn out this way, I probably wouldn't have worried so much; but then again, maybe things turned out this way precisely because I did. Wherever the truth lies, I am sure the X chromosome includes an extra genetic sequence, the 'worry function', which plays a crucial role in human evolution by ensuring that children (especially those with Y chromosomes) survive childhood and reach adulthood with a modicum of civilisation and self-discipline.

I recall reading a magazine article about how archaeologists determined the diet of Neanderthals by analysing their bones. Not long afterwards, I read an article on dendrochronology, the science of dating trees by counting the rings in the trunk. Linking the two, I imagined my sons' bones comprising concentric circles of Kentucky Fried Chicken, McDonald's and Butler's pizza, the only food they were really enthusiastic about. So I salved my conscience by making them take a multivitamin pill every morning before they went to school.

When work took me away from home, Johann had to promise me he would give them their vitamin pill every morning. When I returned, I always asked whether he had. And he would reply: 'Yes, I always gave them their vitamins … but they didn't always take them.'

My worrying about this kind of thing was a source of much hilarity in our home and gave the boys endless opportunity to send me up. They still do some wonderful skits about me as they embellish their memories of various things I did, like calling them while I was abroad, across a nine-hour time differential, to check that they were eating salads and wearing sunscreen. Even I have to laugh at it.

Johann often quoted the legendary 'Jewish telegram': 'Start worrying now. Details to follow.'

'Worrying works,' I responded. 'Every single time I worry about the boys when they write exams, they do fine.'

Paul and Thomas are an intriguing genetic combination: the older has dark hair and dark eyes, looks like me, and has my temperament and his father's brain; the younger one, with blond hair and blue-grey eyes, has his father's looks and temperament, and my brain. Hardly surprising then that our elder teaches mathematics, and our younger is making a career in creative writing. It always surprises me that the same recipe produced two such different people, linked by an unbreakable brotherly bond.

They were unmistakably who they are from the moment they came into the world. Raising them has made me intrigued by the nature/nurture combination. The best advice I ever received was: all parents make mistakes, but don't make the mistake of taking the blame or the credit for what your children do. Fortunately, I was busy enough not to be over-involved in my children's lives. But nothing could prepare us for the curve balls hurled at us when we least expected them.

One night the landline rang at about 1:30 a.m. I jumped out of bed to answer. I was worried that there might be a problem with my parents. A breathy, sultry voice on the other end said, 'Hello, is that Mrs Maree?'

'Yes,' I said. 'Can I help you?'

'I have something important that I need to tell you.'

'What?' I replied anxiously. The tone of voice told me I was in for a shock, and my mind raced through all the possibilities.

'I need to tell you that I am having an affair with your husband' – long pause – 'and I am pregnant.'

I sank into a chair. 'Who are you?' I asked.

'My name is Samantha,' came the reply.

I was dumbstruck for a while. I had never had any reason to believe that Johann had been unfaithful to me, but he could conceivably have had an affair, as men sometimes do without wanting to put their marriage at risk. Were we now on the set of our own *Fatal Attraction* movie?

Before I got married, my mom had given me various pieces of unsolicited advice, including that a 'sidestep' (the direct translation of the German *Seitensprung*, as she euphemistically referred to an affair) is rarely a reason to end a marriage. I didn't agree with her, and I never passed on her advice to Johann – in case he took it.

I certainly did not want to leave Johann, and it had never occurred to me that he might want to leave me. But I also knew he would never abandon a child he may have fathered by another woman. So I fully expected this baby to end up with us. I had conjured this whole scenario up in seconds, because it was inconceivable to me that someone could invent a story like this. Just thinking about the prospect of a third child brought a wave of depression over me. The blood drained from my head.

When I found my voice again, I said to Samantha, 'Johann is here, would you like to speak to him?'

'Yes,' she breathed provocatively.

I went back into the bedroom and sat down next to my sleeping husband. I laid my hand on his arm. 'Johann,' I said, trying to make myself heard above his semi-snore. 'Johann, wake up. There's a woman on the phone who wants to speak to you.'

He hardly stirred.

'Johann, there is a woman on the phone who says she is having an affair with you and you have made her pregnant.'

He sat bolt upright as my words hit his central nervous system like an electric shock.

'What?' he asked.

'Samantha is on the phone. She says she's pregnant,' I said, trying to gauge his response. 'She wants to speak to you.'

Johann leapt from the bed, wide awake now, and told me: 'You take the phone in the dining room, I'll take the phone in the study.' The fact that he wanted me listening in on the conversation reassured me immediately.

'Hello,' he said, curtly.

Samantha's voice got even sultrier. 'Hell-oo-ooo', she purred, 'it's me. I'm sorry, but I had to tell your wife, given the circumstances.'

'Who's speaking?' Johann demanded.

'Oh, is that how it is?' she responded. 'You don't want to know me now?'

'Who are you?' Johann demanded again.

'Are you denying that you know me?' The purr audibly turned to a pout.

'Who is there with you?' Johann said sharply. 'Who has put you up to this?'

The phone clicked and the line went dead.

I felt violated by this telephonic intrusion into our home.

Once more, in the early hours of the morning, Johann and I made a cup of tea and sat next to each other on the bed to reflect on what had just happened.

'Look at my face,' I said to Johann, using the technique I used with the boys when I really wanted to be sure they were telling me the truth. 'Look at my face. Is there any truth to this? I need to know the truth. Are you having an affair with someone?'

Johann replied, 'Helen, you know I'm not. This is someone trying to get at you, not me. There is something else behind it. I am trying to work out what.'

I believed him, but still spent a fitful night trying to think who might have a motive to do something so potentially destructive. If our marriage had been shaky, this kind of intervention could have blown us apart, which was clearly the intention. Even though I trusted Johann, 'Samantha' had planted a seed of doubt in my mind, and the next morning I asked him to reassure me again. I was still in bed and Johann was in the bathroom when I asked the question. I heard him laughing uproariously and asked him what was so funny. He was shaving, and shaking with laughter.

'We both forgot last night,' he said. 'I can't make anyone pregnant. I've had a vasectomy.'

Then we both laughed.

There were other signs of Johann's fidelity that I picked up on without him even realising it. Once he returned from a conference in Berlin, where he had given a paper on the industrial-relations challenges of applying 'Just in Time' principles in the textile industry and the need to keep up with changing fashions. The audience, he told me, had burst out laughing when he said this was not a major challenge in the underwear industry because underwear tended to remain the same. He asked his audience why they found this observation so funny.

'It's because you think women's underwear doesn't follow fashion cycles,' a woman replied. And everyone laughed again.

In the earnest way that only Johann can, he informed his audience that this was not the empirical conclusion he had drawn from observing his wife. Which set them all off once more.

Johann had obviously just assumed that all women are as devoted as I am to what Woollies euphemistically describes as 'cotton briefs' (and which my sister more aptly calls 'bobba underpants') and the matching bras that come at a discount if you buy them in packs of three.

As my sons would say about their dad (their heads shaking in disbelief), 'Fresh from the farm.'

I was gentler. I told Johann he should heed his own lesson of avoiding general conclusions from a representative sample of one. But at least I knew I was that sample. If he had drawn that conclusion about women's underwear, he clearly could not have seen other women in their bras and panties since our marriage.

But back to the hoax calls. After a few more of them, I became convinced that this had something to do with a major court case with which I was involved in my capacity as chairperson of the governing body of The Grove Primary School.

Our opponent: the new ANC government. And already we had them on the back foot.

The case, which brought together a consortium of eighty public schools, took issue with the newly imposed voluntary severance package and redeployment scheme. This was the government's strategy to redistribute teaching posts throughout public schools without anyone losing their jobs. Essentially, it offered lucrative early retirement packages to teachers in order to entice them to leave education permanently, and then proposed to redistribute the remaining 'excess' teachers into the resulting vacancies. It subordinated the educational interests of children to the job-security demands of the South African Democratic Teachers Union (SADTU), and would have been a complete disaster for the public-school system – particularly for poor schools. Furthermore, it was a direct contradiction of the excellent new South African Schools Act, which had just been accepted by parliament, in the formulation of which I and the Grove governing body had enthusiastically participated. This act gave governing bodies a key role in interviewing and recommending teachers for posts.

It was during this period that I was first called a racist. It was from the mouth of Mzwandile Hewu, who was SADTU's provincial chairperson at that time. He was standing outside the arched gate of the school, using a megaphone to address hundreds of SADTU marchers and a large contingent of journalists. They were protesting against the school as a way of opposing our court case.

I had tried to tell SADTU how disastrous the policy would be for the poorest schools, where most of their members worked. I had tried to explain that the consequences for education would be the enticement of the most experienced teachers to leave the system, and the filling of vacancies unrelated to the competencies required. I said middle-class schools would be able to compensate by creating and filling posts funded by fees levied by governing bodies, something that poor schools would not have the means to do.

Their counter-argument was to call me a racist. This was, in the early years of the new South Africa, the ultimate insult, the perfect debate blocker. And it was also a totally new experience for me. In all my years in organisations associated with the mass democratic movement, I had been able to raise alternative points of view, which were debated on their merits. Now, in a democracy, this had become impossible.

Of course, they not only called me a racist. They called The Grove Primary School racist, which was the greatest irony of all. I don't think there was another public school in the early years of our democracy that had done as much to diversify its student body as The Grove had done. But SADTU knew all this, because several prominent SADTU members had enrolled their own children in the school. They used to drop their children off at the school each morning before making their way back to the schools at which they taught, to which they would never contemplate sending their own children. And here they were, seeking to disrupt a school in which children were studying uninterrupted, while their own pupils were left without teaching.

One of the SADTU leaders was Mr Phumzile Makhosana, a warm, congenial man, who was on the provincial executive of SADTU, and whose child was a Grove pupil. Mr Hewu's son went to Wynberg Boys' Junior School, one of the eighty partner schools in our case. The same applied to many other SADTU members.

I applied for a day's leave from UCT so that I could be at the school to deal with this unprecedented protest and to calm anxious parents. I found it fascinating that SADTU members whose children were at The Grove were among the most anxious parents, calling to ask the secretary whether they should bring their children to school on that day. Irony has always been woven into the fabric of South African society, but nowhere was it more evident than in the disjuncture between what SADTU members professed for others and the choices they made for their own children.

So the SADTU march went ahead, circling the school, and stopping at the front gate. They demanded I come out to address them, which I did. I made the mistake of trying to explain the rationale behind our case and to suggest that they should join us rather than fight us, because the government's teacher redistribution scheme would be particularly devastating for disadvantaged schools. It was the first time I had addressed a large protest march and I learnt the lesson there and then. When people are shouting slogans, they are in no mood for a rational argument.

'Now, comrades,' announced Mr Hewu over a megaphone, 'we can see that Comrade Mrs Maree is a racist comrade.'

He had used my married name, because I was known as Helen Maree in the school context, as parent to our children. I also did not want my private role to become intertwined with my professional role at UCT, where I was known by my maiden name, and the symbolic distinction was important.

It soon became quite apparent why. Shortly after the protest march, we had a function for school principals at UCT, which my department organised as part of our outreach and communication programme. After some posturing speeches, the SADTU principals staged a walkout because of my 'racist' presence.

This could have had serious consequences for the university. We were already under heavy fire from many white parents and principals for the pace of 'transformation', and now here was SADTU – which represented most black principals – labelling the director of the department that undertook student recruitment a 'racist'.

It was at times like this that I deeply appreciated Mamphela's clarity and strength. She never faltered. She understood the issues at stake and backed my position fully. She did not fall for SADTU's manipulation. This took real courage in the context. If she had not backed me, continuing my combined role at UCT and The Grove would have been untenable. But Mamphela never wavered. She let SADTU stage a walkout and we continued with our function.

Many years later, in another twist of fate, Mzwandile Hewu found himself working for me! Like many senior ANC cadres, he had been 'deployed' into a senior position in the province when the ANC ran it, after initially being appointed as the manager of the ANC caucus. When the ANC lost power in the Western Cape in 2009, Mr Hewu was palpably hostile to the DA administration at first, but slowly his position changed. When I was preparing to write this book, I asked him for an interview in order to capture his memories of our previous interchanges. He was happy to oblige, and I was absolutely amazed at his retrospective insights.

I asked if he remembered calling me a racist. Yes, he said, disarmingly, of course – 'that is what we called everyone who disagreed with us'. He elaborated: 'We had a culture of not listening to people who disagreed with us. We labelled them racist. Had we said okay, let us talk – we would have found one another because we both had the same aim to improve education. But that is what we robbed ourselves of. We actually should have taken the trouble to understand why you were opposed to that scheme, but we just said, No, they want to retain the old white privileges. We said, Because she is white, she must be prejudiced. We should have said, Let's have tea with her and understand what she is opposed to.

'Today we understand that you were saying, Don't do it this way. We are going to lose our experienced teachers. And that is exactly what happened, especially in maths and science and commerce. Schools ran short of these teachers. Then they closed the colleges; the universities were not producing the teachers we needed. It was a mess.

'It was our biggest mistake not to talk. What you said actually came true. They took our best teachers for a lot of money. We realised that implementation was going to cause havoc in the townships, especially for promotion posts.'

I asked what he meant by causing havoc for promotions posts. He then gave me my first real insight into why SADTU had suddenly changed its mind and started opposing the voluntary severance and redeployment scheme, after vilifying us for doing so.

Mr Hewu explained that the Department of Education and Training, the former apartheid department governing black education, had not advertised posts since 1994 and many teachers were 'acting' in promotion posts, such as principals, vice-principals and heads of departments in schools. However, the redeployment scheme would involve incumbents considered 'in excess' at other schools getting first preference for deployment to the existing vacancies in what SADTU considered 'their' schools. Because the promotion of their members was at risk, SADTU stood firm against the scheme being implemented in relation to senior posts in 'their' schools, and what was more, they succeeded. They demanded a closed vacancy list – i.e. only open to SADTU applicants – to avoid having to accept non-SADTU teachers. And although their demand was unlawful, they won without having to go to court.

I did not know this at the time, and it gave me some insight into the extent to which SADTU has actually run our education system since the dawn of democracy against only one yardstick: the convenience and advantage of its members. Children's educational interests always were, and remain, a distant second for the union. They were fine with transformation as long as it meant that their teachers would be deployed into other schools. But woe betide anyone who added 'and vice versa'.

It was the Grove case that propelled me into politics – but I was not quite there yet. I had a challenging job at UCT and I was also trying to be a good mother. I had not yet realised that there is no such thing as Superwoman. In fact, I suppose I had been conned into believing it was possible to have it all.

My role as chair of the governing body of The Grove had effectively become a second full-time job, and was particularly challenging because of the benchmark court case we were spearheading, in a deluge of negative publicity. As for my day job, because UCT correctly focused on its academic priorities, administrative departments were often under-resourced, to put it diplomatically. This meant working what is euphemistically described in the industrial-relations literature as 'unconventional hours'. My day typically began in the very early hours and ended late, with several 'parenting breaks' in between.

In that sense, 31 October 1996 was just another day at my hydra-headed office:

at work, at school, and at home. I remember the date because it was Halloween, and Paul, who was in Grade 6, had gone trick-or-treating with his friend Warren Minnie in the Claremont street where the Minnie family lived. Johann was due to fetch him at 8 p.m. At 7:30, just as Johann was walking out of the front door with his car keys, Warren's mother, Wendy, called to postpone the pick-up time. The boys had sprayed shaving cream all over the neighbour's garage door, she said, and would have to wash it off before Paul went home.

That prank – and Wendy's phone call – saved my life.

Tom had fallen asleep watching television on our bed. Johann was whiling away the extra thirty minutes before fetching Paul. I disappeared into the study to start my day's third shift, writing a speech for Dr Ramphele to deliver the next day to a large gathering of school principals. It had to be ready by the time the university's executive meeting convened at eight the next morning, 1 November 1996.

It was an important speech. UCT was moving boldly towards inclusivity in a complex environment. Almost everything that happened on the campus made headlines and generated controversy, even things that would seem tame today. We had just adopted a mission statement committing UCT to being 'flexible on access, active in redress and rigorous on success' and were trying to give content to that commitment. We were actively seeking to make ourselves the university-of-first-choice for good students of all races, from all backgrounds, seeking English-medium higher education.

The challenges of bridging the gap between being 'flexible on access' and 'rigorous on success' were enormous and costly. The gap had to be spanned by our strategies to be 'active in redress' both educationally and financially. With a rapidly diversifying student body, huge discrepancies in previous education experience and periodic campus protests, we remained determined also to retain the top students from the best English-medium high schools. It was a tall order.

That was the context of Mamphela's first scheduled speech to school principals. Public interest was high in hearing from the first black woman university vice chancellor. The subtext of the curiosity was an unstated question, bordering on scepticism, about what impact Mamphela's appointment would have on UCT. My purpose in writing the speech was to convince as many of her audience as possible (without doing a direct 'sell') that UCT was on the right course and should be the logical choice for top students, from advantaged and disadvantaged schools alike.

I was still at the point of jotting down preliminary thoughts when I heard the beep of a sensor, which was part of our home alarm system. It indicated that a door was being opened. Johann had heard it too, and walked out of the lounge at the same time as I stepped out of the study to examine the control panel in the passage. It told us the back kitchen door had been opened. Without a second thought, I strode towards the kitchen to close and lock the door. Fortunately, Johann followed close behind.

All I remember was the flash of the knife and the fist clutching it, bearing down at my neck. In a split second, as I ducked, Johann grabbed the wrist bearing the knife, and the battle was on. The dining-room chairs flew as we crashed down on the table. Johann was battling to stabilise the hand holding the knife while he did combat with his other hand. I tried to help by locking my arms around our attacker's legs in a rugby tackle, but a single kick sent me spinning. I returned and went for a more vulnerable body part, the only remaining option in this life-and-death struggle. After about two minutes, which felt like twenty, Johann had overpowered the man, with a little help from beneath from me. The intruder was pinned down, in a pool of his own urine, and some blood, the source of which I could not immediately determine.

Throughout the ordeal, I remember my greatest worry was that Tom would wake up and walk in on this terrifying scene.

Struggling to escape Johann's grip, the intruder used his teeth as a weapon of last resort, biting Johann on his lower neck and shoulder, drawing blood. Most people would have smashed his head on the quarry-tile floor, but Johann turned his attacker's face sideways and instructed me to 'Get some pantyhose and tie him up.'

I dashed to our bedroom, past a sleeping Tom, to my cupboard, and grabbed a pair of pantyhose. As I tried to tie the prostrate intruder's ankles together, he gave me another kick but, locked beneath Johann's grip, this time he failed to dislodge my grip. I then tied his knees. The reef knot I'd learnt in primary school came back instinctively when I needed it.

Then I called the Rondebosch police and opened the front door and the gate by remote control so that they could come in when they arrived. Johann continued to hold the man down. Within a few minutes, the door burst open and a woman sergeant, gun drawn, bellowed 'Freeze!' My first words were a request to her to keep the volume down, to lower the risk of Tom waking up. She obliged, arrested the intruder and left.

Tom slept on. By now it was about 9 p.m. I phoned Wendy to ask if Paul could sleep over at their house because something unforeseen had happened that required immediate attention, and it would be too late to fetch Paul when it was resolved. I did not go into detail, but something in the tone of my voice must have conveyed to the intuitive Wendy that it was best not to ask. Johann and I resolved not to tell the children or anyone else about this episode. We did not want the boys to find out about it, because we thought it might make them fearful in their own home.

The police returned to take statements, while I cleaned up the dining-room and kitchen floors. When my adrenalin levels subsided, I realised I had either seriously sprained or broken the baby finger on my right hand. Johann's neck bites were bleeding too, so we called the doctor, who arrived somewhere between ten and eleven. Tom was still sleeping peacefully.

The doctor gave Johann an injection, strapped my finger, and advised us to be tested for HIV following the tough physical confrontation in what had become a sea of bodily fluids. We showered and made a cup of tea. I took two strong painkillers to lessen the pain in my throbbing finger.

I got back to the speech after midnight. Once again I realised how therapeutic it is not to be able to dwell on a crisis. For me, the best way to deal with a real shock to the system is to have no other option but to face the next hurdle, confront the next deadline. I am not one for trauma counselling, because it just makes me think I have a reason to feel traumatised. I find it more helpful to get on with the next thing.

I finished the speech to my satisfaction at about half past three in the morning and arrived with it, printed in the correct format, at Mamphela's office shortly before eight, after we'd got done with the morning school routine. It felt good to have been able to do that, in the circumstances. Feeling that I had risen to the occasion helped me not to dwell on the experience.

I was a bit shaky, but I got through the day. Above all, I was grateful to be alive.

Not long afterwards, we had our second incident. This time Johann was away at a conference. After fetching the boys from aftercare at The Grove, I took them to the Spur for a burger because it was easier than cooking supper. When we arrived home and opened the front door, a man stepped out of a bedroom into the long passage and faced us from the distance of about three metres. We all froze for an instant. Then the man turned and strolled, almost casually, down the passage. I pressed the panic button at the door. Silence. It wasn't working. Paul, who was twelve years old, immediately went on the attack to protect me and his little brother. He started running down the passage to give chase. I bolted after him to drag him back, hearing the sound of glass smashing in a back room. I got the children into the street, where I alerted a neighbour who called the police. Again they were there in minutes, but did not make any arrests this time. We found two broken windows and many displaced items that the burglars were in the process of removing when we surprised them. The police said there must have been several intruders, judging from the various areas of activity. I was deeply relieved that they had chosen to retreat rather than confront us.

The police undertook to do patrols near our house for the rest of the night. I locked myself and the boys into our bedroom, where we spent the rest of the night in fitful sleep.

The next day I was due to go on a fundraising trip to Johannesburg with Mamphela, where we were going to spend the night. Grace was scheduled to sleep over at our house to take care of the boys. On the way to school that morning, I told Paul and Tom that I was going to cancel my trip to Johannesburg and stay home with them. When Grace arrived for work and I told her what had happened, I asked her to spend the night with us anyway, so that we could support each other. She said sure.

Then I went to tell Mamphela what had happened and why I was not going to be able to accompany her after all. I explained that Johann was away and that I needed to deal with my domestic situation. All the arrangements for her fundraising trip were in place, I told her, including appointments, venues and transport. Her answer was no. She reminded me that I had chosen to accept a challenging job and that I had to fulfil my professional responsibilities without allowing my personal life to intrude. I understood her point, but I felt these circumstances were exceptional.

Looking back, I should simply have refused to go and taken the consequences, but I didn't. It was too late to organise a sleepover for the boys elsewhere. In the pre-cellphone era, arranging anything took far longer and required more logistics than it does today. I only had time to get back home and pack before leaving for the airport. I did not even have time to get the windows repaired. But I did call the departmental driver, Bobby Lewis, who was always willing to fetch the children from school when my work commitments made it impossible for me to do so.

When I told Grace that I would have to go to Johannesburg after all, she said she would feel more comfortable if her then boyfriend, Abel Mputing, came to spend the night with them. I was relieved that there would be a man in the house.

As I drove to the airport, my emotions ran riot. I resolved that I would say nothing until I had my feelings under control. I hardly said a word on that trip, only responding matter-of-factly when spoken to.

At the fundraising dinner, someone made a joke about whether they could really have an honest conversation in the presence of the 'whitey' (meaning me). It was genuinely meant as a joke, but in the circumstances I did not find it funny. If only they knew how much I didn't want to be there. I had to apply all my self-control not to get up, leave the table and catch a taxi back to the airport. That night I hardly slept, vacillating between fury and concern about Grace, Abel and the boys. Today, text messages or WhatsApp would have made things so much easier.

My fury was aggravated by the fact that the only contribution I had made on the trip was to take follow-up notes. Anyone could have done that. It was compounded by the guilt I felt on leaving the boys, having told them I would stay. But, again, I was worrying in vain. I returned home to find them as happy as crickets, having had a wonderful time with Grace and Abel. I did not even ask what time they went to bed. Neither did I allude to the fact that they had a reason to feel let down by me. I had learnt from my mother's guilt not to transfer my feelings to my children. Once you give a child a reason to feel hard done by, they often do, even though it might not have otherwise occurred to them. So my philosophy was: If they did not raise something, neither did I. But if they did, I took their concerns on board and listened carefully, even when I thought they were unfounded.

To her credit, a few days later Mamphela called me to apologise. I greatly appreciated that gesture, and our friendship was back on track.

Working for Mamphela was demanding. Despite our friendship, and that of our children, she was also my boss, and I respected the hierarchy. She was toughest on the people who supported her the most, and we were (mostly) resilient enough to take it. I will never join the choir of those who slam her term as vice-chancellor. The university was strong enough to provide a platform for her two greatest strengths – communicating our vision, and raising the funds required to realise it. Her strengths outweighed her weaknesses, and that is all one can ask of any leader.

However, I often arrived home feeling battered from all sides.

Looking back, I realise just how important this decade was in preparing me for the pressure I was destined to face in my, as yet unanticipated, political career.

All through the Grove controversy, I had been writing about education policy in the media to dispel the default assumption that the issue revolved around 'white racism'. Tony Leon, the leader of the DP at the time, was one of the people who read what I wrote. He contacted me early in 1998 and asked me whether I would be prepared to cast an eye over the DP's education policy and give him my views. I did, and I told him that it needed some work. He asked me to do it, which I did. He then asked whether I would be prepared to throw my hat into the ring for a seat in the provincial legislature, because, he predicted, there was a chance the DP might win enough seats to hold the balance of power, which could put the party into government for the first time. Who knows, he said, you could even end up as the provincial minister of education and then be able to do something about implementing your policy, not just talking about it.

I said I would think about it.

I discussed Tony's suggestion with Johann, who was just emerging from a severe bout of depression which had seen him take off work for several months to recover. He was non-committal, but did not rule out the idea. James Selfe, Tony's right-hand man who had played a crucial management role in the DP since its inception, also worked hard to convince me.

But what propelled me into taking up their challenge was attending an education portfolio committee meeting in parliament, called to discuss new draft legislation that the government was enacting to counter the impact of The Grove's court victory over the disastrous redeployment and voluntary severance plan. The court had found that the voluntary severance package and redeployment scheme was not only unlawful, but it made no logical sense and could only undermine public education.

The ANC's attempt to change the law to legalise this scheme outraged me. Our democracy was so new, and here was the ANC government pursuing National Party tactics. If a court overruled an action as unlawful, their response was to change the law rather than change the unlawful government directives.

The future of the public-school system was at stake, so I attended the parliamentary portfolio committee hearings. I assumed that members of parliament would be fully seized with the issues at stake, well prepared, and able to debate the clauses in the proposed amendment bill and their implications.

I was dumbfounded and disillusioned to learn the opposite. Many of the ANC members arrived dressed to the nines, with their envelopes containing the papers for the meeting (if they had them at all) still unopened. They sat through the meeting doing everything except concentrate on and debate the issues at hand. Mike Ellis of the tiny Democratic Party which had nearly been wiped out in the 1994 election was the one person fully apprised of the situation. He, and he alone, raised issue after issue, clause by clause, to warn of the consequences the amendments might have.

Then and there I knew my decision to vote for the DP in 1994 had been the right one.

At the break, my disillusionment with the rest of the parliamentarians turned to anger. A food trolley was wheeled into the meeting area, laden with delicacies, and I watched as members who had done absolutely no work all morning piled their plates. There was plenty left over. I then observed how several of them took the parliamentary table napkins, loaded them with as much food as they could, folded them up and then deposited them in cavernous handbags, along with several cans of cold-drinks. I was frankly gobsmacked at this literal feeding at the government trough.

But my mind was made up. I was going to get into that arena, because it was the place from which the fight would have to be waged. I called Tony Leon that same evening and said, Yes, I'm going to throw my hat in the ring for the provincial list in the 1999 election.

Then I called my mom to tell her. She was vehemently opposed to my decision and urged me to reconsider.

'You are much too sensitive to be in politics,' she said.

'Not any more,' I replied.

I was relieved that she did not know the half of what the 1990s had brought into our lives. I had told her about events on a need-to-know basis, because I know that a mother's worrying is never done, no matter how old her children are, and my mother was unusually well endowed with the worrying gene.

'Please don't do this,' she begged, knowing from experience that I would do what I believed was right in any event.

And for the umpteenth time, I answered: 'Mom, I have made up my mind. Please accept it.'

As my time at UCT came to an end, I was delighted to receive the vice-chancellor's medal for services to the university. But my most treasured memento from my years at UCT was a letter sent to me by a young man who worked in the Alumni Office, in the department I headed. He had arrived during my term of office, first as a student in part-time employment, and later as a junior employee, full of fire and brimstone and determined to challenge every aspect of 'the system'. He gave me a run for my money, but there was something about him that I related to, and that he responded to.

No accolade that I have received, before or since, has meant as much to me as Will Hlatshwayo's email, dated 25 January 1999.

Dear Helen,
Now that you are no longer directly my boss, I think it is fitting that I let you know something very insignificant.

When I came to the Communications dept I came braced for a war. I had heard a lot of stories told about you and liberals. Mainly bad. I now concede defeat since there was no war to be fought.

Instead of a liberal monster I found a firm but fair manager. You are a stickler when it comes to details, but this applies to all your staff.

There were times when you dwell into some philosophical or moral issue, that I felt you were the mother I never had time to know. There were times when you gave me a serious talk that I had to battle to keep tears back. Within a few months I have learned quite a number of valuable lessons. There is one thing about you: you never undermined the value of any person. It really made all the difference to me. I will always value what I have observed from you.

I have always been a difficult person, growing up an orphan and mainly fending for myself from the age of eleven. I had to grow up even before I reached my teens. Growing up like that makes one feel threatened each time something goes not according to one's liking. Consequently, I must be the most defensive person to walk this planet. And that is my biggest problem. It closes avenues for smooth co-operation with colleagues sometimes. I was glad that somehow you found a way of dealing with me. Although we had some mishaps occasionally, you dealt with it in a professional but understanding manner, displaying far greater maturity that impressed upon me the fact that I still have a long way to go.

I appreciate the respect you showed me, although I doubt I deserved even a quarter of it. I, in turn, respect and admire you, both as a person and manager, although I may not have shown it.

I hope we will remain on good terms forever.

Regards,

Will

It was a wonderful way to round off the UCT years. Will had shown me there is light at the end of the tunnel of the turbulent teenage years – something I would need to keep reminding myself of in my parenting role in the decade that lay ahead.

And, as 1999 drew to a close, Grace gave birth to Chulumanco on 27 December. His name means 'joy' in Xhosa, and rarely was a baby so aptly named. I cannot recall ever hearing him cry. Grace was a natural, relaxed mother to her 'Joy Boy', who brought a new and extra dimension to our family, which compensated somewhat for my repeated absences.

My first foray into representative politics was the start of a new era, and quite different from what I had expected.

8

Yes, Minister

IN THE SPACE of six months, from January to June 1999, I went from being a mom working at a university and chairing a primary-school governing body to being sworn in as MEC for education in the Western Cape provincial government. The position of MEC carried the title 'Minister' under the provincial constitution.

As I raised my right hand to say 'So help me God' in the stinkwood-panelled provincial legislature on 18 June 1999, I reflected on the extraordinary sequence of events that had brought me to this point. The significance of this moment overcame me, and my glasses misted over.

Three colleagues and I were in the process of becoming the Democratic Party's first ever members in a democratic provincial government. I felt the weight of responsibility pressing down on us and the obstacles rise before us. Our performance would be make or break for our party and, in the longer term, for the country.

As always seems to happen to me in times of great moment, I forget the details. I'm sure there was some pomp and ceremony and lunch together with our spouses afterwards, but the only detail I recall was watching the event on TV that night.

The visuals switched backwards and forwards between two high-profile events in which I had been involved, three years apart. The first showed me emerging from the Cape High Court, in 1996, as chair of The Grove Primary School's governing body, having just won the historic court battle for the right of governing bodies to recommend teachers to fill vacancies in public schools. The second showed me being sworn in as provincial education minister that morning, three winters later. And lo and behold – I was wearing exactly the same black-and-red outfit on both occasions! Time to expand my wardrobe, I said to myself.

I had originally become active in The Grove's governing body to make a contribution towards building the quality of public education. My experience taught me that I would have to go into politics to do that effectively. And here I was, being sworn into executive office with a mandate to do just that.

To get there, I had had to get through five hoops, some of which were entirely dependent on the decisions and actions of others. Negotiating each one seemed challenging enough. Getting through all five in quick succession seemed impossible. Until it happened. Sometimes, as the late, great *Sunday Times* editor Joel Mervis used to say, 'all your finesses go right'.

They did for me in 1999.

First, I managed to do well enough in the DP's tough electoral-college selection process to be placed number five on their list.

Then the DP won just enough votes to scrape past the five-seat threshold and get me elected. Our 11.91 per cent of the vote in the Western Cape entitled the DP to exactly 5.002 seats in the legislature, which shows just how close an election outcome can be.

Next, it turned out that the five elected DP members held the balance of power in the provincial government, by a single seat (mine). Neither of the two big parties, the ANC or the renamed New National Party (NNP), had managed to reach 50 per cent, which meant neither could form a government on its own. The era of coalition government had dawned for South Africa, and the tiny DP would be its pioneers.

Then we had to negotiate the terms of a coalition, as a minority partner, to ensure that we could make a visible difference in government and avoid being drowned out by a bigger, more dominant party. We got an excellent 'bride price' when the NNP agreed that four out of the five elected DP members would sit in the provincial cabinet, with plum portfolios, including the two big-budget departments, health and education. These would give us a platform to show what we could do in government.

And, finally, Hennie Bester, our caucus leader, chose me to be one of the DP's ministers, even though I was his most junior caucus member. He weighed up whether to assign me to education or to health, and then I got the call. He told me he was submitting my name to the premier, Gerald Morkel (who was also the NNP Western Cape leader), to appoint me provincial minister of education. I was delighted.

The night of my swearing in, the phone rang during supper. Tom was ten, the age when kids love to answer the phone, and he ran to reach it first. He answered, and I saw him frown.

'Minister?' he asked, puzzled. 'Minister? Do you mean my mom?'

Then he roared with laughter, forgot about the person on the line, and called out to his brother: 'Hey Paul, do you know what they call Mom on the phone? They call her Minister!' Then both boys roared with laughter.

When I got to the phone it was Nat Kaschula, a senior professional in the education department.

'There isn't much respect for your position in your home, is there?' said Nat dryly.

When I had finished the conversation, the boys were still wide-eyed.

'Yoh, Mom, people treat you with respect, hey?' commented Paul. Then he added quickly, 'But we'll make sure you stay humble.'

They certainly did.

So did the demands of the job and the obstacles that stood in the way of doing it. Not to mention the controversies that accompanied it.

It had been a difficult and controversial election campaign. The DP's slogan 'Fight Back!' caused an uproar. The fact that controversy was the strategic intention didn't make it any easier. My family loathed our slogan, and I, too, had my doubts. Of course, the ANC wasted no time in racialising it, claiming the DP was 'fighting blacks'. Our argument that our fightback was against unemployment, crime, corruption, poor education, etc. was swept aside by a hostile media that swallowed the ANC's line whole.

Ryan Coetzee, the twenty-something strategist directing our media campaign, was relaxed, which made me worry even more. I thought he hadn't grasped what we were up against. I was co-ordinating the DP's communication in the Western Cape, reporting to Ryan nationally. It was near torture going through the newspapers early each morning, preparing for our daily teleconference. We were being slammed and censured from every quarter, including newspapers that had in the past been sympathetic to the DP. I did my best to counter the negative coverage, with little impact.

'Our coverage is so negative,' I said to Ryan one morning, 'the outcome of this election is going to be a disaster.'

'Helen,' he said, in his bordering-on-brash way, 'you still don't get it, do you? That is the whole point! We *want* them to fight with us. Every day we want the election to be depicted as a contest between the ANC and the DP. We have achieved exactly that. There are two dogs in this fight, and we are one of them. It makes us look bigger, stronger and more relevant than we are. The campaign is working exactly as planned.'

His strategy succeeded. We shot up the ranks from fifth position nationally in 1994 to second position in 1999, pushing the once mighty National Party down to fourth place. It was a crucial breakthrough. And I had to concede: the campaign that I hated had got me elected.

I have often reflected on the irony of the inverse relationship between our media and our electoral support. In almost all previous elections the DP and its predecessors had been the darling of the English press, and inevitably fared dismally when the votes were counted. Suddenly we were presented as pugnacious aggressors rather than hand-wringing conciliators, and we soared. We stopped being intellectual and ineffectual and began to look tough and serious. Tony called it 'muscular liberalism', and it went down well with people who understood the role of an opposition.

In the 1999 election, those who wanted an effective opposition to the ANC abandoned the NNP and chose us. The NNP was so weighed down by historical guilt over apartheid, and so inherently stuck in racial nationalism, that they still conflated a racial group with a political party. They operated from the premise that the ANC 'owned' black voters, but that the NNP 'owned' coloured and white Afrikaans voters.

We rejected the notion that any party owns any voter, let alone whole groups of voters (even though it certainly seemed that way at times in South Africa). We knew that democracy would fail unless a radically different idea took root: that every individual has the freedom to make an autonomous choice of party affiliation, at every election, based on principles and policies and the performance of the party's public representatives between elections.

We felt no guilt about being strong opponents of the ANC's brand of racial nationalism, because we had always opposed apartheid's.

We knew that if South Africa was to succeed as a democracy, voters would have to understand that a vote is a choice between alternative political programmes, not an expression of loyalty to a racial or ethnic group. Those distinctions are very hard to make in an emerging democracy, but there was no time to lose in getting started.

The election of 2 June 1999 was a good launching pad.

For a while after that historic election, it looked as if the DP might not be part of a coalition government in the Western Cape after all. The ANC (which had 42.07 per cent of the provincial vote) initially approached the New National Party (with 38.39 per cent of the vote) to try to set up an ANC/NNP 'grand coalition' – a move described by the ANC provincial leader, Ebrahim Rasool, as a 'progressive development' and a sign of 'mature politics'.

But when this courtship ran aground, the NNP turned to the DP, putting us in a strong position to demand our pound of flesh in the coalition negotiations. We also agreed to include the tiny African Christian Democratic Party in our shared cabinet.

No sooner had we announced our agreement than the public outcry erupted, in the media, the business community, the churches, civil society; through marches, letters and telephone campaigns.

'You are ganging up on the ANC!' went the cry. And in a classic conflation of a political party with a racially defined category of people, they added, 'You are dividing the whites and coloureds on the one side, against blacks on the other.'

Hardly anyone grasped the fact that the issue was about checks and balances on unfettered power, and not about race.

Today most people understand why we took the stand we did, and many who criticised us then now know that we were right to prevent the ANC from tightening its grip on yet another province. The challenge then, as now, was to build the alternative and ensure that it was non-racial.

But back in 1999 we were under relentless pressure to succumb to the ANC's demands. The business community harangued us; the churches lobbied us; the English newspapers led the charge against what they depicted as the DP's 'demonic dance with the forces of apartheid' (although they had voiced no such criticism of the proposed NNP/ANC coalition before that had reached a dead end!). It was as though the ANC was a big bucket of detergent that could wash the NNP's past sins clean.

It is hard, looking back today, to imagine a time when the ANC had a virtual monopoly on morality in the public mind, but that is how it was back then. The pressure on us was so intense that the ACDP announced it would no longer join the coalition, despite its earlier enthusiasm.

This was one of the many times I learnt a key political lesson: when you have to take a controversial decision, project yourself ten years into the future and look back on the decision from that vantage point. If you 'start from the core principle at stake' (as Helen Suzman always advised), it is possible to see through the temporary dust storm to the destination.

This is not easy in the middle of a furore when you are being bombarded with angry letters and phone calls from the good and the great, all clearly part of an orchestrated campaign. Anglican Archbishop Njongonkulu Ndungane offered to 'mediate' – as if mediation was appropriate to the strategic considerations that determine the balance of forces in coalition negotiations based on an electoral mandate.

The Institute for Democracy in Africa (IDASA) created a public platform for the ANC to state their case before an audience of luminaries, effectively assisting them to mobilise resistance to the proposed DP/NNP coalition.

In the end we were bludgeoned into offering the ANC a position in the cabinet. This was promptly interpreted as an 'insult', so our offer was upped to three cabinet seats.

The various lobbyists and the media did not seem to grasp that, having failed to reach 50 per cent in an election, the ANC had no automatic right to be in power, let alone dictate the terms.

If the ANC had accepted the generous offer of three cabinet posts, there would have been no chance that I, as the most junior member of the DP caucus, would have been appointed to the cabinet. However, the ANC overplayed its hand, rejecting the offer, and demanded that negotiations start again from scratch. This exposed their determination not merely to participate in, but to control the coalition. We drew the line and went ahead without them, despite the public outcry.

Bizarrely, critics accused us of 'excluding' the ANC. They found it difficult to accept that being in opposition is not exclusion; on the contrary, opposition has an essential, mainstream role in any democracy. A strong opposition is essential to good government. Elections presuppose that some parties will end up in government and others in opposition. All political parties have to learn to sit on both sides of the house and play their role. It was a very basic lesson, but if our democracy was to succeed, it had to be learnt early on.

We refused to feel guilty about it. We had never misled the electorate. On the contrary, we were fulfilling our election promise of putting together an opposition coalition in the one place we had managed to bring the ANC below 50 per cent. Eventually, the ANC, very reluctantly, accepted that in the Western Cape they would not be calling the shots in government.

After the thrill of being sworn in, I soon returned to reality.

I had the romantic idea that I would walk into my new office on day one, meet the senior professionals in the education department, and begin implementing my education plan on day two. Instead, I hit a brick wall.

I soon learnt first hand about the 'iron law of oligarchy', which describes the way in which a small group of people usually end up controlling large and complex organisations. The Western Cape government was a textbook case.

There was nothing inherently surprising about this. What did surprise me, however, was that elected politicians were largely excluded from the inner circle. We were generally regarded as a temporary inconvenience that needed to be humoured until the next election and kept meaninglessly preoccupied doing symbolic things like cutting ribbons, proposing toasts, and kissing babies.

When I entered government, it felt like I had arrived on the set of the British TV comedy series *Yes, Minister*, which depicts how bureaucrats allow politicians to think they are in charge, while stroking their egos and stripping them of any real power. Before then, my only understanding of the role and function of the state came from reading and from covering politics as a journalist.

I assumed that in our new, open democracy, the state bureaucracy would embody the rule of law and accountability in action: a functional organisation based on professional merit selection and political non-alignment. It would work according to clear rules, in a structured hierarchy, to implement the policy programme of an elected government and serve the public.

That is the understanding of the state I brought to government. I was hopelessly naive.

I did not really understand the tectonic plate shift required to move from the apartheid mindset to the culture of our new constitution, and the ANC understood it even less. While I never thought the change would happen overnight, I thought we would make rapid progress in shaking off the shackles of a system controlled by a few 'big men' dispensing favours through patronage networks of connected individuals, following arbitrary instructions from the top.

The great risk, I soon learnt, was that in an emerging democracy, 'big-man' politics could quite easily be grafted onto the machinery of the modern state, with devastating consequences for core concepts such as merit selection, political independence, impartial criteria, accountability and due process. Spymaster-turned-public-official Niel Barnard was the Western Cape's 'big man' in his capacity as director-general of the provincial government.

Lukas Daniel (Niel) Barnard, born to a school inspector in Otjiwarongo, South West Africa, was a powerful and feared figure. In 1979, at the age of twenty-nine, he was already a full professor of political studies at the University of the Orange Free State, when he was recruited by the most irascible of all apartheid's prime ministers to start a new national intelligence service. Prime Minister P.W. Botha, commonly known as Die Groot Krokodil, gave Barnard the mandate to identify and weed out apartheid's enemies.

A tall, imposing figure, his full head of black hair, square jaw and set mouth seemed just a few menacing genetic tweaks away from Cary Grant in the movie *Charade*. I never saw Barnard smile, and his eyes were brooding and dark. His physical bearing undoubtedly helped him rise through the ranks of a political system obsessed with genetics and control. He preferred his politicians and colleagues pliant and passive. If they weren't, he set about moulding them into his preferred form by applying Machiavelli's famous dictum 'it is safer to be feared than loved'.

Inspiring fear was Barnard's stock in trade. He made everyone in government, officials and politicians alike, believe he controlled their destiny. This was physically symbolised by his chair at meetings, which was always slightly higher than his colleagues'. If he was determined to get rid of you, he would find a way. He had a suite of strategies, learnt from several previous lives, as supreme commander of apartheid's intelligence service.

For the first time, when the DP landed in government, his control was challenged. We had insisted that our coalition agreement specify that Hennie Bester, the DP's provincial and caucus leader, would have a veto right over DP nominations to the cabinet and, crucially, their dismissal. If it weren't for that, Niel Barnard would have made sure I didn't last long. To Hennie's great credit, he stood his ground to defend me on several occasions. Niel Barnard worked hard to draw Hennie into his web and drive a wedge between us.

I quickly learnt how a patronage system works and why it is so effective, dangerous and inimical to good governance. Here's one example.

I had been invited to sit on a selection panel for a senior vacancy in the administration. I duly read the CVs and accompanying documents, and attended the interviews. One candidate (in my opinion) stood head and shoulders above the rest, in qualifications, relevant experience and strategic analysis. After the interviews, the selection panel was supposed to discuss the candidates' comparative merits. I was the only panel member who provided an analysis. I stood alone. When the votes were counted, one of the weaker candidates was selected by a very wide margin. The candidate I thought was best was ranked stone last. I was dumbfounded.

I am not suggesting that my evaluation of a candidate was necessarily better than everyone else's, but in the absence of any coherent motivation for the successful candidate, I knew the outcome was no coincidence. It was clear we had been involved in an elaborate charade. It was obvious that the decision on the appointment had already been made before we began. We were merely going through the motions.

I sat in the room gathering my thoughts as everyone else left.

One of my colleagues had to be assisted from the room. He had arrived inebriated, but this did not prevent him being eligible to sit on a selection panel for a key position in the administration. As long as he was not too drunk to follow instructions, I supposed, it didn't matter.

Suddenly I was alone, with the scoresheets in a pile on the table, waiting for the secretariat to collect and file them. I decided to take a look. The scoresheets did not record the name of the selection-panel member, so I reckoned I was not violating the principle of a 'secret ballot' (even though, strictly speaking, this did not apply to a selection panel). And besides, the scores are stored for later inspection if needed. I decided to inspect them there and then.

They revealed what I suspected had happened. The selection had clearly been rigged. Every single scoresheet, except mine, ranked the candidates in exactly the same order. And the one exceptional candidate had been ranked last by everyone, except me, to ensure that she did not make it. I was just a useful idiot, going through a charade, being used to give the process a semblance of credibility.

I raised my concerns at a cabinet caucus, to fierce denials. I wondered what I should do next. I had a choice of walking out, or of staying in the fuzzy zone where pragmatism and principle blur. I decided that when I did leave, it would have to be on an issue that had real traction and was not susceptible to the plausible deniability that applies to so many borderline cases.

It does not take much imagination to see how multiplying crony appointments throughout the administration undermines any chance of building a capable state based on each individual's capability and accountability to get a job done. The very process of patronage selection is a form of corruption that violates the rule of law. Cumulatively, it results in a paralysed, beholden bureaucracy whose first priority is remaining in the big man's favour, rather than executing its public-service functions. The Western Cape administration, under Niel Barnard, had the primary objective of protecting a network in power.

I came to the conclusion that both in a political party and in government (and indeed in any organisation), selecting the right person for each job is the most important thing senior managers do. Appropriate selection involves a combination of criteria, applicable to the specific requirements of each job. Achieving diversity is certainly an important criterion in a complex, plural society. The bottom line, though, is this: if you make the right appointments, good governance largely looks after itself. The problem is spotting who has what it takes. It is rarely obvious. The capacity to pick the right people for the right job is a crucial leadership skill. Getting this right in government makes an enormous difference to society.

But when the purpose of selection is control rather than good governance, the right people are often actively sidelined.

Barnard got a grip on provincial ministers by controlling their senior officials, who did his bidding. In turn, he looked after them, and helped them head off their provincial ministers when necessary. He pulled it all together through his control of the premier, Gerald Morkel.

The first problem I encountered as MEC for education was that most of the senior education officials regarded the Western Cape education department as an administrative arm of the national government, and implemented its instructions to the letter. There was little understanding (let alone application) of the hard-won constitutional autonomy that gives provincial governments real power to determine policies that do not necessarily conform to diktats from the centre. There was an assumption, carried over from the previous apartheid dispensation, that national policies trump provincial policies. I never succeeded in convincing the Western Cape education department that this was generally not the case (except in a few circumstances specified in the constitution). I proposed appointing a legal adviser to assist me in my office, which set off a veritable panic in the department.

They had never worked any other way but via instructions from above, which certainly did not emanate from the office of the provincial minister. When I insisted that we implement the policy for which we had received a mandate from the voters, some senior managers resisted. But, of course, they did not say this directly to me. Straight talk was inimical to the organisation's culture. Instead they went to Niel Barnard, who hatched a plan behind the scenes to cover their backs – if they covered his.

I remember once, as MEC for education, undertaking a performance evaluation of a senior manager, only to be told afterwards (by Niel Barnard via the premier) that I was required to change my scoring because it was important that all officials of his rank, across various departments, should fall within a certain range to qualify for the same performance bonus. Otherwise it would cause tension between the officials, I was told.

I asked why, in that case, we were wasting our time with performance appraisals. The answer I received was that the rules required us to go through the procedure before awarding bonuses!

Of course it wasn't long before the official lodged a grievance against me. When I learnt of it (also via the grapevine), I was keen that it should proceed to a full hearing, so that I could produce the evidence I needed to rebut the complaint. But despite my desire to proceed, the process was stopped, with the support of Niel Barnard and the premier.

I took independent legal advice, and was told that there were strong grounds for me to lay a complaint of mismanagement and incapacity against the manager. I indicated to the premier that if the official's grievance was prevented from going to a full hearing, I would lay a complaint myself, which would then go to a hearing in order to establish the facts, which I considered essential.

I then received a letter from Premier Morkel, saying: 'I must instruct you not to lay a formal charge of incompetence or mismanagement against him.'

I began to understand what was going on.

Until then, I had actually been surprised that an official would declare a grievance and then simply allow it to be swept under the carpet without a proper hearing, but it became quite clear that a spurious grievance had been declared, which was never intended to reach a hearing. The purpose was to enable the official to claim 'constructive dismissal', which would then make him eligible to receive the balance of his salary for the remaining years of his contract before taking up a top job outside government, for which he had successfully applied before he resigned!

Minister Geraldine Fraser-Moleketi, then the national minister of public service and administration, initially declined to award the payout. She said, quite correctly, that if the official accepted another job, he should resign. But Morkel sent a second motivation for the payout (after the official had already accepted the other job). The national minister finally relented, but added a rider that Morkel 'would have to justify the payment of the package in the event of enquiries'.

I wrote an enraged letter to the premier when I suspected this kind of manipulation, only to receive an abrupt letter from him closing down the interaction.

I again consulted a lawyer and was advised to put the matter behind me. In major public disputes, the lawyer said, spurious allegations could be made against me to justify claims of constructive dismissal, which would be difficult to rebut. When such claims are sensationalised, it is difficult, often impossible, for the public to discern fact from fiction. However unjustifiable, some mud sticks. I was persuaded, as a new politician and junior cabinet minister, not to drive the matter further.

But I was becoming increasingly disillusioned.

If Barnard disliked me, he loathed Ryan Coetzee, who refused to treat the director-general with the obsequiousness due to an *Obergruppenführer* (the German word speaks for itself, without translation). Barnard considered Ryan irredeemable from the moment he arrived at work, on his first day, wearing jeans and a T-shirt, and addressed 'Dr Barnard' as 'Niel'. Even worse, Ryan had his own opinions, which he argued forcefully. But above all, Ryan was seen as a threat to Barnard's hold on Premier Morkel. Ryan's brief was to assist the coalition government with a communication strategy. He worked in the premier's office and had a direct line to him, something that Barnard resisted strenuously. It put his patronage network at risk.

Ryan, who had been one of the key architects of the DP's success in almost quadrupling our support between 1994 and 1999, had concluded that it was time to take opposition politics to the next level. Small parties competing against each other for the support of the small pool of opposition voters created a diversion South Africa could not afford, Ryan argued. The country required opposition consolidation, on the basis of an agreed set of core principles, to challenge the growing hegemony of the ANC.

Because the DP had whipped the NNP into fourth place in the 1999 election, Ryan proposed forming a new party that would bring together the DP and NNP, in order to take on the ANC in the local government elections of 2000. He reckoned this was the right strategic time to make the move, given the fact that almost every NNP councillor in the country felt jittery about their chances of re-election in 2000. Preserving their positions would trump historical party loyalty, Ryan predicted.

Of course, it was a highly controversial proposal. Most of the DP's members had spent their entire lives fighting the National Party and here was a twenty-six-year-old telling us to merge with them! We had intense debates, and it was fascinating to see who came down on which side. Senior DP MP Dene Smuts was vehemently opposed to the move, arguing that we would merely be strapping the NNP's 'rotting carcass' to our backs. We should let the party die a natural death, she pleaded. She was supported by Mike Waters, the MP who had won the DP's first by-election against the New National Party in an unlikely ward in the white working-class suburb of Kempton Park. We were now in a position to wipe out the NNP at the polls, he stressed. We would create enormous problems for ourselves by absorbing a party that did not share our values.

Counter-intuitively for many people, I supported Ryan's proposal. I thought a merger on our terms, and under the national leadership of the DP, would give us the backing we needed to assert our values in the Western Cape government. This would enable us to move beyond the patronage model based on fear and manipulation that was so deeply entrenched in the NNP's political culture. We would be able to start implementing the 'open, opportunity' philosophy where we governed.

By June 2000, enough debating and background work had been done to enable the DP's Federal Council to approve a proposal to incorporate the NNP into the DP without compromising our political philosophy, brand integrity or organisational culture, to paraphrase a Federal Council decision.

The motivation was that if we were to succeed in turning South African politics into a contest between the ANC's racial nationalism and our open, liberal alternative, we shouldn't be fighting the election on two fronts simultaneously. We had to close down the battlefront with the NNP so that we could focus on the ANC. And this required incorporating the NNP's public representatives, members and remaining voter support into a broader party based on the values of the 'open, opportunity society for all'.

Although the NNP, like the ANC, was primarily a racial/ethnic nationalist party, we reckoned that it was a good time to convert their members and supporters to our liberal philosophies based on constitutionalism, non-racialism and individual rights, protected by the rule of law – rather than continuing to rely on the patronage and protection of a dominant group. In fact, we believed that when a once-dominant group loses power, its members are in a good position to appreciate the idea that their only effective protection lies in strong institutions that defend every individual's rights against the arbitrary abuse of power.

In short, we thought the time was ripe for supporters of the New National Party to make a mass transition from the politics of racial identity and ethnic preference to the politics of principle and professionalism. I was soon to learn exactly why this transition has taken so many centuries (probably closer to a millennium) in countries that now consider themselves established, sustainable democracies.

I always knew it would be a big challenge; I just had no idea how big.

9

The Battle for the Soul of the DA

WHEN WE AGREED in mid-2000 to merge the NNP and DP to form the DA, we thought the hard work was behind us. In fact, it had only just begun. For one thing, it was complex constitutionally. Because the DA was formed before the local government election of 2000, former NNP and DP councillors joined the DA and were registered as DA candidates for this millennial election. The NNP and the DP therefore no longer existed in municipal councils.

It was different at provincial and national level. There the NNP and DP parliamentarians had been elected as representatives of these two parties in 1999 and could not switch to the DA without losing their seats. They had to wait for the next provincial and national elections in 2004 to be elected on a DA ticket. However, they could become ordinary members of the DA in the meantime, while retaining their seats in the name of their party of origin. This required keeping both the NNP and DP alive, in parallel with the new DA. It was also asking for trouble.

It proved extremely difficult to manage the DA, with public representatives elected under the banner of three different parties – the NNP and the DP at provincial and national level, and the DA at local council level. (And in fact there was an additional party forming part of the DA, Louis Luyt's Federal Alliance, with two seats in the National Assembly and one in Gauteng.)

The NNP members of provincial and national parliaments remained answerable to Marthinus van Schalkwyk, the leader of the NNP, and the DP members to Tony Leon. At the same time, all DA members were accountable to the party, led by Tony (with Marthinus as his deputy). These fault lines proved difficult to manage, especially as the NNP was determined to keep the rifts alive and ensure that Van Schalkwyk retained control over NNP members in various caucuses, despite Tony Leon's leadership of the DA.

In the Western Cape, the DP was one third the size of the NNP, and we were treated as such. But nationally, the picture was different. We had almost wiped out the NNP in many other provinces and, I reckoned, if we incorporated the NNP into a single party, albeit under a new name, 'without compromising our liberal ideology, brand integrity and organisational culture' (as the Federal Council resolution stated), we could resolve many of our problems in the provincial government. As DA members, we would work in the knowledge that the NNP and DP were being phased out as separate entities, in order to become a single party under Tony's leadership.

I did not sufficiently consider the risk of an alternative outcome: the possibility of a reverse takeover which would give the NNP a new lease on life, under a new name, in a new patronage-driven party in which they would be the dominant force, controlled by ethnic nationalism and racial mobilisation, cronyism and corruption. In fact, this possibility did not even occur to me.

Thinking back on what happened, it was best symbolised through the memory of a Staffordshire terrier pup we had acquired when Tom was a toddler. After the puppy had been with us a few days, we named him Murphy, because he was the proverbial accident looking for a place to happen. If there wasn't an obvious cause for calamity, he would create one.

One day I walked into the kitchen to cook supper and found the pup gasping in agony, with an enormously extended stomach, and in the grip of something akin to a seizure. I ran to his help, trying to work out what had happened. I glanced at the kitchen counter and saw that the pork roll I was about to cook for supper had vanished. I worked out afterwards that the cat must have knocked the pork off the counter and that Murphy had devoured the whole thing, uncooked crackling and all. We rushed him to the vet. I think he vomited in the car. He survived, but came to within an inch of his life. The vet was amazed that he had made it.

This roughly describes what happened to the DP in our attempts to incorporate the NNP.

We only managed to forestall a reverse takeover by waging the toughest political fight of our lives. Nothing I have experienced, before or since, has even come close to the intensity of the war that was waged for the soul of the DA between 2000 and 2007.

What started out as a battle between the NNP and the DP within the DA eventually ended in a deep rift between Tony Leon and me, which took years to heal. I initially found it difficult to fathom why we were, increasingly, on opposite sides of the fault-line that had rapidly opened like the Grand Canyon in our ranks.

The reason slowly became apparent. Over the traumatic two years that followed our merger in 2000, Tony must have slowly come to the conclusion that in order to save the DP's political philosophy and organisational culture in the rest of South Africa, he would have to sacrifice the Western Cape to the provincially dominant NNP.

While I was happy to respect the election of candidates who commanded majority support, I was not prepared to accept the imposition of racial nationalism and political cronyism in the only province we could govern. I was determined to fight these to the death. Ironically, my opposition to this political culture was my motivation for agreeing to the merger in the first place, but the result was the precise opposite. I expected the DP's open, opportunity-driven culture to become the party's default position. It did not turn out that way.

Looking back, it is clear how pitifully naive the DP (and I especially) had been in our negotiations with the NNP. We acted in good faith and assumed that they would too. We made the enduring strategic flaw that liberals everywhere make, assuming that other people think like us, act in good faith, and match their words with deeds.

We began by negotiating an agreed credo of core principles, as we quaintly believed these would form the basis of future decisions and actions. Tony nominated me and Ryan to negotiate the DA's founding principles with NNP representatives. We met in a cold, bare room in the Marks Building, which housed opposition parties in the parliamentary complex. I was preparing for a marathon session of haggling on crucial points of political principle.

To my surprise, it took us all of one hour to reach agreement. Each potential sticking point just melted away as we happily ticked the boxes. The atmosphere became almost convivial, warming the cold room. Even the DP's strong stand on gay rights – which I thought would elicit resistance from the party still steeped in the principles of the conservative Dutch Reformed Church – was accepted without demur.

I was amazed that it had been so easy – and was later even more amazed that it was so totally meaningless. I don't think the principles were ever invoked again, following the formal establishment of the DA on 24 June 2000. The only reference to them was in the breach, every day, in every way.

In retrospect, it is clear that a reverse takeover had been the NNP's strategy from the start. That was the reason they agreed to the merger at all. We learnt about this later, in a demonstration of the old adage 'the truth will out'. According to Tony's memoirs, a DP colleague was accidentally given the tapes of a meeting at which Marthinus van Schalkwyk, the NNP leader, sought to persuade his most senior colleagues of the merits of doing a deal with the 'liberal English'. The tapes intimated that the NNP would be able to engineer a reverse takeover by enrolling more members than the DP.[*]

Their strategy was clearly based on a book of tricks, devised and authored on a political planet to which we had no entrée. It involved a level of intrigue that many of us had never encountered.

At one point, Ryan Coetzee's laptop was stolen from his office in the premier's suite, and although I cannot prove it, I am prepared to wager that this was an inside job. This became obvious when, before long, his files, both personal and professional, were being selectively leaked to the media. The purpose was to depict a conspiracy between Ryan and Tony to marginalise the DA's deputy leader and former NNP leader, Marthinus van Schalkwyk.

---

[*] Tony Leon, *On the Contrary* (Jonathan Ball, 2008), p. 545

The desired outcome materialised. NNP members reverted to their laager in the face of a perceived threat.

Our political cultures had been forged in different fires. There were many historical factors involved. One was that in order to survive, the DP (and its predecessor parties) had to retain and grow their voter support. In contrast, the NNP took the loyalty of its voters for granted. I recall National Party members boasting that they could even get a broomstick elected, such was the depth of voter loyalty to their brand, based on ethnic nationalism.

This meant that politics in the NNP and its predecessor, the National Party, had degenerated into an internal contest for positions of power, which was often little more than a battle between broomsticks, a kind of political quidditch. Voter support was simply taken for granted.

In the DP, by contrast, there was no point focusing primarily on internal jockeying for positions, because we had so few public representatives. It made far more sense to spend our time winning over new voters so that more candidates could be elected. Unsurprisingly, our external focus on the voters had led to our overtaking the NNP at the polls in the historic election of 2 June 1999. The outcome gave the NNP an enormous fright. Their survival was at stake.

But an organisation in the grip of a 'big-man' culture based on internal systems of obeisance to a leader who dispenses favours and eliminates challengers (rather than improving performance) finds it very difficult to make the changes required when it eventually starts losing voter support.

The NNP's survival strategy was to help create the DA and then use it to entrench and extend, rather than rethink and reform, that culture. Their approach rested on two pillars: firstly, to reinforce NNP dominance of the DA in the Western Cape, where the DP was a third of the NNP's size; and, secondly, to then take over the rest of the party through membership recruitment (which, as it turned out, also included massive membership fraud).

My faith that the DP's principles and organisational culture would automatically become the dominant ethos of the new DA was totally misplaced. And my belief that we could become one seamless new party working on the basis of our agreed values was nothing short of delusional.

In most parties, worldwide, internal party leadership elections and candidate-selection procedures are based, in one way or another, on membership numbers in branches. It is therefore not unusual that, before electoral processes begin, there is a scramble to recruit members to ensure the election of a favoured candidate. But I did not expect it to degenerate into outright fraud aimed at rigging the outcome of an entire election contest. In the NNP, 'membership farming' (to give it a polite name) was an entrenched part of the organisational culture.

No sooner had the DA been established than the NNP component started signing up thousands upon thousands of members, with their eye on the party's next elective congress, where, we now suspected, they were scheming to oust Tony Leon. Members were being 'sponsored' in their thousands to drive an internal coup d'état. The NNP component signed up 55 000 members in a few months, two-thirds of them from the Western Cape.*

In terms of the DA's rules, members had to pay their R10 subscription fee themselves, precisely to avoid membership manipulation through mass sponsorships. The former NNP component of the DA simply ignored this. I recall once, in the Joe Slovo shack settlement alongside Langa, when I was establishing the very first DA branch there, David Erleigh, a particularly manipulative NNP councillor, watched our branch chairperson, Valencia Nkomokazi, hand me a pile of dog-eared R10 notes that members had paid in subscriptions. She asked me to submit the money to the regional office, along with their membership application forms, which I undertook to do.

David was amazed. Had these members actually all paid their subscriptions themselves, he asked. Of course, I answered, that's what our rules required. His tone and body language told me that the NNP was busy with a different strategy. The DA's internal 'rule of law' was easily cast aside if it interfered with the patronage network's self-preservation!

Apart from taking over the party from within, the NNP's second (and related) objective was to ensure their chosen candidates were selected to stand in the local government elections of December 2000.

Reading the documents in retrospect reveals the extent to which we were out-manoeuvred in this process. We were veritable babes in the wood.

Over time it became apparent that every argument and demand the NNP made, on almost every issue, had to be read through the prism of their preparation for candidate selection. To the DP this was an alien way of approaching things, because we tended to debate the intrinsic merit of alternative proposals, usually without hidden agendas.

However, the NNP's 'big-man cabal' knew that if they controlled candidate selection, they could apply Machiavelli's dictum: you can control people if they fear you. And the best way to make them fear you is to control their job prospects.

This naked power abuse was disguised in various cynical ways.

Quoting the Bible was always a favourite ruse. I remember being rendered speechless at a meeting in Malmesbury when an NNP leader closed down a budget discussion by implying that my questions were a sin against divinely constituted authority. Quoting Romans 13, he said: 'The authorities that exist have been established by God. Consequently, whoever rebels against the authority

---

* Tony Leon, *On the Contrary*, p. 557

is rebelling against what God has instituted, and those who do so will bring judgment on themselves.'

End of debate. Thought blocker. No one was prepared to risk divine wrath by debating my points after that.

I kept detailed notes of that meeting, because it produced the clearest set of examples thus far of the total incompatibility of values between the two parties that were trying to make the DA work.

The merger agreement between the DP and NNP included the notorious Clause 14, which got the NNP exactly what they wanted – virtual control over the candidate-selection process in the Western Cape.

Drawn up in August 2000, Clause 14 was based on the assumption that there was insufficient time between the formation of the DA in June and the local election of December 2000 to establish a single candidate-selection process. So each party would draw up their own list, and nominate their own ward candidates, according to their own procedures. Then the lists would be merged on the basis of the 'relative-strength' principle, calculated on the election results of 2 June 1999.

In the Western Cape, this meant that the NNP would be able to nominate two candidates to electable positions on the list for every one candidate nominated by the DP. In much of the rest of the country, it was the other way around.

This agreement shows that the NNP was prepared to sacrifice its councillors in several provinces (where they had lost heavily against the DP in 1999) to secure dominance of the municipalities of the Western Cape, the only province where the DA had the prospect of winning power. That would give them a strong platform of government patronage in the Western Cape and the space to prepare their national takeover strategy in time for the next parliamentary elections, when they would use membership recruitment to control candidate selection in the rest of the country as well. They would then be able to marginalise the troublesome 'Engelse' or 'Progge' (as the original members of Helen Suzman's Progressive Party were disparagingly described) and anyone else who questioned the oligarchy.

The Western Cape NNP was controlled by a tightly knit central group of eight schemers. Each of them had a designated role in herding, growing and controlling the former NNP's power base within the DA.

Leon was the schemer; Pieter the calculator; Erik the leg-man; Kent the street-fighting mobiliser; Anroux the comforter; Kobus the English-hating bully (who, ironically, sent two of his daughters to live in England long enough to acquire British passports); and Sarel the double agent, whose job it was to keep abreast of our counter-strategies. Theuns played an interesting dual role: he was simultaneously the ringmaster and the captive animal. He issued instructions, but if these veered towards internal reconciliation or the middle ground, the cabal threatened to cull him at the next congress. He knew they would. He had a different face and voice for each constituency, but they each had the same nickname for him: Leuens.

The cabal worked together to preserve their levers of control by preventing the development of a strong 'middle ground' which would bring together members of the former NNP and DP on the basis of a values- and merit-based organisational culture.

According to Clause 14: 'In metropolitan municipalities, the first position on the list will be drawn from the party with the greater relative strength and the second position will be drawn from the other party. The rest of the list will reflect the relative strength of the parties in that metropole.'

This meant that the DA mayor of every winnable municipality would be drawn from the ranks of the former NNP. And the power of patronage that mayors can wield in our constitutional system is enormous. That is precisely why the NNP focused on capturing these 'commanding heights' of local government power. It was central to their strategy.

In addition, Clause 14 stipulated that ward candidates would also be allocated on the basis of 'relative strength' with a right to appeal to the provincial management committee, which was firmly under the dominant control of the NNP in the Western Cape. Indeed, all conflicts in candidate selection would be resolved by provincial management committees, leaving the national structures of the DA effectively powerless in the candidate-selection system.

Back then, we did not realise what profound consequences Clause 14 would have. We blithely assumed that candidate selection happened (largely) on a combination of 'fitness for purpose' – a mixture of several factors, including diversity and capacity to fulfil the functions of the job. That was the general rule in the DP. As we gradually emerged from our age of innocence and realised what was going on, we tried to prevent the tensions from boiling over and the party from blowing apart in the run-up to the election of 5 December 2000.

As I write this, I am spending successive weekends serving on a selection panel for candidates for the 2016 local government election. It is a rigorous, professional, performance-driven process, with several components: a score produced on the basis of sustained job evaluation; a test to assess the candidate's understanding of the DA's political philosophy; a writing exercise; an impromptu role-play speech to an audience; an evaluation of the candidate's CV; and an interview. The scores are then bell-curved to ensure consistency between panels. The result is a list that seeks to ensure that merit, diversity and skills reinforce one another to produce the best team of which we are capable. The outcome won't be perfect. No system can entirely rule out manipulation. The result will still be controversial – election lists always are – but the system has evolved over many years and is one of the great achievements of the DA, which may well be unique in the world.

I remember discussing our system once with Angela Merkel, who was amazed. 'How did you get your party to agree to that approach?' she asked.

My answer was: We lived through the alternative of patronage and cronyism, and soon learnt that this is the kiss of death for a political party. That gave us enough motivation to build as many structural bulwarks as we could against it.

The closed crony system slowly killed the NNP, and very nearly the DA as well, even before we fought our first election.

Yet today, one of the Western Cape's great contributions to the party is that we have, largely, transcended the historical differences that once threatened to blow the party apart. We have consciously worked on building a new internal culture, based on a value set that gives meaning to freedom, fairness and opportunity, both inside and outside our party.

It was very different in the run-up to the 2000 poll. At that point, many of us, myself included, had drawn the conclusion that the formation of the DA had been a terrible mistake. But the voters thought differently. On 5 December they demonstrated how much they loved the idea of a united opposition, depicted on our election posters by the formula DP + NNP = DA. The DA achieved a spectacular 22 per cent of the vote, an increase of almost 150 per cent over the DP's 9.6 per cent in the 1999 national election only twenty months earlier. In terms of voter support, we were on a high. In every other way, we were on a downward spiral.

I was too new in politics to interrogate the result. I fooled myself into believing that almost one in every four voters now supported the DA. Despite the challenges we faced, this seemed a vindication of our decision to merge the DP and the NNP. I later discovered I did not yet know how to interrogate election statistics properly. Although the DA won 350 000 more votes in 2000 than the DP had in the previous year's national election, the result was still 700 000 below the combined total of the DP and NNP in 1999. But the real lesson emerged from the ANC vote. Between April 1999 and December 2000 the ANC vote dropped an astonishing 50 per cent – from over ten million to just over five million.

I then learnt never to compare national election results with local election results. National polls advantage the ANC, whose voters turn out en masse. The opposite happens in local elections, when ANC voters tend to stay away. This gives the DA the benefit of differential turnout in local government elections. Results, expressed in percentages, particularly after local elections, tend to create a false impression of the extent of our support. I learnt to interrogate the actual numbers, the voter turnout and the differential. My sense of euphoria, despite our challenges after the 2000 election, was premature, not only regarding the election result, but particularly its consequences.

I learnt a lesson for the first time that I was due to learn repeatedly in the years ahead: in politics, you are at your most vulnerable when you have just experienced a great triumph.

In the afterglow of the quick win, Peter Marais became the DA's mayor of Cape Town. He was a colourful character who courted controversy and loved the limelight. He had a folksy, populist style and a penchant for pomp and power. Tony Leon noted, however: 'I had severe doubts whether he could lead the city and our municipal caucus in an inclusive and goal-oriented manner.'*

Our entire strategy hinged on being able to demonstrate that, where the DA won, we governed demonstrably better, and in the interests of all the people, compared with the ANC. But good governance doesn't just happen. It requires building professional state institutions. It requires strong leadership, working together to achieve a coherent plan, against clear targets and timelines, based on the voters' mandate. Failure to do this cannot be disguised by good public relations.

Peter Marais was more interested in the symbolism than the substance of governance. This caused problems from the outset, which bubbled over in his proposal to rename Adderley Street after former president Nelson Mandela, and Wale Street after his predecessor, former president F.W. de Klerk. Mayor Marais considered the renaming of these two main traffic arteries in central Cape Town, which meet next to parliament, a fitting tribute to the leadership of the two men who had steered South Africa to democracy.

The problem centred on allegations, backed by evidence, that the public-participation process around the renaming proposal had been rigged. A councillor colleague, the straight-talking Belinda Walker (formerly of the DP), brought this evidence straight to Tony Leon. This was seen as a profound affront and challenge to the NNP's provincial hierarchy, which had been bypassed as the conduit for information to reach the leader. Things quickly unravelled from there.

Peter Marais's populist appeal made him the poster boy for the NNP's strategy of mobilising its supporters by casting him as a victim of the evil 'Engelse'. Van Schalkwyk argued that by calling Marais to account for his manipulation of a public-participation process, 'die Engelse' were showing contempt for all people of colour. This is how racial nationalism's divide-and-rule tactics work. An individual's 'misdemeanour' is an opportunity to condemn an entire group. Conversely, if one person feels insulted, it creates an opportunity to make an entire group feel aggrieved and persecuted.

Despite an independent investigation that produced damning findings, Peter Marais was confident of being protected by the carefully engineered NNP major-

---

* Tony Leon, *On the Contrary*, p. 545

ity in all the DA's Western Cape structures, which would shield him from national accountability.

The tension reached breaking point. In an attempt to stave off a split, former president F.W. de Klerk, South Africa's patron saint of strategic compromise, reappeared on the scene to resolve the stand-off. He suggested that an 'out-of-control Marais' should be replaced as mayor by the more compliant and conciliatory Gerald Morkel. That would leave the door open for Marthinus van Schalkwyk to take over Morkel's role of premier. The new premier would then offer Marais a landing in the provincial cabinet soft enough to avoid denting his ego too badly.

The NNP regarded it as essential to defend its last bastion of support, the Western Cape, which was at risk of disintegrating due to divisions within the DA around the role of Peter Marais. If Marthinus van Schalkwyk held the reins in the province where the NNP had carefully engineered control, their consolidation and expansion strategy could work.

But Morkel threw a spanner in the works by refusing to resign as premier.

So the plan to remove Marais from the mayoralty by playing political musical chairs with Premier Morkel failed.

The DA's national leadership was not prepared to leave Marais in the mayoralty. Given that our growth strategy was based on demonstrating that we could govern effectively, something had to be done about what was now publicly described as the 'political circus' in Cape Town. Cartoons of the goings-on in the DA administration routinely featured the major players with round red clown noses cavorting in the arena of the Cape Town City Council chamber.

On 19 October 2001, Tony convened the DA's national management committee in a cold boardroom of the Marks Building to give Peter a stark choice. If he did not resign from the mayoralty, he would lose his party membership, in which case he would forfeit the mayoralty anyway. The committee was split between the DP and NNP members, who faced each other across the table with Siberian-level frigidity. Peter refused to resign and walked out, announcing he would seek relief in court. Van Schalkwyk later left, declaring Marais a victim of a race vendetta, and publicly pledging his support for Marais's legal battle against the decision.

Unbeknown to us at the time, Van Schalkwyk had already prepared a fallback position. Behind-the-scenes negotiations with the ANC were well under way, culminating in an announcement in late October 2001 that a constitutional amendment would be fast-tracked to enable DA councillors to return to their original parties without losing their seats. The purpose of the 'floor-crossing' legislation was to open the door for all DA councillors selected on the NNP's ticket to return to the NNP and enter a coalition (or alternative form of co-operation agreement) with the ANC.

I was not as surprised by the news as many of my DA colleagues were. By this time, I was coming to the conclusion that we had little chance of turning the DA into a party espousing a non-racial, open-opportunity political philosophy. It made increasing sense to me that the nationalists of the former NNP and the nationalists of the ANC should get together in the same party. Ultimately, I came to the conclusion that it was a necessary and welcome development in South Africa's political realignment. People who have the same basic world view should be in the same party.

The NNP Federal Council resolved to end its membership of the DA.

In his capacity as NNP leader, Marthinus van Schalkwyk immediately suspended Gerald Morkel as Western Cape premier (Morkel had been elected on an NNP ticket in 1999). The NNP/DP coalition in the Western Cape collapsed, and the five DP members (including myself) prepared to go into opposition.

We thought the DA would bleed to death following the amputation of one of its legs, despite our strategies to tie an emergency political tourniquet to stop the flow of support out of the party. But then we discovered that the DA could stand independently of Van Schalkwyk. He was mistaken in assuming that the NNP component would meekly follow him into the pact with the ANC. He must have been more shocked than anyone to find his carefully crafted strategy exploding in his face.

The NNP's culture of obeisance to its leader had already been eroded by its association with the DP component in the DA, where we constantly questioned and called leadership to account. In fact, the most glaring of the DA's culture clashes lay in the response of the rank-and-file to leadership, which became apparent in almost every meeting.

Other factors were also at work, though. As I have explained, the NNP component, due to its numerical majority in the Western Cape, was firmly in control of the DA in the province. It was a comfortable place to be, if you came from the NNP. Their dominance could not be transferred to a coalition with the ANC (which was numerically bigger than the NNP in the province). There would, in all likelihood, be no more NNP mayors in ANC-dominated coalitions.

In any event, all the NNP's councillors knew that if they followed their leader Marthinus into any form of alliance with the ANC, they would face a backlash from their voters and probably lose their seats at the next election.

Apart from an aversion, in principle, to joining the ANC in government, the resistance of the DA mayors also made sense through the prism of self-preservation. Some of them drew the correct conclusion that, under Van Schalkwyk's scheme, they would be toast, either sooner or later, a lesson that Van Schalkwyk himself eventually learnt.

As Theuns Botha, who was then executive mayor of Langeberg, said on several occasions: Why would you leave an alliance where you are in the majority to enter one where you will be in the minority? It makes no sense.

The leading DA mayors in the Western Cape (all originally from the NNP component) largely agreed with him. They convened a historic series of meetings at Goudini Spa, outside the town of Worcester, culminating in a mass assembly on 3 November 2001, where they unanimously backed Morkel and passed a motion of no confidence in Van Schalkwyk.

By that evening, opposition politics in South Africa was another country. The DA would survive. The NNP in the Western Cape (the only province where they still had a significant support base) had rejected Van Schalkwyk and his proposed alliance with the ANC.

But something else had also happened at Goudini. It took me a while to realise exactly what.

The NNP in the Western Cape had not only rejected Van Schalkwyk.

They had also captured Tony Leon.

He had them to thank for the DA's survival, the formation of which had been his biggest political gamble, on which he had staked his legacy. From that moment, he was beholden to them.

Starting to realise the enormity of what had happened, and its implications, I stood against Theuns Botha for the provincial chairmanship of the DA in the Western Cape late in 2001, at a congress where Gerald Morkel was re-confirmed as DA provincial leader. I knew I had no chance of winning, but I believed it was necessary, at least, to ensure a contest. I did not have much time to canvass support, but when I spoke to several long-standing and close colleagues, they explained to me that they would be voting for Theuns because of what had happened in Goudini. He had showed loyalty to the DA; we needed to show loyalty to him. I understood the argument, but I went ahead with my candidacy nevertheless.

I asked Gavin Paulse, a former NNP colleague with whom I got on well, to nominate me for provincial chairperson. He happily agreed, until the morning of the congress, when he phoned me in embarrassment, saying he was under intense pressure not to nominate me. It was just another minor manifestation of the way the NNP worked. Anyone who spoke their mind or acted autonomously was immediately pulled back into line. Free choice was a foreign concept in its ranks.

As expected, I was thoroughly thumped in the election, 214 votes to 109.

It was the outcome Tony wanted. It was also the outcome he needed, if he was to rely on the NNP's provincial leadership to counter the pressure and inducements that would be used to lure councillors to defect from the DA during the floor-crossing window period scheduled for the first two weeks of September 2002.

* * *

After the collapse of the DP/NNP coalition in the Western Cape government, Peter Marais was sworn in as premier of the province, as an NNP member in coalition with the ANC, on 5 December 2001, exactly a year to the day after his election as the DA's mayoral candidate.

He relished the combination of vengeance and vindication his premiership represented, which he used as a potent inducement to persuade his former NNP colleagues to join him in their former political home. 'Kom Huis Toe' (come back home) provided a powerful 'pull' to former NNP councillors, a warm, fuzzy family coat to cover a naked, ethnic appeal.

For his part, Tony Leon needed to minimise any possible 'push' that would encourage former NNP councillors to leave the DA when the first defection window opened. This meant that most of the senior DA leadership turned a blind eye to (at best), and often actually facilitated, an NNP strategy in the Western Cape that they had done everything possible to block at national level – a full-blooded reverse takeover in the only province where we were in government at local level. In the process, the DA's national leadership had to condone, and even defend, practices that fundamentally undermined our principles, and our vision of an open, opportunity-driven society for all. Race mobilisation, favour trading, inducements, intimidation and manipulation became the stock-in-trade of the patronage culture that gripped the province.

Our party was becoming a mirror image of the ANC, only targeting different ethnically defined, and politically connected, beneficiaries.

Despite their deviousness, the NNP strategies (from their base within the DA) were no match for the defection inducements that the ANC/NNP were able to offer, using the promise of state patronage, to entice DA councillors to cross the floor.

There is a famous photograph, symptomatic of the times, which shows the DA Western Cape leader, Gerald Morkel, surrounded by former NNP councillors pledging undying loyalty to the DA – only to abandon Morkel and cross the floor in the first few hours after the defection window opened on 1 September. Most of them had been promised lucrative promotions, achieved through increasing the number of sub-council chair positions and turning committee chairs into paid positions. Another major inducement was the promise of re-election at the next local government poll in 2006.

They knew that if they stayed in the DA, they would in all likelihood lose the protection of Clause 14 by the next election, and have to compete for re-nomination on their performance record. In the NNP there were no such requirements. Whatever candidate-selection charade there may have been, the cabal determined the candidates' list on the basis of compliance with their instructions.

The ANC/NNP also ensured that the DA spent the run-up to the defection period mired in controversy. The NNP knew the darkest secrets of its members and were determined to expose those who had remained in the DA, punishing their disloyalty to Van Schalkwyk, while simultaneously doing maximum damage to the DA.

They knew that Niel Barnard, while director-general of the province, had put together his own quasi-intelligence network, which met in a 'bunker' to discuss strategies for entrenching their control in the province. (I always remember the amusing detail that the bunker was furnished with plastic garden chairs so that no listening devices could be attached to them.) The NNP also knew that their members in the DA had received (and laundered) money from the German fraudster Jürgen Harksen. The rest of us knew nothing about either.

To turn this into a public scandal, the NNP/ANC used on old trick inherited from the apartheid regime. They appointed a judicial commission of inquiry to probe the allegations, which would ensure blanket media coverage. A judge was appointed to give the strategy an aura of respectability and independence, which the media swallowed hook, line and sinker, helping to disguise the fact that it was, in fact, a political hit squad. In April 2002, the ANC/NNP appointed Judge Siraj Desai to chair the commission. The idea was to have the DA mired in public scandals and controversies for five months in the run-up to the defection window in September.

If anyone in the DA had really committed a crime, a complaint could have been laid and investigated by the police, culminating in a formal charge in a court of law on the basis of evidence. Because the evidence was limited to certain individuals, and was insufficient to tarnish an entire party, a commission of inquiry was a more expedient alternative. It could be used as a fishing expedition to drag up all sorts of irrelevant details for the purposes of smearing, not collating evidence to secure a conviction. In short, it was intended to be a kangaroo court masquerading as an objective investigation.

It had none of the formal checks and balances of court proceedings, such as cross-examination, the weighing of evidence, a judgment and sentence, or, crucially, the right to appeal. The commission was a perfect propaganda platform for rumour mongering, smears and posturing, which was precisely the intention. The ANC/NNP used it to the full in the run-up to the first defection window. Eventually Judge Desai issued a report which claimed that he had glimpsed inside the DA and seen 'the heart of darkness'. His analysis dominated the media for days and achieved precisely the political outcome the ANC/NNP wanted.

During this period, Hennie Bester became so disillusioned at the level of manipulative intrigue that he resigned as the DP's leader in the provincial legislature, and left politics. I succeeded him as caucus leader. He had also been deputy leader of the DA in the Western Cape, a position that was not immediately filled.

Unsurprisingly, in the face of the tactics and our weakened position, twenty-three of the DA's thirty-two former NNP councillors in Cape Town crossed the floor to the NNP, and the city's DA government fell to an ANC/NNP coalition. So did over a dozen more DA-run councils in the province.

As Gawa Samuels, a former DA deputy mayor (drawn from the NNP's ranks), was famously quoted as saying (when asked why she had crossed): 'I took a decision to stay close to the public purse.'

At the same time, the NNP leadership who remained in the DA had realised what power they could wield by threatening to defect if they did not get their way. This threat had real traction, given that a floor-crossing window reopened every few years, during the first two weeks of September. The NNP members now had a comfortable alternative in their re-established party, which could offer them a soft landing in a governing coalition with the ANC. The DA's former NNP component had learnt how to hold the DA's national leadership to ransom by threatening to split the party a second time, which would have left Tony's legacy in tatters.

It was a weapon they used to the full, especially in their efforts to maintain the national leadership's backing in their battle against the 'Engelse' and the 'Progge' (of all languages and races) in the Western Cape. Ironically, most of the national leadership could themselves be described as 'Progge', but were desperately trying to hold onto the NNP component in the Western Cape to prevent the DA's regression to a tiny opposition party once more.

While the DA was still licking its wounds after the 2002 floor-crossing, Gerald Morkel determined that he would surround himself with 'more effective people' than those who, in his view, had failed adequately to defend his flanks. He proposed appointing, as an adviser, Abe Williams, a former colleague who was on parole after being released from prison a year earlier, having served a third of his sentence for fraud. At a meeting on 19 November 2002, some of us objected to a person on parole for a serious crime being given an influential position alongside the provincial leader of the party. The last thing the DA needed was yet another addition to the cabal whose members already made the archetypal conniving schemer, Frank Underwood, the fictional character from the television series *House of Cards*, look like a choirboy.

After I noted my objection, the normally mild-mannered Gerald Morkel exploded. I took his response down verbatim, in shorthand, because it illustrated so perfectly the incompatibility of values within the DA.

'While I am leader of this party,' Morkel said, 'I am not taking any bullshit from these bloody liberal ideas. I have proposed before that we get fat Abe Williams in here to help, but I am told we cannot have him in here because of his past, all these bloody liberal ideas. I need a champion on my side. I have said this for a long time. I don't want bullshit. We need a fighter who will get out there into the trenches, not sit and tap on a computer.'

What he meant by the trenches, of course, were the internal battle lines between the NNP and DP factions *inside* the DA, not out among the voters, between the DA and the ANC. The irony of the time was that the few people who were actually in the real electoral trenches trying to extend the DA's voter base *were* the 'bloody liberals'.

That is one of the reasons why we kept being outmanoeuvred in the party's internal trench warfare, which the cabal had turned into their full-time occupation. While they were strategising how to win every internal contest (from the lowliest branch secretary to the provincial executive) in order to demonstrate their power over every candidate's future prospects, some of us were out there building the DA's organisational network and brand among the voters, so that we could actually get some people elected. The cabal was happy to let others do this work, as long as they had exclusive power to determine who would actually hold office on the back of these efforts.

By December 2002, as a result of the Desai Commission's report, Gerald Morkel resigned. He was succeeded by Theuns Botha as provincial leader. Kent Morkel, one of Gerald's sons, became provincial chairman. Two members of the cabal were now leading the DA in the Western Cape.

The dirty tricks escalated.

I have records of this period that would enable me to write the definitive, multi-volume political dirty-tricks manual based on real-life case studies.

As I read through my papers again, I seriously thought of contacting the producers of *House of Cards*, proposing to write an entire year's worth of scripts, guaranteeing a new set of dirty tricks in every episode, to keep viewers riveted in morbid fascination and disbelief.

Some of the tactics included:
- concocting and then leaking bogus documents to the media
- multiple forms of financial inducement
- fake group SMSes sent under false names
- circulating additional ballot papers in closely contested electoral contests
- manipulating the composition of meetings and committees
- changing meeting dates and venues
- sending fake messages of the postponement of meetings
- creating new decision-making structures to undermine standard procedures and existing structures
- gerrymandering constituency boundaries
- altering minutes to change the wording of decisions

- forcing re-votes if the 'right' candidate was not elected
- removing ballot papers from voting boxes after they were cast
- packing electoral colleges with family members
- ignoring invoices so that default judgments would be made against the party to reflect badly on key individuals
- undermining the performance-evaluation system
- turning the disciplinary process into a way of persecuting opponents and protecting allies
- making secret tape-recordings of meetings so that snippets of what people said could be used out of context to whip up fear and frenzy when it was needed for political purposes

And many more.

In addition, there were the stock-in-trade favourites such as membership fraud, direct personal threats, circulating false rumours, and playing the race, religion and language cards till they were worn through with overuse.

As I said, I could write a book, with a chapter on each.

Let me take just a few examples.

Shortly after the DA lost Cape Town in the floor-crossing of 2002, the DA caucus in the city met on 28 October to elect members of the city's executive committee, to which the party was entitled. There were seven candidates in total from either side of the divided caucus.

Ballots were cast according to a single transferable vote system, designed to avoid manipulation to the greatest extent possible. It worked for a while, before the cabal figured out how to crack it.

According to this system, each voter had to rank ALL the candidates in order of preference, otherwise they would record a spoilt ballot. The computer works out the result according to votes weighted in rank order.

The result was totally unexpected. At the top of the list emerged Brian Watkyns, a soft-spoken, effective councillor and former DP member, popular with almost everyone. Danny de la Cruz came second. Gerald Morkel, the provincial leader, came third. There were only two positions to fill.

The cabal was stunned. It was an early signal that, as soon as the caucus could openly express their preferences in a secret ballot, they did not follow instructions.

The cabal immediately moved to rectify this 'mistake'.

That night, Kobus (the Bully) Brynard phoned Brian and tried to persuade him to step down in favour of Gerald. This was followed by further phone calls in an orchestrated sequence. Brian's response was: The caucus has voted. There was a result. I stand by it.

Another caucus meeting was convened the next day, at which the previous day's vote was extensively discussed. After NNP members had exerted extreme pressure on Brian, he agreed to stand back from the top position in favour of Gerald, the caucus leader, but insisted on taking the second position, as he had been elected ahead of Danny.

Of course, Danny de la Cruz objected vehemently to this. At which another member of the NNP grouping, Ken Lategan, proposed that the caucus should agree to give Morkel the top slot and that the caucus should re-vote for the second position.

This proposal was put to the vote in the caucus. By show of hands, they resolved to accept the proposal of a re-vote on the second position. The fear factor had been reintroduced. The vote was much more closely supervised the second time around. Brian and Danny were the only two candidates. Danny won.

So the (unduly) elected DA candidates for the remunerated exco positions were Gerald Morkel and Danny de la Cruz.

I was a member of the provincial legislature and, for this reason, was not a member of the Cape Town council caucus.

People were not supposed to leak information of caucus proceedings. But this development was so egregious that colleagues informed me about it on the night of the second caucus meeting. I insisted that we could not let the precedent stand. A valid vote had been held on 28 October, with a legitimate outcome, and could not be overturned unprocedurally the next day just because the cabal didn't like the result.

The matter was referred to the provincial executive, chaired by Theuns Botha. Both Gerald Morkel and Danny de la Cruz were members of the committee. There were so many conflicts of interest in this saga that it boggled the mind, but this seemed to be a non-issue in the ranks of the former NNP. Instead of abiding by an electoral outcome, their first instinct, of course, was to try to find out who had leaked the information to me from the city caucus!

Their second instinct was to try to squash the matter, but working with Pierre du Preez, the incorruptible, straight-talking chair of the Pinelands branch, we made sure it was referred to the DA's Federal Legal Commission (FLC) for adjudication.

Kobus Brynard argued that Pierre had no *locus standi* to bring the matter, as he was not entitled to know what had transpired in the caucus meeting!

I always found it deeply ironic that James Selfe tried to persuade me to drop the case, while the chairman of the FLC, former NNP MP Tertius Delport, ruled in our favour.

By the time of Delport's ruling, the ANC had changed the city's system of government and had thrown Gerald and Danny off the city's executive committee, replacing it with a mayoral committee. But the FLC nevertheless – correctly, in my view – ruled that the Cape Town caucus had acted incorrectly, that they owed Brian an apology and had to make good his financial loss, which amounted to R142 242.

In the interests of our almost bankrupt party, the soft-spoken Brian accepted R65 000 (to cover his accumulated overdraft) payable over five months.

These kinds of shenanigans became routine. We were determined to challenge them one by one.

In this context, it is appropriate to say a few words about James Selfe, whom I had always assumed would be a close ally of mine on these matters. James has all the bulldog qualities produced by the British public-school system: stoicism, doggedness, determination and, sometimes, an overdose of pragmatism. Each facet of his personality was essential to his job as chair of the party's Federal Council and Federal Executive. He had played a key role in recruiting me into the DA. He was central to the DA's survival during the darkest days, and resolutely drove the process of building it into a model of functionalism – as he continues to do today. He has been the party's essential common denominator through three successive leaders.

I shouldn't have been surprised when, as the party's internal rift grew, he fell in line behind Tony. But I was. After I became leader, in 2007, I wanted James to remain in these two key party positions, because he was so good at them, but we had an honest conversation first. He said to me that he regarded it as central to his role to always back the leader. He would do the same for me as he had done for Tony. And he did, even in the most difficult circumstances. Now he is doing the same for Mmusi Maimane. It is part of what makes James's role in the DA's development so pivotal.

But back to the soapie and one more example of the many in my files.

On Friday 24 January 2003, a political reporter writing for the Cape's Afrikaans daily, *Die Burger*, left me a message to call him back urgently. He told me he had obtained a leaked DA memo. It was on a DA letterhead and had been compiled by Theuns Botha, then the DA's provincial leader, for the attention of the DA's provincial director, Hanna Langenhoven. The letter asked Hanna to be flexible in her preparations for the forthcoming provincial congress so that we could accommodate the possibility of forming a new coalition if required. The implication of the letter was that members of the NNP, now in coalition with the ANC, wanted to re-cross the floor to realign with the DA at the next defection opportunity.

The reporter said he did not know the source of the leaked letter, which had arrived at *Die Burger*'s office by fax. He had spoken to Hanna and Theuns, who were both deeply shocked that this highly confidential internal memo could have been leaked. He asked for my comment.

I had no knowledge of this development (I was not in the provincial inner circle) and needed time to find out, so I asked if he could phone me back in a few minutes on my landline. He said he had to leave a function and return to his office and would phone me back from there. I immediately called Theuns for a briefing on the background. Theuns said he was busy on another line and would call me back.

The reporter called first. I told him I needed to hear the contents of the leaked letter before commenting. He read it to me. Contrary to the dismay reportedly expressed by Theuns and Hanna, I thought the letter would not harm us, because it hinted at the extent of the problems within the NNP and the likelihood of new defections from their ranks, back to the DA.

I told the journalist I was unaware of any plans for a new coalition, but that I did know that many NNP members were very unhappy in their alignment with the ANC and wanted a way out. Peter Marais, the person for whom Marthinus had split the DA, had himself been expelled by Marthinus. So, his colleagues were asking, what had all the fuss been about? They had concluded that they were now stuck in a coalition with the ANC to satisfy Marthinus van Schalkwyk's ego and hunger for power.

Facing a backlash from voters with the election only a year away, the NNP members now wanted to find a way back to the DA. This was the interpretation I suggested to the reporter.

I then pertinently asked him: 'As an experienced journalist, you will obviously know that it is important to ask yourself: Who leaked this memo and with what motive? Whose purpose is this serving?'

As it turned out, it was a most ironic question.

I concluded that the letter must have come from a person who wanted to facilitate former NNP members rejoining the DA. Perhaps someone in the DA office had leaked it to an NNP member, who leaked it to the journalist, I ventured.

The journalist said he thought just the opposite; he thought this memo played directly into Van Schalkwyk's hands, as it would now enable him to show that the DA was exploiting the problems of the NNP and trying to drive a wedge into their ranks. This, he said, would have the effect of driving NNP members back into the laager – or, alternatively, help the NNP smoke out the DA sleepers in its ranks.

When I asked the reporter why he thought this was the news angle (rather than the extent of the confusion and chaos in the NNP suggested by the letter), he said that I clearly did not understand how the NNP members would interpret this development. The instinctive response would be to demonise the DA and close ranks behind Marthinus van Schalkwyk. If there was any story at all, he said, it was that *'die DA probeer munt slaan uit die NNP se probleme'* (the DA is trying to take advantage of the NNP's internal problems).

The reporter's account of Theuns and Hanna's dismay over the leaked letter tended to reinforce the interpretation that they had the same perception as he had about the news angle. *Die Burger*'s readers would see it in the same way, he said.

I sought to argue the opposite; alternatively, that it was actually a 'non-story' and that they should beware of driving hidden agendas through leaked documents. We rang off.

Theuns then phoned me back. I summarised my conversation with the reporter, saying that it was unfortunate that the angle of the story was likely to be how the DA was trying to manipulate the conflicts within the NNP. Theuns said that *Die Burger* would do anything to discredit the DA, and we would have to hold tight and see what happened. He seemed genuinely concerned.

The journalist then phoned me back to say that after consideration, he and the political editor, Willem Jordaan, had decided NOT to run the story that Saturday, because there were too many unanswered questions about its source and intentions. He would conduct further interviews to get to the root of the matter. I expressed my view that it would be wrong to play along with what I thought was the NNP's agenda in getting hold of an internal DA memo and leaking it. He said he would phone various NNP people to test this thesis.

I phoned Theuns to tell him that *Die Burger* would not run the story without further research. I thought he would be relieved at the news, given the angle that the reporter was likely to take. Instead, I was greeted by a stunned silence on the other end of the line. After a short interaction, we ended the conversation.

About thirty minutes later, Hanna phoned me. I thought she was also worried about the leak and how *Die Burger* would report it, so I filled her in on my conversations with the journalist. She listened in silence. Then, she said, running the story would actually benefit rather than undermine us, because it would sow confusion in the NNP's ranks. I told her this had been my initial interpretation, but that I had changed my mind in light of the journalist's analysis of the relevant news angle, which would almost certainly backfire against us.

After some strong innuendo on Hanna's part, it suddenly occurred to me that she actually *wanted* the story to appear. After a few more sentences, it dawned on me that there could be even more to it. I then asked her directly whether she had leaked the letter herself and, after a long hesitation, she admitted that she had. On further probing I learnt that it was not an authentic letter at all. Hanna had written it to *appear* authentic (with a fictitious section appended to a list of valid instructions to the DA staff) for the express purpose of leaking it to *Die Burger*. The aim was to have the leaked letter published to escalate divisions within the NNP's ranks, as they would all suspect each other of wanting to cross the floor back to the DA.

Hanna had been instructed to try to achieve this and was getting on with it. She thought that she had done her job well, particularly in getting the reporter to believe that she was horrified about a leak of a confidential memo from her own office by her own staff. She said she thought I had been informed about the strategy. Theuns had apparently told her that I was in the loop, as were Robin Carlisle, James Selfe and Tony, according to Hannah. But I had no clue and didn't know whether the others had either.

I told Hanna I was pleased that I did not know the truth when the reporter cross-examined me. I said if this deceptive strategy was known as widely as she suggested, it would certainly surface at some stage. It would be a scandalous story if the DA were exposed as writing fictitious letters, 'leaking' them, and dissembling shock and horror, for the purposes of misleading the public.

It struck me with a deep sense of irony that the journalist had actually been right to conclude that the letter was proof of the DA trying to exploit the difficulties in NNP ranks, but in ways that neither he nor I suspected.

Die Burger did not run the story.

Theuns and Hanna were angry because I had messed up their strategy. We agreed to differ.

By then I knew that the DA was failing. We were supposed to be offering an alternative to dishonesty and intrigue, but we were gradually being engulfed by the same things. For me, even worse than the treachery of some NNP members were what I saw as the double standards of the DA federal leadership. I reported every one of these infringements (which made Peter Marais's fake signatures on a street-renaming petition seem tame by comparison), but was dismissed like a goody-goody schoolgirl telling tales on her friends.

For my part, I began to regard Tony and the coterie of young men in his office as a nest of narcissism, impenetrable to other perspectives, and intoxicated on their own importance. Anyone who didn't agree with them was an idiot, a goody-two-shoes or an adversary, depending on the issue. I had no direct line to Tony. I gave up trying to work through David Maynier, his chief of staff, who approached everything as if it were a military manoeuvre and tended to impute motives and agendas where they did not exist – to the point that one had to develop a motive and an agenda (as well as a strategy) to get anything across to the leader. Increasingly, I just kept my distance.

I only understood their office culture many years later when, on an international flight, I watched a few episodes of *The West Wing*, the television drama series depicting the cut-throat politics of the American president's office. It suddenly dawned on me: Tony's office had been modelled on the White House's West Wing, and each of the bright young politicos that surrounded him was playing a role in the series as if they were vying for an Emmy.

While Peter Marais had lost his job for manipulating a public petition (admittedly a serious offence), the DA leadership was now tacitly condoning, or ignoring, far worse infringements. They feared the cost of confrontation with the cabal and the risk of splitting the party again. It therefore became impossible for the DA to hold anyone in the party to account for poor performance or misconduct. If you did, people would drag disciplinary procedures out until the next floor-crossing, and then blithely defect to another party. Whatever the colour of the accused, they would claim they had left the DA because of racism (what else?), a trend that had been started by Van Schalkwyk himself.

This dispensation made it virtually impossible to run a party along the lines of competence and accountability. Floor-crossing enabled personal expedience to trump every other consideration.

This was another issue on which many of us liberals (with notable exceptions) had been hopelessly naive. We assumed that floor-crossing would be driven by principle. We thought it would happen as it does in established democracies. Only in exceptional circumstances, if the party had deviated from its electoral mandate, would someone cross the floor, without losing his seat, to remain accountable to the voters, rather than being held ransom by party bosses.

This is how floor-crossing in a democracy is supposed to work in theory, but in practice it didn't. Not in South Africa, anyway, where the list system meant it actually had precisely the opposite effect. It gave the party bosses new manipulative levers to offer promotion prospects and other inducements to defectors from other parties. Politics became a cesspit of self-serving expedience.

I often asked myself how it had come to this. My main reason for supporting the merger of the DP and NNP into the DA had been my belief that it would make the DP's 'open, opportunity' culture dominant in the party. This would enable us to transform the way we governed the Western Cape, as well as put us in a strong position to win municipal councils across the country in our bid to establish firm foundations of democracy and good governance. It turned out exactly the other way around. The break-up of the DA left the NNP members who stayed with us in the seats of real influence and power because of the sword of Damocles they constantly held over the head of our leader.

Ironically, this tendency merely intensified as the NNP's component of the DA shrank.

After the crossover of September 2002, the Nationalists were numerically weaker. 'We used to outnumber you two to one; now we are closer to 50/50,' Theuns Botha commented to me at the time. This was particularly the case in the greater Cape Town metropolitan area, where the former DP component now actually had a marginal majority. The rural areas were still strongly rooted in the old NNP.

I was hoping the new power balance would facilitate the transition to a closer co-operation based on the values we claimed to espouse; that it would encourage us to evaluate each other on the basis of contribution and effort, not on past affiliation, language, religion or colour. I was wrong. I underestimated the difficulty of making the transition from the protective cocoon of group solidarity to an open, opportunity-driven system – a transition that has taken hundreds of years in most societies, although few (if any) have faced the challenges we do.

To many former NNP members, the rough equivalence of numbers merely aggravated the 'us vs them' mentality. The NNP component of the DA was determined to claw their way back to an unassailable position, dominating the province. So they made a calculated move. They divided the province into three regions: the Cape metro and two rural regions, east and west. The purpose was to achieve equivalence between regions in decision-making, which would again enable the cabal to mobilise enough support to outnumber the 'Progge'. In the now looming likelihood that we might win the DA's internal struggle for the metro, they needed to control the two rural regions in order to outnumber us 2:1 in provincial decision-making. However, this coincided with a move in the DA, nationally, to put a greater emphasis on votes cast for the DA in various constituencies and regions as the determining factor in all internal party processes. And as the Cape Town metro region produced 66.4 per cent of the DA's vote in the Western Cape, the proposed regionalisation backfired on the cabal. We were now in a stronger position than before.

Early in 2003 I was elected chair of the metro region by a slim majority, despite a number of tricks employed at the AGM to try to prevent this outcome (including the distribution of fake ballot papers).

The shift in the balance of power sent the cabal into overdrive. Their primary mobilisation method was the fear factor. They used my election to strike terror in the hearts of former NNP councillors and members in the metro. As a result, every time I took a strong line on a point of principle in order to stop manipulation or dishonesty of some kind, it would be used to 'prove' that I was implacably opposed to the interests of the former NNP component, always with an additional racialised twist (of course).

It was a classic lose-lose situation. If I stood firm, the strategy to manufacture fear and resistance escalated. If I compromised, it was interpreted as a sign of weakness and the cabal took the gap to advance their position. They were trying to hold a sword of Damocles over my head as well, seeking to control me in the same way as the national leadership.

It created agonisingly difficult decisions as I sought to persuade people that we would all be better off if we adhered to our value set. I sometimes had the impression that people preferred the closed, controlled environment of enforced conformism, because this created a secure future. In an open, opportunity-driven system you have freedom, but you also face risk. And the worst risk for a mediocre politician is to face a competitive process for re-election.

Once the cabal had generated an irrational level of fear in the people they sought to control, they would warn the DA national leadership that, because of me and the other 'Progge', Afrikaans-speakers of all races would leave at the next floor-crossing. Then they would demand concessions, usually successfully, which often undermined our carefully balanced and fair internal systems.

With each concession, the cabal demonstrated its power to bend the system in favour of those beholden to them. This was the safest route to re-election, irrespective of past performance. The cabal had hit on a winning formula that kept us on a constant treadmill.

I was determined to show the former NNP component that we had no intention of marginalising them; that we wanted to build an inclusive party in which everyone would feel comfortable, on condition that we all adhered to our foundational principles and worked hard. Those attempts, in retrospect, were my biggest mistake. Every concession to address their artificially manufactured fears was manipulated and used by the cabal to extend their advantage and leverage. The advance and retreat of this trench warfare could be measured in metres, like the battle lines of the Somme in the First World War: three forward, five back, four forward again … and so on.

The grisly details are fascinating for true politicos, who analyse such minutiae like pathologists over a cadaver, but they are both boring (and probably nauseating) to normal human beings, so I will just focus on the big battles, which were also the site of the biggest betrayals. And I will do my best to explain them so that they are understandable to readers who are not versed in the arcane complexity of political structures and processes.

The election of 2004 was approaching. It was an election for national and provincial parliaments. The DA was at its lowest ebb ever – deeply divided, politically paralysed, strategically directionless. It was the worst time to have to draw up election lists.

Tony established a carefully balanced technical committee – on which I served together with several others, including people who understood the statistical technicalities of various electoral models – to devise the fairest possible candidate-selection system. We spent many hours working out a method that would be manageable, while also avoiding a simple 'winner takes all', majoritarian outcome. We wanted our lists to be broadly balanced and not allow a faction with a narrow majority to wipe out significant minorities. This, we believed, would be best for our attempts to build internal cohesion and unity around principles and policies, not race.

I learnt an enormous amount about various voting systems during this period, but I had to really apply my mind to a field I had previously known almost nothing about. I spent many hours studying the documentation and asking for explanations telephonically.

My children still do a wonderful skit of me discussing various complex formulae on the phone while the supper burns (yet again) in the background.

I will spare readers the gruesome details of electoral mathematics.

Even the great cosmologist Stephen Hawking used only one equation (Einstein's $E = mc^2$) in his popular book on the origins of the universe, *A Brief History of Time*, after his publisher warned him that every additional equation would reduce the book's sales by 50 per cent.

Actually, $E = mc^2$ seems pretty simple in comparison with the system of checks and balances we devised to limit attempts by cabals (of whatever origin) to manipulate the compilation of election lists. If a cabal nevertheless succeeded, they would have had to put in a very deliberate, determined, calculated and collective effort to do so. It could not happen casually, individually or accidentally.

The cabal, of course, promptly started a deliberate, determined, calculated and collective effort to find ways to beat the system (while we, of course, worked among the electorate to bring in the votes).

The multiple checks and balances depended on certain interrelated factors.

Despite Stephen Hawking's law of diminishing reader returns, I must try to give a simple overview, both for the historical record and for the politics addicts who may read this book. It will only take eleven paragraphs.

The system involved setting the most accurate possible seat target number for both the national and provincial parliaments, based on our tried and tested poll-projection methods. An electoral college would then select the candidate list in batches, by single transferable vote, to achieve the most balanced possible outcome, proportionally approximating the relative strength of votes cast between regions in the last election.

The cabal must have spent hours studying the system to come up with their battle plan, which only revealed itself slowly. They started as usual, by convincing many in their faction that the new formula was a deliberate and devious plan to prevent them from being elected. Again, the starting point was rumour mongering and panic manufacturing.

The next step was to convert fear to resistance, so that they could demand concessions. And, as usual, to show there was nothing to fear, I argued that we needed to concede, often against the advice of some of my strongest allies. It was like feeding steaks to the crocodile in the hope that it would become vegetarian (as Tony once accurately noted).

Having prepared the groundwork, the cabal then insisted that we (1) change the regional composition of the electoral college away from votes cast (60:40) to a 50:50 metro:rural formula; and (2) abandon the requirement of selecting the list in batches (which would be necessary to ensure incremental proportionality).

In order to reassure us that these concessions would not materially affect the outcome, they guaranteed that 66 per cent of positions within the 'real seat target number' would go to the metro to reflect and distribute public representatives on the basis of voter support.

What we failed to foresee was that they planned to artificially inflate the seat target number after we had made the other concessions. By doing so, they could easily promise the metro 66 per cent of an inflated seat target number, but ensure that most of these seats fell below the electable threshold. Most of the metro candidates would therefore be unelectable.

It was devious beyond comprehension. And the arguments used to promote it were disingenuous beyond imagination. To this day I wonder what kind of evil genius is required to work these things out.

But what really worried me was this: the only way they could have inflated the seat target number was with the support (let me avoid the word connivance) of the national leadership, because the national leadership had to set the seat target number. It caught me totally by surprise at a Federal Council meeting where I was unprepared for the guillotine when it fell.

I felt sick to the stomach.

Once the cabal had rigged the system, they had to ensure that enough electoral-college delegates voted in the 'right way'.

Perhaps the most telling story is that of Councillor Basil Lee of Grassy Park, and a delegate to the electoral college. According to Basil, Leon van Rensburg had handed him a list of instructions on whom to vote for, but Basil promptly tore it up and said he could think for himself. Within thirty minutes he received a call from Gerald Morkel, who remained extremely influential in former NNP circles.

Basil's version of the conversation, which I recorded, went like this:

Morkel: Do you like being a councillor, Basil?

Basil Lee: Yes, I do.

Morkel: Well, you will be out of office in the next election.

Basil Lee: Why?

Morkel: Because you refuse to vote for the list.

Gerald then told Basil that if he wanted to remain in politics, he had better go, by the next day, to Leon van Rensburg and pick up his list.

It was as blatant as that.

Basil refused and reported the conversation to me, which I recorded verbatim. He reconfirmed this interaction when I phoned him to verify the contents of the conversation during the course of writing this chapter.

Basil showed enormous courage in the circumstances. He knew that anyone who didn't comply with the cabal was quickly marginalised. This applied particularly to moderate former NNP members, and former independents, who resisted the dictates of the cabal in their determination to build the DA in the middle ground – people like Claude Ipser, Nicky Holderness, Felicity Purchase, Fanie Jacobs, Chris Hattingh, Hein Herbst, Andrew Loubser and Dan Plato.

It is frankly impossible to build a functional political party, let alone a capable state, when candidates are selected or rejected on this basis. I was in despair about the possibility of salvaging the DA.

The metro ended up with a guarantee of 66 per cent of a completely unachievable provincial seat target of twenty-two seats. The actual election result showed just how outrageously inflated this was.

The DA in the Western Cape won a mere twelve seats in the provincial legislature. The entire metro ended up with five MPLs for two-thirds of the province's voters, living in the Cape Town metro. And three of those five MPLs were drawn straight from the NNP's faction. Those who understood and implemented DA values had almost been wiped out.

So much for all the promises and assurances. And the great irony was that I had been cast as the aggressor, the person to fear. I soon learnt that what the cabal had accused me of, they were actually guilty of themselves.

This outcome, of course, dramatically weakened my position in my own region, which was precisely part of their plan. My allies had been right when they warned me that my attempts to build the moderate centre of the party through accommodating people's concerns, by making concessions, would only be used against us.

It did not help to argue that I had spoken in favour of compromise in order to demonstrate good faith and prevent the cabal using us as the proverbial bogeyman. In the end all I achieved was to undermine my own metro constituency while strengthening the cabal and failing to build the middle ground.

I had been hospitalised during the election campaign after being diagnosed with an ovarian cyst, double the size of a tennis ball, which the doctor was concerned might be malignant. I needed a full hysterectomy urgently. Fortunately, the growth was benign, but a hysterectomy is a major operation and it took me out of action for a large part of the election campaign. I was probably suffering from exhaustion as well, and my family was being totally neglected.

I still remember with great guilt a conversation I should have had, but never did, with our elder son sometime during this period. It was late at night. I was half asleep in bed, my mind churning over political developments. Paul came to sit on the edge of my bed and initiated a conversation that must have been very difficult for him.

I was in no position to take anything more on board, let alone an issue of emotional intensity. 'Don't worry about it,' I mumbled, and turned over. He left, and for years afterwards I thought of how different things might have been had I woken up and listened to the conversation he was ready to have with me, but that I was unable to absorb.

It took months to recover from the setback to my health. I had taken a decision to leave the province and throw my hat in the ring for election to the National Assembly, where I was made spokesperson on education.

The 2004 general election result was disastrous for the DA in the Western Cape. Although we could not do an 'apples vs apples' comparison between two national elections, because 2004 was the first the DA had fought, the combined provincial total of the NNP and DP in 1999 had topped 50 per cent, enabling us to put together the short-lived coalition. The NNP's acrimonious exit from the DA had hurt us badly in the province, although the impact was far less in the rest of the country. In politics, you can't afford to dwell in the past. You have to try to learn the right lessons and move on.

As soon as I was back at work, we were already preparing for the 2006 local government elections, in which local branch membership played a crucial role. The year 2005 was therefore the critical preparatory year where membership recruitment would determine much of the composition of the branch and list electoral colleges for selecting the eligible pool of councillors.

Buoyed by their internal success in manipulating the candidate-selection process for the 2004 election, the cabal sprang into action to recruit members by the thousands. The auditor afterwards described it as the most corrupt process he had ever seen.

The national leadership of the DA, paralysed by threats of a new round of defections looming in September 2005, again turned a blind eye.

Next, the cabal worked hard behind the scenes to get rid of the Western Cape's three regions. Whereas three regions had suited them in the candidate-selection processes for provincial and national parliaments, they did not maximise the cabal's potential for controlling the selection of municipal council candidates (for reasons of the formulae, which I do not need to explain in detail). So with the support of the DA's federal leadership, and behind the metro region's back, moves were put in place to scrap regional electoral colleges and give the power to provinces, working with local management committees.

However, this arrangement did not suit one of the cabal's members, who faced opposition from his own local management committee. As a result he broke ranks, opening a gap for me to develop a constructive relationship with him that helped us turn the tables. I learnt that when dealing with a cabal, a point will eventually come where self-preservation and the collective agenda collide. And in those circumstances, self-preservation usually wins. As they say, there are no permanent friends in politics, only permanent interests.

I convened a regional council at Nooitgedacht, Cape Town, on 18 June 2005 and, taking on a divided cabal, managed to reduce the fear factor and beat back the proposal of province (backed by federal) to reduce or eliminate the role of regional electoral colleges in candidate selection for the 2006 local government elections. It was a stunning victory. Divisions in the cabal paralysed its capacity to mobilise and the meeting swung behind us, 163 votes against two abstentions.

But this victory was, as they say, academic. I knew that in the face of widespread membership fraud in the province it would be impossible to establish electoral colleges at all, at any level in the party.

My father died on 29 June 2005, and I remember the combination of grief and outrage burning in me so intensely that it felt like the beaker in a chemistry experiment we had done at school, when sodium was dropped into water, releasing hydrogen at intense and explosive temperatures.

It had generated in me a burning determination to destroy the cabal within the DA – or be destroyed in the process. The status quo could not prevail.

By the time I returned from Dad's memorial service, where my son Paul had played Massenet's 'Meditation' on his violin with incredible depth and passion, my resolve had hardened.

Turning the other cheek and making compromises had always backfired; I had learnt it was impossible to find viable middle ground or make honest compromises. I had to fight fire with fire.

The first thing I did was set up my own advisory group of nine people, carefully chosen for their ideological compatibility with the DA's founding values. Their integrity, discretion and courage would go head to head with our opposite numbers. We resolved that we were now going to take on our opponents on every single issue. I was told, in no uncertain terms, that the era of compromises was over. I concurred.

We belied our steely determination by choosing the whimsical code name Some Day, perhaps hoping that eventually the DA might emerge from this nightmare, and also to indicate that we met on Sundays, without having to mention it in our communication.

There was Ian the statistician; Debbie the lawyer; Anthea the level-headed realist; Rose the expert administrator; Denise the head girl with a human heart; Demetri, whose sharp focus always brought us back to the main point; Belinda the razor-tongued terrier; Owen the scathing wit; and Liz, always organised and dependable.

We met at different venues, usually each other's homes, our conversation lubricated by a glass of good wine. The jovial atmosphere belied our deadly serious intent. We became experts at planning, calculation and execution.

There was no point in working hard to win elections if the Democratic Alliance had become just another corrupt, racial-nationalist, closed, crony party. We first had to fix ourselves.

We spent an entire meeting discussing the question 'Is the DA redeemable?'

This is the photograph that my Granny hung above her bed in her small Hillbrow flat. She is second from the right in the middle row. Her husband, the grandfather I never met, is on the far right in the back row. They are with the Marcus siblings and spouses, together with the Marcus parents, Ernestine and Hermann in the front row (middle). It was only in the course of writing this book that I learnt how many of them were murdered in the Holocaust (Shoah).

Helene Marcus Zille, the grandmother after whom I was named, with her two young sons, Heinrich (left) and Wolfgang (my father), shortly after her husband Walter Zille's death in 1922.

Emilie (Mila) Cosmann, my mother's mother, who we knew as Ama, with me on her lap at six months. I still have clear memories of wearing that poncho, a gift from my Aunt Otta in Buenos Aires.

Christmas 1951: Me, as a baby, in the arms of my father Wolfgang. Next to him is my Apa, with my cousin Anne on his lap. They sit opposite our Ama. This was inside our corrugated-iron lounge (seen behind the Christmas tree), furnished with second-hand garden furniture and a rocker.

With my mother's father, Carl Maximilian Cosmann, our Apa and paterfamilias. He devoted his life after the Holocaust to reuniting his family in the diaspora.

My mother Mila, left, sits alongside her mother Mila (my Ama), and her mother-in-law Helene (my Granny). My younger sister, Carla, sits on Ama's lap while I am fascinated by our Great Dane puppies.

Mom and Dad, with Carla and me, sitting in front of our newly constructed house in 1956/57.

This photo was taken in 1960, by which time our brother Paul had joined the family.

A studio shot of me at about ten years old.

Practising the piano at home on the Bechstein my parents had bought me. I battled with the piano because of my short fingers, which were unable to stretch an octave, and also because I had cut off the tip of my right index finger in an accident involving our electric mincing machine.

This is a photo of me in 1967 (when I was in Form 4 or Grade 11), emulating my skinny model hero, Twiggy. I got the make-up and hair right, and then set out to achieve the same body shape, with almost disastrous results.

I achieved the pinnacle of my ambition when I was selected for the drum-majorette squad in 1970. By then I was already caught in the cage of anorexia.

Two years later (1972) as a student at Wits, on my way to beating anorexia.

After pulling out of my degree at UCT for health reasons, I completed my studies at Wits. Here I am on graduation day.

As a journalist at the *Rand Daily Mail*, finding real purpose and meaning in my life for the first time.

In my late twenties, sitting on the floor of my bachelor flat in Berea.

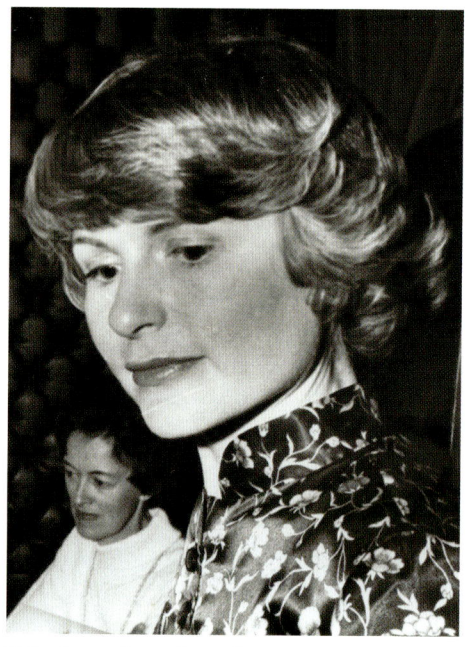

This photo, from about the same time, was taken at a party.

Matt Franjola, at around the time he arrived in my life. We spent almost three fun-filled years together.

Matt and me at a fancy-dress party. I can't remember what we were dressed up as, but it clearly had a raunchy connotation. Matt was wearing his aviator glasses.

My wedding to Johann Maree in December 1982. We are with my parents and Carla. Unfortunately Paul, my brother, could not come from England for the wedding.

Addressing the delegates at the Black Sash national conference in 1989.

With my two sons, Paul and Thomas, shortly after Tom's birth, just as my second post-natal depression was kicking in around October 1989.

Tom's bath time was often a family occasion.

With Tom and Paul on the ferry en route to Robben Island in 1993.

Paul was in Grade 7 and Tom in Grade 1 at The Grove Primary School when this photo was taken in 1996. During my tenure as chair of the school governing body, The Grove led a consortium of eighty public schools in a successful court challenge against the ANC government's voluntary severance and redeployment scheme.

Photo: Karina Turok

We analysed the option of using the floor-crossing window in September 2005 ourselves to relaunch the Democratic Party, but after examining that option from every angle, we rejected it. If we had been stupid enough to go into alliance with the former NNP, we had to be stupid enough to make it work (to quote former DP leader Colin Eglin, who had, by then, retired from politics).

Then, how to save the DA? There was only one way forward: if we were to save the party from within, Tony Leon would have to go. And some of his top lieutenants with him.

I had already received an email tip-off, from Bill Johnson, former Oxford don and executive director of the Helen Suzman Foundation. He'd told me that Tony was planning to step down as DA leader, but was holding on because he was concerned about the possibility that I might succeed him. The reason why Tony opposed my candidature, as he explained to Bill, was his fear that there would be a mass exodus of the former NNP members out of the DA if I succeeded him. I knew this was a possibility, but I was clear on one point: if people did not accept the DA's core philosophy, it was best if they found a more compatible political home elsewhere.

Floor-crossing did not spook me the way it did Tony. On the contrary, the departure of 'crosstitutes', as they were commonly called, usually had quite a cleansing effect on our system.

So by mid-2005 the situation could be summarised as follows: Tony was determined he should stay. Some Day and I had resolved he had to go.

The stakes were high. We applied our minds to a viable strategy.

Then I got a call from Tony Leon.

He wanted me to come and see him, he said, about the local government election, scheduled for early 2006. I went. He asked me to run as the DA's mayoral candidate in Cape Town. I was taken aback. I was ensconced in parliament, away from the poisoned pit of the province and working on the portfolio I loved most, education.

Sensing my resistance, Tony assured me that we were unlikely to win Cape Town, given the fact that we'd only managed to draw 27 per cent of the vote in the metro in the 2004 election – just over half of what we had managed only four years earlier. However, Tony added, Ryan's polling indicated that my candidacy would maximise the DA's vote. And there was a chance that we could end with a hung council and form a coalition with other parties. In that case, we might have a chance of regaining the city.

Besides, he said, he was worried about the fact that Kent Morkel (who was chairman of the DA in the Western Cape) had announced his availability to run as the mayoral candidate. From my experience of Kent Morkel's capacity for manipulation, I had to agree with Tony. If Kent became mayor, his leadership of the city would make the Peter Marais circus look like a curtain-raiser. His nomination, against the backdrop of a cupboard of skeletons, meant that the party would be mired in controversy throughout the election.

I told Tony that local government was not my area of expertise. I would be inheriting a poisoned chalice in the form of an administration largely hollowed out of expertise under the disastrous tenure of the ANC's NomaIndia Mfeketo as mayor of Cape Town. If I became a councillor, I would sacrifice the accumulation of my pension, and I would be returning to an arena of factional warfare. I was worn out, my health had taken a serious knock, and I just did not see my way clear to doing it.

Tony asked me to think about it. I said I would, and revert. Then I convened Some Day to discuss his proposal. We came to the conclusion that there were two reasons why Tony had approached me.
1) He obviously genuinely wanted to maximise the DA's vote in Cape Town, regain the city if possible and make sure it was governed properly.
2) He sensed that I was gearing up to make a move against him and wanted me out of parliament. The parliamentary caucus had always been the traditional platform for the DA's federal leader; it had not been considered possible to do it from another base.

Having been briefed by Bill Johnson, a third reason was ineluctable: with me out of the way, Tony would see his way clear to step down, with a better than even chance of preventing me from succeeding him.

Now I had to make up my mind on how to respond.

We spent two Some Day sessions discussing one theme: Would it be better, in our attempt to achieve our strategy of salvaging the DA's core value set, for me to remain in parliament, or to become the mayoral candidate for Cape Town? We discussed this from every conceivable angle.

We concluded that being the mayoral candidate would be a strong signal at a time when the NNP thought they had wiped us out and had the province firmly under control. And furthermore, if the outcome resulted in no party achieving over 50 per cent, as seemed possible, we might be able to put together a coalition with the Independent Democrats (ID), the party most likely to achieve a balance of power. The ID had been founded by Patricia de Lille in 2003, when she crossed the floor from the Pan Africanist Congress. A coalition with the ID would cause a shift in the balance of forces inside the DA in the Western Cape, the province where this was most needed. If we could achieve this, we would be in a better position to accomplish our mission. The rest of the party was not at risk of values erosion – at least not then. We finally agreed that the mayoralty could be even more important to our battle for the soul of the DA than the national leadership.

Some Day concluded that I should accept. It was worth a try, we thought, and more likely to succeed than taking on the national leader, which was an impossibility so close to an election.

I went back to Tony and said yes, but only on condition that I received the unequivocal support of the federal leadership if I ran for mayor and that, if I won, the DA would make up the balance of the pension I would lose. I did not want to be led into yet another trap under false pretences, only to be let down at the eleventh hour.

Tony gave me his word and I believed him, despite the fact that he had failed to give us support on any of the other critical issues when we'd so desperately needed it. I also knew of his additional motivation, and had also been informed, by Bill, about Tony's attempts to seek opportunities in the USA once he stepped down from the DA leadership. He needed me out of the way first. Making me mayor opened the possibility of doing so.

The cabal had other ideas, however. They thought it was possible both to prevent me from becoming the mayoral candidate *and* from becoming Tony's successor. They set about trying to change the formula for selecting mayoral candidates, and James Selfe expressed his support for Theuns Botha's plan to scrap the regions.

Tony, however, was backing me for mayor, even if he was making a virtue of necessity in his circumstances. But, to give him his due, when the chips were down and the party was staring into the abyss of a potential Kent Morkel mayoralty, Tony drew the line and did the right thing.

I had to smile at the irony when Tony asked me to help him get Kent out of the way as a councillor and potential mayoral candidate (so that Tony could get me out of the way of succeeding him). Tony's plan was to get Kent selected to fill the vacancy in the provincial legislature left by the resignation of Danny de la Cruz (whose wife had won the Lotto, enabling him to retire).

After Some Day had decided I should run for mayor, we were determined to give it our best shot. We switched strategy and poured our energies into winning the mayoralty rather than ousting Tony.

The cabal switched focus too – to getting rid of any regional role in candidate selection of councillors.

From Pieter, the alienated cabal member, I learnt a lot about how they worked. Each had a role. They analysed every single member of every caucus (including their financial problems, their interpersonal conflicts and their individual aspirations). This 'intelligence' was essential to the cabal's manipulation strategy. They knew the human configuration and fault-lines of every party structure in the finest detail. They used an elaborate colour-coding system, and assigned a 'handler' to people to bring them in line and keep them there. They analysed who sat next to whom in meetings, and who spoke to whom at tea breaks and made sure they knew that they were being observed. I saw Excel spreadsheets with more markings and highlighted colours than I knew existed. I could see for myself just how much work and co-ordination the cabal's closed, controlled system required. It was terrifying to observe this autocratic tendency emerging in our own party.

Because of the extent of the membership fraud in 2005, it was impossible to convene a proper electoral college according to the candidate-selection regulations. The result was an electoral college dominated by delegates of only two out of the city's 103 wards – and both had been seriously tainted by membership fraud – while thousands of DA members in properly constituted wards were disenfranchised. Furthermore, family networks of Kent Morkel and Kobus Brynard dominated the cabal's faction of the selection process, so that the choice of candidates could be tightly controlled.

As a final insult, the provincial executive resolved to block the release of the membership audit in order to cover up the enormous manipulation that had taken place.

The metro region objected. We appealed through the structures, requesting the Federal Executive to set up a candidate-selection process, as they were empowered to do in the event of a deadlock. But the federal response was clear: although there had been serious irregularities, it was too late to do anything about it.

The real reason for turning a blind eye to this travesty was that the federal leadership knew what the cabal's response would be if their carefully manipulated electoral college was nullified. They had threatened to split the party again, and Tony believed that they would.

On the other hand, the DA's federal leadership always assumed that the cabal's opponents would act rationally and reasonably in the interests of the party. In doing so, ironically, we allowed practices and precedents to become established that could have profoundly damaged the party had we not eventually succeeded in turning the tables.

The result was a deadlocked electoral college in which the provincial leader, Theuns Botha, had the power to exercise a casting vote for every ward candidate in Cape Town. The provincial executive had resolved to allow him to do this without even listening to the candidates' interviews! Travesty and farce are far too mild to describe the violation of fairness and due process this involved. We would almost certainly have won a court action to set aside this candidate-selection system if we had gone this route. But we would also have missed the election.

I fought back hard – and publicly – against some of the most gratuitous attempts to remove some of our best-performing ward councillors, and succeeded in some cases, buoyed by the public outcry in various wards.

The worst thing about all these internal machinations was that it threatened to establish the NNP's tradition of 'inward focus' in the DA – eradicating the DP's traditional outward focus on the voters.

In our Some Day meetings we reflected on the long-term costs of my tendency to default to compromise, and said we might be harming the party far more by backing down, but we had no other option if we wanted to fight the election. Our hope lay in the selection of the mayoral candidate, which was done according to a different formula.

True to form, the cabal then turned its attention to controlling the mayoral electoral college, with Kent Morkel deployed to capture some of its members through his usual chicanery.

I discovered this quite by chance when a member of the electoral college, Mzuvukile Rasta Mfengwana, casually mentioned to me in conversation that he had been contacted by Kent Morkel to discuss a business proposition shortly before the mayoral electoral college meeting. I warned Rasta that the 'business opportunity' would be conditional on his opposing me in the electoral college, after which the offer would disappear as miraculously as it had arrived.

To his very great credit, Rasta refused to be co-opted. But it was just another indication of how the cabal worked.

Given the composition of the electoral college and the dirty tricks campaign, my selection as mayoral candidate was by no means assured.

The cabal put up Lennit Max, who had just crossed the floor from the Independent Democrats to the DA two months earlier, but I managed to beat him 22 votes to 16 with Tony Leon's canvassing assistance behind the scenes.

My supporters and I (including Some Day, whose existence and identity were secret) went to a local restaurant and pooled our pennies to buy a bottle of sparkling wine to celebrate.

I felt like a gladiator who had survived a confrontation with a pride of lions in the Colosseum. But I had not done it alone. Some Day had bonded as a team. And Tony Leon, for all his equivocating, understood when the chips were down what was at stake. I had always respected him as a leader and empathised with the acute dilemma he faced in his efforts to hold the DA together. I had also felt the cold steel of the cabal's sword in the nape of my neck. And I had faced the wrath of my support base for making concessions.

From the moment I was selected as the DA's mayoral candidate, Some Day knew we would have to do whatever it took to win the municipal election in March 2006, because it would also mean winning back the DA for the values on which it was founded.

It was only because we eventually succeeded that I can look back today and say that, despite all the agony it involved, the formation of the DA was worth it. It enabled us to short-cut history.

Although there is no doubt that the NNP would have steadily continued its decline, even if we had remained separate parties, it would not have gone quietly. For several successive elections we would have been fighting on two fronts, making progress extremely difficult and far too slow for the urgency of the time. If I had known beforehand what forming the DA would entail, I probably would have chosen the longer route. But once we were in it, we had to win it. Another major bust-up would have sent us back to square one, not merely to 1999, but probably back to 1994, when we had had a mere 1.7 per cent of the vote.

Finally, it is valid for readers to ask an important question. Against the background of this ghastly phase of the DA's history, was it hypocritical of me to appoint some members of the cabal to senior positions within our administration when I had the power to marginalise them instead? A few of my allies remain angry with me to this day because they thought I was too accommodating, just as I was once angry with Tony.

My answer has two parts. One is that politics is the art of the possible. It is essential for a leader to try to hold a party together, to draw its opposing forces closer, in an attempt to consolidate core principles. I have tried to do this, and I think it is fair to say that when these principles were violated by those entrusted with high office, I did not hesitate to act against them. But I was never motivated by a desire for political revenge.

The second (and more important) part of the answer is that people can and do change. As former NNP members (and even members of the cabal) came to experience our values in action, they genuinely preferred the 'open' way of working. Once we had won this battle, we could allow our internal culture to flourish, which many former NNP members found liberating. But, as I am learning again, retaining and building on this culture is a continuous battle inside a political party. The fight is never finally won.

Today, I can confidently say that the vast majority of our members and public representatives who came from the NNP have internalised and adopted the vision of an open, opportunity society for all. This is the story of a truly remarkable transformation in the space of a decade.

When all is said and done, a political party, based on a coherent political philosophy, cannot grow unless it converts its opponents. This happens through exposure, experience and convincement. Sometimes it also requires confrontation and compromise. The balance is always delicate and difficult.

Perhaps the greatest lesson I learnt in this period is that the distance between success and failure in politics is often measured in millimetres. And this tiny difference always depends on good strategy and Herculean effort.

10

'Hamba Kwa Langa'

A TWO-FRONT WAR IS a battle waged on two separate geographical fronts simultaneously. It is also a good description of my life between 2000 and 2007. As the battle for the soul of the DA raged inside the party, the ANC was consolidating its single-party hold on South Africa.

A resolution adopted at the ANC's Mafikeng conference in 1997 on cadre deployment laid bare its plans to capture state institutions and turn our constitutional checks and balances into appendices of the ruling party. The fig leaf used to disguise this strategy was 'affirmative action'. Anyone who opposed cadre deployment could therefore neatly be labelled 'racist'.

In truth, 'cadre deployment' was a strategy the ANC had learnt from the Stalinist South African Communist Party. The SACP understood the power of patronage. They knew that control over positions and promotions enabled the 'centre' to entrench total control over the party, its members and all other institutions. They described this totalitarian system by the oxymoron 'democratic centralism'.

Top positions in the institutions of state rapidly degenerated into a loyalty rewards programme run by a deployment committee accountable to the 'big man' in power.

The academic name for this form of patronage is 'patrimonialism'. It is a sure recipe for destroying the rule of law, preventing the emergence of a capable state, and entrenching cronyism and corruption throughout government. This combination of factors always undermines economic growth and job creation, making it impossible to tackle our biggest problem, pervasive poverty.

Yet, here we were in the DA, South Africa's major opposition party, waging a debilitating war with ourselves. We were trapped in the realpolitik of the present at a time when history required us to be on the battlefront of the future.

The only way we could prevent South Africa's slide into a failed state was to build a culture of accountability. In a democracy, this requires voters who are prepared to switch their vote in order to change their government. Power-abusing governments can only be reined in if they fear losing the next election.

But the opposite was happening. The ANC's support base had grown in every election and, after three rounds of floor-crossing, the ruling party had almost 75 per cent of the seats in parliament – over 10 per cent more than the ANC won in the first democratic election of 1994.

Although few observers realised it, as South Africa's economy entered a boom cycle, we were on a slippery slope. There was only one conclusion. The DA had to grow. And to do so, we had to extend our support among black voters.

Tony recognised this. He asked me to establish a beachhead into new territory – the ANC's strongholds of Langa, Nyanga, Crossroads, Gugulethu and Khayelitsha. I was allocated a constituency comprising twenty-eight wards, every one of which was hostile space for the DA. Because these wards fell on both sides of the N2 national road, we called them, collectively, the 'N2 constituency'.

As constituency head, I was a general without an army. Actually, without a single soldier. My first job was to recruit my first member as the first step in the proverbial thousand-mile journey. The few friends and acquaintances I had in my constituency were staunch ANC loyalists who had regarded my move to the DA as an act of betrayal. This made me appreciate just how brave people in these wards would have to be to make the move from the ANC to the DA.

It is no exaggeration to say that I would be putting them and their families at risk by asking them to join the DA. I asked myself whether I could, in good conscience, recruit members under these circumstances. But then I thought of the alternative. If we allowed the ANC to turn townships into 'no-go zones' for opposition parties and claim 'ownership' of black South Africans, our democracy would be stillborn. The stakes were high, but it was essential to try.

If there is one indicator that shows how far our democracy has advanced since then, it is the establishment and growth of DA branches in ANC-dominated areas. Today we probably have more properly constituted branches in the N2 constituency than the ANC has!

But back then, people literally took their lives in their hands if they openly identified with us. I still marvel at their bravery and sacrifice in helping to plant the seeds of multi-party democracy in the most barren soil. They had what astronauts call 'the right stuff'.

I remember recruiting my first member as though it were yesterday. I had been referred to her by a friend, Dr Mary Roberts, who did locums in various township clinics.

'Why don't you speak to Lungiswa Gazi?' Mary suggested. 'Her house was burnt down in Khayelitsha because she opposed the ANC. She may be interested.'

I had my doubts about contacting someone who had already paid such a high price for her political convictions. If my house had been burnt down, I thought to myself, I would want to avoid a repetition. But I didn't have many options, so I resolved to give it a try.

Through Mary, I got Lungiswa's address. She lived in a semi-detached 'train house' in one of the offensively named 'Native Yards' in Gugulethu – NY74.

One Saturday, late morning, my pale-blue hatchback Kadett pulled up outside her gate at the end of a path that led up some steps to a stoep and her front door.

Before I met Lungiswa, I made my acquaintance with Bobby. He was lazing in front of the door, in the sun, one eye open, the other shut. Every time I touched the gate, he emitted an ominous growl. I had expected some hostility from people – but the dogs?

A little girl from the neighbouring yard hung over the low fence separating the small plots. 'Go in,' she urged. 'Go!' I laughed and shook my head. I was prepared to take risks with people, but not with dogs. The child bounced out of her yard, took me firmly by the hand, opened Lungiswa's gate and marched me up the garden path, all the while talking sternly in Xhosa to Bobby. He clearly understood, because he stopped growling and watched us, one ear erect, the other at half-mast, a caricature township mongrel.

The little girl positioned herself firmly between me and Bobby as I knocked on the door.

There was the sound of splashing water, and within seconds the door swung open, revealing a very large lady in a very small towel. It only just managed to cover the three key points.

I gulped, apologised profusely and said I would come back later. I looked down, hoping the girl would rescue me from another tricky situation, but she was already skipping out of the front gate.

'No, no,' Lungiswa insisted. 'Come in!'

I stepped inside and she closed the door. Pulling up a chair next to a large metal tub in the centre of the room, she instructed me to sit down. Then she dropped the towel, revealing her full glory, got back into the tub and reclined in two inches of soapy water. 'I don't want my water to get cold,' she explained. 'It already takes me four kettles to get this much.'

It was only then that I noticed another woman in the darkened room, also scantily clad in a towel. She had just finished her bath. Now it was Lungiswa's turn.

I was experiencing what sociologists call 'culture shock'. Friends taking their ablutions together. I soon came to love the spontaneity and authenticity of the world I was about to become part of.

At the time I felt rather inhibited to initiate a political conversation in those circumstances. After all, I had not come to talk about beauty products.

Lungiswa did not know me from the proverbial bar of soap with which she was scrubbing herself. I introduced myself, amazed that she would let a complete stranger into her 'bathroom', but interpreted it as a sign of acceptance. She then introduced her friend Koliwe Gubangca, who, still wrapped in her little towel, pulled her chair closer. They were fascinated to hear the purpose of my visit.

By the time Lungiswa had finished her bath, both she and Koliwe had signed their membership forms.

From that moment, we were in contact almost every day. Lungiswa advised me to start recruiting in Langa, where, she said, many people were 'fed up' with the ANC. She introduced me to another friend, Valencia Nkomokazi, who introduced me to Mambhele Makeleni, who introduced me to Reginah Lengisi, who introduced me to Timothy Mbiza, who introduced me to Siphokazi Ngomu, and so on, until we had the twenty-five people necessary to form a branch. It was exhilarating and not nearly as daunting as I had feared.

Or so I thought – until we became big enough to attract the ANC's attention.

Then I observed a pattern emerging, which has become standard throughout the country. The ANC ignores opposition as long as it remains tiny and irrelevant, but when it grows to the point that it poses a challenge, their tolerance evaporates. The vacuum is filled by any method required to crush the challenge, including violence and intimidation.

Before long we had 300 members in the Langa branch. On 3 February 2001, the branch in Ward 52 Langa became the first new DA branch in my constituency. We hired a marquee and invited the DA's newly elected mayor, Peter Marais, to speak at the launch. We slaughtered a sheep and brewed *umqombothi* and had a marvellous feast under the electricity pylons along the N2 highway.

Then our problems started.

Mambhele Makeleni was our star organiser and membership recruiter. A tall, slender lady with a spontaneous laugh and intermittent teeth that had never known the luxury of dental care, she lived in a one-roomed shack #18 Zone 25 in Langa, which doubled as a crèche during the day. Her worldly goods stood in a little pile in one corner. She hardly spoke any English. Whenever she left her shack, she always wore her signature black beret.

Less than two weeks after our launch, members of the ANC-aligned South African National Civic Organisation (SANCO) started harassing Mambhele to the point that she had to leave Langa and go into hiding because she feared her life was in danger. She always returned after a night or two, but then the cycle would start again.

After a while, a new and even more insidious pattern began to emerge. The Langa police became part of the pattern of persecution. Mambhele was arrested on Friday 24 August 2001 following a SANCO complaint that she had 'stolen R5 under false pretences'. The ANC issued a press release, arbitrarily increasing the amount Mambhele was alleged to have stolen to R42 – without any substantiation.

She spent the weekend in jail and appeared in the Bishop Lavis court on 27 August, where she was released on bail, pending the next hearing, set for 10 September. I was totally astounded that this matter even reached a court. I had been taught in my legal-theory course at university that *de minimis non curat lex* – the law does not concern itself with trivialities. But before her second appearance on this ludicrous charge, Mambhele was rearrested, again on a Friday (7 September), this time on a charge of stealing five tins of milk.

I instituted my own investigation and learnt that Mambhele's crèche was part of a feeding scheme in the area to which milk was allocated by the clinic. I managed to get her released from police cells on the basis of a sworn statement from a senior manager at the clinic explaining that the milk had been legitimately allocated to her.

Then I learnt that laying a spurious charge against an opponent on a Friday afternoon (preferably before a long weekend) was a favourite ploy of the ANC's in Langa. This ruse would give the police an excuse to arrest the person and keep them in jail for the entire weekend, as a bail hearing could only take place on the first working day of the following week. Once people had suffered a few rounds of such victimisation, their opposition to the ANC usually crumbled.

But not Mambhele. I have never quite understood what drove her. She was one of the world's few instinctive democrats. She reacted vehemently against authoritarianism. Every autocratic action by SANCO or the ANC begat an equal and opposite reaction from her. She inspired her little band of followers, which included Reginah Lengisi, a woman of similar mettle who spent years living in the community hall, with scores of other people, after their shacks burnt down in a fire.

Mambhele and Reginah became magnets for others experiencing intense frustration at the way they were being treated by the local 'chiefs' masquerading as democratically elected councillors and community leaders. Their way of staying in power was to enforce their authority, not by earning respect through responsiveness and service. It was beyond the realm of possibility, back then, that an ANC public representative could be voted out of office in a Xhosa-speaking community. If any form of accountability existed at all, it was to the party bosses, not the people.

As I recruited members to form branches in different wards of the N2 constituency, I kept asking myself the question: Why would people join us? The stakes were so high and the personal danger so real.

The impetus was usually a local issue such as corruption in housing allocation, the authoritarianism of the local ANC councillor, or conflicts in the local ANC branch (typically over competition for positions). When anger over any of these issues welled up sufficiently, I would offer an alternative, and some people were brave enough to take it. Others tried for a while, but retreated when the going got too tough. The strongest remained. It was necessary to separate the men from the boys, although in this instance the proverb is wholly inappropriate.

It was usually a few strong women, like Mambhele, Reginah and Valencia, who formed the core of a sustainable branch. I was always on the lookout for people of similar quality.

Mambhele's story is a good example of what they had to be prepared to endure in order to stay the course. Many tried. Few lasted.

Mambhele and Reginah remain party stalwarts to this day. Valencia, tragically, was murdered in a robbery in her thriving small business. None of them sought public office or positions in the party. They just believe in our cause. Reginah still attends our public events, with her tightly wound doek, slow gait and broad smile.

On 10 September 2001, Mambhele appeared in the Bishop Lavis court again, and a group of her supporters walked the 5.6 kilometres to be there for her. I could not go, as I was attending the Council for Education Ministers meeting in Cape Town in my capacity as the provincial MEC for education. But Kululwa Mpongo, a newly elected DA councillor from Mitchells Plain, with whom I had started working closely, was there to provide support.

After a brief appearance, the case was postponed yet again. I suspected this was part of the harassment pattern. But, in a completely unexpected move, the magistrate issued a court order prohibiting Mambhele from returning to her home, 'for her own safety', following a threat by SANCO to burn her alive if she went back to Langa.

I managed to get a copy of the court order, which was attached to a copy of the charge sheet (which, interestingly, did not specify any charge).

The magistrate noted, in his written order, that SANCO had informed the prosecutor that they would 'burn' Mambhele if she went back to Langa. Instead of ordering the arrest and prosecution of the individual who had made this threat, the magistrate issued an order for Mambhele not to return to Langa until the matter was finalised, despite the fact that she had told the court she had nowhere else to go.

SANCO had achieved its aim of driving her out of Langa. Now, the DA members suspected, SANCO would destroy her home and occupy her site, banishing her from the area permanently.

When I came out of my meeting, I noticed that I had missed many calls. I followed up and found Mambhele and her supporters standing in the rain outside the Mowbray Civic Centre, not knowing what to do next. I took Mambhele to my home, and we agreed that a few DA members would stay in her shack until we could sort out the gross miscarriage of justice. Little did I know that it was just the start...

The DA members in Mambhele's home were immediately targeted, and despite my calls, the police made little effort to protect them.

In one of my many interactions with the Langa police station during the next twenty-four-hour period, a policeman asked me: 'What do you expect if the DA comes to organise in an ANC area?' He accused me of 'asking for trouble' and said I shouldn't be surprised at what was happening. My activities in the area were just creating more work for the police, he said. Especially over weekends, because they did not receive overtime pay.

I began to understand why the police preferred to arrest the ANC's rivals before the start of a weekend – it saved a lot of effort and trouble that would otherwise be required in order to preserve the peace. And in the circumstances, it was easier to arrest the victim than the perpetrators.

The police had little appreciation of their responsibility to defend basic constitutional rights such as freedom of association.

My house in Rosebank was about four kilometres, as the crow flies, from Mambhele's shack. Driving that short distance, I felt as though I was travelling backwards in a time capsule, with our hard-won freedoms growing more distant with every kilometre.

As I turned off the N2, into Langa's Bonga Drive, I left behind the 'world's most progressive constitution' and entered a realm where the local ANC councillor became the substitute for the tribal chief, whose word was law.

I was to experience, over and over again, how easy it is for the vocabulary of democracy to provide a thin veneer for authoritarian tribal practices – which few commentators dared question because of the towering moral authority of the ANC. I was, once again, exposed to the other dimensions of South Africa's 'liberation party'.

As I began my search for a lawyer, SANCO struck again, on 12 September 2001. It was about 9 p.m. when I received the call to say they had returned and tried to break down Mambhele's shack. I tried to resolve the issue telephonically, but soon realised I would have to get there, and fast. The police were refusing to arrest the people attacking the house, saying they couldn't 'arrest a crowd'. They also insisted that the DA members should go to the police station to lay a charge first. But our members refused to leave the shack unguarded, knowing it would be broken down if they did.

I drove to Langa at 10:30 p.m.

When I arrived, I found a group of eight DA supporters protecting Mambhele's shack being taunted by about fifteen SANCO supporters. I asked the police to disperse the crowd and prevent the SANCO supporters from intimidating the DA members, who had a right to protect the property. Some youths in the crowd shouted racial insults at me and made lewd sexual suggestions in Xhosa. One of the policemen said they could not disperse a crowd that was not committing a crime, as 'there is freedom of movement in this country and people can be where they like'.

I noted the irony in the police perception that this freedom applied to SANCO and not equally to the DA. There seemed to be a tacit assumption that we were 'trespassing' on SANCO's territory. I also made the point that freedom did not include the right to destroy property and intimidate people.

Shortly afterwards a policeman, whose name I only recorded as Mashaba, turned to the DA supporters and said, 'Why don't you leave? I am tired. I want to go home.'

I countered that this was not a minor party-political squabble, but a violation of fundamental constitutional rights. Nevertheless, I could understand his frustration. To the police, competitive political activity in a climate of intolerance was an unnecessary additional burden, especially when resources were tight. If the DA just stayed away, the police wouldn't have to face this extra hassle.

I saw it from a different angle, however: establishing competitive politics in ANC strongholds was essential for South Africa's future.

After a stand-off of about an hour, a person identified only as a senior SANCO leader arrived on the scene and asked the SANCO supporters to leave, which they did. The police then insisted that Councillor Mpongo and I ask the DA supporters to leave as well, because their presence was a magnet for SANCO to return. I agreed to the request, on condition that the police took over the role of guarding Mambhele's shack and its contents.

After some negotiation, our members reluctantly concurred. When they had left, I took Kululwa home to Mitchells Plain before returning to my own home, a round trip of about thirty-five kilometres. In the early hours of the following morning, shortly after I had fallen asleep, my cellphone rang. It was Captain Annett from the Langa police station. He informed me that he was sending the police home and removing Mrs Makeleni's possessions from the shack for safekeeping. 'We have to fight crime, not guard property,' explained Captain Annett. 'If people want to have their property protected, they must get private security.'

I reflected on the profound irony of the fact that Mambhele had indeed organised private security – her friends and fellow DA members – but that the police had insisted they leave the area without arresting the SANCO members who were intimidating them. I reflected on the fact that attacking people and property was one of the crimes the police were supposed to prevent.

The cynicism of suggesting that a destitute woman hire private security to protect the home from which she had been unjustly barred (and the extent to which the police casually acknowledged their failure to protect her rights) was extremely disturbing to me, and I found it difficult to sleep for the rest of the night.

The next morning, 13 September, I cancelled most of my appointments so that I could deal with the crisis in Langa. After fetching Masonite boards to repair Mambhele's shack, Kululwa and I returned to the scene. A crowd soon gathered and subjected us to taunting and abusive language. They became increasingly aggressive, so I drove to the police station to inform them that we intended to repair the damaged shack. I asked for their protection while we were doing this. I also enquired what progress had been made in arresting the persons against whom we had laid charges in relation to the previous day's violence.

I spoke to Captain Annett, who was approachable and professional. However, after listening to him for a while, I became concerned at what I was hearing and asked whether I could take notes of our conversation. He said that I could and offered me a clipboard and paper for this purpose. I took down his words verbatim, in shorthand.

The instinct to write things down is a hangover from my years in journalism. I am finding this habit very useful in retrospect, as I wade through piles of notes and reports on almost every important encounter, like the one with Captain Annett.

To cut a long story short, his description confirmed my impressions that:
1) The police accepted the notion of SANCO hegemony and proceeded from the assumption that representatives of other organisations should be considered responsible for any 'trouble' if they tried to organise in the area against SANCO's wishes.
2) The police were actually aiding and abetting the political objectives of SANCO and the ANC by trying to get the DA to leave the area rather than taking prompt action to stop intimidation and destruction of property and protecting the right to freedom of association.
3) Instead of enforcing the law, the police relied on SANCO to give instructions to its followers. If SANCO refused, or failed to persuade the crowd to back off, the police were either unable or unwilling to stop their criminal activity.

During my discussion with Captain Annett, Kululwa interrupted us to say that she had received a call from one of our colleagues stationed at Mambhele's shack, informing her that SANCO was resuming its demolition operation.

After initially claiming there was no police vehicle available, the police eventually agreed to accompany us to the site, but by the time we got there, it was too late. Mambhele's shack was flattened. The handmade DA banner she had sewn for our Langa launch in February 2001 had been strung up on a pole with a sign below saying, 'Magogo, Hamba Kwa Langa' (Granny, get out of Langa).

It was truly devastating to see the remains of Mambhele's meagre possessions trampled and strewn about (including a framed certificate for a course she had completed, smashed to the ground).

I asked the police if they were going to arrest the people responsible for this. The SANCO supporters, numbering around thirty, began to chant that they all wanted to be arrested. Without saying anything further, the police jumped into their vans and left the scene, leaving Kululwa and me at great risk in a very hostile crowd. To taunts and threats, we got into my car and left. To this day I am sorry that I did not take that first DA flag with me, but I knew I had to make a quick getaway.

SANCO and the ANC had succeeded in sending an unambiguous warning to other DA members in Langa.

After staying with me for a while, Mambhele went to live with Lungiswa in Gugulethu. Her trial on the charge of 'stealing R5 under false pretences' was postponed again and again until the magistrate, a Mr Musi, struck the matter from the roll on 12 February 2002 because 'the state neglected to subpoena state witnesses for trial'. The reason for this, I knew, was that there were no credible witnesses in this vexatious case. SANCO had achieved its objective of driving our star organiser out of Langa, so they let the matter lapse.

Thus began Mambhele's nomadic existence. She often lived with Lungiswa, then in a shack in Khayelitsha, until eventually, having made it to the top of the housing waiting list, she was allocated the first formal house she had in her life, in Delft, at the age of sixty. She was ecstatic.

Having succeeded in evicting Mambhele, SANCO turned its sights on Reginah for her leading role in protecting Mambhele's shack. A week later, Reginah was 'summonsed' to appear in a SANCO 'court' on Tuesday 18 September 2001.

I was determined to give Tony Leon some idea of the challenges we were facing trying to build DA branches in ANC areas, so I asked Tony's chief of staff, David Maynier, to accompany Kululwa and me to the 'court', which had been convened in a small business centre in Langa that also housed the ANC offices.

On the way there we passed other DA members walking towards the building. I stopped to speak to them and learnt that they had also been summonsed to appear. I asked why they did not merely ignore the summons. SANCO, I told them, had no powers to establish a court or to summons anyone to appear before them. They shook their heads and said, 'Look what happened to Mambhele. She refused to co-operate with SANCO, and now she can't live in Langa any more. It is better to go.'

The 'sentence', they said, was usually that the person had to renounce their DA membership (which, I gathered, several of our members had already done). Reginah Lengisi, with a backbone of steel, was not one of them.

David, Kululwa and I entered the 'court' just after 6:30 p.m., as the meeting was about to start. Our appearance took the chairperson and about fifty onlookers, all packed into the small venue, by surprise. They instructed us to leave, saying it was a private meeting.

I saw Reginah, the accused, seated on a raised platform, looking more alone than I have ever seen anyone in such a crowded venue. The atmosphere was reminiscent of a medieval lapidation, a witch-stoning ceremony, when people participate enthusiastically in the execution of a miscreant accused of misleading the community. The police station was two blocks away, but the rule of law was a foreign concept.

I answered in (my very broken) Xhosa that I had heard DA members were being put on trial and that this was a violation of their rights. I said SANCO was breaking the law and violating the constitution.

At that, mayhem broke loose. The SANCO group began singing, shouting and toyi-toying. They demanded that we leave immediately.

We refused to go. I continued trying to state our position, but could not make myself heard above the noise. The crowd stopped taunting Reginah and began accusing Kululwa of being a traitor by working with whites.

Then the lights went off, and in a room without external windows, it was dark, with only a dim light visible through the open door. I learnt afterwards that switching off the lights is a strategy to ensure that the perpetrators of violence cannot later be identified – just like an execution by stoning, where it is impossible to identify exactly who inflicted the fatal blow.

When the lights go off in a situation like this, there is no time to lose. You go, and fast. Fortunately, we were close to the door. Recognising the signal, Kululwa pushed us backwards, out into the corridor, and we left the building in a hurry, to racial taunts.

Driving down the street, I noticed an ANC councillor, Danile Landingwe, rushing to the venue. He was a tall, imposing, educated man with whom I had a good rapport. I had worked with him on some housing-development projects. I knew he would be as appalled by a kangaroo court as I was. I stopped the car to tell him what was happening. He said he already knew. He was on his way to the 'court' because he had been phoned by someone present telling him to get there quickly, as lives were in danger. I suggested that he *should* get there quickly, as Reginah Lengisi was still there, without any support. I asked him to explain to SANCO that they were acting illegally. He replied that this 'logic' would not carry any weight with them, but he undertook to use his authority to prevent physical violence.

The 'court' proceeded, and Reginah was sentenced to renounce her DA membership; alternatively, to leave Langa and go and live 'in Rondebosch with the whites'. She emerged physically unscathed and more determined to press on building the DA than ever.

I phoned Frank Raymond, a DA member who ran a legal practice in Somerset West. It was the first of many occasions that I called on his commitment to defending constitutional rights. He never once turned me away, and never once submitted an account for his services.

When the history of South Africa's democracy is written one day, a generous chapter must be devoted to the unsung heroes, principal among whom are the lawyers, like Frank Raymond, Elmarie Neilson and Stuart Pringle, who did this kind of *pro bono* work in the most difficult circumstances. They were responsible for making the constitution meaningful to many people whose rights would otherwise have been trampled underfoot.

Frank told me that we needed to get a court interdict to stop this harassment, but that we would have to name specific respondents who posed a direct threat to DA members in Langa. Simply citing SANCO and the ANC would not be enough.

Getting the names proved a challenge but, in the end, with a lot of groundwork done by Lungiswa, Valencia and Reginah herself, we got together twenty confirmed names.

But before we even made it to court, SANCO had their sights trained on Timothy Maduna.

Apart from being charged with 'joining the DA', Timothy was accused of witchcraft because an ANC councillor, Xolile Gophe, had had a car accident in strange circumstances, and because a female SANCO member had accused Timothy of bewitching her so that she 'went mad'. When Mr Maduna asked the 'court' who was making these allegations, the 'presiding officer', a Mr Gugushe, said that the 'court' could not reveal the name of the complainants, but took up cases anonymously on their behalf!

He then ruled that not only Timothy, but ALL DA members had to leave Langa by the following Thursday. SANCO had a full list of their names because they had managed to take the DA membership book from Mambhele's shack. They announced publicly that every single DA member was banished from the area.

Many of our activists understandably renounced their membership at this point. The alternative, of continued harassment until they were driven out of the only homes they had ever known, was an unbearable price to pay.

I began to despair that it would be possible to build a democracy in South Africa. Constitutional rights were meaningless in Langa and, I assumed, in many other ANC strongholds. The police, who were supposed to be the arm of the capable state protecting the rule of law, were clearly complicit in its violation.

Just four kilometres away, my experience of the Rondebosch police was entirely different. They were prompt, professional, committed and impartial. What accounted for the difference? It was difficult to say. Certainly not race, as there were police officers of both races at both stations. The only answer I could come up with was ANC hegemony. This, I knew, was the greatest threat to South Africa's future.

At about this time, I learnt about the concept of an enclave state – a state that is entirely surrounded by the territory of another state. I concluded that South Africa's formerly white suburbs were enclave states, enjoying the protection of the constitution and the rule of law, while people living just a few kilometres away did not. Yet they continued to vote for an ANC government who were capturing and abusing the institutions that should have been protecting citizens' rights. Instead, under the ANC, they were protecting rights violators.

I grappled with a big question: Would the institutions of a constitutional state be able to extend their reach beyond the enclave to reach *all* South Africans? Or would the authoritarian grip of tribal feudalism engineer a 'reverse takeover' and capture the institutions of democracy throughout the country? The race was on. And the DA started with a serious handicap.

The ANC had found a foolproof way to counter our growth. Their circular argument followed four basic steps (and still does to this day). Their tactic is:
1) Brand the DA a 'racist, white party'.
2) Isolate and intimidate any black person who is brave enough to identify with the DA.
3) Then (to 'prove' that the DA is racist) cite the fact that it battles to attract the support of prominent black leaders.
4) Go back to (1) above.

The more successful we become in attracting significant support from black people, the more hysterical these claims become. The truth, of course, is the exact opposite. The ANC's claim of 'ownership' of black people's political allegiance, and its determination to prevent them from exercising free political choice, is patronising and racist in the extreme. It is the perfect smokescreen behind which to legitimise the ANC's capture and manipulation of state institutions to entrench an increasingly autocratic form of single-party dominance.

Under Frank's guidance, we soldiered on, along the legal route, and on 9 October 2001, Mr Justice Nathan Erasmus granted an interdict in the Cape High Court prohibiting nineteen prominent members of SANCO in Langa from harassing and attacking members of the Democratic Alliance in the area. The order was made final by Mr Justice Essa Moosa on 13 October 2001.

Throughout the crisis in Langa, I was facing a similar pattern of problems in my efforts to establish the DA in Crossroads, about ten kilometres down the N2 highway from Langa.

Among my first recruits in this area was Mzuvukile Mfengwana, a strongly independent-minded young musician, thin as a whippet, with no front teeth and a huge head of dreadlocks (which earned him the nickname Rasta). He was soon joined by Ms Agrenett Kwana, a portly, outspoken young woman who was angered by the alleged corruption in housing allocations in the area.

It wasn't long before they also became the target of harassment. The local ANC councillor, Depoutch Elese, confronted them both about their DA membership, on different occasions early in 2001, pointing his firearm at them.

They laid a complaint at the Nyanga police station, but nothing came of it. Follow-up inquiries by me yielded no results. Eventually, I suggested we revert to the 'enclave state', and I took them to Caledon Square police station in central Cape Town (where the rule of law still generally worked) to lay a charge. We also submitted a complaint to the speaker of the City of Cape Town. The culmination of our efforts was the suspension of Councillor Elese from the council for a period of three months, without pay.

It was a minor victory in our attempt to extend principles such as the rule of law and public accountability to Crossroads.

But it was only the start.

Despite the ANC councillor's tactics, there was a groundswell of support for the DA in Crossroads because of widespread perceptions of corruption in housing allocations in the area, which were being manipulated by the ANC councillors. I undertook a research project to establish details of the allegations and submitted a ten-page report, with full details of the names of people who had allegedly illegally benefited through the allocation process, as well as the site numbers of the plots involved. Many of the unlawful beneficiaries were family or friends of Councillor Elese and the previous ANC councillor, Melford Gwayi.

It was essential to stop this patronage system at source, because this is the root cause of the failed state. If state benefits are provided on the basis of people's personal connections and political allegiance, rather than objective criteria, it is impossible to build a capable state that applies the rule of law.

I called for the community-based project-management committee (which had been hijacked by the ANC councillor) to be disbanded and for the establishment of a formal commission of inquiry (with powers to subpoena witnesses) to investigate the allegations of corruption, and propose remedies in order to institute a fair and objective system.

Inevitably, I became the target of a smear campaign, not only by the ANC locally, but of their institutions nationally. At the forefront of this campaign was the National Intelligence Agency (NIA). Hennie Bester, our DA leader in the provincial parliament and the provincial minister of community safety, was entitled to see their security briefings, and he alerted me to the fact that I was under investigation. I saw a report that fingered me as the source of the problems in Crossroads.

The report noted: 'It is common knowledge that the Provincial Minister, Ms Helen Zille, has been meeting with a group of Boystown residents she believes have by dint of their political allegiance been denied audience by the local ANC Councillor Depoutch Elese.'

The report went on to give a totally distorted analysis of the situation, blaming those exposing corruption for delaying the development. It concluded: 'By meeting with this group and compiling a list of "grievances" and cases of corruption, Minister Zille has not only elevated its status but also created the impression that anyone can stop development in order to attract attention to their cause no matter how petty. The result is that the people of Boystown are confused and a potent climate for violent conflict has been created.'

It took me straight back to the apartheid era, when security police informers submitted deliberately distorted reports that provided the rationale for state action against anti-apartheid activists.

There was nothing 'petty' about the levels of corruption that characterised housing allocation under the ANC that I was trying to expose in Crossroads. It was essential to root it out, even if the project was delayed.

As the economy – and optimism about the future – started to soar in South Africa, I (in my counter-cyclical way) began increasingly to despair about the possibilities of making a successful transition to democracy. But in between all the bad times, there were moments of real hope.

One occurred on 25 March, when I convened my first DA rally in an ANC ward at the Mfesane Hall in Crossroads. We invited Tony to address us, and the hall was packed. I was amazed that so many people came, despite the climate of fear and intimidation in the area. It made me realise that, from the ground up, we would defeat single-party authoritarianism. Many of the people who came were not DA members, but they wanted to hear what the DA could do to assist in ensuring a corruption-free housing-delivery process. That was the key issue that drove up our membership in Crossroads.

Soon after that, we converted a broken-down structure in Boys Town into the first permanent DA office in a shack settlement. The building project was led by Eric 'Kabila' Njonga, who was a stalwart from the start.

The office soon became a magnet for people wanting to report their problems. One was Mrs Nomahobe Tom. Of the many cases that came to me in the course of my work in the constituency, few indicated the extent of the police's failure to serve the people as clearly as hers. Her case stretched back to 1998, when, on 29 June, she had seen her husband shot at point-blank range by the ANC councillor Melford Gwayi in a dispute over alleged housing corruption. There were several other witnesses to the shooting, including a Mr Hitler Ngxekana and Mr Themba Marhwanqana.

Mrs Tom opened a case at the Nyanga police station. When it went to court, it was Mrs Tom's word against Councillor Gwayi's. The investigating officer had failed to get statements from the other witnesses (who were available and willing to give evidence, but had never been approached). Mrs Tom was convinced that this was a deliberate tactic to ensure the ANC councillor's acquittal, which duly transpired. Mrs Tom was enraged, as were others in the community.

Years later, when I started organising in the area, she came to me for assistance. I approached the Independent Complaints Directorate (ICD), which had been established to investigate public complaints regarding police misconduct. The ICD promptly sent the complaint back to the police to investigate themselves! Predictably, the investigation ran into a dead end.

In April 2001, I approached the Legal Resources Centre for help in getting the trial reopened. A Mrs Fortuin told me that they could not accept the case, as it was an individual matter (not a class-action suit) and did not fall within one of their focus areas (which included 'land, housing and development'). I then wrote a motivation to explain why Mrs Tom's case was indeed a class-action suit, on the basis of the pervasive corruption in housing allocation, as well as ineffectual, partisan policing. The former, at least, fell right into the LRC's priority area.

However, they turned me down. From my interactions with the LRC through Mrs Fortuin, I just got the impression that they were uncomfortable to be seen to be taking on the ANC (especially on behalf of a 'white' opposition party). Such was the Zeitgeist.

I then took my case to the senior public prosecutor at the Wynberg court, where the matter had been heard. This was the only office that took the matter seriously, and they sent me the first decent reply to my queries – sixteen months after I had first taken up the case on behalf of Mrs Tom.

An S.J. Wilson had clearly been through the file carefully. That level of effort was a rare phenomenon indeed. Wilson wrote:

> The accused, Melford Gwayi, SHC 152/99 was acquitted in Wynberg Regional Court B on 9/12/99.
>
> Magistrate Kotze concluded his judgement by saying 'the court is faced with good evidence on the side of Mrs Tom and evidence from the defence side which reasonably might possibly be true, a situation which causes reasonable doubt. The court is obliged to give the accused the benefit of the doubt, for this reason the accused is acquitted on all charges.'
>
> In terms of section 106(1)(d) of the Criminal Procedure Act an accused can argue he has been acquitted, if the State were to charge him again. The question is whether the acquittal is 'on the merits' or on a technicality. It is clear from the judgment the accused was acquitted on the merits of the case and therefore cannot be charged again. It is indeed a great pity that the two witnesses, Anthony Marwanqana and Hitler Gxekana [sic] were not available at the time of the trial.

This letter should have been all that the ICD required for investigating and taking action against the police officers who investigated the case. But I had learnt that submitting complaints to the ICD was like sending them into outer space. They went into orbit beyond the reach of gravity and never returned to earth.

A more urgently needed but more useless state institution would be hard to imagine. Every time a complaint was submitted about the incidents I encountered, they were dismissed on the grounds that I had a 'political agenda' and was therefore creating problems for the police. Of course, I was politically engaged in trying to establish DA branches in the township, but this was a constitutional right – and indeed a necessity – for the future of South Africa's democracy. Neither the police nor the ICD seemed able to accept that point of departure. They regarded me as a troublemaker.

I should have brought a civil case against the police in relation to the appalling detective work in Mrs Tom's case, but with the number of cases I was dealing with, and the refusal of the Legal Resources Centre to take up the issue, I felt stymied.

Not long afterwards, a DA member, Mr Ndayi, was shot dead at a housing protest, allegedly by the new ANC councillor in Ward 36, Depoutch Elese. I was not going to allow the police to use the same trick twice, so I made sure the witness statements were properly gathered.

Then, out of the blue, Elese's bodyguard made a 'confession', claiming it was he who had fired the fatal shot. The bodyguard was duly charged, pleaded guilty and sentenced to a prison term. All the eyewitnesses to the scene were convinced that the bodyguard had agreed to take the fall (in return for some reward when he left prison), given the fact that they said they had seen Councillor Elese pull the trigger.

By this time, I had set up another branch, in Philippi, and the normal pattern of harassment began. This time it was spearheaded by the ANC councillor Mzwandile Matiwane, who was probably the nastiest of the lot.

Going through my files, it is difficult to decide which examples I should choose to demonstrate how dire the situation really was.

There are the cases of Koliswa Sigonya, Nontombana Sicetsha, Makazi Topo, Nongejile Mapunguza, and that of a Mr Tiyesi. I took notes of their accounts of their clashes with the councillor or his henchmen, who allegedly assaulted his opponents, some extremely seriously. One person lost much of her hearing as a result of an assault; another was so badly injured that he stayed in hospital for a month; a third was brain-damaged. The cases arising out of these assaults included CR 711/11 2001, CR 714/11/2001 and CR 518/11/2001. And in every case, Councillor Matiwane was allegedly protected from prosecution by the local police at the Philippi East police station.

Once, when I went to investigate the progress of a case (CR 359/1/2001) against Matiwane, I was shown on a computer screen in the charge office that the 'accused' was 'undetected'. I asked what this meant. They said they were unable to locate the accused. I asked how this was possible, given the fact that Councillor Matiwane was a well-known figure and his whereabouts and place of work were a matter of public record. I received no reply. When I left the station, a policeman followed me and told me under his breath as I got into the car that whenever an ANC councillor was charged, the police would simply enter 'undetected' onto the computer. That was the only credible explanation I ever received.

I raised the issue in the provincial parliament, on 24 June 2002, and the provincial minister of community safety dismissed my complaint, demanding to know who had told me this. Needless to say, I did not pass on the information or a policeman would have lost his job.

But the story that most clearly illustrates the manipulation of the criminal justice system is the one involving five new DA members in Philippi: Sakhele Kula, Andile Burwana, Shaun Kalako, Phakamthe Mpi and Victor Malangabi.

It started when Mr Shaun Kalako, a disabled man who was the community liaison officer for a development project in the area, was instructed by the councillor to ensure that certain of his pals got jobs on the project. Shaun refused. On 28 September 2001, Shaun was assaulted with a sjambok, allegedly by the councillor. Shaun then laid a complaint against the councillor at the Philippi East police station. After lengthy delays, during which he was told that the docket was lost, the matter was placed on the roll for trial on 23 April 2002, at the Philippi court.

On Monday 25 March 2002, Shaun and four friends joined the Democratic Alliance. Two days later, on Wednesday 27 March, all five of them were arrested by the police on a charge of 'pointing of a firearm' (despite the fact that only one was alleged to have actually pointed the firearm). The complainant, a Ms Sipayile, described herself as Councillor Matiwane's secretary.

By now I knew the pattern. I called on Elmarie Neilson for assistance, which she gave, *pro bono*, with great commitment. She came out to Philippi the next morning to arrange a bail hearing. In such cases, she said, the police have the discretion to grant bail, and there was no need for a court hearing.

The investigating officer, Inspector Cornelissen, said it was impossible, however. He gave every possible excuse, including that there was no police van available to transport the accused. As we found a way around each obstacle, Inspector Cornelissen finally informed us that it was impossible to arrange bail, as the matter had been referred to the Serious and Violent Crimes Unit because a 'crime against the state' had been committed.

Later on that day, Inspector Cornelissen heard he had been promoted to the rank of captain, and I could not suppress a nasty suspicion that his tendency to equate the ANC with the state had something to do with it.

Even if Councillor Matiwane had been the complainant (which he was not), the alleged crime of pointing a firearm would not have constituted a crime against the state. The concept of the separation of party and state, so fundamental to any democracy, was entirely absent.

Captain Cornelissen's intention was clearly to keep the men in jail over the Easter weekend. Elmarie was having none of it. Working directly with the court, she arranged a special bail hearing on Good Friday, despite the protestations of the prosecutor that he would be in church. Elmarie compromised and agreed that the bail hearing would be held in the afternoon, after church.

On Good Friday morning, I received an SMS from Elmarie to tell me the bail application would be heard at the Wynberg court at 2:30 p.m. I went to Philippi to collect the men's wives. We arrived in Wynberg, and at around three o'clock the hearing began. We were amazed to find that the police had changed their tune entirely. It would not be necessary to get a magistrate, they said, as they had decided to grant bail. I concluded that they obviously did not want the magistrate to hear about their manipulated attempts to keep the men in jail over the Easter weekend. Bail was set at the ridiculously high amount of R800 each, which Elmarie and I shared between us, with a contribution from the wives.

Then we were told that bail had to be processed at the Philippi East police station, which was about twenty-five kilometres away, so we would have to return there. And, insisted Captain Cornelissen, the men could only be transported by police van.

We waited two hours, phoning the police station repeatedly, each time being told the van was 'five minutes away'. I was about to called the provincial minister of community safety, Leonard Ramatlakane, to complain when Captain Cornelissen said that although he was not technically allowed to do so, he would take the men back in his car. I followed in my own car. When I got to the police station, I established that no van had been dispatched to fetch the men at all. Every time I had been told the van was 'five minutes away', it had been a lie.

Then we had to wait in a queue for the bail to be processed. The waiting room at the station was like a scene from a horror movie. A woman hobbled about in a torn shirt, saying she had been raped and complaining that the police had refused to take her statement. When I enquired why not, I was told that she was 'under the influence'. Eventually, she was attended to, in a room full of men.

At last we reached the front of the queue, only to learn that the Philippi East police station did not have a bail book and could not process the bail. Someone who gave their name as 'Kakudi' told us to go to Nyanga police station, where the bail could be processed. We arrived at Nyanga police station at 6:45 p.m., where an Inspector Davids told us they also did not have a bail book. They, in turn, referred us to the police station at Gugulethu, but by this time the police van in which the men were being transported had left and there was no official vehicle available. The vans, I was told, were taking policemen home at the end of their shift. I asked them to radio a van. They said the radio was broken.

I was tempted to take the men in my own vehicle, but having been warned that I could be charged with an offence if I did, I decided not to. Being the leader of the opposition in the provincial legislature, I did not want to offer the police the excuse of laying a criminal charge against me, which would have provided the perfect red herring to divert attention from the travesty of justice that I was trying to expose. So we had to wait until one of the vans returned after providing a free taxi service to policemen. We arrived at Gugulethu at 7:30 p.m.

Again, the charge office was a scene from a horror movie. Another badly beaten woman was staggering around in tears, covered in blood. I tried to speak to her, but she was in no state to respond. The police said they were going to attend to her when they had completed the change of shift – something that should have been finalised at least an hour previously.

Eventually, at 8:15 on that Good Friday night, the Gugulethu police turned their attention to us … only to inform us that they, too, had no bail book.

At this point, I exploded. The target of my pent-up fury was an Inspector Dosi. He replied, in great indignation, that it was not Gugulethu police station's problem to be trying to find a bail book for Philippi East. I said it was a scandal that none of the three police stations had a crucial, basic necessity such as a bail book. He shrugged. I was told the problem could not be solved until Tuesday morning, because 'there are no logistics' over the weekend.

At that point the door from a back office opened and a Captain Ntandane walked in. He saw me and instantly turned a few shades paler. He recognised me from a previous episode in the Gugulethu police station, one that had become national front-page news.

Almost two years earlier, when I was provincial minister of education, I had called the Gugulethu police from a nearby school to ask them to dispatch a van urgently to deal with a break-in. The station's phone just rang and rang. After several futile attempts to call them, I drove to the police station. There I found the police officers in various states of repose, watching an episode of the TV soapie *The Bold and the Beautiful* in the charge office. I interrupted and asked why no one was answering the phone. The phone was out of order, they said. So I stood there, in the charge office, and pressed redial. The phone on the counter sprang to life, ringing loudly, much to the officers' chagrin. It turned out that they simply ignored the phone during screenings of *Bold*, as the popular soapie was widely known.

I reported the matter and it became a big news story, followed by disciplinary action.

I suppose Captain Ntandane did not want to risk a repetition, so he sprang into action and eventually produced an ancient bail book from the previous century (literally). We were finally able to bail the men out.

After taking them home, I drove home myself.

'You're in late,' said Johann.

'Another day at the office,' I replied.

The date that Councillor Matiwane was due to stand trial for assaulting Shaun Kalako, 23 April 2002, was approaching. There was a great deal of interest in the case, given the widespread experience in the community of the councillor's abusive and violent behaviour towards his opponents.

Suddenly, out of the blue, on Friday 19 April, Captain Cornelissen went back to court, claiming that Shaun and Victor had broken their bail conditions; he asked the court to issue warrants for their rearrest. Although Elmarie's name and contact details were noted as the 'attorney of record' and although the case was brought before a magistrate, no one informed Elmarie that her clients' bail was being revoked. None of the accused had been informed of the hearing to revoke bail either, so they had no chance to respond.

On Sunday 21 April 2002, at 5:50 in the morning, Shaun and Victor, who were due to give evidence against the councillor two days later, were rearrested. I had no doubt at all that their arrest had been engineered to make sure they could not appear in the witness box to give testimony against Councillor Matiwane.

I immediately contacted Elmarie for assistance. She was as shocked as I was. Her files record that she had tried to call Captain Cornelissen, but that 'the investigating officer then switched off his cellphone, so that it was impossible to arrange a bail hearing. The men asked for permission to call me but this was refused.' On Monday 22 April, Elmarie dropped her other commitments so that she could be in court, but Captain Cornelissen refused to bring the complainants to have the matter heard, and so the men had to spend two more nights in prison.

Mission accomplished. They would not be available to testify against Councillor Matiwane.

On Tuesday 23 April, Elmarie went to observe the case against Matiwane – where she intended to make a statement to the court to explain the circumstances of the witnesses' absence – only to find that the case would not go ahead ... because the police had not brought the docket to court!

While the police continued to protect Councillor Matiwane, the case against Shaun and Victor and the other DA members for allegedly 'pointing a firearm' proceeded to a hearing. Through masterly cross-examination, Elmarie exposed the complainant as being in collusion with Councillor Matiwane and that the two were acting with a political agenda. The accused DA members could provide watertight alibis, which included an employer's testimony that they were at work at the time of the alleged offence. The magistrate correctly noted that there was 'much more to this than meets the eye', especially given that the accused were witnesses in the case against Councillor Matiwane.

This was clearly another abuse of legal procedure to defeat the ends of justice. It was routine in ANC-dominated constituencies. The rule of law was honoured in the breach, just as it had been under apartheid.

There is just one more example I should extract from my files. It is the occasion when, on 29 October 2002, Mr Fihla, a stalwart in our Crossroads branch, called me at around 9 p.m. to warn me that the ANC was stockpiling weapons in a pink shack in a settlement called New Rest. The DA branch was expecting an attack against them the next morning. I asked Mr Fihla if he had been to the police. He said he could not go to the Nyanga police station (dubbed locally as the ANC headquarters) and that the Philippi East police station was too far to walk.

I called Philippi East and spoke to an Officer Januarie, who said he would call his station commander, Senior Superintendent Jonas, who would contact me. Senior Superintendent Jonas did so, and referred me to a Senior Superintendent Manci to deal with the situation. I had butted heads with Senior Superintendent Manci on a previous occasion, but because Jonas had pronounced his name incorrectly, I did not recognise him as the same person.

I spoke to Senior Superintendent Manci, who said that if they were to search the shack, they would have to have a sworn affidavit that would justify issuing a search warrant. I asked whether they would be prepared to fetch Mr Fihla from his home, as he was not well and could not walk that distance. Senior Superintendent Manci replied that Philippi East, as a satellite station, had no vans.

There was no alternative but to go out myself and fetch Mr Fihla so that he could make a statement. I was gratified that Senior Superintendent Manci said he would also return to work to deal with the matter.

When we arrived at Philippi East, I was told that Senior Superintendent Manci was based at Nyanga. Mr Fihla simply refused to give a statement at Nyanga, so Mr Manci obligingly agreed to come to us at Philippi East. Mr Fihla gave the sworn statement necessary for the issuing of a search warrant. We waited for all the documents to be completed, but were told (once again) that the Philippi East police station did not have the necessary documentation to issue a search warrant. However, Senior Superintendent Manci assured me that they could easily get it from another station and would do so to complete the process once we had pointed out the pink shack to them. Because he had been so helpful up till that point, I accepted his word.

We drove in front of Manci, into New Rest, where Fihla pointed towards the pink shack. We then left the police to complete the operation while I turned back to drop Mr Fihla at his home in Crossroads. On the way, I managed to drive straight into a ditch that I had not seen in the dark. The elderly Mr Fihla and I battled in vain to free the wheel, but fortunately some locals came to help us, and eventually, my heart pounding, I could drive on, drop him and go home.

Next morning I called the police station to ask what they had found in the raid. I was told they had not conducted the raid because they arrived at the shack and found it locked.

'Well, why didn't you open it?' I asked. 'You had a sworn affidavit from an eyewitness that it is being used to store weapons in preparation for an attack. That enabled you to get a search warrant.'

I was furious that I had put both Mr Fihla's life and my own at risk by doing what we had done so late at night and in dangerous circumstances – and then finding the next day that it had all been in vain. I wrote another complaint to the ICD, with the same non-result.

Reading through these files again, in the context of contemporary news reports, I reflected on the extent to which the current debate on 'whiteness' and race trivialises the real 'black pain' that so many people experience in our country. The middle-class commentators, who obsess about issues such as whether they are seated behind a pillar blocking the view at an upmarket restaurant, or whether they have to make an effort to attract the waiter's attention, reflect the narcissism of our times.

The people I was working with had real problems. One of them was Eliot Maki, who had recently come from the Eastern Cape to join the DA, having experienced similar brutality for opposing the ANC councillor in his home town. One day, buying furniture at Russells, Eliot recruited the salesman, Mzuvukile 'Archie' Figlan, who later introduced me to an energetic youngster named Masizole Mnqasela. I asked them to help me launch the first DA branch in Khayelitsha, where they lived.

Masizole, like others before him, had joined the DA in protest against corruption in a housing-allocation process in Makhaza Khayelitsha, where lists were (once again) being manipulated by the councillor, Thobile Ludidi. Ludidi's ANC rivals in his ward started using this against him, and knowing his time as ANC councillor was up, he tried to join the DA to become our candidate in the 2011 local government election. Masizole and I discussed his approach and decided it would be too great a liability. (Eventually, in mid-2012, Ludidi was convicted of fraud for illegally selling plots belonging to the city.)

Masizole had been the first to expose this, many years earlier. He also took on Ludidi for controlling access to jobs at the newly opened Score supermarket in Makhaza. At first, Masizole told me, Score objected to Councillor Ludidi's interference, but later on they just had to accept that 'this is the way things work if you want to operate in Khayelitsha'. Masizole said he was not prepared to simply accept the system of political patronage extending its tentacles into private businesses.

In 2002, Masizole concluded that it was too difficult to wage this fight on his own. He needed some organisational muscle to help him expose the ANC's corruption, and decided the DA was the right place to be. He was twenty-one years old.

He went to the DA's office in town, where he was referred to Archie Figlan, who brought him to my house in Rosebank. A compact, good-looking young man, he had all the confidence and conviction of youth, backed by a determination to change the world. I knew that, if he also had staying power, he could make a big impact in Khayelitsha.

Our biggest obstacle to progress in this huge new residential area was the Khayelitsha Development Forum (KDF), which had declared the DA a 'white party' and unwelcome in Khayelitsha. But according to the KDF constitution, any political party that was legitimately constituted, with branches in Khayelitsha, could be represented on the KDF, which provided a forum for discussing development in the area. It was essential to be represented on the KDF if the DA were to have a legitimate voice in Khayelitsha and a platform to expose corruption.

Our next step was to start DA branches. We launched our first Khayelitsha branch in Masizole's mother's house together with Mzuvukile, Xolile Gwangxu and twenty-three others who were angry enough about the housing corruption to agree to join the DA. I formed a close bond with Masizole's mother, a warm, homely woman who always seemed genuinely pleased to see me. She idolised her son, and whenever I came around, she was feeding someone. She was the closest approximation to a Xhosa-Jewish mother I have ever met. Masizole got his spunk and forthrightness from her.

Masizole and I then attended the KDF's next meeting and argued that as the DA was now properly constituted in Khayelitsha, we should be admitted into the KDF. There was vehement opposition – but support came from an unexpected and influential quarter, the respected KDF chairman, Mr Zamayedwa B. Sogayise. He had enough inherent strength, and respect in the community, to go against the run of play.

He told the meeting that he had been principal of Uxolo High School in Khayelitsha while I was still the provincial minister of education. He explained how one of his young educators had been shot and paralysed and how I had visited him in hospital and supported the school. He managed to persuade the delegates that some people in the DA cared about Khayelitsha and that the party should therefore be allowed a seat on the KDF. He turned the tide, and it took great courage in the context to do so. Masizole became our delegate on the KDF.

He and Archie then set about extending the DA's network of branches in

Khayelitsha. One of their first recruits was a 'big catch', a prominent ANC activist named Nomboniso Thiyiwe. She lived in a shack with her elderly mother Nomsa and five children in the nearby Ward 99. Within a few weeks of joining the DA, she had recruited the twenty-five members necessary to form a branch. Her shack became an effective DA office, and our numbers grew. Nomboniso was very popular.

Then, on the night of 28 August 2003, tragedy struck. Shortly before an official branch launch, in the dead of night, her shack burnt down in a ferocious fire that engulfed the structure in minutes. She managed to save her elderly mother and two of her children. The other three – Siphesihle, Zizipho and the toddler, Asemahle – were burnt to death.

I was in Johannesburg when I heard the news the next day. I had come to know the family well and was devastated. I went straight to the airport and caught a flight back home. It was early evening when we touched down and I rushed to Nomboniso's address, overcome by a combination of grief and guilt, feeling partly to blame for the tragedy.

I found Nomboniso, her mother and the two surviving children in a neighbour's shack. We were both too shocked to discuss much. She wanted to stay where she was. She told me that the police who had come after the fire on the night of 28 August had promised to return the following day to take a statement, but had not done so. Instead, a bulldozer had arrived and flattened the site, removing all the debris, including a layer of topsoil. She was convinced that the purpose of this was to remove any evidence of the incendiary liquid on the ground that she believed had been poured over the shack before it was set alight. There was no other explanation, she told me. There were no open flames in her shack, no paraffin and no candles, because she had electricity. The fire must have been deliberately started.

I could not believe that the police had allowed a potential crime scene to be so severely disturbed.

Nomboniso did not want to go to the police immediately, as it was already dark, but she asked me to come back the next day, which I did. We then went to the Site B police station, where we found Inspector Ntsinde.

Nomboniso, with extraordinary composure and control under the circumstances, explained why we were there. She wished to ensure that there would be a full police investigation, as she was convinced the fire had been started by an arsonist. She even suspected a particular individual. Inspector Ntsinde replied that a docket had been opened. A case was being investigated.

I had my shorthand notebook and pen with me and I started taking verbatim notes. The conversation that followed was surreal.

Ntsinde: 'They opened a case. It was registered on the computer. Then the CID and the detectives have to follow it up. If they do not come on Monday, you must contact us again. What is the address?'

Nomboniso: '37402 Ntonga Street.'

Ntsinde: 'But it is not our job to come to you. It is your job to come to us.'

Helen: 'What is the case number?'

Ntsinde: 'It is 1664/08/03.'

Helen: 'What is the charge?'

Ntsinde: 'The charge is Inquest.'

I was puzzled. Then I said, 'Yes, we would like there to be an inquest, but in this case we would also like to lay a charge of arson. We suspect arson.'

'You cannot have a charge of arson when people died,' said Ntsinde. 'Arson is when clothes and furniture are burnt. When people died, you have an inquest.'

I then explained that by the time the inquest had taken place there would be no evidence left. Most of it, I pointed out, had already been removed. I said it was important to have an urgent forensic investigation into what we believed was the likelihood of arson.

Eventually, after making no progress, Ntsinde took us to see Inspector Johnson in a back room. We told him we wanted a case of arson to be investigated. Johnson said he could do nothing without the docket. A detective called Du Toit had the docket and he was not on duty. I asked for Du Toit's number, but Johnson said he didn't have it.

'Over the weekends, if the shifts are off, we don't work because we don't get paid overtime. It is inappropriate to come over a weekend to inquire about a case. If you open a case on Thursday, why do you come and moan about it on Saturday if it is so important?'

I asked what I could do to take the matter forward and was told to see Senior Superintendent Beneke at Harare police station.

Then Nomboniso asked a question. 'I was told on Thursday night,' she said, 'that Inspector Taylor would be investigating the case. Why is it now Inspector du Toit?'

Johnson replied, 'Don't be difficult. I know you are in an emotional state, but don't be difficult with me.'

I protested, saying she had merely asked a question and was entitled to a decent answer.

'She has an attitude,' he said. 'You did not see her face when she spoke to me. She has an attitude.'

I told him I had never heard a police officer speaking to a bereaved person in this brutal way, without doing anything to assist in the circumstances.

As Nomboniso and I were leaving to go to Harare to try to locate Senior Superintendent Beneke, we distinctly heard Johnson say, loudly and unmistakably, 'Fok hulle!' (Fuck them). I turned back and informed Inspector Johnson that I was going to lay an official complaint against him. Then we left.

We were just getting into my car when I was approached by a policeman who introduced himself as Inspector Burger. He asked if he could help us. For the third time that day we explained the situation. He apologised for the inconvenience we had experienced and asked if he could accompany us to the Harare police station. I welcomed this.

At Harare police station, Senior Superintendent Beneke was extremely helpful and respectful towards Nomboniso. When she had finished recounting her story, he said he would find out from Inspector du Toit why he had failed to dispatch an investigating team. He left the room to try to track him down. He returned to say that Du Toit was out of town.

On the face of it, Beneke said, it sounded like arson, and if this was in any way substantiated, the police would open a case of murder. He asked Nomboniso if she knew anyone who had a grudge against her. She said it could either be the result of her political affiliation or professional jealousy because I had put her in contact with funders for the crèche she ran alongside her shack.

Beneke and Burger were the only two policemen who showed real concern. As we left, Beneke said, 'My concern remains. We review crimes every day. Yesterday morning Inspector du Toit was supposed to visit the scene and get the statement, then open a docket. I am very disappointed that Du Toit did not go to the scene yesterday morning.'

Later that afternoon, when I returned to Ntonga Street to bring some provisions, I found a Captain Williams there. He had a forensics expert, a Mr Nimbe, with him, who had a sniffer dog. The dog had identified a patch of soil that smelt of paraffin, which was located near to where the shack's kitchen had been and where the blaze had started. Although at least six inches of topsoil had been removed, the traces of the flammable liquid were still there. Soil samples were taken, and we were very grateful that Senior Superintendent Beneke had arranged assistance for us on a Saturday afternoon.

I was asked to speak at the funeral service on the afternoon of Saturday 6 September 2003. The DA branch helped me prepare the speech in Xhosa, to ensure that I expressed their pain and conveyed their condolences idiomatically and appropriately. But one serious area of disagreement arose. The community wanted me to say that even though everyone was grief-stricken, the children's death had been God's will. I said I could not say this, although I understood that this would probably be a source of great comfort to them. They were shocked that I did not think that the fire had been God's will. I considered compromising, because this event was about them, not me, but eventually I concluded I just could not say it, because it clashed too vehemently with my concept of God, and raised more questions for the bereaved than answers. It was one of the most difficult speeches I have ever made.

I often try to think back on the funeral scene, but my mind draws a blank. I know we pitched a marquee on the flattened plot where the tragedy had occurred and that a large choir sang soaring hymns in magnificent harmonies. I can't even recall the children's coffins, perhaps because the sight of a tiny coffin is such an assault on the natural order of things. The only thing I recall was Nomboniso, draped in her black blanket of grief, swaying backwards and forwards with a vacant expression in her eyes, while her mother, her burn wounds bandaged, wept beside her.

On the television news that night, there was an account of events, which quoted a police spokesman saying that 'no foul play was suspected'. I contacted television news to ask which police spokesman had made the statement, and was told that it was a Superintendent Barkhuizen. I contacted Superintendent Barkhuizen on Monday 8 September. He told me that a neighbour of Nomboniso's had said she had first noticed smoke and flames coming from inside the kitchen area. This contradicted everything that I had heard prior to this point. And I knew that the investigation would run into a dead end, which it duly did.

It took us several weeks to recover from this tragedy. Tony Leon came to visit Nomboniso, and we held a service on her flattened site. Slowly our organisation came to life again, but, understandably, Nomboniso withdrew from political involvement. She was never the same again.

Masizole remained driven and persuaded me that the DA needed to invest in loudhailers (an essential part of political infrastructure in Khayelitsha). We agreed, and we affixed these to the roof rack of my ancient Opel Kadett. Masizole would drive around Makhaza calling people to our weekend meetings. And before long, Masizole started spending more and more weekends in jail, having been arrested on the Friday, in a repeat of the ubiquitous pattern. In this way the police were spared the inconvenience of having to keep the peace around our meetings (without getting overtime payment, to boot!).

A station commander called Shivuri at the Site B police station hated the DA and created real problems for us. As Masizole noted, 'The Site B police cells became my home over weekends.' Frank Raymond was also kept busy bailing him out.

Masizole was young, bold and outspoken. When a vacancy arose in our Cape Town caucus, I discussed him with Mzuvukile 'Archie' Figlan. Both of us thought that Masizole had the backbone required to be a councillor. Looking back, I can hardly believe it, but at that time the DA did not have a single black councillor in the City of Cape Town! It was beyond time to change that. Masizole would first have to go through our rigorous selection process, which involved appearing before the electoral college, an intimidating experience for anyone, let alone a twenty-one-year-old.

The NNP's cabal, needless to say, opposed his candidature with everything they had.

I helped Masizole prepare for the crucial electoral college, where he had to make a three-minute speech and answer tough questions on the DA's political philosophy and policies. When I brought him some important background documents to go through, he told me that he couldn't read them because he didn't have glasses and could not afford to buy himself a pair. I took him to an optometrist, where his eyes were tested, and he acquired a smart pair of glasses.

Masizole went to the electoral college well prepared. He made a good speech, answered the questions well, and won the nomination on 18 October 2003. It was a crucial breakthrough.

The next evening I visited him in his backyard shack abutting his mother's house in Khayelitsha, where we planned our next steps in building the Makhaza branch and further structures in Khayelitsha. I left his house at about 8:30 that Sunday night. It was dark. As I rounded the corner, I saw two men semi-running towards the intersection. Thinking they were in a hurry, I slowed down to let them pass, but one stopped in front of my car and held up his hands to block me. The other approached the side window with what I thought was a rock in his hand. In an instant I realised I was being hijacked. I managed to swerve my new car (I had just acquired an Opel Corsa), avoiding the man in the road, and put my foot on the accelerator. I heard two loud bangs, and concluded the car had been stoned.

Stonings happened now and again in the course of my work, and my old car had several 'dings' to show for it, but I was irritated that it had happened so soon to my new car. I drove at speed, hardly stopping at intersections, until I was back on the N2 highway. As the adrenalin subsided, I became aware of a deep ache in my lower back that I could not explain.

I got home and told Johann that our new car had been stoned. He took a torch and went out to check. 'No, you weren't stoned,' he said, 'you were shot.'

I realised that what I had thought was a rock in the hands of the man who came to my window was actually a gun. He must have taken aim and tried to shoot me as I drove off. There were two bullet holes in the Corsa's back door. One of the bullets had gone through the driver's seat, but had been sufficiently slowed down by the tightly woven springs to pierce the fabric and hit my lower spine without penetrating my skin. There it was, protruding through the twisted metal and fabric. I had a massive, rapidly spreading purple bruise on my butt, the result of subcutaneous bleeding. Johann took a photograph, which is for family viewing only (or consenting feminists in private).

I immediately went to the Rondebosch police station to lay a complaint and asked them to come back with me to Khayelitsha straight away to look for the perpetrators. I had quite a clear memory of the face of the man who had come to my window. They said no, the matter would have to be investigated by the Khayelitsha police. I knew that the trail would end there, and I was right. No one was ever arrested.

A lot of theories emerged as to how I managed to avoid serious injury in that incident.

'I knew you were thick-skinned, but this is ridiculous,' someone quipped. (I am sure it was Johann, but he swears blind it wasn't.)

A few gave credit to Divine Providence, and several drew the conclusion that 'God must have a plan for you.' I hoped so, because there was still a lot to do.

When I asked our family doctor, Geoff Baron, how he could explain that the bullet hit me but did not penetrate my skin, he said with a straight face, 'It ran out of kinetic energy.'

That Wednesday, three days later, was Masizole's first council meeting. It was a big moment. As he arrived to take his seat in the chamber, he was met, and arrested, by two policemen dispatched from the Khayelitsha Site B police station. He was charged with assaulting Linda Sambata, an ex-girlfriend and the mother of his child. Masizole protested his innocence, but I was genuinely in a quandary. What if he had actually assaulted her? If this were the case, the DA would have to suspend him, which would be an awful way of ending the tenure of Cape Town's first black DA councillor, before he could even attend his first council meeting.

I went to see Masizole at the Site B police station, to find Frank Raymond already there. Frank assured me that Masizole was being framed. Linda had phoned Masizole earlier in the day and left a voice message explaining that she was being pressured by the ANC councillor Ludidi and others to make a false statement implicating Masizole so that the ANC could have him politically neutralised.

The ANC knew that Linda was heartbroken after Masizole ended their relationship, so they offered her a chance to seek revenge by making a false claim against him – not thinking, of course, that she might phone Masizole and warn him. Masizole saved the message and played it to Frank, who spoke to Linda, who confessed that she had laid the charge under duress, on the instructions of the ANC. When Frank reported this to the police, they warned Linda that if she withdrew the complaint, she would face a charge of defeating the ends of justice – which duly transpired. Frank then defended Linda in court and managed to get the case dismissed because of the pressure Linda had faced and her fear of reprisal if she refused the ANC's 'request'.

Predictably, though, there were no consequences for the ANC representatives who had connived to defeat the ends of justice for political purposes.

Not too long afterwards, Masizole and I decided to convene a mass meeting at the Desmond Tutu Hall in Makhaza to introduce the new councillor to his immediate community in Ward 96. We got a good little crowd there, and while we were doing the obligatory introductory singing, dancing and 'viva-ing' we heard a tremendous noise, banging and shouting, outside. Councillor Ludidi had arrived with a crowd to break up our meeting. As was his wont, Ludidi hung around the back while his henchmen, led by Telelo Moni, actually perpetrated the violence on his behalf. Moni ushered the protesters into the hall, overturning the chairs and attacking people. Nolitha Nyoka, who was prominent in the ANC Women's League, jumped onto the stage and began dragging me outside, saying she was going to put me on a taxi to send me 'back to Constantia, to the whites'. I saw Moni hit one of our branch secretaries, Bongi Buso, in the face, shattering her spectacles.

By now there was a free-for-all brawl on the square. Both Ludidi and Masizole had drawn firearms, and I heard a shot ring out. It was only a matter of time before someone was killed. At last the police arrived, sirens screaming. They got out of their van – and promptly arrested Masizole!

I protested vehemently. Bongi Buso showed her broken spectacles and bruised face, and pointed to Moni as the perpetrator. Eventually, he was also arrested, and both Masizole and Moni were driven off to the police station, while the police ordered the rest of the crowd to disperse, which we did.

I got into my Corsa and drove to the police station, where I met Frank Raymond. We were both there to support Masizole, who was charged with pointing a firearm, while Moni faced charges of assault. Both men were detained in police cells while Frank organised bail for Masizole.

As they sat together in the cell, Moni complained to Masizole that, unlike the DA, the ANC had failed to support him, even though he was acting on Councillor Ludidi's behalf. By the time they had finished their discussion, Moni said, 'I think I should rather join the DA.'

Not long afterwards, amazingly, he did! Moni became a DA stalwart in Khayelitsha, along with someone else who had been part of the ANC crowd that attacked our meeting in that hall. This was Bonginkosi Madikizela, who is now the DA's deputy Western Cape leader and Western Cape provincial minister of human settlements.

Despite these accounts which focus on our battle to establish fundamental rights – and our clashes with the police in the process – I should stress that my constituency work involved much more than regular visits to police stations and courts (and dodging the occasional bullet). I was also called on to provide ambulance services from time to time, sometimes in the dead of night.

At times I transported some interesting passengers … Every time we had a branch launch, we would buy a live sheep, which I would fetch in my car. The animal would sit meekly in the back, looking out of the window as if it was enjoying the view. It gave me an insight into the English idiom that compares a calm, unwitting walk into disaster with 'a lamb being led to the slaughter'. During the short drive I bonded with each sheep and felt deeply guilty every time I dropped it off at the party venue. I always had to leave until the deed was done, which was a source of much mirth among our members.

I learnt to drink *umqombothi* from old Sunbeam polish tins, and how to eat offal in steaming pots (despite its aroma). I put an effort into improving my Xhosa. But I focused specifically on the work required to entrench the concept of the rule of law, because this was make or break for every citizen, and for the country's future.

We have made substantial progress since the day I recruited Lungiswa in her bath in Gugulethu in 2000. In fact, South Africa today is another country, and despite the roller-coaster ride, we are moving in the right direction. Part of our progress was the hard graft, on the ground, moving from ward to ward, recruiting members, enduring setbacks and disappointments, surviving harassment and providing the alternative that gradually some 'early adopters' wanted. Back then, progress was so slow as to be imperceptible, but by the end of 2003 we had built a credible network of branches in the N2 constituency. We had a base from which to fight our first electoral battle. But, as I was about to learn, there is a big difference between building branches and attracting votes. The former is much easier than the latter.

Our expectations of the election were sky-high, but we were soon brought down to earth. Despite all our efforts, we ended up with 0.4 per cent of the votes in the N2 constituency. Although I was getting used to the hard knocks of politics, it was still a blow. All the work we had done, all the risks we had run, had merely taken us to the base of the foothills of the challenge. Mount Everest still lay on the distant horizon.

I had just been elected a member of the national parliament, and as the N2 constituency head, I would have to lead the trek forward.

11

An Unlikely Coalition

'WE HEARD ABOUT this white woman who was infiltrating our areas. We heard she was starting branches and recruiting members for the enemy. We had to stop her. We had to keep Khayelitsha a no-go zone for the DA.'

Bonginkosi Madikizela, impeccably dressed in a mauve tie and matching pocket handkerchief, was sitting in my lounge in January 2006, reminiscing about the circumstances that had led to our first meeting three years earlier. He had been a leading member of the ANC in Khayelitsha, implementing the ANC's strategy of keeping the DA out.

Even though I had been on the receiving end of this strategy for years, I was still surprised at his use of the word 'enemy'.

'That is the language we use,' he said. 'That is how the ANC views opposition.'

The attempt to drive out 'the enemy' had brought us face to face for the first time at that fateful Makhaza meeting in the Desmond Tutu Hall, where Masizole Mnqasela, who had just been elected as the first black DA councillor in Cape Town, was trying to set up the first DA branch in Khayelitsha and Bonginkosi was among the leaders of the ANC shock-troop that stormed the meeting. His strategy, he told me, was to get hold of the microphone and take over proceedings. The ANC was going to use the platform to warn Khayelitsha residents not to join a 'white party' that planned to bring back apartheid.

'We wanted to drive you out with words, not violence,' he assured me, but the combination of adrenalin, crowd psychology and hegemonic instinct created an uncontainable eruption that sent chairs, fists and projectiles flying in every direction.

Now, three years later, Bonginkosi was sitting opposite me, sipping tea in my lounge in suburban Rosebank, in the run-up to the local government election scheduled for 1 March 2006. He needed assistance, he said.

An important part of politics is to expect the unexpected, to divine a changing landscape and adapt to its contours. I sensed this was an important moment. Bonginkosi's surname underscored its significance. Madikizela – a name that belongs to the pantheon of South Africa's political royalty. The maiden name of Winnie Madikizela-Mandela, the most famous, and notorious, of Nelson Mandela's three wives, and Bonginkosi's aunt. A name synonymous with the ANC.

Here was Bonginkosi Madikizela, great-grandson of the paramount chief under the great warrior King Sigcau of the Amampondo, telling me that the ANC now also described him as an 'enemy' because he dared to differ with the official party line. Branch meetings had become war zones, and a colleague was in hospital after being hit on the head with a brick during one such altercation.

He and several colleagues had complained to the party's national leadership, and when they received no response, decided to contest the local election as independents. Time, however, was tight. They needed help, especially with fundraising for T-shirts and posters.

At the time I was desperately trying to raise funds for the DA's own election effort, and it seemed absurd to consider fundraising for candidates who would stand against us.

'What's in it for the DA?' I asked.

I will never forget his answer.

'We will take enough votes from the ANC to enable the DA to win the election.'

I had become inured to unanticipated developments, but I never ceased to marvel at the thread of irony woven through the fabric of politics. Here was ANC royalty promising to get me elected mayor of Cape Town, while a large faction of my own party was doing everything possible to prevent it.

Here was a young man, leading a group of independents, standing for election without resources or organisation, just six weeks before the polls, confident of drawing substantially more votes than we could after six years of intensive groundwork.

Bonginkosi took me through his mental calculations. He was clearly on top of his game. I compared them with the DA's statistics and was amazed by the correlation. We both agreed that no party would get over 50 per cent and that Cape Town would be governed by a coalition. The big challenge would be to ensure that the smaller parties gravitated to a DA-led coalition rather than an ANC-led coalition. Given the histories and political philosophies of the smaller parties, this shift would be highly unlikely. The independents could help by shaving a few percentage points off the ANC's total. If the DA emerged as the largest party, it would make a critical difference, he argued.

'Why do people have to vote for us via you?' I asked. 'Why can't they just vote directly for us?'

'Because of the trust factor,' he said. 'The ANC has convinced people that the DA will bring back apartheid. More and more people want to vote against the ANC, but they need a party they trust.'

His words felt like a stick in the eye. The very notion that the DA might bring back apartheid sent a searing pain through my head. Reluctantly, I conceded that the ANC's racial mobilisation, and the fear of recreating a hated past, had worked.

'I'll see what I can do,' I said.

In the remaining six weeks Bonginkosi and I saw each other often, sometimes in the dead of night at rendezvous points in Khayelitsha. He had to avoid being seen with me. The closer the election came, the more I knew he was right. We would stand or fall by the success of the independents in Khayelitsha. They got their posters and pamphlets.

And they also got almost 18 per cent of the vote in the Khayelitsha wards they contested (compared to our dismal 3.2 per cent). Their performance in those Khayelitsha wards gave them 2.2 per cent across the metro as a whole. Bonginkosi had been right. If they had not shaved this sliver off the ANC's total, as it turned out, we would not have been able to put together a majority coalition.

Although they did so well on their home turf, none of their candidates was elected, as they did not actually win their wards and could not benefit from the proportional vote because they had not formed a registered party. All the same, they managed to reduce the ANC's support sufficiently to enable us, for the first time in South Africa's history, to remove the ANC from a seat of power through the ballot box.

Of course, other factors contributed too – including human error and the forces of nature.

One of our big campaign platforms was the ANC's neglect of the fire and disaster management service in the city. On the weekend before the election, a tourist threw a cigarette out of a car window, lighting a wildfire that raged for days, engulfing the Table Mountain range, burning down houses and killing a person who was caught in the inferno while on a walk. The ill-equipped fire service was not up to the task. It underscored the points we had made throughout our campaign – the ANC administration had allowed a once great fire-fighting force to collapse. Our message settled on the city, along with the veil of smoke and ash.

Then, to drive the point home further, the electricity went down, with blackouts escalating (specifically in Cape Town) as the election approached. Our message reverberated through every darkened home and empty business: the ANC had decimated the electricity generation and reticulation capacity in the same way as the fire service.

On the night of 28 February, during a brief respite from 'load-shedding', I sat down to watch the last evening news bulletin before the election.

The lead item was the minister of public enterprises, Alec Erwin, speaking at a hastily convened news conference to announce that a loose bolt in the generator of the nuclear power plant outside Cape Town had been responsible for the city's 'rolling blackouts'. Then he added ominously, 'It is a matter of great regret that this is, in fact, not an accident.'

Erwin went on. 'I should also indicate that any interference with any electricity installation is an exceptionally serious crime. It is sabotage. Sabotage is everywhere. We need to be very clear that the bolt in the generator was not an accident.'

The matter was being investigated, he said, by the National Intelligence Agency and the police, and charges would be laid 'against individuals who, we believe, are responsible for this'.

On the eve of the most closely contested local election in our democracy's history, the implication was clear: the ANC's opponents were prepared to resort to sabotaging a nuclear facility to reinforce their narrative of ANC governance failure. The ANC was no longer responsible for bad governance, but the victim of sabotage.

I was aghast. The DA would now enter the close election race not as the party capable of reversing ANC decline, but as potential suspects in an act of sabotage that could have endangered the lives of thousands of people by damaging a nuclear power plant for electoral advantage. The haste with which the minister's news conference had been convened, eighteen hours before the polls opened, left us with no time to reverse the situation.

The media swallowed the minister's line entirely, reporting the 'sabotage' of Koeberg as fact.

On election day, the dominant issue in the newspapers was that saboteurs had made it through the Koeberg nuclear plant's security to throw a bolt into the main generator. All the commentators weighed in.

Mike Kantey, of Koeberg Alert, said the potential threat to Cape Town from sabotage at Koeberg was 'enormous'. The Wildlife and Environment Society said it was 'reprehensible' that saboteurs could 'threaten the safety of hundreds of thousands of Capetonians' living in the shadow of the nuclear power station. And so it went.

I made a few preliminary enquiries, which convinced me that there was no sabotage involved. The National Energy Regulator of South Africa could not confirm sabotage, and a person I trusted who was in contact with a senior Koeberg executive emphatically denied it. I felt confident enough to issue a statement the next day rejecting the allegation of sabotage out of hand. 'For the ANC to cry "sabotage" the night before crucial local government elections shows just how desperate it is to disguise its incompetence and mismanagement,' I said. 'The real problem is that the ANC elite has let South Africa's crucial infrastructure progressively collapse as it works out who gets the lion's share of the next empowerment deal.'

The newspapers opined about politicians 'squabbling' at a time that the public was at grave risk because of sabotage at Koeberg. I asked myself why so many journalists took the lazy route of reporting a 'row' rather than establishing whether the allegation of sabotage was true and exposing it for the political ruse it turned out to be.

The real scandal, of course, was either (1) that a cabinet minister had been prepared to put out an unfounded scare story of enormous proportions on the eve of an election in order to counter the narrative that his government had neglected the maintenance of a crucial facility; or (2) that the National Intelligence Agency had misled him.

Either way, it was a sensational story.

On election day, I was assigned to my constituency, the N2. My brother, Paul, had come down from Johannesburg to support me and drove me from polling station to polling station in my blue Kadett so that I could jump out and check that everything was proceeding smoothly, without unnecessary delays. The ANC's yellow T-shirts overwhelmed every voting station.

One of our members in Crossroads phoned to tell me that the ANC was handing out identity documents at their local party office, so that people without identity documents could go and vote. Suspecting possible fraud, I asked Paul to drop me at the ANC office. I walked in and saw a home affairs official issuing standard green identity books from a large box. I took a few quick photos with my rudimentary phone camera before being physically manhandled off the premises. I dashed for the car and jumped in as Paul sped off. It all added to the adrenalin rush of the day.

I complained to the Independent Electoral Commission, but nothing came of it.

Despite everything, we still managed to emerge from the election as the largest party in Cape Town, with 42 per cent of the vote, compared to the ANC's 38 per cent. It seemed like a stellar result, but compared to the local election in 2000, when the newly formed DA polled 53 per cent in Cape Town, the election outcome showed we were still struggling to recover from the devastating impact of the DA's messy divorce back in 2001.

But the most significant aspect of the 2006 election result was that no party had reached 50 per cent in the City of Cape Town. There would have to be a coalition government.

The precise outcome of the election was significant, because it determined the possible permutations of our coalition options. If the goal of a coalition is to secure stable governance, the compatibility of the partner parties' political philosophies is also relevant. We had two weeks to navigate this new and uncharted terrain before the election of the mayor and speaker on 15 March.

We studied the breakdown of the 210 seats in council:
- Democratic Alliance (DA) (open society, market economy): 91 seats
- African National Congress (ANC) (national democratic revolution): 81 seats

- Independent Democrats (ID) (social democrat): 22 seats
- African Christian Democratic Party (ACDP) (Christian fundamentalist): 7 seats
- Africa Muslim Party (AMP) (Muslim fundamentalist): 3 seats
- United Democratic Movement (UDM) (breakaway party from the ANC): 2 seats
- United Independent Front (UIF) (ANC left-wing breakaway): 1 seat
- Freedom Front Plus (FF+) (far right, from the remnants of the right-wing breakaway of the old National Party): 1 seat
- Universal Party (UP) (no explicit political philosophy): 1 seat
- Pan Africanist Congress (PAC) (Africanist philosophy): 1 seat

Our obvious coalition partner was the Independent Democrats, led by the fiery, feisty Patricia de Lille. We were the closest in political philosophy. If we added our 91 seats with the ID's 22 seats, we had a combined 113 seats of the council's 210 seats – a comfortable majority. We were the only two-party combination that could do this. As far as I was concerned, it was a no-brainer.

Except the ID didn't agree with my analysis.

I did not get to meet Patricia de Lille, their leader, who was the celebrity politician of the time, but I spoke to her mayoral candidate, Simon Grindrod, who told me the ID's aim was to put together a mayoral committee, with a ceremonial mayor and a three-party coalition, including the ANC. The ID would not go into a coalition with the DA alone.

The DA's election manifesto had supported a proportional, multi-party executive committee under a ceremonial mayor, and the media understandably roasted us for ditching it. Our problem was that, given the election result, it clashed with another election commitment we had made, namely that we would, wherever possible, enter coalitions with other opposition parties to replace the ANC in government. Cape Town offered us that chance. We could put together a coalition, which would force the ANC to go into opposition.

We faced a dilemma. We were the biggest party, with 42 per cent of the vote; but if we went into a coalition with both the ID and the ANC, we would hand power back to the ANC through their alignment with the ID. In a three-party government that the ANC and ID demanded, they would together form the bigger block and out-vote us on every issue.

So we had to break one of our election promises, as we had not foreseen a situation in which it would be impossible to keep both. Ryan Coetzee clinched it with this argument: 'It cannot be right that a party that wins an election is forced to hand back that victory voluntarily through a coalition agreement. That would be a bigger betrayal of our voters.'

We told the ID that we would not include the ANC in our coalition, and the ID promptly vindicated our decision by choosing to back the ANC's mayoral candidate.

Game over, I thought.

Not so fast, said Pauline Cupido, the Western Cape leader of the African Christian Democratic Party. She had convened a meeting of the other opposition parties (apart from the ID), and six of them were prepared to negotiate with the DA, she said.

I thought it was a crazy idea. The six parties were more ideologically distant from us than the ID, and would therefore be even less inclined than the ID to come into a coalition with us, I thought. And even if all six parties were willing to vote with us, we were not guaranteed an overall majority. If the remaining party, the PAC, voted with the ANC and ID, we would have a dead heat.

It would be impossible to hold together a workable coalition in those circumstances, I argued. It would mean that if any 'one-man party' felt aggrieved for any reason, that party could simply vote with the ANC and our government would fall. Any such coalition would be lucky to survive two weeks.

I prepared to return to parliament.

The negotiating team, comprising James Selfe, Ryan Coetzee, Kent Morkel and Theuns Botha, gave it a try. Their mandate was to negotiate coalitions not only in Cape Town, but across the province. As the mayoral candidate, with a direct vested interest in the outcome, I could not be involved in the negotiations. However, I asked Tony to include Ian Neilson, a long-standing councillor with a profound grasp of local government issues, in the negotiating team for Cape Town. Ian had the inside knowledge required to understand what was necessary for governance to actually work. Both he and I were reluctant to take power for the sake of taking power. Once we were in government, we would have to be able to govern well.

The first piece of advice Ian gave us was that we should avoid going into a coalition unless we secured two key portfolios: finance and corporate services. These were transversal functions, essential for resuscitating the council from its internal malaise and near-bankruptcy.

On 14 March 2006, the evening before the mayoral election, I got a call from James Selfe. 'We have sealed a coalition deal with everyone except the PAC,' he said.

The deal was this. I would be the executive mayor. The ACDP would fill the position of deputy mayor. The DA would get five mayco positions (including finance and corporate services) and every other party would get one, except the Freedom Front Plus, which would get the speaker's position. The UDM had insisted on having the community safety portfolio, and the Africa Muslim Party had insisted on the economic and social development portfolio.

I was amazed that our team had pulled it off, but I downplayed it. I just didn't believe that all six of the other parties would actually vote for us when the chips were down in the council chamber. In the context of the time, when the DA was still widely perceived as a white party that would bring back apartheid, this would be nothing short of miraculous. And apart from anything else, the ANC would, up to the last minute, find a lot of gravy to splash around among the smaller parties.

But James seemed confident. He cautioned, however, that there was one more important step to take. If the coalition was to win, the PAC's single councillor would have to abstain. If he voted for the ANC, we would end with a tie. 'Please speak personally to Bennet Joko, the PAC councillor,' said James. 'Ask him to abstain and let me know what he says.'

'I'll try,' I answered.

I figured that if the UDM and UIF were prepared to enter a coalition with us, then almost anything was possible.

I now had to urgently contact Councillor Joko to have the kind of conversation that one can only have face to face. I needed to read his eyes and his body language. I did not know where he lived, but I knew Masizole had worked with him in the past, so I called Masizole. Sure, said Masizole, he would show me where Bennet lived. So I fetched Masizole, and we pulled up outside Bennet's place in Town Two, Khayelitsha, at about 9:30 that night, thirteen hours before the crucial mayoral election was scheduled to begin.

Masizole had Bennet's phone number, and I called him from the car, parked outside his house. 'Mr Joko, this is Helen Zille, the DA's mayoral candidate. I am sitting in my car in your street, with Masizole Mnqasela. Would you be prepared to speak to us?'

The door opened and a curious face, phone clutched to his ear, peered around the corner. We were about two metres apart, speaking to each other on the phone. We both laughed. Bennet greeted me warmly and invited us in. It was the first time I had met the tall, handsome young man who now held the future of the city in his hand.

'Would you like some tea?' he offered.

'Yes, please,' I said, knowing how many tricky situations throughout history have been resolved over a cup of tea. I stopped short of making a pun on his name (Joko being my favourite South African brand of tea), because I remembered my mother's advice: 'If ever you can make a joke about someone's name, rather don't. You can be sure they will have heard it a thousand times before.'

Bennet set about making the tea. He explained that his wife was in bed. She had just come back from hospital, that very day, with their newborn baby daughter, Azania. Would I like to see the baby?

'I would love to,' I said, 'as long as I am not disturbing them.' We went into the adjoining corrugated-iron room, and there in bed next to her mother was a tiny, brand-new human being. I apologised for intruding on such an important and special family night, but the Jokos were relaxed, and Azania was fast asleep. While Bennet made everyone a cup of tea, Azania's mother and I clucked over their baby.

Then Bennet, Masizole and I sat down in the adjoining room and engaged the crucial topic of the mayoral election the next morning. I explained our canvassing results, and showed him the numbers. He pored over them.

'Mr Joko, I am not here to ask you to vote for me,' I said. 'I understand that this would go against the PAC's position. But I am asking you please to abstain from voting tomorrow.'

'Why are you assuming I wouldn't vote for you?' he asked.

'Well,' I replied, nonplussed, 'our political philosophies are so different that I did not think it was appropriate to ask you to vote for me.'

'Never make that assumption,' he said. 'The DA at least approached me to discuss a coalition. And now you have actually come out to speak to me personally. The ANC hasn't even made contact, because they just assume that I will vote for them. They are in for a surprise.'

His response surprised me too! Then he confirmed that the PAC had, in fact, taken a decision to abstain, and he said he would abide by that decision.

I mentioned that the ANC was likely to offer all sorts of inducements before the vote the following morning.

'I am also expecting that,' he said. 'But I give you my word, I will abstain.'

I knew I could trust him.

As I drove home, it dawned on me that within eleven hours I could be mayor of Cape Town.

I called James. 'Mission accomplished,' I said.

I knew the ANC would pull out all the stops to swing at least one of the coalition partners away from us, which was all they needed to do, so I was prepared for any eventuality.

When I got home, at about eleven o'clock that night, I found Johann at his desk.

'Johann,' I said, 'there is actually a chance I could be elected mayor of Cape Town tomorrow. Would you like to come and watch the proceedings?'

'I can't,' he answered. 'I have to take the car for a roadworthy test.'

I was used to this kind of response. Johann's commitment to maintaining the domestic infrastructure of our lives meant that bills got paid, cars got serviced, licensed and roadworthied, lightbulbs were changed, drains unblocked ...

'Okay,' I said. 'Pity.'

Then I thought about it some more. No, I decided. For once Johann is going to put duty aside and come and share this occasion with me. I went back to the study we shared. 'Johann,' I said, 'when we are old, we won't remember getting the car roadworthied, but we will remember the day I was either just elected mayor of Cape Town – or just lost. Either way, it would mean a lot if you were there.'

He got an attack of the mutters. 'It's not easy to get an appointment to roadworthy the car, you know,' he said pointedly. 'It will mean I will have to wait again for several months before the next slot comes up.'

'Then the car will just have to wait,' I said, before sitting down at my desk to write a few paragraphs, which would be the first words I would utter from the podium as mayor if I won the election.

Next morning, on the Ides of March 2006, we set off for the City of Cape Town chamber, which is constructed like an amphitheatre surrounded by gallery seating for public viewing. We had agreed that Tom could take the day off school as well (which, unlike his dad, required no prodding at all). Paul had work to do at university, and I thought it best not to distract him.

I steeled myself for disappointment. It was beyond the realm of possibility that our six prospective coalition partners would withstand the ANC's pressure to switch sides.

On the way to the Civic Centre I heard that one of our councillors, Theresa Thompson, would probably not be at the meeting at all. Her sister had been murdered thirty-six hours earlier, shot dead by her husband. Theresa was dealing with an unimaginable crisis. I felt terrible for her. But it is not often that the future of democracy and a personal tragedy collide so starkly. We had planned for every eventuality, except something like this. I called Theresa to commiserate. Audibly devastated, she nevertheless volunteered to do her best to be at the meeting. 'Your family comes first,' I said lamely. 'But please do your best.' I felt awful even saying that.

We arrived at the council chamber. The Democratic Alliance still sat in the opposition benches. We kept a close tally of the councillors arriving. The well-worn phrase 'every vote counts' had never (in my experience) been so literally true.

Theresa wasn't there. The meeting started promptly at 10 a.m., chaired by the city manager, Dr Wallace Mgoqi. Up first were a few routine agenda items to constitute the meeting. Then Dr Mgoqi announced the next order of business: the election of the speaker. As the customary bells chimed, signalling a vote was about to be held, Dr Mgoqi announced: 'The doors will now be locked. No one may enter or leave during the course of the vote.'

I had my eyes trained on Theresa's empty seat.

That's it, I said to myself. The cosmos has intervened. It was not meant to be.

I gave one last glance at the closing door at the top left-hand corner, just in time to see Theresa slip through before it latched. The cosmos had indeed intervened, but contrary to my expectations! If our coalition held, and the PAC abstained, we would win by a majority of one vote in a 210-member council.

Looking back, the minutes of this meeting make fascinating reading. I have never seen entries like this at a large meeting before or since.

APOLOGIES

Absent: None

The following Councillors submitted their apologies for late arrival:
None

The following Councillors submitted their apologies for leaving early:
None

Everyone was there. After the collective oath to 'affirm faithfulness to the Republic of South Africa and obedience to the constitution', the election of the speaker commenced.

It was immediately apparent that the ANC and ID had a joint game plan.

The ANC nominated one of their councillors, Gavin Paulse (a former DA member who had crossed the floor to the ANC in 2002) as the speaker. Then, to my surprise, the ID also nominated a candidate, but not one of their own. They nominated a DA councillor, Leon van Rensburg, who was the informal intellectual leader of the DA councillors who opposed me. The ID/ANC strategy was to confuse the DA caucus into voting for one of its own high-profile members, against the FF+'s Dirk Smit, our coalition's agreed candidate for speaker. If just two of our number got confused and voted for Leon, we would lose. Fortunately, Leon declined the nomination.

Then Councillor Dumisani Ximbi of the UDM nominated the FF+'s Dirk Smit. To understand how counter-intuitive this was in the South Africa of the time, try to imagine Michelle Obama nominating Ted Cruz. I had to pinch myself.

Then the vote started and the ballots were collected. Our vote-counters moved to the central table. The ballots were poured out and counted in neat piles. Our observers watched closely for every possible trick. The piles grew. My lips and throat were dry. My water glass was empty. I glanced up and saw Johann and Tom looking down on me with binoculars from the gallery. It felt good to have them there.

The first thing I heard from the central table was the ANC demanding a recount. My heart leapt because it meant they were unhappy with the result. The recount began, but the tally remained the same.

Gavin Paulse (ANC): 104 votes

Dirk Smit (FF+): 105 votes

Abstentions: 1

I knew who had abstained and I smiled at Bennet Joko across the floor. He smiled his broad gap-toothed smile back.

The atmosphere was electric. Until that minute, the ANC and the ID had been confident of victory. The buzz in the council auditorium rose to an intense chatter.

The newly elected speaker took over the chair.

'Just move quickly,' I said aloud – but to myself. 'We are on a roll. We dare not lose momentum now.'

The meeting adopted the rules of order, and just as we were going to move to the mayoral election, the ANC asked for an adjournment so that they could caucus. I knew why. They wanted to apply last-minute pressure and offer inducements to the other seven parties. They needed only one to break from our coalition and vote for them, in order to take power.

I was mentally willing the speaker to reject the request.

But, erring on the side of ultra-fairness in his first big decision, he allowed the adjournment.

That's it, I thought. They will now bring in the big guns and make offers that can't be refused.

'It's over,' I SMSed Johann in the gallery. He sent me a string of encouraging messages. I also got a message from my sister Carla, who was in Johannesburg with my mother. I messaged her back, giving details of the delays and risks.

Mom usually had a whisky in the evening, but this occasion was an exception. She had brought her sundowner forward to late morning. Carla urged us to get on with the proceedings, as Mom was on her third whisky and was rapidly losing focus. I messaged back that the proceedings were out of my hands and urged her to keep the whisky out of Mom's.

Ryan Coetzee was in the gallery, keeping Tony informed. Tony had decided not to come, he explained to me later, because the precariousness of our situation required us to reduce any possible distractions or feelings of animosity towards the DA. Inevitably, as leader of the party, Tony was a controversial figure, and he did not want his presence to provide a push factor that might nudge one of our allies to switch sides.

It soon became apparent how generally unexpected the outcome of the speaker's election was. Council staff poured out of their offices and hung over the balconies to find out what was happening. The ground-floor concourse, where a huge screen had been erected for public viewing, had had rows of empty chairs until that point. Now they were suddenly filled to capacity. Hearing of the unexpected outcome of the speaker's election, people drained from the building to watch the mayoral vote on the big screen. Work came to a standstill. The atmosphere felt almost radioactive.

The minutes of the meeting record that the adjournment lasted fifty minutes. In my memory it was much longer. Sitting in my seat in the fishbowl chamber, I saw ANC bigwigs approaching each of our coalition partners. Kent Morkel was doing an outstanding job of insulating them from enticement. Some of our prospective coalition partners remained in the chamber, refusing to move. The Africa Muslim Party was frog-marched out of the chamber by the ANC into a caucus room. I got an unconfirmed message that President Thabo Mbeki was calling people to speak to them personally, persuading them to change sides.

When at last the meeting reconvened, I had prepared myself for defeat. I thought the ANC would never have agreed to continue the meeting if they thought they would lose. It seemed implausible that the coalition would have held through that length of time and that strength of bombardment.

It is better that we go down now, before we even start, than collapse after a fortnight of chaos, I told myself.

The speaker then called for nominations for mayor of Cape Town.

Anthea Serritslev nominated me, and someone else nominated the ANC's NomaIndia Mfeketo, the incumbent. Ballots were distributed and the voting started. The only thing I could do (apart from vote for myself) was wait. I remember worrying about the fact that I had no lipstick with me. I laughed inwardly at my psychological diversion strategy. In an 'atmosphere article' the following day, journalist Michael Morris described my face as 'inscrutable', a thin veneer covering the turbulence I felt inside.

Once again, the ballots were poured out on the central table and the count began. The wait seemed endless, until Martin Fienies, the leader and sole public representative of the Universal Party, who was observing the count, glanced over his shoulder and gave me a big wink. He spoke with his eyes and I listened with mine.

When the ANC demanded a recount, I knew the coalition had held.

What I did not yet know, though, was that we had actually increased our majority. I had won by a full three votes! The final tally was DA: 106; ANC: 103 (with one spoilt ballot).

Not only had our coalition (and Bennet in his abstention) stood firm, but someone from either the ANC or ID had broken ranks and voted for me. That meant the ANC/ID coalition got one vote less than they should have (103) and we got one vote more than we expected (106). In the context, it felt like a landslide!

The buzz radiated from the chamber. The Civic Centre – which had stood still for the duration of the vote – became a hive of activity. The outgoing mayor's spokesperson rushed down the corridor, yelling into her cellphone, 'Cancel the champagne, cancel the champagne!'

Patricia de Lille, the ID leader, who had watched the proceedings from the gallery, left with her entourage. Her gambit of backing the ANC had backfired.

I sat frozen in my seat, wondering where the extra vote had come from. I guessed it was Sheval Arendse, a member of the ID with whom I had previously worked quite cordially. But he was adamant that it wasn't him. In fact, it was impossible for any ID member to have broken ranks, he told me later, because they had agreed to check each other's ballots to ensure compliance with the controversial decision to back the ANC.

So, I concluded, someone from the ANC must have voted for me, and I am still fascinated to know who it was. I have spoken to someone who says he knows who it was but won't tell me. I respect that.

I received the chain from the city manager, and I made my first speech as mayor (without lipstick). Then, in a daze, the partner parties decamped to the mayoral office. It was deserted except for a temporary contract worker answering the telephones. Every staff member in the mayor's office had been a 'political appointment' and had abandoned ship.

The celebrating DA caucus filled the void, however. I felt like the proverbial dog that chased the tyre of the bus and managed to catch it.

What were we going to do now? How were we going to make this unlikely coalition work, across divergent ideologies that stretched from the far left to the far right, from the Crescent to the Cross? At that moment we were too hyped to think about practicalities. We had an impromptu celebration, and as the afternoon wore on, everyone left, except me. I sat in the vast mayoral office, behind the huge, empty mayoral desk, looking out on the spectacular view of Table Mountain and the city bowl, and asked myself: What the hell do we do now?

I remembered with relief that the Friedrich Naumann Foundation, the German liberal foundation that had supported the tiny DP with training and mentorship, and now partnered the DA, was prepared to assist us in charting a way forward. I knew they would bring in the world's best authorities on coalition management to assist us. The first thing I did the next morning was follow up the Friedrich Naumann offer, and was relieved to know that help was already on its way.

Next, from my desolate office, I wrote to the Cape Town city manager, Wallace Mgoqi, asking him to assign the city's best administrator to advise me on what the law allowed in terms of setting up an office and assist me in drawing up an organogram. My only stipulation was that the person be an excellent manager and be politically non-aligned.

A few hours later there was a knock on the door and in walked the man I probably least wanted to see.

That's the guy who almost cost us the election, I thought to myself.

'The guy' was Brent Gerber, the deputy electoral manager in Cape Town, reporting to the city manager.

'Congratulations,' said Brent. 'The city manager has sent me to advise you on setting up your office.'

I glared at him, still angry at the fact that, in his capacity as deputy electoral manager, he had disqualified one of our ward candidates, Miriam Ngcono, before the election in Ward 13. We had mistakenly filled in two identical forms for the same candidate, instead of two different forms. Given the pressured circumstances, I felt it was a miracle that we'd only had one administrative slip-up, and I thought he was being unfair by disqualifying her. We had been expecting about 2 000 votes in that ward, which was enough, in a close contest, to determine the outcome of the election as a whole.

Brent had remained unmoved by my entreaties. 'I am sorry,' he replied. 'I have to apply the rules fairly and equally to everyone. Otherwise I would endanger the election.'

He explained the appeal mechanism, but I did not take it further because I had to concede he was right. Our mistake cost us dearly. We were now facing the consequences in such a finely balanced coalition.

In our first cordial meeting since that initial encounter, Brent advised me on how to structure a small, diverse, effective office. Carin Viljoen was appointed chief of staff. She was an outstanding manager and administrator who built a strong, responsive, functional system which complemented my more intuitive leadership style. Her first task was to go through the piles of abandoned files and unanswered correspondence that were stuffed into drawers.

Brent also suggested I employ someone to manage 'stakeholder relations'. I would get hundreds of letters, mostly complaints, he warned, and it was very useful to have someone who would take a personal interest in following up the issues and interacting directly with the people involved. I thought Bonginkosi Madikizela would be the right person for the job. We decided to test the idea through a contract post of a year. I will never forget my conversation with Bonginkosi when I asked whether he would consider filling it. He was unemployed at the time.

I described the purpose of the job, and its various aspects, to him.

He replied in his formal way, 'But Madam Mayor, I am not a member of the DA.'

I didn't see what that had to do with it.

'I am not asking you to vote for me,' I said. 'I am asking you to do a job of work for the city.'

At moments like this it became clear to me how alien the idea of the separation between party and state still was in South Africa's political culture – even though it is a key assumption underlying our constitution. I had grown up with this idea in my mother's milk. Bonginkosi accepted the job offer.

Within days Brent was in my office again, this time to tell me our government was about to fall.

The city manager, Dr Wallace Mgoqi, had declared three vacancies, to replace the Africa Muslim Party councillors who formed part of our coalition. I was aghast, especially when I heard the 'back story'. The AMP had been internally divided about whether to join the DA coalition or throw its lot in with the ANC and ID. Dr Wasfie Hassiem, the AMP's leader, and Dr Gulam Sabdia, its chair, stood firmly with us. But another faction of the party had different ideas. They had written a fraudulent letter to the Independent Electoral Commission saying that Wasfie and his two colleagues had been struck off the AMP's list and would be replaced. The city manager wasted no time in declaring three vacancies. Unless we could reverse this declaration, our coalition government would fall.

I asked Brent to investigate whether the move had been procedural. (It didn't take me long to figure out that government processes are so complex that one can often find a procedural flaw if one wants to reverse a decision.) Brent returned with encouraging news. According to the IEC head office, the only member of the Africa Muslim Party authorised to submit names for the party's list was Wasfie Hassiem. The attempt to remove and replace him and his colleagues had been unlawful. Mgoqi initially refused to backtrack, saying that the vacancies had already been declared and could not be reversed. I said we would fight it in court.

In the end the IEC nullified the fraudulent attempt to oust the three AMP councillors, who were reconfirmed as duly elected. It occurred to me that I would now have to cope with conflicts, divisions and factions in our coalition parties as well as my own!

This episode also convinced me that Wallace Mgoqi would have to go. It was untenable to have a city manager who appeared to have connived with the ANC behind our backs to get rid of us. It was a simple matter to terminate his contract, as its extension, shortly before the election, had also been unlawful. The mayor had done so unilaterally, by unlawfully usurping a power of the full council.

Mgoqi challenged this in court, arguing that if his appointment had been unlawful, the election of the mayor (over which he had presided) must also have been unlawful, and therefore our government would fall. The court dismissed his argument.

But the city manager's attempt, in the first week of our term, to bring down our government was an early indication of how precarious our situation was. Throughout my term in office, when I got home, often late at night after a fraught day, one of my sons would generally greet me with the words: 'Hi Ma, are you still the mayor?' They didn't know how close to the bone that question often came.

The boys' sense of humour provided the perfect foil for the pressures of work. One Sunday morning, around mid-April 2006, I was having a cup of tea and reading the *Sunday Times*, which had a banner headline saying 'RASOOL SET TO TAKE DOWN ZILLE' (or words to that effect).

Tom walked in, half asleep. I was engrossed in the newspaper. He looked over my shoulder inquisitively. 'Look at what's happening now, Tom,' I said, referring to the headline.

'Ja, cool, Ma,' replied Tom. 'I see Snoop Dogg's coming to town. Can we get tickets?'

He was referring to another front-page article (plus full-colour picture) of a gangsta rapper from California called Snoop Dogg, whose Cape Town concert was scheduled for 1 May. It was Tom's way of telling me to get things into perspective. I laughed, folded away the paper, and we had breakfast together.

But after that first attempted 'coup', I made arrangements to appoint a lawyer in my office, one who had expertise and experience in local government, to advise me. I did not want to be caught off-guard again.

As challenging as it was to keep our coalition partners on board, it was even more complex to bind the DA's internal factions together.

Appointing DA members to the mayoral committee was a delicate and controversial balancing act, but essential to bridge the deep divisions in the DA caucus. I kept one of the ten mayco seats in reserve for the ID, but they turned it down again.

The ID's decision to side with the ANC was followed by an outcry of epic proportions from their voters, who felt betrayed. This knocked the ID hard, and several of their caucus members openly questioned whether they had made the right decision.

But we had our own problems.

The next issue that almost brought down the multi-party government was a toilet. The deputy mayor, from the ACDP, wanted a private toilet, so he instructed the staff to turn one of the offices next to his suite into a private bathroom for him. The quotes came back: installing a bathroom in a corner of the building that did not have plumbing infrastructure (on the sixth floor) would cost R1 million in alterations. I just laughed it off and assumed everyone else would too.

Then the speaker, Dirk Smit, came to my office. He was the spokesman of the multi-party forum that our coalition partners had formed to represent their collective interests in our government and prevent 'domination' by the DA. I was surprised to learn that they had spent a full meeting discussing the deputy mayor's proposed private toilet.

'This is a serious issue and you need to treat it as such,' said the speaker. 'I am not exaggerating when I tell you this could bring down the coalition.'

I thought he was joking. I called a mayco meeting and realised that he was right.

It was my first lesson in the realpolitik of coalition management. Coalitions are more vulnerable to issues of style than of substance. During the first year of our term, the size of offices, toilets, cars, drivers, protocol and overseas trips were more frequent topics of contentious debate than major policy decisions. It took a while, but we eventually all agreed that spending R1 million to construct a private bathroom was indefensible.

The coalition survived.

Of course, we also had enormous policy and administrative issues to deal with. The city's middle management had been hollowed out, ANC cadres had been deployed to many top positions, and the finances were precarious. Above all, the tender system was susceptible to serious abuse and manipulation. I was amazed to learn that the ANC had restructured the administration to make the same 'cadre' responsible for both procurement and legal compliance. This made it relatively easy to gloss over abuse of the procurement process. Unsurprisingly, the person who headed both offices was widely known as Mr Ten Per Cent. It was alleged that this was the cut he required to swing a tender in the desired direction.

After a rudimentary investigation, it was clear that his services would also have to be terminated, and some matters referred to the police for investigation (which, predictably, went nowhere).

This step also brought our coalition to the edge of the precipice. One day Dumisani Ximbi, the UDM's mayoral committee member for community safety, arrived in my office with some colleagues. He suggested that we leave 'Mr Ten Per Cent' alone. As it turned out, Mr Ten Per Cent had a brother who was a UDM councillor in another Western Cape council, Stellenbosch, where he held the balance of power in coalition with the DA. If we terminated Mr Ten Per Cent's contract, I was warned, his brother would bring down the government of our neighbouring municipality, and the UDM might be forced to withdraw from Cape Town's multi-party government as well, which would bring us down too.

Councillor Ximbi was not threatening me. On the contrary, he was trying to help me pre-empt this blackmail attempt.

I called Brent Gerber.

'We have a problem,' I said (a phrase that I was to repeat to him on innumerable occasions over the years).

Within minutes, he was in my office. He went to investigate.

It turned out that the charges against Mr Ten Per Cent were serious and I could not back down. I went to discuss the risk with the DA leadership in Stellenbosch, and they understood that I would have to stand my ground on investigating serious allegations of corruption in the administration, even if both our governments fell.

Once we had agreement on that, I could continue the investigations into Mr Ten Per Cent, who was finally dismissed on 22 January 2007. By that time we had done a lot of preparatory work and the UDM, both in Stellenbosch and Cape Town, held firm in our respective coalitions.

Our approach to dealing with the countless governance and administrative challenges would be a good subject for my next book, about how to build a 'capable state' in South Africa. This book deals with my personal and political battles to stay high enough on the greasy pole of public office to be able to play a role in building a capable state at all.

Needless to say, the coalition and its travails was a subject of intense interest to the media, with the DA getting the lion's share of the attention. Our partners in government kicked back hard against the DA's growing public profile. The UDM even wrote us an official complaint and issued a statement on the matter. I learnt that in any coalition the largest party stands to gain the most, and the smaller parties tend to appear subordinate, much to the chagrin of their leaders and voters. I made a particular point of helping our partner parties build their profiles, because this was essential to the survival of the coalition.

It wasn't long before we were facing the next move to bring down our government.

Richard Dyantyi, the ANC's provincial minister of local government, wrote a letter giving me notice that he would issue a proclamation changing the structure of Cape Town's government from a mayoral committee to an executive committee. This would reconstitute our government, marginalising our six coalition partners, and creating a new three-party executive committee in which the ANC, DA and ID would be represented in the ratio 4:4:2.

The intention was obvious – to give the ANC and ID a majority in the executive and oust me from the mayoralty. The ANC's shenanigans had unintended consequences, however. Instead of dividing us, it helped solidify our very fluid coalition. When our survival was at stake because of the ANC's dirty tricks campaign, we bonded.

Our voters also rallied behind us, and we decided to do something that would enable them to identify, publicly, with our cause.

We organised a march for 26 October 2006. We called it the 'Save Democracy in Cape Town' march, aimed at protesting against the ANC's attempts to topple our government by abusing the Municipal Structures Act. The issue dominated the news for several weeks.

But my fight with the ANC was, as usual, far easier to handle than the internal dynamics of our coalition or the battles inside the DA. As we organised the march, the DA's robust and abrasive internal culture collided with the vulnerabilities of our coalition, creating perfect conditions for spontaneous combustion.

The DA made it clear at the start that they would only contribute funding towards a DA-branded event. I explained that it would have to be a multi-party event (to cement our coalition), largely funded by the DA (because our partner parties had no money, and we could not spend city funds on a political protest). When the multi-party organising committee vetoed a DA-branded poster, the tension grew.

The temperature went up another few degrees when we discussed speakers. Because the DA had agreed to carry most of the costs, they wanted a proportional amount of speaking time. This was strongly opposed by the other parties, who argued that the purpose of the protest was to defend the multi-party coalition. In the end we agreed that everyone would get a five-minute slot, and that Tony would speak first, followed by all the other parties in alphabetical order. I, as mayor, would say a few words at the end on behalf of the multi-party government (effectively giving the DA two slots).

Security also featured strongly in our preparations. It was crucial to enable the UDM, which had registered concern about the DA's high profile in the coalition, to handle the security (which was their portfolio in the coalition government). They did not like the DA opening parallel channels with the police or second-guessing their advice.

On the day of the march, the UDM confirmed we had been given the 'all clear' from the police, despite earlier fears that the ANC was planning to disrupt our protest. Hundreds of people arrived at the starting point spontaneously, having been apprised of the march through the media, which had been dominated for weeks by the political machinations in Cape Town.

The loaded buses (paid for by the DA but used by all parties) arrived at the top of Keizersgracht. There was a festive atmosphere despite the seriousness of the issue we were facing. The minute-by-minute programme stipulated that party leaders would lead the march down Keizersgracht at 11:45 a.m.

Then suddenly, on the day of the march itself, Russell Crystal, who was in charge of the DA's events team and worked from Tony Leon's office, exploded onto the scene with all the finesse of an enraged bull elephant.

Russell is one of the few people I have encountered in my professional life with whom I have simply been unable to establish a productive working relationship. I suppose he sensed how I felt about his role as an undercover security policeman during his student years under apartheid. But I have learnt to forgive a person's past. The real reason that I could not work with him was his rare talent for turning any routine situation into a crisis, replete with exaggerated hand gestures and a steady flow of expletives.

He knew nothing about the six preparatory meetings we had held to reach consensus on the carefully crafted programme and protocols, so it wasn't too much of a surprise when, just before the march started, I received an instruction from a DA staffer (which I was told emanated from the South African Police Service via Russell) that the march was cancelled. This was news to me – and to the UDM's Bongani Maqungwana, whose role on the organising committee included police liaison.

Before long, one of Russell's staffers was walking around with a megaphone, instructing the marchers to get back onto the buses so that they could be driven to the end point and listen to the speeches without marching.

I was angry but not surprised at this unilateral brushing aside of all the preparatory work we had so carefully negotiated. What an irony it would be, I thought to myself, if the coalition collapsed over the arrangements for a march to express solidarity with the multi-party government.

I immediately convened the multi-party committee on the central island of the Keizersgracht, with people milling around, increasingly impatient to start. All the coalition partners reacted strongly against changing the arrangements. Their party leaders were already there and ready to march. Bongani Maqungwana and I spoke to the police, who said that while they could not guarantee our safety, there was no immediate threat.

After further rapid consultations with the multi-party committee, we decided to go ahead with the march, in order to reaffirm that peaceful protest is a constitutional right, not a favour granted or withdrawn at the whim of the police without good cause.

Russell was still issuing instructions from head office, so I sent a message via his staffer on the ground that we were waiting for Tony but that we would start the march without him if he took much longer. Our coalition partners said they would march anyway, even if the DA chose not to.

I did not know what was being conveyed to Tony, except that the message would be amply embellished.

When Tony still had not come almost twenty minutes after the scheduled starting time, and the marchers were growing more and more irritated by the delay, we began. We had a smooth and safe passage to the steps of the Wale Street legislature, receiving only support and encouragement from people along the way.

We were about to begin the speeches when Tony arrived, looking like thunder, having walked the short distance from parliament to Wale Street. After a brief introduction by me, Tony spoke for thirty minutes.

Overall the march was a success. At our seventh multi-party steering committee meeting the next day, to evaluate the event, there were complaints about the DA's high-handedness, but no direct threat to the coalition. The fair share of media coverage for all the leaders had stabilised rather than endangered our government.

I thought it was over, but I was naive. Russell wrote a report, full of pomposity and bluster, addressed to 'the Leader' (as most DA staffers deferentially referred to Tony). The report makes almost comical reading in retrospect:

> Firstly, please accept my most sincere apologies for the circumstances in which you found yourself during the Save Democracy in Cape Town March/Rally on Thursday 26 October 2006. I am well aware that my responsibilities in organising national events include, *inter alia*, ensuring that the status and dignity of the Party Leader is maintained and promoted at all times. During the conceptualisation and execution of hundreds of such events, I have always made absolutely sure that those events are conducted in such a way so as to prevent any external or circumstantial influences from impacting negatively on the profile of the Leader.
>
> The same applied to this event. However, while my focus was on dealing with the numerous external factors that threatened the successful implementation of this event, for the first time in the 9 years that I have done this job (including the rather difficult period when Marthinus van Schalkwyk was the Deputy Leader of the Party) I discovered that I also had to deal with an internal disregard for, and '*undermining*' of, the role of the Leader of the Party by another senior local DA leader participating in the event. I feel all the more responsible for this oversight as I should have known what was likely to transpire as in the weeks preceding the march it was clear that, despite Ryan Coetzee's unambiguous direction to all concerned (including Helen Zille) that this event was a DA-led Multi-Party March/Rally, Helen kept referring to it (both internally and to the media) as a 'City march'. For this oversight I once again most sincerely apologise.

And so the blather continued ...

Of course I sensed what was going on. Tony had by then informed his inner circle (including Russell Crystal) about his intention to step down, and it did not take long for the news to reach me.

Of all the people in the party determined to prevent me from becoming leader, Russell topped the list. He adopted a belt-and-braces approach to ensure I stood no chance. The march and its aftermath was the perfect opportunity to fuel resentment against me for having 'undermined the Leader'. This didn't bother me much, because I was coming to the conclusion that there was no way I could manage the coalition government while driving an effective turnaround strategy in Cape Town and lead the DA simultaneously.

And then I got some news that had all the elements of a major conspiracy theory, except it turned out to be true. A Senior Superintendent Stephanus Johannes Vorster, of the South African Police Service, had information that the ANC provincial government had issued a political instruction to the police to derail the march. Furthermore, a Superintendent Botha had apparently received orders from one of his seniors, Director Peter Jacobs (a former Umkhonto we Sizwe operative) to find a reason to arrest me. When asked afterwards why he had not arrested me, Superintendent Botha replied that he could find no legal reason to.

This story seemed bizarre, but, because the march had gone ahead and I was not arrested, I ignored it. A year later, when I was arrested by Police Director Jeremy Vearey, another former MK operative, during a march in Mitchells Plain, Senior Superintendent Vorster came forward again, and was prepared to make a sworn affidavit which assisted me in getting a settlement from the police for unlawful arrest.

A senior ANC politician also confirmed Vorster's story. Requesting anonymity, he informed me that I had been arrested on the instruction of the former provincial MEC of community safety, Leonard Ramatlakane. The ANC then turned on Ramatlakane because the strategy had backfired so badly, resulting in enormous publicity for me and growing support for the DA. But that is a story for another chapter.

Looking back, the information that slowly emerged between the two marches gave me a different perspective on the events of 26 October 2006 at the Save Democracy in Cape Town march. I understood the police's behaviour – and other developments – in retrospect. The police had been trying to create a situation where they could prevent the march from proceeding, and then be able to say I had failed to obey the legitimate instructions of a police officer. Russell, wittingly or unwittingly, had played along with them. I was not in the least bit surprised.

In comparison to these machinations, resolving the attempted coup in Cape Town proved altogether easier and more pleasant, thanks to my repeated interactions with the courteous and soft-spoken national minister of local government, Sydney Mufamadi. I held a meeting with him and he agreed that it would be unconstitutional for the province unilaterally to alter the system of governance in the city. He arranged a meeting between Richard Dyantyi, the MEC for local government, and myself. The result was that the province agreed to back off, with Mufamadi's encouragement. As a face-saver, we were asked to create two additional sub-council positions, pulling together wards that would have an ANC majority in them, so that the ANC could at least fill the positions of two sub-council chairs.

I discussed it with my colleagues, who agreed it was a relatively small price to pay for greater stability in our fragile government, and we said yes. We had survived again.

On the other side, the manoeuvres inside the DA continued unabated. And they were coming to a head.

A month earlier, just as we started planning our multi-party march, Tony Leon had appointed Athol Trollip to head up an internal commission of inquiry to investigate and make recommendations on how to resolve the DA's internal conflicts in the Western Cape.

My question was, why now? The DA in the province had been deeply divided for years and we were, at last, making good progress to resolve the problems. Relationships were better than they had ever been. Since becoming the mayor, I had worked hard to defuse people's unfounded fears that had been deliberately fuelled for factional purposes. Of course I knew the answer to this question about the commission's timing. Those of Tony's confidants who were officially in the loop of his 'step-down' plans knew that his two most likely successors were Athol Trollip and me. I found it impossible to explain as a mere coincidence the appointment of one of the front-runners to investigate another. A bigger conflict of interests would be hard to imagine in politics.

Several other parliamentarians interpreted the appointment of the commission in the same way. An MP who was also a member of the Trollip Commission contacted me and asked if I was aware of what was actually going on. Perfectly, I replied.

I was called to appear before the commission on 26 October – the very afternoon of the city's Pro-Democracy march.

During the long preceding week of meetings with Minister Mufamadi to forestall the Cape Town coup, I also spent a lot of time preparing my twenty-two-page submission for the Trollip Commission. I knew the commission would compile a report that would be presented to the Federal Executive and Federal Council, the party's highest decision-making structures. I needed to present my case with absolute clarity so that I would not leave an undefended gap that would enable my opponents to reinforce the myth that I was a divisive influence.

When I arrived at the Marks Building in the parliamentary complex to appear before the commission, Russell was still fulminating in Tony's office suite. I could hear him raging down the passage. The air positively bristled with indignation at my insubordination towards The Leader during that morning's march. I faced the panel in a frosty atmosphere.

Following three days of hearings, Athol produced a balanced report, 'on-the-one-hand-on-the-other-hand', which (in my view) did not penetrate to the heart of the issues we needed to address in the province.

Inevitably (and without an ulterior motive on Athol's part), the mere existence of the commission was used to drive the line that I was dividing the party in the Western Cape. This was ironic indeed, given my role in holding together the multi-party coalition, and the repeated compromises I had to make to bridge the divide in the DA's own fractured provincial structures.

Then something happened, the significance of which I did not understand until later.

Troye Lund, a journalist from *Finweek*, called Robert MacDonald, my spokesman, to request an interview with me. There was nothing unusual about this. The story of the election, our unlikely coalition, and our battle to remain in government dominated the news during 2006, to the extent that the National Press Club named me 'Newsmaker of the Year' for 2006/7. At that time, I was doing up to five media interviews a week.

Robert organised a time for the interview and I arrived at the appointed place with unwashed hair and in no state to be photographed for the magazine's cover, which I discovered was the intention. A waiting stylist did her best (in the absence of hair-washing facilities) to fix my hair and make-up. Even after the interview ended, I was unaware of their intention of running a cover story with the headline: 'Move over Tony. Why Zille would make a better leader of the Opposition'.

The article had been prompted by what it described as 'corridor talk' about succession in the DA ranks in parliament. Troye had been assigned to the story and had interviewed both me and Ryan Coetzee (and others who chose to remain anonymous). Tony Leon was approached but was unavailable for comment.

I did not pick up any indication of the article's angle in Troye's interview with me, except the routine question that inevitably came up everywhere: Was I thinking of running for the leadership of the DA when Tony stepped down?

My reply was: 'I am concentrating on being mayor of Cape Town.'

The article speculated that I would not run. 'Knowing how she throws herself into projects until she sees them through, speculation is that she would not make herself available for such a position until she'd achieved what she'd set out to in her Mayoral role.'

That pretty much summed up my own position.

The magazine was due to hit the streets on Monday 27 November 2006.

I was scheduled to leave Cape Town for Johannesburg in the late afternoon of Friday 24 November, and then travel to Mogale City, where I was to speak at a fundraising dinner on the same platform as Tony. As I was preparing to leave for the airport, I had a call from a colleague saying Tony had been informed that *Finweek* would be running a story suggesting I should succeed him as leader, and that he suspected me of planting the story.

I was dumbfounded. There was enough tension between me and Tony without the added suspicion that I was behind an attempt to undermine him in order to boost myself in the media.

The flight up to Johannesburg, in the middle seat of a row of three on a budget airline, was the worst of my life. My stomach churned. The air-vent above my seat was broken and it was steaming hot. The baby next to me screamed the whole way. I had to use the time to write a speech in Afrikaans to motivate people to donate to the DA. And I had no illusions about what sort of reception awaited me at the other end.

As soon as I walked into the venue, the atmospherics overcame me. I escaped to the toilet. Anchen Dreyer, a close colleague and the constituency head, followed me, trying to establish what was going on. I told her about the bomb that I suspected was about to explode, and she urged me to calm down, come out and speak to Tony. Russell was stalking up and down like a wounded tiger waiting to pounce. Tony glared at me in a way that told me he was not going to engage in pleasantries.

What Tony did not know was that I had, since mid-2005, been apprised of his vacillating intentions to step down. But I had no prior knowledge about *Finweek*'s intention to write an article promoting me as the next leader of the DA. I would have had no interest in such an article, anyway, given the fact that I had no intention, at that stage, of running for the leadership. And given the fact that our relationship was at an all-time low, there was no way I would have deliberately sought to exacerbate the situation, especially as there was absolutely no point in doing so.

It was obvious Tony did not believe me. I can't really recall how I made it through my speech or the rest of the agonising evening, my stomach in a knot over an article I had not yet seen.

That weekend Tony announced his intention to step down, convinced that I had deliberately driven him into a corner. He was wrong, but I could understand why he thought differently. Certainly, had I not been the mayor facing such complex circumstances, I would have been strategising to oust him, because I believed this was in the interests of the party.

The year limped to an injured close. The DA was gearing up for a succession battle and no one yet knew who the candidates would be. Several people asked me to make myself available, but I said no. Although by then Some Day had disbanded, I called them together again to seek their advice. They were divided. Some believed I should run; others warned that it would be disastrous to try to do both jobs. As for myself, I was too exhausted to think straight. Johann urged me to take a complete break and come back rested in the new year.

'If you can avoid it,' he advised, 'don't make a life-changing decision when you are at a low point.'

So I postponed thinking about it.

We spent Christmas at home, and in January 2007 set off to spend time at our shared holiday cottage on the Keurbooms River. The boys always took bets with each other about how long I would remain on holiday before going back to work. 'I'm staying till the day before school starts on 17 January,' I insisted. Famous last words.

We had been at Keurbooms a few days when we heard Athol Trollip announcing his candidature on the radio. He gave an excellent interview, and I concluded that he would be an outstanding candidate for the leadership. Any residual desire to take up the challenge was draining away. This feeling was reinforced just two hours later, when Brent Gerber called me.

'Get back to Cape Town immediately,' he said. 'Your government is about to fall.'

12

'We Can, We Must, and We Will'

IN POLITICS, FRIENDS come and go, but enemies accumulate. This old aphorism is part of every politician's experience.

Making enemies in politics is unavoidable and inevitable. It is also necessary. Every time you take a decision, someone somewhere dislikes it. They then tend to gravitate towards others who disliked your previous decisions, and together they build what former president Thabo Mbeki famously described as a 'coalition of the aggrieved'.

After a mere nine months in the mayor's office, my enemies were accumulating fast.

Top of the list was a stocky, larger-than-life character named Badih Chaaban.

When I get around to writing my political soapie, I am going to have to dilute Badih's attributes, because depicting him as he is in real life would be literally unbelievable. Badih looked and spoke like someone auditioning for the lead role in a Mafia movie. His trademark duckbill cap disguised his receding hairline. His greying three-day stubble had the opposite effect on his jowls, which curved like parentheses below a jutting lower lip. He often enhanced his look with accessories, such as a cigar drooping from the corner of his mouth, and a gorgeous blonde from his arm. I learnt her name was Diana. She was in her early twenties, about the same age as Badih's daughter, Lee. Diana had married the rough-talking Lebanese immigrant after a whirlwind courtship of three months. She spoke only Russian, and I shuddered to speculate what circumstances had brought her from a village somewhere in the former Soviet Union to seek a better life in Cape Town, where she ended up with Badih Chaaban.

Badih (pronounced Buddy rather than the more appropriate Baddy) was the major funding conduit for the Africa Muslim Party, channelling money from dubious sources. He described himself as Muslim, but was also a self-confessed compulsive gambler and heavy drinker, who boasted about his links with the Cape Town underworld's most notorious figures. His favourite recreational activity, outside of strip clubs and gambling dens, was smoking a strong form of dagga called hydroponics. He considered a sentence incomplete without at least one expletive.

Under the ANC's tenure in the city Badih had accumulated some prime property leases, allegedly through his dealings with Mr Ten Per Cent, but he fell out with the administration when the flow dried up. The tap was turned off after the National Intelligence Agency wrote to the ANC-governed council in 2004, urging them to stop awarding Chaaban tenders. According to the NIA's letter, widely quoted in the media when it surfaced early in 2008, Mr Mfundo Majozi, the then acting head of the NIA in the Western Cape, had warned the ANC-led city administration as early as December 2004 that 'Chaaban ... is involved in a wide range of organised crime activities, including dealing in false passports, the drug trade, money laundering, prostitution, human trafficking and murder'.

Mr Majozi's letter also revealed key details of how Chaaban operated, allegedly using his cousins, Michael and Omar Mouneimne, as 'front men' to tender for other parking areas.

'It is recommended that counter measures should be taken to prevent Chaaban from getting more tenders,' Majozi was quoted as saying by the Independent Group on 7 February 2008. I quoted directly from this letter in a legal communication with Premier Rasool, also dated 7 February 2008, making the case for why the city had considered it essential to investigate Chaaban.

On the same day, Professor Pierre de Vos, in his blog *Constitutionally Speaking*, echoed my thoughts exactly when he wrote:

'Now, I wonder how can it be possible for any politician to survive such allegations and even head a political party without being hounded out of office by his colleagues. More importantly, I wonder whether the police have investigated these claims at all and if not why not. Moreover, if they had investigated it or would investigate it, would they actually have the skills and capacity to unravel the very strange world of Mr Chabaan [sic] to determine whether he is guilty of any of these crimes or not?'

Chaaban, full of his normal bluster, denied everything and threatened to sue the NIA for 'fabricating' this information, but he never did so. Beyond his braggadocio, his inaction spoke even louder than the NIA's words.

Neither I nor the DA (with one key exception) knew anything about Chaaban's background when we sealed the coalition deal that included the AMP. At that stage he was not even on the AMP's election list, so there was no reason to undertake a 'due diligence' investigation into him. He worked behind the scenes. His aim, which gradually revealed itself, was to control the city's substantial property holdings and the tendering system for the 2010 World Cup. He was not working alone, but on behalf of his underground network. Their plan unfolded in stages. With help from the ANC (and a key figure in the DA) he came within a whisker of succeeding.

Badih's opportunity came when the AMP won the balance of power in the 2006 election. As the AMP's major funding conduit, Badih first tried using his leverage to influence property leases under the control of the Department of Economic and Social Development. He thought he could achieve his aims without breaking cover, because he held the AMP's purse strings. When he failed, and his funders started getting irritated by the lack of results, Badih forced his way onto the AMP's list by engineering the resignation of an incumbent AMP councillor and insisting on filling her place. Now, he thought, he could exercise more direct influence.

When the news broke that the AMP was changing its list to bring in Badih Chaaban, Theodore Yach, a socially conscious businessman and leading light behind the City Improvement District concept, which transformed the centre of Cape Town into the safe, clean place it is today, came to see me. So did Derrick Bock, its chief operations officer.

'Are you crazy?' they said. They strongly advised against Chaaban becoming a councillor because of what they believed to be his involvement in criminal activities.

I went to speak to Wasfie Hassiem, the AMP leader, and told him what I had heard about Badih. Wasfie already knew. His problem was that Badih was a major funding source for the party and therefore called the shots. I was in no position to influence the composition of the AMP's list.

Within days of Badih's arrival he was trying to exercise undue influence on the city's property department. Wasfie, as the executive councillor responsible for economic and social development, summoned the director of property management to his office, where he introduced her to Badih and another business colleague involved in parking contracts in the city. Badih advised her that he was interested in extending their business and wanted a full list of the city's properties.

The young director returned to her office in a state of shock, determined to muster support from her executive director, Mansoor Mohamed, and the city manager, Achmat Ebrahim. They told her they would back her. She returned to Wasfie to say that what Badih was asking for was illegal. Backed by her superiors, she stuck to her guns: no deal could be done without going through a legally compliant tender.

Ian Neilson, the mayoral committee member for finance, also moved quickly to put in place a transparent and accountable tendering system that made manipulation almost impossible.

Badih was not accustomed to these kinds of obstacles. He had to hatch a new plan. He needed more power. He was soon angling to become deputy mayor, displacing the ACDP from the position. He went about it strategically. He approached me at a function, full of schmooze and smooth talk about the difficulties the coalition was facing as a result of my opposition to building the new Cape Town Stadium in Green Point (I wanted to extend and refurbish Newlands Stadium instead, at a much lower cost).

Badih said my position was causing a backlash among voters, who interpreted my stance as hostility to the World Cup and racism (of course). He proposed to help me and the coalition partners out of this tricky situation. His solution was that I should delegate the World Cup to the deputy mayor and give him the job, replacing the ACDP. He said it in a jovial way, which gave me the opportunity to treat it as a joke, but I knew that he was flying a kite – and I made sure he knew his offer had sunk like a stone.

Within days he was negotiating with the ANC, supporting their final push to take over the city. They waited until I was taking a break to make their move. On a relaxed day in Keurbooms, I received the call to return to Cape Town urgently.

I was in my office early next morning, where I phoned Wasfie Hassiem and said we needed to talk. He came quickly, and did not dissemble. He conceded that the AMP was in negotiations with the ANC, but there was nothing he could do about it. He was trapped. I felt bad for him because I knew he wanted to remain part of our coalition, but he could not rein in the out-of-control Badih. I had no alternative other than to 'relieve the AMP of its role in our coalition government', as the political cliché has it.

Our coalition now had fewer than 50 per cent of the council seats (103) while the ANC, ID and AMP together had 106 seats. The government had fallen, and we prepared to leave office.

There was still time, however, to try Plan B. In a last-minute bid to save the coalition, I convened a meeting of our remaining five partners.

The Independent Democrats, I said, had suffered a sharp decline in support following their strategic misjudgement to back the ANC's NomaIndia Mfeketo for mayor. They needed to salvage the situation, which meant they might now be amenable to an offer to join our coalition. The meeting mandated the speaker, Dirk Smit, and me to approach Patricia de Lille and offer her another opportunity to join us. If she agreed, we could reconstitute the coalition with a comfortable majority.

Our coalition partners had one reservation. They were worried about their own positions, because the ID/DA could constitute a majority coalition without them. The smaller partners would become superfluous. I gave them my word that, if they continued to support our policy direction, we would keep them in the coalition, because they had supported us at a time when we needed them. We would not drop them now. However, I gave no guarantees about which specific positions they would fill. I had to retain the freedom to reshuffle the mayoral committee if I needed to. They accepted this.

Dirk and I met Patricia and her right-hand man, Simon Grindrod, at the Westin Grand Hotel on 17 January 2007, where we sat in the corner of a semi-lit large dining area, during the lull between the breakfast and lunch rush. It was an unlikely public space to have such an important discussion, but we did the deal within minutes. I got the impression that Patricia was relieved to have a way out of the cul-de-sac she was in. She was friendly and warm.

The ACDP had agreed to step down from the deputy mayoralty in return for a position on the mayoral committee and another sub-council chair. The ID would get the deputy mayor and a mayco position. They also wanted the important economic and social development portfolio and I agreed to Simon Grindrod taking the portfolio. The ID's Charlotte Williams, nicknamed Pocahontas because her pretty features and flowing locks resembled the cartoon depiction of the legendary Native American, became the deputy mayor.

Apart from salvaging the ID's support base, the reconstituted coalition also had enormous advantages for the DA. We could no longer be held to ransom by each one of five tiny parties if they did not get their way. The coalition was now as stable as it was possible for a coalition in our circumstances to be. In retrospect, Badih had done us a favour – but only after bringing us to the brink of collapse, and Cape Town to the edge of disaster. If Badih's plan to become deputy mayor with responsibility for the World Cup had succeeded, my fear was that the City of Cape Town's tendering system would have turned into an extension of Cape Town's underworld, overnight.

Instead, the city now had a stable coalition government, with partners committed to governing well. I am always amazed at how short the distance is between such divergent outcomes in politics.

Badih was down but not out. This was a setback for his ambitions, but not a final defeat.

My personal situation, on the other hand, had changed substantially.

John Steenhuisen, an instinctive politician and the DA's young, energetic, razor-sharp KwaZulu-Natal leader, recognised immediately how the political terrain had shifted. He gave me a call. Given the change in the coalition's circumstances, would I now consider running for party leader, he asked. Sensing my hesitation, he invited me to come to the province to talk to some of his colleagues before I took the final decision.

On 2 February 2007 I flew to Durban, my mental decision-making dial pointing towards red. John remembers me pitching up in a City of Cape Town tracksuit, which was hardly a strategic move if I intended winning hearts and minds in KwaZulu-Natal. This didn't occur to me at the time. I wanted to be comfortable.

After two standing-room-only meetings in Durban and Pietermaritzburg, and a lovely supper at the Steenhuisens, my dial was turning in the direction of green.

When I got back to Cape Town, I called my long-time friend, Ian Davidson, the DA's Gauteng leader, with whom I had worked closely in politics since our student days. He was level-headed and direct, with clout in the party. I asked for his opinion because I knew he would give it to me honestly. 'Of course you should run,' he said.

We had had three weeks of unprecedented calm in Cape Town's coalition government, and I started to think it might just be possible.

I consulted each of my close colleagues, including the Some Day group, individually. They encouraged me strongly. My growing core of allies in the Western Cape did the same.

With my dial turning solid green, I kept Johann in the loop.

'I think you should first work out how it will be possible to combine these roles,' Johann said. 'I can do what it takes to support you on the family front, but I cannot say more until I understand properly what the two other roles entail and whether it is possible to combine them.'

We decided to have a discussion with two men involved in the other spheres of my life – the city government and the DA – to analyse whether and how the roles could be combined.

Thus it was that Brent Gerber and Ryan Coetzee accompanied Johann and me to a pizzeria in Newlands to have one of the most important discussions of my professional life. Ryan was the DA's chief executive officer. I did not know whether he would support my candidacy, as he was very close to Tony, but I valued his straight-talking style. I knew that, even if he opposed me, he would tell me truthfully whether the roles could be combined and if so, how.

Brent, who by this time was a director in the mayor's office, was an excellent systems thinker and I knew that if it was possible to design a management system to combine both roles, he would do it. I wanted Johann and I to make a final decision with the full facts on the table.

I started with Ryan. He said it was doable, depending on how we structured it. Doing both jobs would require a sound relationship with the parliamentary caucus leader, excellent interactive communication with head office and provincial leaders, attending caucus meetings and other leadership meetings, lots of delegation, and devoting my weekends to travelling around the country from province to province, to attend DA events. I would also have to devote a lot of time to fundraising.

Brent had arrived with a proposed organogram, office structure and time analysis, gleaned from my diary. He concluded that I was spending too much time in one-on-one meetings on operational matters and produced a list of issues he said I could delegate. He had also devised a rudimentary dashboard system, which he said would enable me to keep my finger on the pulse of all the city's projects at the click of a mouse. He had designed an interactive office model, which would enable me to have a DA office alongside the mayoral office, in a system that ensured that the city would carry no DA costs. The DA would rent the office, cover the costs of infrastructure, and pay vehicle mileage spent on DA business. He had worked out a simple system to manage that, too.

That night, over a glass of wine, Johann and I discussed the pros and cons. It would take a heavy toll on the family but Johann said he was up for it. That night we decided: Yes, I should run.

On 1 March, exactly a year after the local election, my friend and colleague, the DA's chairman Wetshotsile 'Joe' Seremane, announced he would also throw his hat into the ring to succeed Tony as DA leader. I phoned to congratulate him.

On 15 March 2007 – a year to the day after being elected mayor of Cape Town – I announced my candidacy. Athol had a two-month campaigning head start, and Joe two weeks. The race was on.

Outwardly, Tony maintained his neutrality, but his confidants and allies did the legwork.

Publicly, it was the retired academic Bill Johnson who proclaimed to anyone who would listen that it would be impossible for me to do both jobs simultaneously. The chatterati largely agreed with him. On the night of 16 March, Bill and I had a brief conversation about it. I wrote to him the next day, setting out some of the background systems we had devised to enable me to do both jobs.

He wrote back:

> Really, I can say what I think in a few very simple statements. I thought and still think you'd make the best DA leader. And I don't think, either in principle or in practice, that this job should be combined with that of executive mayor.
>
> If you think of it, there has to be a reason why no one in South African history (or British or American history) has ever attempted what you're thinking of attempting. One has to respect that history. Also, Tony has, for all his faults, been an exceptional leader who took a small shattered party and built it into the main Opposition. It will be a hard act to follow and one can predict that even if you gave the leadership your full-time best there would be times – lulls, down-periods, whatever – when people would start making that comparison.

Bill (correctly) predicted that the attempts to destabilise our government would continue, while the job of DA leader would be much more demanding than I anticipated. 'You can guarantee that moaning about the trouble starting with Zille having two jobs will start right away and just go on and on.'

He was right about that too, because he initiated much of the moaning, and kept it going for years, as he searched for evidence that he had been right, and I had been wrong.

As the 2007 leadership election approached, James Selfe, the chairman of the Federal Executive, did Tony's legwork inside the party, mobilising support for Athol and liaising closely with Theuns Botha, who continued the NNP cabal's scare tactics by threatening to leave the party with his supporters if I became the leader. Tony was, understandably, desperate to avoid the party's disintegration, which threatened to cost us the City of Cape Town for a second time. The party would not survive that. I, on the other hand, had long experience of the cabal's capacity for panic-mongering, and I did not anticipate any of their horror scenarios eventuating. Looking back, I realise I underestimated their threats. They were not as empty as I assumed.

Their strategy first surfaced in a letter that appeared in *Die Burger* describing my candidacy as a threat to the future of Afrikaners.

I shrugged it off as just another 'attack letter', to which I had become accustomed, but an Afrikaans MP, Willem Doman, called to warn me that this was the start of an orchestrated campaign. He advised me to be wary because it was more serious than I imagined. I did not realise how big the iceberg was beneath that tiny tip until much later (after I had become premier of the Western Cape and long after the cabal had disintegrated).

The extent of the threat was contained in a dossier leaked by a former cabal member seeking revenge on Theuns Botha, who was by then the DA's Western Cape leader and provincial minister of health. His former colleague was languishing in the political wilderness, consumed by jealousy. He wanted to create a context in which I would 'relieve Theuns of his position' in the provincial government. So he sent me documents that revealed the extent to which Theuns had been involved in a plot to thwart my leadership campaign, and to destroy the DA if I won.

When I read the dossier I concluded that Tony's fears of this happening were well founded, and not as exaggerated as I had assumed.

The leaked dossier contains a series of letters between Theuns Botha, the DA's Western Cape leader, and Dan Roodt, the right-wing founder of the Pro-Afrikaans Action Group (PRAAG). The dossier also includes instructions from Theuns written to his network inside the DA.

The letters set out an action strategy to prevent me from becoming DA leader; and in the event that I did, to destroy the DA as a result. This would require breaking away from the DA and starting a new party, modelled on an unreconstructed racial nationalist view of political organisation in South Africa. The new party (tentatively referred to, in one letter, as the Republican Party) aimed to bring together Afrikaans-speakers (both coloured and white) with Zulu-speakers, led by Jacob Zuma, who had been fired as deputy president and was in the political wilderness (temporarily, as it turned out).

A coalition between Afrikaans-speakers of all races would destroy the DA in the Western Cape, the argument went. And if this new party brought together

Afrikaans-speakers across South Africa and sought common cause with a Zulu-based party, led by Jacob Zuma, they would be able to engineer a change of government nationally. This seems bizarre, until one realises how far the planning went.

According to Roodt, a preparatory meeting had already been held with Jacob Zuma as a prelude to this development.

James Selfe did not know about this background. He was only aware of Theuns's threat to leave the DA if I became leader. James was keeping close contact with Theuns, at Tony's request, to prevent this eventuality. None of us, except those in the cabal's tight circle, knew about the plan, which would proceed in three phases: Plan A, and two fall-back positions, if required.

The letters show that, initially at least, Theuns was confident that he could prevent me from becoming leader, in one of two easy steps, which he describes as follows:

- Force [Zille] to withdraw her candidacy through a public intimidation campaign and the associated risk.
- Ensure that she loses at the congress by making the party so frightened of the consequences that they do not vote for her (the DA across the whole country survives on the success of the Western Cape). [Direct translation from the Afrikaans.]

Theuns spells out Plan A: Use public debates between the DA leadership candidates to trip me up and generate intense media controversies aimed at alienating the DA's Afrikaner support base. This would lead the party to conclude that the risk of electing me would be too great.

However, bemoaned Theuns, this plan could no longer go ahead because of a decision, taken at a Federal Executive meeting in Durban, that candidates would only address internal DA meetings. This meant that the campaign would not be driven in the public arena. According to Theuns, most of the DA's leadership believed that an open, public process would benefit me because of my media profile. Only Tony had backed Theuns's position in support of public forums 'but his influence is on the wane – he hates Helen Zille,' the letter stated. Theuns concluded they would have to move to Plan B, to 'unmask Helen Zille for who she really is'.

They would now have to use other strategies to cause as much media controversy as possible about the threat my leadership would allegedly pose to Afrikaners. They would start the campaign online, and generate sufficient outrage for the print media to give the story legs.

As a basis for this vilification strategy, Theuns authored a document about me, to provide guidelines for those participating in the campaign.

This profile describes me as a micro-managing control freak – 'Autocratic, domineering, manipulating (German, but not actually Nazi)'.

Other bullet points read:

- [She] was an activist in the hated Black Sash
- Was an activist who accommodated ANC terrorists in safe houses
- Was the cause of Tony Leon's resignation as party leader – stabbed him in the back (a looooong story for another day)
- Was an activist in the former UDF – an ANC front organisation
- She baffles with bullshit. Die meeste mense word deur haar gemesmeraais (most people are mesmerised by her)
- Amongst those who know her she is someone who can lie without blushing
- Agterbaks (Luisgat – geen beter Afrikaanse woord nie) [I searched in vain for a translation of *luisgat*, but it does not exist. The literal translation is louse-arse.]
- Married (as a spinster) to an Anglicised Afrikaner. He WAS Afrikaans but is now a raped Afrikaner as in 'very British Boer'.

And on and on it went.

This formed the background briefing document for the controversy-generation campaign, which I have learnt over the years is standard stuff in internal party contestation.

To set the ball rolling, Dan Roodt wrote Theuns an email dated 28 March 2007, alerting him to an attack piece he had written and placed on his organisation's website, to generate public controversy. And he made this request of Theuns: 'Can you please encourage your people to use pseudonyms or whatever and write letters and articles and we will place them?'

Referring to Theuns's pejorative character sketch of me, he offered, 'I can also conduct an anonymous interview with you or distil the opinions that you expressed in your last letter. Let me know what you prefer.'

Roodt also reported positively on a meeting with Jacob Zuma: 'Our discussion with Zuma was very successful. I think he is increasingly marginalised within the ANC itself, because he came alone without any supporters or advisers except Liesl Goettert who is an Afrikaner.

'If we can establish a new Afrikaner and brown [coloured] centric party, and Zuma breaks away from the ANC to look for Zulu support, the two parties (Afrikaners/coloureds and Zulus) [can] govern the country, because they have the numbers…' The letter concluded: 'Come, let's see if we can unleash a bit of a storm on the internet, as we have discussed previously.'

Just over an hour later Theuns forwarded Roodt's letter to Leon van Rensburg,

Erik Marais, Kent Morkel, Kobus Brynard and Kobus Marais. The latter was not part of the cabal, but was a close confidant of Theuns.

Theuns's accompanying message read: 'Manne, die bal is aan die rol. Sorg dat julle aanboord kom en dadelik deelneem. Maak net 100% seker dat julle anoniem is. Dankie Theuns.' (Guys, the ball is rolling. Make sure you come on board and participate immediately. Just make 100% sure that you remain anonymous. Thanks, Theuns.)

When I received the dossier of correspondence, many years later, I took it home and showed it to Johann, who roared with laughter. 'Manne, die bal is aan die rol!' he bellowed, between guffaws, until the tears of laughter rolled too. To this day, in the Maree Zille household, whenever Johann wants us to get going, he announces, in the same tone of voice: 'Manne, die bal is aan die rol.' And then, as befits a 'very British Boer', he mistranslates it into English – 'Guys, the balls are rolling' – and we laugh again.

But the cabal was deadly serious. If this vilification campaign did not get enough traction to stop my election, they would move to their final fallback.

This involved Theuns leading a walkout of the DA with white and coloured Afrikaans-speakers, during the floor-crossing scheduled for September 2007. The plan was to team up with smaller parties such as the Independent Democrats and the Independent Civic Organisation of South Africa (ICOSA). Roodt's task was to prepare for a form of co-operation with a strong Zulu-based party, through forging links with Jacob Zuma.

After I received the dossier, all those years later, I resolved to speak to Theuns about it. I raised the issue in a relaxed, unthreatening context. The relationship between us had, by that time, become cordial and professional and he was doing a good job in his portfolio. I did not tell him that I had only just received the documents. He assumed I had had them for a long time. My body language and tone reflected the fact that I was interested in the background, rather than angry. Theuns made light of it, too, saying it was deep history, and that people's fears had been genuine. He said it was big of me to appoint him to the key health portfolio in the cabinet despite our past history of conflict. At no stage did he deny the authenticity of the documents, some of which had originated from his personal email address. We agreed to draw a line under it.

Oblivious to what was unfolding behind the scenes, as far as I was concerned the leadership campaign in 2007 went well, and was conducted in a cordial spirit between Joe, Athol and me. We all spent some money, but nothing like the amounts that are spent on internal campaigns today, and we kept the contest largely in-house, following the Fedex decision. We travelled across the country, addressing DA congress delegates to promote our candidacies. The debate around me hinged on whether it was possible to combine the roles of leader and mayor.

The word went around that Tony had addressed 500 events across South Africa during 2006, and spent 70 per cent of his time fundraising. I said, quite honestly, that I could not manage that time allocation, but that I doubted those figures were correct (unless meetings included Tony's parliamentary appearances), since there were only 365 days in a year.

Sporadic attack letters appeared, but the strategy to trumpet the threat my candidacy allegedly posed to Afrikaners never made a major impact. It simply lacked credibility. Most people realised it was entirely opportunistic. The strongest case against me was the difficulty of doing justice to both jobs, something I too was worried about. I said we could turn my dual role into a positive for the party, because inevitably, I would have to delegate a lot, foregrounding other faces and voices. This could have the beneficial effect of profiling the DA's growing diversity.

As the campaign progressed, I sensed increasingly that Ryan had broken ranks with Tony's inner circle and was going to support me for the leadership. We had developed a strong, forthright relationship which I valued.

I had a team of excellent canvassers countrywide and they sent me regular results of their canvassing. John Steenhuisen came up with the idea for a bumper-sticker – 'KwaZille Natal' – which injected humour into the campaign. Ian Davidson, in his methodical manner, managed the Gauteng campaign, and incorporated the surrounding provinces in a comprehensive phone canvass. I was particularly touched by the efforts made by Rene Kitshoff to mobilise support for me, in hostile territory in the West Region of the Western Cape. She succeeded beyond my expectations, and canvassed every congress delegate individually. I also had a core of support in the Eastern Cape led by two prominent figures in opposing DA factions, Eddie Trent and Tertius Delport. And in the Western Cape, Marius Swart and Pierre Rabie, previously closely associated with Theuns Botha, gave me their support.

When 6 May 2007 dawned, I was pretty confident of victory.

I had stayed over the previous night in my mother's cottage in Emmarentia in Johannesburg. I hardly slept thinking of what the future would hold, and wondering whether I would manage the two enormous jobs. Probably from sheer exhaustion, I developed a painful eye infection. My sister-in-law, Isabel, a medical doctor, prescribed antibiotic eye-drops to contain it. My hair had been cut short and I could not manage it. When I arrived at the venue my supporters dragged me to the bathroom and tried to improve my look. My right eye was still red, rheumy and sore, and visibly shrunken in comparison to the other one.

Johann required no prompting to fly up to Midrand. He wanted to be there. Carla took Mom to the conference centre. Mom had never heard me speak in public before. That made me nervous.

But just before balloting started, another campaign bomb exploded. Afrikaans delegates received an SMS, that purported to come from a friend of mine, Councillor Pat Hill, warning that a victory for Zille would be a 'nail in the coffin of the Afrikaner'. The message caused a stir. Pat was one of my allies and, the argument went, if he had broken ranks with me to warn delegates of the consequences of my leadership, then there must be something to worry about. The voting delegates were abuzz with the news.

Pat, who was not a delegate to congress, flatly denied having sent it, and I knew he was telling the truth. It was just another dirty trick, although I did not understand how they had hacked Pat's cellphone. One of my first requests, after I had been elected leader, was for the party to undertake a forensic investigation into the origin of the fake SMS. It proved impossible to track down. I do not know whether this final fraudulent attempt to derail my election changed anyone's voting intentions. I still won comfortably, securing 72 per cent of the vote against Athol's 22 per cent and Joe's 6 per cent.

Both my opponents were gracious in defeat, and congratulated me warmly. From that day onwards, throughout my leadership, I only received support from both Athol and Joe, even in the most trying circumstances.

I could see that Tony was less than ecstatic with the result, but he also congratulated me sincerely, despite his understandable concern about what would happen next, given that threats of a mass walkout still hung heavy in the air.

Joel Pollak, Tony's speechwriter, with whom I had also developed a rapport, had written me a powerful acceptance speech, in which I praised Tony's immense contribution to democracy – a tribute I genuinely meant. He was a great leader, ideal for that time, place and role. I now had the terrifying responsibility of leading the party on its next mile. I knew that if the DA did not succeed, South Africa's democracy would fail.

The speech ended with seven words which subsequently became my informal personal slogan: 'We can, we must, and we will'. There was a lot of cheering in the hall from my supporters, but the celebration was by no means universal.

Johann joined me and Tony on stage for the victory photos. I then linked up with Carla and Mom, gravitating towards family as I tend to do on occasions of great significance. Mom was sitting on a chair, clearly overwhelmed. Carla told me Mom had gone missing during my speech and was eventually tracked down crying in the bathroom. She was overcome by emotion, she said.

I made the mistake of thinking that once the madness of the campaign was over, things would revert to 'normal' (whatever that was in my life), but the pressure was only just starting. The next weeks passed in a blur, from one media interview to the other. I dropped into bed exhausted every night. I woke up each morning, looked at the diary, and got onto the treadmill again. I didn't dare look at my diary the night before. If I did, I couldn't sleep.

I woke up one morning to find that my media spokesman, Robert MacDonald, had scheduled an interview with BBC's HARDtalk, a programme famous for presenting the world's toughest interview. There it was, a HARDtalk interview slot, tightly squeezed between a host of other appointments. There was no time to prepare and no place to hide. Stephen Sackur pummelled me, but I fought back. I was especially delighted when the BBC named my interview among their 'Best of 2007'. That is one of the accolades that has meant most to me in my political career.

There was only one journalist who gave me a tougher time, and that was years later when my son Thomas was a financial reporter for CNBC Africa. He made sure no one would ever accuse him of asking me 'sweetheart questions'. I still wake up sweating at night when I remember the interview he did with me thirty-six hours after a quarterly labour force survey had been released (which I hadn't read yet). I had to tread rhetorical water like crazy on live television to prevent myself from drowning.

13

Of Crosstitutes and Criminals

WITH THE GOVERNING coalition in Cape Town stabilised, we had to start fixing a failing and near bankrupt municipality while laying the foundations for a best-practice model of local government. But the immediate challenge was the floor-crossing 'window' due to open in September 2007.

At that stage I was still blissfully unaware of the 'mass exodus' plan hatched by Theuns and his cabal. A central figure in this plan was Kent Morkel, the DA's Western Cape chairman, and scion of a political dynasty that liked to style itself the 'Kennedys of Cape Town'. Kent was a wily street-fighting mobiliser, and he had been tasked with turning this strategy into action. I subsequently learnt that he had travelled the length and breadth of the Western Cape in the run-up to the floor-crossing (while he was still our provincial chairman), trying to recruit as many public representatives as he could to join him in crossing the floor to start a new party, predominantly for Afrikaans-speakers, even though he mainly spoke English!

It also later emerged that Kent was 'doing business' with Badih Chaaban.

Badih was planning a floor-crossing himself, to start his own party, with the aim of holding the balance of power in Cape Town once more, on behalf of his underworld network. His aim was to team up with the ANC in a governing coalition. He would then demand his pound of flesh, and reckoned the ANC would be less fastidious than we were about legal compliance.

Without realising it, I was facing a pincer movement from two directions: Kent Morkel (focusing on recruiting DA members to defect) and Badih Chaaban (who initially targeted councillors of Patricia de Lille's Independent Democrats). The ANC would work with anyone who could remove the DA from office. Together they planned to topple the Cape Town coalition by reducing its numbers to below 50 per cent, through defections.

Oblivious of the extent of the danger, I just got on with my work, which included time devoted to making all councillors feel genuinely included and comfortable in the party. I appointed a balanced mayoral committee that included our coalition partners as well as the DA's internal factions; we managed a fair and equitable spread of competent sub-council and committee chairs. I met small groups of councillors regularly, in a relaxed environment over evening drinks in my office, to discuss their issues. I tried to be as accessible as possible to all members of the DA and our partners, and had an 'open-line' policy, even if my diary did not allow this to extend to an 'open door'. I worked very long hours, seven days a week, backed by a remarkable team of dedicated people, both in the mayor's and leader's offices. Their co-ordination and professionalism made my task far easier than I had anticipated – certainly much easier than my previous dual roles, such as raising two children at the same time as starting my consultancy in the early 1990s!

In the four months following my election as leader of the DA, most of the manufactured and exaggerated fears about the consequence of my leadership evaporated. Our message found internal traction and people kept their eyes on the prize: winning more electoral support for our vision of an open, opportunity-driven society for all. The reflex of racial nationalism was weakening.

Then, out of the blue, I got a call from Willem Veltman, a Cape Town businessman of Dutch origin I had met on several occasions in the course of my work. He warned me that Badih Chaaban was raising funds in order to bribe councillors to cross the floor and join him in starting a new party, with the aim of holding the balance of power in the council. I had suspected it, but this was the first alert I received. I needed to speak to Willem directly. This was too important a conversation to have over the telephone.

I reported the matter to the speaker and asked him to accompany me to Willem's house to find out more. The speaker needed a statement in writing for the purpose of possible disciplinary procedures. So Willem told his story and I wrote it down. The speaker is a commissioner of oaths, and Willem was prepared to take the oath. The date was 16 April 2007.

Using the Dutch idiom, Willem said he knew Badih Chaaban 'by face' and had once sat next to him on Greenmarket Square. Badih was 'busy raising money from shady characters in Cape Town to facilitate floor-crossing in September. This would unseat the present mayor and Chaaban would then take over the city and would reward all the people who contributed to his fund,' Willem stated under oath.

Then Willem added a warning: 'I have come to the conclusion that Chaaban would not hesitate, in a dispute, to kill his opponent ... he is extremely dangerous ... I have come to the conclusion that political life will become very difficult in the period leading up to the floor-crossing and if he does not succeed with this plan to get a position of power in the city and is not able to reward those who contributed to his plan, he will be under enormous pressure to deliver somehow. This makes me extremely anxious about the safety and sanctity of life of key people in the city structures. That is why I contacted the Mayor.'

Similar allegations started surfacing in other places, primarily from ID councillors. Rumours were swirling in the corridors.

Then suddenly, as if to corroborate the warnings I had received, Cape Town's underworld was hit by a seismic event. This was the assassination of Yuri Ulianitski, kingpin of the city's underground mafia, which controlled gangs, gambling, drugs and human trafficking. He was generally known as 'the Russian' because the cops could not pronounce his surname. He was revered, feared and fawned over – and finally shot dead in an ambush on a suburban street. On the night of 29 May, Yuri was travelling home from a restaurant in his midnight-black Audi Q7 4x4 with his wife and young daughter. His assassins left no room for error. He was hit twenty times. Four-year-old Yulia was hit only once – killed by a bullet through her brain. Her mother, Irina, was severely injured.

The next day in the council meeting I watched Badih. He was like a cat on hot coals, jumping up and down in agitation, regularly leaving the chamber to take and make phone calls. The relationship between Badih and 'the Russian' had become extremely tense in the months before his death, because Ulianitski had accused Badih of taking his money without delivering on his promises.

On 31 May the media reported police sources saying that before Ulianitski's death he had threatened to make public the names of politicians he was dealing with in relation to properties in the Cape Town central business district. Police sources said Ulianitski's relationship with the politicians had soured when the politicians failed to deliver the results he wanted. The implication of the police statement was that 'the Russian' had been eliminated before he could expose the politicians involved. The speculation revolved around Badih Chaaban.

J.P. Smith, the young and energetic councillor for Sea Point, who knew all about the activities of Cape Town's underground networks in his ward, had alerted me to what was going on. At the time he told me that the person who knew more about these developments than anyone else was a young journalist called Aly Verbaan, who had extensive experience and inside knowledge in reporting on Cape Town's criminal underbelly. She had researched the subject extensively.

When, unexpectedly, I got a call from Aly, I assumed she had been prodded to call me by J.P. Smith. The purpose of her call was to warn me. Ulianitski, she said, had called and threatened her with death, because she was writing about his network. Then, he'd added, Zille would be next. According to Aly, Ulianitski regarded me as the greatest barrier to his ambition of controlling the city's property leases and its tendering system. 'They are after you, and your family too,' said Aly. 'Take this seriously.'

As these things often turn out, it was Ulianitski who was assassinated first, probably in a hit orchestrated by one of the many people he threatened. The rule in his world was eat or be eaten.

I reported these developments, as they occurred, to the speaker. By this time, I was really worried. The speaker commissioned a 'threat assessment' from George Fivaz & Associates (GF&A), a reputable private investigation company (Fivaz had been appointed as democratic South Africa's first police commissioner by President Nelson Mandela), to determine whether Badih was capable of carrying out these threats. Their report provided even greater cause for concern, as Badih was found to have regular meetings with Cyril Beeka, a bouncer and notorious underworld heavyweight with close links to alleged Mafia boss Vito Palazzolo. The report confirmed that Badih had also worked closely with Ulianitski before his assassination, as well as a notorious gang known as the Moroccans.

They were not playing games.

I also kept James Selfe in the loop, and the DA took out hefty life insurance policies for me and my children.

Towards the end of May, Simon Grindrod arrived in my office. He explained he had a tape-recording of Badih Chaaban trying to bribe an ID councillor, Trevor Trout, to cross the floor to join a new party that Badih was launching in time for the floor-crossing window due to open on 1 September. The name of this new party, said Simon, was the National People's Party (NPP) – a clever play on the abbreviation NNP, by which the former New National Party was known. Before its demise, the NNP had been the strongest party in the Western Cape and would still resonate in the hearts and minds of many voters, Badih reckoned.

At last, I thought, we may have something concrete. I asked Simon to give the recording to the speaker and I too was given a transcript, which, unbeknown to me at the time, turned out to have been selectively edited. In the process of writing this book, I managed to get hold of the unexpurgated tape and read the full transcript. The three-way conversation, between Badih, Trout and Abdullah Omar, an ID councillor whom Badih had already signed up to defect, is very revealing.

Omar makes it clear that Trout is in financial trouble, and that Badih can help him out. Badih boasts about his close business links with the Moroccans and the Chinese mafia.

Badih explains that his floor-crossing offer to councillors involves R30 000 cash (for a councillor with leadership qualities) and a guarantee of two more terms in office. (It was rather quaint that he assumed his party would get enough electoral support to ensure two more terms for defectors.) He also offered a sweetener to early recruits of between R5 000 and R10 000 per month in the run-up to the floor-crossing, 'as a welcome to the party'.

Badih said he was making excellent progress towards his recruitment target among members of the ID, and still had 135 days to reach it before 1 September. He was confident of doing so. The target was twenty defectors from the DA's coalition – enough to bring the government down. As it turned out, he had a little help from a prominent, well-placed friend inside the DA.

Badih predicted that both the DA and the ID would implode at the floor-crossing. He described me as a 'fucking stupid bitch' and Patricia de Lille as a 'Hottentot kaffir'. The thread that emerges, between expletives, is that women cannot run a government. Then he throws in some seriously anti-Semitic comments for good measure.

Because Trout was from the ID, Badih laid it on particularly thick when he spoke about Patricia, the ID leader. 'Your leader unfortunately, she made every fuck up. Firstly, when you are a woman and you want to be like a man, you need to be at that level. You can't just fucking come from the kitchen, jump, fucking … [inaudible] then you end up "I am the fucking national president." My balls! Let's see what happens after September, what fucking national president?'

Then the bombshell.

Badih boasted that he had met Kent Morkel, the DA's Western Cape chairman, that very morning and that Kent was working to recruit floor-crossers at the DA end. The plan was simple: if Kent brought enough DA defectors, and Badih attracted enough ID defectors at the floor-crossing, they could bring down the DA coalition and enter their own coalition with the ANC to get the positions they had long coveted. All he wanted, Badih said, was the deputy mayor's position and the mayco member for economic development, with its portfolio of prime properties.

Badih said Kent Morkel's role in the deal was to 'break' me inside the DA. They both agreed on that. But, said Badih, he differed with Kent on how to deal with Patricia de Lille. According to Kent, if they were targeting coloured people for the crossover, they had to take her seriously. 'This is a woman that Kent Morkel is trying to tell me: "*You know … don't discount Patricia*" … I said this fucking woman is a moron.' But, says Badih, he had been persuaded that she had a 'brand' and that their strategy required her support base. That was why he wanted to attract it.

Looking back, I am truly amazed that those who listened to the tape at the time did not pick up the various references to Kent Morkel, and his role behind the scenes, of which I was totally unaware. And most puzzling of all, why had I not picked up these references when I read the transcript given to me at the time? Surely the references to Kent Morkel would have jumped out at me immediately? After all, he was the DA's provincial chairman, and I would have definitely followed up Badih's claims that he was meeting Kent in order to 'break' me and plan the collapse of our administration in Cape Town. Surely it would have occurred to me immediately that there was something seriously wrong if Kent was attending meetings with James Selfe and other DA leaders to discuss how to deal with the Badih crisis – while behind the scenes he was also secretly meeting with Badih? Something didn't make sense.

I extracted the transcript of the tape I had been given at the time, from my files. To my absolute amazement, it had been purged of all Badih's references to Kent Morkel. Why? Someone must have edited the transcript carefully before giving it to me, but who? And on whose instructions? The people who had organised the tape-recording, and transcribed it, were clearly trying to keep me in the dark about the interactions between Kent and Badih.

I wanted to investigate. I was no longer in contact with Simon Grindrod, who had given me the tape, so I asked Dirk Smit, who was still the speaker, why Badih's four separate references to Kent Morkel, captured on the tape, had been deleted from the transcript provided to me back in 2007. He replied that his office had been instructed to keep strictly to its brief, separating party and state. The speaker's investigation had nothing to do with party political dynamics. His job was to investigate Badih Chaaban's violation of the council's code of conduct. Kent Morkel was a member of the provincial parliament, not a councillor, and investigating or reporting on Kent would have been beyond the speaker's mandate.

It was an admirable example of the separation of party and state, but I still wonder whether there was something more to it than this. After all, giving me the unexpurgated transcript would not have required the council to take any further action against Kent Morkel. It would merely have put me in the picture. I would have followed up the issues relating to Kent in party structures. And in all likelihood, I would have uncovered the plotting, within the DA, that was going on behind the scenes in the run-up to the floor-crossing. Someone, somewhere was trying to keep this away from me.

After everything I had already experienced, Kent's treachery in the run-up to the 2007 floor-crossing still came as a shock all those years later. A lot of further developments fell into place after that.

Badih was charged with several counts of breaching the council's code of conduct for trying to bribe councillors, for his racist and anti-Semitic comments, and for insulting Patricia and me in extremely crude terms. He was found guilty by the multi-party disciplinary committee, who recommended his expulsion from the council. In terms of the law, however, the proposed penalty had to be ratified by the ANC's provincial minister of local government, Richard Dyantyi. This is where it got stuck. The ANC needed Badih to cause havoc in the DA-run council. And they needed him to remain there as a future partner to form a new ANC-led coalition in the city. So the ANC protected him, despite a meticulous disciplinary process leading to a conviction and the recommendation for his expulsion. The rule of law be damned, if it stood in the way of the ANC seizing power.

Badih at least had to face a disciplinary hearing in the council, even though the ANC squashed it at provincial level. Kent got away scot-free.

Everyone knew that Kent Morkel had never given up his ambition of becoming mayor of Cape Town, and Badih coveted the deputy mayoral position, with responsibility for oversight of the World Cup preparations. They had found each other, like a moth seeks out a flame, or perhaps more appropriately, a fly finds a dung-heap. Their venality and their ambitions converged. But they had to avoid being caught. Badih had his own delicate way of informing Trout what would happen if he breathed a word about the conversation.

'If someone fucks with us, we will fuck him,' explained Badih on the tape. 'And we're not talking about going to court. If you're a member of us, we will protect you. But if someone tries to betray us, we say no problem, one: we take your life away ... It [the information] comes back to us! So no one must try and fuck with anybody! We're serious about the future of this country and about our future.

'Remember, there's been a lot of money injected in this project ...

'And there's been a lot of lives at risk, and there's been a lot of sacrifices and people have put in things ... And we can't allow a rat amongst us ...

'So I've got to say to everybody else, that if we catch a rat, we kill a rat. Simple.'

Understandably, after this little warning, Trevor Trout was terrified of exposing Badih Chaaban, but his leader, Patricia, knew he had gone in with a recording device, and Trevor duly handed it over. He was then given professional protection by the city. Trevor was particularly nervous of exposing the fact that he needed Badih's help to rescue his business, and tried to separate this aspect of the taped conversation from Badih's attempted bribery.

After receiving the tape, and legal advice, the speaker came to me and told me we would have to take this matter very seriously. People's lives were potentially in danger. The matter needed further investigation.

By that stage, James Selfe, the chairman of the DA's Federal Executive, had become very concerned at what was happening. On the advice of Theuns Botha, the provincial leader, he held a meeting with Philip du Toit, representing GF&A, on 21 May 2007. When James learnt shortly afterwards, from the council speaker, that the city was legally obliged to undertake its own investigation, he concluded there was no point in having two parallel investigations, so he did not accept GF&A's quote and left the investigation to the speaker's office instead.

On 1 June the speaker interacted with two representatives of GF&A, Niel van Heerden and Philip du Toit, and did all the preparatory work through the supply-chain management system so that they could be lawfully contracted. The speaker found that GF&A had already been registered on the city's supplier database since 2003 – when the ANC governed the city.

I had nothing to do with the process of procuring the services of GF&A, although I knew it was under way. But I kept asking myself why we were having to undertake this investigation at all. If so much about Badih's dealings and connections were 'common knowledge', what were the police doing about it? After all, the NIA had warned the city of Badih's nefarious activities. And police sources had issued a statement on the circumstances behind the assassination of Yuri Ulianitski, the Russian, which strongly pointed to his links with 'politicians'. Had they even questioned Badih about this? And how come Badih was able to manoeuvre himself into a position where he came within a whisker of capturing the city's property-leasing and tender system? Why did *we* have to deal with the danger Badih posed? Wasn't this the job of the criminal justice system?

Badih seemed to know he was immune. He never stopped. After the council meeting on 27 June, he sent me what he described as a 'love letter'. 'Your hair looked good today, but in 80 days you will be history. Tick ... tock ... tick ... tock.'

He meant this warning to be ambiguous. It could either mean I would no longer be the mayor or that I would no longer be alive. But there was no time for philosophical or existential questions about the meaning of Badih's love letter. He posed a clear and imminent danger, not just to the coalition, but potentially to people's lives, as the GF&A report stressed.

Badih soon picked up that the speaker was having him investigated, and arrived unannounced in the speaker's office for a chat. His purpose soon became clear. He invited the speaker to accompany him to one of his nightclubs.

You have to picture Dirk Smit, the speaker, to appreciate the hilarity of this little scene. Dirk Smit is the stereotypical patriarchal Afrikaner, an enormous man, his round head a smaller replica of his body, straight brown hair parted on the left, short back and sides. His weight gave him a ponderous walk, but you could still see signs of the young athlete who had once excelled at boxing. He had been raised on the East Rand, in the former Transvaal, in a poor, strictly Calvinist home by his loving, strait-laced grandmother. Here he was, the Honourable Speaker of the City of Cape Town, being invited to a den of iniquity by the representative of Cape Town's underworld.

There were no flies on the speaker. He knew exactly that Badih was trying to compromise him so that he could be forced or bribed to abandon the investigation.

'Sure,' he said. 'I presume I can bring my wife?'

'Are you mad?' blurted Badih.

'In that case,' replied the speaker, 'I must regretfully turn your invitation down.'

Philip du Toit gathered as much evidence as he could by interviewing the DA and ID councillors who had come forward to say that Badih had tried to bribe them. On the speaker's instructions, he then took the evidence to the police. On arriving at the Cape Town central police station, he spoke to Superintendent Les Ziegelaar. Du Toit reported back to the speaker that, on the basis of Ziegelaar's response, there was scant hope of a proper police investigation.

Du Toit subsequently made a sworn affidavit of what had transpired: 'On Tuesday the 26th June 2007 I met with Superintendent Les Ziegelaar at Cape Town central police station where I provided Les Ziegelaar with the affidavits that I had taken from the councillors as well as the recordings that were handed to me. He said that this whole issue is politics and that I must understand that if a case is registered and his superiors request the docket and he never hears about it again then I must understand that it would be out of his hands.'

Du Toit's experience with Les Ziegelaar was corroborated by my own, when I went to the police station, at a later stage, to enquire about progress with the investigation into Badih. He was entirely unhelpful, and said the matter was out of his hands. The speaker also had an independent discussion with Ziegelaar and drew a similar conclusion.

We could clearly not rely on the police to assist us – an experience that was corroborated over and over again in later years when the ANC openly broke the law in trying to bring down the DA government. We would lay a charge, and it would mysteriously disappear.

Of course, back then, I was as yet unaware of an even greater immediate danger to our own ranks, in the form of Kent Morkel. Kent enjoyed recognition in our party as a key architect of our coalition government, but had now joined forces with those trying to bring us down. As DA provincial chairman, he sat in all our meetings and was party to all our plans. And, as I later learnt, he was also 'doing business' with Badih.

After the floor-crossing, allegations emerged about large sums of money passing between Chaaban and Morkel, although both denied it. Badih only dealt in cash, so one would never find a paper trail. It emerged that, as Philip du Toit started his investigation into Badih's corrupt dealings, he received an agitated phone call from Kent, who wanted to inform him that he had done a business transaction with Badih, in which he had received R800 000. Du Toit interpreted this as Morkel trying to pre-empt the discovery of this transaction during the investigation. Morkel was keen to separate this 'business deal' from the floor-crossing bribes Du Toit was investigating.

Again, Du Toit relayed none of this information to the DA at all, insisting that the speaker was his client and he would deliver a report to him relating only to his precise brief.

It was only after the floor-crossing that the beans started spilling from every conceivable source, each corroborating the other. Badih's behaviour was so outrageous, and his treatment of people so abusive, that one by one they turned against him. Juan Duval Uys, Badih Chaaban's previous spokesman, claimed to have personally conveyed an amount of R100 000 in cash from Badih to Kent Morkel. Uys also explained how Badih allegedly laundered this money. Badih, said Uys, would send him to the GrandWest Casino in Goodwood to cash in thousands of gambling chips, worth R1 000 each, in order to pay floor-crossing bribes and related costs to the total cumulative value of R9 million. (He did not say whether the chips were genuine or counterfeit.)

Badih never denied Uys's account.

Uys later claimed that he could prove, on the basis of hotel booking confirmations, that Badih had brought two Senegalese 'witchdoctors' to Cape Town to perform rituals for two weeks in an attempt to drive the DA-led coalition out of office. This included the ritual slaughter of 'a cow for Zille, a sheep for Grindrod and a goat for Smit. A chicken was slaughtered for Mohamed,' the newspapers reported.

The targets of these rituals were the people who stood in the way of Badih's ambition to capture the city's property-leasing and tendering system. I was the mayor, Simon Grindrod was the mayco member for economic development (including the city's property portfolio), Dirk Smit was the speaker and Mansoor Mohamed was the city's executive director of economic development. We all laughed when we read this account in the newspaper, but I could see that Mansoor was a little indignant that Badih considered his role in preventing corruption as worthy only of a slaughtered chicken!

Then there is the story of David Sasman, an ID councillor and an early recruit to Badih's cause. Sasman stayed away from council meetings for months, on the basis of a psychiatrist's letter saying that he suffered from agoraphobia and that close proximity to people unleashed panic attacks. The truth emerged when Sasman inevitably fell out with Badih. During the months in which Sasman was supposedly terrified of going outdoors and being among other people, he was actually criss-crossing the province recruiting councillors for the floor-crossing on Badih's behalf. When Badih became suspicious of how Sasman was spending the liberal allowance he had been given to bribe councillors, Badih had him followed.

Badih then accused Sasman of spending time in nightclubs and other places of dubious repute instead of doing his job. A fight ensued, during which Badih flung a coffee cup which hit another colleague and cut his head. Sasman got away more lightly. He was only hit by flying documents. But he nevertheless laid a charge of assault and *crimen injuria* against Badih for calling him a dog and a bastard – extremely mild language in Badih's vocabulary. Badih appeared in court and was convicted.

What an irony, I thought. With allegations of felonies circling him, and a vocabulary of curses, including racism, anti-Semitism and misogyny, that would warrant a new thesaurus of crude language, he was eventually convicted for throwing a coffee cup and describing colleagues as 'dogs' and 'bastards'.

As the date for floor-crossing drew closer, Badih became more desperate. The floor-crossing legislation required at least 10 per cent of a caucus to defect in order for any defection to be valid, and he needed seven more defectors to make up the numbers, he said. Patricia had thwarted his plans by expelling her compromised councillors before the defection window opened. If they were expelled in time, they would lose their seats and be of no further use to Badih's new party. The ID would then be able to retain the seats and replace the expelled councillors with loyal ID members.

So Badih, through middlemen, approached Theuns Botha. Theuns reported the approach to the DA national leadership and agreed to the meeting, in order to tape Badih Chaaban. During the discussion, Badih offered to give Theuns R200 000 and the 'services' of a twenty-two-year-old woman if he agreed to help him get the councillors he needed to cross the floor.

Badih, of course, denied these allegations. He had no interest in dealing with Theuns, he said. 'I am opening a coloured party. Where would I get with a boer like this?' he asked rhetorically. He claimed it was Theuns who had called him to a meeting.

Giving his account of the meeting, Badih said: 'He [Botha] said: "If I help you get DA councillors, what will I get?" I said: "What do you want?" He then lifted two fingers and said R200 000. I thought it was so cheap. I mean, is he selling sheep?' The offer of a twenty-two-year-old woman, Badih explained, was merely an attempt to determine whether Theuns was gay.

Theuns referred the matter to the police. He said he had not reported the offer immediately because he wanted to be able to take the conversation with Badih further.

At the council meeting on Wednesday 29 August, forty-eight hours before the defection window opened, Badih caused so much disruption that he was ordered by the speaker to leave the chamber. He told journalists he'd wanted to leave, and being expelled was the best way of doing so. Asked why, Chaaban replied, 'Because I still have recruiting to do.' He made it clear to journalists that his efforts to wrest the city were a joint effort with the ANC. Behind the scenes he had been meeting Mcebisi Skwatsha in a 'last push' to wrest the city during the floor-crossing, he boasted. This was confirmed later when an informant, with first hand knowledge, stepped up to tell me about these interactions.

What an irony! The same Mcebisi Skwatsha for whom Johann and I had rented the yellow Toyota, and who we had supported in the struggle, was now working side by side with a mafioso to remove me from office. But as the Mafia say in the movies when they are about to put a bullet through your brain: 'This ain't personal. It's business.'

Skwatsha, who was in charge of the ANC's floor-crossing preparations across the Western Cape, hinted shortly before the defection window opened: 'People will fall off their chairs when we announce what is to come.' He was right.

The ANC said that while they did not have formal agreements with any particular party, they were prepared to work with others to unseat the DA. This left the door wide open.

As the defection window came closer, the media was intensely focused on the intrigue surrounding floor-crossing. The political battles intensified, and the stories of clandestine meetings and offers grew more and more bizarre.

Badih was getting desperate. By then he had found common cause with Anwar Isaacs, a city official with a slightly dubious reputation, to help induce councillors to cross the floor. On 30 August, Anwar met two DA councillors, Yasir Pearce and Bahia Vlotman, and offered them R50 000 each and a sub-council chair position if they defected to the NPP. Yasir and Bahia immediately reported this offer to me, and were prepared to make sworn statements. These statements formed the basis of a disciplinary hearing against Anwar Isaacs. He was found guilty and dismissed. Badih, as usual, got away scot-free. Although all these matters were reported to the police, nothing ever came of them. On the contrary, in a scandalous development that I discuss in the next chapter, the ANC prepared the way for Anwar, Badih and Kent all to get immunity from prosecution!

The ID, for its part, 'outed' several disloyal members and moved quickly to expel them. Patricia warned the rest that accepting a bribe constituted a violation of the Prevention and Combatting of Corrupt Activities Act, which carried serious penalties. This, together with Badih's increasingly erratic behaviour, led some of them to have a last-minute change of heart.

Badih had anticipated this risk. His plan to pre-empt it required councillors to hand in the official, signed defection form before receiving their monetary incentive, which several of them did. Badih planned to submit the forms to the Independent Electoral Commission as soon as the defection window opened. When some councillors changed their minds, they tried to get their signed defection forms back from Badih, but failed. Reports emerged of tussles and fisticuffs as councillors tried physically to wrestle back their forms from Badih.

ID members who had already submitted their signed defection forms to Badih found themselves trapped; they could not confess their bad faith to their own party, because they would have been immediately expelled. They came to my office. As they were councillors claiming entrapment by someone I considered a criminal, I asked my legal adviser, Koos Cilliers, to advise them. It was far more important to collect evidence on Badih than to trap them, especially as they seemed genuinely clueless as to what was going on.

Koos worked hard to turn the situation around. On the advice of senior counsel, he concluded that a signed defection form could be nullified if the relevant councillor informed Badih Chaaban before the window period opened. They would also have to submit their retraction to the IEC before Badih submitted their signed defection forms. It was a race to the finish.

Koos helped the ID defectors and called in the help of Kobus Brynard, a DA member of the provincial legislature. Unbeknown to Koos (who was my apolitical legal adviser), Kobus was the cabal's English-hating bully and lawyer.

At about 10 p.m. on 31 August, Koos thought that the situation had been salvaged. He then discovered that they had entered the wrong party name in their legal notices to rescind the councillors' defection decisions. They had filled in 'New People's Party' instead of 'National People's Party'. This meant that all the documents were invalid. They had to be compiled and signed again. Koos raced against time to redraft the affidavits and have them signed. He finally managed to complete the rerun at 11:26, as the witching hour, midnight on 1 September, approached.

Relieved at having made the deadline, Koos set off home.

Kobus, however, had another task to finalise.

By the next morning, 1 September 2007, Kobus Brynard had cleared his DA office on the fourth floor of the legislature building and defected – to the ANC! Together with Kent Morkel! A colleague discovered their deserted offices when he failed to reach them on the phone that morning and went looking for them.

The DA was stunned at the news of Kent's and Kobus's defections to the ANC, a move engineered by none other than Mcebisi Skwatsha, when he had befriended Kobus on a delegation abroad. Mcebisi had been spot on when he predicted that developments in the defection period would get us to fall off our chairs.

Kobus always professed hatred for 'the English' but had appeared to hate the ANC even more. In fact, he often described me as being not only pro-English, but pro-ANC as well. This combination was the worst slur he could think of. He was the last person on the planet I expected to join the ANC's ranks.

On the other hand, anything was possible with Kent Morkel.

Defecting to the ANC would certainly not have been Kent and Kobus's first preference, though. They would far rather have stuck to the original plan of starting a new party for Afrikaans-speakers and holding the balance of power in the city, enabling them to dictate the terms of a new coalition, and grab the mayoralty as the price for putting the ANC back into local government in Cape Town. They couldn't execute this plan because they didn't manage to recruit DA defectors in sufficient numbers to reach the 10 per cent threshold to make the defections valid.

Defection was easier in the provincial parliament. With only thirteen DA members, Kent and Kobus together exceeded the required 10 per cent.

But the DA's city caucus was another matter. With ninety-one members at the start of the floor-crossing and ninety-three by the end, Kent and Kobus needed ten councillors to leave in order to validate any of them. They couldn't attract that number before the defection window opened. So Kobus and Kent (from the provincial legislature) crossed the floor alone, determined to recruit the councillors they needed during the remaining two-week window period.

I remember exactly where I was when I heard the news that they had left. It was mid-morning on 1 September 2007, and I was being driven in CA1, the mayoral car, back to my office, around the circle in lower Adderley Street, Cape Town's main road. Rose Rau, our regional director, called me with the news. We were both ecstatic. I can rarely remember a better day in politics.

Unfortunately, the ID lost six councillors, and one prior to the floor-crossing, bringing their number down to sixteen. But because four councillors had joined the DA from different parties, our coalition suffered a net loss of only three seats overall. Badih and Kent would still have to persuade sixteen more councillors to cross the floor to bring us down. Ten would have to be from the DA to meet the 10 per cent threshold.

I felt confident they would fail, but my colleagues were not so sanguine. The news of Kent's defection, in particular, caused panic in the ranks of the DA. He was a master mobiliser – better at wheeling and dealing than any politician I have known before or since. We knew he would work flat out during the two-week floor-crossing window to recruit the sixteen councillors he still needed to topple our governing coalition (which, ironically, he had helped establish), and now he had the ANC's clout and purse to back him up.

Everyone drew the same conclusion: Kent still harboured his lifetime ambition of becoming mayor of Cape Town, and if he could recruit enough DA floor-crossers in the city during the defection period to bring us down, the ANC would reward him with this grand prize. He would require a coalition partner to do it, which was where Badih Chaaban came in. Still determined to become deputy mayor, Badih was waiting in the wings, leader of the newly formed National People's Party, for the opportunity he coveted.

But, they learnt, there was no longer much appetite for defection among DA councillors. The odds were too high that they would end up as beached whales – the graphic description of councillors who lost their seats because they fell short of a 10 per cent caucus defection required to make their walk-over valid. The DA, with its growing internal cohesion, seemed a better and safer option.

Fears of the consequence of my election as leader had receded rapidly. The DA was growing fast; no one had been victimised. On the contrary, everyone was treated fairly and judged on their merits, not their ethnic identity. We were getting (mostly) good media coverage, and a majority of councillors correctly concluded that starting a new party would have minimal prospects of success. The DA's prospective floor-crossers retracted one by one.

Meanwhile, I was desperately trying to continue with my work despite all the shenanigans going on around me. I felt like a horse trying to run a race on a hard surface scattered with marbles. Getting a grip on the substance of my job was proving really difficult in this environment.

I had been invited to join an anti-drugs march in Mitchells Plain organised by the People's Anti-Drug and Liquor Action Committee (PADLAC). This organisation had distanced itself from a vigilante organisation with a similar name, PAGAD (People Against Gangsterism and Drugs), which was notorious for taking the law into its own hands when confronting drug dealers, having lost faith in the police to do so. PADLAC, in contrast to PAGAD, described itself as a 'passive resistance' organisation.

Deeply aware of the ravages caused by drugs in the Mitchells Plain community, I agreed to join the march. The ANC immediately accused me of supporting vigilantism. I rejected this slur, and asked, in return, why the police were not doing more to curb drug dealing in the suburb. PADLAC applied for the necessary permit to march, and got the go-ahead for 9 September 2007. I joined them. Although the issue was serious, it was a welcome break from the tension of the defection period.

As we marched, community members pointed out the houses of various drug dealers. They were instantly recognisable – upgraded, smart establishments, clearly distinguishable from the poorer surrounding houses. The drug dens all had walls, with additional perimeter security and closed-circuit television cameras, to give prior warning of pending police raids. The drugs, I was told, were immediately flushed down the toilet in the event of a police search. I saw one hopeless young addict walking away from one of the drug dens, only to be stopped and frisked by the police monitoring the march. The police confiscated his small packet and arrested the boy, who looked no older than fourteen. Why don't the police raid the premises, I asked.

I got no answer.

A little further on, at another drug house, one of the fellow marchers, Armien Maker, knocked on a suspected dealer's gate, which directly abutted the sidewalk. The police immediately arrested Armien, shoved him into the back of a waiting police van and took him to the Mitchells Plain police station. I asked why he had been arrested. No response. I then demanded to be arrested too, but the police ignored me. I then diverted the march and led it to the Mitchells Plain police station to enquire what law Armien had violated and to demand his release. On what planet did knocking on a gate that verged onto a public sidewalk warrant arrest, I asked. I was told that one of the conditions of the march was 'no stopping'. Armien had stopped to knock. That was why he had been arrested!

Here was law-abiding Armien being arrested for stopping in the street while Badih was working with the worst criminals in town to bring the government down. I thought I had gone crazy. I made my views known, politely but firmly. This gave the police the excuse they were looking for to arrest me as well.

The next day the *Cape Times* reported the circumstances at the Mitchells Plain police station as follows:

'In ugly scenes, police dragged screaming women and teenagers into the charge office as relatives and bystanders tried to intervene. An incensed Zille walked to the police station and was taken to an office.

'She emerged minutes later, saying she had not been arrested, only to be called back, when – in the presence of her lawyer, Stuart Pringle – she was formally taken into custody.'

I was released later that night.

The media now had a new story, which dominated the news for days, and backfired badly on the ANC. If there was one incident that hastened the swing of support in Mitchells Plain away from the ANC towards the Democratic Alliance, it was the police's heavy-handed action at the PADLAC anti-drug march, followed by my arrest.

Superintendent Stephanus Johannes Vorster came forward again, showing enormous courage given his circumstances. He wrote an affidavit that helped me secure a settlement from the police for unlawful arrest, with the legal assistance of the indomitable Frank Raymond.

Turning our focus back to the floor-crossing, we waited for the dying minutes of 15 September 2007, the close of the defection window, the adrenalin pumping in anticipation of a last-minute surprise. But Kent and Kobus had missed their target, although we never found out by exactly how much.

Thus Cape Town stepped back from the brink of having Kent Morkel as mayor and Badih Chaaban as deputy mayor. We could breathe again.

Kent and Kobus, the two DA defectors, never forgave Theuns Botha for staying in the DA despite his promise to lead his support base out of the party. As the provincial leader, Theuns would have had a lot of clout, and together with Kent, the provincial chairman, would have been able to wield a lot of influence. Together they may have achieved the 10 per cent of DA crossovers they needed in the city.

Theuns's (apparently last-minute) decision to remain in the DA was a big setback for the defection plans. Kent and Kobus were particularly angry because it was Theuns who had hatched the plan to start a new Afrikaner party (together with Dan Roodt). As the DA in the province grew stronger, he had changed his mind. He knew, as Western Cape leader, that if the DA kept on its growth trajectory, he stood a good chance of becoming premier of the province. He began to waver, and then to play both sides.

With the cabal broken, Theuns and I worked on repairing our relationship. I certainly approached this project in good faith, and I sensed he did too. Now, I thought, surely the ANC would have to accept that they could not snatch the city back, even by foul means. At last we would be able to get on with the business of governing without all these distractions.

To smooth the way, I also did my best to establish a cordial relationship with Ebrahim Rasool, the ANC premier. Because of my own history, I sometimes felt a greater affinity to certain people in the ANC than I did to some in my own party. Ebrahim Rasool was one of them. I thought we could end the ANC's enmity by establishing a firm basis for co-operative governance between the DA-governed city and the ANC-governed province.

I was wrong. The ANC was riven by its own internal factionalism, and Rasool was on the ropes. He decided the best way to salvage himself inside his own party was to succeed where previous attempts had failed and to end the DA's dominance in the City of Cape Town.

I gradually realised something was afoot, but I did not suspect that the latest and most serious assault on our coalition government had only just begun.

Early in January 2008, I accepted an invitation to attend an event abroad. When I returned home, Johann told me about a weird experience he had had. The phone had rung in our study, and when he answered it, he heard what sounded like the click of a tape-recorder reaching the end of a tape, then rewinding. He listened for a while. To his amazement, he heard the 'playback' of a conversation Grace, our housekeeper, and I had had in the study before I left.

I was asking her please to ensure that the boys drank their orange juice and ate their salads while I was away. As it was school holidays, I asked her to let them sleep as late as they wanted in the morning. Johann wrote down details of the conversation as it was replayed. Grace and I remembered the conversation exactly, as Johann later reported it to us.

None of us realised that a phone could record a conversation happening in a room without anyone actually being on the phone. Although it was a serious invasion of privacy, we laughed at the thought of the hundreds of mundane conversations some poor sod was having to listen to somewhere – which I later learnt happened in an office in the suburb of Bishop Lavis. We automatically assumed the 'bugging' was the work of the National Intelligence Agency, under ANC instructions – yet another example of the abuse of a state institution for party political purposes.

Looking back with what I know today, our phone could have been tapped at the instance of almost any of my opponents. It was soon to become apparent how many of them had contacts in private investigation agencies able to undertake such surveillance. Whoever was responsible, they were clearly on a fishing expedition, trying to find anything they could possibly use against me politically. I knew they would find nothing, but I still regarded the invasion of the constitutional right to privacy as a serious matter.

Johann and I made an appointment to see the minister of intelligence, Ronnie Kasrils, on 14 February 2008. I remember it exactly because while we were waiting in the minister's reception room a rather dishy radio journalist phoned me and asked me to be his Valentine. 'Why do you call when my husband is sitting next to me?' I asked him.

Anyway, there we were, with our old-style green round-dial telephone in a plastic Pick 'n Pay packet – exhibit number one. Ronnie was welcoming and warm and confirmed that technology existed that could pick up a conversation in a room through the telephone. He gave us the assurance that there had been no official or legal authorisation to intercept our phone or bug our house. I had known Ronnie for a while, and I believed him. 'However,' he added, 'I cannot give you the assurance that some rogue operative has not tapped your home through your phone line.' He told us he could not tell from physically examining our phone whether it had been tapped. The device would have been secured to a part of the phone wire on the pole outside the house. Anyone with the requisite technology could have installed it.

As we left his office I said to Johann, 'It feels as though we are back to the state of emergency in the 1980s.'

'No,' said Johann. 'We are in a much better space than that. Back then we were doing things that would have landed us in jail. Now we aren't. And we are protected by the constitution.'

But it was still an uncomfortable feeling, not knowing where in the house we could talk privately.

We assumed we were still under surveillance. We presumed that it was unsafe to talk in the house, so if we wanted to discuss anything privately (usually a family matter), we went into the garden, a precaution we maintained for a long time.

Johann and I often sat in bed talking and laughing about what the 'spooks' would make of our conversations. Like the one we had – next to a telephone – about political 'dirty tricks'. I had been explaining the tactics some of my opponents were using against me, and expected Johann to be shocked to the core. Instead he tried to console me by saying my travails were mild compared to those recorded in the Old Testament. He then gave me a rather graphic example about Saul's tactics, born out of jealousy, to get rid of his emerging rival, the young David. When Saul's daughter, Michal, fell in love with David, Saul said David could marry her if he went forth and returned with the foreskins of 100 Philistines. Saul naturally assumed that David would be killed in the process of harvesting them, but David returned with 200 foreskins – double the number required! – and duly won the hand of the beautiful Michal.

It was Johann's way of saying I should be grateful that I only had my comparatively minor challenges to worry about.

It was the first time I had heard that story. At Rivonia Laërskool we had had Bible study every day, and I am sure that I would have remembered that one. On reflection, I thought our Calvinist teachers must have taught the Bible selectively. However, I warned Johann, if *I* didn't know the story, very few NIA agents would be acquainted with this section of the Old Testament either. If they were listening to our conversation, they might jump to the wrong conclusions. 'Don't be surprised,' I said, 'if the police arrive here soon with a search warrant to look in the fridge for Philistine foreskins.' We both laughed.

When I look back today, I have an open mind about who may have been tapping our phone. It may not have been the NIA at all. It could just as easily have been any of my opponents, including those inside the DA, undertaking what my colleague Theuns Botha once referred to as routine political espionage. 'You know,' he was quoted as saying by journalist Deon de Lange of *Independent Online* on 12 October 2007, 'in politics, we make use of professional espionage and investigation services all the time.' This statement raised some eyebrows, but, in retrospect, not as many or as much as it should have.

Despite everything that had happened, I was still pretty green in politics. I was about to learn some lessons that surprised me even more than the various Old Testament stories I had never heard before.

14

Zillegate

The next phase of my life was ushered in by two apologies. One came from Badih Chaaban to the people of Cape Town. The other was from Badih's spin doctor, Juan Duval Uys, to me.

I was heartily amused to wake up one morning to see an advertisement in the *Cape Times* with a bold headline and the NPP's colourful logo:

> **APOLOGY**
> NPP regrets failing to liberate our 3,3-million Cape Metro residents from the Zille regime. Your shackles will be removed in 2009.
> – Badih Chaaban, NPP President.

A while later I got a letter, also with a bold headline 'APOLOGY'. It read:

Dear Mrs Zille,

I need to apologize for everything I have said since September 01 2007 on behalf of Badih Chaaban's NPP, that revolts [sic] around your integrity.

The most stupid decision I ever did in my life, was to follow Badih Chaaban and to join his movement which he registered with the IEC as a political party. The mere fact that such a person could sneak into South African politics, itself is a disgrace to our country.

Whatever I stated in my capacity as Spokesman for Chaaban and the NPP with the intention to insult you, was done as per direct instruction from Badih Chaaban. I am deeply remorse [sic] and need your forgiveness in this regard. I will only be at peace if you can forgive me for my assistance in this, as you stand as innocent victim of intentional verbal assault. As Chaaban's and NPP's spokesman I made myself available to be abused for the shady objectives of others.

I thank GOD that I came to my senses.

The example you set as a politician is amazing and you stand as a true inspiration to all in this country.

Yours Sincerely,
Juan Duval LT Uys

There was such an element of burlesque about all this that it was hard to take it seriously, and yet I had been warned repeatedly that we should not treat it glibly. Badih seemed like a buffoon, people warned me, but he was dangerous. And he was working with others who were even more so. They had pumped a lot of money into his project and wanted results.

After the diversion of the floor-crossing drama, I put my head down to get on with the real business of governing the city. We had to put together an integrated development plan, backed by a budget; we had to rescue the city's ailing finances, get people paying their municipal bills again, so that we could advance basic service delivery. We needed to fill the huge holes in middle management (not to mention the potholes across the city), and get systems and structures working again.

To ensure stability in the coalition, I met regularly over a meal with Patricia de Lille, a practice we have continued to this day. We developed a strong and forthright relationship. I also had to work very hard to keep the DA's factionalised caucus behind me, often the most difficult job of all.

Our recent defectors, especially Kent Morkel, kept his DA contacts alive and worked overtime to continue destabilising us. Having been the party's provincial chairman, he knew all our internal fault-lines and the background of the investigation into Badih Chaaban.

Unlike me, Kent had been present in the meetings with James Selfe and Theuns Botha to deal with the Western Cape's floor-crossing threats. He had been party to the DA decision to abort the GF&A investigation and leave it to the city. His job now was to deliver to the ANC a full-blown DA scandal that could be linked to me.

I believed they would search in vain. At that stage, I still assumed that there actually had to be a real scandal before it could be sensationalised.

Once more I was wrong. In politics a scandal can be created out of smoke and mirrors. And as usually happens with mirrors, the real scandal is often the reverse of what it seems.

The ANC provincial premier, Ebrahim Rasool, needed a scandal involving me to deflect attention from his own. He was facing a multi-party investigation in the provincial parliament into whether he had lied to the house after claiming that the auditor-general had condoned overspending, of R200 000, on security upgrades for the home of one of his ministers.

Of course, Badih Chaaban had still not been arrested or questioned, despite all the evidence handed to the police. Given the extent to which the police did the ANC's bidding, it was clear that Badih enjoyed protection in high places.

Meanwhile, on 28 September, Philip du Toit, the investigator who had probed and reported to the police Badih's alleged criminal actions during the floor-crossing, was arrested and charged with armed robbery and hijacking. The charges were serious enough for the police to keep Philip in jail and for the magistrate to deny him bail.

This development knocked me sideways. Here was a private investigator, from a reputable company, being arrested for serious crimes. I knew something was afoot.

Philip's house was raided and his computers and all his tape-recordings confiscated. In a highly unusual move, the provincial police commissioner, General Mzwandile Petros, personally supervised the operation.

The police claimed they needed Philip's equipment in order to investigate a charge of hijacking and armed robbery against him, charges which were eventually dropped.

The charges against Philip provided an excuse for the police to raid his house, to confiscate his equipment and recordings, as they continued their search for a scandal that could bring down the DA government in Cape Town.

I was convinced they would find nothing.

But I was concerned about Philip. I had learnt never to make assumptions one way or the other, especially in the shady semi-underworld of spy vs spy. Was there any substance to the charges against him, I asked. Philip's advocate, Johan Nortje, told me there wasn't. I accepted his word.

Philip had been in jail for almost a month when I, in my capacity as DA leader, set off early on the morning of 24 October 2007 to attend a function in Worcester. I took the newspapers to read in the car because I was perturbed to see a banner headline in the *Cape Times* which read: 'CITY COUNCIL IN SPY SCANDAL'.

The report was written by a top reporting team, which showed that the editors regarded it as a serious investigative assignment.

It began. 'The Democratic Alliance-led Cape Town council is at the centre of a potential spy scandal that includes unexplained payments to private investigators for work originally sourced by party bosses to guard against floor-crossing loss of power.'

I had to read the article a few times before I grasped the nub of the issue. The 'scandal' involved allegations that the city had paid an account that should have been settled by the DA. The amount involved was R80 000, the newspaper alleged.

The *Cape Argus* took the 'scandal' further that afternoon, announcing:

'Premier Ebrahim Rasool has summoned top police management for discussions on the clandestine investigations carried out by a former NIA informant for the ruling DA-led coalition.'

Then Rasool added: 'I am shocked at these allegations that show to what extent Mayor Zille may have wanted to go to remain mayor of the City.'

I had to laugh at this. This 'scandal' showed precisely the opposite. It showed to what extent the ANC was prepared to go in order to topple a legitimately elected government in the city, and to reverse the outcome of a democratic election.

Rasool said he planned to have the matter investigated. That was the first hint of what lay ahead.

The exposé had been carefully timed to coincide with a cabinet meeting scheduled for the same day, 24 October. Premier Rasool invited Mzwandile Petros, the provincial police commissioner, to brief the cabinet on his investigation into Philip du Toit and its implications for the DA coalition in the city. Neither Rasool nor Petros saw anything wrong with the police briefing politicians about an ongoing investigation – and then presenting untested allegations to the media to create a 'scandal' against their political opponents.

One would have thought that the commissioner of police, at least, would have understood the basic tenets of the rule of law. But by then I had become accustomed to the provincial SAPS behaving as if it were the coercive arm of the ANC. Nevertheless, I was still amazed at the brazenness of it all.

After the cabinet meeting, Premier Rasool held a press conference and released a statement saying: 'Following the shocking allegations that the Mayor of the City of Cape Town and the DA Leader is involved in matters of espionage, the hiring of private intelligence from the apartheid era, and that taxpayers' money was used to fund DA activities, I invited Commissioner Petros and the police leadership to Cabinet. They briefed cabinet today, 24 October 2007.'

Then, without a shred of evidence, Rasool stated as a fact that: 'The Mayor was aware and complicit in the illegal act of surveillance through audio and video recording of people without their consent ... I appeal to the Mayor and DA leader to come clean and co-operate fully with the police.'*

What was he talking about? I was battling to get a handle on this scandal.

After a while it came together: the ANC was alleging that the DA had wanted to undertake a political investigation to determine which of its councillors were about to defect. Instead of paying for the investigation themselves, the DA had palmed the investigation off onto the city, the ANC alleged.

I went to the speaker's office.

'Did this happen?' I asked.

'No,' he said emphatically. He then picked up a file from his immaculately neat desk, opened it, and read in Afrikaans: 'Item 13, schedule 1 of the Municipal Systems Act: If the chairperson [speaker] of a municipal council, on reasonable suspicion, is of the opinion that a provision of this code has been breached, the chairperson MUST authorise an investigation of the facts and circumstances of the alleged brief.'

---

* Premier statement dated 24 October 2007

The speaker read the words aloud. Twice.

Then he added: 'I was given concrete evidence that a councillor of the city of Cape Town was trying to bribe other councillors. They were not even from the DA. This councillor was violating both the Systems Act and the Prevention and Combatting of Corrupt Activities Act.'

Then he turned back to Item 13, schedule 1 on the paper in front of him and repeated, 'It says here that in such circumstances I MUST investigate, not MAY. I was obliged to investigate. So, when the DA found out about this, they decided not to do another investigation. What's wrong with that?'

His argument made sense to me. I explained it to the journalists. They were having none of it. They would not let the facts stand in the way of their 'speaking truth to power'! If it didn't look like a duck or quack like a duck, they were going to find proof that it was, in fact, a duck.

I asked the city manager to send me the invoices and other relevant documents relating to the GF&A investigation. I drew up my customary timeline. When one is dealing with a crisis in politics, it is essential to know how events unfolded, and in what sequence.

I established that James Selfe, Theuns Botha and Kent Morkel had met Niel van Heerden and Philip du Toit of GF&A on 21 May 2007, to discuss a possible DA investigation into Badih Chaaban's bribery efforts in Cape Town.

GF&A invoiced the city R1 400 for this initial briefing session.

Their invoice also listed:
- Consultations on 22 May 2007 with four councillors, who Badih had tried to bribe (R1 400).
- An 'investigation' with a witness on 28 May (R350).
- Another investigation with a witness on 31 May (R350).

All those meetings had been undertaken without any contract having been signed between the DA and GF&A. In fact, the DA had not yet accepted a quotation. It turned out that these meetings, for which GF&A had billed the city, had been held before the speaker had briefed them on 1 June to undertake the investigation into Badih.

There could be a problem here, I said to myself.

Even if the DA had decided not to investigate (because the city was legally obliged to), GF&A may have wrongfully charged the city for meetings preceding the city's contract.

I calculated the total amount involved. It added up to R3 500.

If I included a pro-rata amount for phone calls and mileage claims, it came to no more than R4 000.

Where on earth did the newspapers get R80 000 from, I asked. I finally concluded that this was the cost of the entire investigation, from beginning to end. The newspapers had simply accepted Rasool's word for it that this investigation should have been done by the DA, but had been palmed off onto the city.

But, I conceded, even if the city had paid a small amount that should have been paid by the DA, it would obviously have to be recovered. I also resolved to investigate how this had happened.

I was more than slightly cynical at the ANC's sudden zealousness about the separation of party and state, when they were busy capturing and abusing every possible state institution to undermine a legitimately elected council where we were in government.

I requested a formal answer from GF&A, in writing, explaining the invoice. The request was sent in the name of the city's executive director of finance, Mike Richardson.

GF&A replied that the four interviews, conducted before they were formally contracted to the city, had been material and relevant to the investigation. That is why the city had been billed for this work. There had been no double payment. If they had had anything to hide, GF&A argued, they would have changed the dates on the invoice. They did not – because even though the interviews were done before the formal contract was signed with the city, all the material was valuable and useful to the speaker's brief. The interviews would have had to have taken place in any event. There was no double-dipping and no fruitless and wasteful expenditure.

This argument also made sense to me.

I had by then learnt that any attempt to reverse the 'twist' journalists have collectively put on a story is like trying to reverse the vortex of a tornado. It gathers pace with a life of its own. Any subsequent development, in order to be considered newsworthy, must accelerate the spin's momentum in the 'right' direction.

There was only one journalist who consistently saw through it all.

He was Dave Marrs, the Cape editor of *Business Day*. Unfortunately, he was an editorial writer and columnist, not a news reporter. He dealt with the issue in an occasional column, bringing some much needed perspective to the uproar.

He hit the nail on the head when, on 29 October 2007, he asked: 'Why would [the ANC] be crying foul over a city council investigating allegations of serious criminal activities by one of its sitting members? Could it be that there is a can of worms arising from the [ANC's] flirtation with Chaaban that it would prefer kept from public view? It does seem odd that Western Cape police commissioner Mzwandile Petros is personally leading an investigation into ANC Premier Ebrahim Rasool's allegations of spying and abuse of public funds, yet the police seemed strangely reluctant to act after being handed copious amounts of evidence against Chaaban. Stranger still that Petros is said to have personally supervised the arrest of the private investigator who had been monitoring Chaaban on the council's behalf.'

As far as I have been able to ascertain, no other journalists picked up these fundamental points from the get-go.

The city took out a full-page advertisement to set out the facts, because we simply could not get our points across amid the sound and fury that had gripped the fourth estate. We also sent the premier's office all the information he required. We made it clear we had nothing to hide and would play open cards with him.

It made no difference.

Every day the media would be drip-fed a new snippet of salacious news from the premier's office.

Next was the allegation that the city had used illegal means to obtain information. That worried me. A mistaken payment was one thing. We could recover the money. But illegal espionage was another matter entirely.

So, again, I asked the speaker: Were any illegal means used – either in contracting GF&A or in the investigation itself? He told me that GF&A had been registered on the city's database during the ANC's tenure; that the investigation was considered urgent because of a potential threat to life; it had therefore been contracted through a legally compliant tender deviation. And, he stressed, he had received an absolute assurance from GF&A, in writing, before the start of the probe, that they would only use legal methods of investigation. He showed me the contract and I was satisfied that, if any illegal methods had been used, it was not on the instruction of the speaker nor anyone in the city. GF&A would have to account for this aspect.

For their part, GF&A assured the speaker that the investigations had been conducted within the law. Conversations had been taped, but never by an outside third party. I learnt that it is perfectly legal to secretly tape a conversation between two people, if the person doing the recording is a party to the conversation.

This had been the case with all the recordings, I was assured.

Before long I was satisfied that nothing illegal had transpired, certainly not on the instruction of anyone in the city. But to make absolutely sure, and to cauterise the slow bleed, I asked for an independent investigation, to be undertaken by a retired judge, to probe every aspect. We needed an independent legal expert to give an opinion on whether the city had paid for a DA account and, if so, how much, and whether illegal surveillance methods had been used. I asked Fiona Stewart, my lawyer, to choose the appropriate person.

She advised me to approach retired Judge John Foxcroft. The judge replied that the Constitutional Court's guidelines precluded him from undertaking the investigation. Judges were advised not to lend the weight of their office to proceedings outside the formal criminal justice system that could potentially have political implications, he explained. The principle of the separation of powers prevented him from doing it. I understood the logic of his argument, which was to stand me in good stead later.

Fiona then approached senior advocate Josie Jordaan, whom I had never met before. He accepted the brief and was given independent, open access to any material or individual he required to get to the facts.

Rasool rejected this move with contempt, saying it was akin to investigating myself! Most commentators swallowed this line, saying that, as the accused, I could not appoint the judge and jury.

Rasool demanded my immediate resignation, which made nationwide news.

By this time 'Independent' Newspapers had christened the scandal 'Zillegate'. It made a salacious headline.

The next big news break focused on the number of spy tapes confiscated from Philip's house. Under the breathless headline 'POLICE SIFT THROUGH 300 ZILLEGATE TAPES', the Independent Newspapers reported on 27 October: 'Police investigators are trawling through a staggering 300 secretly taped conversations, mostly involving politicians, in Cape Town's Zillegate spy saga. Police said it would take weeks to listen to all the conversations, taped between May and September.'

Three hundred tapes? Was this possible, I asked.

Complete nonsense, I was told. At most, about twenty interviews with councillors had been conducted.

Then came the next big news hit. The recordings were 'explosive', Rasool alleged, providing hard evidence that we had been spying on our coalition partners.[*]

Within minutes, all the coalition partners demanded to know whether this was true. After the speaker had assured me it wasn't, we met our governing partners to reassure them. Then I had to deal with my own party, the DA. That was always the hardest part.

When you are the leader, everything that appears about you in the press reverberates through the party. The DA (unlike the ANC) tends to be very sensitive – even skittish – about any criticism that appears in print. They, understandably, interpret the news as the average newspaper-reading voter would and assume that it must be true.

So I had a lot of explaining to do. Although the party accepted my word, there was deep discomfort. Liberals are instinctively wary of the underground world of espionage and secret dealings, as indeed I am myself, because there is so much room for abuse. But if the police refuse to act against a real threat, what is one supposed to do but hire a private investigator from a registered and legal company?

---

[*] *Cape Times*, 27 October 2007

I managed to hold the coalition and the party behind me – for the time being.

It got more and more difficult as Independent Newspapers (in particular) ratcheted up the scandal. In exasperation, I went to the mayoral spokesperson, Robert MacDonald. 'It seems as if Rasool is dictating stories to these journalists,' I said. 'Why can't we get our point across? What is going on?'

I did not know how ironic my question would turn out to be until much later.

Patricia, the leader of our key coalition partner, insisted on listening to the tapes. Rasool, sensing the chance to divide us further, agreed and enabled her to do so. The police played her pre-selected excerpts.

I was no longer flabbergasted that the police commissioner was prepared to assist the premier to drive his political agenda by releasing excerpts of evidence in an ongoing criminal investigation in order to divide his political opponents. The media didn't bat an eyelid about this blatant abuse of power. They were on tenterhooks to know what Patricia had heard on the tapes.

She emerged from the meeting to say that the quality of the recording was so poor she could hardly make out what was being said. She informed me personally that she did not believe we had spied on her. I gave her the assurance that her conclusion was correct.

On 29 October 2007, I wrote a letter to Commissioner Petros, rejecting his selective release of the recordings and requesting to hear the tapes as well.

For the first and only time in all my years in government, I got a full response on the same day. The meeting would take place at ten o'clock the next morning, Petros wrote.

'The meeting will be facilitated by the Investigating Officer, Superintendent Piet Viljoen, who will be contacting you telephonically to finalise the necessary arrangements.'

Viljoen phoned and we agreed to meet at the Bellville police station.

Fortunately, I had the presence of mind to inform my lawyer, Fiona Stewart, before I set off, who insisted on coming with me. Thank goodness she did.

When I arrived at the police station, we were ushered into a room full of electronic equipment. Within minutes I realised my request to listen to the tapes had been used as a ruse to get me into a full-blown police interrogation. There were four policemen. They were determined to find something on which they could pin a criminal charge against me. The four policemen present were exploring three options: (1) that I had deliberately passed a DA investigation onto the city for payment; (2) that I had ordered my colleagues in government to be spied on; or (3) that I had knowingly condoned illegal activity.

I answered all the questions honestly, knowing that they would find nothing.

They were playing good cop, bad cop. Ken Speed came across as kind and supportive; Piet Viljoen was the bludgeoning bully. Two others hovered menacingly in the background, dropping in a word from time to time. I could see how the psychological tactic worked. Thank goodness I had Fiona next to me.

Every now and then they would play a crackly excerpt on the tape-recorder and ask me to comment on it. I could barely hear what the person was saying, nor glean the context of the comments. Viljoen and Speed tried to explain them, but I said I could not comment on their interpretations of snippets I could hardly make out. I knew they were on thin ice, and I was not going to let them drag me along too.

The questions ranged far and wide. They asked why I had supported an investigation into Badih. I explained the warnings and threats, the murder of Ulianitski in suspicious circumstances, the reported threats to my family …

My family. I must have said it in a way that caused them to change tack. They knew they had hit a soft spot.

Viljoen proceeded to bulldoze his way down that route.

It was a knife in my heart. I had been seeing so little of my family during this period. I knew Paul was facing challenges at university and I was never there for him. The only time I saw him was sometimes at around 3:30 in the morning, in the kitchen, when he came home after his band had finished a gig, at about the same time that I was getting up to start my day. We would have wonderful short conversations as I made my morning cup of tea and he ate the leftovers from supper before dropping into bed.

I hardly saw Tom, who tended to be asleep at that hour, waking only after I had left the house. Because he did not spontaneously share his feelings, I felt even more neglectful of him. He had seriously injured his knee playing rugby and, because he was so stoic, our doctor did not diagnose how serious the injury was until much later, when it was beyond complete surgical repair. I felt that if I had been around more, my motherly instinct would have picked it up.

As Piet Viljoen relentlessly pursued this avenue, the tears rolled down my face. I could understand how police interrogation could break a suspect. I thanked God for the fact that we were now in a democratic South Africa, where we all had rights, even if the police still regarded themselves as an extension of the ruling party. My thoughts went back to Steve Biko, alone, in solitary confinement, no access to lawyers or medical treatment or a court, facing brutal physical violence. I felt nauseous.

Piet Viljoen was not even pretending to be independent any more. He boasted that the evidence he had gathered had cost the DA dearly at the Desai Commission of Inquiry (appointed to damage the DA after the split of 2001). What was more, he said, he would do the same to the DA again now.

He subsequently denied having said it, but both Fiona and I remember it clearly.

It stood out because it was the first hint we had of what lay ahead. If the police could find no evidence that would stand up in a court of law, they would appoint another kangaroo court – under the guise of a commission of inquiry – to damage the DA, and specifically me, as much as possible.

Rasool was worried because the parliamentary ad hoc committee had found him guilty on three counts of knowingly misleading the provincial parliament. He must have been relieved, though, that the newspapers treated this as a minor side issue compared to the daily new Zillegate revelations.

I recalled Bill Johnson's warning. He had predicted that the ANC would target me to distract my attention from my two jobs and that I would fail at both. It was happening exactly as he said.

But life had to go on. Johann was a quiet pillar of support. I didn't tell him much more than he was reading in the newspapers, because I just could not talk about it after having dealt with it all day at the office. We spoke about domestic issues. I remember worrying that he wasn't disciplining the boys enough. Johann didn't tolerate me 'backseat-driving' his parenting methods.

The Western Cape provincial congress was held in Mossel Bay on the weekend of 3 and 4 November, where Theuns Botha was comfortably re-elected provincial leader against Lennit Max, himself a former police commissioner. At the same congress, Theuns announced that he would not be available as a candidate for the premiership in the forthcoming election, scheduled for 2009. He was standing aside for me. I was surprised, but unsure whether this was the right move. There was so much work to do in the city, and holding the turbulent coalition together was a full-time job.

The prospect of my being the DA's candidate for premier drove Rasool to redouble his efforts to discredit me. He would not survive politically if he lost the province to the DA.

I tried not to think about the unfolding intrigue too much. I just had to focus on the job for which I had been elected. I decided to leave the legal issues to Fiona and the media to Robert. I even stopped reading the newspapers for a while to get my equilibrium back. Being an avid newspaper reader, it was hard, but I could no longer afford to be distracted.

I flew to Johannesburg for a DA fundraising trip and stayed over on the night of 6 November 2007 at a hotel near Bruma Lake. As I was falling into bed, exhausted after several long meetings (in which, inevitably, I had to explain Zillegate to sceptical audiences), I got a call from Advocate Johan Nortje, Philip du Toit's lawyer. He had just seen Philip in prison, and he needed to warn me urgently. Two policemen (one known by the nickname Skippy and an A.J. de Beer) had come to see Philip late at night in his cell. They told him that he would be granted bail only if he was prepared to sign a statement implicating me, according to Advocate Nortje.

He was required to 'confess' that I, in my capacity as DA leader, had commissioned the investigations into Chaaban for political purposes in the run-up to the defection period, and that I had then told GF&A to bill the city.

A statement like that would open the way for me to be charged with fraud.

Philip had refused to make this statement, and as a result would be in jail for some time, Advocate Nortje explained. Philip was getting desperate, as he had been in a crowded cell since 28 September on what turned out to be trumped-up hijacking charges. I could understand his desperation, but I was getting pretty desperate myself.

'Is Philip telling the truth about these policemen?' I asked.

'Yes, I believe he is telling the truth,' Advocate Nortje replied.

'What can we do to get him out on bail without him having to falsely implicate me?' I asked.

'We have to expose what is going on,' Nortje answered.

'Well, the media aren't particularly open to hearing what I have to say at present,' I pointed out, 'but I'll try.'

I knew there was no point in contacting Independent Newspapers, so I called *Die Burger* late that night, and they managed to get the story into the newspapers the next day.

The police vehemently denied the allegation.

I hardly slept all night. I kept waking out of my fitful sleep imagining banner headlines reading 'Zille Arrested for Fraud'. Neither the coalition nor the DA would be able to stomach that. Nor would my mother. As the current 'investigation' of finance minister Pravin Gordhan unfolds, I know what he is going through. I have been there.

Philip's account was given credence the very next day when the police took the unprecedented step of holding a media briefing to keep the 'scandal' going. None other than Piet Viljoen, by then the acting head of the Organised Crime Unit, addressed the media. He announced that the police were investigating a case of 'fraud' against the DA. He stopped short of mentioning me by name, but Philip's account dovetailed perfectly.

The report continued: 'At the media briefing, investigators outlined their investigation into the Cape Town Spy Saga, dubbed "Zillegate" that's seen the DA being accused of using ratepayers' money to spy on former Councillor Badih Chaaban.'[*]

I was amazed that I was being investigated by the Organised Crime Unit – when someone I considered to be a real villain was getting away scot-free.

The story had become big enough to appear on the front pages of many national newspapers. Mom read them every day at her cottage in Johannesburg,

---

[*] 'DA Under Investigation by Police', News24 Archives

and was beside herself. I phoned her regularly, trying to be cheerful. She never once doubted me, but was enraged with the newspapers, including her normally beloved cartoonists, for the way they depicted me. Inevitably, she would end these conversations in tears, advising me: 'Helen, please get out of politics. You are much too sensitive to be in politics.'

And she didn't even know the half of it!

Although I was feeling the pressure, I wasn't suffering half as much as she was. As a mother myself, I could empathise.

Johann, of course, knew the full story and was his usual imperturbable self, which helped me retain my equanimity.

On 15 November, Advocate John van der Berg successfully appealed the denial of bail for Philip. Judge Roelof van Riet found that Magistrate Noma-Afrika Kokwe had erred in denying bail, and released Philip. The hijacking and armed robbery charges were dropped. It had all been a ruse to keep him in jail and put pressure on him to implicate me.

(Not that Philip du Toit was an angel, mind you! He was later found guilty on unrelated charges of perlemoen smuggling. He lived a colourful life and was dating a Ukrainian stripper. And he had lied about being an NIA agent – he was in fact working for their 'rivals', the Scorpions. In short, he was the secret agent from central casting!)

But both Advocate Nortje and I believed Philip when he told us what had transpired in prison (against the background of what we had already experienced).

I took Philip and Advocate Nortje out to tea at Starke Ayres nursery, near my home, to thank Philip for not falsely implicating me, and Advocate Nortje for helping him to stand firm. A cup of tea and a piece of cake seemed a puny gesture in the circumstances, but I wanted them to know I appreciated it.

The police could find no evidence against me that could form the basis for a criminal charge in court. They had even secured my cellphone records from my service provider and tapped my phone for months (as I later found out), to no avail.

So they had to move to Plan B.

On 29 November 2007 Rasool announced he would establish a judicial commission of inquiry into allegations of possible maladministration, corruption and fraud in the city. He appointed Judge Nathan Erasmus, head of the Judicial Inspectorate of Prisons, for the job.

A few days later Rasool announced that a hotline had been opened, enabling anyone who wanted to give evidence to make contact. At the front of the queue was the coalition of the aggrieved, ranging from Anwar Isaacs (who had recently been fired from the city), Kent Morkel (who had defected to the ANC) and Les Ziegelaar (who had failed to drive the investigation into Badih Chaaban). They should all have been facing charges of corruption or defeating the ends of justice. Now they were lining up, a political hit squad, earning brownie points with the ANC by helping to destroy the DA and me. However irrelevant or untrue their testimony might be, they could come and spill their guts, unrelated to any specific charge, and help drive the ANC's smear campaign. What was more, they could do so on national television.

The commission secretary was Zithulele Twala, the brother of Mzukisi Twala, regional editor of the South African Broadcasting Corporation's television news. The Twala brothers could now work together to ensure live broadcasts of the juiciest evidence.

There was only one problem. If Anwar Isaacs and Kent Morkel were to step up to the witness box and give evidence, they would have to admit to their own illegal activities in the process of trying to slander the DA. Anwar had been fired for acting as Badih's intermediary and bribing councillors; Kent had also been involved in questionable 'business dealings' with Badih. Les Ziegelaar would have to explain what he had said about kicking 'political' investigations upstairs so that they would vanish into thin air.

They could end up in trouble.

To prevent this, the premier had conveniently included an indemnity from prosecution in the commission's terms of reference, making it possible for them to escape the consequences for their illegal actions while slagging me and the DA off at the same time. Neat.

It was all so patently obvious.

The media welcomed the commission, chaired by an honourable judge. Now we could get to the truth, the editorials opined.

But the story was soon overtaken by far bigger developments in Polokwane – the ANC's elective conference and the ousting of its leader, Thabo Mbeki, by his arch-rival and sacked deputy president, Jacob Zuma. This was a tectonic plate shift in South Africa's politics.

It also changed the ANC's balance of power in the Western Cape. Rasool, an Mbeki supporter, was further weakened. This only encouraged him to shore up his shaky support base by redoubling his efforts to destroy me.

I discussed the situation with Fiona. She agreed that these developments would give the Erasmus Commission greater momentum. She also believed it constituted a blatant abuse of power for ulterior political motives.

Advocate Jordaan submitted his findings. He found that the investigation contracted by the speaker had been legal, and necessary; he found that I had played no part in it. He found that the city had not paid a DA account. We gave Jordaan's report to the premier and offered him carte blanche to inspect any document or interview any person he wished to clarify any aspect of the matter. We had nothing to hide.

The province could have had no possible 'reason to believe' that we had done anything wrong. They required a 'reason to believe' that we had done something seriously wrong, in terms of the Municipal Systems Act, before they could institute an inquiry.

What more information could they get from a commission – unless they had another motive?

'The commission will provide a poison-dripping tap that will continue non-stop till the next election,' I said to Fiona. 'And if they repeat their lies often enough, more and more people will believe they are true. We have to turn this tap off.'

Fiona agreed. She said even though the commission was vulnerable on substantive issues, we should first look at the technicalities. Based on an opinion from Advocate Owen Rogers, she advised me to challenge the establishment of the commission, on the basis of the Municipal Systems Act and the Western Cape Commissions Act.

The commission suspended its hearings until the case was decided. Our application to declare the commission improperly constituted succeeded.

All the while, we were still waiting for the provincial minister of local government, Richard Dyantyi, to validate the council's decision to expel Chaaban – five months after the recommendation had been submitted to him. There could no longer be any doubt at all that the ANC was protecting him.

Having lost the case to establish the commission, I hoped Rasool would have come to his senses and use the opportunity to back off quietly. I hoped his lawyers would warn him that even if he complied with the legal technicalities in reconstituting the commission, it would still be vulnerable to challenge. If we could show that he had acted irrationally and in bad faith (which the lawyers believed we could), it would severely damage him.

As it turned out, the province's lawyers did warn Rasool against reconstituting the commission, but he ignored them. His political motive in destroying me made him throw caution to the wind.

The negative publicity had taken its toll, just as the ANC had hoped. On 19 March 2008 the DA lost a by-election in what should have been a safe seat – Macassar, Mitchells Plain – to our coalition partners, the Independent Democrats. I felt the loss deeply, and personally. The negative publicity I had been attracting was letting the party down and setting back our efforts to win the Western Cape in 2009.

Then, on 20 March 2008, Rasool wrote me a letter, saying, 'I have decided to appoint a commission of inquiry and to avail myself of my authority in terms of section 127 (2) (e) of the Constitution for this purpose.'

He had reconstituted the Erasmus Commission.

The constitution required him to act rationally and in good faith. That would inform our next line of attack. I believed we had all the evidence we needed. Fiona agreed.

But I knew we would pay a price. The media would howl in indignation and accuse me of a cover-up. They more than met my expectations.

I came to the conclusion that the ongoing negative publicity would destroy the DA's chance of winning the province in 2009 if I were the party's premier candidate. I discussed the dilemma at one of my breakfasts with Patricia de Lille. Then I made her a proposal. I didn't have a mandate from the party. I first wanted to clear it with her.

'The ANC is determined to destroy me,' I said. 'They won't stop until they have. This commission is going to drag on for months, and the media are going to play along with it. By the time the election comes, they will make sure I am thoroughly discredited, despite the fact that there is no basis for the allegation.'

I continued: 'If I am the party's premiership candidate, it will add fuel to the fire. They will just redouble their efforts. They cannot afford to lose the province as well.'

Then I 'popped the question'. How would she feel if we merged our two parties and she became the premiership candidate in 2009?

Patricia didn't dismiss the idea out of hand. I told her I had not yet broached the issue with the DA, but I wanted an indication from her before I did. I said the advantage of entering the election as a united force was that we could tackle the ANC and not have to fight the election between each other as well. Our experience in the city had shown that we could work together.

Patricia thought about it, but declined. I guessed the negative publicity surrounding me was getting to her too. The ID stood to gain the most out of the DA's relative decline – as our defeat in the Macassar by-election had shown. It was a trend we both thought would continue into 2009. Most polls projected that the ID would hold the balance of power in the province after the election. If that happened, Patricia would be able to hold out for the premiership anyway, I speculated.

With my proposal rejected, I knew I would just have to grit my teeth and get through this dip myself.

Then, out of the blue, I received a phone call – on the mayoral landline, as I recall – from a woman who introduced herself as Tatiana. She asked if she could come and speak to me. She had something important to say. My instincts told me to cut the red tape and accommodate her. 'Can you make it this afternoon?' I asked. I rearranged my diary.

At the appointed hour a woman walked into the mayoral waiting room. She was a knockout in her early twenties. From the marble-smooth skin to the cherub curl of her lip, the bounce of her thick blonde hair and the surface tension of her curvaceous hips, she oozed sex appeal. Her shape was enhanced by tight white jeans and a simple blue cotton top. As she walked down the foyer of the mayoral suite, I could see what it meant to turn heads.

I did a double-take myself and invited her into my office.

'I have something to tell you about Badih Chaaban,' she said, in a matter-of-fact way.

Tatiana's story poured out.

She had been Yuri Ulianitski's mistress, and Badih Chaaban's personal assistant.

She had met Yuri while waitressing at a gambling den belonging to Mark Lifman, routinely described in the media as 'one of South Africa's biggest underworld bosses'. Yuri had pursued her relentlessly, sending twenty-four long-stemmed red roses every day to the Waterfront restaurant where she worked when she wasn't at the poker club. Her former husband, another underworld figure, Dr Olli Tavares (who she married when she was seventeen), died when he was thrown out of a high building in Sea Point in a dispute over money. He had been associated with notorious gang boss and alleged double agent, Cyril Beeka.

Tatiana knew the inside story of the plot to capture the tendering system in the city. She told me how the underworld met to strategise its 'takeover' in time for preparations for the FIFA World Cup scheduled for 2010. As gangsters apparently do worldwide, they planned to have a politician 'on the inside' to help swing things their way. Badih was supposed to be that man.

At first I was cautious. Was this another trap, I asked myself. But I listened, saying as little as possible in case the conversation was being taped.

Tatiana told me she had resigned from Badih's employ because he pursued her relentlessly for sexual favours. She told me about his cash businesses, about his conversations with 'someone called Skwatsha' and another person I assumed to be Anwar Isaacs (from the description she gave). She told me Badih had a poster of me in a room in his house, at which he threw darts. And many other things besides. She showed me the most obscene phone messages he had sent to her in the early hours of the morning. She said she could not live like this any more and thought I should know what was going on, and the risk the city faced.

There was something deeply vulnerable, intelligent and gentle about this young woman, but it was also clear that at the tender age of twenty-one, she had been around the block a few times.

'Would you be prepared to put this all down in a written statement and swear to it under oath?' I asked.

'Yes,' she said without hesitating. I became worried for her.

'I'll get my lawyer to contact you,' I said. 'Thanks very much … and let me know if you face any problems.'

We exchanged phone numbers and Tatiana then left my office suite, with everyone's eyes following her.

I immediately called Fiona. She made an appointment to see Tatiana, and popped into my office afterwards, her eyes on stalks. Now we had it all down in a sworn affidavit, from someone with first-hand knowledge. Our investigation into Chaaban had been more than justified, and the police's failure to act against him inexplicable.

Our challenge on the constitutionality of the Erasmus Commission could not be heard by a judge from the Western Cape division, because it affected one of their number, Judge Nathan Erasmus. So two judges were seconded from the KwaZulu-Natal division, Judge Kevin Swain and Judge Chris Nicholson, to hear the case.

For my part, I tried to turn my mind to other things. I had been invited to New York to address the General Assembly of the United Nations on 'Urban Governance: Lessons Learned and Challenges Ahead'.

I can't remember clearly how this invitation came about; I recall a meeting with someone in Cape Town who represented the United Nations Commission on Population and Development. They were grappling with the problem of developing cities, where governments often regarded urbanisation as a negative phenomenon and were trying to stop it. I said we had to embrace urbanisation as an inevitable, potentially positive phenomenon, and I explained what Cape Town was doing to accommodate it.

As I recall, an invitation followed shortly afterwards.

Brent Gerber and I flew to New York. Brent's luggage never arrived. He must have been the first person to enter the plush United Nations lounge wearing a tracksuit and takkies, the clothes he had worn for the sixteen-hour flight. I had the equivalent of a VIP pass, so they did not challenge him, but Brent did himself no favours when the waitress asked him what he wanted to drink. 'Passion fruit and lemonade,' he replied. Her jaw dropped, and she stepped backwards to get a decent distance between herself and this weirdo. The look on her face told me she thought he had made an indecent proposal. I quickly intervened to explain that in South Africa this was a popular drink. She didn't look convinced. Brent had to order something else.

(When I looked online afterwards to find out what a granadilla is called in the United States, I saw that 'Passionfruit online' is what is known as an 'adult site').

I told Brent he was 'fresh from the farm' and forbade him from ordering passion fruit again in New York.

I gave my presentation to the full General Assembly and held a press conference on 10 April 2008, both of which were well received.

I then flew home, into the eye of a new storm.

At that time I had a weekly slot on the popular radio station Good Hope FM with Nigel Pierce, a local shock jock. Inevitably, the interview turned to the Erasmus Commission and my opposition to it. He wanted to know why I had challenged it. After all, it was being chaired by a judge.

To which I replied: 'Some judges allow themselves to be used, and unfortunately Nathan Erasmus is one of them.'

I had hardly put the phone down at the end of the interview when the world erupted around me. Here was the leader of the Democratic Alliance and the mayor of Cape Town attacking the integrity of a judge! This undermined the very foundation of democracy, the separation of powers and the integrity of the judiciary. We were entering one of the public-outcry cycles with which I was becoming familiar.

The story now had fresh legs. It was all over the newspapers and radio.

The DA, in particular, reacted very negatively. I had undermined one of the fundamental tenets of liberal political philosophy: respect for an independent judiciary.

The chief of staff in my DA office, Gavin Davis, wanted to speak to me. We sat in the leader's office in the DA's Cape Town headquarters. He leant forward, which indicated that I needed to listen carefully. He had something weighty to say.

'You have to apologise,' he said. 'You cannot survive this unless you do.'

'No,' I replied. 'What I said was true, and I am not going to withdraw it. Or apologise. I would rather resign.'

'You're in trouble,' Gavin said. He was a strong ally of mine and I knew he had my interests at heart. 'The party is reacting extremely negatively and this was an unforced error. You did not have to say that.'

'I did,' I said. 'A judge cannot claim the protection of his office if he is prepared to preside over a legal process this flawed, especially after a police investigation found nothing against me. He is allowing himself to be used. And I said so.'

Gavin had learnt by the tone of my voice that I was not going to budge, but he warned that it would be very hard for my leadership to recover.

'Be that as it may,' I said. 'I'll ask the party to let our court challenge run its course. If I lose, I'll resign.'

The DA gave me the time I wanted, but they were deeply disturbed by the flood of negative publicity my comments attracted.

The chatterati were one thing; the scathing criticism of a professor of constitutional law at the University of Cape Town was quite another.

Professor Pierre de Vos wrote a 'Thought Leader' column (dated 16 April 2008) that hit particularly hard. It was titled 'Zille Zillier Zilliest'.

Democratic Alliance (DA) leader Helen Zille has been very successful at cultivating the image of a no-nonsense, straight-shooting politician who sticks to her principles – no matter what. Her party has over the years also (rightly) lambasted the ANC for covering up the arms-deal corruption and for making statements aimed at undermining the independence and impartiality of the courts.

But in the wake of the appointment of Judge Nathan Erasmus to head a commission of inquiry into allegations of illegal spying and other shenanigans around the floor-crossing period, Zille seems to have thrown all these principles out of the window and, in the process, has probably irrevocably tarnished her image as Mrs Clean.

First, she has instructed her lawyers to take legal action to try to stop the Erasmus commission from doing its work, claiming that the commission was set up with a political motive merely to tarnish the image of the DA and the coalition government it leads in Cape Town. This kind of argument sounds awfully familiar. Is that not the kind of thing that ANC politicians say when they try to rubbish investigations of corruption against its own members? And when ANC politicians make such claims, is it not the kind of thing the DA leader shouts and screams about?

One would have thought that if the DA – and Zille in particular – had nothing to hide, it would welcome the chance to clear its name through such a commission of inquiry. By trying to stop a judge from finding out whether some DA politicians had broken the law, Zille seems to suggest that the DA has something to hide and that the party will do everything in its power to make sure that the truth does not come out.

This makes Zille and the DA appear shifty and dishonest – exactly the opposite of the image the DA leader is trying to project. It also makes Zille look like a rank hypocrite for always finding fault with the secretive ways of the ANC as far as corruption and maladministration is concerned, yet then to try to stop an inquiry into corruption when it deals with her own party. She has every right to challenge the legality of the commission, but politically, this is a very stupid move on her part. After all, people in glass houses should not throw the first stone.

This kind of thing went on for weeks. Syndicated columnist William Saunderson-Meyer provided this example on 19 April 2008 under the headline 'Zille's Spectacular Own Goal'.

> Zille is making a political mistake that will cost the DA dearly. She is adjusting her principles in front of the very voters she promised she would run a clean and accountable administration. Zille is in danger of giving the impression

that she is just another double-dealing, slimy politician, no different from the ANC bunch that the DA dislodged in Cape Town ...

There is a principled solution. If the DA has evidence against Erasmus, present it. If it is unhappy about the terms of reference of the commission, argue for them to be broadened. In the meantime, the DA should prove its commitment to the rule of law by submitting to it.

Oh, and a grovelling apology to Erasmus wouldn't come amiss.

On and on it went, day after day. My mother read it all. She wanted explanations. I gave them and, unlike most others, she grasped them instantly.

I knew this case would be make or break for me, but I tried to put it out of my mind. If we lost, I would be finished as the DA's leader, a year into the job. I would undoubtedly have to resign the mayoralty as well.

In the meantime, I put my head down, as I always did in a crisis, and lost myself in my work. I slogged day and night with my colleagues to get the city up and running efficiently. Gavin had his hands on the tiller at the DA leader's office and helped me keep the ship steady.

Then, on 12 May 2008, I read a news item that nearly made me fall off my chair. It was datelined Henley on Klip, which is a picturesque small town on the Klip River situated between Johannesburg and Vereeniging in Gauteng.

'Mystery surrounds the attack in which a Good Samaritan was murdered and a witness before the Erasmus Commission and her father were cut across the throat.

'Some men broke into the house of Tatiana Jacobs-Croucamp, 21 ...'

This was Tatiana, the young woman who had plucked up the courage to tell me the full story about Badih Chaaban, and put it down in an affidavit.

The report revealed that, after having her throat cut, she had managed to drive herself and her badly injured boyfriend, Tony Zizar, by car to a Vereeniging hospital 'where both were treated for cuts to the throat'.

'Police spokesperson Captain Shadow Mashobane confirmed that police had found a bloody knife near the parked car at the hospital. Police are investigating whether it was used to attack Jacobus-Croucamp and Zizar. Another knife, gloves and a beanie (hooded cap) were found on the crime scene.'

I immediately phoned Fiona.

'They tried to kill Tatiana!' I blurted.

I was convinced that the Western Cape underworld had tracked her down to Gauteng to murder her for snitching on them, as Badih had boasted he would when he tried to bribe and threaten Trevor Trout.

I tried in vain to make contact with Tatiana. The number she gave me had been discontinued. I concluded the last thing in the world she wanted was to make contact with me and risk further retribution. I let it be, but I felt dreadful, because I thought I was the cause of this attack. At least she had survived. That was some consolation.

During the course of writing this book, I tried to contact Tatiana again, without success. Then I hit on an idea! When Google fails, try Twitter. Early in July 2015, I sent out a tweet asking if anyone knew how I could contact Tatiana. Before long, I managed to get her contact number and she came to see me. Now almost thirty, her hair was darker and her blue-green eyes sadder, with life's light lines beginning to encroach on the corners of her voluptuous mouth.

She told me her story in an unsentimental and powerful way. It is how I hope she will write her story herself one day. She described her mother as 'utterly, unnecessarily beautiful', which had played a role in propelling her through six failed marriages and a descent into the hell of alcoholism. Tatiana left home at sixteen, finishing her matric at a cram college while supporting herself. Finding work came too easily to her, having inherited her mother's utterly unnecessary beauty. Soon she was earning more money working at clubs than a university graduate could hope to do in the first fifteen years of a career. It was there that Tatiana's life 'collided' with Cape Town's underworld, as she described it. She had a beautiful command of English.

I realised, once more, that exceptional beauty is not an asset for a woman seeking a purposeful life, as Tatiana now clearly was. She was sensitive and intelligent, and wanted to develop these attributes. When beautiful women are very young, it takes enormous strength of character and good guidance to avoid taking the path of least resistance. I sensed she had the character but had lacked the guidance.

I asked her what had happened to her at Henley-on-Klip. I was relieved when she replied it had nothing to do with the retribution of Cape Town's underworld or Badih Chaaban. Someone was trying to murder her, she said, after a property deal went sour. There was clearly more complexity to her life than I understood.

But back to 2008, where Rasool was waiting in limbo, increasingly impatient for our court challenge to conclude so that he could finally get on with his commission. If he destroyed me, he would be a hero in the ANC. Without this leverage, he was becoming increasingly beleaguered within his own party.

Bizarrely, we were still often invited to events together, as premier and mayor, where we sometimes spoke from the same platform. It was a surreal experience. Rasool was an outstanding public speaker, and always advocated open-mindedness, inter-faith dialogue and multiculturalism. I enjoyed listening to his speeches, because they encapsulated my own sentiments on these issues.

On one such occasion, he alighted from the stage at the Cape Town International Convention Centre, after we had both spoken, and I asked him directly: 'Premier, why do you promote these values in public and do the exact opposite in private?'

'It's a complicated world,' he replied.

It was definitely too complicated for me to fathom.

Inside the DA, we were preparing for the 2009 election. We undertook a major research project, under Ryan Coetzee's guidance, to determine the potential support for our core values of freedom under the rule of law, non-racialism and opportunity. We decided to relaunch the party towards the end of the year to herald the transition from our being a party of opposition to becoming a party of government. We hired experts to redesign our logo, and we decided to switch our party colour from yellow to blue. That would distinguish us neatly from the rest.

The conflict within the ANC escalated, which caused a major earthquake in the party.

The pre-shocks started in the Western Cape in July 2008, when ANC national chairperson Baleka Mbete announced that Rasool would vacate the premiership of the Western Cape. He had effectively been fired.

He was spared the embarrassment of being forced to resign, as he probably would have been just weeks later, when the high court handed down a devastating ruling against him.

I will never forget that Spring Day, Monday 1 September, when judges Swain and Nicholson ruled the Erasmus Commission unconstitutional, because it had been set up with an ulterior political motive.

The court also found that the appointment of a serving judge (Nathan Erasmus) to chair the commission was incompatible with the principle of separation of powers and was therefore 'unlawful and invalid'.

The judges found that Rasool's motive had been an 'improper one' of seeking to embarrass his political opponents, in particular the Democratic Alliance.

Because the premier's actions had been arbitrary and unlawful, his commission was 'set aside'.

As had so often happened before, people who abused their power to target me went down first.

But this wouldn't have happened without a strong, independent judiciary, one that refused to bend to the prevailing political winds. I understood, yet again, how crucial it was to do whatever necessary to preserve and protect the rule of law.

The very next day, De Vos published another 'Thought Leader', with the headline 'Zille Maybe Not So Zilly'.

Maybe I owe an apology to Helen Zille, leader of the Democratic Alliance? I harshly criticised her earlier this year for challenging the constitutionality of the Erasmus Commission of Inquiry set up by Premier Ebrahim Rasool, arguing that she appeared shifty and less than honest. I was particularly scathing of her criticism of Judge Erasmus ...

But yesterday a bench of judges agreed with Zille that Rasool's motive had in fact been the 'improper one' of seeking to embarrass his political opponents, in particular the Democratic Alliance (DA), which leads the city. Judges Kevin Swain and Chris Nicholson, sitting in the Cape High Court, also said the appointment of a serving judge to chair the commission is incompatible with the principle of separation of powers, and is therefore unlawful and invalid.

Luckily I did not comment on the legal validity of Zille's argument – otherwise I would have had serious egg on my face. However, in as much as my comments might have been interpreted as suggesting she does not have a case, I definitely owe her an apology. The Court, presented with all the facts, found that this Commission was set up with a political motive and thus that Rasool had tried to abuse the judiciary for short-term political gain.

De Vos went on to say that he still believed I should not have criticised Erasmus in the way I did, but I was grateful that he had the guts to acknowledge he was wrong and apologise.

Of course, none of the other columnists did. They moved on. Lovely job, being a columnist. You have enormous power to shape public opinion, but never have to take accountability for misleading them (unlike the politicians who they hold accountable for wrong judgements every day).

On 25 July, Lynne Brown was sworn in as premier. I had known her for years, and respected her quiet fortitude and straightforwardness.

For the first time in two years, I got the sense that the ANC accepted they had lost the 2006 election in Cape Town, but the battle had cost countless hours and many millions of rands. I often reflected on the irony of how an account of R3 500, paid by the City of Cape Town, started a 'scandal' that almost brought down our government, to the background chorus of a baying hack-pack.

Now, I hoped, we could get on with governing.

And we did. With a vengeance – a subject that I hope to cover in another book.

The news cycle moved on as another catalytic development hit the country on 12 September, when Judge Chris Nicholson handed down judgment in a much more significant case in the high court in Pietermaritzburg, KwaZulu-Natal. His decision to set aside the raft of corruption and other charges against Jacob Zuma was to change the course of South Africa's political history. The reason was a technical one: according to Judge Nicholson, the National Prosecuting Authority had not given Zuma a chance to make representations before they had charged him, as he said was required by the constitution. But Nicholson went further, stating that there had been 'political meddling' in the case, which had been overshadowed by a 'baleful political influence'.

Judge Nicholson's judgment left the door open for Zuma to be re-prosecuted once the procedural flaw had been rectified, but Mbeki was destroyed. The judgment led directly to the ANC's decision to recall him on 20 September.

I reflected on a remarkable coincidence: Judge Nicholson, whose judgment two weeks earlier had saved my political career, had now destroyed Mbeki's.

I felt really bad for Mbeki. I had met him several times during my period as DA leader, and I had found him amenable, approachable and reflective, not the aloof, forbidding figure he had been made out to be by his opponents.

I recalled my first one-on-one meeting with Mbeki soon after my election as party leader in 2007. It was a big media event, signalling a thaw in the frosty relationship between the president and the leader of the opposition. As the scrum of photographers clicked away, in the beautiful ante-room of Tuynhuys, the presidential office near parliament, President Mbeki leant over and straightened the collar on my cerise-pink silk blouse. I interpreted this as a protective gesture, to shield me from media commentary on my skew neckline. When the journalists left, we settled in for a chat, which was cordial and friendly, recalling our first meeting in Bermuda all those years ago. But I could see he was on his guard. After all, I was his political-opponent-in-chief – or so I thought until I realised that that role was reserved for people inside his own party.

I assumed our discussions were confidential, so I did not speak publicly about their content. Over time a relationship of greater trust developed. Even as the media portrayed Mbeki as a race-obsessed AIDS denialist, I came to see many facets of his reserved nature, which was often mistaken for haughty aloofness. Regarding his approach to AIDS, it was clear to me he wanted to balance treatment with prevention, at a time that the loudest voices in the AIDS lobby insisted sex was a private matter and no business of the state, despite the public and budgetary consequences.

But the president could never get to the point of talking plainly about prevention, and the behaviour change this required, because (I assumed) he was concerned that talking about intergenerational sex with multiple concurrent partners would reinforce the pejorative stereotype (as the African-American Dr Edward Rhymes put it) that black people are 'rampant sexual beasts, unable to control our urges, unable to keep our legs crossed, unable to keep it in our pants'.[*] In any event, our discussions gave me a much more nuanced understanding of his position than the caricature portrayed in the media.

Mbeki's greatest political challenge by far lay in his own party, and over time

---

[*] Cited in *ANC Today* 4 (42), 22–28 October 2004

I came to appreciate and understand this conundrum more and more. I reached the conclusion that his seeming obsession with race mobilisation disguised a much bigger battle within the tripartite alliance around economic policy. It became clear that his overriding mission was to save a market-based economy in South Africa as the foundation for growth and poverty reduction – against massive resistance in his own party that was coagulating like a large clot, around the figure of Jacob Zuma. Mbeki was not immune to the temptation of using race to mobilise the troops and keep them behind him. But his real focus was the economy, and for this reason he needed the DA to grow, although he could never say so outright. But he knew that I knew.

I remember one conversation in particular, long before the idea of 'state capture' became a topic of media speculation, when we spoke about the death of Brett Kebble. He told me that the investigation into Kebble's 'assisted suicide' had become a tool in the ANC's internal battle for control. There were factions in the police, he said, that were prepared to let a murderer off the hook if he was prepared to give evidence against the police commissioner, who had to be removed because he was a Mbeki ally. I listened aghast during some of these discussions, and sometimes I did not know why the president was telling me these things. I deduced that he wanted to give me a framework within which to understand developments. Because I got to know him personally, I never had the disdain for him displayed by some of my colleagues. He was a complex figure, certainly, but nothing like the autocratic ogre portrayed in the media.

Judge Nicholson's judgment on Mbeki was overturned a year later by Judge Louis Harms, who concluded that his interpretation of the constitutional right to representation before prosecution was incorrect, and that Nicholson had 'overstepped the limits of its authority' in raising allegations of political meddling.

But, back in 2008, after what came to be known as those eight fateful days in September, political events started snowballing. They were so momentous and so pivotal to the future of the country that I barely registered that I had made it to the final fifty out of a starting pool of 820 mayors, worldwide, who had been nominated for the biennial title of World Mayor.

I do not know who nominated me. That's nice, I thought, to get into the top fifty.

I didn't think about it again. The next thing I knew, I received notification that I was in the top eleven. (Eleven is a rather arbitrary number, I thought to myself.) Anyway, that was even nicer. A few weeks later I found myself in the final three. I then had to answer a long series of questions, online, and undertake a telephone interview. And then the news came through: I had been the unanimous choice of the urban think tank for the World Mayor award!

On 13 October 2008 the *Mail & Guardian* reported:

> The mayor of Cape Town, Helen Zille, has been awarded the 2008 World Mayor prize by City Mayors, an international urban-affairs think tank, a statement said on Monday.
>
> Editor of *City Mayors*, Tann vom Hove, said Zille had dedicated her professional life to improve the well-being of South Africans.
>
> 'Helen Zille was the judging panel's unanimous choice for the 2008 World Mayor prize. This amazing woman was making a difference and giving people hope.'
>
> 'Her only equals in South Africa are Desmond Tutu and Nelson Mandela,' the statement said.
>
> Zille is also leader of South Africa's opposition, the Democratic Alliance.

The City Mayors' statement listed Cape Town's achievements in the two years since the Democratic Alliance had ousted the ANC. I was particularly tickled by the fact that I had pipped the mayor of the world's most organised city, Zürich, to the title. I called to congratulate Emar Ledergerber, mayor of Zürich, who had given me a good run for my money.

It had been one of the rare uplifting weeks in politics.

The turmoil in the ANC was coming to a head. The tide was turning.

On Wednesday 8 October 2008, Mosiuoa 'Terror' Lekota, ANC chairman, served 'divorce papers' on his divided party. He walked out, together with Mbhazima Shilowa, and they announced the formation of a new party, the Congress of the People (COPE), amid an unprecedented media fanfare in Sandton, Johannesburg, on 1 November 2008.

The ANC was dramatically weakened, but the DA was also in trouble. Just eight months short of a general election, there was a vibrant new opposition party on the scene, born in a blaze of publicity, and heralded as the 'real thing' – a credible opposition challenge to the ruling ANC.

The DA's relaunch on 15 November, at Constitution Hill in Johannesburg, where we formally changed our colour and our logo, was a small and muted affair by comparison. It was met with some scepticism by journalists who had been swept along in COPE's wide slipstream as the party prepared for its founding congress in Bloemfontein on 16 December, the Day of Reconciliation.

This chapter cannot end without answering a question. What happened to Badih Chaaban, who had turned my life upside down for more than two years? He wasn't arrested, let alone charged. In fact, the ANC eventually gave him the mayoralty he so desperately craved, promoting him to the position of mayor of the Winelands District Municipality, where his party, the NPP, had brought the ANC to power in a coalition after the defection window of 2007.

By this time, nothing could amaze me any more. Not even the kind words

Badih directed at me after his inauguration: 'She [Helen Zille] is premier – the highest position in the province and I'm a mayor. I hope we will not fight again. I got to like her actually. She has a role to make sure I don't stray out of line and I don't think I will, and I've got to get on with my business of running this municipality. I hope we will not fight again.'*

I had survived another turbulent year in politics. But there was no rest ahead. The next year, 2009, was an election year, and we aimed to win the Western Cape.

---

* Aziz Hartley, Independent Newspapers, 3 July 2009

During my time as director of development and public affairs at the University of Cape Town, we organised a public-speaking event for the first lady of the United States, Hillary Clinton. Left to right: Professor Martin West, deputy vice-chancellor; Thenjiwe Kona, a departmental colleague responsible for events; Hillary Clinton; Helen Zille; Mamphela Ramphele, the vice-chancellor; John Martin, deputy vice-chancellor.

My favourite photo of Dad, with Carla's cat, Loverboy, on his lap.

In 2006 I became mayor of Cape Town, and two years later I was surprised – and delighted – to win the World Mayor Award.

With Tony Leon at the Gallagher Estate Convention Centre in Midrand on 6 May 2007, shortly after I was elected his successor as leader of the Democratic Alliance.

At my first meeting with President Thabo Mbeki, he lent forward to straighten my collar. It was a gesture of warmth and collegiality.

Above: Our extended family: Thomas and Paul with Grace Voyiya Mputing and her son Chulumanco, on Chulu's first day at The Grove Primary School. He is now at high school at Rondebosch Boys.

Right: Paul's graduation after completing his degree in applied statistics and psychology in 2007. Thomas is on the right.

Carla, Paul and me celebrating Mom's ninetieth birthday on 18 January 2009.

Grace watches her daughter, NgoweNceba, taking a ride on the back of Kaizer the Rottweiler.

Campaigning in 2009, the year I became premier of the Western Cape on 6 May. This was my lucky date. I had been elected DA leader on 6 May two years earlier.

Chatting to President Zuma at an event in Johannesburg in the run-up to the 2010 World Cup.

German Chancellor Angela Merkel flew in to Cape Town to watch the quarter-final match between Germany and Argentina in the 2010 World Cup. She took the opportunity of visiting a German-funded project in Khayelitsha together with Mayor Dan Plato and me, wearing my favourite 2010 coat.

The iconic 'three women' election poster which contributed to an outstanding national result of 23.9 per cent of the vote for the DA in the 2011 local government election. Flanking me in the poster are Patricia de Lille and Lindiwe Mazibuko.

The 'other woman', Mamphela Ramphele, and the infamous kiss. This was shortly after we announced that she would be the DA presidential candidate in the 2014 election – before the plan unravelled.

Mmusi Maimane and I take a break in the back of a car during campaigning for the 2014 general election. I was probably sending out a tweet. Mmusi was our candidate for premier in Gauteng.

With the Eastern Cape team (left to right) Nosima Balindlela, the former ANC provincial premier with whom I had confidential conversations for a year before she moved to the DA; Veliswa Mvenya, who has grown the DA exponentially in the former Transkei; and Athol Trollip, our provincial leader, with whom I worked well despite our repeated electoral contests against each other.

Putting up the first poster of the 2014 general election campaign at the national poster launch in Greenmarket Square on 24 April 2014 in Cape Town.

Finalising my State of the Province speech in 2014 as Janine Schouw styles my hair.

Outside the North Gauteng High Court, where I had come to collect the so-called Spy Tapes on 4 September 2014, after waging a five-year legal battle to have them released by the National Prosecuting Authority and Jacob Zuma's legal team. The tapes were pivotal in our attempt to demonstrate that the NPA had acted irrationally when it withdrew corruption charges against Jacob Zuma. On my left is DA spokesperson Phumzile van Damme, and on my right is Ntomboxolo Makoba, the leader's spokesperson.

Arriving with Mmusi Maimane and the rest of the DA caucus on the red carpet at the opening of parliament in February 2015. We were dressed in black to symbolise our mourning for the failure of political leadership and the consequent unravelling of the economy.

15

Moral Equivalence

Shortly before every national election since democracy, a new opposition party has emerged in South Africa, giving political pundits something to believe in. Each time, the new party is hailed as the real deal, a viable alternative to the ANC. Three additional words, 'unlike the DA', are sometimes implied, sometimes explicit.

While the DA was respected as an effective opposition, it was rarely taken seriously as a potential alternative government, primarily because we had a white leader. This analysis helped reinforce the ANC's line that we were a 'white party'.

An ex-brigadier of an apartheid homeland army, if he was black, was assumed to have greater legitimacy as a political leader than an anti-apartheid activist who happened to be white. South Africa's political debate has been stuck in this groove since the dawn of democracy.

In the run-up to every election, political analysts genuflected before the new black-led party, which offered renewed hope as the 'real alternative', while the DA had either 'painted itself into a corner', 'reached its support ceiling', or whatever.

Before the 1999 election, the great hope for the future of democracy was the United Democratic Movement, founded by Bantu Holomisa, who had been expelled from the ANC just two years after joining. Holomisa teamed up with former National Party minister Roelf Meyer. Five years later, in the lead-up to the 2004 election, came the feisty trade unionist Patricia de Lille, the unrivalled darling of the media, who left the moribund Pan Africanist Congress to form her own party, the Independent Democrats. President Nelson Mandela described Patricia as his 'favourite opposition politician'.

Eight months before the 2009 election, a turbocharged version of the 'new hope' phenomenon burst out of the starting blocks, directly into the home straight of an election campaign. The acronym for the new party, Congress of the People, was COPE. It came drenched in ANC symbolism, its name borrowed from the original Congress of the People, the mass gathering held in Kliptown in 1955 to collate the Freedom Charter.

COPE's new leadership looked like a who's who of the ANC's old: Terror Lekota (former ANC national chairman), Mbhazima Shilowa (former general secretary of

COSATU, Willie Madisha (former president of COSATU) and Smuts Ngonyama (the ANC's former communications chief).

The only new faces were white. Lynda Odendaal, a brand-new recruit to politics, made her debut as COPE's 'second deputy president' at its inaugural congress in Bloemfontein on 16 December 2008. The party's leadership needed 'minority' representation, and women. With Lynda, they could kill two birds with one stone. Unsurprisingly, she didn't last long. Lynda soon jumped ship, like the UDM's Roelf Meyer, to join the ANC.

For whites seeking redemption, the ANC was a bucket of powerful detergent in which to dip their stained fabric. Quick immersion could remove the marks of an apartheid past. By the time Lynda landed in the bucket, however, it was at least twenty years too late. It was more like wallowing in a mud hole.

By 2009, fifteen years after the advent of democracy, it was gradually becoming 'progressive' to oppose the ANC (as long as you weren't DA!). As a result, most commentators predicted that COPE would pose an even greater threat to the DA's support base than it did to the ANC's. DA voters, the argument went, would now be able to vote for a potential 'alternative government' rather than merely an 'effective opposition'. They would seize that opportunity in their numbers, the pundits predicted.

On 1 January 2009, Helen Suzman, the DA's iconic figure, died. It was the end of an era. There was a curious disjuncture in the way commentators and politicians across the spectrum hailed her prescience and foresight, while dismissing the party that continued to run with her baton. I felt secure in the knowledge that future generations, looking back on our role, would one day revise their assessment, just as they had of Helen Suzman. Even though she had not been politically active for years, we felt her loss keenly.

Early in 2009, the ANC moved quickly to scrap the floor-crossing provision in the constitution, fearing that, for the first time, they might become the victim rather than the beneficiary of defections.

COPE, seeking to differentiate itself from the ANC, chose the respected Bishop Mvume Dandala as its presidential candidate. Dandala was the former Presiding Bishop of the Methodist Church of South Africa (which had more than three million members) and former head of the All Africa Conference of Churches.

We faced the 2009 election squeezed on two sides. We were caught between an exciting, new party with a renowned church leader as its public face, and a 'new-look' ANC led by a charming traditionalist.

Zuma's ascension had tilted the ANC's internal see-saw away from the Xhosa-speaking heavyweights (often referred to as the Xhosa Nostra) to the numerically dominant Zulu.

This opened up a huge new potential support base. The ANC entered the 2009 election poised to absorb the Zulu traditionalists of the once powerful Inkatha Freedom Party in the province of KwaZulu-Natal. The ANC believed that what they lost on the COPE swings, they would regain on the Inkatha roundabout. Despite the tumultuous developments which tore the ANC asunder just eight months before an election, the party's support dipped by only 3.8 per cent in 2009 compared to their peak in 2004.

The DA, on the other hand, had no natural reservoir from which to draw new votes. On the contrary, there were now even more parties competing for the limited pool of opposition supporters. We found ourselves fighting on several fronts for a share of a complex market that defied clear definition. It was difficult terrain in which to grow, but we had no option. If a party stops growing, its leader (like the rider on a stalled bicycle) falls off, as Tony Leon always warned.

The arrival of COPE undoubtedly slowed the DA's momentum, but did not reverse it. After a bruising campaign, we grew nationally from 12.37 per cent in 2004 to 16.66 per cent in 2009 (polling 2.9 million votes, a million more than in 2004). I liked to say we had grown 33 per cent since the previous election. It sounded better than 4.3 percentage points. Most people didn't seem to know the difference anyway.

But we paid a price for our relative success. Our final campaign call – 'Stop Zuma' – may have been prophetic, but it was also deeply polarising. The year 2009 was our most racially divided election, even more so than our controversial 'Fight Back' campaign ten years earlier. Jacob Zuma was overwhelmingly popular among black South Africans.

COPE produced a strong showing, pulling 7.2 per cent of the vote, but came nowhere close to displacing us as the official opposition nationally. The new party did, however, achieve official opposition status in four provinces, an outstanding achievement.

The DA was the only party other than the ANC to win a province, taking the Western Cape with a clear majority (51.46 per cent). This was a breakthrough. Comparing apples with apples (the 2004 with the 2009 general election) we had grown by over 90 per cent in the Western Cape. It was the voters' positive verdict on DA governance in Cape Town and several other local municipalities. I was delighted with the result. I was sworn in as premier by Judge Dennis Davis, judge president of the Labour Court, and Dan Plato took over from me as mayor of Cape Town.

Winning a new sphere of government was pivotal to our strategy. It gave us the momentum we needed. We were now, indisputably, a party of government, not merely a party of opposition. This enabled us to show, rather than tell, that we could govern better, for all the people. This would enable South Africa to continue making the crucial transition from the politics of race to the politics of policy choice, without which no democracy in a multi-ethnic society can succeed.

If we hadn't won the province, we would have been far more vulnerable to the argument that we had now reached our final ceiling, and that COPE would surge forward, carried by the growing opposition to Zuma's ANC.

This didn't happen. The question is, why not? In fact, why didn't any of the 'real deal' opposition parties manage to convert their initial promise and popularity into a viable organisation with growing support?

Most analysts would say they succumbed to infighting, exacerbated by floor-crossing. When internal differences arose, there would either be a fight to the death or the disaffected would just cross the floor at the next opportunity, lured by the promise of ANC patronage.

I maintain that these were symptoms and aggravating factors, but not the root cause of their problems.

All political parties have their factions, internal battles and leadership contests, which at times become bitterly divisive, but comparatively few have built the internal institutions that are necessary to manage the tensions that arise across these fault-lines.

The DA's greatest achievement, and comparative advantage, is the development of these internal institutions, over decades. This is the real reason the DA has survived and grown for so long, despite remaining in opposition (a major feat anywhere in the world). Most political parties that maintain their momentum in a democracy enjoy spells in government. Becoming a party of government is a relatively recent experience for the DA.

Our internal battles are just as fierce, our contests just as ferocious, but we play by agreed rules. What's more, there are consequences for failure to do so. Our systems incentivise the outcomes we want, and our structures support them. The party's organisation is strictly separated from the internal political battlefield. Our disciplinary systems function independently of the political power hierarchy, so that prosecution for misconduct in the DA cannot be used for purposes of political persecution. Performance is measured on objective criteria and agreed benchmarks.

Perhaps above all, our candidate-selection system is structured to prevent it from degenerating into a manipulative patronage scheme, where leaders reward friends and penalise opponents. We don't always succeed, but we come closer than any other party I know of.

It is hard to become a public representative for the DA. Over the years, between elections, we have evolved a system of candidate selection that weighs past performance (against a range of criteria), as well as the more traditional elements of politics – speaking ability, policy proficiency and public profile. Our selection process has separate stages, with built-in checks and balances that seek to minimise block voting wherever possible, although we have never managed to eradicate this entirely. We improve our systems between every election, in the short window, when tensions ease.

We are far from perfect. Our systems are often flawed. But the very fact that we recognise how important these factors are, and that we try to solve our problems by improving our systems, distinguishes the DA from other political parties.

The DA's way of operating is the antithesis of the ANC's patronage system, which centres on a leadership clique dispensing rewards or retribution to keep people in line. Their ultimate lever is the compilation of election lists. If you fall out of favour, you are history.

Of course, the temptation to abuse power exists in every hierarchy, including the DA, but we consciously do our best to minimise it. That is one of the keys to our long-term survival.

When a patronage party loses power, they discover somewhere along the line that the purpose became peripheral to the perks. When there are no more jobs and goodies to hand out, they fall apart, as the ANC has in the Western Cape. The same thing happened to the old National Party, where leaders were traditionally treated like Moses descending Mount Ararat with tablets of stone. Their word was law. I vividly recall that when the New National Party finally rose in revolt against the decision of their leader, Marthinus van Schalkwyk, to join an ANC-led coalition in 2001, they had to search for a copy of the party's constitution to find out how to challenge him.

This would never happen in the DA. People refer to our constitution and rules every single day. No leader is above them. And there is open debate on almost every issue. It's a good start.

If there is one thing I would like my leadership of the DA to be remembered for, it is that I advanced this 'holy trinity' of attributes and consolidated them in the party's culture, through facilitating the development of strong internal institutions. This does not mean I did it alone, or that the job is done. As Francis Fukuyama warns, history has an up-escalator and a down-escalator. Every generation of politicians has to reinforce, and sometimes reconstruct, the culture of democracy and the institutions on which it rests.

During my tenure at the helm, between 2007 and 2015, the DA also worked to make these values part of South Africa's culture, primarily through what became known as our 'lawfare' programme (about which more later).

The biggest survival test for political parties in a democracy is how they weather the process of selecting candidates for elections. Every five years, elected representatives go through the painful process of reapplying for their own jobs, competing for an electable position against their colleagues as well as newcomers. This gives rise to a condition we call 'electionitis', which reaches epidemic proportions in the eighteen months before each poll. And because elections for different spheres of government alternate in staggered five-year cycles, parties find themselves in the grip of raging electionitis every two years.

For parties less robust than the DA, this disease often proves fatal. This is why so many opposition parties, for which people hold out so much hope, succumb so soon. COPE, for example, could not even convene an internal elective congress without splitting.

But the major reason for the premature demise of most opposition parties is that they have been built almost exclusively around individual, charismatic leaders. They never manage to lay stable institutional foundations, let alone build them into effective structures and systems, or entrench sound governance based on agreed rules. Arbitrary decision-making by party leaders has grave consequences for political organisations operating in democracies.

I have little doubt that the same fate will befall Julius Malema's Economic Freedom Fighters, except it will take a bit longer and will leave more blood on the battlefield.

It has become a cliché to say that Africa needs big institutions, not big men.

And Africa's political parties need to build strong 'internal institutions'.

Having inherited strong foundations from Tony Leon, I resolved to ensure the DA became a model African political party. I was driven partly by conviction, and partly by necessity. I did not have the time to be hands-on, let alone to micro-manage our systems as my opponents had warned I would.

Ryan Coetzee and I agreed that my job as DA leader would focus primarily on promoting our vision and values, communicating the key messages (internally and externally), and raising a significant proportion of the money required to achieve our electoral goals. These tasks kept me busy enough.

I gave direction to debates in the appropriate party structures, but only intervened in operational matters when our agreed rules, structures or systems were violated, or when I judged there was an overriding need to do so, in the interests of the party's electoral prospects. And I always did so within the rules.

Usually, I just let people get on with their jobs, maintaining an 'open-line' policy that enabled them to speak to me when they needed to.

Appointing the right people in the right positions proved crucial. I called it 'fitness for purpose'. I depended a lot on the excellent young people who ran the leader's office, like Gavin Davis, Frits de Klerk and Geordin Hill-Lewis. They had to make thousands of decisions every day and respond to hundreds of people a week. Crucially, they required the discernment to know which to refer to me.

It was primarily the quality of the professional staff at the federal head office and in the provinces that turned the DA into the 'blue machine' it is today. They have been ably led by successive chief executive officers, Ryan Coetzee, Jonathan Moakes and Paul Boughey.

James Selfe, together with the ultra-efficient Elsabe Oosthuysen, provided the nexus where the party's political process and its professional staff came together. James had chaired the Federal Council and Federal Executive since the DA's formation. This continuity provided the stability and institutional memory that proved pivotal, as successive leaders and chief executives came and went.

And, throughout, we had the invaluable support of the Friedrich Naumann Stiftung, the German foundation named for the great liberal leader of the late nineteenth century, which supports the development of liberal parties worldwide.

My main job in our evolving strategy was to make sure we governed effectively where the voters had elected us to do so. That meant focusing, first and foremost, on my 'day job', initially as mayor, and after the 2009 election as premier. This also gave tremendous scope for the leader of the parliamentary caucus, as well as provincial leaders, to build their profile and play a leadership role in the party.

When Tony stepped down as leader of the opposition in 2007, the interregnum leading to the 2009 election was filled by the experienced Free State parliamentarian Sandra Botha, before she became South Africa's ambassador to the Czech Republic.

After the 2009 election, the position of parliamentary leader was contested by Athol Trollip and Ryan Coetzee. I supported Ryan, with whom I had built a strong and functional relationship. Athol won. It had been a divisive battle. Ryan was expected to win, until a final switch in support of some caucus members the night before the vote. Some of the research staff, whom Ryan had mentored, had actively supported him, against the party's rules. Now Athol was in charge of the parliamentary operation. It took some time for the party to get back on an even keel again.

As in the past, when we had been on opposite sides of electoral contests, Athol and I moved on quickly and developed a strong, productive partnership. We met every Wednesday evening for a drink, so that we could talk through what lay ahead in the parliamentary caucus meeting the next morning. Even these short engagements made a big difference to the smooth interface between our offices. We never experienced the 'two centres of power' problem I'd been warned of, despite the fact that we were both strong personalities.

Ryan resigned from parliament to become chief adviser in my office in the provincial government. He made as big a difference to re-imagining our role in government as he had to re-engineering our party.

We had the numbers to govern the Western Cape on our own, but we decided to offer a position in the cabinet to the Independent Democrats and COPE, who had two and three seats in the forty-two-member legislature respectively. The

ID accepted a cabinet position; COPE turned us down, wishing to carve out an independent identity.

I had to fill the remaining nine cabinet positions by matching the portfolio with the skills of individuals in our twenty-two-member caucus. Our success in government would depend on getting this fit right. And I also had to be mindful of the 'balance of internal forces' between contesting groups and factions inside the DA in the process of constituting a cabinet.

I scoured the CVs of the twenty-two elected DA members of the legislature and found the best fit possible in the circumstances.

I was prepared for the inevitable fallout. Except I did not anticipate its force and extent. It reverberated throughout the country, and lasted for years. In fact, today, seven years later, it is still often raised by my critics. The reason for the furore was that all nine of the DA's cabinet members I appointed, as well as the one from the ID, were men. People responded as if I had personally rejected every woman in the Western Cape. Was there not one single woman in the whole province who was good enough to sit in my cabinet, critics asked. 'There are thousands,' I responded. 'Unfortunately, they did not make themselves available for our election list.'

Most critics seemed unaware that I was not free to choose from the entire Western Cape female population. I had to pick a cabinet out of the pool of twenty-two DA members who had been elected to the provincial parliament, of which only three were women. There were far more women on our list for the national parliament than the provincial legislature. In the DA we allow freedom of choice for candidates to put themselves forward for the list of their choice.

The public criticism was justified, at least in part. Although the DA rejects quotas, it taught me a lot about ensuring greater gender diversity in our processes, from the start.

Nevertheless, the political opportunism of my opponents rankled, as they tried to turn it into a major scandal. Tony Ehrenreich, the ANC and COSATU provincial loudmouth, threatened to go to court to overturn my cabinet selection and call a general strike unless I apologised.

Everyone who was anyone in the ANC accused me of sexism, and worse.

Irritated, I said this criticism was rich coming from a party that had never had a woman leader in its hundred years of existence and was led by a 'self-confessed womaniser with deeply sexist views, who put all his wives at risk by having unprotected sex with an HIV-positive woman'. I originally wrote this sentence in a letter to the *Cape Argus*, in response to ANC criticism. As the furore gathered momentum, my spokesman released the letter as a press statement.

With that, we leapt from the frying pan into the fire.

I had expected the statement to cause a flurry. Indeed, it was intended to. I was sick of the rank hypocrisy of those accusing me of sexism.

I did not anticipate the uproar that followed, however. There was unmitigated outrage from almost every quarter, friend and foe alike. Initially, I was puzzled (since I had stated the bleeding obvious), but then I began to understand a phenomenon that sets in after the election of a new national leader. It is a process of societal adjustment, of realignment, where people instinctively fall in behind a new power hierarchy. It is expressed in the old adage 'The king is dead. Long live the king'. I had bucked this convention.

If I had attacked Zuma using the same words during the election campaign, no one would have noticed. The fact that I said it afterwards, about a newly elected leader, just as everyone was adjusting to the new order, made it unforgivable (even if it was true).

On and on the furore went, as if nothing else was happening in South Africa, let alone the rest of the world. The ANC competed with its alliance partners and affiliates to release the most extreme statements of condemnation. When I read a news report of the ANC Youth League saying 'Zille has appointed an all-male Cabinet of useless people, the majority of whom are her boyfriends and concubines so that she can continue to sleep around with them', I knew it was time to take another short break from reading newspapers. I needed to restore my equilibrium.

Reading the newspapers formed part of our morning routine. Either Johann or I would jump out of bed, make tea, fetch the newspapers and open the blinds so that we could prepare for the day ahead. Usually, I read the newspapers while Johann did his meditations. When I needed a break from the media, I would leave the papers unopened in a pile, prop my laptop on my knees and work on my email correspondence instead. Johann would get to the papers after his meditations, and inform me if there had been any new development about which I needed to know.

This was the bedroom scene on an autumn morning in late May 2009.

Johann suddenly burst out laughing.

'What's so funny?' I asked.

He pondered the article he was reading for a second, and said: 'This is actually serious, but it's so outrageous, it's funny.'

'What?' I asked impatiently, trying to get on with my emails.

Johann proceeded to read aloud a report of a media briefing held the previous day at Luthuli House, the ANC's headquarters in Johannesburg, where the MK Military Veterans Association presented its considered analysis of why I had appointed an all-male cabinet.

'The real reason,' said MK Military Veterans Association Chairman Kebby Maphatsoe, 'is so that its members are kept close enough to satisfy her well-evolved wild whore libido.' Then he added: 'They [the men] are also kept in her power corridors isolated from other women, so as to satisfy her and her alone; hence the exclusion of other women as they pose undesired sexual competition to her undying lust for sex with her male groupies.'

Maphatsoe then moved on to the political relevance of these observations: 'She is a fascist of the worst kind, who, after evidently sleeping with more than her fair share of white males in her preferred lifestyle of serial monogamy, now turns around and demonises those who are honest to their cultural preferences,' he noted. If I did not 'refrain from this anti-African and racist behaviour', the Military Veterans would 'not hesitate to launch a political programme aimed at rendering the Western Cape ungovernable'.

The general secretary of the South African Communist Party, Dr Blade Nzimande, was quoted next, saying, 'I'm worried if Helen Zille is still together upstairs.'

The ANCYL repeated the line about my appointing my lovers and 'concubines' and threatened 'militant action' against me if I continued to 'speak hogwash'.

Johann and I looked at each other in astonishment. Then we both burst out laughing.

'These guys have actually done you a favour,' said Johann. 'They have confirmed your point about where the real sexism lies.'

His words provided some consolation. So did those of the ANC secretary general, Gwede Mantashe, who described the comments as 'a marked departure from the ANC's approach to political engagement'.

Mantashe's statement had little discernible impact, however. The Military Veterans announced they had started a 'systematic movement to remove [me] from office' (*Cape Argus*, 28 May). The ANCYL vowed to reveal the names of my lovers, as one banner headline boldly announced. They had evidence of whom I was sleeping with, they claimed (*Sowetan*, 18 May).

Hundreds of Military Veterans marched to my office dressed in camouflage gear and demanded that I appear before them. My strategically sussed secretary, Donnae Strydom, had arranged for me to be elsewhere. When Minister Bonginkosi Madikizela went to collect their memorandum, they refused to give it to 'one of Zille's boyfriends'.

Although I had stayed out of the fray for at least a week, the media treated the matter as one of 'moral equivalence' between me and the ANC. In other words, we were equally culpable. The DA remained silent, although the DA Youth showed it agreed with the 'moral equivalence' line when it urged me to stop the rhetoric and focus on delivery. Their statement appeared under the headline 'ZILLE RECEIVES "REPRIMAND OF SORTS" FROM DA' (IOL, 14 May 2009).

In the midst of all the turmoil, I received a call from a councillor colleague, Carin Brynard, who asked if she could bring someone to speak to me urgently.

I needed to be warned. We had to meet in private. We arranged a time and place. Carin introduced me to a police officer, who was clearly worried. 'If anyone finds out I have come to speak to you, I will lose my job,' the officer said. 'I just need you to know that for months your telephone calls have been intercepted and transcribed at the headquarters in Bishop Lavis.' The officer then handed me a dossier that included excerpts of conversations I had conducted over the phone. This was irrefutable evidence that my calls had indeed been intercepted. I asked the officer whether a judge had authorised the interception – which would otherwise have been illegal – and I was told that, indeed, it had been properly authorised, which meant that there was a judge helping the police to help the ANC to undertake a fishing expedition to find anything they could to discredit me.

I thanked the officer and undertook not to reveal who had passed this information on to me.

I asked the DA parliamentary office to submit questions to the minister of intelligence, but this produced nothing concrete. If I could have quoted my source as well as the information, the scandal of the bugging would have dwarfed the outcry over my alleged sexism. I was getting used to the Kafkaesque world where nothing was what it seemed. Every manufactured public scandal was actually designed to disguise the real scandal.

Jacob Zuma stood above the fray, more popular than ever.

It was in this unconducive climate that I tried to persuade the party to challenge the decision of the National Prosecuting Authority to drop charges against President Zuma on over 700 counts of corruption, bribery, money laundering and racketeering. The decision to withdraw the charges was announced by the acting national director of public prosecutions, Advocate Mokotedi Mpshe, on 7 April, just two weeks before the 2009 election.

Mpshe announced that the case against Jacob Zuma would not proceed because 'an intolerable abuse has occurred which compels a discontinuation of the prosecution'.

'As an officer of the court,' Mpshe continued, 'I feel personally wronged and betrayed that on a number of occasions I have given evidence under oath, that there has not been any meddling or manipulation of the process in this matter. It is with a great regret that I have to say today that in relation to this case, I cannot see my way clear to go to court in future and give the nation this assurance.'

He had come to the conclusion that there had been political meddling in this case after listening to a tape-recording, provided by Jacob Zuma's lawyers, of a wire-tapped telephone conversation between Advocate Bulelani Ngcuka (former national director of public prosecutions) and Leonard McCarthy (former head of the independent corruption-busting Directorate of Special Operations, better known as the Scorpions).

In the recording, made in the last quarter of 2007, Ngcuka and McCarthy discussed the timing of recharging President Zuma, in relation to the ANC's Polokwane elective conference scheduled for December, where Zuma was set to challenge Thabo Mbeki.

Mpshe's logic was less than convincing. Firstly, it was Mpshe himself who had decided that the prosecution should go ahead, on the basis of the evidence before him. Secondly, it had been Mpshe who had determined the timing of the announcement. Neither Ngcuka nor McCarthy had the power to do so, which meant any conversation they may have had on the matter was purely academic and could not have influenced Mpshe's decision. Indeed, Mpshe had not even known about the conversation when he took the decision to recharge Jacob Zuma. Yet here was Mpshe, effectively saying that undue influence had been brought to bear on a decision about the timing of recharging Zuma – a decision that Mpshe himself had taken. Unless he was admitting having succumbed to some other form of undue influence, his lamentations concerning 'intolerable abuse' made no sense at all.

In fact, Mpshe's reasons were so disingenuous (the constitution would use the word 'irrational') that I knew immediately we would have to challenge them.

Furthermore, I could not quite understand why it was improper for an investigator and a prosecutor to be discussing the timing of a case against an accused. As long as they don't tamper with any evidence, they both have the same role in a criminal justice system – to ensure the conviction of criminals on the basis of unearthing and presenting the facts. It is not as if either of them was going to serve as a judge, or a defence lawyer.

There was something seriously wrong going on. I realised our battle with Jacob Zuma was only just beginning – yet there was a strong sense in the DA that it was time for a moratorium on hostilities, after the racially polarising impact of our 'Stop Zuma' election campaign.

I had to persuade a combat-and-controversy-weary DA that we would have to gird our loins once more for a legal battle to test the constitutionality of Mpshe's decision to withdraw the charges against Jacob Zuma. I argued that we could not shy away from what I believed would turn out to be 'the most important review case in our democracy'. We could not allow Jacob Zuma and his allies to capture the National Prosecuting Authority for their own ends.

The DA's Federal Executive gave us the mandate to proceed. Thus began our lawfare programme.

In the meantime, within six months of my having been excoriated for my comments on Jacob Zuma's sexism and sexual behaviour, the wheel turned 180 degrees, when the news broke that the daughter of one of Zuma's close friends had given birth to the president's twentieth child, a little girl. Whatever I may have said about the president six months earlier paled into insignificance compared to the vitriol now spewed at him from every quarter.

The baby's grandfather, Irvin Khoza, one of South Africa's soccer czars and co-chair of the committee responsible for organising the FIFA World Cup scheduled for June/July 2010, was quoted as saying he felt 'betrayed' by his friend Jacob Zuma. That was the mildest statement of all.

Having been effectively told to 'shut up' about Zuma's behavioural example by the party eight months earlier, I now took my gap. On 4 February 2010, I wrote in my newsletter:

> The latest controversy surrounding President Jacob Zuma illustrates a consistent thread running through his presidency: power abuse.
>
> Zuma believes he is above the law and social norms. He believes that – by virtue of his position – he can get away with anything.
>
> This attitude applies to Zuma's financial dealings, his relationships with women, and to his relationship with his citizens. If any institution of state gets in his way, it is effectively neutered. If any government campaign requires him to change his behaviour, it is ignored.
>
> Behind his undoubted warmth and charm, this is the real Jacob Zuma. It is also the real ANC.

I described his appeals to culture as a ruse to avoid accountability. And then I turned to the most mismanaged issue in our democracy – preventing the spread of HIV and AIDS.

> The truth is that Zuma has set us back at least a decade in the fight against HIV/Aids. His actions will have a far more negative impact than even the Aids denialism of Thabo Mbeki. Getting bogged down in esoteric theories and quack science would have had far less impact on people's behaviour, than a leader who by his own example, justifies unprotected sex. The inevitable response of millions of young men will be: 'If the President can do it so can I.' This attitude undermines the entire edifice of the government's HIV/Aids prevention programme. It will destroy many lives. And it will cost the taxpayers millions in treating people who contract HIV/Aids as a result.

During the many public and sometimes vitriolic clashes I have had with Jacob Zuma, there was one person who was always unfailingly pleasant, warm and gracious towards me, and that was – Jacob Zuma! To the point of unnerving me entirely. I would have felt better if he had counter-attacked. Or even just cold-shouldered me. I was prepared for that. Yet, he was always charm itself. After every interaction with him, I felt deeply guilty about criticising him.

I remember my first one-on-one conversation with Jacob Zuma as though it was yesterday.

It took place on 25 May 2009, at the height of our very public confrontation over the composition of my cabinet, during which I had used his sexual proclivities as an example of the way the ANC generally regarded the role of women.

I was due to fly to Pretoria early next morning to attend my very first national cabinet lekgotla. A cabinet lekgotla is the quarterly meeting, convened by the president, at which the full cabinet meets the provincial premiers to discuss items of national importance.

The day before the meeting, I was in Khayelitsha at a preparatory event for the World Cup. One of my colleagues came running up, saying he had just had a call from my office to say that the president was about to call me on my cellphone. His office had requested my number. Seconds later my phone rang. I answered. There was the unmistakably warm voice of President Zuma.

'Good afternoon, Mr President,' I said.

'Good afternoon, Premier,' he said jocularly, as if we had never had a disagreement in our lives. He was full of levity and laughter. 'Tomorrow you will be coming to the presidential guest house for your first lekgotla,' he continued.

'Yes, Mr President,' I answered.

'You will be the only DA person there,' he said.

'Yes, I know, Mr President.'

'Well, I just want to let you know that you should feel completely relaxed about that. Please do not worry about it. You will be very welcome.'

That was it! That was all he had phoned to say.

I was totally astounded. In an enormously pressured schedule, in the third week since his inauguration as president, he had taken the time to track down the cellphone number of his most outspoken critic, with whom he was involved in a bitter and highly personal public spat, to put her mind at ease about a meeting he thought she might feel apprehensive about.

I had spent an entire election campaign telling voters to 'Stop Zuma', and here he was saying I will be welcome at the presidential guest house and ensuring I did not feel apprehensive.

That was my first direct, personal experience of the legendary charm of Jacob Zuma. Apart from being amazed, I felt deeply guilty about saying nasty things about him (let alone the court case we were planning to get the charges against him reinstated).

But I couldn't let my emotions trump reason or my constitutional function.

I went up to Pretoria the next day actually looking forward to meeting him and talking to him personally. I arrived at the imposing state guest house with Brent, who by that time was the Western Cape's director-general, in a small hired car. We looked out of place among the limousines that sailed around the circle to drop ministers at the end of a pillared walkway which led to the conference facilities at the presidential guest house.

There was a spread of food, including a variety of fruit, and tea in beautiful thin china cups. When President Zuma arrived, a hush fell on the room, as he greeted people.

At that, and every subsequent meeting, he greeted me as if he had been missing me, and called me *intombazana* (young girl) – which he meant as a compliment, and which I interpreted as one. He was so profoundly, unconsciously patriarchal that it was actually endearing.

At the very next lekgotla, we were invited to a braai at the president's residence to socialise after a full day's work. As usual I was the only DA politician there. We ate and then the music started. I was chatting in a small group when I felt a nudge on my arm. I turned to see President Zuma, who with a small, chivalrous nod of his famous head asked me to dance. I gulped. I could see by his stance he meant ballroom, not bop.

'Mr President,' I stuttered, 'I would love to, but I can't dance.'

'Don't worry, I will lead you,' he replied. He placed my left hand on his right shoulder, held my right hand aloft with his left, and we were off, around the makeshift dance floor. I was all left feet, sweaty palms and palpitations. My right hand must have been crushing his left hand, I was holding on so tightly.

'Relax,' he laughed. 'I will steer you.'

Within seconds I realised what an accomplished ballroom dancer he was. I tried to follow his lead. Occasionally, I almost tripped us both, but he made light of it, paused momentarily to recalibrate, and then set off again, hardly missing a beat.

By this time, almost the entire cabinet had their cellphones out to record this dance. I tried to look relaxed, smile and make small talk.

'Where did you learn to dance so well, Mr President?' I ventured. 'I also need lessons.'

'It's a funny story,' he replied.

The story kept me entertained for the rest of our dance. As a young man he met a young lady he fancied and asked her out to a dance on a Saturday night. I think he said it was in Durban. She was obviously more worldly than the young man from Nkandla. Poor Jacob suddenly confronted an unexpected sight – twirling couples executing complex ballroom routines. He was too embarrassed to ask the young lady to dance (I assured him I knew what he must have felt like), so he and his date stood on the perimeter and watched. It did not take long for another beau to approach his date and whisk her off, while Jacob stood holding her coat for the rest of the evening.

'The very next Monday morning, I went and enrolled at Arthur Murray dance studios, where I learnt to dance,' he told me.

'I know where I'm going this coming Monday morning,' I answered.

He laughed. 'You will enjoy it,' he promised.

I flew back to Cape Town still having flashbacks of almost tripping up the president on the dance floor. Those moments were captured in scores of cellphones – I'm amazed that none of them ever appeared in the newspapers!

When I got home I had made up my mind that Johann and I were going to go for dancing lessons. He had grown up in a community where dancing was considered a sin. Now his excuse was that his knees gave him too much pain to dance.

He was scheduled for a double knee replacement.

'When you have your new knees,' I said, 'there are no more excuses. You and I are going to take dancing lessons. I have to be able to dance properly with the president when I go to lekgotlas.'

I told him the story.

'I just can't help liking Jacob Zuma,' I said. 'He's nicer to me than almost everyone in the DA.'

That was true. The DA is tough on its leaders. You have to earn their respect. You have to justify your proposals and ideas. They call you to account when things go wrong (and sometimes when they don't).

But not Zuma. He always made me feel comfortable, in whatever circumstances.

After that, every time I went to a cabinet lekgotla, Johann would say he expected me to return as President Zuma's next wife.

I learnt something important from Zuma's approach to leadership: to leave as much of the fighting as possible to others. It is important to distinguish between the battles that only you can fight and those that others can, and should. I had always assumed that only cowards ducked out of fighting their own battles, but I learnt it is not necessarily so. Wise political leaders limit the number of enemies they make to the essential and unavoidable (there are more than enough of those). You must let your allies fight some of your battles. It is a leadership skill I never mastered. President Zuma had it down to a fine art. He was a living manifestation of Dale Carnegie's time-honoured philosophy that making friends is the most effective way of influencing people (and benefiting from them).

But this alone is no substitute for other leadership attributes, as Zuma was soon to learn.

I had never been to a lekgotla chaired by President Thabo Mbeki. At my first tea break on the first day of my first lekgotla, I heard cabinet participants comparing lekgotlas run by Mbeki and Zuma. Mbeki made you stick to the point, they complained. Zuma let you speak your mind. It was so liberating.

They liked it before tea on the first day. With each passing day at each successive lekgotla, I sensed a growing impatience with the waffle and self-indulgence that passed for discussion, as Zuma's underlings tried to impress him by saying a lot about nothing. I got the sense that more and more participants were starting to miss Thabo Mbeki.

Yet, however great the crisis of the moment, Zuma was supremely relaxed and always warm and friendly. I believed him when he said he did not listen to his critics, otherwise he would have 'that disease white people call stress. I don't have it because I know better.'

Because of confidentiality provisions, I am not allowed to say what specifically was discussed or quote anything said at these meetings, but I can say how they said it.

I was given an opportunity to speak every time I requested one. I regularly challenged the ANC line. President Zuma would be jocular and warm. Then the attack dogs would go for me one by one, each given a longer leash by a smiling chair. Each speaker ratcheted up the volume and ferocity. I got to know the pattern early on.

It was also apparent how different our governance model was in the Western Cape from those of other provinces and the national government. We had worked hard to establish a transversal model of government, working together to achieve overarching shared government goals. National departments tended to work in silos, protecting their turf from encroachment by other departments. It really hampered the process of building a capable state. I could never really work out how other provinces functioned.

As the World Cup approached, Zuma nicknamed me Vuvu-Zille (after the blaring monotone plastic horn known as the vuvuzela). It was the perfect, humorous put-down to my sustained criticism.

The World Cup proved a pleasant respite. Despite all the challenges, we were ready for kick-off in Cape Town on 11 June 2010. The Fan Walk became a centre of celebration for everything we had achieved. South Africa put on a show for the world to remember. Even the criminals took a break for a few weeks, and crime dropped to record lows. South Africans reminded themselves of what we have the capacity to be.

One of the political highlights was the visit of Henry Kissinger, United States secretary of state in the Nixon years. I felt quite chuffed that he specifically asked to see me. He wanted to ask a question: How was the DA managing to build a party based on common values, that transcended racial and ethnic boundaries in a deeply divided society? He said he had told both President Nixon and President Ford that this goal was impossible to achieve in Africa, yet here was the DA doing exactly what he had predicted could not happen. I had to think very hard about my answer. But he left me in no doubt about the enormity of our challenge, and that we would have to contradict every historical precedent in order to achieve success. He reminded me that no other party, anywhere, had succeeded in doing what we were setting out to do, so shortly after a transition to democracy. Those kinds of statements kept me awake at night.

Fortunately, I had a lot of distractions.

By that stage, Johann and I were living in Leeuwenhof, the premier's residence, even though we had resolved, after my election, not to move there. We changed our minds after the 'premier's security' moved onto our Rosebank property, and my sons' friends had to 'sign in' to visit them. The boys then insisted that we leave. 'That is why they have a residence for the premier,' said Tom.

Soon afterwards, my soccer-crazy Argentinian cousin, Bobby Herzveld, and his wife Erna came to stay with us at Leeuwenhof for the World Cup, and we enjoyed an evening together with Angela Merkel, the German chancellor, who flew in for the quarter-final match between Germany and Argentina in Cape Town on 3 July. We had a great time together watching the other quarter-final, between Spain and Paraguay, on our family television.

In the middle of the World Cup, a big local story broke. On 30 June, a former journalist for the *Cape Argus* newspaper, Ashley Smith, decided to 'unburden his soul' and confess that he and his political editor had secretly moonlighted as embedded, paid spin doctors for the Western Cape premier, Ebrahim Rasool. The political editor was Joe Aranes, a former member of MK and a strong ally of the premier.

According to Smith's confession, they were given money in brown envelopes, via a communications consultancy, also headed by a former MK operative and close ally of the premier, who had been awarded a multimillion-rand communications tender through unconventional means by the provincial government. The company had recruited the help of serving journalists.

'Prior to the 2005 ANC Western Cape conference,' Smith's confession read, 'it had become clear that Rasool's political life was on the line and it was around this time that I started receiving calls to meet with Rasool at Leeuwenhof, the premier of the Western Cape's official residence ... These meetings were often held at irregular hours, often late at night. Always present at these meetings were the three Inkwenkwezi [communication company] members.'

Some of the meetings were attended by Rasool's political allies, said Smith, who sought indemnity from prosecution for his confession.

The newspaper went through an agonised *mea culpa*, pointing out that Smith had faced disciplinary charges in 2005 but had resigned before they reached a conclusion. Aranes, facing a lesser charge, had been stripped of the title of political editor.

Nevertheless, the paper's ethos had, by then, become established. Aranes's popularity and charisma continued to permeate the newsroom. Most English-language newspapers had 'transformed' their reporting staff rapidly, taking on board activists who had previously promoted the underground ANC in the 'alternative' media; these senior journalists were supplemented by newly minted activists, fresh from college.

This meant that many of the newspapers found themselves still stuck in a struggle syndrome, with the ANC on the moral high ground. With a few notable exceptions, journalists found it difficult to move to a more independent and critical appraisal of the developments in the new South Africa. And when it came to the internal struggles in the ANC, they chose sides.

All this I already knew. The new revelation, which came with Ashley's confession, was that there were payments involved.

And there were some indications that this practice may have continued far longer than the paper conceded. In 2009 it emerged that Vukile Pokwana, the former accounts director of the communications company through which payments were channelled, alleged that the payments had continued for many years after 2006. This was never finally confirmed or disproved. The company was wound up and Pokwana relocated to the Eastern Cape.

After the DA won control of the province in 2009, a forensic investigation revealed that communications tenders to the value of R80 million had been irregularly awarded to three communications companies, and twenty-three officials faced disciplinary charges. We also laid charges with the police, but, as usual, these ran into the ground and nothing came of them.

I had long suspected that something was going on at the ironically named Independent Group of Newspapers. We would get fair coverage until a political confrontation erupted. Then it appeared to me that the newspapers defaulted to the ANC's spin. This slowly changed as the ANC's abuses became more and more egregious.

Crucial to bringing these abuses to light – and to the courts – was the DA's fighting cases like the 'Spy Tapes', in which we challenged the NPA's withdrawal of corruption charges against President Zuma. In my weekly newsletter, *SA Today*, I argued: 'If, as we suspect, the charges were withdrawn for political reasons, the NPA will be shown to have subverted the core constitutional principle it is mandated to defend: equality of all before the law.'

The NPA and the presidency did everything possible to stall the day of reckoning. They challenged our *locus standi* (standing in law) to bring the case at all. They argued that a decision to withdraw a charge could not be reviewed by a court; they dragged proceedings out further by failing to comply with court orders until we had won yet another court order to compel compliance. It was the most comprehensive legal filibuster I had ever encountered, and rested on a cynical abuse of the bottomless pit of state funding.

No doubt the Zuma circle hoped we would run out of funds, or staying power, or both. With every delay we became more determined to see the case through to the end. We had to stop the creeping capture of state institutions by politicians, which had become the hallmark of Jacob Zuma's term in office. We had to make sure that all South Africans understood that the institutions of state were created to protect them from power abuse – not to protect the powerful from accountability.

On Friday 29 April 2016, after seven years and eight court hearings, costing the DA approximately R10 million, the deputy judge president of the North Gauteng Division, Judge Aubrey Ledwaba, shredded Mpshe's justifications for dropping the case.

Reading the full judgment, on live television, Judge Ledwaba confirmed what we had suspected from the start: 'Having regard to the conspectus of evidence before us, we find that Mr Mpshe found himself under pressure and he decided to discontinue the prosecution of Mr Zuma and consequently made an irrational decision. Considering the situation in which he found himself, Mr Mpshe ignored the importance of the oath of office which demanded him to act independently and without fear or favour … Mr Zuma should face the charges as outlined in the indictment.'

Judge Ledwaba also made a costs order in favour of the DA, enabling our lawfare programme to proceed with similar precedent-setting cases.

There are still some unanswered questions arising out of the case, such as: where did the pressure on Mpshe come from? That question cries out for an answer, and a separate prosecution!

But even without that answer, the judgment will reverberate through every office of state where an incumbent is required to swear loyalty to the constitution. There is no ambiguity. This oath must always supersede any other loyalty. It was crucial to establish this benchmark at such an early stage in our democracy.

The Spy Tapes case was the first in a long line of legal actions that we initiated in order to expose and prevent power abuse. Between 2009 and mid-2016, we launched 103 court cases, with a success rate of over 90 per cent, to defend the independence of state institutions and embed the separation of party and state into precedent-setting case law. Some actions were mounted in defence of the rights of our members and public representatives against the wanton abuse of state power, to which ANC office-bearers in various spheres of government across the country had become prone.

We defended freedom of speech, upheld the power of the public protector, sought to secure the independence of the public broadcaster and the oversight powers of parliament. We compelled the electoral commission not only to manage elections, but to ensure they were free and fair. We fought the abuse of state funds for party political purposes. We defended due process of law, at every level. And we always defended the principle of rationality in the exercise of political power.

Several non-governmental organisations took up the same baton, most notably Freedom Under Law, the Helen Suzman Foundation and the F.W. de Klerk Foundation.

Our primary aim was to prevent 'state capture': the practice of powerful politicians turning supposedly independent institutions of state into political instruments to pursue their own agendas, protecting their allies, prosecuting their enemies and enriching themselves. State capture is the root cause of the failure of democratic transitions across our continent and in many parts of the world.

Our lawfare programme was designed to help prevent this in South Africa. History will record how important this was. The independence of strong state institutions – the capable state – is a *sine qua non* for the success of democracy.

James Selfe, whose office managed the DA's legal affairs, steered the lawfare programme with the dedicated help of Mervyn Smith, the party's meticulous legal adviser, for ten years. Mervyn had rendered his services *pro bono* when we couldn't afford to pay him (which was more often than we liked to admit). His name belongs in the pantheon of legal heroes of the new South Africa, but because he was challenging the hegemony of the ANC, it will take somewhat longer for his crucial contribution to democracy (and that of many others) to be adequately recognised.

Nevermind, as we say in South African patois. The wheel turns. Inexorably.

16

Damned If You Do

WITHIN A MONTH of Rasool's brown-envelope scandal, it was the DA's turn to be mired in controversy once more. We had just held a successful elective conference. I had been re-elected leader, unopposed. Wilmot James, who had entered parliament for the first time a year before, was elected chairman, succeeding the long-serving Joe Seremane. And the congress elected three deputy chairs: Anchen Dreyer, Dianne Kohler Barnard and Ivan Meyer.

Three women and two men in the top leadership elected at congress was a good gender balance, but despite the fact that several black candidates had stood for the position of deputy chair, none had been elected. (Wilmot as chair and Ivan as deputy would have been classified by apartheid as coloured.)

There was an outcry, and the DA was once again depicted as a party for 'minorities' which was not 'for blacks'.

I should have foreseen this and tried to pre-empt it, but I did not like interfering in internal party elections. The election outcome was a consequence of our voting system. Almost every congress delegate had voted for a diverse slate, which obviously included a black candidate on each ballot. But because there were so many black candidates (as opposed to candidates from any other demographic category), the vote was split between many candidates, with the result that none made the threshold. It was a serious strategic error. At the very least, I should have warned the nominees of this risk before they all stood against each other.

I vowed that I would never allow this to happen again. I started working seriously on diversifying the party's leadership and getting a 'succession pipeline' in place. It was time to take the next big step in what Tony Leon had called 'the politics of addition' in order to grow the DA.

Patricia de Lille had rejected my advances once before, but she and I largely interpreted political developments in the same way. This time the circumstances were more propitious. She was in a weaker position following the 2009 election. Instead of benefiting from public disaffection with the ANC, the emergence of COPE had deprived the Independent Democrats of a new voting pool. Even Patricia's right-hand man, Simon Grindrod, one of the party's vice-presidents, had quit the ID for COPE before the elections.

Patricia was feeling the squeeze, and when I approached her again to merge with the DA, I got a different response. We were having breakfast in one of the top floors of a downtown hotel, watching the city shaking its morning feathers and coming to life. We had reached the stage of our relationship when there was no more need for introductory small talk. Patricia agreed with my argument that there was no point in remaining separate parties, but she did not want to take the step alone. She was clearly concerned about the reaction to her merging with a party that the ANC had branded 'racist'.

We approached COPE. Terror Lekota was keen. We had an initial meeting with their leadership that we thought went well. We all signed the paper napkins on the tables at the restaurant after a discussion we believed would turn out to be historic. That is where it ended. COPE was too divided to reach agreement on how to relate to the DA.

Patricia needed forward cover. We approached a prominent South African from a similar philosophical tradition to Patricia, Dr Mamphela Ramphele, former vice-chancellor of the University of Cape Town and former managing director of the World Bank. She was also a friend of us both. She understood the bigger picture.

Mamphela was enormously encouraging and helped Patricia and me plan and execute our historic merger. We tried to persuade her to make the move as well – we liked the symbolism of three women taking this historic step together.

Mamphela said, 'Not yet.' She had other work to do first. That was when I picked up that she might be planning to enter politics at some later point. It was a so-called 'no-brainer' that the three of us should take this step together, in our view, but the time was not yet ripe for her, she said.

On 15 August 2010, in the afterglow of the World Cup, Patricia and I formally merged our parties, with a view to bringing Mamphela on board as soon as the time was ripe.

Of all the issues I have been criticised for, the proposal to bring Mamphela on board as the DA's presidential candidate in the 2014 elections was – with justification – one of the most controversial. It was, indeed, one of my biggest mistakes. Intentions don't count in politics. Only results do.

So, why did I do it? People said I had worked with her at the University of Cape Town and should have known it would end badly. Perhaps I am just less sensitive than those who found her difficult to work with because of her imperiousness and incapacity to take advice. I had experienced these character traits at UCT but I had learnt to work around them. Mamphela was also courageous and outspoken and could get to the heart of new issues in seconds. She could take the pressure, which is absolutely critical in politics, and she could argue a case she believed in from any platform, to any audience. She was an excellent delegator, and an even better fundraiser. She was well versed with a broad range of policy issues. She could take hard decisions.

And she was black.

Every time I concede that this was a factor that I took seriously in wooing Mamphela, I am accused of 'window dressing' or 'buying a black face'. I find this weird. The ANC demands affirmative action on the basis of race; yet if the DA concedes that race is one among many criteria we seek in order to strengthen our leadership, we are accused of window dressing. Damned if we do, and damned if we don't.

There is no doubt, given South Africa's history, that being black is an important attribute in politics, especially for the DA. The ANC clearly wanted us to retain white leadership so that they could continue to vilify us for being a white party. The corollary of this was that they set out to destroy every prominent black member of the DA, describing them as a 'puppet' or 'token' leader – often with added volume from an eager commentariat.

Only the most courageous could take the heat. Mamphela had that courage.

True, part of her toughness manifested in high-handedness and a lack of empathy for the people close to her, and I had been on the receiving end of both of these things more times than I care to remember. But it had never destroyed me. It had made me stronger and taught me not to take myself too seriously. And anyway, I reckoned, academics are notoriously sensitive. Politicians are much tougher. They face a battering every day.

I knew that only a strong organisation could survive Mamphela in its leadership, but I judged the DA to be strong enough. And I knew that Mamphela would respect the independence of our internal institutions. She was brilliant at delegating any job that someone else could do. Above all, with her in our leadership, we could never be accused again of wanting to bring back apartheid. I had to rid the DA of that albatross, if it was the last thing I did.

So, after Mamphela had so warmly and enthusiastically facilitated the marriage of the DA and the ID, and appeared with Patricia and me on shared platforms, I assiduously continued trying to draw her into a threesome.

My mind was on the 2011 local government elections, and the 2014 national and provincial government elections that would follow. I had to ensure that the party was well placed to make good progress and break out of its 'minority' mould.

I wrote to Ryan Coetzee, with whom I always discussed strategic questions. The date was 12 September 2010, the anniversary of Steve Biko's death.

> Hi Ryan,
> We were going to talk succession –
> In 2014 we have to make a significant breakthrough in provinces outside the Western Cape, and I do not believe I have the wherewithal as national leader, to achieve that for the Party.

We will have to elect a new leader in 2012, to give that person a chance to establish a brand before 2014. This issue is preying on my mind more and more and I would like us to put some serious thought into this.

To which Ryan replied:

Hi Helen

This is what I think.

The party needs desperately to break out of the minority space in 2014.

It is ultimately not possible to do full justice to both the party job and the WC government job (although you've managed to an astonishing degree, in part by driving yourself harder than is healthy or wise, if you don't mind me saying so).

You're right that if you're not going to lead in 2014 then you should go in 2012, and give someone else two years to build a profile.

Your replacement must, however, be a real vote winner, or have the potential to grow into one in two years, because otherwise the entire project is imperilled which would be a disaster.

Your replacement should ideally be black, but if push comes to shove, it is more important that the leader has the skills, judgement and political orientation necessary to succeed in the job than that he or she is black.

I agreed with all of the above. In any event, the party as a whole, not Ryan nor I, would make the choice of a new leader at a congress. My job was to ensure a pipeline of available candidates who already had some experience and came as close as possible to fitting the bill. There was never going to be a perfect person. We just had to get close.

I was always on the lookout for quality people to bring into the DA. And obviously, given our situation, it was important that we attracted potential future black leaders who believed in our vision and values.

Our Young Leaders programme was oversubscribed and doing an excellent job, but there was a big gap in the middle-age category of politicians, forty to sixty, from which leaders are traditionally drawn. Ideally, what we needed was a person who had come out of the struggle, and who had enough courage to leap across the race chasm because they understood that the best thing we could do for the future of democracy was to build the DA.

Mamphela understood all those things with resounding clarity. I instinctively felt it was a matter of time before she would take that leap. She was slightly past the 'middle-aged' category, formally classified as a 'senior citizen', but very few people tick all the boxes in politics. And some of the world's greatest leaders, including Nelson Mandela, were senior citizens before they assumed the mantle.

I knew it would be much easier to return to this discussion if we did well in the 2011 local government elections. The better we did, the more people would see us as a legitimate and viable alternative.

As we were going through the excruciating process of candidate selection for the 2011 election, I got a call from Ian Davidson. He was the chief whip of our parliamentary caucus, on whose judgement I relied a lot. He was helping me identify potential mayoral candidates.

Two months earlier, he had accompanied me to try to persuade Bobby Godsell to make himself available. Bobby, who had chaired the Progressive Party Youth when both Ian and I were members in the early 1970s, had a high public profile after his recent role as board chairman of Eskom. His contretemps with its dysfunctional management before his resignation was celebrated as a principled move after a valiant attempt to improve Eskom's governance. Bobby had a reputation as a leader, manager and excellent communicator. He could cross political fault-lines. I thought he fitted the bill. When he finally said an emphatic no, however, we had to cast the net wider.

Ian was also a member of the broader candidate-selection panel in Johannesburg. He phoned me to say they had interviewed an excellent candidate. 'I think we may have found a mayoral candidate,' said Ian. 'You need to come up to Johannesburg and meet him.'

That was on the Monday. On Friday morning Ian and I arrived to have breakfast with Mmusi Maimane at a Rosebank hotel.

The foyer was filled with young business executives, all fancy gadgets, flashy watches and shiny shoes, purposefully on the move. A tall young man emerged from the crowd, crisp white shirt and plain tie against a dark suit. He recognised me. 'Good morning, Mrs Zille,' he said with comfortable formality. 'I'm Mmusi.'

Over a light breakfast he told Ian and me about himself. It couldn't have been a better story, from his childhood in Soweto, his parents' sacrifice to educate him, his academic achievements, his vision for the future of his young family, and for all South Africans.

It is very hard to judge someone at a first meeting but, going on first impressions, he certainly had the 'right stuff' to be our mayoral candidate for Johannesburg.

There were big risks. He was a complete novice in politics. That is always a serious issue. But he was perceptive enough to know that. Mmusi was more concerned about it than I was, but eventually he was persuaded to throw his hat in the ring. He stood against an experienced and excellent councillor and party stalwart, Jack Bloom, who would have made an outstanding mayor. But the majority of the selection panel swung behind Mmusi's charisma, flair and communication skills (backed by his obvious intelligence) – all crucial attributes in politics. And, of course, he was black. That was indeed a factor, and anyone denying it would be lying. But the fact that he was black was not the ONLY factor. It was an additional 'plus', on top of a host of other attributes.

Jack Bloom, having worked so hard for our cause and sacrificed so much, was gracious in defeat, and continued to work with determination and passion. That kind of response always won my profound respect. He knew as well as the rest of us that we had to grow the pipeline of potential future leaders and this was one of the ways of doing so, offering platforms for young, talented people to build their profile and hone their experience. The mayoral candidacy provided that for Mmusi, even though his starting point was very near the top.

In Cape Town, our selection process identified Patricia de Lille as our mayoral candidate, against incumbent Dan Plato, who had succeeded me when I became premier in 2009.

After Dan's defeat, I appointed him to the provincial cabinet, as minister of community safety, where he could maximise his exceptional interactive skills with local communities and develop an effective system of police oversight. He remained a committed colleague, never showing any bitterness, always moving on to the next challenge with equanimity, never harbouring a grudge. A magnificent and rare attribute in politics.

Election times helped me see a lot more of my Johannesburg family, as I passed through the city a lot and stayed overnight with Carla and Mom. Mom was always in a froth about my dancing at rallies, which she watched with growing mortification on television. Like my sons, she began by begging me not to.

I tried to explain that I could not simply stand there while everyone around me was dancing. She was not persuaded. She thought my sense of rhythm deficient. I did not dance with a smooth flow, she complained. Lydia Puleng Thulo, Mom's carer, and her young daughter Keabetswe, tried to help me improve my steps on the carpet of Mom's bedroom, with Mom acting as choreographer-in-chief from the vantage point of her bed. It provided some light relief during the tense and exhausting campaign. Every time a television camera captured me dancing at a rally, I had a little laugh thinking about Mom watching this at home. It always surprised me that she was so distressed by it.

During the election campaign I spent a disproportionate amount of time in Nelson Mandela Bay metro (comprising Port Elizabeth, Uitenhage and Despatch). This urban conglomeration, in the ANC's heartland, offered us a real chance of winning a metro outside of the Western Cape – the next big step we needed to take. A victory there would do a lot to change perceptions of the DA. We threw everything at it. I visited the metro seven times and campaigned on the ground, including on election day itself.

After voting early at my voting station at St Paul's church in Rondebosch, Cape Town, I flew back to Port Elizabeth to help ensure DA supporters came to the polls.

That evening I flew to Johannesburg en route to the Independent Electoral Commission centre in Pretoria, to begin the marathon forty-eight-hour waiting session as the results trickled in from around the country. As I got off the plane from Port Elizabeth at Johannesburg's O.R. Tambo airport, a man caught up with me in the arrivals hall and said, with a sense of breathless urgency: 'Mrs Zille, the DA just has to win Nelson Mandela Bay. You just have to win so that we can get the city back on track.'

'We have a good chance of winning if every single DA supporter votes before nine tonight,' I answered. 'I trust you voted before you left today.'

'No,' he replied without hesitation. 'I don't vote, I pray.'

I was momentarily stunned. Here was a man telling me we had to win in Nelson Mandela Bay, but he was not prepared to cast his ballot to help us. Did he pray that everyone else would go out to vote, I wondered.

'Why don't you do both?' I suggested. 'Many of us pray *and* vote. They are not mutually exclusive activities.' I thought I was quite polite in the circumstances.

'You wouldn't understand,' he said, with the tone of an impatient parent trying to bat away an inquisitive child's umpteenth unanswerable question.

'You're right. I don't understand,' I said. 'It is people like you who make the DA lose elections. Your prayers, I'm afraid, are no compensation for actually voting. Unfortunately, the votes are tallied in Pretoria, not in heaven.'

The ANC duly won Nelson Mandela Bay by 51.9 per cent – dropping almost 15 percentage points (or 24 per cent) in comparison to the last local elections in 2006. But they just scraped home. The DA, in contrast, achieved a spectacular result. As the media reported: 'The DA managed to win 154 472 more votes in 2011 than in 2006 – an increase of 112.67%. This lifted their share of the vote from 24.39% to 40.13%.'

It was really good, but not good enough. We fell just short of what we needed.

I kept kicking myself that we had not supported COPE's campaign in the same way that we had supported the independent candidates in Cape Town in 2006. We had assumed that COPE would be able to retain at least half of the 17 per cent they had captured in the 2009 national and provincial election. If they had retained a base of support in 2011, we would have been able to form a governing coalition of opposition parties in Nelson Mandela Bay, as we had done in Cape Town in 2006. But COPE slumped from 17 per cent in 2009 to 4 per cent in the local elections of 2011, enabling the ANC to just cross the 50 per cent mark they needed for an overall majority. And in politics, a miss is as good as a mile.

Still smarting when I got home from Pretoria after the final count, I asked Johann which verse in the Bible could be interpreted as an injunction not to vote on earth. He assured me there wasn't one. On the contrary, he said, Romans 13 could be interpreted as encouragement to vote for a just and fair government.

Despite our disappointment in Port Elizabeth, we did extremely well in the 2011 election, polling 23.9 per cent of the vote countrywide, which meant 3.2 million people had cast their votes for the DA (compared with 1.6 million in 2006). The DA/ID coalition paid off handsomely in Cape Town, where the DA, with Patricia as our mayoral candidate, drew over 60 per cent of the vote. We had grown more than 40 per cent in the city since 2006. It was a triumph.

Watching Patricia being elected and inaugurated as DA mayor, I had to pinch myself. If anyone had told me back in 2006 that she would one day join the DA and hold high executive office under our banner, I would have thought them certifiable.

Mamphela, justifiably, felt some pride in the result, having midwifed the merger between the DA and ID.

Not long after the election of 18 May, she popped in to see me at Leeuwenhof.

'I'm ready,' she said. 'I'm ready to join the DA.'

I remember it clearly because I wrote down her exact words.

'The DA has now almost reached 25 per cent. All I have to do, by the next election, is bring the required 26 per cent and we have a new government.'

I laughed. 'Mamphela,' I said, 'I wish it were as simple as that.' It was not the right time to explain the impact of differential ANC turnout between local and national elections.

She laughed too. It wouldn't take her long to find out how hard one has to work in politics for every single vote.

After she left, I called Ryan. 'The game is on,' I said.

We had a year to prepare before the party's next congress in 2012. If Mamphela joined us and played her cards skilfully, she could be a strong leadership candidate by then. But I was not sure she knew how hard she would have to work for every single vote inside the DA as well. Tough leadership elections are part of the DA's internal culture. She could not assume the outcome would be a foregone conclusion.

17

Varying Shades of Bad

THE BIG QUESTION for political decision-makers is always: compared to what? I don't know who first said it, but every political leader soon finds out what it means – and that it is true.

Most decisions are not a choice between the best and the worst option; nor even between good and bad. The most common decisions in politics are between varying shades of bad. And it is often impossible to predict the impact of different choices without the wisdom of hindsight. This means it is difficult to know which decisions will merely be bad, which will be worse, and which will be disastrous. There are so many unpredictable factors that are completely beyond one's control.

I often found myself misquoting Churchill when I took a difficult decision. 'This is the worst possible option in the circumstances – except for all the others.'

There are many complex layers in political decision-making, few of which are visible to the outside observer. It is like evaluating the complex internal layers of an onion by the flimsiness of its skin.

These thoughts come to mind when I think back on the repeated efforts I made to bring Mamphela Ramphele into politics.

Looking back, we all agree it turned out to be a mistake, perhaps my biggest mistake as DA leader, for which I take responsibility.

I do not intend to justify it. Just contextualise it.

So I return to the question: compared to what?

At the time there was a lot of talk about the DA needing a 'Clause 4 moment'. This was a reference to a historical turning point in British politics, when Tony Blair turned the Labour Party into a viable option for a majority of British voters in the mid-1990s. Up until then, Clause 4 of the Labour Party's constitution, dating from 1918, espoused the nationalisation of industries (in Marxist jargon). Given the historical record of Marxist economics, the majority of voters regarded this as a barrier to voting Labour. In his 1994 speech to the Labour Party conference, Tony Blair announced that the party needed a new statement of aims and values, and by 1995 the reference to nationalisation had been dropped.

This opened the door for many voters to see Labour as an alternative government. And in 1997 Labour won the election.

The lesson we learnt from it was that Tony Blair had identified the biggest obstacle preventing the majority of Britons from voting Labour; he took steps to remove it; and he reaped the results within the course of one decade, the 1990s.

Now, as we approached the 2014 election, the DA also needed a redefining moment. We needed to break out of our minority mould and convince the electorate that we were the party through which South Africans could build an inclusive future, not resurrect a hated past. We all agreed that the equivalent of a Clause 4 moment for the DA would be when the party elected an outstanding black leader with vote-winning appeal. I saw it as part of my job, as the current party leader, to create conducive conditions for that moment to arrive.

The need was blindingly obvious. But it was also controversial. Some critics, inside and outside the party, regarded it as a violation of our commitment to non-racialism. Surely we should just look for the best candidate, irrespective of race, they said. In principle, yes, absolutely. In practice, it was not that simple. We were doing a good job in opposition, but we had to win elections if we wanted to save South Africa's democracy and defend the constitution.

Ironically, those at the forefront of demands for the DA's 'transformation' labelled every emerging black DA leader as a 'token', seeking to prevent the very development they claimed to demand. This neatly exposed their motives, but it didn't make it any easier.

I kept reminding the party that we were in a race against time to prevent the ANC from capturing all independent state institutions through cadre deployment, and then institutionalising corruption to the point that we would become a criminal state. Jacob Zuma was determined to neutralise any state institution that got in his way.

The biggest obstacle in the DA's way, all our polls were telling us, was that the majority of voters regarded us as a 'white party'. The ANC had obviously drawn the same conclusion from their research, which is why they only drove a single, simple message. 'The DA is a racist party that defends white interests. They will bring back apartheid.'

All of our policies and actions told a different story, but we could not break the sound barrier. And in any event, we had to show, not tell. We had to win elections. And to do that, we had to move fast to diversify our leadership.

I was painfully aware that 2009 had been our most racially polarised election ever.

I wanted the DA to be in a position, by our 2012 elective congress, to have the choice of an outstanding slate of nominees in order to elect a diverse leadership team. And ideally we needed to find the right person, with the required attributes and name recognition, to clinch our Clause 4 moment at the top.

Of course, there are many thousands of South Africans who fitted the bill. The trouble is that not too many of them were queueing up to contest for leadership positions in the DA! I asked several prominent people to consider doing so, and while some indicated support for the DA's values and policies, they said the time was not ripe for such a move.

Many black leaders knew only too well what the consequences would be if they openly aligned themselves with the DA: vilification, marginalisation in their community and family, forfeiting their struggle credentials. They knew politics was a terrain of great uncertainty, with no clear career path; and for most of them it would have meant a considerably diminished pay packet.

In the discussions at the time, it was clear that people could not envisage a day, in the foreseeable future, when the ANC would lose power. If they wanted to work for change, they were better placed inside, rather than outside the ANC. If the ANC chose the right leadership, they believed, the party could put South Africa back on track. They felt it their duty to use their leverage inside the party to influence its course. I learnt that people don't easily move out of the warm embrace of power. As the ANC always warned its internal critics, 'It's cold outside.'

The DA was caught in a classic catch-22 situation. On the one hand we battled to get many of our own supporters to go to the polls, because so many people did not realise how important it was to vote, or because they had some weird ideas and beliefs. On the other hand, the carefully manufactured perception that the DA was a racist party serving white interests prevented the very people from coming to us who could change that perception! All the ANC had to do was use every opportunity to intensify it.

Mamphela was one potential exception to this rule. She had been prepared to publicly support Patricia de Lille's decision to join the DA, when many others were accusing her of selling out. She had backbone, name recognition, charisma, credentials.

So when Mamphela told me, in my lounge at Leeuwenhof, that she was ready to join us after our 2011 election success, I was delighted.

I could tell she was firing on all cylinders. After talking politics, we turned to family. We talked about our boys who had been such good friends as children, and how happy we were that they were both launched in life. She told me how wonderful it was to be a grandmother. By the end of the conversation my own granny hormones were truly pumping. We had connected again, just as we once did when we were both thirty-something moms trying to balance children with careers.

Apart from our long-standing friendship, it would have been political suicide for me to reject her. Can you imagine what the response would have been if I had turned down a woman of her stature, profile and struggle credentials when she had offered to help transform the perception of the DA? I would (correctly) have been accused of trying to block a potential competitor.

I had no intention of doing so. On the contrary, I thought my leadership was approaching its sell-by date, given the challenges the party faced and the fundamental makeover we required. We needed new blood. Of course, Mamphela knew she couldn't expect a coronation as leader when she joined. She would have to contest for the position; but all the planets were aligning in her favour. At the time, her public standing was generally very high among the category of people known in political jargon as 'news multipliers'.

Mamphela, Ryan and I discussed how best to approach her 'coming out'. The plan was that early in 2012 she would announce that she was joining the DA. We would then embark on a countrywide tour to give her speaking opportunities on various platforms throughout the country, introducing her to party structures, and enabling her to use her oratorical skills to build a support base. This would be timed for our 2012 congress, which, we proposed, might take the form of a relaunch, enabling her to run for office.

I asked Mamphela to nominate someone who could work on the details with Ryan. She nominated a young professional, Marc van Olst. We were all sworn to secrecy, to the point of encrypted emails. We knew the plan would be derailed if it leaked. We would only go public when everything was nailed down.

Ryan and Marc got going.

At the end of June, Ryan reported back on the timing. Different views had emerged on the right moment to make the move, in order to juxtapose it with the ANC's elective conference scheduled for December 2012. We were confident we could find a way to work around these issues. Ryan mentioned there was also 'talk about a social movement', but he did not know how this related to the discussions we were having. I left him to resolve the issues with Marc and return with greater clarity and a more detailed plan.

I had other things to worry about. Apart from trying to run a provincial government, I was preoccupied with the fact that the DA parliamentary caucus was heading for mid-term leadership elections. We had never had mid-term caucus elections before – this was an innovation, and it threatened to be very divisive.

The wounds from the previous caucus leadership election, in 2009, when Ryan had lost to Athol, hadn't healed, and the mid-term election was widely regarded as a deliberately engineered opportunity to settle a score. This added to the tension.

That context would make things very difficult for Lindiwe Mazibuko, the candidate who was being primed to challenge Athol. Many caucus members saw her as a potential 'revenge candidate' who would be nominated to beat Athol, because Ryan could not.

Lindiwe had turned thirty-one in April that year, and had been a member of the parliamentary caucus for just over two years. Her name was seldom mentioned without the qualifier 'rising star'. Indeed, her ascendancy in the DA had been meteoric.

I had met her several years earlier, while she was an honours student in communication studies at the University of Cape Town. Her thesis included an analysis of the DA's (and my) media profile. Like many students of the time, she was working on some sort of capitalist conspiracy theory involving the media and the DA! As part of her research, she came to interview me. I did not agree with her thesis, but I was bowled over by her incisive intelligence and vibrant personality.

A short while afterwards I was told she had recorded an entry on Facebook saying something like: 'Help! I'm beginning to agree with the DA.'

Shortly thereafter she applied for a position as a researcher in the DA's parliamentary team. Ryan chaired the interview panel and appointed her. She did a good job.

In 2009 Lindiwe threw her hat in the ring to become a member of parliament, on the KwaZulu-Natal list, the province from which she hailed. She came in at number three on the list and was duly elected as an honourable MP on 22 April 2009.

It soon became apparent how quickly she mastered new policy areas. The articulacy with which she could argue almost any case, from our perspective, prompted me to appoint her as party spokesperson, which is usually reserved for more senior parliamentarians. Lindiwe ticked all the boxes. And she now had the platform to raise her profile. She made such an impression that she became the face of the 2011 election campaign, where she did almost all the television debates normally done by the party leader. She rapidly garnered a large following. She was firmly among the favourites in the succession pipeline I was trying to build.

When Lindiwe made her move to become caucus leader, it sent a strong signal that she saw herself moving in that direction. She was doing a job that I could never have mastered at such a young age, but aiming for the caucus leadership so soon, I thought, might risk overreaching. Life experience is almost more important than any other qualification for the complex job of maintaining a functional team, pulling in the same direction, in a context of constant competition for influence and power, not to mention South Africa's many other fault-lines.

At that stage our talks with Mamphela were not advanced enough for me to introduce her as a factor into the conversation. If she joined the DA, I envisaged the possibility that she would contest and fill the next parliamentary vacancy, and possibly run for the caucus leadership at the appropriate opportunity. If that happened, there would be yet another divisive internal election – a very disruptive event in the life of a caucus.

Without being able to go into these background details, I suggested to Lindiwe that she stand back and let Athol complete a full term. She declined. She was determined to run. And win. It was her right to do so, and while I could suggest that she stand down, I certainly could not pressure her to do so.

I then concluded that if she ran, she would have to win. We were still feeling the reverberations of our 2010 congress when not a single black candidate had been elected to the party's top leadership. I did not want a caucus election to provide further grist to the ANC's mill. We needed to move closer to our Clause 4 moment, not further away from it.

Then, as inevitably happens in tense moments, I got a call from a journalist.

He had received a tip-off, he said, that I was backing Lindiwe to take out Athol Trollip in the mid-term election, and that there was huge dissatisfaction in the caucus because of this. Did I have a comment? In the course of our brief conversation it transpired that he had received an email from a source who wanted to remain anonymous.

'Please forward that email to me,' I asked. 'When I have read it I will comment in detail.'

The journalist removed all the sender's identifying features and sent it to me. It read:

> A little scoop for you. Helen Zille, having pushed De Lille in as mayor of Cape Town, is now trying to do the same in Parlt. She has told the DA parliamentary caucus that she wants Atholl [sic] Trollip to resign so that Lindiwe Mazibuko can take his place. This would effectively be the end of Trollip's career, so he has refused. The result is that there will be a hard-fought election in October. Helen is really pushing her luck after the euphoria of the local elections:
>
> Lindiwe is very much her protege and still very young. There are plenty of very talented young whites in the DA and it is quite nakedly racial to try to promote Lindiwe like this.
>
> Helen could lose. She doesn't sit in the Caucus in Parlt and there is great discontent there over the way she hardly ever bothers with it. Both of the women DA ambassadors who went off to posts told me that they were just so fed up that they could never even see Helen to talk about important business, and that's why they wanted out. Then, when Helen tried to impose Wilmot James (another Cape Town pal) as Parlty leader the Caucus made it clear it wouldn't accept it so then she put up yet another CT protege, Ryan Coetzee, and to Helen's fury he got soundly beaten by Atholl Trollip. Lindiwe, as you know, is yet another CT protege and at least Trollip comes from the Eastern Cape.
>
> Fact is, Helen is utterly Presidential, is ignoring the fact that the DA is a federal and democratic party and is trying to ensure that every single position of power is held by a member of her small Cape Town clique. As you will know, such a thing would have been utterly unacceptable in either the old NP or PFP, the main constituents of the DA.
>
> I did not, of course, tell you any of this.

I read through this email and then applied my investigative-reporting skills to find who had deliberately distorted facts and then 'leaked' them in order to manufacture outrage.

I scanned the document to find any telltale phrases or unusual words, or contextual issues that might help identify the source. I soon found what I was looking for.

The abbreviation used for Parliament was Parlt. I had never seen that before. Nor had I seen the abbreviation Parlty for Parliamentary.

So I searched the hundreds of thousands of emails stored on my computer to find any previous occurrence of those two abbreviations.

They immediately popped up – in emails from Bill Johnson. No one else had used the abbreviation in correspondence with me.

I compared the emails. The gossipy style, the syntax, and even the end note, followed the formula. I had no doubt. It came from Bill, serving as a conduit, asked or unasked, for people in the caucus. Of course Bill, an academic and political commentator, was not bound by caucus confidentiality, so there was nothing further I could do.

It was clearly intended as a juicy story to drive the narrative that I was not coping with both jobs and that I was trying to 'remote-control' the caucus through deploying my proxies. That certainly was not my perception of the dominant mood in the caucus at the time, but it was indicative of what I was to face further down the line.

The email's information was objectively wrong in material respects.

For example, I did not want Athol to resign. In fact, my preference was for Lindiwe not to run for the caucus leadership so soon. A mid-term election was optional, and if we did not have one, no questions would be asked, no feathers ruffled and no new controversies generated. Secondly, Lindiwe was a member of parliament from KwaZulu-Natal, not the Western Cape. It was also pure conspiracy theory to suggest I was trying to deploy a provincial cabal into leadership positions, although I certainly was trying to diversify the leadership team by supporting available talent to get into positions from which they could build a profile. I wanted them to be in a position to contest for leadership positions as they arose.

But when it became clear that the mid-term election would go ahead, and that Lindiwe would run, I concluded we had to make sure she won. Our opponents were always looking for 'proof' that we were racist. And they would seize on this. If she had been good enough to be the face of our 2011 election campaign, why was she not good enough to lead the caucus, they would ask. Had she merely been a token?

I discussed the issue with a few of the party's leadership figures, and we resolved to ask Athol to withdraw his candidacy, for the worst of all possible reasons – that we thought he would win. We asked James Selfe to speak to Athol. James told me afterwards it was a very difficult conversation. Athol listened to James's case, framed in his normal cautious and diplomatic way. There was a pause in the conversation before Athol said: 'Let me get this quite clear. You are asking me not to contest the caucus leadership because you are worried I will win?'

'Yes, bluntly, that's it,' said James.

Athol laughed. 'You can't be serious. Let our democratic process run its course.'

When James told me about the conversation, I said we couldn't fault Athol's logic.

The battle was on.

David Maynier, the DA's shadow minister of defence, chaired Lindiwe's campaign like a military operation. They met according to a strict schedule, raised funds, hired a public-relations consultancy to manage the media, and held weekly press conferences. This broke the mould of the DA's normal below-the-radar internal elections. The public campaign introduced the culture of American primaries into the DA's internal electoral process. My chief of staff, Geordin Hill-Lewis, had just been elected the youngest-ever member of parliament in South Africa's history at the age of twenty-three. He and other young people threw themselves into Lindiwe's campaign with determination and enthusiasm.

One day Geordin came to speak to me. They had tallied their canvassing, and if they allowed for a 'lie factor', there was a risk of losing. The campaign team had decided I had to get involved. I was very reluctant, beyond doing what I had already done, which was suggesting to both candidates that we should avoid a divisive, race-charged contest at that stage. Geordin insisted, and reminded me of what we had been through the previous year after the congress. I concluded it was time to expend some political capital to diversify our leadership. It was certain to be a highly controversial move.

That was the start of what came to be known as 'the Leeuwenhof Express'. Geordin scheduled appointments for me with individual MPs who were marked on the canvass sheets as 'doubtful'. He drove them to Leeuwenhof for our one-on-one conversations, where I did whatever possible to convince them of the importance of repositioning our party, which required us to give Lindiwe the opportunity. I faced stiff resistance. My colleagues said she was too young, too inexperienced, and that Athol was doing a good job and didn't deserve to be treated this way. It was hard to contest any of this.

However, I said there was an overriding imperative to change the DA's brand, and we knew how good a national spokesperson Lindiwe had been. Although I agreed it was slightly premature, I was confident she was ready for the next step. Of course, the fact that she was black was an important factor. I accepted that a thirty-one-year-old white person, who had been in parliament for just two years, wouldn't stand a chance of being elected caucus leader. But we were not living in normal times, and I knew Lindiwe had the intellect and the political instinct to do it. Not once in her campaign had she played the race card. She was asking people to vote for the attributes she could bring to the position.

In the end, most of the people I spoke to agreed to vote for her. And then even some people who had sworn their allegiance to Athol decided to swing behind Lindiwe. I knew my own credibility was on the line. For the future of the party, it had to work out.

One of my attempts to persuade a colleague to vote for Lindiwe went seriously pear-shaped. It was my interaction with my long-standing young colleague, Masizole Mnqasela, a strong Athol supporter. He was not part of the 'Leeuwenhof Express'. He had been marked on the canvas sheet as 'against' Lindiwe, not 'doubtful'. I took Masizole out to Nelson's Eye steakhouse for dinner to try to convince him. We had a meal in the private back room, and I suggested why I thought he should vote for Lindiwe. He told me directly that he would not. I was backing the wrong horse, he argued. I was glad he felt free to tell me this directly, and that he did not dissemble.

However, I did not appreciate the fact that he took his campaign against Lindiwe onto the airwaves, announcing on national radio that she was not black enough to attract the support of black voters. For good measure he added that by trying to persuade caucus members to vote for Lindiwe, I was running the party like a spaza shop. I hauled him over the coals for introducing Verwoerdian classifications of 'real' blackness into the campaign, based on the way Lindiwe spoke English with an accent that reflected a privileged education. He countered that Lindiwe's team was fighting the battle in the media and he had the right of reply. Things got messy. He faced internal disciplinary charges, which were dropped when he apologised.

The battle became bitter because it was so public. There were difficult moments, such as a decision by David Maynier to withdraw Lindiwe from a potentially complex press conference on domestic workers' rights at the last minute (to which Athol as caucus leader had assigned her).

And, once again, many of the professional communication and research staff in parliament openly sided with Lindiwe, partly because of their loyalty to their former colleague, Ryan, who had lost to Athol in 2009.

Contrary to our rules, Gareth van Onselen, executive director of innovation and projects, and Ryan's close friend, was actively involved, writing 'attack' documents for Lindiwe's campaign to use against Athol. It created an untenable situation. I felt my absence from parliament intensely.

There was blood on the floor before a single vote had been cast.

Gavin Davis, newly appointed executive director of communications in the

DA, started preparing for the aftermath of the election scheduled for 27 October 2011. He reasoned that, in order to enable the DA to recover, both Athol and Lindiwe should appear together at a press conference after the vote, in a show of unity. Whoever lost would concede defeat and congratulate their opponent; whoever won would pay respects to their opponent, and sketch out a vision for the future. He went to see Athol and Lindiwe separately to put this proposal to them. Athol replied that, although it would nearly kill him, he would do it for the sake of the party. For her part, Lindiwe refused point blank. I could see a problem approaching.

I will never forget the caucus election. It began in an atmosphere of electric tension. Lindiwe, who was clearly ahead at that point, made a relaxed speech about the Mazibuko clan's history and about every South African's place in a shared future. Athol was angry, stung at the way his long-standing colleagues were being turned, one by one. While I could genuinely understand what he was going through, his election speech on the subject did him no favours. He intimated that he had been the target of a conspiracy, led by me, to oust him to ensure Lindiwe's election, so that Ryan could return to parliament to run the show. He came across as angry and bitter, which I suppose he was at that moment.

After the speeches, both candidates left the room and we had a discussion in caucus on their merits. Dene Smuts, firmly in Athol's camp, made a strong speech, referring to a statement I had made about the need to diversify our leadership. I had described the process of nurturing young talent in our ranks as 'growing our own timber'. Dene flayed me for asking the caucus to vote for a 'sapling from the grow-your-own-timber' nursery. It was a powerful piece of oratory.

In the end Lindiwe won by a differential of 9.5 votes. Athol, true to his word, gritted his teeth, appeared at the press conference, and was gracious in defeat, once more. He had done nothing to deserve being treated like that.

His wife, Angela, sent me a letter, which cut to the quick. It read:

Dear Helen,

From one woman, wife and mother to another, I would like to tell you how I feel about the DA's latest election. I'll start from January 1999, when Athol undertook to run the election campaign in the Eastern Cape. We moved off the farm and rented a small flat in Gonubie to run the campaign, I did the fundraising. From that time Athol has dedicated almost every minute of every day to growing the DA. He has travelled the length and breadth of the Transkei, opening branches, taking wheel chairs to some remote settlement on some impassable track in the remotest corner of the Transkei. (Athol now has to sell this vehicle, which due to the mileage and road conditions is worth less than the balance of the payments, because of his drop in income.) I have spent the last 12 years of my life pretty much alone. My children were at boarding school, and sadly their father missed out on most of their hockey and rugby matches. I was there alone, always. 'Sorry darlings, Dad is at a meeting.'

In 2005 we sold our farm so Athol could commit 100% to his career. My son was the 6th generation on that farm.

When he moved to Cape Town as an MP and was elected as the Caucus Leader, his time was even more compromised. I spend every week alone, coming home from work to an empty house, knowing that I am making a sacrifice for the country. Many a weekend, I am alone, but I know my husband is doing an important job for the party and the country. He comes home, and sleeps on the couch so he can take a call from radio uMhlobo Wenene at midnight to do a radio interview. I pay for groceries at the till at the Spar with my credit card, the teller says 'Mrs. Trollip, do you know Athol Trollip? I heard him on the radio last night.'

All the time, I am thinking, it's worth the sacrifices, because the DA is different. But now I think, is the DA any different from the other political parties? Power is everything at any cost. When I call on my customers who are DA donors they ask me, 'What happened to the phrases that we've heard so often at fund raising breakfasts and dinners, "fit for purpose", "the DA delivers because it puts the right people in the right positions, regardless of colour, creed or religion"?' They tell me they are extremely disillusioned, what do I tell them?

I am extremely proud of the way Athol has accepted this outcome, considering his passionate personality, but I think it is totally unjust.

Yours sincerely

Angela

I wrote back, what, in retrospect, seems an inadequate response.

Dear Angela,

Thanks for writing to me. I genuinely appreciate that you set down your thoughts and put them to me. And I can totally understand how you feel. Yes, I understand that people regard what happened to Athol as unfair and unjust. Many of us, in this transition period have had very similar experiences at crucial stages in our career development ...

Athol has been extremely magnanimous in his response to this matter. And his commitment to the DA's vision and values remains undiminished. Everyone has seen that clearly, and he has been greatly enhanced as a result.

Furthermore, all of us who have been in politics for years, know what sacrifices a spouse and family have to make in the process. The loneliness, the single parenting, the unilateral decision-making – it is hugely difficult and only the strongest relationships survive it, usually not unscarred. I am more than aware of the sacrifices you and your family have made.

Where I disagree with you, is your perception that Lindiwe is not 'fit for purpose'. Yes, she is exceptionally young, and has very limited experience, for such a weighty position. But the way I analysed it is as follows: Parliament is our most crucial national platform. As we move to 2014 we have to work very hard to 'own' the concept of diversity. There will be 3-million new voters, among the 'born-frees' in 2014. Lindiwe is the most articulate communicator in our party, bar none, and giving her the opportunity to use that platform can achieve a lot for the party. She has the opportunity of a lifetime. She must use it or lose it ...

The tough thing about politics is the insecurity. No position is ever secure. You can be in one day and out the next – not because you did a bad job, but because the terrain shifted. I have experienced that very often. Making major life choices on the assumption of a secure and clear career path is absolutely impossible in politics. It is genuinely a gamble.

It is hard to say these things without sounding patronising, but Athol will continue to be a highly valued and respected colleague, who leads by example every day.

Please be assured that I am not lifting my own position out of the succession stakes: It is right there on the table, and I will happily step down next year for a person who can combine the attributes we require to attract more votes than my leadership is able to, in the next election.

I felt terrible. Few people had made the sacrifices for the party that Athol and Angela had. Much the same could be said about Ian Davidson, my long-time colleague and adviser as chief whip, who had stood so solidly behind me in every political contest. He had built a sound relationship with Athol as well, and they were on the same ticket for re-election, with Sej Motau, a former journalist colleague of mine, as their candidate for caucus chair. At times like that I really hated the choices politics forced me to make, but I did so on the basis of what I genuinely believed was the party's best interests at that time and place. It is a miracle that so many friendships survived these decisions.

Finding a new leader to take my place would be next on the cards.

First, however, I had to make sure that the new parliamentary set-up worked. This required, as a start, a seamless interface with my office.

I immediately sensed resistance. Not anything overt, just implied.

However, I was relieved to hear that Lindiwe had asked my outstanding chief of staff, Geordin, to assist her in setting up an office. That would lay the groundwork for good communication, I thought. I immediately arranged for him to be seconded to her, and suggested that we consider setting up a shared office, in the parliamentary building, where Geordin could manage our complementary roles seamlessly. Lindiwe rejected that suggestion, and I accepted that she wanted to build her own platform, clearly differentiated from mine. Fair enough.

Within three weeks I got a call from Geordin. Lindiwe had fired him from his position managing the transition in her office, he said. I was dumbfounded. Why, I asked. Geordin said Lindiwe felt the recruitment process (with advertising, interviews, etc.) was not moving quickly enough. Neither had he secured sufficient media coverage for her early on, when David had advised that a 'big splash' was required.

Unbeknown to me, although the caucus election was over, David continued driving the military operation into the next phase of Lindiwe's campaign. I mistakenly thought she and her team would regard the parliamentary leadership as a destination, at least for a while. Instead, it soon became clear it was merely a stepping stone, on which to land one foot, fleetingly, before taking the next leap, to the DA's national leadership, and then to the Union Buildings in the 2019 election.

I received reports of dinner parties at which the composition of a new national cabinet was discussed, but I laughed it off. I thought it was obviously done in jest. No one would seriously be measuring the curtains in the West Wing of the Union Buildings shortly after being elected the DA's caucus leader!

Throughout I realised how important it was for me to avoid anointing a successor. There is always opposition to someone making her way up the ladder more quickly than her competitors. This resistance is compounded by perceptions that she may be favoured by the current incumbent. My job was not to back any one candidate, but to ensure there was a strong slate of potential leadership candidates. Lindiwe was undoubtedly in pole position. From the moment of her election as caucus leader, the succession race was on.

I hadn't expected it so soon, or so intensely.

'They have drunk the Kool-Aid,' a close confidant said of Lindiwe and her team, referencing the cult suicide that occurred in 1978 in a jungle compound in Guyana, and which had become an American political metaphor. In modern political parlance it refers to a situation in which people begin to hold a firm, if unrealistic, belief without critical examination, which ultimately has serious consequences.

Lindiwe's advice was to consolidate her position in the leadership race from the start by stamping her authority onto the caucus, and to ensure she was never seen as a proxy for me. When he was president of the ANC Youth League, Julius Malema had once cruelly described her as my 'tea girl' – a label she had actively to disprove in order to shed it. Within a month of her election, she challenged our established practice of having both the federal leader (me) and the parliamentary leader (her) at some press conferences. She said this was unnecessary and simply confirmed the narrative that she was my 'tea girl'. The clear assumption was that I should stand back, which I then did, when appropriate.

I understood it was essential for Lindiwe to build a separate platform and use it to the full. Her success in doing so was also essential for the party's repositioning as we sought to grow our voter base. But, apart from differentiating our roles, we needed to align our offices so that they worked seamlessly and co-operatively together.

Before Geordin left Lindiwe's office on the day she fired him, he gave her some unsolicited advice. She had to fix the sense of permanent crisis and panic that pervaded her office, he said. Otherwise it would destroy her.

I thought it was a symptom of initial insecurity, a response to the massive internal and external expectations that accompanied her election. I was convinced things would soon settle. I urged colleagues not to escalate disagreements.

The most marginal issues were generating resentment, sometimes igniting a firestorm of angry email correspondence that eventually landed on the desk of the chief executive officer, Jonathan Moakes. Sometimes they landed up with me. I started getting worried.

I tried to calm the waters. I wrote to a colleague asking that Lindiwe be accorded the space and time she needed. 'She is finding her feet and testing the boundaries. I have full confidence that she is intelligent enough to realise she has overstepped them, as I often have in the past. It is hard as a young, female leader, starting out, because you feel you have to stamp your authority on the situation at the start, even when you are surrounded by loyal, competent people. I will raise the issue at the appropriate time in the appropriate way – but as you are the first to recognise, now is not that time. She feels she needs to get out of my "shadow" although I have never cast one over her.'

Routine press statements became a battleground over who would be quoted saying what. MPs started complaining about encroachment on their portfolios.

Even the way we spoke to each other in the corridors of parliament changed. Lindiwe became 'Madam Leader'; Watty Watson was 'Chief Whip'. And David was addressed as 'Media Whip', a newly created title. What was going on?

This was followed by a move to turn the parliamentary leader's office into the centre of the party's communications network, as it had once been under Tony's leadership. Ryan's re-engineering project had deliberately changed this structure, placing the federal communications nerve centre in the national head office with satellite teams working in parliament, the provinces, the regions and my office. The advantage of instant electronic communication meant that we could evaluate and prioritise national and provincial coverage, and target our media, to the right places, by the right people. The system was working well.

Lindiwe and her office wanted to change it. They did not tell me, because they wanted to act independently. I soon saw that David was continuing their campaign, based on the 'Bush doctrine' – if you aren't with us, you are against us. This approach was also applied to staff members who had remained non-aligned in the leadership battle. In the binary 'for or against' narrative, they were pigeonholed as 'against' and had to be moved out.

David had also been Tony Leon's chief of staff, and wanted to revert to the system he had known and could control. He was backed by Gareth van Onselen, who had run parliamentary communications under Tony's tenure. Their binary 'with us or against us' philosophy was reflected in their approach to their work: control or catastrophise. That soon led to tensions within Lindiwe's close-knit circle, as the pragmatists tried to defuse the growing tensions.

The plan was to bring Gareth back, to run parliament's core media operation. This required organisational restructuring. I was informed about it as a fait accompli. I drew the line, and said that any restructuring would happen through the proper processes.

The battles over the media continued over the most ridiculous issues. There was a major conflagration over the headline on a press statement – something that would normally go unnoticed by almost everyone.

I was at a bit of a loss as to how to deal with this, because every attempt I made to assist was seen as interference. I kept hoping and believing that things would settle.

Meanwhile, my occasional meetings with Mamphela continued, and things seemed to be on track. When we met in October 2011, she was accompanied by Sid Luckett, a long-standing friend of Johann's. Sid was a fine person, but I had always known him to be allergic to the DA. I was somewhat surprised that he appeared to support our plans now. How times change, I told myself. Mamphela said that Sid would take up the discussions where Marc van Olst had left off.

I learnt, much later, that times hadn't changed at all as far as Sid was concerned. He had opposed Mamphela's plan to join the DA from the get-go.

The first inkling I had of this was on 10 December, when Mamphela again arrived to see me with Sid. She said she wanted to postpone implementing her plan to join the DA so that she could first build the Citizens' Movement in an attempt to transform people 'from being subjects into becoming citizens'. I asked her how she proposed going about this. She explained she would hold community meetings in which people would be encouraged to face their 'woundedness' and move beyond it.

The notes I wrote after the meeting reminded me that 'she also made it clear, without actually saying so, that she did not want to join the DA'. Sid had clearly convinced her.

She said she would see how things unfolded in the future.

It was a big setback. But as no one except Ryan and James Selfe knew anything at that stage, there was no major damage, internally or externally. We could adjust.

On 13 December 2011, I appointed Mmusi Maimane to the position of party spokesperson, left vacant after Lindiwe's election as caucus leader. He was the obvious choice for spokesperson, after his strong showing as our mayoral candidate in Johannesburg.

Two days later, I was struck by an editorial in *Business Day*. It gave me some sense of how advanced the succession battle already was. I knew that Lindiwe's campaign team, and David in particular, had fostered close ties with an editorial writer at *Business Day* in the run-up to the caucus election, and this was an indication that the extended team was probably still mobilised. The editorial began by welcoming Mmusi's appointment as spokesman, saying he had the qualities required for the position, which was a 'launcher of political careers'. It pointed out that both Lindiwe and I had held the position previously. However, the editorial speculated, there 'may be a more underhand motive behind this appointment'.

> It has been suggested that placing Mr Maimane in a prominent position will serve as a counterbalance to Ms Mazibuko's increasing influence in the party. She has apparently wasted no time in flexing her newfound political muscle and carving out her own space both within the parliamentary caucus and the public eye, making it clear that she is hungry for the party's top position.
>
> It is no secret that the DA's greatest challenge is to transform its image to attract more young, black voters, and the appointment of articulate individuals like Mr Maimane and Ms Mazibuko, who have shown that they can more than hold their own in the political arena, will certainly go a long way towards achieving that goal.
>
> What remains unclear is the effect their rapid elevation will have on the internal dynamics of the party. Ms Zille has been expected to stay on as party leader after the 2014 elections, to be replaced by a suitable candidate in the run-up to the 2019 poll. However, Ms Mazibuko's popularity and rising support both within the party and among the electorate has prompted some in the DA to wonder whether the plan should not be expedited.

The first thing that struck me about this editorial was the perception that trying to ensure a strong pipeline of succession candidates was being interpreted as 'an underhand motive'. Everyone knew I had supported Lindiwe for the caucus leadership, but everyone also knew I did not support coronations. I, and almost everyone else in the DA, preferred political competition.

There was no doubt among all who read this editorial that it was flying a kite, to see whether it was possible for Lindiwe to reach the top slot before other potential competitors got out of the starting blocks.

The succession race had begun in earnest. We were a year away from a DA elective congress, scheduled for the end of 2012.

Back in the caucus, the rebellion against the new Mazibuko/Maynier regime was escalating. As the editorial correctly noted, Lindiwe had wasted no time in flexing her newfound political muscle and carving out her own space. What remained unsaid was the extent to which her style was alienating her colleagues, including some of her strongest supporters. The more I hoped matters would settle, the messier they got.

On 16 December, a public holiday known as the Day of Reconciliation, Marianne Thamm, an author and journalist, popped round to see me. She told me she wanted to follow up on what she had read between the lines in a recent newsletter I had written on a string of DA by-election successes. The paragraph that interested her was 'Our role in the DA is to read the signs correctly, spot the trends, and position our party in the non-racial centre of the political spectrum. If we get this right, we will govern South Africa before the end of the decade. There is more reason to be optimistic about the future of democracy than ever before.'

Marianne said I seemed to be hinting at something. I said I had been speaking openly about political realignment for many years. Then Marianne got to the real point she wanted to discuss with me. She had been talking to a fellow journalist, Fiona Forde, who had told her that Mamphela was planning to join the DA and that she would subsequently make a bid for the leadership. I nearly fell over. Where had she heard this, I ventured, without giving anything away. Mamphela had told Fiona herself, Marianne said.

I was astounded. Mamphela had sworn me to secrecy and had allegedly told a journalist! This must clearly have happened before she came to see me on 10 December to tell me about her change of heart. I did not say anything about the latest development. I merely confirmed that Mamphela and I had discussed it, but it would be premature to speculate about anything at this stage. It was very early days.

Johann and I ended the year in Keurbooms, where I experimented with a new app called Twitter, which I enjoyed. It was my entrée into the world of social media. I used it as an alternative form of SMS. I did not understand the concept of 'going viral' (and I thought a troll was an ugly little dwarf with outsized ears who lived in a cave). I didn't remotely grasp the essence of technology's first mass-outrage-manufacturing machine. And I made the cardinal error of assuming that people who made the effort to follow me would be my friends.

My office had always kept me away from Facebook, but somehow I managed to dodge them with Twitter. Ideally, it should have been the other way around. As a colleague, Jacques Maree (no relation) finally explained: Facebook is like a home game – the crowd is usually on your side; Twitter is an away game – the crowd is largely hostile and willing you to make a mistake so that they can pounce. And there is nothing playful about it. Cyber-stalking is magnified manyfold in the case of politicians. We are so used to vitriol, however, that we tend to forget how excruciatingly sensitive 'normal' people are.

I have always enjoyed verbal sparring – playful jousting without landing weighty blows. I took to Twitter because it provided a platform for this kind of superficial engagement. In fact, condensed repartee is one of the few things that Twitter's 140-character limit lends itself to. When, before long, I became the target of some heavy pummelling, I assumed a return jab would be acceptable in Twitter culture. The trouble is that the punch does not only connect with its intended target; it lands on the timelines of hundreds of thousands of followers. Any one of them can choose to take offence, even if it was not meant for them. It truly amazed me how many people are out there, searching cyberspace for any opportunity to feel insulted. Or to manufacture outrage. What's more, when the mob mentality combines with anonymity, there are no holds barred. Those are the unwritten rules, and they take years to learn, normally through making mistakes. Or simply by refusing to accept arbitrary rules and double standards.

And nowhere are race classification and double standards as entrenched as they are on Twitter.

I started on Twitter without realising any of this. I strode forth where angels fear to tread, lustily engaging the debate on whether Cape Town was 'racist'. After an interchange with singer/actor Simphiwe Dana, I finished with a jibe, picked up from a column by Jacob Dlamini in *Business Day*. I said: 'You are a highly respected black professional. Don't be a professional black. It demeans you.'

All hell broke loose.

Lindiwe was one of the people who was angry that I had provoked this controversy, and I understood why. She made fair points.

Then, early in 2012, came the first real caucus explosion. Lindiwe reshuffled her shadow cabinet, a move interpreted as a strategy to take revenge on supporters of Athol Trollip. The backlash was instant and strong.

The Times reported it as follows on 2 February 2012: 'DA parliamentary leader Lindiwe Mazibuko has flexed her muscles, making wholesale changes to the shadow cabinet and handing her old rural development portfolio to her predecessor, Athol Trollip.

'Mazibuko, who allocated new portfolios to many experienced MPs, said of the wide-ranging changes: "Ultimately, this decision is mine."'

Those were exactly the same words she had used to me, when she had presented me with her planned reshuffle as a fait accompli shortly before announcing it. Normally, the parliamentary leader would discuss a proposed reshuffle with me, analysing the pros and cons of every detail, as well as the timing, until we had reached agreement on the way forward. I got the sense that Lindiwe had taken the decision and didn't want interference.

The news report continued:

'Some of Trollip's backers during the bruising campaign for the DA parliamentary leadership have either been reassigned to new portfolios or demoted.'

There was unadulterated fury in some sections of the caucus, but I knew that intervening would be the worst possible response on my part. It would press all the wrong buttons and I would be accused of treating her like a 'tea girl'. I had to back off.

Communication between our offices became sporadic and abrupt. I began to realise how much I had taken for granted the ease of interaction with Athol and Ian, when I was kept regularly apprised of the major issues, of the forthcoming legislative programme, and especially of impending risks. During that period there really was no problem with the party leadership being separate from the parliamentary leadership. The bridges were strong. Ian had the experience in the role of chief whip to keep his finger on the pulse and ensure he kept both Athol and me informed. We picked up the phone whenever we needed to, and the quality of the professional staff in our offices did all the rest. We wanted each other to succeed, and the cogs of the party's gears were linking well.

I had simply taken all this for granted. Like knowing that electrical appliances will work when you switch them on. Until the electricity fails. Good internal communication is the electricity supply of a functional political party.

In the new set-up, a lot of this crucial personal interaction ceased. Geordin was soon *persona non grata*; Lindiwe did not want Janine Schouw, my stylist, to advise her about her wardrobe (but changed her mind later, when the ANC and the media focused on her clothes, her body, her hair, in an outrageous display of South Africa's ingrained patriarchal culture).

Lindiwe's chief whip, Watty Watson, although an experienced parliamentarian, was new to the post as well, and it was always going to take a while to master all the intricacies of the complex position, especially in relation to the legislative load which was escalating rapidly as we moved into the second half of the five-year term. And with new MPs now reassigned to critical portfolios, as well as alienation growing in the caucus, there was an accident waiting to happen. I felt powerless to prevent it – because, ironically, trying to prevent it would actually cause the conflagration. I just hoped our systems would be strong enough to cater for human error.

And then, on top of it all, the structure of caucus meetings was changed, leaving very little time to discuss pending legislation, which is the core function of the caucus.

As the resistance within caucus to the new leadership gathered momentum, some of my colleagues came to see me and told me directly: You persuaded us to vote for Lindiwe. It was a mistake. It was premature.

The occasional attempt I made to resolve issues evoked stronger and stronger resistance. I soon sensed there was a Berlin Wall between us, of the kind that I first experienced when David Maynier had been Tony Leon's chief of staff. I could not get through to Tony then, and I could not get through to Lindiwe now. Our discussions became superficial and I could sense she was going through the motions. We were talking past each other.

I got involved in another Twitter spat (a twar) that was, in my view, deliberately blown out of proportion. Nevertheless, a twar at that crucial time did not help the general ambience much.

The contretemps arose out of the fact that 600 additional learners had arrived unexpectedly at a school in Grabouw called Umyezo Wama Apile during the first quarter of 2012. For almost three preceding years we had been trying to acquire an ideal piece of land for a new school from the National Department of Public Works to accommodate learners whose families were arriving from the Eastern Cape in significant numbers. We were all extremely frustrated by the bureaucratic blocking we had experienced, arising primarily out of the inefficiency of the National Department of Public Works.

By then the school had become so overcrowded as to be dysfunctional. I faced public criticism and the Twitter trolls, who are always looking for a way to go in for the kill. It was ironic that the tweet that got me into so much trouble was my response to a jibe which came from someone I liked, and with whom I chatted a lot. This was a local entrepreneur named Vuyisa Qabaka. He started accusing me of doing nothing for black learners in the Western Cape. I was mightily irritated at his taunting, especially as I knew just how much of our infrastructure budget was being devoted to accommodating learners coming from the Eastern Cape – while the national budget for this purpose kept going to the province from which so many learners were fleeing, and where 300 schools had just been closed.

So I sought to shut him up, within Twitter's 140-character limit, by tweeting: 'While ECape education collapsed, WC built 30 schools – 22 new, 8 replacement mainly 4 ECape edu refugees. 26 MORE new schools coming.'

My point was to show just how much we were doing for Eastern Cape children – but I had left the door open for ANC and other hostile trolls to falsely conclude that Eastern Cape children were not welcome in the Western Cape. This was ironic because the very point of the tweet was to make the opposite point.

The controversy raged for weeks. It was beyond my comprehension. To me, there was nothing pejorative or racist in the word 'refugee'. Indeed, the word was intended as an affirmation of the learners and an indictment of the authorities that denied and trampled on their rights to education in their province of origin.

I apologised – and meant it. But when all was said and done, I thought Justice Malala, the author and television talk-show host, hit the nail on the head with his commentary.

> What would you do if you were a parent with a child in one of the [Eastern Cape's] schools? I know what I would do. I would take my child out and put them in a school elsewhere. I would uproot myself from my friends, relatives and home. I would become an 'education refugee', as the opposition Democratic Alliance's former leader put it before she was roundly condemned by the ANC for allegedly being racist. But there is no other way to put it.*

On 24 April 2012, Mamphela launched the Citizens Movement for Social Change in a blaze of publicity attended by a who's who of the business and academic elite and a few top politicians. She attracted some outstanding staff, and her legendary fundraising skills had brought in millions.

Then, suddenly, in July 2012, Mamphela was back in Leeuwenhof, speaking to me. She came alone. She said she was no longer working closely with Sid Luckett. She was ready to resume our discussions where we had left off before Sid had arrived on the scene.

This vacillation was out of character. I hadn't experienced it throughout our years of working together. When Mamphela took a decision, she stuck to it, sometimes perhaps even too inflexibly. But I made allowances for her current situation. I understood what an enormous step this would be for her, given her past, and what courage it would take. I was prepared to suck up a lot of stuff in the process. No one else with her struggle credentials was even remotely prepared to consider what she was prepared to do.

I had always suspected that Mamphela's change of heart between 6 October and 10 December the previous year had something to do with Sid Luckett's persuasion. In the process of writing this book I phoned Sid to ask him if my hunch was correct. He confirmed that it was. He told me that when he started working with Mamphela in September 2011, she had decided to join the DA. This was still the situation when we spoke at Leeuwenhof on 6 October. And by 10 December, he had persuaded her at least to postpone her plans.

'I felt very strongly she should stay out of party politics,' said Sid, 'and I told her so.'

Seven months later, after she and Sid had fallen out (allegedly over the man-

---

* Justice Malala, *We Have Now Begun Our Descent* (Jonathan Ball, 2015), p. 357

agement of the Citizens Movement's finances), Mamphela was available once again to resume where we had left off seven months earlier.

We agreed that this time we had to discuss the options formally and properly, with a team on both sides and a regular schedule of meetings, proper records and the necessary documentation.

I put my team together: Wilmot James, party chairman; Lindiwe Mazibuko, the parliamentary leader; James Selfe, chair of the Federal Council; Ryan Coetzee, the party's chief strategist; and Jonathan Moakes, the chief executive officer. Mamphela's team comprised Prince Mashele, a research consultant and master's graduate in political science; Brutus Malada, a political consultant; and Dr Moeletsi Mbeki, a well-known political economist and commentator (who also happened to be former president Thabo Mbeki's brother).

We held our first meeting on 18 August 2012 at a beautiful old-world guest house with high ceilings in Oranjezicht, Cape Town, two days after the Marikana massacre. The circumstances could not have been more compelling. Everyone recognised the urgency of the times, captured by Mamphela when she said, 'If we want to arrest the decline, we must sprint as we build.'

She said a new political force was necessary, built on the foundation of the DA's formidable machine. She said that she and her followers did not simply want to be absorbed into the existing DA – they wanted to be part of building a new brand.

This was a different approach from the one we had discussed previously. But it was a proposal we were prepared to explore. The urgency of the times demanded it.

There were seven meetings, in all, including a smaller technical task team mandated to draw up documents between plenaries. James Selfe kept scrupulous notes of every meeting.

The converted Victorian guest house provided a homely ambience. Whenever we arrived, I could sense a buzz among the manager and staff, as if they sensed history was being made behind the closed door of the small conference room. They kept us well nourished for our task, with lovely home-bakes at tea and delicious plates of home-cooked food at mealtimes. The atmosphere could not have been more convivial.

Prince Mashele drafted the first position paper. He titled it 'Strategic Perspective for South Africa: Repositioning the Democratic Alliance for greater leadership responsibility'.

Ryan shortened the document and gave it the title 'The DA's Path to the Future'.

Mamphela's team inserted references to colonialism and imperialism, and the need to change the extractive nature of the South African economy. And they also wanted us to showcase the DA as a party of competent governance. So far, so good.

I had learnt by this time that Lindiwe could be inscrutable, and that she tended to back away from confrontation, so I could not really gauge how she was responding to our process, which, if successful, would provide her with stiff competition (at the very least) in her bid for the top job. But she participated in the discussion in her normal articulate and incisive way.

Mamphela for her part, exuding confidence, never thought of anyone as an equal competitor.

By mid-September we had made sufficient progress to start preparing the ground publicly. I addressed a meeting of the Cape Town Press Club on 27 September and spoke about the urgency of political realignment, the obsolescence of current party boundaries and the need to reshape political formations as a choice between constitutionalism and populism. We had to build a new force at the centre of South African politics to bring together all South Africans who supported constitutionalism, non-racialism and a market economy, and understood the importance of defending independent state institutions. Leaders and parties who supported these values would have to be prepared to give up part of their individual identities to form a greater entity, capable of challenging for power. It was essential given the urgency of the times.

My exact words were:

Giving up a small part of our political identities will be worth it if we can build a new political vehicle to put South Africa on course and stay the distance.

I will continue to devote my life to the attainment of that goal. I have staked my political leadership on it. And I am prepared to work with all like-minded political leaders to achieve it.

If we can transcend the political formations that keep us trapped in the past, future generations will look back and thank us.

The speech was well received, with excellent media coverage. We now had the wind at our backs.

I felt confident that with the now formalised talks with Team Mamphela, we would have something new and exciting to offer the electorate in 2014 that could start bridging the racial divide that separated the electorate.

At the same time, I supported Lindiwe building her profile by leading the DA's charge on a range of issues, including Nkandla. She lodged the formal request with the public protector to investigate and rule on the expenditure of public money on the president's private residence late in 2012.

But September 2012 also brought a blow. Ryan came to tell me that he had accepted an appointment as strategic adviser to Nick Clegg, the leader of our sister party in Britain, the Liberal Democrats. I had come to rely on Ryan, both to generate strategic ideas and as a sounding-board for my own. Whether we agreed with each other or not, our interactions were always honest and productive, sometimes even brutal. I valued Ryan's ability to see to the heart of a situation.

The night he told me he was going, I sat in bed and cried. I told Johann why.

'Hmm,' he said, 'it's an interesting experience sitting in bed next to my wife, who is crying over another man.' I had to laugh.

We continued to work together on what I had dubbed the 'M-Plan' (after Mamphela), echoing the famous secret original Mandela Plan, which mobilised the ANC at street level to challenge for power.

By the end of October, and hours of discussion, our M-Plan had crystallised to the point where we even had a proposed name for the relaunched party. We suggested it should simply be called 'The Democrats', signalling that it was a political home for all genuine democrats.

According to James's notes:

1. MAR [Mamphela's initials] and HZ would together announce their joint commitment to establish a new entity based on the four pillars outlined in HZ's Press Club speech.
2. Prior to that, the technical team would meet and arrive at consensus on
   - The values, attitudes, principles and behaviour
   - A process to establish policy
   - The system of representation
   - Method of choosing candidates
   - Continuous evaluation of public representatives
   - The separation of professional staff from elected office-bearers
   - The retention of the current NHO checks on money and expenditure
3. Failure to agree on these matters would involve in MAR going it alone, and that we will meet again after the election in possible pacts or coalitions.
4. However, assuming agreement, both parties would commit to consulting structures and stakeholders, and the broader public. Over time, others may endorse the initiative and give it momentum.
5. In the meantime, the technical team would finalise a new constitution, leadership arrangements, fundraising protocols, a launching congress and so on.
6. The DA would at some stage during this process have a congress to resolve to renew/relaunch/rebrand itself as part of a new political formation called 'The Democrats'.
7. 'The Democrats' would be launched as a political party on 16 June 2013 at a suitable venue.
8. The technical sub-committee would finalise all details by the end of the year.

Meanwhile, on the broader political front, the Nkandla scandal was gathering momentum. Unable to get answers to crucial questions in parliament, we decided to go to the homestead and see for ourselves. Our decision caused an outcry, and strong resistance, even in the DA's ranks. It would be regarded as disrespectful by the voters of KwaZulu-Natal, we were warned, to be marching on the president's home.

Our KwaZulu-Natal leader, Sizwe Mchunu, declined to accompany us on the walk, and I said it was a matter of individual choice.

We deliberately kept the Nkandla delegation small, to minimise the risk of aggravating a controversy that could boomerang. But we could not let the issue slide, especially as we were not getting decent answers to questions about Nkandla in parliament. We had to keep the questions alive and find ways of ensuring that we eventually got the answers.

There were about eight DA leaders who participated in our walk to Nkandla.

We walked along a public road, surrounded by undulating hills in the most beautiful countryside, dotted with the thatched rondavels so typical of rural South Africa. I noticed corrugated-iron shacks springing up too, a blight imported from urban South Africa that was rapidly destroying what, to an uninformed outsider, looked like a rural idyll. The people around here lived in abject poverty.

I recall the first moment I saw Nkandla. It looked like a sprawling conference centre and golf estate, stretched across the shoulder of a wide hill. This was the president's private home, effectively built with public money. At that moment, in that setting, I understood what had happened in South Africa. The cattle herder from Nkandla had used a constitutional democracy to turn himself into a paramount chief, to whom people across the country owed their allegiance. This justified spending public money on himself. It explained why he saw state institutions as an extension of his power, to use against his enemies and protect his friends. The people were accountable to him, not the other way around. That perspective lay at the root of his failure to comprehend constitutionalism. It was all so clear, walking down that road on that beautiful day.

I was thinking about how much work lay ahead to embed constitutionalism into South Africa's culture when the large police contingent asked us to move to the verge to make way for several buses that came rattling past. Their passengers were adult men, some in ANC T-shirts, all of them carrying traditional weapons, which they waved menacingly out of the windows. They were local villagers, being transported to a point further down the road where they alighted and formed a barrier to prevent us from reaching the spot, outside a school close to the homestead, where we had received written permission from the relevant authorities to congregate. We saw the men alight from the buses and block the roadway a few hundred metres in front of us, waving their weapons menacingly to show they meant business.

The police, wearing riot gear, instructed us to turn around and abort our march. I asked them why they had failed to instruct the buses to turn around instead. We were the only people who had permission to congregate. The mini impi clearly constituted an illegal gathering. There were armoured Nyala personnel carriers, two trucks with water cannons, and a helicopter in the area. It was obvious they expected problems.

I tried to explain that we were on a public road, that we had permission to be there, and that no one could prevent us from exercising our rights. This argument was lost on the police, who insisted that we turn around, for the sake of our safety. I looked ahead and saw the impi's numbers swell with the arrival of surrounding villagers.

Here were the desperately poor people of KwaNxamalala (as the area is known), who lived without even the most basic services, congregating to defend their leader's honour. They gazed upon the president's opulent, publicly funded private residence every day, and instead of being angry with what it represented, were deeply proud that a local lad had made good and had become South Africa's paramount chief.

My constitutional assumptions represented colonialism writ large, aggravated by the fact that I was white.

The newspapers reported, with obvious *schadenfreude*, that we had been forced to retreat, and the DA became the focus of criticism for being confrontational!

Once again, the subtext was that a 'white' party did not understand the predominant Zulu culture and that our stand, no matter how justified in constitutional terms, was counterproductive. Yet Julius Malema's later actions on Nkandla, which were purely theatrical and unconnected to getting information that the EFF had failed to extract through the parliamentary process, were publicly applauded. I realised once again that we were judged by a different yardstick, which constrained us in fulfilling our functions.

I understood all of this – and how urgent it was to reach our Clause 4 moment fast, but the idea of standing down at the 2012 congress in November was clearly premature. I stood for re-election as leader, unopposed.

Lindiwe's team had drawn the conclusion that they would not be able to win, so it was better for her not to run at all, at least not yet. Being part of the DA's M-Plan team, she clearly understood the possibility that Mamphela would seek a leadership position for one five-year term. By that point Lindiwe would be in her late thirties, which would give her the advantage of a few more years of experience and a chance to recalibrate her approach and become the strongest contender for the leadership after that. I sensed that she had reached that conclusion, but I could not discuss it with her because our relationship was no longer conducive to those kinds of conversations.

Wilmot James invited Prince Mashele and Brutus Malada to the congress, and they were highly impressed to see the blue machine in action, as well as the diversity of the DA's membership and newly elected leadership. It was all systems go.

By the end of the year, the Western Cape countryside was burning, as rival union organisers sought to outflank each other with their own 'M-Plan' – 'bringing Marikana to the Western Cape'. It was a devastating strike in which farms and infrastructure were destroyed and thousands of jobs lost. Dealing with this crisis absorbed my efforts and energies. It also added huge renewed urgency to our talks, which were still happening in secret.

James and Prince and their colleagues in the technical task team were forging ahead with the agreement. James had passed every draft on to the rest of the DA team, and we assumed Prince had done the same with Mamphela's team. The two drafters-in-chief met again on 27 December after a short Christmas break. James gave the thumbs-up from our side.

Prince then mentioned that his team members had not read the agreement, but he knew them well enough to be able to say that they would agree with 99 per cent of it. The 1 per cent on which he said they would disagree was, however, a deal-breaker. It involved an additional requirement: the complete disestablishment of the DA, because of perceptions that a new party would not succeed if it were simply perceived to be the DA under a new name.

We had repeatedly said that the DA would not, and could not, simply fold up its tent and go out of business. We had more than three million voters, a large national organisation and 1794 public representatives. And apart from her brand, which was important, we were not sure who Mamphela and her small group of colleagues were bringing to the table. She kept having a range of consultations, but she would not say with whom.

We were prepared to relaunch and recast the DA, but not disband it.

We had all previously agreed on that point, I thought.

James made it clear that this expectation would be a serious obstacle. Prince understood why. He thought we could find a way around it. He and James agreed that the final agreement would have to be agreed in detail, clause by clause, and that the refinement process had to start in the week beginning 14 January 2013. James worked on the draft. He consulted the rest of us. We were fully prepared. Prince volunteered to take care of the meeting logistics. We waited for his call.

In the meantime, I was also meeting Mamphela to finalise the timing for our announcement that would follow the finalisation of the agreement.

The communication process would be extremely complicated and risky. The

DA team had stressed from the outset that without a two-thirds majority from the 130-member Federal Council, representing the DA's highest decision-making body between congresses, we would not be able to proceed.

We had to plan a public announcement immediately after our Federal Council meeting, on the assumption that we would manage to get the necessary support (which was a bold assumption). If all went well, we planned to announce our relaunch as 'The Democrats' at a major public event on 16 June. We knew it would be a big story, and we agreed that an element of surprise would be helpful when making a public announcement. We needed to prevent premature leaks from the Federal Council discussion, which made the timing important.

I went to Mamphela's home in Camps Bay on 10 January 2013, and we discussed how to manage the announcement. She was absolutely adamant that we had to make it before the State of the Nation Address (SONA). This would give us maximum coverage and open a new political debate, which would overshadow what the president had to say. I said time was very tight, as the SONA was traditionally held early in February, and we still had a lot to finalise and agree on. She was optimistic we could do it.

Then she told me that she still wanted to consult with a range of 'civil society' leaders to explain the plan to them in advance. I strongly advised her against doing this. If she did, it would be in the newspapers in minutes and we would not be able to shape the message. And if the DA first read about it in the newspaper, without contextualisation, it would massively complicate the situation. I needed her to understand that we could not simply take the DA's support for granted. The DA had strong internal institutions which had to be respected.

Mamphela said she would be very cautious; she would ensure confidentiality. I said these things never worked out that way. I also anticipated that some of the leaders to whom she would be speaking would try again to dissuade her from our agreed course of action. We had come so far, and I did not want us to create unnecessary hurdles now.

She assured me she had things under control. As I left, she asked me to let her know exactly when the State of the Nation Address was scheduled.

When I got home, I looked at my diary and sent her a text, confirming that the SONA was scheduled for 14 February 2013.

Mamphela replied: 'Wow! Very little time! We need to aim for 12th. Thanks dear! Let's go!'

The clock was ticking. Every minute counted.

Mamphela's absolute insistence that we announce on 12 February caused a problem. Our Federal Council was scheduled for 15–16 February (after the SONA). We would have to bring it forward to 9–10 February, and if we got adequate support, we would make the announcement on Tuesday 12 February.

Rearranging the Federal Council involved an enormous logistical effort, and provoked questions throughout the party, especially as we were unable to give a coherent reason for this major change in schedule.

In the meantime, James was waiting for Prince's call to arrange the final clause-by-clause drafting meeting in the week beginning 14 January.

Monday 14 January 2013: Radio silence.

Tuesday 15 January 2013: Radio silence.

James and I discuss what we should do. Prince had insisted on organising the logistics and we don't want to barge in and take over. We agree that James should call Prince. Prince says there's a problem, but not serious. The meeting will only have to be postponed by a day.

Wednesday 16 January 2013: Prince calls to say the meeting has been postponed indefinitely but he is not mandated to say why. I contact Mamphela and ask her what is going on. She says she cannot tell me immediately. My anger boils over, but I try to control it.

Thursday 17 January 2013: Mamphela and I see each other at a function. I step aside with her and ask her what is going on. She says I shouldn't worry, she will see me on Monday 21 January.

Friday 18 January 2013 (Mom's ninety-fourth birthday): I write to Mom and worry about the M-Plan. I spend the weekend worrying.

Monday evening, 21 January 2013: The DA team gathers at Leeuwenhof and waits for Mamphela. She arrives with a new colleague – Associate Professor Mills Soko of the Graduate School of Business at the University of Cape Town.

Mamphela explained that Prince Mashele and Moeletsi Mbeki had fallen out over an issue entirely unrelated to the 'The Democrats' project and that Mills would be Prince's replacement. Mills would finalise all the documents with James Selfe. I was taken aback at the latest changing of the guard, and extremely stressed about the time frame, but I was somewhat comforted by Mills's formidable reputation and focused approach.

We were due to have our Federal Executive meeting on Friday 25 January – that very week. The meeting of the Federal Executive, the party's top leadership, preceded and prepared for the full Federal Council on 9–10 February. The Federal Executive would have to consider the draft M-Plan agreement clause by clause, but first we had to reach consensus on it. Mills was new to the discussions, and needed time. It seemed impossible. As we tried to fathom the way forward, I asked for a separate caucus with the DA team.

We retreated to Leeuwenhof's red lounge, which was tastefully furnished in shades of burgundy and olive. In the middle, from the chandelier, dangled a gaudy pink heart made of sparkly beads and wire. Johann had bought it for me from a street vendor the previous Valentine's Day and had hung it in the room to surprise me. I had left it there because it was so wonderfully out of place. It added a touch of levity and farce symbolic of my job to the formal space.

We sat beneath the dangling pink heart discussing our options. We had put in so much work, done our research and concluded that a rebranding relaunch with a new leadership configuration was the right move. This was a serious obstacle on the road, but should we allow it to abort our journey? We concluded we would have to move the date of our Federal Executive as well, to 1 February.

It is virtually unheard of to shift important meeting dates around in the DA. The schedule is fixed a year in advance. Yet here we were, rescheduling our second major meeting in as many weeks, without being able to explain why. I don't think Mamphela and her team grasped how much political capital we were expending simply by adjusting meeting dates in the DA's structured organisational environment. In these circumstances we would, inevitably, enter these crucial meetings on the back foot. That would make things more difficult.

Nevertheless we agreed that the project was important enough to warrant it.

We also set up a meeting of DA provincial leaders on 29 January, to talk through the proposal before the Federal Executive. The provincial leaders were pivotal to the direction the discussion would take in the Federal Executive. By that stage, they were also very curious. They concluded something really big was about to happen. But we remained tight-lipped.

I undertook to keep regular contact with Mamphela to ensure everything was in place. She committed Mills to calling James the next day to set up a schedule for finalising the detailed proposal for a relaunched party under our proposed new name.

Tuesday 22 January 2013: Mills doesn't call. Now what? James will deal with it.

Wednesday 23 January 2013: Radio silence. I send an early SMS at 7:07 a.m.: 'Hi MAR. Can we pls have Mills's tel number so that James can call him. Tks HZ.'

She sends me the number. Later, at 2:35 p.m., she sends a text, the formality of which bothers me: 'Good day Helen, could we see each other for an hour or so tomorrow afternoon or evening? Best wishes MAR.'

I reply at 4:03 p.m.: 'Yes I can clear my diary at 16h30 for an hour. Your place or mine.'

At 6:06 she replies: 'Yours pls.'

At 7:07 I ask: 'All organised. Can I bring James Selfe?'

At 7:26 she replies: 'No only you and I. Thanks.'

That was cause for real concern. I wondered why.

Mamphela arrived punctually, her normal confident and relaxed self. I did not sense there was a problem. I offered her something to drink and she chose water. She took a few sips. The way she put her glass on the side table told me she was gearing up to tell me something she knew I didn't want to hear.

Then she began a long and convoluted explanation that took forever to get to the point. It was completely out of character. In a nutshell, she said that she and I were 'engaged', but unfortunately she would have to launch a new party on her own on 12 February. The DA was no longer part of the plan. At least not in the initial stages.

I could not believe it, and I told her so. We had been working on a detailed plan for eight months, we had a final draft document just awaiting the last details and ratification, we had rescheduled two crucial DA meetings to fit her time frame, and she was just wiping it off the table. And going in a completely different direction. Why?

She then told me she had been presented with research done by someone called Jos Kuper. The research, she claimed, showed that if she launched a new party on her own, she could potentially attract about 60 per cent of the vote. On the other hand, if she aligned with the DA, the maximum the relaunched party could draw would be between 30 and 40 per cent of the vote. If we did it her way, we would win the 2014 election, she argued.

I could not believe what I was hearing. I told her she was dreaming. It would take a miracle, I said, even on the basis of a complete relaunch of the DA, for us to get over 30 per cent, combined! She told me that I was so trapped in small thinking that I could not get my head around a new vision.

Without actually using the word, I intimated that she was deluded, and that if she launched a new party, she would be lucky to reach a percentage in double figures. She countered that Barack Obama had only started his bid for the US presidency with 1 per cent support, and it had escalated from there. Jos Kuper's figures had shown her that she could do the same thing.

I then told her in so many words that she was dreaming, and she told me to stop patronising her. I went further and said she clearly didn't understand electoral politics. I said all she could hope to do, even if she teamed up with us, would be to add a few percentage points to our vote. She thought I was myopic.

We both ended up furious. I was no longer containing myself, as I had learnt to do over the years, working around her. As she left, in her chauffeur-driven car, I told myself it would be the last time I would meet her. I was up to my neck with being led by the nose. My emotions were as mixed as my metaphors. On the one hand I was relieved to be rid of her. On the other hand, our Clause 4 moment would be pushed back yet again, and South Africa was in a race against time.

Later I sat in bed, looking over the sparkling lights of the Cape Town skyline, and poured my heart out to Johann.

'"Tis better to have tried and failed than never to have tried at all,' he said, misquoting Tennyson.

'I've invested a lot trying to reposition the party and it keeps backfiring,' I replied. 'There is an enormous cost to trying and failing in politics. If I fail to diversify the DA's leadership sufficiently and successfully, it will be at an even bigger cost to the country. The irony is that, if I fail, I will remain the leader. If I succeed, I won't. But the worst of all possible worlds is having to remain leader with massively diminished political capital because my plans backfired on the party. And then it will be even harder to drive a new vision.'

I told him, for the first time, that my close allies were really angry and blaming me (with some justification) for the deteriorating situation in the national caucus.

And then, on top of it all – Mamphela!

If Mamphela, of all people, who agreed with our analysis and had lots of guts, found it impossible to take this obvious step, even in a relaunched and rebranded version of the DA, what hope did we have of growing at the rate required to prevent South Africa becoming a failed state?

'Why is it so hard? Surely this step is as obvious to other people as it is to me?' I moaned.

'If you hadn't tried, you would never have known it wouldn't work,' replied Johann.

I was too tired to work out that double negative. It was just the start of a political year, and I already felt thoroughly spent. Shattered.

The next day I met my DA colleagues on the M-Plan team. They were stunned too. We had been taken for complete idiots. I apologised to James that he had spent the whole of his Christmas holiday working on a detailed document that was cast aside so lightly.

Mamphela sailed on.

I had to explain to the provincial leaders' meeting, and the Federal Executive on 1 February, what we had planned and why it had gone so wrong. I managed a cool façade, saying it was probably for the best. We had dodged a bullet. But I still felt betrayed and shaken.

Should I even have tried to bring her on board, I asked myself. Which again raised the question: compared to what? If I hadn't responded positively when Mamphela had said (repeatedly) that she was available, I would have been sidestepping a rare rebranding opportunity.

On Saturday 2 February, I had been invited to attend the gala dinner to commemorate F.W. de Klerk's historic 1990 speech. The event was at the Radisson Hotel, where I was asked to say a few words. I needed a diversion, and looked forward to it.

Moeletsi Mbeki was there. I could hardly bear to look at him, but managed to greet him civilly. He indicated that he wanted to speak to me. He drew me aside to explain what had happened behind the scenes. He knew I was angry, he said, but he needed to inform me that we were being led into a political ambush.

I said I didn't know what he was talking about.

Then he switched to conspiratorial mode. Prince Mashele, he whispered, was an NIA agent and had been on a mission to destroy us. The NIA wanted Mamphela to join up with the DA in order to damage her political credibility. Then, according to the NIA's plan, we would make the announcement on 12 February, so that Zuma could destroy us both in his State of the Nation Address two days later. 'The Democrats' would be stillborn, he claimed. Prince had almost pulled off this diabolical strategy by persuading Mamphela to go along with it, said Moeletsi. That was why she had been so insistent on a 12 February announcement. Fortunately, he said, she had seen through it in time.

It was another absurd story. ANC leaders who had been in exile always seemed full of them.

I was sick to death of it all, but I held back. All I said was that I did not believe that Prince was an NIA agent and that I could no longer expend energy on the matter.

I heard the real background story only later. Moeletsi and Prince had fallen out with each other over the controversial findings of an opinion survey they had conducted among trade union shop stewards. Prince wanted to release the findings; Moeletsi didn't. That is where Moeletsi had come to the conclusion that Prince was an NIA agent, deliberately attempting to leak the findings because his 'handlers' had allegedly told him to do so.

And their battle had spilt over into the M-Plan team. Moeletsi had convinced Mamphela that Prince was an NIA agent and that she should not fall into his trap set to destroy her – to join forces with the DA.

I wondered why Mamphela kept listening to these siren calls when it seemed to me so patently obvious what would be in South Africa's interests. I was furious with the people who kept whispering in her ear at critical moments, convincing her to unravel months of work – first Sid, and then Moeletsi. It was so unlike her to vacillate in this way.

Circumstances were not getting any better in the DA's parliamentary caucus either. I raised my concerns about the gathering anger and unease directly with Lindiwe, but she genuinely believed the rumours were being put about by a few disgruntled people. Lindiwe tended to withdraw in the face of problems; my style was to tackle them head on. We continued to talk past each other, when we spoke at all.

February 12 came and went, followed by Zuma's State of the Nation Address two days later. It was dismal. I have rarely felt lower in my life.

On Monday 18 February 2013, Mamphela launched what she described as a 'political platform', and called it Agang, Sotho for 'Let's Build'.

People were puzzled by the concept of a political platform, but I knew what

Mamphela was getting at. She saw it as a life raft onto which other opposition parties would all jump, as Agang became the voters' preferred vessel, in line with her understanding of Jos Kuper's research.

Mamphela's new approach echoed a proposal that Moeletsi had made at the outset of our team discussions, in August 2012, but that everyone (including Mamphela at the time) had roundly rejected. He had wanted all the opposition parties to come together, around a new catalyst, which, he suggested, Mamphela would provide. Prince disagreed with Moeletsi, and won the argument. Once Moeletsi had manoeuvred Prince out of the way, with his 'agent' story, he could resurrect his 'platform' idea. Mamphela was by that time entirely convinced that the tide was coming in strongly for her, and that the DA would be swept along by the current that would reach its flood by the 2014 election. The DA would then join her, on her terms, rather than the other way around.

I asked myself what kind of Kool-Aid she was drinking. I had little doubt it was Moeletsi's. In the end, after everything had collapsed around her, Moeletsi denied having had anything to do with the formation of Agang, and I know Mamphela was deeply stung by this.

All of us involved knew that Moeletsi was integrally involved. Indeed, he was the key person who persuaded her to abandon the work we had done over many months, and to launch the nonsensical idea of a 'platform' to draw together all opposition parties.

Soon after Agang's launch, it seemed as if the smaller parties might gravitate towards her. There were news reports about COPE and the UDM (with whom Moeletsi had also been speaking) wanting to join 'the platform'. I had a sense of déjà vu. Here we were, going into yet another crucial national election with a new and potentially exciting competitor, feeding off the same limited opposition pool. There was no way on the planet that Agang was going to take a meaningful slice of the vote from the ANC. I was at a loss. How were we going to break this destructive cycle?

The Nkandla scandal was gathering momentum. So was conflict in the ANC. In June, expelled ANCYL leader Julius Malema, facing charges of money laundering and racketeering, announced that he was holding preliminary discussions and canvassing the start of a new party called the Economic Freedom Fighters to contest the 2014 elections. So now we would face another competitor in the opposition space, which would be targeting disillusioned ANC voters.

I seriously asked myself: should I rather just let it be, and abandon my efforts to break out of the minority mould? That is what some of my DA colleagues had always argued – that we would never attract a significant number of black voters anyway, that it was pointless to try, and that we should rather remain a small watchdog party for minorities.

I had always strongly rejected that option, arguing that if we wanted a non-racial future, we would have to build a non-racial party that could win elections, not simply remain in opposition. Now, with Agang and the EFF on the scene, we would be squeezed from both sides, and could end up with as racially polarised an election in 2014 as we had had in 2009.

While I was preoccupied with these thoughts, the DA's caucus pot boiled over.

A report appeared in the *Sunday Independent* and the *Sunday Tribune* on 21 July 2013.

> The long knives are out for DA parliamentary leader Lindiwe Mazibuko, with even former key lobbyists conceding she could be removed after next year's general elections. Described as arrogant and autocratic by members in the caucus, senior party members this week rued what they described as her poor leadership and management style.
>
> Mazibuko's office was not available to comment this week.
>
> After a bruising contest in which she went head to head with respected veteran DA MP Athol Trollip for the position, largely splitting the caucus, Mazibuko now faces serious challenges from inside her own party, in addition to the regular fire she comes under from the ANC.

After reporting a range of criticisms, the article described how unhappy the caucus was that I had intervened to support Lindiwe in the caucus election.

I now seriously considered returning to the national caucus after the 2014 election. My advisers warned me that this would have very serious consequences in the public discourse. It would be a massive public humiliation for Lindiwe, and reconfirm the 'tea girl' narrative. On the other hand, I could not allow things to continue as they were. Putting up another candidate was an equally risky option, especially as it opened the possibility of the race issue re-emerging in a far more virulent form.

At a personal level, I felt disappointed and somewhat guilty that Lindiwe, who once seemed unassailable as my natural successor, had become a victim of her own initial success and premature promotion. I remembered the cardinal rule in politics: peak late.

I concluded that, all things considered, there would be less risk in my returning to parliament than remaining in the province. But I also had to seriously consider the impact of a succession struggle for the premiership. Our brand was that we were competent in government where we won elections. While I did not regard myself as indispensable, we were just consolidating our position and preparing for lift-off.

This was my lowest moment in politics. Every option seemed inordinately risky. My political choices seemed to hover between worse, worst and too ghastly to contemplate. And the only people who were absolutely sure about what I should do were the commentators who would not have to face any consequences for being wrong. Some were convinced I should move to parliament. Others were equally adamant that I should remain in the province.

My mother's health was deteriorating and she went through bouts of depression, now managed by medication. I saw her every time I went to Johannesburg. She had developed emphysema from a lifetime of smoking, and was confined to bed, on medication that was leading to rapid hearing loss. I could no longer talk to her on the phone, so I started writing to her.

In my sixties, I learnt something profound about my mother. She was a poor listener (even when she could hear properly) but a brilliant reader. Instead of arguing with her when I was a teenager, I should just have written letters to her. Then I would have got my points across, and she would have read and reread my letters, till she understood them.

We were both glad we discovered this technique towards the end of her life. By then she had the insight to know that she had been incapable of listening to what her children were saying to her because her head was so full of her own convictions on every issue. She usually jumped to the wrong conclusion and refused to change her mind. When I started writing to her, she truly grasped the essence of what I said. Then she would engage with what I had told her, rather than what she thought I should have said.

Writing to her became a wonderful form of therapy for me as well, and I have files full of the letters I sent her, which became a detailed diary of events at a crucial and difficult time. And when I went to Johannesburg she always had rich and insightful advice to offer.

But no advice or empathy could save me from the double conflagration that lay ahead.

18

The Plane Crash

OF ALL THE topics South Africans find difficult to have a rational conversation about, affirmative action tops the list. Whatever we call it – employment equity, black economic empowerment or corrective action – it means just one thing to most people: preferment on the basis of race. And most South Africans believe you can only take one of two possible positions on this issue. For or against. Like a switch that can either be on or off. There is nothing in between.

This makes it difficult to have a nuanced debate on this complex and crucial topic. Our history of legalised racial oppression makes it all the more important to have this discussion, but also all the more difficult. For years it was virtually impossible for anyone to be taken seriously when they ventured an opinion, unless they regurgitated the ANC's line. Slowly, like so many things in South Africa, this binary approach is changing. It is one of many intangible ways that our democracy is maturing.

Today, for example, most people, including ANC supporters, recognise that Gold Fields' acquisition of a new mining licence, in return for a R25-million stake in the deal for ANC chairperson Baleka Mbete in 2013, was a bribe, not broad-based black economic empowerment. A respected New York law firm confirmed this. That acknowledgement, and the accompanying outcry, was a big step forward towards debating more ethical, and truly broad-based, forms of redress that South Africa urgently needs.

Yet bribe-based black economic empowerment still continues throughout the economy (epitomised by the many Zuma–Gupta enrichment schemes), while Mbete, far from being shamed by her Gold Fields millions, has announced she will be running for president to succeed Zuma.

How is this possible?

Cheryl Carolus, Gold Fields' chairperson and a former ANC luminary, answered this question when she said the company had acted 'in full compliance with the law'. She was right. Our current law legalises corruption, as long as it is covered with a BEE fig leaf, however flimsy. It is this perversion of BEE that the DA has been exposing and opposing for more than two decades.

Since our transition to democracy, big business has bought favour from the ANC elite to the tune of R500 billion in share-transfer deals, thus complying with the legal requirement of 'black economic empowerment'. Gold Fields even admitted that they received a memo from government listing the people who should be 'empowered'. The memo might as well have said, 'If you pay all the powerful people on this list a bribe of the required amount, they will co-operate with you and protect you politically.'

Over time, this elite enrichment project was exposed for what it was, and the debate moved towards changing it into *broad-based* black economic empowerment (BBBEE).

The DA has always supported genuinely broad-based black economic empowerment, a position Tony Leon had spelt out as early as 2003 in a seminal speech titled 'Empowerment must create jobs, not just allocate jobs'. We also accepted, in principle, that the points-based codes of good practice (the tool for measuring BBBEE compliance) could be compiled in non-racial terms. This was the approach we had always championed. The ruling party seemed to be coming around to it.

We were enthusiastic about this development, assuming initially that this shift might be real. It started full of promise but turned out to be purely cosmetic. The passage between initial prospects for a new, genuinely broad-based approach to redress and the eventual disillusionment was very difficult for the DA to traverse. We started out giving the ANC the benefit of the doubt. We had been encouraged by discussions with leading ministers who seemed to recognise the disastrous results of bribe-based black economic empowerment, and genuinely wanted to change it. But we soon found out that the ANC had set up the classic political oxymoron: the broader BEE's name became, the narrower the criteria for beneficiaries. Behind the 'broad-based' façade, the favoured few could become even wealthier through their political connections.

Navigating the political rapids, from initial enthusiasm to disillusionment, would have been difficult for the DA in the best of circumstances. But we had to do it in the worst. We were trying to change the false perception that we, as a party, were defenders of white privilege against black aspirations. And we were in the run-up to a crucial election, which was why the ANC deliberately focused the debate on this most divisive of issues, by introducing two race-based bills in parliament early in 2014.

They were the Broad-Based Black Economic Empowerment (BBBEE) Amendment Bill and the Employment Equity (EEA) Amendment Bill. The difference between them is crucial, and caused a lot of confusion, not least among leading members of our own caucus.

- The Broad-Based Black Economic Empowerment Amendment Bill dealt with patterns of ownership in the economy, and incentives to broaden economic participation.
- The Employment Equity Amendment Bill opened the door for the imposition of coercive racial quotas in the workplace.

I knew that the management of these two bills through the parliamentary process would be crucial for our positioning in the election. The risks were enormous. In a normal, collegial environment, we would all have got together, analysed the challenge, and forged a strategic approach that we would then execute across all the DA's platforms, including parliament. But things weren't working like that.

I had reason to be optimistic, however, when I learnt that the parliamentary research team, under Phumzile van Damme, had initiated a system of summarising bills on a template which compared each clause with DA policy and offered a suggested position for the caucus to take. I asked if I could be on the mailing list to receive these templates. This should have been a routine matter, but, I was told, there was serious unhappiness in the caucus leadership at what they regarded as my 'interference'. I thought it would be obvious to everyone that summaries of important legislation should be sent to the party leader as a matter of course. I should not even have had to ask. And, in any event, the province also had to take a position on most bills before parliament, making it important to align provincial positions with those of the parliamentary caucus. The template analysing legislation would be useful at every level.

Complex, race-charged legislation in the run-up to the election required particular vigilance and, as party leader, I had to keep my finger on the pulse. We needed a coherent, united response to prevent a reversion to the binary 'light-switch-on-or-off' dichotomy. But the growing divisions inside our own parliamentary caucus, and the increasing self-imposed isolation of its leadership, made the required co-ordination difficult and eventually impossible. The inevitable conflagration came. I called it a plane crash, after author Malcolm Gladwell's analysis, in his book *Outliers*, of how a sequence of individually minor errors can result in a conflagration. The DA caucus plane crash followed a long and bumpy flight during which one system after another failed.

I still sometimes lie awake at night wondering how I could have prevented this. Almost two years later, in March 2015, I read the horrific account of the captain of the ill-fated Germanwings airline banging on the cockpit door after having been locked out, before the plane crashed into the Alps. It was a greatly magnified version of the powerlessness I felt at times, back in 2013, to prevent the DA's legislative plane crash.

The Broad-Based Black Economic Empowerment (BBBEE) Amendment Bill was up first. This bill fell within the portfolio of trade and industry. Wilmot James was our shadow minister of trade and industry, with Geordin Hill-Lewis as his deputy. Appropriately, they led the discussion in the relevant party structures on our response to the bill. Wilmot, in his capacity as the DA's federal chair, was also the leader of the party's policy process, so he had a central co-ordinating role.

We all accepted that this was a pivotal strategic moment, which, if used skilfully, could help the party's repositioning. The BBBEE Amendment Bill was very short. It made fronting (a form of fraud to gain BBBEE points) a crime, and set up a commission to monitor this. And, as an afterthought, it sought to accommodate a recent high court ruling that Chinese South Africans were legitimate beneficiaries of BBBEE.

How would the DA respond to this bill?

In its essence it was about preventing fraud and including the Chinese as BBBEE beneficiaries. We had no objections, in principle, to this.

If the goal was to broaden access to the economy for disadvantaged people, and if more BBBEE points were allocated to companies for investing in skills, small business development and job creation – none of which had to be defined in racially exclusive categories – we could support this approach. If the strategy effectively targeted genuinely disadvantaged people, the vast majority of whom would inevitably be black, we would not have to entrench apartheid-era race classification in law. This is what our policies proposed. On this basis, we could support the bill.

The first draft of the new codes of good practice looked distinctly ropey and would undermine the stated intention of the bill. I was worried about enabling legislation that gave the minister power to impose a retrogressive set of codes, but Geordin reassured me that the codes were being refined and that things were moving in the right direction. We had to encourage this trend, he said.

As a safety precaution, to ensure that we were not making the wrong assumptions about the ANC's intentions, Wilmot and Geordin held a meeting with minister of trade and industry, Rob Davies, to ascertain government's plans for the final codes. Davies assured them that his plan was to do precisely as we had hoped – to promote genuinely broad-based empowerment and prevent corrupt methods of elite enrichment.

Of course, it is extremely dangerous to accept one's opponent's word in politics regarding their intentions. If the codes were going to encourage genuinely broad-based empowerment, increasingly on a non-racial basis, it would be hard to justify our opposition to the bill that enabled this. We wanted to encourage the government's movement in that direction, while reducing the perception that the DA was 'racist'.

Wilmot and Geordin entered the debate in the portfolio committee with a positive inclination that seemed likely to result in our supporting the bill.

Suddenly, however, a snag arose, on the most marginal issue. The high court's recent ruling that Chinese South Africans, who had been the subject of past discrimination, could also be valid beneficiaries of BBBEE necessitated their specific inclusion in the law. And this created a problem of definition.

Until then, the law had been silent on this crucial question, allowing people to 'self-define' their race in order to benefit from BEE. But the inclusion of Chinese people required a greater degree of specificity regarding the categories of people who could qualify as beneficiaries. The law would have to define which categories of people could legitimately claim to belong to a designated group. The question inevitably arose: would people have to undergo an evaluation reminiscent of the notorious apartheid pencil test in order to qualify for a BBBEE deal?

All sorts of alarm bells started ringing.

Geordin wrote to Wilmot and asked him to convene a broader DA task team or study group to discuss this crucial issue. He received no reply. He wrote again. Still no reply.

Then one day, out of the blue in a meeting of the trade and industry portfolio committee, Wilmot proposed an amendment to the bill that would define which people could qualify to be beneficiaries of BBBEE. He reached back to definitions framed under apartheid, and concluded that people who would have been excluded from the franchise (or were only entitled to a qualified franchise) because of their race could be defined as black. The only way one would be able to determine this would be to use definitions contained in the Population Registration Act, which had formed the cornerstone of apartheid and had long since been consigned to the scrap heap of history. It was this act that provided the foundation for apartheid's ugly edifice, including the pass laws, the Prohibition of Mixed Marriages Act, the Group Areas Act and the Immorality Act, culminating in the loss of citizenship itself. I was genuinely surprised that Wilmot might have proposed this because I was aware of previous positions he had taken that 'disadvantage, not race, should guide redress' (in a statement on 8 March 2011, 'The ANC has abandoned non-racialism').

The implications of the DA proposing the reintroduction of the race classification that formed the basis of apartheid hit Geordin between the eyes. Right there, in the committee, he sent Wilmot a message cautioning him about the likely consequences of his proposed amendment. Afterwards Geordin contacted me and warned that we had to deal with the party's position on this issue as a matter of urgency. He told me he had written to Wilmot about two months previously, asking him to set up a study group, but had received no response.

Now what to do? It should have been no problem to just pick up the phone as any colleagues would do in a functional, collegial organisation, but the parliamentary leadership did not see it that way. They regarded any suggestion on my part as interference, and would batten down the hatches to keep me out.

By this point I was aware that the Employment Equity Amendment Bill had also been tabled, creating a mini crisis of its own. Having inserted myself, despite resistance, onto the research department's mailing list, I studied the template analysing the EEA Bill clause by clause, and realised there was a serious problem.

A new researcher had confused insertions in the bill for deletions. This resulted in proposals that we should support clauses in the bill that contradicted our policy. The implication of our research department's memorandum was, for example, that we should support a clause that could make national demographics mandatory in employment equity programmes across the country. In other words, it would resurrect the terms of the hated Population Registration Act and open the door for racial quotas. If people were classified 'coloured', for example, a category that constituted 9 per cent of the national population, they could qualify for only 9 per cent of senior jobs, irrespective of regional demographic variations.

We could, obviously, never support a bill that opened the door for this kind of racial engineering. This approach, we hoped, had been consigned to history with the ending of apartheid.

I assumed the research department must have made a mistake, although it was a logical follow-on from Wilmot's definitions. After my query the error was corrected and we seemed back on track again.

But if our parliamentary processes had been working, it would not have been left to me, reading my email, to pick up this rather fundamental issue.

This near miss heightened my anxiety about the future management of the passage of these crucial bills. We just had to have a face-to-face meeting to discuss the issues in detail. So I took a deep breath, knowing what the response was likely to be, and wrote a letter to the caucus leadership on 6 May 2013, asking Wilmot, in his capacity as leader of the policy process and as shadow minister of trade and industry, to set up the necessary task team to discuss our approach to both bills.

In it, I proposed a framework in terms of which we could assess the bills, as follows:

1. We support the need to redress the legacy of apartheid.
2. The best way is through sustained economic job-creating growth, education and skills training aligned to the needs of the economy.
3. We have spent at least R500-billion on narrow-based 'BEE' in the past 19 years. This has not created new jobs or broadened the base of the economy to any significant extent.
4. The empowerment results have been dismal: We have only managed to 'over-empower' a small politically connected elite.
5. We need to redress both the legacy of apartheid as well as crony-based BEE, which merely continues the legacy of apartheid, by excluding the majority of disadvantaged South Africans.
6. We need to start by asking what the REAL barriers are to black advancement in the economy.

7. Anything that prevents job creating economic growth is a barrier to black advancement in the economy.
8. Anything that prevents first time job seekers getting jobs is a barrier to black advancement in the economy.
9. Anything that undermines education and training, and that mis-aligns this with the needs of the economy, undermines black advancement.
10. Once the requirements of growth, jobs, education, training and alignment with the economy are met, it will create opportunity on a grand scale. This will primarily advantage black South Africans and do more for BEE than any initiatives undertaken by the ANC thus far.
11. Within this context we need to incentivise business to ensure opportunities, training and promotion for disadvantaged South Africans.

I warned that there were great hazards attached to both bills. Whatever the stated intention, it appeared, at that stage, that they could both compound the problems of corrupt, narrow-based enrichment, quotas and cadre deployment, rather than encourage broad-based empowerment and economic inclusion. So I proposed that we oppose both in their current forms. There was as yet no clear indication that the codes would promote job creation and training, and I was wary of accepting the ANC's word for it.

Of course, this is what the ANC wanted us to do, because as soon as we opposed the bills they would claim we were against black advancement (when the very opposite was true). And the volume the ANC would put behind its simplistic racial slur (and the media's seeming inability to grasp the nuances of the debate) would make our repositioning much more difficult. My recommendation to the caucus would therefore carry a cost.

All things considered, I have always believed it is better to be proven historically correct than politically correct in an expedient moment. That was why, on the information then available, I proposed opposing both bills, irrespective of the short term electoral cost.

But I could not dictate a caucus position.

Because I did not want the caucus leadership to become further estranged, arising out of my proposed position, I ended my letter with a request to Wilmot:

> we must be on the same page on this crucial issue. I think we need a task team to meet and discuss all of the elements that we require to flesh out and communicate this approach, inside and outside Parliament. May I ask Wilmot please to convene another meeting with all the people in the top address list (not the copied list) to attend.

The DA's director of communications, Gavin Davis, responded to my letter by suggesting that as soon as the task team had met and determined our approach, we should hold a press conference to spell out our opposition to these bills on the basis that, by hindering growth and job creation, they would have the effect of curbing black advancement.

After which, on 8 May, Lindiwe sent a formal response telling both Gavin and me, politely but unequivocally, to butt out of caucus affairs. She told me to trust the process and put my faith in Wilmot and his team:

> At this stage none of us is better informed than they are on what our position on these two bills should be. Furthermore, our two MPs have until now based, and will continue to base, their inputs in committee and in the media on the fundamental principles for which the party stands – that is the role with which we have entrusted them.
>
> As with every single bill that the DA processes through the National Assembly, the decision about how we will vote on these bills will be made by the parliamentary caucus. Sej and Wilmot can present to the caucus when they are ready to give a draft position. We will debate it in caucus, and make a decision accordingly ...

That was as unequivocal a rejection of my proposal as it was possible to give.

Unsurprisingly, given the parliamentary leader's response, Wilmot did not act on my request and the study group/task team did not materialise.

There was clearly a major confrontation building up. I was still at a loss to understand why. Sitting around a table to discuss minefields in the runway ahead seemed such a simple, collegial thing to do. Why was it causing issues?

Because doing simple, obvious things had become so difficult, I asked Fedex for a mandate to formalise a policy committee that could be convened to discuss policy issues when the need arose.

My proposal was accepted unanimously.

Wilmot did not challenge me in the meeting, but he wrote to me afterwards, on 3 June 2013:

> Dear Helen
> I was looking forward to having a face-to-face conversation with you and I am sorry that this did not happen. It leaves me then simply to write an e-mail as you ought to know where I stand: I was elected on a platform to direct policy-making and created a small team consisting [of] Frouwien Bosman and I – with occasional part-time help to do the job. We have made good progress in carrying out our mandate. At the last Fedex the governing structure for all policy was peremptorily changed and now we have something for

which Frouwien Bosman and I did not sign up. I do not believe having such a structure is necessary and I am unconvinced that the redesign serves the best interests of the party. We should simply settle the BBBEE/AA policy sui generis. If you proceed with the new structure, I would have great difficulty being part of it given its status (it looks and feels like a POLITBURO); and though Frouwien will no doubt speak her mind, she has told me in the strongest terms that she will consider her options. I hope we can arrive at a good solution tomorrow.

Best wishes, Wilmot.

I could not understand this logic. In what universe could the inclusion of a political party's elected leadership and key professional staff in the policy-making process be described as a Politburo? It seemed to me that having an exclusive, impenetrable two-person group, reporting to the parliamentary leadership and keeping others out of the process, was more deserving of such a loaded description.

Nevertheless, I decided, as I so often did, to de-escalate the issue, in the hope that bruised egos would soon recover. I went on to convene the study group, now with a mandate from the Federal Executive.

The BBBEE Amendment Bill was first on the parliamentary programme. The DA's policy committee held two meetings in quick succession to discuss it. At the first, Wilmot again proposed his apartheid-based definition of race in order to amend the bill, which almost everyone else rejected. Wilmot's position puzzled me because at around that time, on 23 June, he said in a lecture at Lilliesleaf farm that the DA would use disadvantage, not race, as the criterion for redress.

Tim Harris, who had previously been the shadow minister of trade and industry, and who was now shadow minister of finance, gave a presentation on the bill and why, in principle, without the racial definitions, he believed we could support it. It opened the possibility of codes that could largely be applied non-racially. In the category calculating the limited percentage of points allocated for 'ownership' of enterprises, the DA wanted to rely on racial self-definition, without opening the door for racial identity to be imposed by the state. We were also determined to prevent a situation in which a politically connected elite could be re-empowered repeatedly. Tim convinced me that the BBBEE Amendment Bill could potentially be a step in the right direction, redressing apartheid's legacy without imposing racial classification.

At our second meeting we reached agreement on our position and the strategies for communicating what we knew would be a counter-intuitive take on the BBBEE Amendment Bill.

This was a complex position to communicate in this most challenging of all policy debates and at the most difficult of times.

We needed a slogan that would break the sound barrier and explain where we stood. Tim proposed a simple slogan: 'The DA supports BEE.' Some members of the committee supported this simple, direct approach. I (and some others) felt this would merely allow the debate to revert to the simplistic light-switch approach. It had to be more nuanced.

Geordin hit on what I thought was the perfect slogan: 'The DA supports BEE that creates jobs, not billionaires.'

That summed up our position perfectly.

We had navigated the first rapids. I assumed that the second set of rapids, dealing with the Employment Equity Amendment Bill, would be easier. All the relevant role-players were aware of the complexity of the issues and, as I thought, were on the same page. I was keen to repair relationships with the parliamentary leadership, and wanted them to navigate the next passage. They had reassured me that the parliamentary study groups and relevant checks and balances were in place and working. There had been so much resentment of my 'interference' that I resolved to stay out unless I was alerted to the fact that something was going wrong – in the same way that Geordin had pressed the metaphorical panic button on the issue of resurrecting apartheid definitions of race.

I now had to trust the process. But I underestimated the difficulties that lay ahead.

The Employment Equity Amendment Bill proved far more difficult to deal with. In contrast to the BBBEE Amendment Bill, it dealt with the legal and regulatory environment to advance the ANC's notion of 'representivity' in the workplace. To the ANC, 'representivity' meant that employment profiles in companies should, ideally, reflect the exact ratio, in racial terms of the broader population – despite the acknowledged disaster of public education for the poor, and the massive skills shortage in the country.

This 'representivity' approach also required racial definitions to be entrenched in law; it created heated debate around whether national demographics or regional demographics should be used as a yardstick. The low point of this debate, conducted over years, had been the assertion by the then director-general of labour, Mzwanele Jimmy Manyi, that there was an 'over-supply' of coloureds in the Western Cape, and that if they wanted jobs, within the allocation 'allowed' by their 9 per cent proportion of the population, they should move to other provinces.

That was the extent of the Verwoerdian logic and racial engineering that the ANC was prepared to resort to in the name of 'representivity'. The inevitable consequence would have been plummeting investment, shrinking growth, fewer jobs, greater unemployment, escalating racial tensions, and more and more adversarial contestation over the dwindling number of jobs available. It was surely obvious that our policies needed to massively encourage investment, growth and jobs, rather than the opposite. The more jobs there were, the more all South Africans would be included in the economy.

Another important factor was that the Supreme Court of Appeal had ruled that representivity quotas were unconstitutional – because they created an impenetrable barrier for people on the basis of race. This meant that we had to be especially vigilant that this bill did not open a regulatory back door for the implementation of a quota system.

While the DA opposed quotas, we strongly supported diversity, encouraging a mix of race, gender, cultural and other attributes throughout society's organisations and institutions, to promote South Africa's quest for an inclusive, open society. It was critical that we understood these nuances and applied them to the bill.

The process was running its course behind the scenes.

We had launched our 'Know Your DA' campaign in preparation for the 2014 election. The campaign's purpose was to define ourselves as diverse and forward-looking in the public mind, with a proud anti-apartheid history. We had to counter the ANC's definition of us as 'racist'. Part of the campaign involved explaining, in clear and simple terms, that we supported black economic empowerment if it was genuinely broad-based. We unveiled a huge DA-branded billboard in Johannesburg, with the slogan Geordin had thought up: 'We support BBBEE that creates jobs, not billionaires.' I got the sense that the media and opinion makers were beginning to understand that we were committed to broad-based black economic empowerment – and that they were starting to see through the ANC's bribe-based version. But it was not that simple. Very few people inside our own caucus understood the complexity of these issues.

Relationships between the caucus leadership and me were, by then, so tense that I had to step back for the sake of holding the caucus together. By this stage I knew that Lindiwe's chances of winning another election for the caucus leadership were rapidly diminishing as the rift between her shrinking inner circle and the rest of the DA's parliamentarians widened.

Most DA public representatives knew that I was preparing to pull back as party leader and trying to pave the way for an orderly succession, and that I did not pose a threat to anyone's aspirations. On the contrary, I was trying to create as many opportunities as I could for future leaders.

While I understood why it was important for Lindiwe to shape her own platform, I could not fathom why this had to include the erection of a 'Berlin Wall' between her office and mine. And why did it prove so difficult to have an open discussion on all these issues? I could not allow these complexities to prevent me from fulfilling my leadership responsibilities, but I did not envisage the issue would come to a head as quickly as it did.

Thursday 24 October 2013 turned out to be a fateful caucus meeting. As usual, I was there (this was my one regular contact point with the full caucus), and I presented my political overview of current developments. I kept to my designated national leadership role and avoided parliamentary matters. Lindiwe spoke, and I do not recall her giving an indication of the enormity of the bills the caucus would be called upon to consider in that caucus meeting before voting on them in parliament that very afternoon.

There were seven bills. The relevant shadow ministers had drawn up memorandums to inform the caucus of the key points in each bill and recommend a voting position. The Employment Equity Amendment Bill was one of them.

I read through the summary of the Employment Equity Amendment Bill (which I received at the meeting for the first time), which indicated that it was innocuous. I was worried, but was acutely aware of the context, including the fact that the bill would be voted on that afternoon. What was more, we only had five minutes (literally) of caucus time to consider seven bills. Wilmot, in his capacity of caucus chairperson, whizzed us through them. It was nothing like the full caucus presentation and debate that Lindiwe had promised in her email of 8 May at the start of the process, when she had informed me in no uncertain terms that my 'interference' in the passage of the bills through the DA's parliamentary system was unnecessary and unwelcome.

The rush was due to the fact that the parliamentary leadership had changed the structure of caucus meetings, inviting an outside speaker to address us after the tea break. This severely truncated the time for the analysis of legislation – the most important function of a caucus. It proved disastrous in the circumstances.

As the caucus gave the nod to one memorandum after the other, in quick succession, I was in no position to raise a credible challenge. I did not know, for example, whether and to what extent the Employment Equity Amendment Bill had been amended in the committee stage. The newspapers had paid scant attention to the passage of this legislation until then. Given the breakdown of my communication channels with the caucus leadership, I had received no information. I also felt it would be inappropriate for me to openly challenge them about the memorandum in front of the rest of the caucus.

So I made an error of judgement. On the assumption that our proposed amendments must have been carried (as many of them had with the passage of the BBBEE Amendment Bill), I kept quiet. It proved to be a costly silence.

With the bills dispatched in a few minutes, the invited speaker was ushered in.

I left. There was too much to do to listen to a random speech on a topic I was not particularly seized with.

In parliament that afternoon, the DA caucus voted in favour of the Employment Equity Amendment Bill. I waited for the reaction. None came. *Business Day* was the only newspaper that seemed to be focusing on this issue, and generally did so in a low-key way. That reassured me somewhat. I felt my more hands-off approach had been vindicated.

Then, on Monday 28 October, Vesuvius erupted. James Myburgh, editor of the influential *Politicsweb*, published an article with the headline: 'Has the DA just put a bullet through its brain?'

I took James's analysis very seriously. He had, about ten years earlier, been one of the DA's best parliamentary researchers. He wrote:

> It is difficult to see what on earth could have come over the DA caucus in parliament to make it reverse its former opposition to this racialist and totalitarian legislation and support these amendments. Helen Zille has in the past described the principle that lies at the heart of the Act as 'Verwoerdian' so why would her party vote for its more stringent enforcement? By doing so the DA has betrayed its supporters, its history, its principles and indeed, the future of South Africa itself...
>
> The Amendment Bill will... cause enormous damage to the cause of broader black advancement, which wholly depends on increased investment, a growing economy, rising educational standards and massive job creation.

My heart stood still. I immediately moved to get a copy of the actual bill that had been tabled in parliament (which had not been available in the caucus). There had been no ameliorating amendments as I had mistakenly concluded after reading the caucus memorandum. The bill that had been tabled in parliament confirmed James Myburgh's analysis.

My first question was: Why had we again received such a defective caucus memorandum on the bill? Who had compiled it?

Responsibility was attributed to the shadow minister, his deputy and the research team.

We had had yet another massive systems failure. My initial evaluation framework had been entirely disregarded. Our preceding discussions might just as well never have happened.

I spoke to Gavin, our director of communications, and Geordin, my chief of staff.

'I am going to have to fix this,' I told them.

The two spent hours trying to persuade me not to. 'There will be a nuclear explosion if you do. Please stay out of it,' Gavin advised. Geordin concurred. I wrote a draft of my newsletter, *SA Today*, in which I levelled with the public. Geordin and Gavin persuaded me not to send it out. It was unlike them to be so cautious, but they warned me that the situation was explosive. It would have the effect of dropping an atomic bomb on the caucus, they kept repeating.

'Okay,' I said, 'then the parliamentary leadership team will have to put it right. I am going to meet them to find out how they intend to do it.'

So on the Tuesday night, 29 October, I convened a dinner meeting in the big back room of the Nelson's Eye steakhouse.

It was one of the most bizarre meetings of party colleagues I have ever attended. The caucus leadership arrived, grim-faced – with a lawyer to represent them. This was a fellow caucus member, Hendrik Schmidt. Instead of adopting a collegial, problem-solving approach (given the fact that I had restrained myself), they were upping the ante! It had come to this.

To say the meeting was tense would be an understatement. The steak knives would have been unable to cut through the atmosphere. Watty Watson, the chief whip, insisted that they had done nothing wrong, and that all the points I had made had been argued by the DA in the portfolio committee and in the members' speeches in the debate. I asked how, if that was the case, it was possible that we could have voted for the bill. They said, on balance and all things considered, they had concluded that it would be preferable to support rather than oppose the bill, and the caucus had concurred. I countered that the caucus would have been unlikely to reach that position if the memorandum on which they had had to rely had not been so grossly defective. I asked how it was possible to present such a flawed memorandum on such a crucial bill. I got no satisfactory answer. The meeting ended in stony silence, without any proposed solution, except the suggestion that I should leave it to the caucus leadership to chart the way forward. I was really stumped as to how I would fix the rapidly unravelling situation.

The next morning, I decided to check what our shadow minister of labour and his deputy had actually argued in the portfolio committee and in the debate itself. Geordin retrieved the minutes of the parliamentary monitoring group covering the portfolio committees and the *Hansard* of the parliamentary debate.

When I read them, I realised that Watty had either misled me or did not know what positions our members had taken. I blew a fuse, good and proper. Our shadow minister and his deputy had raised none of the points we had discussed and canvassed over so many months. They had entirely ignored the framework that we had discussed in the policy committee for evaluating the bills. Far from arguing against quotas, our shadow minister had tacitly supported their introduction by arguing for harsher penalties for failure to comply with targets. A target with harsh penalties is indistinguishable from a quota.

But it was inappropriate to limit the blame to shadow ministers on the portfolio. It would have been like blaming border guards for the incursion of an invading army. The generals had to take the rap. And I, as the commander-in-chief, would have to step forward.

Several commentators described the situation as the 'DA's greatest crisis yet'.

While I exploded behind the scenes, Gavin was trying to pour oil on troubled waters. He wrote a conciliatory letter to the caucus leadership and the relevant senior professional staff, analysing what had gone wrong and proposing a way forward. He ended his letter with a suggestion that a parliamentary 'risk register' be managed by the parliamentary operations director, in consultation with the parliamentary leadership and the director of communications.

This might work in the future, I told Gavin, but how could we fix the mess that we were in?

Gavin did not have an immediate solution, but expended much energy trying to convince me not to put out my newsletter, in which I explained how we had erred and what we were doing to correct it. His strongest argument was that my newsletter would inevitably overshadow the launch of our Gauteng election campaign, which was scheduled for that weekend in Kliptown, Soweto. I took the point. We were already well into a national election campaign and we had to ensure that the launch took precedence over the controversy.

I agreed to hold back my public newsletter but I wrote a straight-talking formal letter on a DA letterhead, to the full caucus, to leave no doubt as to my position on the matter.

> Dear colleagues,
> I write to you about the recent debacle relating to the Employment Equity Act Amendment Bill.
> There were two key failures in this matter:
> First: there was a basic failure by the parliamentary management team to spot a Bill which was sure to be controversial and which needed special attention and focus in its journey through the House.
> This Bill should have been 'triaged' as soon as it was tabled, and the management team needed to have kept themselves completely abreast of the debate in the committee and the progress of the Bill.
> This has exposed the inadequacy of a number of caucus processes which are designed to spot and track these developments: the whip group did not spot it, the whippery did not spot it, and there was clearly no process in place to determine the most important things that require attention from amongst the large number of Bills and issues that Parliament deals with. The five minutes allotted to discuss 7 pieces of legislation in caucus meant that the final back-stop failed as well.
> And, this was despite my having raised the sensitivity around these Bills in correspondence and in meetings months ago; provided a clear framework of how to deal with it; and requested that Gavin be involved in preparing a communication strategy around it. None of this happened.

Second: the spokespersons on the committee failed to identify that the issue was of significant strategic importance to the DA. They did not raise a 'red flag' on the Bill, and they were clearly unaware of the points that I have repeatedly raised and that have been regularly discussed on these matters.

They did not arm the caucus with the necessary facts to make an informed decision. Indeed, if the correct facts had been tabled, we would probably have reached a different position. And being caught on the back foot, we were unable to defend our position publicly. The memo submitted to the caucus was so defective as to be misleading. Indeed, when I read the memo to caucus (which was only delivered at the meeting) I assumed that major changes had been made at the committee stage of the Bill. I could not have been more wrong. But as I was present in caucus I must accept responsibility.

I was also given the wrong feedback about the speeches of our spokesmen in Parliament. I subsequently read them in Hansard – both speeches missed the key issues particularly relating to the deletion of clause 39 and the serious dilution of clause 42.

They did not check that the positions they were taking were aligned with DA policy (which they were involved in drafting), they did not read (or ignored) the comment of the Western Cape Government, they failed to check up on the positions taken by organised business at Nedlac (or misinformed me about it) and they didn't get a 'negotiating mandate' on those crucial clauses as they were being dealt with in committee.

I regard this in a most serious light. I am also aware that my interventions are regarded as 'interference' in the caucus. Nothing could be further from the truth. We are one party, and it is my primary responsibility as the leader to ensure that we act cohesively and pull in the same direction. This is not a case of party leadership interfering with caucus leadership. It is not an 'us' versus 'them' scenario. Please take note: We have all dropped the ball on a major issue and we all need to understand how it happened, and ensure that it is never repeated.

We need to convene a follow up meeting for the caucus leadership to explain how the management systems will be repaired to ensure that this never happens again.

Kind Regards

Helen Zille

The caucus was scheduled to discuss my letter and the recent debacle at the caucus meeting on 31 October. I was relieved that I would not be there, because it would give them greater freedom to talk through what had gone wrong. I had to attend the launch of the Special Economic Zone in Saldanha Bay, where I was to share the platform with Jacob Zuma. It was the culmination of years of work between the national and provincial governments, and should have been a celebration for us all.

But the ANC provincial leader, Marius Fransman, had bussed in scores of people in ANC T-shirts who swamped an official state function. When I stood up to speak, they executed their pre-planned demonstration, drowning me out with prolonged booing until I left the stage.

I recalled a similar experience when an ANC crowd had booed me at a public lekgotla while I was still mayor of Cape Town and Thabo Mbeki was president. Displaying enormous courage, Mbeki stepped forward and explained to the crowd that it was not a political function but a state function, that I was the duly elected mayor of Cape Town, and said that I should be allowed to speak. Jacob Zuma sat benignly on the stage while all this was going on, smiling and laughing and doing nothing to invoke the need to separate party politics from a state function; or protect my right, as premier of the Western Cape, to speak at the launch of a co-operative governance venture. I left the stage and the function.

As I have learnt in politics, when you think things can't get any worse, they usually do.

Those are not great moments in politics, but by then I was thick-skinned enough to take it. The implications for the future of our democracy worried me much more than the personal humiliation.

However, things picked up the next day when I received the following letter from Lindiwe, following the caucus discussion:

Dear Helen,

Perhaps in my zeal to find a solution to and put in place mechanisms to address the current bind we find ourselves in, I have neglected to clarify my position on what went wrong.

For the record, you are absolutely right – there were failures on multiple fronts which led us to where we are today.

- We did not spot the upcoming vote on this legislation soon enough;
- Our whips failed to alert us to it in time;
- Our spokespersons did not brief us adequately on the problems with the Bill;
- The caucus memo was deficient and the discussion on it was too short;
- Had all of these matters been properly attended to, we may have abstained or even voted against the Bill;
- Had the relevant systems been in place, we would have been better equipped to communicate on this Bill in a pre-emptive, coherent manner.

All of these things are true, and as caucus leader, I take responsibility for them.

We had a long and fruitful discussion about this in caucus on Thursday. Wilmot, Watty and I identified the deficiencies in the system. We spoke about how we must be on high alert as the ANC pushes through multiple pieces of legislation ahead of the election in an effort to look like they are delivering. We spoke about how we must change the system to deal with this reality and ensure that we are not caught off-guard again ...

Caucus embraced the fact that we need to have longer meetings, which focus much more on legislation, and that we need to have a standard for the quality and detail of caucus memos about legislation, which will enable us to have more in-depth discussions.

As a consequence, Thursday's meeting was indeed longer, more qualitative, and included over an hour of discussion on legislation as we had seven bills before us once again.

The caucus leadership will be sending out a memo in the coming days to this effect. In the meantime, our focus is on rectifying the deficiencies during the NCOP [the National Council of Provinces, South Africa's equivalent of an Upper House or Senate] process, which we are all committed to.

I do not believe that we should publicly try to reverse our vote after the fact. It will have no effect on our voting record, and will expose us to significant political attacks from the ANC and the VF+.

I was thrilled to get this letter, because it took great courage to have this open discussion in the caucus and to accept responsibility, at least in part. On this basis of shared responsibility, I felt confident that we would be able to restore our relationship entirely and fix the problems in the caucus. However, I felt there was a contradiction between the penultimate and final paragraphs of Lindiwe's letter. I agreed with using the NCOP process to rectify what had gone wrong, but did not see how we could do this without reversing the position we had taken in the National Assembly.

We could not just draw a line under the issue and move on simply because we were worried about how our opponents would interpret a climb-down.

So I took the reins again. At this point in the complex passage of bills through parliament, the focus returned to the Broad-Based Black Economic Empowerment Amendment Bill.

The vote on the bill was scheduled to take place in the NCOP on Tuesday 5 November. We had supported this bill in the National Assembly, because it could theoretically be used to broaden economic inclusion on a non-racial basis. Except that, crucially, since we had taken that decision in June (and just a few weeks before the NCOP vote in November), the ANC had released the final codes of good practice, which showed we had all been taken for a ride. Contrary to Minister Rob Davies' assurances that they would broaden black economic empowerment, the new codes narrowed it even more.

They raised the threshold for qualifying for BBBEE deals from R10 million to R50 million. This meant, for example, that if an ANC leader like Baleka Mbete had 'only' benefited from a BBBEE deal (read bribe) to the tune of R25 million, she could STILL be regarded as 'un-empowered' and therefore eligible to benefit again. This was tailor-made for increasing this corrupt elite-enrichment scheme.

What was more, the codes limited rather than broadened access for the genuinely disempowered, by overemphasising the ownership component on the basis of race and making it compulsory. We had been caught in a cynical political confidence trick, and we could not legitimise it by arguing that 'in theory' the codes might have turned out differently.

It was glaringly obvious to me that we could not support the bill in the NCOP, so, minutes before the NCOP convened, I asked the DA members of the Western Cape delegation to walk out of the proceedings before the vote. The problem was that by that time they had already had a mandate from the Western Cape legislature to support the bill, in line with our original parliamentary position, when it seemed that the codes would be genuinely more inclusive and progressive. But it had not turned out that way. And when circumstances change so fundamentally, my approach is to change our position. I did. The DA's constitution enables the leader to take an instant policy decision in a situation like that. And in any event the NCOP is accountable to provinces, not the national parliament. I could not instruct the whole delegation, but I could advise the DA delegates to walk out rather than vote in favour of this bill.

Lindiwe was incensed.

We were back to the full military stand-off and tension, setting the scene for the biggest fallout over the matter, in the caucus of 7 November.

James Selfe had sent me a note, correctly concluding that the growing public anger on our position was becoming untenable and that my newsletter needed to go out. Geordin and Gavin were coming around to this position, but they kept emphasising that it would be the DA's Hiroshima.

This was the context of the caucus meeting on that fateful Thursday. By that time, I was determined to send out my newsletter publicly, but wanted to tell the caucus first.

The air was ionised as I entered the caucus venue. A slight draft chilled the sweat gathering in the nape of my neck. The normal buzz before the commencement of caucus, like an orchestra tuning up, was muted.

I spoke more directly than I had ever done before, and set out the systems failure step by step, and the history of my attempts to pre-empt this, and the hostility I had encountered. I said it was entirely ridiculous to act as if the parliamentary caucus was an island in the DA entire of itself. It was one of the party's platforms – granted, the most prominent one – but it was 'a piece of the continent, a part of the Maine'. Snippets of the poetry I had studied at university always came back to me in moments like that.

If we had all just acted rationally and maturely, we could have open communication lines and sort issues out without the defensiveness and attempted exclusion that was currently going on.

At one stage, I heard chief whip Watty Watson say under his breath, 'Well then, I'll resign.'

That just pressed the H-bomb's red button.

A chief whip is to the functioning of a parliamentary caucus what an air traffic controller is to a busy airport. He manages what comes in and what goes out and co-ordinates these crucial processes. They're hardly noticed if they run smoothly, but if something goes wrong the result is catastrophic.

I rounded on Watty. 'Yes, I think you should resign,' I said. 'You are the chief whip. You are responsible for internal parliamentary processes and if there was any accountability in this party you would have resigned already. You should not wait to be asked to do so.'

There was a stunned silence. The caucus had never experienced anything like this before. Fortunately, at that point the caucus broke for tea. During the break Lindiwe tackled me and defended Watty, but I was having none of it.

The next morning I sent out *SA Today*.

SA Today: A plane crash that should have been avoided
7 November 2013
The debate in the media over the past ten days has revealed the depth of confusion regarding the DA's position on affirmative action. I take responsibility for this. The purpose of this newsletter is to make our position unambiguously clear.

In a memorandum to the parliamentary leadership in May, I set out the principles that guide our approach to Black Economic Empowerment and Employment Equity and asked our parliamentary caucus to use them as the basis for judgment on these bills. These principles are not new. Indeed they have been our guiding principles on BEE for two decades. And they will continue to be.

I then repeated them all in my newsletter, just as I had in the memo to the caucus on 6 May. I explained the background of the Black Economic Empowerment Amendment Bill. I then turned to the Employment Equity Amendment Bill:

Not only is it based on racial coercion, it will undermine growth, reduce jobs, drive away investment and work against black empowerment. It will be subject to political manipulation, and undermine our chances of building the 'capable state' which the National Development Plan identifies as a top priority.

So, how did the DA come to vote for it in the National Assembly? Good question.

The best way I can answer this is by reference to Malcolm Gladwell's fascinating analysis of plane crashes in his book Outliers (p. 183–185). Gladwell's purpose is to show the importance of communication and teamwork (or the lack thereof) and the accumulated significance of independently irrelevant, small mistakes, that combine to create disaster.

I said this analysis applied 'with eerie accuracy to what happened in the process leading up to the NA vote on the EEA Bill'.

Our representatives on the portfolio committee were inadequately prepared. The many and varied submissions on the Bill were rushed through the portfolio committee in four meetings. The long parliamentary recess intervened before the Bill went to the National Assembly and so we were unable to debate the implications of the Bill adequately in caucus; when it did come before caucus, on the day it was due to be debated and voted on in the house, the explanatory memorandum produced by our spokespeople was defective. To make matters worse, we had five minutes (literally) to consider seven different Bills.

A number of sequential errors. On their own, none would have led to a crash. In a cumulative sequence, they did.

I, as the captain of this plane, must take responsibility. And I do. I believe it is best to acknowledge mistakes and seek to rectify them.

My colleague, DA Parliamentary Leader Lindiwe Mazibuko, has also acknowledged the deficiencies in the caucus management system that allowed for these errors to slip through and compound themselves. She and the Parliamentary leadership have proposed far reaching changes to the way Bills are 'triaged' and managed from their inception through to their discussion in caucus.

That is why we will propose amendments to the Employment Equity Act Amendment Bill in the NCOP and vote against the Bill if we do not succeed in effecting these changes. We will then also vote against the Bill when it returns to the National Assembly. We should have done this from the get-go because this Bill will harm rather than promote redress.

Our position remains exactly as described in this framework. We will analyse every empowerment initiative on a case-by-case basis, by asking the question: does this broaden opportunity for disadvantaged people? Or does it seek to manipulate outcomes for the politically connected? If it broadens opportunity, we support it. If it is used to camouflage yet another enrichment scheme for cronies, we reject it.

Sadly the ANC will pass the Bill into law anyway. But that is no excuse for the DA's deficient handling of it at its inception.

We can and will rectify it during the remaining passage of this Bill. We cannot support an approach that will create more unemployment and poverty and less empowerment for those who genuinely need it. History would be damning in its judgement if we did.

Shortly after this, Lindiwe moved Sej Motau and Andricus van der Westhuizen from the positions of shadow minister of labour and shadow deputy minister. They did have some culpability, but they should not have carried the full rap, in my view.

On Saturday morning, 9 November, *Beeld* newspaper led with the following story:

> **Tension in the DA is running high after this week's 'plane crash' in the official opposition.**
> *Beeld* can reveal that:
> DA leader Helen Zille wanted to dismiss the chief whip, Watty Watson, on the spot because of the past week's chaos in relation to the Employment Equity Amendment Bill.
> The DA's Parliamentary leader, Lindiwe Mazibuko, told Zille during a white hot caucus meeting the day before yesterday, not to interfere in her business.

The report went on to describe me as 'beyond angry', and that I had ascribed the mess to a failure of leadership, management and appropriate systems, given that I had already sent the caucus a framework in May to give guidance on dealing with the bill. It quoted anonymous caucus members as saying 'the status quo cannot continue, and Zille has now seen this'.

Gareth van Onselen, who had resigned from the DA the year before, after I vetoed the plan, hatched with the caucus leadership, for him to take over parliamentary communications, predictably described my apology as 'hollow' and opined that the real reason for the debacle was my inability to manage both the positions of premier and leader. He clearly had no idea how much time and effort I had devoted to this issue – which should never have been necessary if our systems had been functional.

Gareth kept harking back to a mythical era under Tony Leon's leadership, when the DA had supposedly stuck firmly to its liberal principles. Of course, this assertion was entirely laughable, given what we had been through in the Western Cape, culminating in Tony's personal support for the return of the death penalty in the run-up to the 2004 election, after Marthinus van Schalkwyk had led the NNP out of the DA. But I had learnt to ignore Gareth's personal bile and animus, spewed almost every week in the guise of 'journalism'.

Wilmot sent me a hand-delivered note saying he was 'deeply ashamed' at how I had confronted Watty in the caucus. I have not been able to locate the note in my filing system, but its contents are clear enough from the strongly worded reply I sent back on 11 November. I had simply had enough of the parliamentary leadership's deflection of responsibility. I summarised the history of the debacle and concluded:

> We had a perilously difficult passage to traverse. And we failed and we know why: our management systems in Parliament are in shambles. And then we respond like the ANC, defending our allies from consequences.
>
> And now the totally erroneous narrative is developing that we put our toe in the 'Equity' water and pulled it out because it was too hot. Nothing could be further from the truth. If our framework had been applied we would, from the outset, have drawn a clear distinction between the BBBEE Amendment Act and the Employment Equity Amendment Act, held press conferences to explain why, and enabled us to get our points across, without the false perception gaining momentum that we were abandoning both our traditional voters and our prospective voters because we were 'confused'. If anyone had read our policy and our framework, and the submission from the Western Cape government, no one would have been 'confused'. We were crystal clear on the issue. But the chaotic management of our process led to an outcome in which our opponents on every side had wide gaps, and obviously took them.

I had rarely sent such a forthright letter.

But the parliamentary leadership was still clearly in denial about the scale of the problem we faced.

I knew that things would have to change dramatically after the election of 2014. All indications at the time were that I would have to return to parliament. Unbeknown to me, Lindiwe and her close confidants were planning an exit strategy for her.

We limped to the end of the year, concluding our enormously complicated and competitive candidate-selection process, with the gains of our 'Know Your DA' campaign in tatters and the breakdown of relationships seemingly irreparable. Where to from here?

When the regulations under the Employment Equity Amendment Act were released four months later, the confidence trick was clear for all to see. They were draconian and introduced racial quotas, which legal experts immediately slammed as 'unconstitutional'. The regulations required that companies with 150 or more employees should use the national demographic profile as 'a guide' to determine targets for top, senior and professional employees – irrespective of the skills availability. The act imposed harsh penalties for failure to comply. Targets for skilled, semi-skilled and unskilled employees would be determined by calculating the average of the regional profile and the national one.

For companies with 50 to 149 employees, or companies with a higher turnover than a fairly modest threshold (determined by sector), the national demographic would be used only for top and senior management, and the regional demographic for the rest.

Commentators who had cautiously welcomed what they also thought was a new approach by government to employment equity were aghast. Race classification was back with a vengeance.

Writing in *Business Day*, Carol Paton commented:

> The effect in provinces with large regionally based minorities – coloureds in the Western and Northern Cape, and Indians in KwaZulu-Natal – is a profound skewing of opportunities. So although in the Western Cape coloureds make up 49% of the population, the regulations say they should achieve a level of only 9% of representation at professional, senior and top levels.
>
> The same is true in KwaZulu-Natal, where although Indians are 7% of the demographic profile, they should not be represented in a proportion of more than 2.5%. (For many companies this would mean no Indians at senior levels at all.)

This, I thought, would never pass constitutional muster. It was clearly unfair discrimination.

But Carol's article went on to quote Thembinkosi Mkalipi, the deputy director-general of labour market policy in the Department of Labour, saying he did not see it that way at all: 'Two arguments are in the government's favour: that it cannot be discriminatory as the same yardstick is applied to all; and that while coloureds, for example, might be disadvantaged in the Western Cape, they would be advantaged in provinces where their regional representation is smaller than their national one.'

He was back to Mzwanele Jimmy Manyi's argument that there was an 'over-representation' of coloured people in the Western Cape. And the DA had fallen for the ruse in parliament, despite my clear warnings on the matter.

On 29 November 2013 Colin Eglin died. He had been one of the founding members (with Helen Suzman) of the Progressive Party in 1961. He was a person of exceptional intellect, resilient commitment and unsentimental empathy, with an unwavering perseverance to advance democracy in South Africa. With over sixty years of involvement in this cause, and having been a key architect of our constitution, he really understood what he meant when he warned us that we had to be prepared for 'the politics of the long haul'.

I had often sought Colin's guidance in complex political situations.

Less than a week after Colin, on 5 December 2013, Nelson Mandela died. His death was a major transition for the whole country, indeed for the world. Now South Africa would have to move forward without Madiba's guiding presence, even though he had not been able to actively exercise it for a long time.

After speaking at Colin's funeral in Cape Town on 9 December, I travelled to Qunu, President Mandela's home village in the Eastern Cape, to attend his funeral on 15 December.

It was the end of an era.

Two of our democracy's founding fathers were no longer with us. We had to take up the baton and make our country work.

I knew how crucial the DA would be to this project, but with our parliamentary caucus on the verge of tearing itself apart, the urgency of finding a solution weighed all the more heavily.

I needed to take a break. When my mind had cleared, I told myself, things would get better. After all, they couldn't get any worse.

I was wrong.

19

A Deluded Agenda

WHEN I PULL a single, long thread out of the fabric of a particular year, as I did in the previous chapter, it seems as if it was the only thing demanding my attention. Not so. That strand, although important, was part of a richly textured cloth woven from multiple fibres, day by day.

As the drama of the race-based bills unfolded, much else was happening. I always had 'wall-to-wall' diary commitments. Big-ticket items included the World Economic Forum in Cape Town, regular by-elections and visits to all provinces, major statutory meetings, two trips abroad to raise funds for the forthcoming general election, many local fundraising engagements, policy formulation, candidate selection, President Obama's visit, several big speeches each week, and media interviews almost daily. Not to mention the challenge of governing a province – interspersed with random political tremors like the ANC's refusal to relinquish power when they lost a by-election in Oudtshoorn.

Combining the jobs of party leader and (first) mayor and (then) premier was an enormous load, and looking back today, I sometimes wonder how I managed back then.

It was possible at all, only because of the calibre of my support staff on every front: in the leader's office, in the mayor's office, later in the premier's office, and always at home. My biggest weakness is my inability to manage paper, which tends to translate into poor administration. This is why I have always chosen strong managers and administrators to work with.

The role models of an effective colleague, imprinted in my mind from an early age, were my primary-school teachers – strong women, bearing life's crosses and burdens with determination and perseverance, who understood that life isn't fair. Women, in fact, who expect life to be a never-ending series of problems and who take responsibility for solving them, who don't expect to be having a good time, but are delighted when they are. Their day ends when the work is done. Nothing is ever too much to ask.

That is the culture in which I was raised, and it is what I subliminally expect from the people I work with. It's not always easy for them.

When I became the DA leader in 2007, I was based at City Hall, and my office was run by Carin Viljoen. She lived in another town, Malmesbury, about an hour north-west of Cape Town, and she commuted every day. No task was too much for her, no working day too long. She had a great sense of humour but could be tough when she needed to be. My office ran like clockwork. I wanted her to transfer to the province with me when I was elected premier, but she said it would be impossible. She had a permanent position in the City of Cape Town and could not forfeit her pension and job security by taking a contract as the premier's chief of staff.

Brent told me he knew of someone similar, and that was where Lorika Elliott entered the picture. She was an advocate, previously a manager in the ombudsman's office in the City of Cape Town. I had a mental picture of her that was blown away when she walked through the door. Tall and slender, her jet-black hair, with cherry-coloured highlights, was cut in edgy, tousled spikes. Shaggy chic. And totally together.

After an introductory chat, I appointed Lorika there and then, as this was a position I could fill at my discretion. She was every bit as good as Carin, and her legal insights came to stand me in good stead on many occasions, her lateral thinking joining the dots of important, disparate developments.

Every day when I arrived at the office, no matter how early, I would find three women drinking tea or frothy coffee and planning my life. Their meeting started at 6 a.m. Sometimes Brent joined them.

First to arrive at the office (and usually last to leave) was Donnae Strydom, who liked her title of 'The Premier's private secretary'. She took her job very seriously and personally. She unlocked the office before five every morning to prepare for the day, updating the diary, confirming logistics. I never understood how she managed to devote so much time to me, despite having two young sons.

Lorika (chief of staff) and Caroline Knott (parliamentary officer) arrived at work soon afterwards. Over tea or coffee, they put their heads together and discussed every topic relevant to the running of the office and the government. I called them the *Kaffeeklatsch* (a German word describing people who get together for a coffee and a *skinner*), but this little group played a valuable role in pre-empting problems and proposing solutions. They also had a deft way of making me think I was in charge. When I said the three of them formed the nerve centre of government, I was only half joking.

Donnae's loyalty to me at times even surpassed that of my mother. Unlike Mom, Donnae backed me, right or wrong. She followed every news platform and social-media feed to alert me to any relevant development. She guarded me like a watchdog – to the point that we soon called her 'the Rottweiler'. She had an incredible memory and could locate any document that had ever crossed the threshold of the office. She was an exceptionally visual person, and recalled every detail, such as whether I had left the office holding my cellphone or not. She filled the huge lacuna in my life occasioned by my incapacity to manage documents.

She was also a computer wizard. I swear my computer was scared of her. When something went wrong, she would just approach it, and it would stop giving trouble. The computer wasn't the only one. She ran the show, and the diary, and the link with the Democratic Alliance leader's office, with a firm grip. She kept issues of party and state distinctly separate. Every day she produced a full briefing pack for the following day. I would read it in the car and be on top of the issues I needed to face.

Donnae put my family first in the pecking order. When they needed me, she would sweep away any other commitments. Otherwise, it was almost impossible to get her to change a diary appointment.

Her office was the best-stocked spaza shop in Cape Town. Whatever I needed, from shampoo to toothpaste, to a safety-pin, pantyhose or a headache pill, she would be able to produce it like a rabbit out of a hat. She loved gizmos and gadgets, and would always have the latest what-what.

Caroline, who had worked for our cause since the days of the Democratic Party, was a dyed-in-the-wool liberal, a self-confessed cynic and a nitpicker, with a dry sense of humour. I needed her to compensate for another weakness of mine, dislike for detail. Also, I am inherently far too trusting (something that no level of disillusionment has changed). As a parliamentary officer, I needed someone who would read the newspapers closely, who understood the constitution and the law, as well as DA policy, and could interpret developments through that lens. This person needed to know parliamentary rules backwards, and be able to prepare me for debates and questions-without-notice. Caroline was excellent at strategy and tactics, and managed to predict, with uncanny accuracy, what questions the ANC would ask across the floor. So I usually had the facts and figures at my fingertips.

The various spokespersons (for the mayor, premier and leader) were directly in the line of fire of the often hostile media. They also had to deal with my occasional indiscretions. They coped admirably and soon developed skins almost as thick as mine: Robert MacDonald, Martin Slabbert, Frits de Klerk, Trace Venter, Zakhele Mbhele, Michael Mpofu, Jamie Turkington, Cameron Arendse, Melanie Kuhn, Ntomboxolo Makoba – in succession (not all at the same time!). They all got to know what it felt like to be on the receiving end of the 'hairdryer', as they described my occasional bouts of undisguised fury.

I was pampered daily with an endless supply of tea and rusks, as well as a lunchtime soup or salad, depending on the season, by the ladies who ran the kitchen, Lenie Agulhas and Janet Lodewyk. Lenie's special chicken soup made me look forward to winter.

My different offices (and my personal email) received hundreds of letters a week, and each needed to be treated individually and answered with care. Between the two offices I had four full-time colleagues responding to correspondence. I had to rely on their judgement to refer crucial issues to me, but otherwise to deal with routine correspondence. Very few issues ever fell through the cracks.

It is always invidious to name names, but I do have to pick one out. Enocent Nemuramba worked in the DA leader's office. Tall, and slim, with enormous dark eyes, Enocent was the most dedicated and determined person, probably as a result of the enormous challenges that life had placed before him from a young age. He took every letter seriously, and did the research necessary to answer each one properly. He was an excellent writer, and always managed to assure the recipients of his letters that they were being taken seriously, as individuals.

And then there was Janine Schouw, who eventually became like a daughter to me. She had arrived on the DA scene through Donnae, whose Rottweiler instinct had sniffed out the right person for the task, which was to make sure I looked like a 'Premier' and 'Party Leader'.

My colleagues, in both the province and the DA, were worried about my lack of dress sense and my incapacity to manage my thin, straggly hair. I needed to look more 'Presidential', apparently. The late Gwen Gill, an old journalist friend who used to be the gossip columnist on the *Sunday Times*, produced a South African version of the famous 'Mr Blackwell's' annual international list of worst-dressed women. Before long, as my public profile grew, I topped Gwen's local worst-dressed list, which I took as quite a compliment. I was sure that people would interpret it as meaning that I valued substance over style.

My colleagues disagreed. I needed fixing, they told me. I was finally convinced when one evening, after I had given what I thought was a good television interview, my mother called to comment on it. Her opening words were 'Are you STILL wearing that jersey?'

'Yes, Mom, there is nothing wrong with that jersey.'

I then asked her what she thought about what I had said. She didn't recall a single thing. She was fixated on the jersey. That convinced me. I needed to do something.

Initially, I refused to have a stylist and tried to discipline myself. I went for a few shots of Botox around the eyes and started wearing some make-up; I went to the hairdresser, and tried to co-ordinate my wardrobe. The media noticed. They asked why my look had changed. I explained, including about the Botox, which I didn't think was anything to hide. They had asked me a direct question, so I told them. That generated weeks of comment, and resulted in the ANC adding another pejorative adjective to descriptions of me – 'fake'.

But I could never keep up the co-ordinated wardrobe effort and hair for more than a week before relapsing. Sometimes it required me to pop into Steven Phillip's home (my always patient hairdresser) at four in the morning to get my hair styled before leaving for the airport to fly to another province. It took forever to 'get a look together', as the saying went, and life was just too short for these diversions.

In the end I succumbed, and Janine Schouw arrived in my life. She was a trained hairstylist and beautician. Her brief was to try to make me look presentable every day. It was a big ask. She also became an assistant to our excellent logistics chief, Shaun Moffitt, in the DA leader's office. She arrived at my home early, ransacked my wardrobe, found matching things, started 'accessorising', forced me to wear high heels and get my ears pierced. She never took no for an answer. She would say incomprehensible things like: 'We need to create a Wednesday look.' She never used banal names for colours. It was always 'Today we'll do the tangerine.' Or the amethyst. In fact, she knew names for colours that I never knew existed, such as amaranth and mikado (deep pink and rich yellow respectively). And underwear was always referred to as 'undergarments'.

Janine knew how much I hated spending money on clothes, so when she decided I needed some item, she would scour Cape Town and come back with the perfect bargain she had found somewhere in a factory shop. Donnae had, with unerring instinct, discovered Radeen Fashions in the working-class suburb of Elsie's River, and she passed this gem onto Janine, who subsequently sourced all kinds of outfits for me there. It became our firm favourite. Although I am a few centimetres taller than Janine, we are otherwise the same size, so she would try on clothes for me before buying them, and she often lent me items from her own wardrobe. My best 'look' at an opening of parliament was a black dress I had borrowed from her.

One day Janine decided I needed some new shoes. She found two pairs on a sale for R250. I then had to pass the invoice to Johann, who controlled our family finances.

Johann disliked spending money on clothes even more than I did. He did not understand why I needed new shoes every season, let alone two pairs in one go. He wore the same pair of shoes for at least a decade, often more. I tried to explain that R250 for two pairs of shoes was a bargain.

'R250 for shoes?' he protested. 'If you carry on like this, we will soon be spending more on shoes each month than we do on books.' (Books were the equivalent of the 'gold standard' in the Maree household under Johann's financial management.)

Janine had been raised in the traditional way of never referring to an older person using a personal pronoun. Especially not 'you' or 'your'. This was considered impolite. She called Johann 'Professor' and me 'Premier', and it was so ingrained, we couldn't get her to change it. So a typical Janine sentence would be: 'Does Premier want to take Premier's taupe jacket to Johannesburg when Premier leaves on Thursday?' We all ragged her. After a while in her presence,

I would refer to Johann as Professor and myself as Premier as well. It was contagious.

Johann and I still laugh about a Janine vignette which reflects her attention to detail and personal consideration.

It started with an email Johann wrote to me, commenting on my weekly newsletter. He thought he was commenting on a draft I had sent him (as I often did, after which he would send me his critique and proposals for improvement). This time, though, I had not sent him my draft. The deadline was too tight. He received the final version, from 'The Leader's' email (along with about 80 000 other subscribers).

Thinking he was responding to a draft sent personally from me, Johann hit the reply button.

'Hi Love,' he wrote, followed by a critique of my analysis, and proposals for improving my newsletter, ending with 'Love you lots, J.'

It landed in Enocent's inbox.

Enocent did not know 'J' was my husband, because we have different surnames. For some reason, Enocent also assumed that 'J' was a woman. So he gathered the facts necessary to respond to Johann's critique and wrote back to 'Dear Ms J. Maree'.

After an excellent rebuttal of Johann's arguments and defence of my position, Enocent ended his email with the normal 'Kind Regards'.

That evening, when logging the day's work, the staff in the DA leader's office came upon the correspondence. Reagan Allen, Enocent's colleague, who had met Johann at an official function, recognised that the letter came from my husband. He immediately informed Janine of the misunderstanding.

Janine was mortified.

'What will Professor think if Professor assumes it is routine for the office to receive letters from people who address Premier as 'Love' and tell Premier they love Premier a lot?' she asked her colleagues in horror.

She had to take urgent remedial action.

So she wrote the following letter to 'Professor'.

Dear Professor

Your email regarding the *SA Today* was sent to the Leader's address which Premier does not have personal access to. The Leader's email address is administered by our DA Public Liaison Officers, Enocent and Reagan.

Enocent already responded to Professor's email, but he did not realise it was Professor, Premier's husband, as there are many emails from members of the public who declare fondness towards Premier, with good intentions of course.

With this being said, it is not unusual for Enocent to receive an email addressed to Premier as 'Love'.

Reagan however, met Professor before the Young Leader's Graduation last year and ascertained immediately that it was indeed from Premier's one and only True Love.

Warmest Regards

Janine Schouw

Johann printed the letter and emerged from his study with it, laughing until the tears ran down his face. The letter was vintage Janine.

This kind of care, consideration and professionalism, in a myriad guises, were the hallmark of all my offices, and sustained me through the most turbulent of times.

At Leeuwenhof we had Hajirah Mahomed as the estate manager. She was dedicated, hard-working, intuitive and full of initiative. I didn't have to worry about a thing on the home front, from fixing the plumbing to hosting a formal dinner. She was supported by Ragel Beukes, Anna Friesley, Nellie Klaasens and Grace Voyiya, who arrived with me. Ishmael Hendricks had been my driver and bodyguard from the days when I was provincial minister of education. He was succeeded by Jerome Smith. And Herbert Mbuqe was the handyman who could make or fix just about anything. They all became part of the extended Leeuwenhof family.

At the beginning of my tenure, things started off very formally. It was straight-talking Nellie who soon broke the ice by calling Johann and me by Afrikaans diminutives: Proffie and Premiertjie.

We loved those terms of endearment as much as we had previously enjoyed being referred to as 'The Mayor and the Mayonnaise'.

Nellie loved Johann. One day she said to me, in all seriousness, that if I ever didn't want Johann any more, she would take him. I thanked her and said it was comforting to know, but I would keep him for now!

Sadly, Nellie died during my first term. Then Sandra Rhoda arrived to complete the team, and I had brought Grace and her family to live in Leeuwenhof when I became premier. I no longer had to manage the home front, which gave me hours of additional time. Not to mention the hours I gained by being able to work in the car while being driven around by my protectors, with whom I spent more time than with my family. What a luxury! I never took it for granted, and missed it sorely when I was not in executive office.

I had never had it so good in terms of support. The communication lines between my offices buzzed, everyone made sure everyone else was informed, Johann received my diary daily, and was an integral part of the team. I sometimes felt as if I was carried on an airbed of support services that miraculously remained steady on a turbulent sea. I never took this level of support and commitment for granted. And I needed every bit of it as 2013 drew to a close.

With everything else that was going on, I hardly registered receiving a note from Wilmot on 29 November 2013, saying he had once again held a meeting with Mamphela and Mills Soko, at Mamphela's request. The meeting had taken place on 25 November.

Wilmot's note told me Mamphela had referred to the rapidly changing political environment, the risk of an imminent breakaway trade union party on the left, the growth of the Economic Freedom Fighters, and the prospects for positioning the DA and Agang at the centre of the political spectrum. Mamphela was proposing a 'behind-the-scenes pre-election agreement based on [Agang's] comparative advantage of being able to attract the vote of black rural women'.

Wilmot had told her that there was no indication in the polling data of rural support for Agang (neither men nor women) and that the DA and Agang were competing for exactly the same pool of educated, urban opposition voters. On the basis of our polling data, the picture did not look promising for Agang, Wilmot said.

I was intrigued but not surprised that Mamphela had re-initiated contact. I also understood why she would not venture to make contact directly with me. Our last meeting had been the most acrimonious we had ever had, and I had not minced my words. Her approach to Wilmot turned out to be the opening salvo of a volley of attempts to get around me by going to colleagues she considered more amenable, and asking them to persuade me to accommodate her often incomprehensible strategies.

I wrote back to Wilmot on 2 December, saying that the 'only reason that [Mamphela] could possibly want a pre-election behind-the-scenes agreement is to get funding'. I proposed that we each enter the election separately and see how things stood afterwards. It was too late for a merger, and too early for a coalition. If Agang held the balance of power anywhere, we could talk coalitions after the election.

Wilmot conveyed the message to Mamphela. She correctly concluded that I was no longer prepared to be accommodating.

When she realised there was no way around me, she asked me for a meeting on 20 December. I agreed to listen to what she had to say.

At the meeting she repeated what she had told Wilmot: things had changed substantially since the beginning of the year, with South Africa's political situation deteriorating further. The ANC would be in all sorts of trouble if there were a credible alternative which combined both legitimate leadership and organisational capacity. This combination did not yet exist, she argued. We could create it. We needed to do this in the window opened by Madiba's passing, she said. His legacy of 'collective leadership' could overcome political differences.

I told Mamphela I was no longer available to listen to sweeping statements and political platitudes.

Then she (seriously) proposed that the DA merge with Agang, in a new entity that she suggested should be called AgangDA, because, according to her, this would put us 'at the top of the ballot paper'. I told her the ordering of the ballot paper didn't work like that. It was based on a 'draw', with the alphabetical order following the lucky winner.

I said it was, in any event, too late to discuss anything. The DA's processes were almost finalised, our election material was at the printers, and our lists awaited final, limited adjustments by the Federal Executive.

She urged me not to allow 'logistics' to get in the way of progress, because we had to 'hold on to hope'.

I told her that functional systems and logistics were the lifeblood of a political party, and they could not be bent according to leadership whims. The only prospect for her now was to close down Agang, fold up its tent and join the DA. If she was prepared to do that, I said, I could go to Fedex and make the case for her to be allocated an electable place on our parliamentary candidates list. That was all.

She rejected the idea of being 'swallowed' by the DA. I said there was no other option. It was too late for a merger (in any event, Agang had nothing to offer us) and it was too early for talking coalitions, which only happened after elections, in the attempt to build a governing majority.

Mamphela was insistent that something must be possible.

'Well,' I said, 'give me a detailed proposal, without generalisations or fuzziness, with clear, implementable steps, which take account of where the DA is in the electoral cycle. I will put it to our National Management Committee. If they accept it, it will go further to the Federal Executive.'

I knew there was almost no chance of this. Putting the ball in her court was a way of making her recognise it.

The proposal duly arrived, and it was a non-starter. It made no practical, concrete suggestions. Its main thrust was to trumpet Agang's imagined strengths and propose a form of merger, which was impossible at that stage anyway. But in good faith, I sent it to my colleagues on the original negotiating team, including Lindiwe and Wilmot. They agreed with my assessment.

When I reread the correspondence between Wilmot, Lindiwe and me over this period, I am amazed at the collegiality and congeniality that continued between us, at least judging from the tone of our letters, despite the 'plane crash' and its related upheaval only weeks before.

I don't have enough space on my emotional hard drive to store grudges or hard feelings. So, for me at any rate, things returned to normal. And from their letters, I judged they had moved on as well. It was a relief.

What did continue to worry me, subliminally at least, was that, in the context of our urgent need to reposition the DA, it would be big news if word got out that we had rejected Mamphela (however untrue and distorted this spin would have been). The media knew very little about the long lead-up to this dead end, and would have interpreted any new development in a vacuum, without the background context. And I had little doubt that I would be painted as the Caucasian in the woodpile.

After my rejection, Mamphela approached Wilmot again. He asked me whether he should see her, and, after conferring with the wider DA negotiating group, I replied: 'My interaction with them shows that we are all of the same view: the only thing we can feasibly do at this stage is offer Mamphela a good place on our election list. Agang is not viable and has not got traction amongst voters, according to all our polling … Mamphela is a friend so I would like to support her: but the only way I can see clear at this stage, is through an offer of a comfortably electable position, which would, of course, have to go through Fedex – and we would need to persuade Fedex of this. We cannot offer her anything without going this route.'

Even after everything, I thought Mamphela would make a valuable member of parliament. She would be a strong, fearless debater, and that would help our rebranding and the legitimisation of strong opposition.

'So by all means talk to Mamphela,' I concluded. 'But please ensure that you do not raise any expectations above saying it is likely that we would succeed in getting Fedex to agree that she should have a good, electable place on our list.'

Wilmot wrote back on 23 December, saying that Mamphela considered our offer demeaning and had rejected it. 'I heard her out and stated again that the only offer on the table remains an electable place on the list,' said Wilmot. 'I believe we should stick to our offer as it is and wait it out.'

I agreed with his assessment. I copied the correspondence to the rest of the negotiating team, and drew a line under things. After spending a few days with the family in Keurbooms, I flew to Johannesburg to do what my sister Carla described as a 'locum' for her – taking care of Mom while Carla went away for a well-deserved break. Mom's hearing had deteriorated further and, unlike Carla, she was unable to lip-read. Which meant I continued writing letters to her, often sitting right next to her on the bed, where her dogs, Oscar and Heidi, always had pride of place.

It felt good to put all the machinations behind me. I was convinced that if Mamphela's latest approaches became public, it would not be easy to blame the

DA for the failure to take the next step in consolidating the opposition and offering the electorate something new and exciting.

Mamphela, however, did not give up. Having failed to get what she wanted through me and Wilmot, she approached Patricia, Mmusi and Lindiwe. Of the three, only Patricia and Mmusi informed me of the parallel channel Mamphela was setting up with them. They mentioned that she was asking them to put pressure on me to agree to her terms.

Patricia and I chatted. She recalled the work we had done together to bring the Independent Democrats into the DA, and the helpful role Mamphela had played in the process. We remembered the conversations about bringing her in when the time was right, in the next phase of political realignment, to build a new majority in South Africa. It puzzled us both that she had gone in the opposite direction, towards a failing solo political venture, incurring huge debt in the process.

We were also acutely aware that the polls were telling us that South Africans of all races wanted a strong, united opposition party. Indeed, our own history attested to this. Whenever we had taken steps to consolidate the opposition – first with the NNP and later with the ID – our support from voters jumped exponentially.

There were still advantages, we agreed, in bringing Mamphela on board. Patricia (who was also relatively new to the DA's internal electoral processes) wanted me to make it easier for Mamphela to accept our offer. Limiting this to an electable place on our list made it very difficult for her to accept, Patricia ventured.

Early in January 2014, my discussions with Patricia had persuaded me to ask the DA's national management committee to give Mamphela a final chance of accepting an offer to be our presidential candidate in the 2014 election – a big step up from merely being in an electable position on our list. She would be number one on our national list. Given the background context, I thought this was an enormously generous offer. Perhaps absurdly generous.

On 15 January I met with Jonathan Moakes, our CEO, and James Selfe, and after some discussion, we agreed it would be worthwhile to propose to Fedex that Mamphela should be our candidate for president. We knew it would be far more than a hand-up for Mamphela. It was actually a ladder to help her climb out of her hole.

We firmly agreed that if she accepted the offer to be our presidential candidate, it would not automatically translate into any other position. If she wanted to stand as caucus leader after the election, she would have to fight an internal caucus election on her own merits. I assumed that after her history with the DA, she was unlikely to win. I would certainly no longer support her for that position. Her constant, uncharacteristic vacillation and tendency to speak in riddles in pursuit of an outcome she wanted (but tried to disguise) were profoundly disconcerting.

But our polls were telling us we were not going to win the election, so there was no chance of her becoming president. We would be lucky enough to achieve our goal of keeping the ANC below a two-thirds majority, and the small up-tick we expected she would bring us (between 1 and 2 per cent) might just help us achieve that. Every vote counted.

I have often reflected on why I allowed the DA (and me personally) to be messed around to that extent by a single person pursuing a deluded agenda. I would never have tolerated it had she been white. Nor was my relationship with Mamphela the only example of my tendency to allow people to take advantage of me, on the basis of their race and mine. I asked myself whether this wasn't actually a pernicious form of inverted racism, to which white liberals are particularly prone, which manifests in an acceptance of levels of abuse from black people we would never tolerate from anyone else. But then again, South Africa's history creates a particular context that makes it difficult to walk the line between a mutually respectful relationship and an abusive one, on all sides of the deep divides that persist so stubbornly in our society.

Mamphela, of course, was keenly aware of the racial dynamic, and the advantage of isolating me from the rest of the DA leadership in the discussions. She called Patricia 'my sister' and preferred to interact with her. Patricia told me she had relayed our amended offer to Mamphela. I heard nothing. I assumed she had rejected it.

Then, on 15 January, I received an email from a facilitator, who I'll call Daniel, saying that a major donor wished to have a lunch meeting with me and Mamphela to discuss the upcoming election. The date proposed was 4 February 2014. The invitation came out of the blue. I suspected it was yet another attempt to try to get me to accommodate Mamphela on terms more acceptable to her than we had offered. I groaned inwardly, because the donor would have no idea of what we had been through, and what the DA's obstacles to her 'terms' were.

I wrote back to say I would happily have lunch on 4 February, but that it would be too late for the DA to make any accommodation whatsoever. We were finalising our lists in the Federal Executive on 24 January. That would be the very end of the process and nothing could be changed after that. And I was certainly not going to postpone this meeting or any part of the process to accommodate Mamphela. Our election machine was in full swing according to a carefully prepared timetable.

I also sent Daniel a detailed history of our attempts to bring Mamphela on board. It was essential for him to know the background, because I did not want the DA to be blamed for recalcitrance when I drew the line at any further accommodation.

Daniel understood. His aim, he said, was to shift Mamphela, not me; and he would do that by ensuring that she was made an offer it would be difficult to refuse. It involved paying off most of her debt if she would close down Agang and become the DA's presidential candidate. I made it clear that we had made our final offer, which was already over-generous in the circumstances.

I assumed that Daniel had also been in touch with Mamphela, because I heard, via Patricia, that Mamphela was now prepared to consider our offer. Her desperation for the money was beginning to move her.

I wrote to my DA colleagues on 18 January 2014 to keep them abreast of developments:

> Mamphela wants to consider the offer. She had an emergency [Agang] executive meeting in Johannesburg this week and is going overseas today and wanted to meet with me on Saturday 25th. I let her know via Patricia that this would be too late. The final FEDEX is the 24th. Klaar. She will have to decide before then. She knows what the offer is: She becomes our presidential candidate, gets a place on our list and closes down Agang.
>
> I do not even know if we could get this through the FEDEX but we could give it our best shot…
>
> We will not accept anything but a yes or no [from her]. She cannot demand places for anyone else, and no convoluted arrangements or processes. Yes or No.

On 21 January, in the run-up to the preparation of the final list adjustment at Fedex, Johan van der Berg, our excellent statistician and pollster, wrote to inform me of the gloomy results of our latest opinion survey and tracking poll.

> Today's support levels on the 'low turnout' model:
> - All voters: ANC 61%, DA 20%, EFF 8%.
> - Black voters: ANC 75%, DA 6%, EFF 10%.
>
> Key trends since we closed off in mid-December last year:
> - We've been squeezed down to 20% nationally by a combination of wall-to-wall coverage of Madiba in December, the ANC's intense campaigning since January 8 and Malema's strong showing in the media since the start of the year. We've scored comparatively few clean hits ourselves, and it's showing in the polls. The ANC support is up from the mid-to-high 50s in December to the low 60s.
> - Our black support is flat on a lower level than last year, and the EFF has grown steadily to 10% among black voters.
> - Despite the damage to the ANC's brand, they're still able to shift undecided and soft opposition supporters quite quickly with large scale presence events – see the period from 8 to 16 January.

And, with reference to Agang, he said the only constituency where they were showing any traction was among white voters. What an irony! Far from winning a black constituency that was still beyond the reach of the DA, as Mamphela stubbornly believed, Agang was fishing in exactly the same voter pond as the DA.

I was really bleak about our election prospects when Daniel contacted me again to say he was flying down to Cape Town on 23 January to speak to me personally.

I said okay. He told me that Mamphela had been trying to raise money from many of the donors who had traditionally supported her, at home and abroad, but that most of them had turned her down because they thought it was ridiculous to fund two South African opposition parties with the same broad political philosophy. As a sweetener, to encourage the DA's flexibility in offering Mamphela a 'face-saver' to finalise the deal, he said he was mandated to offer a generous donation to the DA as well. It was very tempting, but after giving the matter some thought I declined. The DA had a clear policy not to accept donations in return for favours, even if they had nothing to do with our role in government. Acceding to any kind of quid pro quo would put us on a slippery slope that we wanted to avoid. Daniel understood that.

I documented all these developments very closely in my letters to my mother, which in retrospect make fascinating reading. I explained my motivation for agreeing to this final attempt to assist Mamphela: '[She] had started her party with so much flare and ceremony, and predicted such magnificent results … Despite the way she has treated me in the past, I didn't want her to end her career in debt and ignominy.'

Mamphela returned from abroad on 23 January, a day earlier than she had planned. I assumed this was at Daniel's encouragement, because he was in Cape Town and wanted to see us for a joint meeting before I flew off to Fedex in Johannesburg on 24 January.

After attending a book launch on the evening of 23 January, Daniel, Mamphela and I went together to a nearby restaurant.

Mamphela wanted to reopen discussions on other options, but I simply repeated that I would ask Fedex the next morning for a two-thirds majority to support the proposal that she be our presidential candidate and close down Agang. I said it would prove hard enough to get that through, and re-emphasised that this was our final deadline for the DA's lists. She had to commit: yes or no.

Daniel then made an intervention. He asked whether it would be possible to make space for other Agang members in electable positions on our candidates list, which we were finalising the next day. I resented having the ball knocked into my court again, and replied that it was impossible. I explained that the DA had been through a six-month process, in which 1 432 candidates had competed fiercely with each other, going through electoral colleges, extensive tests, simulation exercises and interviews before being ranked by independent panels. I said there would be a massive outcry in the DA if I introduced random people from outside at this stage of the process, especially since Mamphela had spurned our offers a year earlier.

Those kinds of situations are the most difficult in politics: when one has made every accommodation possible, and one is still expected to go further, or be painted as the spoiler. I drew the line. I said I had no power to offer her a 'number of positions' which she could fill at her discretion on the DA's list.

I was not confident that Agang would have attracted candidates who would be electoral drawcards for the DA. I recalled Patricia de Lille saying that a new political party is like a new pub in town. The first customers it attracts are all the people who have already been kicked out of every other pub.

Nevertheless, I said if Mamphela could give me individual names of outstanding candidates, I would present the names to Fedex, which was empowered to include a limited number of new candidates by a two-thirds majority, if there was a compelling case to do so. But, I warned, Fedex was not in an accommodating mood in relation to Mamphela any longer. It would be hard enough, I repeated, to get her name accepted, let alone any other names.

I was relieved when Daniel finally supported my position. He left Mamphela with a clear condition to which I was a witness: the money she needed would be forthcoming if she agreed to close down Agang and join the DA.

I left the meeting that night knowing I was about to deplete my bank balance of political capital entirely at the next day's Fedex, trying to save Mamphela from an ill-considered political venture I had warned her against.

Late that night I wrote to Mom about the meeting. Referring to Mamphela's response, I said: 'She completely failed to understand how much I was going out on a limb for her ... She is so used to being feted by the rest of the world, that she assumes people should bend everything to accommodate her every whim. I keep asking myself whether, in good faith, I should still try to get her to be our presidential candidate, but she has strengths: she can deliver a message well, she can destroy the myth that we would bring back apartheid; and she can help me unite the opposition and realign politics. Given the fact that she is unlikely to become president, it seems a symbolic risk worth taking.'

The next morning, 24 January, I flew up to Johannesburg, awaiting Mamphela's response. I had told her we would be going through the lists, province by province, and that it was impossible for me to excuse myself from a meeting where crucial issues would be on the table. There could be no further discussions. There was only one question, which needed a one-syllable answer. Would she become our presidential candidate for the election and close down Agang? Yes or no?

Fedex moved through each province's list in turn, approving confidential candidates and putting the final seal on what we believed had been a fair and inclusive process.

At 11:58 a.m., Mamphela's SMS landed: 'Good morning, I have confirmation of acceptance of offer framed as a partnership bringing together your machinery and our grassroots enthusiasm to get our nation's politics beyond divisive identity politics. Thanks. M.'

I nearly screamed with exasperation. I counted to ten and sent a message back that I did not understand what she was saying. I needed an unambiguous yes or no response.

After a few more SMSes, I told Fedex I did not yet have a clear answer from Mamphela, but asked them to approve in principle that she could be our presidential candidate if she would agree to close down Agang. We looked at the results of the polling, which showed that this move could bring a useful and much-needed bounce to our campaign.

Athol Trollip spoke strongly against my proposal. When we put it to the vote, I only just managed to get the two-thirds support necessary. There was still a majority feeling in Fedex that the advantages of having Mamphela as our presidential candidate would outweigh the disadvantages in the current circumstances, but her vacillation could not have created greater problems for me.

I swore the Fedex to secrecy. If this leaked, it would create endless complications and scupper any attempts to finalise the plan.

I let Mamphela know by SMS that the Fedex had approved the deal in principle, and said how crucial it was to maintain confidentiality. We agreed to meet at 6:30 on Sunday evening, 26 January, for her final response.

On Saturday 25 January we held a press conference announcing our candidates (without Mamphela's name or those of the other confidential candidates), after which I departed for the Northern Cape to fundraise and speak at various events.

On Sunday 26 January, the inevitable happened. A prominent report in *City Press* newspaper trumpeted: 'Agang leader Mamphela Ramphele has again been in secret talks with the DA about possible cooperation between the two parties.'

The article quoted Agang spokesperson Thabo Leshilo describing claims of fresh talks as 'ridiculous', while an anonymous senior DA member said the co-operation between the parties 'could involve the DA supporting Ramphele as presidential candidate when these are nominated and elected in Parliament after the elections'.

This report puzzled me. No one from the DA could have suggested that the agreement involved co-operation between the parties after the election, because our condition was that Agang would close down immediately. On the other hand, Leshilo dismissing the claims of talks as 'ridiculous' showed that Mamphela had not shared the latest developments even with her closest inner circle. It spelt trouble.

I flew back to Cape Town on the Sunday evening and went straight from the airport to see Mamphela. She had two colleagues with her, Andrew Gasnolar and Mark Peach. I was joined by Lindiwe, Wilmot and Patricia. I had asked Wilmot to take the lead in the discussions. He had been an academic colleague of Mamphela's at UCT, and could level with her. She still treated me as if I worked for her, which was not conducive to the kind of conversation we needed to have.

Daniel, the facilitator, was back in Johannesburg, waiting on tenterhooks for news of the outcome of our meeting.

Mamphela raised the idea that had been reported in *City Press* that morning, that the DA and Agang should continue 'on parallel tracks' and come together after the election. That made me suspect that the leak might even have come from Agang to force us into a corner, or appear to be the spoilers if we did not accede to her demands.

Wilmot made it unambiguously clear that Mamphela could not be our presidential candidate and continue to lead Agang at the same time. If she was our presidential candidate, Agang could not appear on the ballot paper. If she had a problem with her fledgling organisation in this regard, we would help her by devising a plan to absorb her branches and activists into the DA, but we could not spend interminable amounts of time in the run-up to an election on internal negotiations. This process was now over, and we had to 'take the fight to the ANC'. She, predictably, responded by saying: 'This issue is much bigger than the ANC. It is about the future of SA.'

Wilmot said firmly that we had made our final offer and that he would spell out the common roles and responsibilities in a memorandum of understanding, which he would compile, so that there could be no ambiguity.

I could see Mamphela was not on board, and by the time I left the meeting I had concluded there was no chance of rescuing the situation. What was more, I was no longer interested in doing so. I had promised my family I would have dinner with them, which we hadn't managed to do for weeks.

My colleagues stayed on in Mamphela's lounge and continued the conversation. Afterwards, Wilmot sent me a text confirming my impression that the outcome of their extended discussion was a 'no go'.

No one could accuse the DA of failing to make every possible effort, I consoled myself, but I started the week feeling flat and low. Everything pointed to the inevitability of a disappointing election result. Especially against the 30 per cent target Lindiwe had announced publicly, on at least two occasions, although I had requested the party not to do so. Knowing what our daily polling was telling us, it would be ridiculous to set this target, although my colleagues responsible for the election plan had set 30 per cent as an internal target in order to calculate canvassing and voting benchmarks in each constituency. I understood why this was necessary – to ensure stretch targets to drive the campaign – but I never took it seriously, certainly not for a national election, where the ANC always benefited from huge turnout. (Even in the triumph of the 2016 local government elections, we achieved 27 per cent countrywide – despite the DA's voter-turnout advantage in local elections.)

I didn't suspect an ulterior motive behind Lindiwe's announcement of the 30 per cent target at the time. But when Gareth van Onselen wrote another excoriating column, titled 'The Anatomy of a Lie', he quoted Lindiwe in order to refute my statement that 30 per cent was never a public target. Obviously, failing to meet our target would reflect badly on my leadership. I started wondering if the public statements about the 30 per cent projection had indeed been the result of an oversight, or a deliberate strategy. I never reached a final conclusion, although several of my colleagues did. They had no doubt it was deliberate.

I woke up the next morning, Monday 27 January 2015, to a much needed tonic in the *Business Day* from an unexpected source, its editor Peter Bruce in his weekly column 'Thick Edge of the Wedge'. I am usually not much swayed by either praise or criticism, although I take both on board, but this column was different.

It was headlined: 'Zille a Worthy Successor to Suzman'.

It is interesting to watch Helen Zille enter what will probably be her last general election as leader of the Democratic Alliance. It is way too easy to dismiss her, to snort her away as a passing politician of little consequence or, if you really still hate white people, as the last real political vestige of a colonial and racist past.

But I have just read a wonderful (and refreshingly brief) book by former British ambassador to South Africa (and, then, the US) Robin Renwick (the Lord Renwick of Clifton to you) about the late Helen Suzman. While not filled with shattering revelations, it nonetheless serves as a delightful and encouraging reminder of the immense value of liberal intransigence. 'Like everybody else,' he quotes Suzman saying, 'I long to be loved. But I am not prepared to make any concessions whatsoever.'

And he reminds us in the book (Helen Suzman: Bright Star in a Dark Chamber, soon to be published here by Jonathan Ball) just how relentlessly this doughty woman fought the National Party, the Afrikaner nationalist vehicle that ran this country for 40 years. Whether it was campaigning for better conditions in jails for political prisoners or cleverly using her parliamentary privilege to force facts into the public arena that the government wanted hidden, Helen Suzman made a huge difference to our political trajectory. She died in 2009, just before Jacob Zuma was elected president.

We're a very different country now to the one run by Afrikaner nationalists. We're a much better place and Renwick's book is a good reminder what an utter misery South Africa was under the Nationalists.

But I couldn't help, while reading it, making comparisons between Helen Suzman and Helen Zille, and every time I stopped to make one, Helen Zille passed with flying colours. In whatever sense she might be a successor to Helen Suzman, she is a worthy one. She won't shut up and she won't back down.

For instance, I was initially appalled by the news that the DA was planning a march to ANC headquarters in Johannesburg to protest against the ruling party's poor job creation record.

I realise now that I was scared. Zille's responses to critics of the proposed march have convinced me that, now that it has been announced, it would be a terrible indictment of our democracy if it were to be called off because of the apparent hostility with which it has been received by some officials in the ANC. A peaceful march to the outside of the headquarters of an overwhelmingly dominant party should be met with tranquillity. If I were the ANC, I would invite Helen in for tea when she gets there. It isn't going to change the outcome of the election.

In a way, Zille's job is more complicated than Suzman's ever was. She has many more political compromises to make, and I am still not sure what economic policy the DA follows or how it plans to create new jobs. But she is clearly making a huge and laudable effort to speed up the racial transformation of her party – and with that must come new values, new experiences and new policies. And while we bystanders may sneer and guffaw, it matters in the end. What Renwick's book brought powerfully home about South African (and probably all) politics was how slowly but how ineluctably bad things change and come right.

Liberals will always find themselves on the wrong side of the dominant nationalisms of the day – once it was the Nats and now it is the ANC. But the role is the same; to care about the integrity of institutions, the rule of law and personal freedoms. Even Steve Biko acknowledged the primacy of the individual in his own vision of a democratic South Africa: 'There will be a completely nonracial franchise,' he once said. 'Black and white will vote as individuals in our society.'

One day the DA will be a well-organised party led largely by black South Africans. For me that can't happen too soon. But it will have been individuals like the two Helens who made it possible.

Now and again, a respite from constant criticism and a small dose of affirmation is all one needs to keep going. I hit the day.

At around midday, Patricia called me, requesting me to come to her office urgently. I dropped what I was doing because I caught the sense of urgency in her voice, although she did not offer any specifics. When I arrived at the Civic Centre, I found Mamphela in Patricia's office. They had clearly had a prior meeting. Mamphela said she wanted to pursue an idea of Patricia's that we should 'separate the political from the electoral process'. I said I did not know what that meant. She said we needed to make a political announcement that she would become the DA's presidential candidate, and that we would then work out the technicalities of incorporating Agang's branches, members and volunteers into the DA and get a joint election campaign going.

It fitted in with what Wilmot had suggested the previous evening. Patricia confirmed this. At last Mamphela was talking specifics, and I thought we were making progress.

I wondered what had made her change her mind from the previous evening, but reading between the lines of what she said, I concluded it was her parlous financial situation.

We continued the conversation for a while before I wrote down, in the clearest possible terms, what she was proposing: Mamphela will become the DA's presidential candidate and we will set up a joint task team to manage the incorporation of Agang's branches, members and volunteers into the DA.

I was very careful to insist on the word 'incorporation' so that there could be no argument about 'parallel tracks' or anything else at a later stage. I read the sentence again. Twice. We all agreed.

The next step would be for Wilmot to finalise the memorandum of understanding and set up the technical task team. Mamphela agreed, but said she wanted to make the announcement immediately. The leak in the *City Press* the previous day had caused all sorts of complications for her political platform, and she had to state clearly what was unfolding. This required an immediate public statement, she insisted, otherwise things would only get more difficult. She was experiencing push-back from her party and she wanted to turn our agreement into a fait accompli.

I did not think it was a bad idea to move quickly, because if we could agree on the wording of a statement, and get it out into the open, it would be more difficult for her to renege again. But it really did not suit me to move as quickly as she wanted to. I had a provincial cabinet lekgotla to attend the next day.

I discussed it with the DA team. We decided it best to strike while the iron was hot, and Gavin drew up two statements – one for Mamphela and one for me. We sent her both. She accepted hers without any alteration and suggested a few cosmetic changes to mine. I accepted them. We sent out an announcement that a joint press conference would be held the next day. It caused a media stir.

The plan was that I would announce that Mamphela would become the DA's presidential candidate and that we would set up a joint technical committee to manage the integration of our structures, members and volunteers. Gavin felt the word 'integration' was better than 'incorporation', because it conveyed our intention of building one inclusive organisation. I accepted this advice, and so did Mamphela.

I described our decision as part of the realignment of politics which I had set out to achieve when I became leader of the DA.

> As the ANC breaks into its constituent parts, the DA is building a new political vehicle at the centre of our politics.
>
> The DA leadership is drawn from across the political spectrum. Some of us come from the liberal tradition that opposed apartheid. Others were previously members of the ANC. Some were part of the Pan-Africanist movement. And others have a Black Consciousness background.
>
> But we all share the same values. The belief in an open, opportunity society for all characterized by non-racialism, a market economy, human rights and prosperity for all.

Mamphela's statement echoed my sentiments and committed her to the agreed course of action.

I woke up early on Tuesday 28 January in a buoyant mood and sent a note to my 'old pal' Daniel to tell him we had pulled it off. Next to a winking face, I joked that he should expect an invoice. But my light-hearted mood soon evaporated. As we were putting the final touches to the press conference plans, Geordin, my chief of staff, called to say that Mamphela had twice changed her statement overnight. The final version included a new second paragraph which read: 'In a unique South African innovation, Dr Ramphele will become the DA's presidential candidate while remaining the leader of Agang.'

We were two hours away from a press conference. I phoned her directly and let rip. I had reached the end of a very long fuse. I told her that what she had now inserted into the statement was electoral and political nonsense, as we had explained umpteen times before. Two political parties could not team up with the same presidential candidate and fight each other in an election simultaneously. Agang would have to close down, and its structures (such as they were) and members would be integrated into the DA, if they wished.

Unless she was prepared to stick to our agreement, I told her, I would cancel the press conference and take the consequences.

I then insisted on having a meeting with both our full teams present, before the press conference, so that there would be absolutely no room for misunderstandings afterwards. Mamphela did not think this meeting was necessary. I said it was a non-negotiable precondition for going ahead with the press conference.

We met at the Townhouse Hotel for a final discussion forty-five minutes before the presser was due to start. I put our case on the table absolutely bluntly, and made it clear it would be for the last time. Patricia urged me to cut Mamphela some slack, and said that we needed to 'trust each other'. But I said there was absolutely no room for misunderstanding at that critical point. We would either proceed on the agreed basis that Agang would close down and we would integrate its members, supporters and volunteers into the DA, or we would not proceed at all. We could, at that stage, still cancel the press conference and endure ten minutes of embarrassment. Or go ahead as agreed. The choice was Mamphela's.

She decided to go ahead. I checked once more that there was no confusion. Everyone understood exactly what the position was. We had fifteen minutes to go before the presser was due to start.

Geordin and Gavin had, as usual, prepared a list of difficult questions that might come up, to prepare us.

The very first question they predicted would be put to Mamphela was: 'Are you joining the DA today, and if so, will Agang be wound up?'

At first Mamphela rejected the idea of discussing the questions at the pre-meeting. I, backed by Wilmot, insisted that we go through them.

Her reply to Geordin's question was: 'Today we are announcing that I am the DA's presidential candidate, the other details will be worked out later.'

I said that answer would not suffice; there was no way any journalist, looking for inconsistencies, was going to accept that. This sparked another round of intense discussion, until Mamphela specifically agreed that if this question came her way she would (1) say she would take up DA membership later that week, and (2) make reference to the technical team which would oversee the integration of Agang structures into the DA.

We walked into the press conference through a media scrum, flashes popping in every direction as cameramen stumbled backwards over each in the narrow passage leading to the conference room of the Townhouse Hotel near parliament.

Mamphela was all sweetness and light. I read my script, interspersed with some personal comments about our sons. She read hers. She had included some additional sections, but had removed the paragraph that deviated from the agreement. It all went warmly and well, culminating in The Kiss that subsequently attained so much notoriety.

In the question-and-answer session, no journalist asked Mamphela the specific question we had anticipated, and she managed to get away with a passing reference to the technical committee. I was determined to get in the bit about the DA membership, so I confirmed that Mamphela would be a signed-up DA member before the election.

The public response was mixed. There was the baleful superficiality of much of the media commentary alleging the DA was using Mamphela as a 'rent-a-black-leader in a white party', and that Mamphela had somehow betrayed the voters who believed she could offer South Africa something new. I thought she responded well to that criticism by alluding to similar allegations made against Nelson Mandela when he began negotiating South Africa's transition to democracy.

But, on balance, the public comment was a lot more positive than negative. And many cynical commentators were unusually supportive.

Lindiwe tweeted: 'I'm thrilled about #AgangDA today. I have worked hard alongside DA leadership to bring us to this point #TogetherForChange.'

But the very next evening, facing a barrage of questions on television, Mamphela started backtracking, saying things such as 'Agang is alive and well and active in all areas' and that we were merely trying to 'leverage the strengths of the two organisations'.

That was certainly not what had been agreed.

She also wasted no time in writing to Daniel to say that she had done what was required of her, and now needed the money.

Daniel wrote back to Mamphela, and copied the letter to me. His reply was unambiguous. The agreement with Mamphela was that the money to make good her debts would be forthcoming if she was willing to close down Agang and stand as the DA's presidential candidate. Put another way, he said, the offer was conditional on her leaving Agang and joining the DA. It would be both untenable and confusing, he said, to have the leader of one political party running as a candidate for another.

There was absolutely no room for confusion about what the agreement had been.

I wrote to my DA colleagues saying that I suspected Mamphela had been disingenuous when she put such pressure on us to hold the press conference immediately; her intention was to get the money she needed rather than clarify confusion inside Agang occasioned by leaks to the media.

Every time she spoke publicly, she simply heightened the confusion. On the Wednesday night we had both been invited to speak at the launch of Lord Robin Renwick's biography of Helen Suzman. It was an uncomfortable situation, but Mamphela's nerves of steel allowed her to rise to the occasion. She knew the audience was, in the main, strongly supportive of our announcement, and in her speech she stressed that we were committed to the deal and that there was no turning back. She would continue on what she described as the 'road less travelled'.

I hoped she was creating enough momentum to prevent the wheels coming off.

On the Thursday morning, in a radio broadcast, she was once again singing a different tune, so I called her and told her things could not go on like this. We would have to clear up the matter once and for all by the end of the day. She told me she was in Johannesburg to consult her party structures. She would be back that afternoon. I insisted we had to meet that evening, as I was going away the following morning and would be out of town for the whole weekend. We agreed to meet at five o'clock that evening, 30 January, at Leeuwenhof.

I gathered the DA's full negotiating team, including Patricia de Lille, and we waited for her.

At 5:30 p.m. I called her to find out where she was. She said she was tired and sweaty and had gone to her home in Camps Bay to have a shower. Her casual attitude towards our meeting arrangement really irritated me. I told her bluntly that we were waiting for her. More than an hour after the scheduled start of our meeting, she breezed in, wearing a sparkling black dress, relaxed and smiling as if all was well with the world. She announced that she had just popped in to see us briefly, as she was on her way to the dinner F.W. de Klerk was hosting to commemorate his historic speech of 2 February 1990. I had also been invited to the dinner but had, for the first time, turned down the invitation because of the pressures we were facing and the fact that I had to get up very early the next morning to leave for the Southern Cape.

I pushed her really hard. I said, 'The agreement is that you will close Agang down and be the DA's presidential candidate.' At that point Patricia intervened again and said that we would just have to 'trust' each other and that I shouldn't put Mamphela under so much pressure. The dynamic of support for Mamphela coming from my team made it more difficult, but I stressed there was no alternative. The confusion had to end, because her contradictory public statements were causing us immeasurable damage.

I told her that I was flying to the Southern Cape town of George early the next morning, where I would be interviewed by the television programme *Carte Blanche* at the airport at 8 a.m. I said I would use the interview to bring clarity to the situation and chart the way forward. We had to come up with a plan of action to promote Mamphela's candidacy. The proposal was that we should announce a joint roadshow that would take us around South Africa to set out our vision for the future.

She had no time to talk further, she said, because she had to be at F.W. de Klerk's dinner. I said our media director, Gavin Davis, would draft a statement overnight and meet her at seven the next morning to clear it with her. That would enable me to receive the letter by email when I landed in George, so that I could read it before my interview.

With a wave of her immaculately manicured hand, complete with fire-engine red nails, Mamphela replied: 'I don't do meetings at seven in the morning.'

I had long since stopped being polite. 'I don't care what you do or don't do,'

I said. 'I must receive that statement by eight o'clock tomorrow morning when I land in George.'

She wafted out, on a vapour trail of Oscar de la Renta perfume. As her vehicle purred down the drive, the DA contingent stared at each other blankly. We agreed that Jonathan Moakes and Wilmot James would take responsibility for liaising with Mamphela the next morning, to get agreement on a joint statement, which Gavin would compile overnight.

That night, in a flurry of SMSes, they tried to ensure that they could clear the statement with Mamphela in time for my eight o'clock interview, but she was resolute. She would not meet them that early in the morning. So when I landed in George there was no statement, which meant I had to waffle my way through the *Carte Blanche* interview. I was beyond incensed.

On my way to Mossel Bay from George, I got a call from Jonathan at 9:30 a.m. to say that the statement had at last been fully and finally agreed and signed off by Mamphela. It said we were forming one organisation, the DA, and that we would embark on a roadshow to set out our vision to the country. I was totally exhausted at the laborious process of bringing her on board, inch by painful inch, as if she was doing us a huge favour.

About two hours later I received a call from Mamphela. She was in a total frenzy. I could not hold my phone anywhere near my ear, she was shouting so loudly. The DA had deceived her, she screamed. 'In what way?' I asked. She then accused us of putting out a press statement that was different from the one she had agreed to. I did not know what she was talking about, but I said I would find out and call her back.

I phoned Gavin and asked whether they had put out anything other than the statement to which Mamphela had agreed. He said no. It was exactly the same statement that Mamphela had signed off with Jonathan and Wilmot that morning. I asked Jonathan to double-check that there hadn't perhaps been a mistake. He confirmed that the correct statement, approved by Mamphela, had gone out. I asked Gavin to phone Andrew Gasnolar (Mamphela's aide) to clear up the confusion. Andrew referred him to the website of the *Citizen* newspaper, where there was an article a journalist had written, based on the press statement.

Of course, it was not a verbatim version of the statement. No journalist writes a report parroting a press statement word for word. They highlight what they consider to be the important parts and analyse the implications. I soon realised that Mamphela had confused the statement with the article based on the statement, but I could not bring her to see reason. She refused to believe we had not deliberately betrayed her. After those two conversations, I concluded that Mamphela had finally cracked under the pressure.

As I put the phone down, I decided that this ill-fated venture had to end, whatever the cost. I cancelled my weekend appointments in the Southern Cape and asked my colleagues in the negotiating team to meet me at Leeuwenhof the next day, 1 February, at 10 a.m. I said to them: 'The only question now is how to end it.' Amazingly, we still did not all agree on this. But by that stage I was absolutely resolute. We had to draw a line. 'There is no other question on the table now, except how to end this,' I repeated.

Mamphela had gone to Johannesburg to meet her members once more. We agreed we would fly up and meet her there with Daniel. We would put a DA membership card in front of her and ask her to sign it. Then we would ask her to confirm the terms of reference of the task team that would integrate members of Agang into the DA.

I doubted she would accept. And if she didn't, it would all be over. And she would not be able to point a finger at us.

We arranged the meeting for Sunday night, 2 February, in Johannesburg. I arrived with two of my colleagues, Wilmot (our federal chairman) and Jonathan (our chief executive officer), and she came with two of hers. I got the impression that they were there to monitor her rather than support her. It was immediately obvious that there was no buy-in from Agang for the agreement Mamphela had reached with the DA. With us on one side and her Agang colleagues on the other, she had no more room to manoeuvre.

It soon became absolutely clear that we were on a hiding to nothing. We did not even get to the point of putting the documents in front of her before we agreed there was nothing left to salvage.

The DA moved quickly to put out a statement that night about the latest developments, and we called a press conference the next day. Mamphela did the same.

I acknowledged that the DA's offer to Mamphela had been a mistake, for which I accepted responsibility. I said it was often essential to take risks in politics. Some succeeded. Others, like our venture to incorporate Agang, had failed. I added that well-intentioned mistakes were seldom fatal in politics, just as success was never permanent. The DA had acted in good faith and would have to move on. Lindiwe, Wilmot and Mmusi were part of the DA's panel and we presented a united front to the media.

My real worry, which I did not express, was the extent to which the DA was obviously still regarded as a political leper by so many prominent black South Africans who actually shared our values. Why were we so 'untouchable'? Why was it so difficult for us to become the logical alternative to the ANC? What did this divide mean for the prospects of non-racialism in South Africa? Why couldn't we focus on shared values?

After the 'plane crash' in parliament during the previous term, followed so closely by the Mamphela debacle, I was more anxious than ever about where the DA's future leadership would be drawn from. Not to mention our electoral prospects.

There was no alternative but to 'keep on keeping on', as Helen Suzman would have said. Or KBO (keep buggering on), as Winston Churchill put it slightly more colourfully.

Mamphela was having an even harder time than I was. I knew she knew she was sinking, but I had stopped caring. I also knew she knew what would have been best for South Africa.

She had just not been able to muster the courage to do it.

After Mamphela's announcement of our failed initiative, she told a journalist that she had been 'forced' into the DA relationship by a donor who had facilitated the process. The press went into a frenzy of speculation. One newspaper pointed a finger at businessman Natie Kirsh, originally from Tlokwe and now based in the United States. This speculation was 100 per cent wrong.

Daniel, however, got a fright and drafted a 'holding' statement (in case Mamphela said anything further). In it he explained that he had been approached by the 'DA leadership' to assist in getting the DA and Mamphela together. He had done so, with the background assistance of a donor.

He sent the holding statement to me, requesting my comment. I was puzzled and wrote back saying it was inaccurate. I had not approached him, nor was I aware of anyone in the DA leadership who had. On the contrary, he had approached me unexpectedly in January.

Not so, he replied, in an email copied to Lindiwe and Wilmot. He insisted it was 'entirely accurate' to say the DA had approached him.

He suggested I speak to Lindiwe about an approach she had made in December, over a lunch and later in a telephone conversation after speaking to Mamphela. That was where the approach to me originated. Daniel had also discussed the matter at length with Wilmot over lunch a week later.

I was astonished to learn about this background. As far as I was concerned, Daniel's call to me in January had come completely out of the blue. I had no idea of the lead-up, nor the involvement of other DA leaders behind the scenes.

I joined the dots. Mamphela had set up separate channels of negotiation with my colleagues, who then took the initiative further, before Daniel approached me.

Things would have been so much easier, I thought to myself, had we all just played open cards with one another. When and from where had this 'secret manoeuvre' culture become a feature of the DA, I asked myself. In complex situations it was absolutely essential for me to be aware of all the nuances, undercurrents and connections. I expressed my discomfort to Lindiwe and Wilmot and pointed this out to them. It was vital that I knew what was going on behind the scenes so that I was in a position to make informed judgements in complex situations.

On 5 February 2014 Lindiwe replied:

Hi Helen,
I should have kept you posted, you're absolutely right. I apologise for the oversight. We were all sceptical about Mamphela's approach, but that's why I thought it would be great for someone like [Daniel] to talk some sense into her.
Warm regards,
Lindiwe

Wilmot had at least kept me briefed in detail after his discussions with Mamphela (even though he had not told me about his discussion with Daniel). Wilmot had also given the prospects of success a 'thumbs-down' after leading our discussions with Mamphela on the night of 25 January.

I accepted that they had both acted in good faith, even if I was surprised Lindiwe had told me nothing. The wall separating us was obviously still there, despite us having ostensibly worked so closely together through the latest drama.

I wrote a final letter to Daniel, saying that while I had to accept responsibility for my own decisions, including the Mamphela mess, I felt let down at the extent to which I had tried to accommodate everyone's demands and was left carrying the can on my own in the end.

He replied, saying he assumed that everything had been happening with my knowledge. After some complimentary comments about my decisiveness in cauterising the mess, and the way that I had managed the situation, he repeated a suggestion that he said he had received from 'several sources': 'Use the moment to pass the presidential contender baton to the next generation.'

This indicated just how fast the leadership succession battle in the DA was gathering momentum, and gave me the idea that the Mamphela manoeuvre may have been connected to it in unanticipated ways, which were open to multiple interpretations. I was unsurprised to learn later that David Maynier had also been in contact with Daniel, and I had no doubt it was to draw him into the succession strategy.

Looking back, and knowing what subsequently transpired, one interpretation rises above the rest. By the end of 2013, Lindiwe knew she would not be re-elected as caucus leader after the election. She had already (unbeknown to me) decided to bow out for a while. The election of Mamphela as the presidential candidate and then caucus leader would enable Lindiwe to withdraw without losing face, and set her up for a later return. Mamphela, who would be almost sixty-seven when elected, would in all likelihood only be a one-term caucus leader.

This strategy was clearly far preferable to the alternative of staying on and being beaten in the caucus leadership by a young competitor in the party's federal leadership succession stakes. The 'Mamphela option' was the best way of avoiding this. Once all the information emerged, it certainly looked like one of the military moves her inner circle was prone to.

But back then, I merely assumed that everyone had been acting in good faith, and I did not interrogate anyone's motives. There was no time for this kind of thing. We had an election to run.

As far as I knew then, Lindiwe was still running for another term. In fact, she topped our national list, while I kept my options open about returning to parliament.

I had known all along that I might have to do so, but I was increasingly reluctant to. Despite all the peripheral political drama, I was deeply invested in the project of building a 'capable state' in the Western Cape, where the DA governed, and I was loving every minute of the challenge (as opposed to the Machiavellian machinations of party politics, which I disliked more and more). Our efforts in government were starting to bear fruit, and I passionately wanted to continue.

I also knew that after the election, Julius Malema and his red brigade would have a contingent in parliament, and would use the platform to generate as much sound and fury as possible. It seemed to me strategically unwise to be positioning me, a sixty-three-year-old white woman, as the voice of an alternative opposition force on the parliamentary platform, against Malema. A sixty-seven-year-old black struggle icon would have been another matter entirely, and would have provided an excellent counterfoil to the young populist. But with Mamphela out of the running, we needed a strong, young voice, preferably black, to lead our charge in parliament. I was much more suited to the role of building viable state institutions where the DA governed.

Mmusi Maimane's name kept coming up. He was both on the Gauteng list as our candidate for premier and on the national list to come to parliament. Our critics, led by Gareth van Onselen, made a big deal of what they described as this ambivalence. Were we admitting that we could not win Gauteng? Was Mmusi being groomed behind the scenes for the parliamentary leadership?

I was torn. I had enormous respect for Mmusi, who was a natural, but I was also acutely aware that Lindiwe had not been well served by such a rapid rise to the top slot in parliament, a premature move that had undoubtedly set back her career. I did not want this to happen to a second highly talented young politician.

But our first order of business was to do as well as possible in the election; and we had to compete in an arena with not one new high-profile opposition party, but two!

Then came another blow. Lindiwe announced that she would not be available to work in the election campaign, because she was required to have surgery. Wilmot James issued a statement on her behalf.

It is always difficult to perform optimally with a key player off the field, but I recalled that I had required urgent surgery in the run-up to the 2004 election, so I was as supportive as possible.

We hit the campaign trail, where only adrenalin kept me going. Our election timetable required me to 'do' up to seven events per day across three provinces. It would turn out to be my last general election as leader, and I gave it my all. Five years earlier, in the general election of 2009, we had won 16.6 per cent of the vote, a 34 per cent increase over 2004. We just had to keep the arrow moving upwards. And we could not have had a worse start to our election campaign. We had a lot of catching up to do.

20

Setting the Record Straight

THE YEAR 2014 was a big year, personally and politically. It marked my last election as DA leader and my first wedding as a mother.

My son Paul's wonderful girlfriend Gretl had accepted his proposal when, after a tough hike, they reached the summit of Devil's Peak, which flanks Table Mountain.

They arrived back at Leeuwenhof later that afternoon, in shorts and hiking boots, to show us the single black diamond set in platinum that looked beautiful on Gretl's unadorned, straight-fingered hand. We were delighted. Both teachers, they had met as colleagues at Westerford High School in Cape Town, and together they made a great combination of practical, down-to-earth values and intelligent idealism.

That evening, over supper, I asked Johann whether he could remember his proposal to me. I could immediately see the look in his eyes (half blank, half panic) as he scoured his memory for any hint of where we might have been and what he might have said. It was obvious he had no clue.

'I'll give you a hint,' I said. 'It was near that square in town.' (I couldn't immediately recall the name of Dunkley Square.)

'Oh, yes, Greenmarket Square!' he proclaimed in a tone that told me he was clutching at straws.

'No,' I said. 'When you're in a hole, stop digging!'

I reminded him that we had been sitting outside a restaurant near Dunkley Square having a drink when he asked me to marry him. He didn't produce a ring. We would have wedding bands when we married, he said. It was unnecessary to have two rings.

Johann admitted he had absolutely no recollection of this rather important milestone in our lives. On the other hand, he vividly remembered the moment he decided he wanted to marry me. What followed, he said, was just formality and ritual. We had had a simple wedding.

So I was excited that Gretl and Paul chose to have the real deal at Leeuwenhof. We wanted to make it unforgettable for them. Gretl requested white flowers in the garden, and Joey Napo, the head gardener, and 'Doepie' du Plessis, her deputy, obliged. Everything was white, from the pansies to the petunias and even the cosmos, all in bloom in time for the big day. (The garden indigenisation project that we had initiated when we arrived at Leeuwenhof had not yet managed to make its way through the government's procurement system, so we were still working through the standard supply of petunias and pansies, five years later.)

The combination of the wedding and the election gave me a good excuse not to participate in that year's Cape Town Cycle Tour – I just did not have the time to put in the necessary training. I had done it the year before, and that was enough. In any event, toyi-toying throughout the election campaign gave me all the exercise I needed.

It was relatively easy to plan for the wedding because Paul and Gretl were living in one of the cottages at Leeuwenhof, the result of an unanticipated family rift – occasioned by our dogs.

As with most major family rifts, this one started in childhood (the dogs', not ours).

And, as with most family rifts, it has a long and complex back story.

The boys had wanted a dog since they were very young, and I had always said no. I knew I could not accommodate an extra sentient being in our lives. Dogs need love and care, bathing, feeding, good company and regular exercise. I couldn't guarantee these things; I was away too often. So I set a test for the boys to pass. We put bird baths in the garden. If they could keep them stocked with seed and water on a daily basis for three months, I would be convinced that they had developed the responsibility and reliability required to look after a pet. If they didn't look after the bird baths, I said, the birds in the air could fly away and look for food and water elsewhere. But a pet had nowhere else to go. It had to be looked after at home, by them.

Whenever I arrived home, I would go straight to check on the bird baths. Sometimes the boys came perilously close to achieving a three-month uninterrupted record of regular bird-bath maintenance, but always (fortunately) they just fell short. If I arrived home to soiled water or old birdseed, they would be disqualified and had to start again.

I thought I had perhaps overdone things a bit when Paul, aged eight and in Grade 3, woke me up at about three in the morning on the first Sunday of the July school holidays to say he had forgotten to feed the fish. It turned out that his teacher, Mrs Lowenherz, had given him the responsibility of feeding the fish in their class's fish tank during the school holidays, and they had not been fed since school closed on Friday. I told him fish did not need to be fed every day. He did not believe me, but, after he shed a few tears over the poor hungry fish, I managed to get him back to sleep. At eight o'clock on that Sunday morning, we had to track down the school caretaker to open the classroom so that Paul could fulfil his duties. I could see the relief on his face when we opened the door to the sight of the fish swimming around, seemingly unperturbed by forty-eight hours of non-feeding. My biggest battle for the rest of the holiday was to not overfeed the fish.

Eventually I relented on the home front and said the boys could have a hamster. In fact, they could have one each, as long as they were the same sex. I did not want to have baby hamsters every six weeks. I took them to the pet shop and they bought two hamsters which the salesman swore were both male. Six weeks later, we had a litter of tiny hamsters. Aaaaaaagh!

About a week after the hamsters were born, I had to make a speech at an event, at a rather smart venue. Johann, unusually, was with me. In the pre-cellphone era, we always left a contact number with Grace, in case she needed to call us. Suddenly a person appeared in the hall and called me out, saying Grace was on the telephone wanting to speak to me personally. I ran to the phone. Grace put Tom on the line. Between Tom's sobs, I managed to work out that they had put the hamsters on the eiderdown, to play, and when the time came to put them back into the cage with the mommy hamster, one had gone missing. Crisis.

We excused ourselves from the event and drove home, only to find (needless to say) that they had found the missing hamster and all was well with the world again. This was exactly the kind of disruption that I knew pets would inevitably bring to our lives, but I also understood that the boys needed pets to develop the capacity for care and bonding they had shown with their hamsters that night.

I also used the hamsters to teach the boys some life lessons. For example, when we separated the hamsters (not wanting any more babies), the male would do whatever it took to get to the female hamster to mate with her. He was a veritable Houdini the way he could get out of any space to fulfil his sexual instinct. The female hamster was obliging, until her babies were born – after which she wanted absolutely nothing to do with her man. He did not dare go near her while she nursed her babies. I told the boys, in appropriately accessible language, that they could learn a lot from hamsters about the difference between the roles of the X and Y chromosomes in the evolution of the species.

After the ordeal of the hamsters, Johann was ready to relent on a dog. He thought it would be a better reflection on males. He was wrong.

We had fallen in love with the brindle Staffordshire terrier featured in a TV commercial for tyres. The commercial featured the stocky dog winning a long obstacle race against sleek, pedigreed greyhounds. The Staffie won because of his dogged determination and capacity to overcome any challenge. I liked his style. (The commercial sold us on the dog, not the tyres.) So we all agreed it would be a Staffie. We got the runt of the litter of a super thoroughbred, whose brain seemed to have been bred out of his system. We called him Murphy (he of the pork roll ...). The boys showered him with love, but Murphy had two fundamental incapacities: (1) knowing when he had eaten enough and (2) understanding that our house was his home. We thought that love would conquer all, but his runaway instinct proved too powerful. We got him back a few times, but on the final occasion when he sprinted out of the opening gate, as if racing greyhounds to the finishing line, we couldn't track him down again. Heartbreak. Another lesson learnt: no more thoroughbreds.

To fill the void, we decided to go to the SPCA to find an abandoned dog to take home as our pet. The boys were beyond excited at the prospect. They hardly slept the night before the big day of our visit to the SPCA. There we saw a friendly pavement special whose sparkling personality compensated for her extraordinary appearance (huge ears, tiny body, long hair and two protruding teeth). As usually happens in these circumstances, the dog chooses its owners. When she saw the boys she became so excited that they bonded with her instantly. We expected to pay our dues and take her home, then and there.

Not so. The SPCA said they would have to come and see whether we were 'fit and proper' to own this little abandoned dog. The boys' disappointment at having to leave without their pet was aggravated by her obvious dejection at seeing us go. I explained that this was an indication of how serious it was to own a dog. We had to prove we were worthy. The SPCA would come to check.

On the appointed day, the inspector arrived, with epaulettes on his uniform and a clipboard on his arm. I had told the boys that they would have to be on their best behaviour to pass this test, and they were exemplary. The man with the epaulettes and the clipboard went through the tick-box checklist with me and Johann as he inspected our premises. He even interviewed Grace. Then he left. We had no doubt that we were fit and proper to own an abandoned dog.

About a week later, we received a letter in the post.

'Dear Dr and Mrs Maree,

'We regret to inform you that your application for the dog was unsuccessful...'

I could hardly believe it. Johann and I had had two children without having to pass a 'fit and proper' parenthood test, and here we were being rejected as owners of a stray dog. It was a serious blow to our self-esteem.

I quickly scanned the rest of the letter to find out why. It turned out that the inspector had discovered a tiny hole in our fence. Once we had fixed that hole, he said, he would re-inspect the premises. I had to break this news to the boys, but again it was a good life lesson. They got going and helped their dad fix the fence. The same day we called the SPCA and asked them to send the inspector again. Our home was now ready for the dog.

Mr SPCA duly arrived, with his clipboard, and pronounced on the spot that we had passed! We went and picked up our dog, who seemed overjoyed to see us. The boys called her Allie. But Allie's primary bond was with Johann. She became his shadow. She slept next to his bed on a rug, and when Johann went to the toilet in the middle of the night, Allie would follow. Every time she heard Johann's voice, her disproportionately long tail would wag furiously.

Allie died a sad death when, during a long walk, we took her off the leash at a stopping point so that she could run around while we rested under a tree. She always stayed close by, but this time she darted off after a squirrel into a road and was hit by a car. Tears, trauma, guilt, and our first family funeral in the garden.

No more pets, I said firmly. In any event, I would have been embarrassed to return to the SPCA under the circumstances.

In matric, all Tom wanted was a 'proper' dog. By that, he meant Big. And so Kaizer, the Rottweiler puppy, entered our lives. Paul was already at university and both boys bonded with Kaizer, but he was primarily Tom's dog. When Tom was offered a scholarship to do a postgraduate year at Rhodes, he said he would accept only on condition Kaizer went too. I sent him off to Grahamstown to find appropriate dog digs. Tom found a room in a house full of dog-loving students, where Kaizer made firm friends with a dachshund called Eugene.

Paul, who had stayed behind at home, pined for Kaizer, so he got himself another Rottweiler puppy. I wanted to call him Bismarck, but Paul thought that was tempting fate. And, as it turned out, fate did not require any more tempting. Tom returned with Kaizer and met the puppy, Panza. They got on fine, until Panza's testosterone kicked in. Then it was open warfare. The two male Rottweilers had only one aim in life: to obliterate each other. They almost obliterated my sons, trying to separate two fighting Rottweilers.

We tried everything. Panza, a prime specimen, was neutered. We separated our smallish garden into two sections but, like the male hamster, the dogs worked out ways of getting to each other, but for the purpose of annihilation rather than copulation. The two poles of the Y chromosome.

We got books from the library and strategies from the internet. After everything else had failed, we called in the dog whisperers, and psychologists, who said that, because the dogs were males, they were trying to establish a hierarchical relationship to see, literally, who was top dog. The dogs had to understand that the humans were in charge, and our sons learnt several methods of conveying this.

The canine Y chromosome trumped every strategy, however. There was no option. One of the dogs would have to move to Leeuwenhof (with his owner). The other would have to stay in our family home (with his owner). As I had feared, the dogs were dictating the course of our lives. Tom and Kaizer stayed in the family home. Panza moved, with Paul and his fiancée Gretl, to a cottage on the Leeuwenhof estate, which required some modification of a fence and a gate to give the dog adequate space to exercise without unleashing a reign of terror among the squirrels, guinea fowl and Egyptian geese on the property. Grace had just had a little girl, NgoweNceba, and the huge, terrifying Rottweiler fell in love with this baby and protected her against all comers. It was delightful to see this enormous dog care for this tiny child, when almost everyone else was terrified of him. NgoweNceba would toddle around Leeuwenhof with Panza staying faithfully at her side. Occasionally, he would stop to lick her lovingly all over, and she, in a real little-girl way, would shout 'Sies!' at the top of her voice. He would then wag his long (undocked) tail, which was powerful enough to knock her over.

It proved convenient to have Paul and Gretl at Leeuwenhof as we planned the wedding. I was exempt from most duties due to the election campaign. In fact, the DA was ambivalent about giving me the wedding day off at all – it didn't fit our detailed election grid!

Janine, who understood every fashion protocol ever invented, said she would organise an outfit for me. The rule for the Mother of the Bridegroom, she stressed, is: 'Wear beige and zip your lip.' I duly complied. Janine's word on fashion and etiquette was law.

Family came from around the world, as the diaspora tends to do when we have a big family occasion. Mom, unfortunately, was not well enough to get out of bed for long, let alone take a flight, but we sent her a video. And, of course, she got a letter from me with a blow-by-blow account of the big day.

I just remember the good bits, but when I reread the letters I wrote to Mom, I realise how absolutely frantic life was behind the scenes.

Take a week in February, a month before the wedding. It started on the weekend of 15–16 February 2014 with the DA's Federal Council in Cape Town, where I explained the background to the Mamphela debacle and apologised to the party for my misjudgement of the situation. On the Sunday evening I had to attend a community meeting at a stalled housing project in the shack settlement of Boys' Town, near Cape Town airport, in my capacity as premier. The provincial government was losing hundreds of thousands of rands a month in penalties because the contractor could not continue on the job, given the extent of community conflict. After that I had dinner with visiting international guests.

The three days that followed included (among other things) press conferences, detailed feedback from focus groups in preparation for the election, recording DA election advertisements in English, Afrikaans and Xhosa, meetings with the province's Forensic Investigative Unit to address allegations of corruption, a housing handover, diplomatic receptions, a provincial cabinet meeting, discussions with representatives of organised agriculture, and intensive preparations for the State of the Province Address (SOPA) – the most important speech of my year. SOPA was scheduled for Friday 21 February, after which I had to immediately fly off to Johannesburg for a fundraising dinner that night. On Saturday 22 February, I would campaign in Gauteng before our manifesto launch on Sunday 23 February in Polokwane, Limpopo.

Diary entries reveal only the tip of the iceberg of the work required. Most meetings require preparation time, which often involves extensive reading, as well as subsequent follow-up work.

Sandwiched in between these commitments was the national caucus meeting of Thursday 20 February. It dealt with no fewer than sixteen bills, and I wondered anew how this legislative gridlock had occurred. Some of the bills were highly contentious and ideally framed for the ANC to reinforce false stereotypes of the DA in the run-up to an election.

After the legislative plane crash on the Employment Equity Amendment Bill, I was super vigilant, despite the resistance I still got from the caucus leadership against my perceived 'interference'. We had a near miss when our recently appointed shadow minister of land reform had inserted two paragraphs into the web-based version of our policy without going through the prescribed policy process. It resulted in our taking a position on a bill that would predictably have had profoundly negative consequences for every constituency in this complex debate, and would solve none of the real underlying problems of the government's slow, ineffective and unproductive land-reform programme. I wondered how this lapse in our carefully defined policy process (and revamped caucus systems) could have occurred, but did not openly verbalise my concern. The situation was too fragile. We discussed the need for amendments to the bill in the caucus.

At 1 p.m., the scheduled ending time of the caucus, I had to leave because I had other commitments. Fortunately, we had dealt with the most contentious bills. The MPs remained behind to discuss the rest. Proposed amendments had to be submitted the next morning, Friday 21 February (which was also the day of my SOPA).

On the Friday morning I worked through the final details of the SOPA, while Janine dolled me up.

I assumed that the national caucus would have finalised and submitted the amendments by the deadline.

After the SOPA, I flew to Johannesburg to start my next round of commitments, culminating in our biggest yet outdoor rally, scheduled for Sunday 23 February in Polokwane, when we were to launch our election manifesto.

Early on Sunday morning, I was working on my final speech in the guest house when a decree landed. It involved a change of wardrobe. Janine had decided I would wear blue for the event, but Shaun, the czar of DA event logistics, overruled her. He said if I wore blue it would disappear against the blue background. I had to be dressed in white from the waist up. That would frame well against the background. So that morning Janine rushed out into Polokwane to get me a new outfit that complied with Shaun's requirements. She came back with a tight, stretchy blue skirt and white jacket, and the highest blue high heels I had ever seen.

I was terrified. I hate wearing skirts, especially tight ones, because my legs, thighs and rear are not my best physical features. But Janine vehemently disagreed and was determined to get me into that outfit. I fought back, imagining myself on live television, hobbling in those heels down the long ramp, surrounded by people on every side, making my way towards a bulb-shaped platform at the end, from which I would deliver my speech to the surround-crowd.

I shuddered at the prospect of that stretch fabric finding traction with the pantyhose and creeping up my thighs as I attempted the obligatory toyi-toyi. And I winced when I thought of the vantage point of the cameras, stationed on the ground below. 'No,' I said, firmly.

Janine ignored me, in the way she did when she wanted to let me know that I would not get in the way of her doing the job she was paid for. 'I'm serious,' I said, trying to get her to pay attention. 'No! In other words, Nee, Hayibo, Nein, Nooit, Nyet, Non, Aikona, Hapana. I am not wearing that skirt – or those shoes!'

I still can't recall how she got me into them, but not long afterwards I found myself teetering down the ramp on what felt like stilts, my ample loins girded in blue stretch acrylic. I walked straight into a nightmare.

The event's organising committee had decreed that I had to deliver sections of my speech in Sepedi (as well as English, Afrikaans and Xhosa) to cater for both the local crowd and the television audience. And we were experimenting, for the first time, with strategically placed screens on the ground, serving as teleprompters from which I would read my speech. To the live television audience, it would look as if I was speaking directly to the crowd (and to the camera) without using notes at all.

But I kept my written speech on the podium, in case things went wrong. I come from the generation that does not entrust its fate entirely to technology. 'To err is human – but to mess things up completely takes a computer,' we always said.

It was a blistering hot day in mid-summer. As often happens at such events, the protocol requires a far-too-long speakers' list, which means the programme seems endless to the live audience gathered at the venue. Unlike the television audience, they can't pop to the fridge for a beer during an ad break.

The leader always has to speak last, when everyone in the crowd is thirsty, restless and exhausted.

Every politician knows that the key to a good speech is reading your audience and connecting with them. At a rally, the distance between the speaker and much of the crowd creates a particularly challenging context, severely exacerbated by what is known as the 'multiple audiences' problem. When a manifesto launch speech is being broadcast live, the millions of potential TV viewers have to take precedence over the 12 000 present at the rally.

The two audiences could not be more different. Most of the people at the rally want a celebration of song, dance, aphorisms and slogans. The TV viewers are not a homogenous group. Apart from those who keep the television going constantly, for background noise, there are the commentators and armchair politicians who want to hear what you have to say about policy before they pick it apart. The sceptics look for opportunities to dis politicians. And your opponents are waiting for something to go wrong, preferably a phrase in a speech, that they can bring back to haunt you.

By the time I stepped onto the ramp, the audience was wilting. I was amazed they still had some cheering, singing and sloganeering left in them.

They surged forward, flattening the barriers around the large screens from which I was to read my speech, finding a convenient open space to toyi-toyi right in front of them. I hoped someone would notice that I would not be able to start my speech until I could see the screens. After a while, I was getting desperate. I could hardly wave people out of the way on live television. That would have launched a thousand 'madam' memes.

I tried to disguise my waving arms as part of my a-rhythmical dance moves, until Geordin and Alex Christians got the message and started moving people out of the way of the screens. Someone also rushed up and put an open bottle of water on the podium, on top of my manifesto.

At last the space in front of the screens was cleared and I squinted into them. We had not anticipated the impact of the sun's glare bouncing back into my astigmatic, light-sensitive eyes. I could, at most, discern two or three lines on the screen, where the glare was less intense. That was manageable as long as I was speaking English. I had read the speech several times and individual lines served as a sufficient prompt for me to ad-lib the rest; I just hoped that the person operating the teleprompter would be able to intuit when to scroll down. When it came to the other languages, however, it was virtually impossible to manage without stumbling over the words, especially those I needed to read, syllable by syllable, phonetically. Now and again, a stray cloud would drift over the sun, making it easier to read the text on the screen. I prayed for rain to end the ordeal.

At moments like that I always remembered Mom telling me that Ronald Reagan provided the ideal role model for politicians in a sticky situation. Ronnie, said Mom, rarely had any idea what was going on, but always managed to look as if he was on top of the situation.

So I tried to look casual, as if everything was unfolding as planned. The last moisture in my body rushed to the aid of my burning eyes, and misted up my glasses. A frog was growing in my throat.

At some prearranged point, I was supposed to whip out the manifesto from under the podium and hold it up to the cameras. As I pulled it out, roughly on cue, the open water bottle overturned, gushing all over my leg and foot. I knew

I would need water to make it to the end of my speech, so in mid-sentence, on national television, I bent down to save some before it had all drained away. Because my eyes were watering, my nose also started running, and I tried to work out how to get the tissue out of my bra, where I usually kept it. (I should have anticipated in advance that this might pose a problem on live TV.)

I sniffed and ploughed on. I don't know whether the crowd was more dazed by the heat or by the dense policy speech. They started streaming out of the venue. I had visions of myself speaking to an abandoned field, with only blue plastic chairs and litter, captured by the television cameras to broadcast into millions of homes or put on an endless loop on every newscast.

One of the great disadvantages of a teleprompter is that it removes the speaker's flexibility to skip sections of a speech, or introduce new themes to fit the situation. You just have to keep going, as the screen scrolls down, regardless of the mood of the crowd.

I battled on to the end, with perspiration exuding from every pore, and 75 per cent of the crowd fortunately still left on the field. I have never been more relieved to hear the explosion of the confetti gun signalling the end of the event. The blue paper drizzled down like rain. As the confetti connected with my skin, the blue crêpe felt like real droplets. I was drenched from the ordeal.

When I got to the airport in Johannesburg to fly back to Cape Town I saw a Sunday newspaper with a headline saying that our manifesto had not mentioned our land policy. I knew that was total nonsense because I had written the four-page section myself. I blew a fuse, sick and tired of the ease with which political commentators could so easily dismiss months of work, and nauseated by their cynical superficiality, lack of accountability and personal agendas masquerading as analysis. I had to remind myself, for the umpteenth time, that the advantages of a free press always outweigh the disadvantages. But I was also entitled to that freedom. So I let rip on Twitter.

I understood what had happened. The mix-up during the previous week over our response to yet another botched bill had necessitated the production of an explanatory caucus memorandum that was leaked to the newspaper. Inevitably, on the weekend of our manifesto launch, their report focused on our leaked memorandum instead of our manifesto that had been months in the making. Once more the problems of the caucus were impacting on the party and derailing the broader project. But I also accepted that I should not have reacted so vehemently. I had reached the end of my tether.

When I got back to Cape Town on the Sunday night, I realised I'd better check up to find out what had happened to the legislative amendments on the Land Bill, only to learn that they had not been finalised. I was told there was nothing to worry about, as the deadline had been extended to 7:30 on Monday morning.

But no one could send me so much as a draft of our proposed amendments. So I got up at 3:00 the next morning, downloaded the bill from the internet, and began to draft additional amendments for submission by the extended deadline at 7:30. I could not get hold of our shadow minister, so I sent the amendments to his deputy early that morning, and asked him to make sure they were delivered on time, to the office of the secretary of parliament. But he waited for another caucus meeting to be convened, later that morning, which meant we missed the extended deadline as well. Finally, we were granted an extension on the extension, and allowed to submit amendments at 12:30 p.m. It was a very close call, as the debate on the bill was scheduled for the next day. I knew we could not continue managing legislation in this way.

Apart from the land debate in the national parliament, Tuesday 25 February was also the debate on my SOPA. The debate continued all afternoon, and during the supper break I prepared my reply, which I delivered later that night. By definition it was largely an impromptu speech, which was to be broadcast on television and inevitably got a lot of adrenalin pumping through my system.

When I arrived home later that night, I made enquiries about the debate in the national parliament, and was informed that things had gone as planned. I was relieved.

The adrenalin kept flowing as we combined the campaign with the final wedding preparations. When the big day for Gretl and Paul dawned, we did not have the spectacular weather for an outdoor wedding we'd been hoping for, but a bit of rain, in the African tradition, is a sign of good fortune. It did not spoil our fun. Thomas and Chulumanco were best men, and Megan, Gretl's sister, the bridesmaid, and little NgoweNceba, with Gretl's young nieces, were flower girls. Panza was the ring-bearer. Johann delivered the sermon, and Gretl's dad Christo completed the legal requirements. The photographer, Jilda G, made great use of the 360-degree panorama from the Leeuwenhof roof, which was dramatic, even in light mist. Paul, joined by his schoolfriends, played the music for part of the evening, while Tom directed proceedings as a rousing and amusing master of ceremonies.

It was a veritable family fest.

Then it was back to the last gruelling weeks of the campaign. April passed in a blur of commitments and remote-control management of the province, through my excellent team.

Over Easter I had an invitation to go visit Moria in Limpopo, to experience the annual pilgrimage of members of the Zion Christian Church. I had always been interested in this ritual, which my agnostic father used to speak to us about every Easter. The Zion Christian Church was the largest in the country, Dad explained, and played a major role in the fabric of society.

Every Easter I read about this remarkable pilgrimage and was determined to accept this opportunity to witness this spectacle myself.

I wrote to Mom about it. She said it was her favourite letter and read it over and over again, so I am quoting most of it.

> I have always had a very soft spot for the ZCC because of the man (from the Star branch of the church) who saved my life in Alexandra, many years ago, when I hit someone's dog that ran into the road. The dog was alive, and not seriously injured, but the intoxicated dog-owner was furious and caused a major ruction in the street, and many people gathered and the scene started to get very tense. I was trying to get the message across that I would take the dog to the vet with the owner and pay for the consultation, but the people were having none of it, and temperatures were rising. Then out of the crowd stepped a man with a ZCC star on his green badge, and calmed the situation down, got into the car with me and the intoxicated man and his dog and off we went to the vet. The dog was fine (just a bit bruised) and it all ended up happily. But I felt as if my life had been personally touched by the ZCC.
>
> I also remember dad telling us as children about the sheer scale of the Church's gathering at Moria at Easter. So when the invitation came, I seized it. I was invited with Dr Tutu Faleni of the DA in the North West province.
>
> We flew in a charter flight to Lanseria and then to Polokwane and drove the rest of the way to Moria. I was wearing a blue and white church outfit that I borrowed from Grace [our domestic helper who had a range of churchwear]. On the way one of the women protectors told me my hair had to be completely covered – no strand in sight, and I was wearing a blue beret which clearly would not do. So luckily I had this weird sleeve-like blue DA brand item with me, and I turned it inside out, covered my hair entirely and put the beret on top in an interesting tilted arrangement. It actually looked quite stylish, as if I had planned it that way. And there was not a hair in sight!
>
> Arriving in Moria was an experience I will never forget. After winding through the distinctive rock formations and vegetation of the area, one comes around a corner on a hill to look down upon more buses in one place than one has ever seen before, neatly parked alongside each other on both sides of a vast open space. Buses stretching as far as the eye can see. It takes 15 minutes driving in the car to get past them all. And between the two bus parking areas, a vast space with more assembled people than I have ever seen. Only in photographs of Haj at Mecca have I ever seen anything comparable.
>
> Our driver drove us straight to the VIP entrance, where we had been told to arrive punctually, at our allotted time of 12h00 noon. No traffic jams. Everything went smoothly. In we sailed, got out onto a red carpet at the reception

centre. I had to take off my glasses and get a liberal sprinkling of holy water before being allowed to go in to register. There the registration process proceeded extremely smoothly. My photograph had to be taken, and stored with all my details.

Then we went off to the holding area, which entailed a short drive through a lined 'road' with a full guard of honour of hundreds of men dressed in the ZCC khaki with the distinctive badge. Then we drove up to another red carpet and got out to be whisked into a holding area where there were cool-drinks and seats so that we could wait for the scheduled start of the service at 14h00. I saw a whole lot of Cabinet Ministers, representatives of COPE and other VIPs that I recognised. We had a pleasant chat, until the Bishop Lekganyane's envoy asked me if I wanted a view from the roof. Yes, I said, and we climbed onto the roof, with its huge dome.

Well, Mom, I cannot describe it to you. You have a 270 degree view (trees block the rest) but in the range I could see, it was just people to the horizon on all sides. But not just a mass. People totally orderly arranged in blocks, wearing different colours, and with a street system demarcated throughout the crowd by ZCC marshals lining the routes so that people and vehicles could move freely among them. The 'maidens' (unmarried women) wear blue and white. The mothers wear green and gold. And everyone seems to know where they should sit. There are huge screens throughout the vast terrain, so that everyone can see directly what is happening on the podium at any time. The sound system must be absolutely unbelievable to get to the furthest reaches of that space. There are rows and rows of toilets (all permanent fixtures) and camping areas with the smoke of fires rising. I just looked on in amazement. We in the DA think it is a big deal to organise an event of 12 000. Here, I can really believe it when they say there are 3-million people, although I would have no way of estimating a crowd of that size. And everything running smoothly. No one in a panic about anything. I met the chair of the organising committee who works for Eskom in Polokwane. I wish they could run Eskom like they run Easter at Moria! I asked him how long it takes to organise the event. He said 'about 10 days'. I nearly fell over. I promptly offered him a job in the DA, and he laughed with a warm belly laugh. I was well received.

Then at 12h45 exactly we were taken to a hall for lunch. What a spread. Two different kinds of chicken dish, beef, a range of salads and hot veg; cold drinks of your choice – and then the pudding. Different green jellies and custard to reflect the outfit that the 'mothers' wear. One of the green jellies was the way Aimee Daniels [our next-door neighbour in Rivonia] used to make it, with whipped Ideal milk, so it looked rather cloudy. That jelly always reminds me of my childhood.

Then it was time to go to the VIP stage and await the procession and the start of proceedings at exactly 14h00. This was preceded by the famous ZCC brass band – a full brass orchestra with every brass instrument you can imagine, playing a whole range of marching tunes, and led by Bishop Lekganyane along one of the marshalled 'streets'. What a rousing atmosphere a big brass band creates. And then it was time to start. On the dot. It started with prayers. That went on for 90 minutes. Each line of each prayer was translated into an Nguni language, a Sotho language, English and (amazingly, I thought) Afrikaans. Having had lunch and being extremely tired after very little sleep during the campaign, it was all I could do to prevent myself from dozing off in front of the cameras projecting images of the stage party into that huge crowd. Fortunately Geordin Hill-Lewis was next to me, and kept nudging me to keep me awake. The MEC of something-or-the-other from Limpopo, sitting on my left, was fast asleep throughout, but if I had done that, it would have been a scandal. So Geordin kept me awake.

The Bishop keeps the press out of there. No media. No party politics. Strict instructions. Then after these lengthy prayers, mainly from the Old Testament, the Bishop gets up to speak. He was greeted with a roar that only 3-million adoring souls can make. I sat back, expecting fire and brimstone. How else could a person attract so many people from the furthest corners of SA and from Botswana and other places? Not at all. Calm, measured and even a bit flat, he began his sermon by introducing his VIP guests. Everyone, including the ANC Ministers, got a polite clap. Then he welcomed Julius Malema who was sitting three rows behind me. The crowd exploded in applause and cheers. Oh dear, I thought. Oh dear! As the Bishop continued down the list, my heart was in my throat. That crowd was interactive and expressing its feelings. I was steeling myself for a 'Boo'. As the Bishop came closer to my name (I had concluded he was going down the list in alphabetical order), I was filled with trepidation waiting to hear what a 'Boo' from 3-million people sounded like. But instead they broke into applause and cheering, almost as big as Julius Malema's. I just can't describe the feeling that came over me. A mixture of relief and amazement. And then the sermon began. 90 minutes. Line by line translated into four other languages. In a biblical lilt. And then at the end, departing from his prepared text, he gave a little sermon about the importance of responsibility, of parents towards their children, of children towards improving their education and getting on in their lives, of people becoming doctors and teachers and contributing to society. I was blown away.

The picture is not complete without describing the scenery and background. The rock formation of the surrounding hills is very different from anything that I have experienced before. And the village on the slopes of the hill looks almost exactly like biblical Palestine, with flat roof houses against red earth. Because of the good rains, the area was green and the cloud formation dramatic. It was truly amazing to see this natural arena filled with so many people.

At the end, the Bishop stepped out on the front balcony and the crowd went wild. Then the Bishop walked to the VIP area, covered by the close circuit television and started shaking the hands of people. When he got to me, he hugged me warmly, and all this was shown on screens and the crowd cheered loudly. It was truly amazing. I cannot describe this phenomenon in words. People told me that if the Bishop hugs you, you are blessed for life. Sitting there on that platform I pondered anew the power of religion, a force that brings so many people together in adulation of a man they believe is the messenger of God.

After that, the Bishop led the marching band around through the entire, man-lined 'road network' – and he was twirling his baton like a real professional drum majorette and obviously loving it. I was watching from the roof again, following his progress through that vast crowd which looked as if it was doing a 'Mexican wave' following him wherever he went as people paid homage to him.

Then another huge spread of food and drink as we waited for the Bishop to see us off which he did personally.

We had to catch a plane to Kroonstad for our events of the next day and as it was quite late, the traffic police insisted on the 'blue light' thing to get us through the crowd. I have never allowed it, but believe me Mom, there I just kept quiet and let it happen. And we got to the Polokwane airport in time.

But then, we couldn't land in Kroonstad, because the lights were out on the landing strip so we had to divert to Bloemfontein. No major hassle. We flew to Kroonstad the next morning, and had a series of events in the Free State, where I am a bit worried about the growth of the Freedom Front Plus. Let's see what happens. I am always reminded of Henry Kissinger's words to me when he came to see me in the World Cup run-up in 2010. He said that no party in the world, in comparable circumstances, had ever succeeded in doing what the DA was attempting to do: Build a new majority across deep historical divisions, based on a new value set of defending each other's rights, and enabling each person to determine their own identity with sufficient opportunities to chart their course in life …

The campaign produced a few more adrenalin rushes, such as the moment, in the final rally at the Coca-Cola Dome in Johannesburg, when the teleprompter technology failed entirely. I was speaking on a platform 'in the round' without a podium. Geordin was standing nearby with a hard copy of the speech, following me word for word. When the screens went blank (in the middle of the complex policy section) I had no alternative but to ad-lib. I could see Geordin looking puzzled. Why was I deviating from the text? He looked up and saw the blank screens, realised there had been a technology failure, and immediately passed the speech up to me. The idea was that I should pick up in the text where the screens had left off. But I was enjoying my freedom, so I ad-libbed till the end!

On election day, 7 May, I toured the country, after which I landed in Johannesburg en route to the IEC centre in Pretoria, where the count began. When the first results came in, Johan van der Berg, our statistician, dropped them into his computer model. We would get 22.2 per cent of the vote, he projected. I was devastated. I had been hoping for at least 25 per cent. Then I carried on hoping (against hope) that for the first time in his career, Johan's projections would prove to be wrong. But they were uncannily accurate.

As it turned out, we polled a million more votes in 2014 (a national election) than we had in 2011 (a local election). Objectively speaking, this was an exceptional outcome, but given the ANC's usual huge turnout in a national election, our percentage of the poll was still 1.8 percentage points lower than 2011.

But, comparing apples with apples (the general election of 2009 with 2014), we had grown by 5.6 percentage points, or almost 33.7 per cent. That was an excellent outcome, by any measure, and compared favourably with our progress between 2004 and 2009, when we had grown by 4.3 percentage points off a lower base (which translated into a 34 per cent growth rate). But I was still deeply disappointed.

Our support from black South Africans had been driven down in the final days of the campaign as the ANC brought out its tried-and-trusted 'race squeeze' over Freedom Day and May Day, with blanket television coverage. My heart sank during the final weeks of the campaign as I watched our poll, tracking support from black voters, move steadily south. And on election day itself we also lost an additional few percentage points. This always occurred because of the gauntlet many of our black supporters faced in getting to the polls through a sea of yellow T-shirts emblazoned with Jacob Zuma's face. Our activists had told us of the sense of isolation they had felt when they stepped out of the ANC's embrace. Only the strongest had it in them to put an X next to the DA, even in the privacy of the voting booth, in those circumstances.

When Johan van der Berg had finished crunching the numbers, he told me that for the first time more black voters than white voters had voted for the DA. Of the one million new, first-time DA voters, 600 000 were black. That was, indeed, a turning point. And, crucially, we had brought the ANC below 50 per cent in both Nelson Mandela Bay and Tshwane (Pretoria). That set up a powerful platform for the 2016 local election, where, with the anticipated fall-off in ANC turnout, we were set to win these metro councils. When we analysed the 2014 result closely, I was pleased. I nevertheless concluded that I had taken the DA electorally as far as I could.

At that stage I still planned to stay on for the local election of 2016 and vacate the leadership at our elective congress in 2017. That would leave my successor two years to turn him- or herself into a trusted household name and run for office in the general election of 2019.

After the 2014 election, however, the succession debate was firmly on the cards, and as usual in the DA, people had strong, and contradictory, views.

The debate centred around two questions: when, and who? Our research department informed me that I still had the strongest voter favourability ratings of all DA leaders, partly because I had the highest name recognition. This made it all the more important to step back in time for someone who, once they achieved widespread name recognition, would be able to surpass my favourability ratings in order to push up our vote total. But popularity, though important, is not the only thing that matters for a political leader. I had learnt how extraordinarily difficult the job is beyond the first flush of novelty value. The crux of the job, over an extended period, is building stable, systems-based internal institutions that can survive the long haul amid growing political turbulence; and then, on this foundation, to keep growing voter support.

I arrived home on Friday night, 9 May, exhausted after the election, looking forward to my first free weekend. On Saturday we were going to have a thank-you party for our staff members from our head office, who had worked so relentlessly to achieve the outcome we did.

I can't remember exactly when it was, but sometime between arriving home on Friday and late Saturday morning, I received a call asking whether Lindiwe could come to see me and James Selfe. It had to be on Saturday, because it was necessary to talk before the *Sunday Times* hit the streets on 11 May. We arranged a time for Saturday afternoon, 10 May.

James had mentioned to me during the election campaign that Lindiwe was rumoured to be considering leaving after the election, but I thought it was just another one of the endless rumours that do the rounds in politics. There were no details and I did not believe it. Despite everything that had happened, I knew Lindiwe had a stellar career in politics to look forward to. Even though she was unlikely to win the pending election for caucus leader, she still had a great platform from which to challenge for the national leadership at a later stage. Through several internal electoral losses of my own, I had learnt that the DA has a soft spot for people who lose electoral contests and carry on contributing regardless. Both James and I bore personal testimony to that culture.

Lindiwe arrived the next afternoon. She told me that Jan-Jan Joubert would run a story the next day in the *Sunday Times* about how she had accepted a place at Harvard. From the conversation it was obvious that the process had been stage-managed for months, culminating in the agreement to give the *Sunday Times* the story, as an 'exclusive'. Whatever. At least she had waited until after the election to make her announcement. That was helpful.

I told Lindiwe that it was a good opportunity for her, and said that I could understand why she wanted to take it. I wished her well. I said we would have to convene a teleconference of the Federal Executive, who would get the news only after it had appeared in the *Sunday Times*. There was nothing else that could be done. James's office set the logistics in motion for a teleconference the following day.

I went off to the DA's thank-you party. Part of me was relieved that we would be spared the showdown of what would have been a bitter leadership election in the caucus. But another part of me was terrified that we might be setting up another aspiring young politician for failure by a premature promotion up the ranks. My mind was more preoccupied by this than by the prospects of Lindiwe's departure.

By this time Mmusi Maimane was being named everywhere as the candidate to support for the caucus leadership, but I was acutely aware that, for leaders to survive at the top, it was preferable for them to have climbed each painful step to get there. I spoke to James Selfe. 'We have learnt from experience. We can't do this to Mmusi. Either I must come back to parliament, or someone else needs to stand,' I told him. 'Would you be prepared to?'

I could see how reluctant he was; he preferred working in the background, building the party's systems and structures. 'It doesn't have to be for long,' I assured him. 'Just two years, to give the younger members of caucus a chance to learn the ropes and climb the rigging.'

James said he would think about it.

We did not have much time before the teleconference the next morning. I informed the Fedex of Lindiwe's decision to take a sabbatical at Harvard, conveyed to me the previous afternoon. The announcement had already been made in the media, and I wanted to give the Fedex an opportunity to discuss it. The discussion was brief. We wished her well, and agreed that I would be the media spokesperson on the matter.

I was intrigued at how quickly the meeting moved on to a discussion about who would fill her vacant parliamentary seat. The king is dead. Long live the king. The KwaZulu-Natal representatives made a strong play to be able to fill what they considered to be their seat, as Lindiwe had been elected via the province's list. The next seat in our system had been allocated to the Eastern Cape, however, so KwaZulu-Natal lost a member of parliament and the Eastern Cape gained one.

I spent the afternoon doing a series of interviews, across all media platforms, defending Lindiwe's decision. I had concluded it would be a thirty-six-hour story.

Until that afternoon. I realised we were in for something more when I picked up a tweet, sent at 3:56 p.m. from someone called Cameron Modisane, saying: 'Gareth van Onselen says he knows the reasons why Lindiwe Mazibuko is leaving the DA. I cannot wait to read his column tomorrow. Hehehe.'

That was the first indication I had of the further roll-out of the ongoing media strategy, initially launched for Lindiwe's campaign as parliamentary leader, and subsequently sustained at strategic moments. The military tacticians worked from the premise that if no enemy actually existed, it was necessary to create one.

I was not at all surprised to learn about what I surmised would be Gareth's attempt to undercut our thus far successful attempts to manage the caucus transition.

I wrote a note to Lindiwe's inner circle:

Dear colleagues,
Please see the tweet I picked up below. I trust that I, the Fedex, and the public have been told the truth about the reasons for Lindi's taking a sabbatical.

I noted that if Gareth, who was known to be close to Lindiwe, came up with a different story, Lindiwe would face the credibility gap between what she had told the party and what Gareth alleged her 'real reasons' were. No one who knew the relationships between the relevant individuals would fail to conclude that this was part of a predetermined plan. And it would reflect negatively on Lindiwe, I warned.

The intention was undoubtedly to damage me and Mmusi, but like all previous strategies it rebounded and did most damage to Lindiwe. I was surprised they could not have foreseen that. And the collateral damage the party would suffer seemed not to feature in their calculations.

I also wrote a note to Lindiwe, referring to the tweet:

Hi Lindiwe, I presume this indicates that Gareth is about to make some revelation tomorrow of which I am unaware. Do you know what it is? If he says something different from what you have said it will do irreparable damage, not least of all to your own credibility. Please let me know urgently. Helen

I did not hear from her, so I gave her a call. She professed to have no knowledge of Gareth's intentions and said she could not control what Gareth wrote; of course, the latter was true.

Early the next morning there was a slight social-media flurry when Gareth van Onselen released his column – only to have it immediately withdrawn by the new editor of *Business Day*, Songezo Zibi. It must have been a bit too tendentious and libellous for him to stomach, even if it came from a 'columnist', who is usually given greater licence than a staffer. So when the article appeared again, it had a postscript:

> This column was up briefly on the website early on Monday morning. In the interest of our and Gareth van Onselen's editorial credibility, we agreed to make amendments that do not alter the substance of Gareth's original column. Even in the case of external columnists, which Gareth is, we have to take care not to fall foul of the Press Code. By agreement between the Business Day and Gareth, we now publish this edited version.

I can only imagine what the original version must have been like, because the revised version was long, ponderous babble:

> On Sunday Democratic Alliance (DA) parliamentary leader Lindiwe Mazibuko announced she would not be returning to Parliament post election. She set out her reasoning in an article for the Sunday Times newspaper, in which she argued she intended to study abroad in order to broaden her prospects. She suggested she might return to the DA at some point in the future.
>
> From that statement, a singular fact is significant: faced with the prospect of leading a growing party in the National Assembly as the constitutionally recognised leader of the opposition, Mazibuko chose instead to return to university.

He described the internal culture of the DA as 'poisonous', and continued:

> There exists a single, dominant and authoritarian personality at the heart of the party. With that there exists too an organisational culture that has become weak and entirely subservient to the wishes of its leader; as a result, intolerant, paranoid, fearful, vengeful and malicious ...
>
> A truly poisonous environment is one where people constantly suspect each other and where individuals are no longer engaged with on the merits of the case they present, but with regards to who they represent and whether their views might advance or damage one's prospects if associated with.
>
> Ultimately, the condition of the organisation itself becomes a lie. Everyone becomes complicit. It is healthy, they tell themselves, because that is what I must believe to succeed.
>
> All of these things are always present to some degree in any political party – they are the nature of the beast. But in an environment where they take on extreme proportions they become defining. More importantly, unchecked they become the way of things. They are all well set inside the DA ...
>
> In an environment where difference is isolated, marginalised and relentlessly

persecuted the result is a kind of slow torture. Your political life is sucked from you. What you believe becomes the source of despair, not encouragement ...

The evidence for this is overwhelming. It appears from discussions with DA members that Zille had placed a party staffer loyal to her in charge of all parliamentary communication (an example of DA cadre deployment, the elected parliamentary leader of the opposition could not sign off the communication of her own caucus).

The relationship between those two became entirely politicised, with the head of communications, a staff member, relentlessly undermining Mazibuko's communication and denuding those platforms available to her of their worth. Certainly they deteriorated to the point that they were irreconcilable.

Mazibuko's staff have been systematically isolated and marginalised inside the party. Zille's faction no doubt leaked correspondence to the media about the DA's affirmative action foul up, damning Mazibuko. Later it was reported Zille would threaten to fire Mazibuko's chief whip over the debacle, despite heading the caucus meeting where the initial decision took place. Her primary issue in the election campaign, Nkandla, would be given to Mmusi Maimane to drive on television and defend in court. And all the while, a campaign would be driven to elevate Maimane as a future leader of that caucus.

Mazibuko was sidelined out the DA's election campaign, reduced to a bit player on posters, adverts and party events. It is true Mazibuko was sick for some of this time, but these kinds of decisions are made months in advance of the actual campaign.

In her place, a golden highway was paved for Maimane, Zille's heir apparent and the ultimate yes-man. The party's Gauteng campaign was used to create a platform for his progression and he will now, inevitably, be anointed parliamentary leader – the first time a DA politician has become parliamentary leader without ever serving in parliament, testament to Zille's inability to maintain unity in her own caucus ...

The interests of the party became internal, not external. And it was done because Mazibuko did not see eye to eye with Zille on many things and posed a potential threat to her future control of the DA. Zille's response to that, and the response of those loyal to her, was to hound Mazibuko out of the party. Those who did not hound, relented meekly before her ...

When a single, dominant and authoritarian personality is seemingly at the zenith of their powers, the truth is they are usually at their weakest. But they cannot see that. A yes-sir culture, supplemented by much fear, means the truth is kept from them. They are told only what they want to hear. Unhappiness wells outside the paradigm they have created for themselves. All of this is fuelled by an intense paranoia, which manifests in yet more authoritarianism and, thus, more fear, making the likelihood they will ever properly engage with reality all the more remote; that is, if anyone ever has the courage to present it to them in the first place.

For these people, there will be no lessons to learn from Mazibuko's decision. Even the question of why studying was more an exciting prospect than leading the opposition in parliament will escape them. They are not interested in the answers to such questions outside of denying their legitimacy. Introspection has long since been replaced by post-rationalisation and, by that standard, things have never been better.

The DA knows this. It knows I know all its secrets. I know the truth. It has never had to deal with a journalist who has insight to and access to the party to the degree I do. It drives Zille crazy. For years it has grown fat off the leaks and discontent that have served to undermine the ANC. If I wanted, I could print every set of DA federal council minutes for the last year, its strategic plans and internal communications. But I don't. Instead I try to present credible arguments, based on the DA's public statements. I play fair. The DA will have none of it. It simply does not do criticism.

On and on it went, until it concluded:

> It is a testament to Mazibuko's immense dignity and strength of character that she left in the way she did. Despite being viciously and brutally maligned and alienated inside the DA, she chose to leave with her head held high and not a single grudge to bear. Take a moment to appreciate the deep care and concern one must have for a cause to swallow so hard to protect the reputation of the one person who has effectively destroyed any positive outlook you once harboured.

I read it and laughed. What irony! This attack on my supposed intolerance of criticism had been penned by none other than the person known inside the DA as the Ayatollah of Liberalism. His distorted understanding of liberalism as a fixed ideology became The Cause, around which a small cult coagulated inside the DA. Like all cults, it brooked no opposition, and was actually the antithesis of liberalism.

Everyone in the DA knew that my colleagues challenged me all the time. I listened to their arguments, and I often adapted or even abandoned my positions as a result. The great sin of inflexibility I had committed was to once have said no to Gareth's plans, hatched without consulting me, for him to take over the rump of the DA's parliamentary communications. And when I said no to him, I meant it, and nothing would move me.

When it came to the reasons for Lindiwe leaving, almost everyone in the DA knew exactly what they really were, and laughed at Gareth's attempt to hammer reality into his narrative. We had been considerate, and circumspect, I thought, not to allude to the REAL reasons, and to let Lindiwe go to Harvard on a high note, presented as someone seizing the opportunity of a lifetime.

My instinctive response to Gareth's hatchet job was to shrug. Anyone who knew anything would merely take it from whence it came, I reckoned. But several colleagues stressed it was essential to set the record straight.

Gavin Davis, who had just been elected to parliament, wrote a devastating, simple response.

Setting the Record Straight
By Gavin Davis
In his article on Monday, Gareth van Onselen asks why somebody would rather go back to university than lead the opposition in Parliament. But what if the real choice was between returning to university and the prospect of losing the parliamentary leadership?

Predictably, Van Onselen doesn't explore this particular possibility.

Lindiwe Mazibuko's proximity to Van Onselen is well known. It is highly unlikely that he would not have consulted her on his column before it was published. And, at the time of writing, she had not refuted his claims.

So let me take the opportunity to set the record straight.

All political parties have internal tensions. It was the case with the Democratic Alliance (DA) under Tony Leon, it remains the case under Helen Zille and it will be the same under the next leader of the party. As Van Onselen himself points out, it is the nature of the beast.

It is true that Mazibuko and Zille's relationship did become strained towards the end. But not irretrievably so. And certainly not because of what Van Onselen describes as authoritarianism on Zille's part.

When Mazibuko was elected parliamentary leader, she insisted on having her own, expanded staff complement. She had her own platforms and carte blanche to position herself as the counterpart to the president of the republic. Zille strongly encouraged this, and ensured she had every opportunity to build her profile.

Mazibuko was given ample space to lead the caucus as she saw fit, immediately reshuffling the shadow cabinet and making subsequent changes without consulting the party leader, as is the convention. This generated strong resentment within the caucus.

If anything, Zille was criticised for being too 'hands off' in her dealings with the parliamentary management team. This was brought into sharp relief with the Employment Equity Bill debacle. The fact is that Mazibuko ignored advice on how to deal with the bill, which is how we ended up in the embarrassing situation that we did.

It is ironic that Van Onselen refers to my appointment as communications director at the DA as 'cadre deployment' when he himself had been deployed to that position prior to me. Zille had nothing to do with my appointment. I applied for the job when the position became vacant and I was interviewed by James Selfe and Jonathan Moakes. Furthermore, when I was appointed, Athol Trollip was the parliamentary leader, not Mazibuko. It is therefore false to insinuate that I had been sent to Parliament to exert control over Mazibuko. I arrived in August and she was elected in October.

The first task I set myself was to repair the damage wrought by Van Onselen – my predecessor – in his internal war against Trollip. This had started when Ryan Coetzee, Van Onselen's mentor, lost the election for parliamentary leader against Trollip. That particular battle had caused deep divisions in the caucus and created a culture of mistrust between MPs and staff. My next job was to professionalise communication in Parliament and align it with the rest of the party. This entailed a restructuring process and filling the numerous vacancies that Van Onselen had simply not bothered to fill.

Like Van Onselen before me, I was empowered to sign off all party communication (including Parliament). This was not new. It was done in terms of a system designed by Ryan [Coetzee] and enthusiastically implemented by Van Onselen when he was in that position. As time went on, I delegated this responsibility more and more to other staff members. When it came to Mazibuko's office, I rarely signed off on any of her communication, leaving that to her chief of staff.

The claim that Mazibuko's staff were isolated and marginalised within the party is simply unfounded. I happen to have an excellent working relationship with her chief of staff. Indeed, it was me who suggested to Mazibuko that he be promoted to the position of director of operations in Parliament. Such was my faith in his abilities, I soon left Parliament to take up an office at the DA's national headquarters so that he could be in charge. Although I worked closely with him on a daily basis, I rarely got involved in the day-to-day running of Mazibuko's office or the parliamentary operation in general.

The most disingenuous claim is that Mazibuko was shut out of the election campaign. The fact of the matter is that Mazibuko was on sick leave for six weeks of the campaign. When she recovered, she was given speaking opportunities at all major events and her campaign team had free rein to set up events for her, which they did. She did an excellent job of driving the Nkandla issue, although it was unfortunate that her illness prevented her from travelling to Nkandla to lay charges (which is why Mmusi Maimane went instead). Mazibuko featured on our national posters and represented the DA in the last two SABC election debates. The latter was my suggestion in recognition of Mazibuko's brilliant debating abilities.

What many people do not know is that Mazibuko was the first in our party to be asked to avail herself for the nomination of Gauteng premier candidate. She declined, later telling people that she turned it down because she saw it as an attempt to 'sideline' her. Had Mazibuko been chosen as the Gauteng premier candidate, the same resources would have been put behind her. The decision to focus on Gauteng was a strategic one taken by party structures on which Mazibuko sat, and agreed; it had nothing to do with who the candidate was or any future internal elections. To say otherwise is paranoid and delusional.

It is amusing to read that Van Onselen thinks he 'drives Zille crazy' with his almost daily diatribes against the party. It tells us a lot about his motives for driving a one-sided agenda in the media. He gets a kick out of it. He thinks that what he writes has a huge impact on the party and its leader. But the truth is, it doesn't. Most people in the party simply roll their eyes when they hear his name. He has been reduced to an embittered former party hack, obsessed with settling scores with his erstwhile opponents in the party.

Zille has grown the support of the DA from 12% when she was elected in 2007 to 22% just seven years later. This is testament to her hard work, strategic insight and ability to keep the party united, despite the best efforts of some to sow division. She expects people to work hard, but gives them space to do their jobs.

Make no mistake, Zille is a strong leader. But she is strong enough to listen to criticism and accept or reject it based on her own assessment of the evidence. And she is strong enough to risk personal failure if she believes it is in the party's interest to take a risk. These qualities explain why she has stayed the course when others have stumbled at the first hurdle.

Ouch.

I had warned Lindiwe's closed circle that she would be hurt the most if they publicly contradicted her stated reasons for going to Harvard.

If the rest of us, who knew the truth, were prepared to go along with her reasons, it was amazing that they wouldn't – until I realised that this was actually part of The Plan. They thought they could spin it in order to turn Lindiwe into the victim, and harm me and Mmusi. And they also assumed no one would respond to their fallacious reasoning by setting the record straight.

I had long since realised that the military strategists in our caucus could not see beyond their next manoeuvre. Their tactics seemed to be inspired by Inspector

Clouseau rather than Sun Tzu. They wanted a free passage to charge headlong into any battle they chose, on their own terms, and cried foul if anyone fought back. And when their backs were against the wall, they resorted to the media duo we had dubbed 'Jan-Jan Onselen'. The partnership between Gareth van Onselen and Jan-Jan Joubert cried out for the elision of their names.

Wilmot James announced in the media that he would be 'leading the charge' against Gavin's rebuttal of Gareth in the Federal Executive that Friday. He said, publicly, that he was furious with Gavin for publicly defending himself and the party against Gareth's public attack. I couldn't follow the logic.

The minutes of the Fedex meeting show that the only charge Wilmot actually led was against Gareth van Onselen, whose 'obsession with excoriating the DA,' he said, was 'just part of a pattern of his unending triumphalist critiques'. Wilmot added that he was 'deeply pained' that the party had reacted.

I said it was quite acceptable for people to exercise the right of reply to a manipulated public attack, but we agreed that the debate should now end. Under the circumstances we had a frank and open discussion in the Fedex, as we normally did. It was, I felt, an example of how an open system should work.

Athol, inevitably under the circumstances, asked me some potent and pointed questions about Lindiwe. He well knew how much political capital I had spent on her behalf, and how the situation had degenerated. He was still smarting at being forced out of the parliamentary leadership. He had turned out to be right, and I had been proven wrong. I presumed he was seeking to underscore the point when he asked me to look back and reflect on how things had turned out as they did. I accepted that he deserved his moment to say I told you so.

In reply to Athol, I conceded that I had, indeed, worked hard to promote Lindiwe's career. In fact, I said I had never done as much to promote any person's career in the DA before. This was an objective, evidence-based fact.

Traversing known ground, I reminded him that when Lindiwe had originally said she wanted to run for parliamentary leader at the mid-term, I advised her against it, because I believed Athol should be allowed to finish a full term and that her chances would be enhanced by waiting just another two years, without launching what many thought was a premature challenge. But when she said she was determined to run, I had backed her because, in trying to diversify the party, I felt it was important for her to win.

I said I was surprised when, shortly after her election, a 'Berlin Wall' was erected between our offices, and major decisions with significant implications for the party were taken without reference to me or the broader leadership. I had been surprised that, when I offered advice, it was not only ignored but regarded as unacceptable interference, and when serious mistakes followed, I stepped forward and took responsibility. This was nothing new. It was evidenced by the record.

I said that I had tried to keep communication channels open and support her as best I could at all times, but that I had experienced repeated resistance.

During the course of the recent election campaign, I had heard a rumour that she intended to go abroad as soon as the election was over. I didn't believe this could be true, but because Lindiwe was on sick leave, and because I had been told this information in confidence, I let it pass. I just did not think it was possible.

When it turned out in fact to be true, and that a newspaper had been informed before the DA leadership, the full picture fell into place. It was quite clear by then that she was going to face defeat in the election for parliamentary leader, and wanted to avoid this. That was understandable, I said, but I would have preferred her to have levelled with me and told me about her plans when she applied to go to Harvard eight months previously. This failure to keep me and the rest of the leadership informed characterised her approach from the moment she was elected. I found it puzzling, but I continued to work to heal the rift.

Lindiwe had given her reasons for going to Harvard to the Fedex only after they had read about it in the *Sunday Times*. I had wished her well, and spent the day talking to the media defending her decision.

Gareth's intervention and the subsequent events were well known to the Fedex, I said. I did not need to traverse the ground again. We discussed the facts, dispassionately. I made an effort to ensure that not a hint of anger surfaced in my voice or my demeanour, although it would not have been unreasonable for me to have felt aggrieved, both by what had happened, but particularly by the way it had been conveyed and escalated during the week. We all agreed that we would draw a line under it and move on.

I should not have been surprised that the very people who were so enraged that Gavin had kept the issue in the public eye by exercising his right of reply would have been precisely those who escalated the public conflict, by leaking distorted information under cover of anonymity.

The next day was Saturday 17 May, and I was about to leave Leeuwenhof to attend a rugby match in my capacity as patron of Western Province Rugby, when Jan-Jan Joubert sent me an article he had written for publication in the *Sunday Times* the next day. He wanted my comment. He sent it at 3:38 p.m., saying his deadline was four o'clock.

His text read:

DA leader Helen Zille has launched a bitter attack on Lindiwe Mazibuko, her party's former parliamentary leader with claims she had 'made' and 'saved' her many times.

Zille also told the party's federal executive meeting on Friday at OR Tambo City Lodge outside Johannesburg that she had opposed Mazibuko's candidature for parliamentary leader against Eastern Cape leader Athol Trollip.

But, she said, she had supported Mazibuko once her candidature had been declared in 2011 because she could not run the risk of a black candidate losing.

Sources said the meeting started with Zille delivering a speech which first focused on the DA's election performance and growth and then turned to Mazibuko's departure and the possibility of national spokesperson Mmusi Maimane succeeding her.

Zille then launched the scathing attack on Mazibuko – who did not attend the meeting – saying Mazibuko should have told her earlier about her decision to study.

Zille also claimed Mazibuko had constructed a 'Berlin Wall' between herself and Zille, and repeated her belief – as stated in the media this week – that Mazibuko would have lost a parliamentary election to Maimane ...

If it had not been for the first paragraph, and the adjectival untruths and exaggerations, it would have been fairly accurate. There was no 'bitter attack'. The only bitter attack all week had been Gareth van Onselen's against me and Mmusi. I did not, at any stage, say I had 'made' or 'saved' Lindiwe, although I did say, truthfully, that I had done a lot to support her in getting to where she was.

The article failed to mention the context of the discussion – that I was answering questions posed to me by Athol Trollip. There was no scathing, bitter (or any other form of) attack; I knew I had to be rational and clinical, although there was every reason to be angry, not only at the substance of Lindiwe's decision but the way it had been conveyed.

It was truly bizarre. The account had been embellished to the extent that it was unrecognisable from the actual discussion in caucus.

I wrote a quick reply, delaying other people by my late departure for the match. I said the impression conveyed by the article was entirely misleading, and I set out the facts.

Next day, Sunday morning, it was Johann's turn to go downstairs to make tea and get the newspapers. While the kettle was on the boil, he returned to the bedroom with the *Sunday Times*. He held it up from the door, and I read the thick black banner headline: 'Mazibuko Nothing Without Me – Zille'

Of course, I had never implied, let alone said, any such thing.

'This headline will destroy you,' said Johann.

'That is precisely the intention,' I replied.

I had stopped being surprised.

The *Sunday Times* had tucked my comment away on an inside page, so that they could claim they had published 'the other side', thus trying to prevent a challenge to the press ombudsman.

In discussion with my colleagues we were left in no doubt as to where the manipulated leaks had emanated. I suggested to James Selfe that it would be preferable to run Fedex like a press conference, by opening up the proceedings to the media, rather than have such twisted versions of our discussions selectively leaked to the papers afterwards, in pursuit of personal agendas in the succession battle. It was particularly ironic that those who most decried the debate going public did the most to stoke public controversy, under a cloak of anonymity, while actually objecting to anyone else stating their views on the record.

Almost everyone in the DA knew exactly what was going on.

On the same day, Sunday 18 May, I wrote my newsletter on 'The abuse of media to drive internal agendas in the DA' in order to set the public record straight. I rebutted the *Sunday Times*'s false attacks, based on selective and twisted leaks from the Fedex. I said that, contrary to the impression given in the *Sunday Times* report, the Fedex meeting was a full, open, frank discussion of adults seeking to deal with a situation and move forward. I went on to say:

> It is very rare that political parties can have discussions of this depth and maturity. It is unfortunate that some members of this body are furnishing the media with selective 'leaks' in order to advance their own succession agendas, both in the Parliamentary caucus and in the Party.
>
> What is most concerning is the way that some media platforms are being abused by so-called journalists and columnists who are embedded in a particular faction of the DA, and using their media 'cover' to advance a factional ascendancy in the DA's succession battle.
>
> Because, when everything is peeled away, this is about who will become the next Parliamentary leader and the next DA leader when I step down.
>
> Up till recently, Lindiwe was seen as my natural successor. Although I believe it is wrong for any leader to anoint a successor, I also believed that Lindiwe had the attributes required, and I did everything in my power to assist her ascendancy up the greasy pole.
>
> She was also backed by a close circle of 'insiders', chief among whom was Gareth van Onselen, who worked on Lindiwe's internal campaign team when she defeated Athol Trollip in the mid-term election in 2011. Gareth, who worked in the DA's media department, became notorious for his obsessive vendettas and divisiveness within the party. His initial aim was to destroy Athol Trollip. Once Athol had lost the Parliamentary leadership to Lindiwe, and returned to lead the DA's Eastern Cape caucus, van Onselen then turned his guns on Mmusi Maimane, who was emerging as Lindiwe's greatest potential challenger.
>
> When I refused to create a new job that Gareth wanted, heading up the DA's parliamentary communication (because I knew he would only use it to continue driving his vendettas) he left the DA.
>
> He has now found other platforms in Business Day and the Sunday Times, which give him the 'veneer' of independence that everyone in politics knows

to be a farce. Certainly, everyone in the DA knows what his agenda is, and now it is becoming apparent to the public too.

Jan-Jan Joubert's proximity to certain personalities in the DA is less well known, but no less entrenched. Jan-Jan's profile in almost all the publications he has worked for is that of an 'embedded' journalist. He and Van Onselen have found kindred spirits in each other, as they promote some individuals in the party and denigrate others.

Their main target here is Mmusi Maimane. They turned their guns on me when they became concerned that I might back Mmusi in the Parliamentary caucus leadership election. Their strategy is to paint me as a dictator conducting a reign of terror. Every honest person in the DA knows that this is patently untrue.

It was time to draw a line in the sand, I said. By having confidential discussions behind closed doors, we were merely playing into the hands of those who wished selectively to manipulate leaks to drive their factional agenda.

I said to James Selfe that opening Fedex meetings to the media would be better than reading deliberately distorted accounts in the newspapers afterwards. The Clouseau circle had not yet realised they had been beaten and would merely continue their strategies to the detriment of the party. We were not going to counter-leak anonymously, so rather open the meeting, I argued.

James disagreed. He said he thought the boil had been lanced. He had a sense that, after the final kick we had just experienced, things would settle down. I took his advice.

I asked James whether he had thought about the caucus leadership. He told me he had given the matter careful consideration but did not see himself on the front line of the looming conflicts in parliament. He still preferred a background role, holding together the DA's internal institutions and systems.

His decision was a blow. James Selfe and Elsabe Oosthuysen were as close as two people could come to being indispensable to the smooth functioning of the DA's internal institutions, and so it seemed best for James to remain where he was.

It appeared increasingly inevitable that, unless I returned to parliament, the caucus leadership contest would be between two newly elected MPs, Mmusi Maimane and Makashule Gana. They were both talented young politicians whose greatest risk, like others before them, was that they might be destroyed by peaking too early.

I knew that Mmusi would be easily elected, ironically carried into office by the unremitting vilification campaign against him by 'Jan-Jan Onselen'. The only way the duo might succeed in destroying him was by propelling him into the leadership too early.

I convened my inner circle to propose that I move back to parliament, rather than take up my seat in the province. We had a long discussion about it. We wrote an exhaustive list of pros and cons, and debated each one. They persuaded me against it, and I was finally convinced that, under new management, the caucus could become functional again. I remember our final discussion during that fateful week, when I faced them across the table and simply said: 'Don't fuck it up. Our party can't survive another plane crash.'

I also swore that I would never become openly involved in an internal succession election again.

In my capacity as premier of the Western Cape, I attended President Zuma's second inauguration on 24 May 2014. At the luncheon afterwards I sat next to a member of Zuma's cabinet with whom I had developed a trusting relationship during the struggle years. We spoke about the differences between President Mbeki and President Zuma, the complexity of managing the ANC caucus, the 'two economies' theory and the development state.

But then he turned his attention to the DA. He told me, frankly, that the ANC was 'hoping like hell' I would go back to parliament. He said the ANC believed that if I left the Western Cape, the DA's 'good governance' alternative, which was proving an increasingly powerful narrative, would start to unravel.

I did not tell him I had already decided to stay in the province, against much public advice. I only said I was not indispensable, but that I thought it was the wrong time to leave the province, having only completed half a job. He said that, from the DA's perspective, I was making the right decision, but it was bad for the ANC. Of course, that was the outcome I wanted.

It was now inevitable that, in his very first year in parliament, on 29 May 2014, Mmusi Maimane would be elected DA caucus leader. I thought it was probably unprecedented anywhere for an established opposition in a parliamentary democracy to choose a first-time MP for this crucial position, but our context created an unprecedented imperative. We were in a race against time, in a complex country, to save democracy.

It was going to be anything but easy-going for Mmusi. He already faced his own 'coalition of the aggrieved' inside the party, primarily because of his rapid rise through the ranks. The crab-in-the-bucket syndrome was alive and flourishing in the DA. The people from whom he might have expected the strongest support were already doing their best to pull him down, led by some of his Gauteng colleagues, who saw their own ambitions thwarted by his rapid rise. And, as often happens in politics, his strengths – dynamism, intellect and charm – became his greatest liabilities, as his opponents sought to portray him as a 'hollow man'. It was an ideal symbol for professional jealousy.

I was sworn in as premier for a second term on 26 May 2014.

Mmusi was elected caucus leader, unopposed, on 29 May. Anchen Dreyer, the veteran Progressive Federal Party MP who had played a key bridging role over many years, was elected caucus chair, with Richard Majola, an MP from the West Coast, as the deputy chair. John Steenhuisen, our former provincial leader in KwaZulu-Natal and Durban caucus leader, was appointed chief whip.

The transformation was immediate. The wall came down, which enabled me to step back. Issues were discussed openly, obviating the need for any unwelcome interventions. Within weeks we were back to the relaxed collegial atmosphere we had once known.

The relief felt like a detox. I had a throbbing tension headache for weeks afterwards as the toxins drained from our system. With my defences down, I got one serious cold after another, but I could now afford to let my body revolt.

Within a few months the parliamentary platform was humming again. Air traffic control, through the whippery, was working efficiently. Bills were triaged and when necessary red-flagged, processed through study groups, discussed and worked through the caucus, which started focusing on legislation and ceased to be a pseudo-academic seminar. Communication with our government in the province resumed so that we could align our position on legislation.

For the first time in ages, a political year ended off better than it had started.

In November I travelled to Frankfurt, Germany, to receive the Friedrich Naumann award for freedom, a great honour which had immense symbolic significance for Mom.

When I returned, I decided to defer my decision on when to step down to the new year. There was no immediate urgency. In fact, I needed to see how things panned out over a few months before making the decision. I cordoned off my private life and went to Johannesburg to see Mom.

She was not in a good way. She was about to turn ninety-six, and was battling on bravely, but privately she confided in me that she longed to die. Her older sister was about to turn 103, and she was worried about lasting that long too. I told her, comfortingly, there was no chance of that. Unlike Mom, her sister had never smoked. Carla was doing such an amazing job of looking after her, said Mom, and she did not want to come across as ungrateful. At first I made light of her wishes, but I realised I had to take her more seriously. My letters did not seem to be helping much any more. I could see that she had lost the will to live because she was losing her interest in politics. She hardly ate.

Yet, despite her failing lungs and her inability to walk even the shortest distance unaided, her heart still pumped strongly and her brain was crystal clear. She learnt a poem off by heart every day – to keep her neurons connected, as she explained – and went through books of complex word puzzles. She was constantly plugged into an oxygen tank.

For years, we had expected every Christmas to be her last. We knew that Christmas 2014 would be.

21

The End of Two Eras

MOM'S END CAME quickly, yet so slowly. The night before, we sat around her bed as she sipped Amarula and ate some salmon, cooked to perfection by Carla. Afterwards she did her word puzzles and recited poetry from her favourite authors, Heinrich Heine, Erich Kaestner and Kurt Tucholsky. My brother Paul followed in her poetry books. If she got a word wrong, Paul would say, scoldingly, '*Strafarbeit*,' meaning 'punishment homework' (the equivalent of a school detention). We all laughed.

Heidi and Oscar, my mother's dogs, lying on her bed, sensed she was nearing the end. Looking at them, I could understand where the word 'hangdog' came from.

Paul told Mom that her name would live on in future generations. He used the plural, metaphorically. Being her normal, absolutely literal self to the last, she replied, in all seriousness, that it would create confusion if more than one of her great-granddaughters were called Mila. We didn't roll our eyes, or laugh, as we normally would have done. We just conceded that it would indeed create a problem, but said we would handle it. She seemed relieved to hear that. It was good to be together.

Twenty-four hours later she was slipping into a coma. She tried to tell me. At first I thought she was telling me to comb my hair, but eventually I got it. Despite her heaving lungs, she was at peace.

Her life had come full circle. She had watched us take our first breath, and we were there as she took her last. It felt right.

We grieved silently, without guilt or regret.

The dogs went frantic when the undertaker arrived. They didn't bark. They just ran around in despair. They knew she wasn't coming back.

We stood around Mom's empty bed, the three siblings, and Lydia and Keabetswe. That small space had contained her life, for three years. It was surrounded by the photos, drawings and the small things she loved most, especially the books, disintegrated from overuse and held together by elastic bands.

We sat on her bed. Paul picked up her word puzzle book. The last word she had grappled with was 'elbigilletninu'.

'She got it wrong,' said Paul.

Carla looked over his shoulder. 'No, she didn't. That is "unintelligible" backwards.'

What a final word to grapple with as your life is slipping away!

We took Mom's favourite books to be rebound.

We planned a memorial service in Carla's garden. We had a few brief tributes and read out two of her favourite poems by Heinrich Heine.

Heine was the writer with whom Mom identified most. He gave voice to much of her own life – a baptised Jew, a man of faith who had never belonged to any formal faith community, who was repelled by the politics of his own country and battled throughout his life to find an identity in exile. I chose to read a poem reflecting his conviction that people are not defined by creed, dogma or ethnic origin, but by kindred spirits who cross their life path and, through shared values, form a bond of love that extends beyond death.

Mom knew the whole poem by heart. I just read two verses, in German. The poem is called 'Wo?' ('Where?')

> Wo wird einst des Wandermüden
> Letzte Ruhestätte sein?
> Unter Palmen in dem Süden?
> Unter Linden an dem Rhein?
>
> Immerhin! Mich wird umgeben
> Gotteshimmel, dort wie hier,
> Und als Totenlampen schweben
> Nachts die Sterne über mir.
>
> *
>
> Where at last will this wandering end
> and a quiet place be marked as mine?
> Under palms in the Southern sun?
> Under lindens on the Rhine?
>
> It makes no difference. God will wind
> his heaven round me there as here,
> and like the lanterns of the dead,
> at night the stars will hover near.

My sister-in-law, Isabel, gave us each a pill to help us get through the ceremony. We needed it.

It was the end of an era.

I returned to Cape Town, straight into the February routine – the opening of parliament and the State of the Nation Address, the DA's Federal Council, the State of the Province Address, and then the round of biennial DA provincial congresses, at which I spoke: Limpopo, Mpumalanga, Northern Cape and Free State. After the provincial budget process, I undertook two DA fundraising trips, one to the UK and the other to the United States. And always, in the background, there was the routine work of governing the province.

I welcomed the pressure. It took my mind off other things.

And of course, it was all systems go for the DA's biennial federal elective congress, scheduled for May.

I had been nominated again as leader, unopposed. The assumption all round was that I would lead the party until the local elections in 2016 and then step down at the 2017 congress, in time for the general election of 2019. Based on this assumption, we deduced, Lindiwe and her strategists (chief among them being David Maynier) had hatched the 'Harvard' plan to avoid the setback of a caucus electoral defeat, planning her return in time to drive a campaign to succeed me as leader at the 2017 elective congress. I learnt later that they had arranged with James Selfe for Lindiwe's name to remain on the top of our electoral list, despite her resignation, which would ease her re-entry. I had not been informed of this, but the reason for the arrangement was obvious when it emerged.

This analysis was reinforced by this group's reaction when I announced I was bowing out before the 2015 election. They immediately thought I had taken the decision to pre-empt their strategy. The truth is far more prosaic.

I was fundraising in the US at the end of March when Athol Trollip announced his candidacy for federal chairman at the 2015 congress. He was going to challenge Wilmot James. In the current party climate, it was likely that Athol would win. The prospect of Athol and me in the DA's two top positions would be welcome grist to the ANC's race mill. I knew that one of us would have to stand down, and it wouldn't be Athol. He had made his sacrifices. It was time for me to make mine.

Gavin and Geordin – who had emerged as my closest advisers precisely because they told me what they thought I should hear and not what I wanted to hear – came round to discuss the situation on the afternoon of 8 April. We agreed that it would create an impossible situation if both Athol and I ran. They said Athol had been approached twice to stand back until the 2017 congress, but had declined. I said we could not push Athol again. It had to be me. But first we did our 'pros and cons' exercise. The two lists were roughly equally balanced, but by the end of our meeting, I had made my decision. I would stand down as party leader. There was a month to go before the congress.

The short time span also had both pros and cons. The downside was that my announcement would take the party by surprise. There would be only one month for candidates to mobilise for a succession battle. The great advantage, though, was that everyone would be spared the debilitating impact of a long, enervating contest. I was due to be elected unopposed at the congress of 2015, but the battle for succession was already in full swing, and would have rapidly gained momentum over the remaining two years, subsuming the party's attention when we needed to focus on the all-important local government election of 2016.

The biggest potential negative of my decision lay in the 'unknown unknowns', the unforeseen consequences. By definition, you cannot foresee an unforeseen consequence. But they always arise, and critics then claim to have predicted them.

I knew that if the succession worked, history would judge my decision to have been the right one at the right time. If it did not, I would be blamed for stepping back prematurely for the wrong reasons. That is how the rear-view mirror works. What you see in the past depends on where you stand in the present.

After a glass of wine, Gavin and Geordin left. I went upstairs. It was the end of another era for me. I sat on our bed, from which several premiers before me must have reflected on their own ending eras, and watched the evening deepen over the Cape Town skyline etched against Table Bay. Johann came into the bedroom to get his jacket and a small pile of books next to his bed. I could see he was in a hurry.

'Love,' I said, 'I've just made a final decision to step down from the DA leadership at Congress.'

'Great,' he said. 'I'm off to house church now. Bye.'

'Did you hear what I said?'

'Yes, you said you are stepping down as DA leader. I said that's great. You've been trying to do that for years. You finally have!'

'Well, it's still a momentous decision and has lots of implications,' I said.

'We'll chat about them later. I'm going to be late.' And with that he rushed out of the door, leaving me thinking about the scores of times I must have rushed out of the door when he may have wanted to speak to me.

I phoned James Selfe. He thought I was making the wrong decision. I said I would sleep on it. Next morning I chatted to Johann, and he believed strongly that my decision was the right one. That reinforced my position. Paul Boughey, James Selfe, John Steenhuisen and two outsiders whose opinions I valued joined Gavin, Geordin and me the next morning, and within ten minutes it was a fait accompli. After a brief discussion, we agreed to convene the Fedex for Sunday 12 April, in Johannesburg. We would not say anything until then (and it was one of the rare occasions that a decision did not 'leak').

The Fedex meeting, at a hotel near O.R. Tambo Airport in Johannesburg, had been scheduled to last an hour. It lasted two and a half. About 75 per cent of the Fedex members were strongly opposed to my decision, no doubt for vastly divergent reasons. But by then, I was unmovable.

The night before the Fedex meeting I sent my statement with a covering letter to my cabinet colleagues and to the staff in my offices. I asked them to treat it confidentially. It was important that they should hear the news from me, not via the media, before I stepped into the press conference.

Just before the press conference was about to start, I had a really weird experience. As I sat down at the table, before the gathered media (who had been waiting a long time), I looked up and saw Pieter du Toit from *Beeld* newspaper take his phone out of his pocket. He had received a message. I saw him read it. He looked up at me – and intuitively I knew he had already received the press statement, sent from someone in the small circle of people who knew what I was about to say. It was interesting for me to observe, in real time, a pattern of media pre-emption that had played itself out for so long.

My statement, dated 12 April 2015, said:

One of the many things I have learned during the last eight years, is that it is easier to lead a sphere of government than a political party. In executive government office, the rules are clear; in party politics one works on intuition, advice and instinct.

A relevant example is the leader's 'term of office'. In South Africa, there are term limits for presidents, premiers and mayors. But not for leaders of political parties. So, when I became Mayor of Cape Town in 2006, and later Premier of the Western Cape in 2009, I knew that I could serve a maximum of ten years in each position – divided into two five year terms, (as long as I was re-elected).

It goes without saying that I intend to complete my second term as Premier of the Western Cape, to which I was elected in May last year. This term is due to end in mid-2019.

As a Mayor or Premier (and of course a President as well), the constitution and the law define your duties and set clear parameters on what you may and must do (and, by extension, what you may not).

Leading a party is quite different. Although parties have constitutions and decision-making structures, much of the job of the leader boils down to decisions and actions informed by intuition; one has to 'read' a situation, and try to get as 'close to the reality' as possible before reaching a conclusion. The leader of a political party does this many times every day, in complex, rapidly-changing contexts, often bombarded by contradictory advice. And whether the decision turns out, over time, to have been right or wrong, there are always people who oppose it. That is the nature of politics.

It is in this kind of context that I have had to decide whether or not to stand for another term as leader at this year's Federal Congress on 9 May. I have led the DA for eight years now, and have worked closely with many outstanding people. From the start, I resolved that the outer limit of my term as party leader would be ten years, not because the party's constitution prescribes this (there are no term limits) but because I believe every political party needs renewal and fresh blood after a decade, no matter how well the incumbent team has performed.

So, from the day I was elected on May 6 2007, I knew that if I was re-elected at subsequent Congresses, the outside limit of my leadership term would be the 2017/8 Congress. In the last few years I have often asked myself whether I should stay till then, or whether the party would benefit from fresh blood to remain exciting and relevant, and grow its support base to build the non-racial centre of South African politics.

Facing the upcoming congress I have spent months wondering whether it is time to go now, or whether I should wait two more years. While May 2015 may be slightly too early, the greater risk is that May 2017 may be slightly too late. And I would rather err on the side of being ahead of my time.

This decision has, paradoxically, been a long time coming – but when the time was right, it was taken quickly, even suddenly. On Thursday last week, I took a firm decision that I would not stand for re-election as leader next month.

The overriding reason has been what I believe are the interests of the DA.

It is essential for a political party in opposition to grow in every election. While I believe we would have carried on growing beyond our current 4-million support base in next year's 2016 election under my continued leadership, I am convinced our prospects will be even better under a fresh team, armed with the new 'Values Charter' we will adopt and launch at Congress. As we all know, South Africa is in a race against time to save our constitution and ensure our democracy succeeds. We cannot waste a single minute or a single vote.

An advantage of my late decision is that the campaign that will determine the DA's next leader will be short and sharp, given that our elective Congress is four weeks away. This avoids the potential for a debilitating contest that deflects attention and effort away from the party's core functions, which inevitably happens when a leadership race drags out for long periods of time.

If I had been re-elected as leader next month, the succession race would have begun the next day and been the focus of attention for two years till the next congress, sapping the energy we need to harness in order to win votes, so that we can govern South Africa in the best interests of all its people.

Of course, I will continue working unceasingly to consolidate democracy in South Africa. This has been my life's work. I shall continue to do so as Premier of the Western Cape until 2019, and in appropriate ways, where I may be needed by the DA beyond that.

As usual, with every difficult decision, there will be those who agree with it, and those who do not. But as I know the party, we will all swing behind the team that is elected on May 9. We will also give advice and speak our minds in the appropriate forums.

And whether we agree or not, we will support our new leader in the way that I have always felt supported, and for which I am deeply grateful.

Of course, the commentators had a field day. The announcement could not simply be presented for what it was, a straightforward decision based on the evaluation of the pros and cons in a specific context. The Afrikaans newspapers reported, accurately, that I had made my decision because of my conclusion that it would create a difficult situation for the party if its two top leaders were white.

Jan-Jan Onselen developed a conspiracy theory to the effect that I had been 'stabbed in the back' by my closest advisers; and Richard Calland concluded I had 'outlived my usefulness' for the party's inner circle. Yadda yadda yadda ...

At the time I was 70 per cent certain that stepping down was the right decision, and 70 per cent is a high 'certainty ratio' in politics. Looking back, I am now 100 per cent certain it was the right decision. I got the timing absolutely right, which was both coincidental and circumstantial. I had fortuitously avoided the fate of most politicians, captured in the aphorism 'There is no comfortable end to a political career; only death or disgrace.'

My exit from the DA leadership was not only comfortable. It was heart-warming.

The party gave me a send-off I did not expect and will never forget. They invited my family to go to Port Elizabeth to experience it. I had no idea what awaited me, and because I knew how busy the boys were in their nascent careers, I told them they should not take the time to come. Dad would take photos, I said, and give them a blow-by-blow account. But Paul and Tom insisted, and so did Gretl.

I only learnt about their role in the proceedings shortly before they walked onto the congress stage – to do one of their inimitable send-ups of their mother. I had to agree with Tony Leon, who wrote to me afterwards: 'The most wonderful moment of the past two days was the marvellous double-act of your sons. You and Johan must be so proud of them.'

That was what my own recently departed mother would have called an 'English understatement'.

The boys' loving, ribbing humour made me laugh and cry simultaneously. When they were done, Janine made me blow my nose and reapplied my make-up, because my own final speech as leader lay ahead.

I heard the tributes but could only really take them in when I took time to read them afterwards. The situation was too overpowering.

Somehow the DA had managed to track down Bulelani Mfaco, who in his strong, gentle voice told the congress 'the story about Helen Zille, a white woman giving refuge to my gogo and other women when the apartheid government was hunting them down'.

Allister Sparks, my mentor and editor, whose political analysis had influenced me so much as a teenager, and who had taught me to write when I was a cadet journalist, compared my contribution with that of the DA's icon, Helen Suzman. He said:

> I know Helen Suzman is your iconic figure, and rightly so. I knew her, too, as a close friend. Dame Helen (you all know, of course, that Queen Elizabeth made her a Knight Commander of the Commonwealth) was indeed a courageous warrior in her long, lone fight for human rights in the very darkest of the apartheid years. She was brave and she was tenacious and she was magnificent. But Helen Suzman didn't pay much attention to political strategy and tactics. By her own admission, that wasn't her thing: she left that to Colin Eglin.
>
> But it's been very much Helen Zille's thing, and it's been very much the required thing in this post-apartheid era when Helen the Second has focused on how to build a viable opposition to challenge a Government that has the overwhelming advantage of being seen as having liberated its people from the oppression and exploitation of apartheid.
>
> That's one helluva challenge …
>
> When it comes to strategy, the most innovative decision ever undertaken in South African politics was Helen Zille's decision as DA leader to remove herself from the national Parliament to focus on local and regional politics. Nothing like that had ever been done before in a Westminster-style democracy. It was a strategic masterstroke, designed to demonstrate the DA's competence as a governing party, not just an opposition party in the talk-shop of Parliament. Such innovation requires not only brains but courage.
>
> Now we have another strategic move. Knowing when to step down is one of the toughest decisions any leader can face. Most get it wrong because their egos get in the way. But with the singularly important local government elections due just a year from now, that I believe will see the beginning of an era of political change through coalition government in our country, I think Helen has timed her departure exactly right. That, too, has required courage as well as judgment.
>
> Finally, I cannot conclude this tribute without including Helen's husband, Professor Johann Maree. He has also been a friend for many years. In fact he educated one of my sons who is now also a professor in the same field of labour relations. Johann has played the difficult role of Prince Consort with grace and dignity. I know, too, that while keeping in the background he has also occasionally been a discreet and valuable adviser to Helen.

And I also read Tony Leon's powerful tribute. It had a special meaning to me, given that the pendulum of our relationship had swung on such a wide arc – from confrontation to co-operation and collegiality.

The party which I was first elected to lead back in 1994 had fewer than 350 000 voters, just seven Members of Parliament, and a few dozen city councillors. Thirteen years later when I stood down as the first leader of the Democratic Alliance, the party had 2 million voters, 57 Members of Parliament, 1 100 municipal councillors and control of 20 municipalities.

I thought that was a fair legacy. Maar, soos ons sê hier in Die Baai, kyk hoe lyk ons nou!

Today, as the second DA leader makes way for the third, she and you can be very proud that she hands over a party of 4 million voters, 102 MPs, 1 656 councillors, and in control of one Province and 28 municipalities.

I once noted that the success of any leader is the success of that leader's successor. On that basis, I can say, without contradiction or dispute or second-guessing, this: –

The movement which Helen Zille, with your assistance, has built over the past eight years, is bigger, more united and today stands on more winning ground than we ever dared imagine or dream possible back in July 2000, 15 years ago, when we founded this Party...

You might know that we have not always agreed on single issues, or on every personality or on each tactic. But then we do belong to a party whose first name is 'Democratic' and which is an 'Alliance' of different interests and many communities.

But I have always believed in the true wisdom of the words offered to history by the great American President, Theodore Roosevelt. He said back in 1910, incidentally a decade before women had the vote in America, these immortal (and rather masculine) words:

'There is no effort without error and shortcoming; but who actually strives to do the deeds ... who spends himself in a worthy cause; who at the best knows in the end the triumph of high achievement, and who at the worst, if he fails, at least fails while daring greatly, so that his place shall never be with those cold and timid souls who know neither victory nor defeat.'

In celebrating Helen's leadership, not even her mightiest opponent, and no one certainly in the Twittersphere, could ever accuse her of being one of 'those cold and timid souls'!

But more than this, while it is relatively easy for a leader to deal with the triumphs of success, I want to turn for a moment to that much truer and sterner test which every leader must face: failure and defeat.

With all the successes on the scoreboard racked up by this Party and its outgoing leadership, it is easy to gloss over the real challenges, in the darkness of our recent past, which this party had to overcome. I want to remind you today of one of them.

Tony then spoke about the time, near the end of 2001, when Marthinus van Schalkwyk led the New National Party out of the DA and into the arms of the ANC:

> The very idea of opposition was in the balance; floor-crossing, political treachery, a rigged judicial commission presided over by an ANC judge was set up to destroy us. The siren calls of high office and cushy salaries were on offer by the ANC to some 'cold and timid souls' in the DA. Some jumped ship, double-crossed their voters and betrayed their mandates.
>
> As the leader of the DA, I had to push back against this with all my might and with the great and loyal assistance of so many of you in this hall today. In the Western Cape legislature, I knew that the one person who had our corner covered and who could never be swayed by the temptation of retaining high office by sacrificing her ideals was the leader of the opposition there, Helen Zille.

This gave me a new perspective of our internal conflicts at the time. Tony and I had disagreed on how to deal with the aftermath of the NNP's walkout, but we were always covering the same corner: the corner of an open and free society, under the rule of law, where a capable state ensures that each person has real opportunities to improve their lives through their own efforts. Tony called it the 'power of an idea', which was far preferable to the 'idea of power'.

And he ended with a word of advice to the person who would be elected later at the congress as the 'third leader of the Democratic Alliance'.

> He must adapt tactics and change strategies to grow this movement further, to reach out to more people, to offer rescue to poor communities in distress, taxpayers and property owners under siege, businesses in failure and so many people who have given up on hope that the promise of 1994 can ever be redeemed. He must honour the past, but he must not live in it.
>
> But more than this, he must convince with the power of his conviction. He must tell the truth: nationalisms of whatever stripe divide and exclude and as history has proven, in the end, always fail. Again he must hoist aloft the banner of a non-racial rainbow nation, built on freedom, cemented by individual choice, anchored in a growing economy and always in service to the many, not the few. He must rebuild that constitutional bridge. And he must live as Helen Zille has led: that public office is a place of principled achievement, not a place to acquire wealth or a hideout for criminal misbehaviour.

As I read it, I thought back on the crowd that day, packing the Boardwalk Hotel Convention Centre in Port Elizabeth. I thought of the new leadership standing on the stage: Mmusi Maimane, Athol Trollip, the three deputy chairpersons, Desiree van der Walt, Refiloe Ntsekhe and Ivan Meyer.

Of course, journalists and observers did the obligatory racial headcount of the congress participants as well as the leadership. And, they pronounced, the DA's demographic composition was fundamentally changed. But what mattered most to me was that the hall was full of blue people – people who understood the power of the DA's idea and were prepared to mobilise behind it, because we knew, in the words of our first leader, Jan Steytler, quoted by Tony: 'One day South Africa will be governed according to our principles because it is the only way it can be governed.'

Reading through my own farewell speech in hindsight, it seems rather pedestrian compared to the others.

If politics were only about policy, the DA would have been in government long ago. Building a new majority based on shared values in a complex, plural society was a 'tough ask', I said, 'which is why our opponents won't even try it'.

'It's far easier to drive people apart than to unite those who have been historically divided.

'It's far easier to focus on diversions and grandstanding than to address the real reasons for poverty and inequality.

'It's far easier to chant slogans in parliament than to do the hard yards, fighting year-in and year-out, for accountability through our democratic institutions.

'It's far easier to play the race card whenever someone makes a point you can't answer, rather than engage them with an honest and open mind.

'It's far easier to look after your politically connected friends, and pretend that this is transformation, than to broaden opportunities for all the people.

'It is far easier to keep blaming the past than to try to fix the present and build the future.'

The DA was the only party that took this difficult route, I said, because we understood the truth of the most famous political aphorism in South Africa's struggle history: 'There is no easy walk to freedom. We mustn't pretend it has suddenly become easy now.'

In fact, I knew it was only going to get harder, because the real battle for the future would actually be between two mutually incompatible philosophies, symbolised by the DA's constitutionalism and the EFF's populism. The dividing line between them ran right through the middle of the ANC. The 'liberation movement' was at war with itself, and its inevitable decline just a matter of time.

Mmusi Maimane was elected by a very wide margin, and I felt the parachute of leadership drop me gently to the ground. I slipped out of the harness. The celebration for Mmusi that followed provided a brief interval before the harness of office would be strapped tightly to his ample shoulders. I looked at Natalie, his wife, who was new to politics and slightly overwhelmed by the occasion, as well as Kgalaletso and Daniel, their children, and wished the young family the strength and resilience they would need, more than they could ever know, to survive the years ahead.

We had to do what no party in a modern democracy had ever done before. We had to overcome historical barriers of race, ethnicity, culture and prejudice to bring together a new majority based on values, principles and policies. By building the DA, we had come much further than I could ever have imagined, in the first two decades of freedom, to entrench and defend the rule of law and accountability as the bedrock of our democracy.

From now on, my contribution to the idea would focus on the third crucial component that had become my passion: building a capable state to demonstrate, over time, what the DA's policies could achieve for every South African.

If the purpose of life is to find a meaningful purpose, I had found mine.

22

The Problem with Race Politics

IN THE FIFTEEN-MONTH run-up to the 2016 local government election, it became increasingly clear how well-timed my exit as DA federal leader was.

Parliament became the centre of media attention once more, primarily because of the antics of the EFF, and the ANC's ham-fisted attempts to silence their unruly, red-overalled opponents. As the confrontations across the floor escalated, the once moribund parliamentary television channel became as popular as the country's best-loved soapie series. And, as the EFF demolished parliamentary process and decorum, many commentators opined that Julius Malema had become the real leader of the opposition.

It was an enormously challenging context for the DA. We had to provide a compelling counter-narrative, by demonstrating the importance of building crucial institutions such as parliament, not destroying them. It was essential, during this period, that the DA's federal leader should be a member of parliament. This was no easy entrée for Mmusi. It was a baptism of fire as he tried to shape a distinct and differentiated role while building the DA's profile. The media gave blanket coverage to Malema's theatrics and Zuma's evasiveness. Mmusi had to forge an alternative brand of tough, dignified civility. In a growing confrontation between two extremes, it is difficult for these undramatic attributes to be noticed. But Mmusi's powerful oratory, delivered in his comfortable style, and backed by John Steenhuisen's agility in the key role of chief whip, provided the ideal counterfoil.

Every time I watched their performances on television, I was relieved to be on the other side of the small screen. But there was an additional, even more compelling reason why I was grateful to have relinquished the hot seat.

The years 2015 and 2016 turned out to be a period of unmatched racial toxicity and polarisation, primarily driven by social media. Apart from the escalating capture of state institutions by the ANC, and South Africa's spiral of economic decline, the growing climate of racist invective was creating profound pessimism about the possibility of building an inclusive society. Many times I thought we were reverting to a new form of apartheid, a society defined by race, where demography would once more become destiny.

It started at the University of Cape Town, when Chumani Maxwele, a thirty-year-old student, flung a container of human excrement over the statue of Cecil

John Rhodes (which had stood in a prominent position on the campus for over eight decades), while a news photographer waited nearby to capture the image.

Maxwele had made the news before, when he was arrested for flipping a finger at the siren-wailing motorcade of President Zuma in 2010. I had sought to help him secure legal assistance at the time. From our interactions then, it was clear he relished the limelight. And when he was awarded a damages claim for unlawful arrest, I expected to hear from him again.

So I was not surprised when his name was linked to the front-page photo of sewer sludge dripping from the stony gaze of the arch imperialist, staring across the African hinterland. The news surged through the cyber-circuit of thousands of mobile phones, launching the #RhodesMustFall movement. The statue, in prime position on the symmetrical central campus, was the ideal symbol to galvanise a new generation of student activists to occupy buildings, invade meetings and set the terms of engagement with university administrators.

The fact that Rhodes had originally bequeathed the land along the slopes of Devil's Peak and Table Mountain to establish the world's most beautifully located campus was an aggravating rather than mitigating factor. For the student protesters, it begged the question: how did it become his to bequeath in the first place? Rhodes had only lived in South Africa for thirty-two years, initially in Durban and then mostly in Kimberley as a diamond prospector, amassing untold wealth and influence. He was elected to the Cape parliament and became prime minister of the Cape Colony at the age of thirty-seven, acquiring prime tracts of land including the Groote Schuur Estate. His statue served as a daily reminder of his colonial project.

Within weeks of its undignified 'baptism', the statue of the man who, in his prime, was depicted as a colossus astride Africa, one foot in Cape Town and the other in Cairo, was dangling at the end of a steel cable as it was lifted off its plinth by a crane and secreted into storage, perhaps never to emerge again.

I understood the case for moving the Rhodes statue to a less prominent spot, but I knew its removal could not eradicate history.

The #MustFall frenzy demonstrated how ahistorical populist history can be. As their rebellion gathered steam, student leaders began accusing the Mandela generation of prematurely abandoning the liberation struggle – as if students' lives would have been better had the ANC hung on for a military victory against the apartheid regime (and as if this was ever even a possibility).

#RhodesMustFall struck a chord because it offered students the romanticised prospect of completing their parents' unfinished revolution. The ensuing #MustFall movement emerged in various incarnations on campuses countrywide, and exploded into a full-blown revolt when the announcement of steep tuition fee increases provided the lightning strike in a perfect storm. #FeesMustFall swept through campuses, culminating in the siege of parliament on 21 October 2015 and an assault on the administrative seat of government, the Union Buildings, two days later, where students breached the perimeter fence and burnt barricades, sending up palls of acrid smoke over the amphitheatre in which Nelson Mandela had been inaugurated as South Africa's first democratic president in an international celebration twenty-one years earlier.

Within hours, after meeting university principals, President Jacob Zuma waved the metaphorical white flag. He did not emerge to address the crowd. Remaining in his office for his own safety, he told the nation via television that there would be no fee increases for 2016.

The wheel of history had turned. The students had drawn blood. #MustFall caught on.

As is the case with many populist causes, it was rooted in a real and valid issue – the accumulation of unaffordable debt by South African students. A young person leaving university owing upwards of R250 000 will be shackled by debt for decades, even if they are lucky enough to get a job. They will then typically also have to meet demands for support from an extended family, where a university education for one member is often regarded as a pathway out of poverty for the rest.

Students were justified in telling the ruling party to live up to its campaign promise of more affordable education (especially in a context of billions disappearing down the hole of rampant corruption). #FeesMustFall provided a rare South African moment when supporters of all parties rallied behind a single cause.

The unity of purpose during those initial heady days was short-lived. As the year-end exams approached, student solidarity splintered between those who wanted to write their exams and regroup in the new academic year and those who were determined that the exams would not be written until further demands were met.

In a leaderless movement, everyone's ideas demand equal attention. Without a centre of gravity, divisions multiply, factions form, and the distance between them grows. Every issue becomes contentious, such as the photo of the Wits SRC president, Nompendulo Mkhatshwa, wearing ANC headgear, on the cover of *Destiny* magazine, where she was depicted as the face of #FeesMustFall. This caused outrage in the rest of the movement as others asked who had given her a mandate to be presented as the leader of an organic, egalitarian movement of communal interests.

Before long, #FeesMustFall spawned #FeesWillFall and public support evaporated as groups of students threw stones, damaged motor vehicles, disrupted examinations and set buildings alight.

But fees were not the only, nor even ultimately the main, issue at stake. Indeed, when you scratched the surface, listened to the discourse, and read the blogs and newspaper columns, it emerged that the movement, in its various manifestations, was a thin veneer for something else.

The official Facebook site of #RhodesMustFall explained: 'The statue was the natural starting point of this movement; its removal will not mark the end, but the beginning of the long overdue process of decolonising this university. In our belief the experiences seeking to be addressed by this movement are not unique to an elite institution such as UCT, but rather reflect broader dynamics of a racist and patriarchal society that has remained unchanged since the end of formal apartheid.'

To be sure, there is still a great deal of 'racism and patriarchy' in South Africa today, some of it truly stomach churning. One just has to scan the public commentary under online news reports to get a taste of it. Another prominent example was the primitively poisonous Facebook post of a woman named Penny Sparrow, who called black people monkeys after observing the litter left on the beach after New Year celebrations at the beginning of 2016.

But for students (many of whom would have been barred from enrolling at their university of choice under apartheid) to suggest that nothing has changed in the past twenty-two years shows why their generation is known as the 'born-frees'. Yes, we should by now have been far further along the road to a prosperous and inclusive society. As our progress stalled, the search for scapegoats started. The #MustFall movement soon assumed the vanguard of this trend.

Ironically, it was led primarily by a young emerging middle class which has, arguably, benefited more from the demise of 'formal apartheid' than any other sector of society. Presenting themselves as the persecuted, they gradually turned themselves into persecutors, intimidating others and denying them freedom of choice, or even the right to an alternative opinion. There is a wonderful new term for this tendency: crybullies.

What's more, they never explained what they meant by decolonising the university. It certainly did not entail abandoning high-end fashion labels or the latest technological gadgets. On the few occasions when I could ask the question directly, I was told it meant Africanising the curriculum, but I have not yet seen a coherent analysis of precisely what this would entail across the various disciplines of an international institution of higher learning. Providing an answer would have been a valuable contribution to the national discourse on transformation.

Instead, #MustFall, in its many manifestations, was accompanied by a rash of newspaper articles describing South Africa's core problem as 'Whiteness', the face of twentieth-century colonialism. Decolonisation is the essential corollary. Taken to its logical conclusion, this line of thinking would define whites as alien in South Africa and its institutions.

I learnt that the concept of whiteness is rooted in critical race theory, a line of thinking which, ironically, comes directly from the United States of America, which supporters of the #MustFall movement despise as the epicentre of global capitalist imperialism. Critical race theory proceeds from the assumption that 'whiteness' is a profound social problem. It is the underlying reason why, in the United States, proportionally more black youngsters are in jail, get poorer average test scores or are more likely to be abandoned by their fathers. The 'pathology of whiteness' is closely aligned to the 'violence of whiteness', which provides the impetus behind the movement #BlackLivesMatter.

Of course black lives matter. But don't dare suggest that #AllLivesMatter. Critical race theorists will accuse you of 'wilful colour-blindness' and of 'deliberately taking race out of the conversation'. If a white policeman shoots a black youth, all whites share culpability, but not vice versa. Woe betide anyone who draws a general conclusion about black people on the basis of an individual's actions.

The purpose of critical race theory in South Africa is not to build an inclusive, non-racial society, which many of us thought was the aim of the liberation struggle. It is to entrench race as the prime social marker, the determinant of pain and privilege, victimhood and villainy. Four legs good, two legs bad.

It resurrects, with a vengeance, the real pathology of divided societies – broad generalisations about entire categories of people based on skin colour, religion, language or ethnicity. It seeks out reasons to promote a new form of social exclusion, based on the sins inherited from previous generations, sins that must constantly be resuscitated in order to reinforce the divisions on which critical race theory feeds.

What began in the United States as an attempt to empower a marginalised minority is becoming, in South Africa, a tool to justify the unbridled hegemony of a racial majority, to classify and pathologise minorities on the basis of racial generalisations, and so discount and delegitimise any contribution they try to make. Individuals aren't evaluated in their own right, on their own merits, or their contribution to society. They are merely a function of their colour.

Critical race theory rejects non-racialism, because it supposedly denies the 'centrality of black pain'. The #RhodesMustFall mission statement dismisses the South African constitution's conception of racism as 'fundamentally racist because it presupposes that racism is a universal experience, thus normalising the suffering of those who actually experience racism'.

In other words, only whites can be racist and only blacks can experience the suffering of racism. That is why 'whiteness' is the problem that must be eradicated. And don't try to debate this thesis. As a Yale student famously said during a controversy about the appropriateness of wearing certain Halloween costumes: 'I don't want to debate. I want to talk about my pain.'

The only acceptable whites in South Africa, according to critical race theorists, are those who retreat in the face of this kind of argument. Some argue that whites must acknowledge that their very presence in the country is shameful and destructive, and that the only way to deal with this is silent self-flagellation. Apart from self-criticism, whites have nothing to contribute to the political debate.

During the #MustFall movement, I learnt a whole new race-laced vocabulary arising out of the 'violence of whiteness'. I read about 'authentic blackness', 'ontological blackness', 'cultural appropriation', 'racial micro-aggression', 'the phenomenology of personal experience' and the 'commoditisation of black pain' (among others).

From my experience with anorexia, I know that it is useful to give a condition a name, because this helps to describe and deal with it. When I thought about these terms, I concluded that some of them can indeed make a contribution to the important debate we need to have about race, despite their academic pretentiousness.

Take the concept 'racial micro-aggression'. All of us have experienced toe-curling situations similar to that of a senior colleague who attended a diplomatic function in Cape Town last year, representing the provincial Department of International Relations. Waiting for the speeches to commence, he helped himself to some snacks and mingled with the crowd. It didn't take long before other guests were helping themselves from his plate. Because he was black, they assumed he was a waiter carrying a serving plate.

This type of profiling is common on many fronts of our manifold social cleavages. Almost every woman in a senior position, for example, has been mistaken for the receptionist in her office. It is therefore useful, even necessary, to have a name for these experiences so that we can discuss issues that would otherwise fester below the surface. We need to become conscious of our assumptions, so that we anticipate and avoid these divisive and embarrassing interactions.

I part company with this analysis, however, in its assumption that racial micro-aggressions are a one-way street. The 'phenomenology of personal experience' means that we all make assumptions about each other, drawing pejorative general conclusions from individual encounters, often under a cloak of academic jargon.

A good example comes from Ms Wanelisa Xaba, a master's student at one of Africa's best universities, situated in what she describes as 'the white colony of Cape Town'. She explains her world view as follows:

> We live in a world of white supremacist heterosexist patriarchy under capitalism – google that term, because it is a thing. And it is powerful. It determines which bodies from which races, gender, sexuality, weight, size and ability get to be defined as human. White people don't see you because seeing you means seeing themselves and their illegitimate existence in this country. To recognise you means to recognise that their existence in this country is a direct result of psychological and cultural genocides, looting and the killing of our ancestors.

> Every material and immaterial privilege that white South Africa enjoys today has centuries of blood dripping from it, which they cover with denial. To recognise you means that they understand that their very presence in this country is violence to the generations of African people who suffer intergenerational trauma inflicted from colonisation until now.[*]

Author Malaika Wa Azania provides a real-life example of what this theory means in practice. She survived the violation of being invited to the Franschhoek Literary Festival in 2015 to discuss themes in her book *Memoirs of a Born Free: Reflections on the Rainbow Nation*. The venue of the discussion was the local Congregational church, and it was chaired by Jonathan Jansen, the vice-chancellor of the University of the Orange Free State.

For reasons she does not explain, Ms Wa Azania voluntarily accepted this invitation, but reflecting on the experience in a subsequent article in the *Sunday Independent* of 31 May, she wrote:

> There is no space more expressive of white violence than the Franschhoek Literary Festival, held each year in the small Western Cape town that remains one of the bastions of white supremacy ...
>
> I was a participant in two panel discussions: one on student activism and another on woman writers breaking free from cages. I should have known from the minute that I walked in that I was entering a violent space. The church was filled to capacity by a white audience, with sprinkles of black faces (I counted five in total ...)
>
> I should have known, merely by the fact that one of the worst apologists of our times was chairing the session, that black thought was going to be sacrificed at the altar of white appeasement.

At first I thought her article was a spoof, but on rereading it, I realised she was serious. I wondered who had elected Ms Wa Azania the spokesperson for 'black thought'. I reflected on why she was so upset at having drawn a capacity crowd, and what her response would have been if no whites had bothered to pitch up to listen to her. What would she have said if the facilitator of the discussion had been white, rather than a renowned black intellectual? As for the demographic mix, did she expect the organisers to coerce more black people to attend her talk if they voluntarily chose not to?

Asking these questions would be regarded as proof of my whiteness, an accusation designed to end critical analysis. It is the ultimate conversation stopper.

To be fair, Ms Wa Azania does propose a solution to the problem of 'white

---

[*] *The Daily Vox* (online), 27 March 2015

violence'. No surprises here: it involves the allocation of more money from the state and the private sector. Would this include donations from 'white capital', I wondered. While not specifically addressing the colour of the money, Ms Wa Azania stressed that both the state and the private sector would have to 'dig deep' to 'fund the infrastructure required for local and African literature to flourish'.

> Until these two things are done, the literary space, in terms of festivals like Franschhoek and the very value chain of publishing, is going to continue with its normalisation of violence, exclusion and the intellectual onslaught on black bodies. And that would be too heinous a crime.

As I reflected on the article and its proposal, I asked myself: Who, exactly, is commoditising black pain?

Not to be outdone in the whiteness survivor stakes, Professor Xolela Mangcu has written extensively about what he describes as the 'suffocating whiteness' of the University of Cape Town, where he is an associate professor of sociology. He copes with his situation by going beyond merely commoditising black pain. He actually commercialises it.

He is quite frank about it. In a delightfully irony-laden article in *Business Day* of 2 November 2015, he describes how he got to where he is today. It is quite clear that the only time white liberals have been of any value in his life was when they were paying his bills.

He tells the story of how, as a fiery young student and proponent of black consciousness and scientific socialism, he managed to win a generous scholarship after being interviewed by three of South Africa's wealthiest industrialists. He managed to compress his studies into two years at the prestigious Massachusetts Institute of Technology, while living it up in one of America's most elite suburbs.

According to Mangcu, those who funded this interlude in his life epitomised 'enlightened liberalism'. This, I presume, is different from 'whiteness'.

I learnt from critical race theory that, while negative attributes of individual whites prove the generalised problem of 'whiteness', any positive action attributed to a white person is deemed an individual exception.

Now, in 2015, lamented Mangcu, the situation was much more difficult for black students than it was at the height of apartheid. 'The policy issues the students are dealing with now – decolonising the curriculum, changing the composition of the professoriate and finding money for free higher education – are far more complex than bringing down an oppressive regime,' he concluded.

Then he bewailed the second reason for the challenges facing black students – 'the absence of the big-hearted liberalism of those three men who interviewed me and allowed me to define my own way with their money'.

'What we have instead,' he said, 'are business leaders who are penny-pinchers and university vice-chancellors who are more adept at disciplinary measures against students than in understanding where they are coming from and where they might want to go.'

As I finished reading the article I could feel a wave of whiteness washing over me. Basically, what Professor Mangcu was saying was this: the only good whites are those handing money to blacks (as if depicting black people as permanently dependent on hand-outs isn't a classic and humiliating example of race profiling). Furthermore, black socialists can be bought off if white liberals pay for them to spend time in elite institutions while living in the most exclusive suburbs of global capitalism.

When I thought about it again, however, I realised that he had a point. Isn't that precisely what many black economic empowerment deals crafted under present government policy are all about?

And as for vice-chancellors, I concluded that Mangcu's real problem was that most of them are now black and do not fall for these manipulative ruses any longer. Instead, they devote hundreds of millions of rands (far more than any of their predecessors) to student financial aid, and are forever fundraising for the purpose. Many individuals and companies continue to support access to universities for poor students, in far greater measure than Mangcu's three 'acceptable' white liberals did in his particular case.

I refer Professor Mangcu to the website http://www.politicsweb.co.za/news-and-analysis/how-wits-is-funded, where he will learn that the private sector provided R523 million in financial aid to students at the University of the Witwatersrand in 2015. UCT disbursed R440 million in student financial aid in 2015, a large proportion of which came from donors and corporate sponsors.

But drawing evidence-based conclusions is not a strong feature of critical race theory. It is all about personal feelings, based on the 'phenomenology of experience'. As Professor Achille Mbembe of the University of the Witwatersrand explains, 'Under the pretext that the personal is political, this type of autobiographical and at times self-indulgent petit bourgeois discourse has replaced structural analysis. Personal feelings now suffice.'[*] In other words, telling your personal story is an acceptable substitute for academic research. You, yourself, constitute a random, stratified research sample of one, from which to draw general conclusions about 'blackness' and 'whiteness'.

Mangcu ended his piece by advising students: 'Take the assistance that will come your way from the government and the private sector, but hold your own.'

No one can accuse Mangcu of not following his own advice. He continues to seek out any assistance he can get, especially from eateries around Cape Town,

---

[*] *Africa Is a Country*, online commentary, 19 September 2015

where he conducts participant-observer research on the racial micro-aggressions of whiteness.

There was the famous 'Spinachgate' case, which involved a lunchtime fracas at a restaurant that had advertised a 'special' including a side-order of spinach which was not available when he ordered it. After an argument with the manager, he was exempted from paying the bill and asked to leave. He likened the incident to the way 'black people were made to internalise oppression in the 1960s until Steve Biko came along'.

On another occasion, a newspaper reported on an altercation between Mangcu and a coffee-shop chef named Claudine Adams about the consistency of an omelette. According to Mangcu, the chef commented that he probably didn't know how an omelette was made, and proceeded to 'lecture' him on the subject. As a black person, he said, it was depressing not knowing how his day would turn out. 'You can't predict if a racist experience will mess up your day.'

The owner of the coffee shop, one Irvin Frank, had a different version, however. He said Mangcu had called the chef a 'coloured servant' whom he did not want to deal with and had ordered her to get the manager. He said Mangcu had been at the restaurant a few times and was always rude to the staff.

I'm not suggesting whose version you should believe, but in case you think that calling someone a 'coloured servant' can be classified as a racial micro-aggression, think again. According to some critical race theorists, racism cascades from lighter to darker skins, not the other way round. This means that a black man can call a woman of mixed descent a 'coloured servant' without being racist or patriarchal. But not the other way round.

I took a particular interest in all this because, at the time, a popular lobby was driving a social-media campaign seeking to represent Cape Town as a racist city. To be sure, there were some gross examples of 'racial profiling' to support this theory, such as the occasion a white man jumped out of his car in Kenilworth and assaulted a forty-four-year-old black woman on her way to work, on the assumption that she was a prostitute 'working the street'. No history of 'personal phenomenological experience' of sex-workers in his area could explain, let alone justify, this kind of behaviour. It was roundly, and rightly, condemned by everyone, black or white, as he faced charges of assault and the law took its course.

That was clearly a case for the criminal justice system. But to deal with less 'cut-and-dried' cases, I invited anyone who had an experience of racism in the city to contact my office, and I undertook to ensure the complaint was investigated. I received around ten complaints over three years, and almost all of them were based on individual experiences in upmarket restaurants and places of entertainment. One young man, for example, messaged me after midnight on New Year's Day to complain that a white patron had jumped the queue and been served ahead of him at a club in Green Point. I duly followed up by writing to the bar's proprietor, who was convinced it was a parody letter purporting to come from the premier. I had a hard time convincing him (short of actually presenting myself in person) that it was really me making the enquiry. Suffice to say his account of the event differed substantially, and I learnt, yet again, how hard it is to get to the truth of these situations.

The difficulty of getting to the truth is one of the founding assumptions of academic research conducted in humanities faculties worldwide. For this reason, it is surprising that the new discourse emerging from many South African humanities faculties seems to accept, as a given, that 'whiteness' is the biggest barrier to black advancement. But has anyone seriously tested this thesis? Is there anyone doing research into the other potential barriers, such as the role played by some teachers' trade unions, or the impact of the failure of millions of fathers to maintain and parent their children, or the epidemic of teenage pregnancies? And why does our discourse not focus on the factors that are deterring investment, growth and job creation? It is far easier to focus on the problem of 'whiteness'. Indeed, researching the impact of whiteness may be one of the few ways that white social scientists can avoid accusations of 'whiteness'.

Fixating on this issue detracts attention from where we should be focusing – on decent basic services for people, including education and health care; and creating conditions for economic growth, so that people, especially poor people, can use their opportunities to get jobs and improve their lives. The fact that Cape Town does this more effectively than any other city merely intensifies the allegations of racism from the restaurant-and-club-frequenting elite.

It is tempting to roll one's eyes and regard this debate as a marginal zone occupied by narcissists determined to turn every window on the world into a self-reflecting mirror. But don't be fooled. Critical race theory, in its South African variegation, has become a fig leaf for scapegoating. There are many examples worldwide of failing governments and political parties adopting similar theories to turn minorities into scapegoats in order to mobilise and unite a divided support base, or cover up their own policy failures.

Blaming 'whiteness' is no longer peripheral to South Africa's discourse. It has become mainstream, and is even considered 'progressive'.

It really worried me when these assumptions started emerging in the DA's own internal debates. At times it appeared as if some among the new generation of DA public representatives felt a greater need for affirmation from their trendy social-media and student peers than to defend our principles. They sometimes fell into the trap of accepting broad race generalisations when there was an advantage to be gained for the rising black elite, while expressing outrage at such generalisations when there wasn't. Thus, some argued, 'black' should remain a proxy for disadvantage when it comes to preferential access to universities, irrespective of an individual's background; but it would be outrageous to assume that 'black' might be used as a proxy, say, for predicting the risk of HIV infection. This risk measure was once actually used by the South African blood transfusion service, when it lacked reliable alternative methods of preventing HIV-positive blood being used in the infectious 'window period' before a donor's AIDS antibodies could be picked up in a test.

There was general outrage about this practice because it was based on a racial generalisation; namely, that black people were more likely to engage in unsafe sexual practices and therefore have a greater risk of contracting HIV. Each person, the argument went (and I endorsed this), is entitled to be evaluated on their individual behaviour. If judging individuals on their own merits is a principle, which I believe it is, we must apply it consistently, and not default to racial generalisations when there is a sectarian advantage to be gained from it.

Standing firm on this principle, especially if you are black, requires enormous courage in the current circumstances, just as it did for Helen Suzman to swim against the stream fifty years ago. It takes no courage at all to be hip and happening. It is always easier to appease your opponents than to defend your principles. And, as I have learnt, it always comes back to haunt you.

It is unsurprising, therefore, that whites are not the only (or even the main) targets of the assault on 'whiteness'. The most virulent criticism is reserved for black people who challenge the primacy of race discourse. They are labelled 'inauthentic blacks' at best, or 'house niggers' at worst. Those who, because of the advantages of a good education, speak with 'white accents' are labelled 'coconuts' (black on the outside and white on the inside), or 'clever blacks', whose sin is having given the pathology of whiteness a non-racial face. Coconuts can only atone by becoming virulent proponents of race-laced discourse, more Catholic than the Pope. Some race evangelists believe they even have the right to interfere in people's private lives, to the point of advocating the termination of interracial friendships and relationships.

To his great credit, despite the most virulent race-baiting, Mmusi Maimane has never wavered in his defence of non-racialism. His persecutors have even seen fit to condemn his marriage to a white woman and, incredibly, this issue even emerged as a factor in his election campaign for the leadership of the DA when some people implied that this showed he was 'not black enough'. Deciding who qualifies as an authentic black is a right that critical race theorists have appropriated for themselves. To qualify, a person has to live life according to the predetermined script. It comes close to a new form of tyranny. Facing such vitriolic attack, Mmusi had the backbone and the guts to stand firm, distinguishing himself as a rare leader.

Ironically, the zealots who assume the right to police interracial relationships don't hesitate themselves to seize upon any relationship that will bring them a personal advantage, whether it is a scholarship endowed by the arch-colonialist Rhodes, or a fellowship established in memory of Ruth First, a white woman who was blown up by the apartheid security police for her part in the struggle for a non-racial, more egalitarian society. If you point out these contradictions, prepare to be met with the full wrath of people who cannot credibly and rationally explain them. This discourse brooks no opposition.

This is the reason I was particularly struck by an article in *Business Day* (reproduced by the *Rand Daily Mail* online on 22 September 2015) written by a history lecturer at Rhodes University, Nomalanga Mkhize. Picking up on what Professor Achille Mbembe has described as the 'me-too-ism' of black pain, she notes that the 'new politics of decolonisation' has the tendency to speak through political narratives of 'self', illustrated by personal examples. The me, myself and I version of history.

The victimhood narrative emanating from the black middle class, Mkhize argues, cannot merely be attributed to the 'inherent narcissism of students', but also to

> the subtle influences of the university lecture hall and what is sometimes called the humanities 'way of speaking'.
>
> Many of the students are drawing from what I call a 'grammar of the particular' or 'particularism' in advancing their arguments for the problem of black alienation on campuses. Particularism is a method of approaching social research in which a single case is given an exaggerated sense of visibility and importance because the research is narrated through story-like form and the use of the word 'I'.

And then comes her conclusion:

> The students' shortcomings in articulating a radically open universalism is partly a reflection of the intellectual failures of South African universities. Part of that failure occurs because the humanities are also attached to a tradition of vanguardist leftism in which the most significant processes of human life are those codified as resistance and struggle. We continue to impart outdated radical theories that purport to answer the universal problems of humanity, by for example 'smashing the ruling classes'.
>
> I am not bashing theory; we can make no universal claims without it. All I am saying is that if the students sound overindulgent, it is partly because our universities are failing to import new, compelling ideas to grapple with complicated African realities.

I can hardly think of a more timely and apt critique. Since apartheid ended, nineteenth-century European Marxism has been replaced by a crude form of American critical race theory as the dominant 'liberation analysis'. Both have profoundly constrained our capacity to address the complexities and challenges of development on our continent. Why is it so hard to learn from the world's history and broaden our horizons?

In the midst of all of this, I travelled to Mexico City to stand for re-election as deputy president of Liberal International (LI). LI is an umbrella organisation of over 105 political parties across six continents, including thirteen from Africa, that seek to build inclusive, open societies on the foundation of constitutionalism, the rule of law, independent institutions and market economies. It was a great relief to be able to escape from the cage of South Africa's race discourse for a while, into the environment of 'radically open universalism' which Liberal International represents. I travelled with my friends and colleagues Stevens Mokgalapa and Michael Cardo. Together, we formed part of a larger African delegation comprising representatives from Sierra Leone, Côte d'Ivoire, Senegal, Democratic Republic of Congo, Morocco, Ghana and Kenya, among others. We spent time together in animated discussion about how to achieve our shared commitment to open democracies and flourishing economies across our continent. My whiteness was no barrier to full and equal participation. Arguments were evaluated on their merits, not damned on the basis of their origin. And my whiteness was entirely irrelevant to my candidacy for deputy president. I felt free and equal in a way that I had not felt at home for a while.

We discussed the challenges facing democrats in situations as divergent as Thailand and Cuba. We heard optimistic analyses about the outcome of the recent Argentinian elections which forced the first-ever presidential run-off and opened the door for a credible liberal challenge to the populist corruption of 'Kirchnerism'. Venezuelan delegates were optimistic about the pending legislative elections scheduled in their country, and I was fascinated by their first-hand accounts of the devastation wrought by Chavism's corruption, nationalisation and unsustainable public spending after the commodities bubble burst in 2014 and oil prices plummeted. For four full days I relished the context of a debate in which the issues were the issue.

Then it was time to return home. During the twenty-five-hour flight I read the *Financial Times*, which led with a story describing the resurgence of the American economy. 'The Bureau of Labour Statistics reported the strongest rate of job creation thus far this year, as payrolls expanded by 271,000,' the *FT* reported. Why, I asked myself, are the only ideas we import from the United States related to gurrl feminism and critical race theory? Why can't we learn about how to grow an economy that creates jobs?

Arriving home after the very long flight, across an eight-hour time difference, sleep eluded me, so I whiled away the time lying in bed scrolling through my Twitter timeline.

There is nothing guaranteed to bring one crashing down to earth more quickly in South Africa than the phenomenon known as 'Black Twitter'. It involves an unending stream of race-baiting and invective, the purpose of which is to make you betray your 'whiteness', after which the pack-hunt begins.

Having been in Mexico, I had dropped my guard. While engaging in random conversations with some of my Twitter followers, I was interrupted by someone calling herself 'Mcebo's Baby Mama'. This handle is revealing. The phrase 'baby mama' is an Americanism adopted by Black Twitter to describe the mother of a man's child, who is not his wife or exclusive partner. And the name Mcebo is linked in the public mind with the surname Dlamini. Mcebo Dlamini shot to notoriety when he was removed from his position as president of the Student Representative Council at the University of the Witwatersrand for declaring his love for Hitler. Then, for good measure, Dlamini described Jews as 'devils' and a university principal as 'a house negro posing as a vice-chancellor'. Shortly afterwards, Mcebo Dlamini emerged as part of the collective leadership of the #MustFall movement.

Given this background, I shouldn't have been surprised when Mcebo's Baby Mama let me know: 'I hate you so much @HelenZille. I really do.'

I ignored her.

She then broadened her attack: 'I hate white people so much' – accompanied by five emoticons of crying faces for dramatic effect.

I ignored her.

Then someone else joined the conversation, and light-heartedly referred to 'Ma Hadebe' (which I associate with a line in the iconic Brenda Fassie song 'Vul'indlela'). I quoted the line back, in Xhosa. At which Mcebo's Baby Mama interrupted once more with: 'Voetsek you cultural appropriator.'

This term describes critical race theory's rejection of the use of any element of black culture by outsiders. In South Africa, it is used as a lever of social exclusion, to remind minorities that they don't belong. This label works in the same way as racism. It is reserved for the exclusive use of the melanin-advantaged to describe the melanin-deprived.

Silly me. Here I have been, for over a decade, trying to master the extraordinary complexity of the beautiful Xhosa language, as a miniscule contribution I thought I could make to nation building. Rather than assume fellow South Africans should engage with me in my language, I wanted to try to speak at least one of theirs and deepen my understanding of our different cultures. To critical race theorists, this is a sign of deep disrespect, one of the sins of 'whiteness', called 'cultural appropriation'.

After her third barb, I looked more closely at the profile pic of Mcebo's Baby Mama, and noticed that she had 'corn rows' behind which dangled a few plaits.

So, to demonstrate the contradiction in her calling me a cultural appropriator for tweeting in Xhosa, I replied: 'And I see you are wearing a weave. Cultural appropriation much??'

To which Mcebo's Baby Mama responded: 'It's not a weave you despot.'

The battalions of Authentic Black Twitter went into overdrive of righteous outrage over my tweet, working into the wee hours to expose my 'whiteness' and limited knowledge of weaves. The topic trended between midnight and three in the morning on 4 November 2015.

Unsurprisingly, the next day the online version of Independent Newspapers ran a story reinforcing the interpretation that my response to 'Mcebo's Baby Mama' had been personal and racist.

The lesson for whites is simple: if you want to be counted among the ranks of what Mangcu calls 'enlightened liberals', never venture a different opinion or ask a challenging question. And never answer back. In other words, be the very antithesis of an enlightened liberal.

I knew I was home, and that the open universalism of the Liberal International debate in Mexico belonged in the past.

When the news broke that the vice-chancellor of the University of Stellenbosch, Professor Wim de Villiers, was proposing that the university senate accede to the #MustFall movement's demand for English as the primary medium of instruction, instead of Afrikaans, I thought about the issue at length. English is the dominant language of instruction at twenty-three out of twenty-five universities in the country. Afrikaans is the majority language in the Western Cape. And it is a constitutional right to have mother-tongue education where reasonably practicable. Any rights-based society realises that a right is not something that can be imposed on people; it is something that cannot be taken away. Now Professor de Villiers was asking the university community to voluntarily sacrifice that right. Would history regard his proposal as a bold move to promote inclusivity, or a surrender to the hegemonic project? I have no doubt that Professor de Villiers and his supporters believe it is the former, but I'm afraid it will turn out to be the latter. One need look no further than the rhetoric of the #MustFall movement, who seem to be oblivious of the profound irony attached to their demand to 'decolonise' the university by replacing an indigenous language – Afrikaans – with English.

At around this time, during a rare year of frequent international travel, I flew to China, where I had been invited to make the opening speech at the International Shanghai Food and Wine Festival. The scale of the place was mind-boggling, as was the attention to detail, at a ceremony bedecked with flowers and ribbons, with immaculate ladies in traditional dress attending to the array of VIPs.

I waited for the deputy mayor of Shanghai to make his scheduled appearance, and was then informed he would not be coming. He had been arrested that morning because of 'serious breaches of discipline'. I felt a shiver down my spine as I made my speech.

Two nights later, in Beijing, I was woken at two in the morning by a phone call from my legal adviser in Cape Town, Fiona Stewart. She was calling to warn me of the possibility that I might be arrested when I returned home. It related to a charge laid against me by the ANC, alleging that I had appointed an 'agent' to spy on members of the opposition. It turned out that what one newspaper was quick to describe as 'Zille's spy' was a person contracted through the procurement system in the province, shortly after the DA came to power in 2009, to check the cellphones of cabinet ministers following the State Security Agency's failure to provide us with written assurances that they were not being bugged.

I thanked Fiona for warning me, and told her I was completely relaxed. Let them arrest me, I said. We have a constitution, and an independent judiciary. I will appear in court, I will get bail, and I will have a fair trial. I have done nothing wrong, I have broken no law, there was no spying, I have nothing to fear.

I went back to bed reflecting on the enormous privilege of being a citizen of a country about which I could say these things with confidence, irrespective of how much I irritated the ruling party. I thought about the incarcerated deputy mayor of Shanghai. Maybe he had committed a crime. Maybe he hadn't. No one would ever really know. He could not rely on due process of law to establish the facts, as I could.

The next stop was Mumbai, a city developing at the same pace as Shanghai but in an entirely different way. I was overwhelmed by the sights, sounds, smells and sheer scale of the place. We ate a magnificent curry at the famous Leopold's Café, which was the scene of a fatal grenade explosion during the 2008 terror attacks on the city. I looked around, thinking of what the scene must have been like on that fateful night almost exactly seven years earlier. And I thought of the terror attacks that had just claimed 130 lives in Paris, as the world held its breath for further assaults.

Outside, the street was full and festive, alive with vendors, traffic, animals; a bustling hive of activity in a cacophony of different sounds. Suddenly a loud explosion sent me rocketing out of my seat. I was convinced that the next terror attack was under way, and we were caught in the middle of it. The waiter roared with laughter. That was a firecracker, he said. It's the end of Diwali. It took a good time for the adrenalin level in my system to return to normal.

When we landed back in Cape Town, the first paper I opened contained an article on Diwali under the headline 'Whiteness Sours the Joys of Diwali'. I knew I was home.

I felt open universalism evaporating and the tide of race discourse rising.
And then I thought of the deputy mayor of Shanghai.

For all my awe at the speed and extent of Chinese economic development, I knew that we South Africans had made the right choice to opt for democracy and a rights-based constitution as the foundation on which to build our future. Now we just had to make it work. I came home fired with enthusiasm to continue that project, an enthusiasm that not even 'Black Twitter' could dampen.

The DA faced the enormous challenge of defending our vision of 'one nation with one future', and providing an alternative narrative, particularly for young people swamped with populist messages promoting institutional destruction and racial hatred.

As I sat watching the results of the local government election streaming in on the night of 3 August 2016, I felt not only vindicated, but elated. Firstly, the outcome was a magnificent affirmation of our strategy to build the DA's brand of good governance on the foundation of our cities. But most of all, this election showed me what a huge support base there is in South Africa for the DA's message of an inclusive, non-racial society, redressing the inequities of apartheid by providing real opportunities for all. Nelson Mandela's vision still resonated, and the Democratic Alliance had become its heir.

We had overtaken the ANC in Nelson Mandela Bay and Tshwane, and pulled the party below 50 per cent in Johannesburg, Ekurhuleni and Mogale City, as well as many smaller municipalities. One newspaper editor, clearly taken aback by the result, noted it was clear that Twitter did not reflect the will of the electorate. She had, at last, seen through the echo chamber of social media and its manipulation.

In Nelson Mandela Bay, the major city in the ANC's heartland, the DA won 47 per cent of the vote, and formed a government in coalition with the UDM, COPE and the ACDP. Athol Trollip, our Eastern Cape provincial leader, became mayor. I remembered trying to persuade Athol to stand for mayor in the 2011 elections, but he had declined. The result was agonisingly close, but the ANC still scraped home. If he had accepted, he might well have been entering his second mayoral term! In Tshwane and Johannesburg, the DA's Solly Msimanga and Herman Mashaba became mayor, but in both cities the balance of power is held by the EFF.

I knew the future of our politics would, from now on, be a contest between competing political philosophies, represented by the primary colours of our three largest parties: Blue, Yellow and Red. Not a racial contest between black and white. South Africa had indeed taken a short cut through history. I was thrilled to have been a part of it and even more thrilled at the prospect of the journey ahead.

But I also realised how vulnerable we were, even (or especially) in our moment of triumph. Every victory in politics opens a new front in an ongoing war. I could think of no bigger battle than what lay ahead: having to depend on the vacillating support of our arch-rivals to govern a major metropolis in a minority government. But I had learnt that in politics, your enemy's enemy is often your only, if fleeting, friend.

That would be another battle for another day. For once, I was content to savour the moment.

23

The Struggle for Economic Freedom

WHEN THE NEWS broke on the evening of 9 December 2015 that President Jacob Zuma had fired finance minister Nhlanhla Nene, the rand fell from R14.5 to the dollar to R15.39 by the following morning. Shortly afterwards it hit its record nadir of R16.04. Against the pound, the exchange rate reached R24:1. During the same period an estimated R170 billion was wiped off equity markets, much of it in losses to pension funds. Worse was to come.

It took this tough lesson for South Africans to confront James Carville's legendary campaign slogan, devised for former US president Bill Clinton's successful 1992 election: 'It's the economy, stupid.'

But for some, the currency collapse still wasn't enough to override the race default. Only whites, they argued, were fazed by the collapse of the rand and the stock market, as though black South Africans are somehow immune to the effects of inflation, job losses and shrinking pension funds.

The consequence of Nene's firing was also a timely reminder to South Africans that, in a global economy, markets tend to hold corrupt leaders to account, even (and perhaps especially) when voters don't, with dire consequences for everyone.

The question is whether enough of us will learn these lessons, or merely redouble our efforts to divert the debate into our traditional comfort zone of race polarisation. A classic of this genre, penned by Kelly-Jo Bluen, appeared in *Business Day* on 14 December. It began in fine form, as follows:

> When President Jacob Zuma removed Nhlanhla Nene, white pearl-clutching Perth packers, Zimbabwe analogists and apartheid apologists took to the internet, newspapers and all other places to voice their discontent.
>
> Falling under the rubric of #ZumaMustFall as a concept, a march and a hashtag, cynically appropriated from #FeesMustFall, much of the white commentary has ranged from explicit racism to the curated dog-whistle racism that often characterises white narratives about black governance. The last-straw-end-of-days-apartheid-nostalgia in much of the commentary reveals a myopic focus on white interests ...

Social media was awash with similar sentiments. The most absurd was a post that accused the markets of rejecting Des van Rooyen as Nene's (weekend) replacement when, despite his name, Van Rooyen turned out to be black. The markets did not seem to mind Nhlanhla Nene being black, but logic has never been the strong suit of race defaulters.

Of course there is still a great deal of racism in South Africa and we must face it and deal with it. Racists (of all colours) are a danger to South Africa's future, not because of their numbers or their power, but because of the extraordinary damage they inflict on others. The anger and divisions they sow prevent us from doing what needs to be done, as compatriots, across the ideological spectrum, to address our poverty crisis.

And the situation is further aggravated by the surfeit of opportunists who deliberately search for (or even manufacture) 'proof' of racism in every possible context. However difficult it is, we need to create a magnetic field of arguments powerful enough to pull the debate away from the G-force of race, towards jobs. This is the make-or-break issue for South Africa's future.

The central question for our politics is how to secure economic freedom for all South Africans. There are two clear choices: the DA's model of economic growth, education and expanded opportunity, or the EFF's model of asset confiscation, nationalisation and institutional destruction? The ANC's internal divisions have made it ideologically incoherent on the subject. The real contest for South Africa's future is between Blue and Red.

Our obsession with race not only deflects us from focusing on jobs, it actually results in decisions and actions that destroy jobs. And, even worse, it provides a smokescreen for policies that undermine South Africa's capacity to create jobs and beat poverty. In other words, our race obsession is delaying economic freedom.

The race reflex is what we have to counter. And there is an encouraging depth of consensus in the political centre on what is required to do so.

Most people acknowledge that it will be impossible for tax-based wealth redistribution alone to reduce poverty, given our current ratio of about 6 million registered personal taxpayers to 16.9 million social-grant recipients. The number of people on grants was almost double the 8 992 000 South Africans in employment at the end of 2015.[*]

We have to begin by turning that ratio around so that there are more people in work than on welfare.

And almost everyone, from socialist to capitalist, agrees that if we want more jobs, we need sustained productive economic growth.

Another point on which we all agree is that an economy cannot grow without investment, from both the private sector and the state. The state's primary investment role in the economy is to construct infrastructure that improves people's lives and creates the conditions for entrepreneurial activity and private-sector

---

[*] Source: http://www.tradingeconomics.com/south-africa/employed-persons

investment that drives sustained growth. I have not encountered any rational analyst, of any ideological persuasion, who disputes this.

This is a strong shared platform on which to build. Surely we can't be stupid enough to allow the racist lunatic fringe to prevent us from doing so?

The National Development Plan (NDP), released in November 2011, spelt out the issues we need to address, if we are serious about growth, which is why I welcomed it in my capacity as DA leader; and why we sought to compare its proposals with our own plan for 8 per cent growth and jobs. Interestingly, we found a lot of overlap. At last, here was a concerted effort, led from the presidency itself, to focus the country on the right questions, with proposals for an emerging national consensus. The NDP was endorsed by the cabinet and accepted by all parties in parliament at the time. This represented enormous progress.

Today we only hear the occasional rhetorical reference to the NDP. It has been almost entirely superseded by 'Zumanomics' with its reliance on nurturing racial resentments and anti-market rhetoric as a smokescreen behind which to hide various forms of corruption.

It is my analysis that the NDP is being ignored because implementing it would have stopped Jacob Zuma's giant Ferris wheel of corruption in mid-rotation, leaving his network of family, friends and political associates dangling helplessly in their gondolas. So the network destroyed the NDP before it destroyed them. It is as simple as that.

The NDP's proposals required us to grow jobs in the only sustainable way a democracy can: on the foundation of investment, education, skills development, productivity and competition to stimulate and meet consumer needs and demands. At its core it understood, and described, the role of a competent, professional state based on the rule of law as a precondition for economic growth.

This provided the framework within which Nhlanhla Nene operated. He was fired because, like the NDP, he put the brakes on Zuma's Ferris wheel.

Nene did this, among other things, by preventing South African Airways chairwoman Dudu Myeni, who was 'close' to Zuma (as the delicate phrase has it), from renegotiating an aircraft leasing deal to bring on board a secret 'middleman', at great cost to the state, without adding any public value.

Next, like Pravin Gordhan before him, Nene refused to approve the nuclear deal with Russia, on the basis of the cost. This infuriated President Zuma and his network, particularly the notorious Gupta brothers Atul, Ajay and Tony, who had actually invested in a uranium mine, secure in the knowledge that they would make a mint when the Russian-built nuclear facility came on stream. They could not allow Nene to continue in office and thwart their plans. According to all media reports (that have not been convincingly refuted), the Guptas were the driving force behind the decision to fire Nene and replace him with the much more compliant Van Rooyen. Cries of 'state capture' reached a crescendo as the currency and markets collapsed.

The truth is that many institutions of state were captured long ago, by the ANC faction under Jacob Zuma. Because South Africans so regularly conflate the party and the state, very few people understand what this means and how serious it is. The state comprises a range of institutions, intended to protect the public from power abuse by politicians in public office, and from criminals of all kinds. These institutions must, among other things, adjudicate disputes and conflicts, according to the law, independently, without succumbing to political influence. Zuma's determination to capture these institutions and to turn them into an extension of his corrupt inner circle proceeded largely unnoticed until the Guptas captured Zuma and, through him, any state institution they wanted to manipulate. Then the outrage at 'state capture' broke the sound barrier.

The markets reacted vehemently to the corruption these developments revealed.

The network, however, rallied around the president, in order to preserve the system so aptly described in the following quote attributed to Kgalema Motlanthe, former president and deputy president: 'Almost every project is conceived because it offers opportunities for certain people to make money. A great deal of the ANC's problems are occasioned by this. There are people who want to take it over so that they can arrange for the appointment of those who will allow them possibilities for future accumulation.'

Motlanthe's words provide a prism through which to understand how the Zuma ANC Ferris wheel works – how it is engineered; how passengers get (and stay) on board; how they extend the duration of each ride by selecting (or defending) the hands on the controls; and how they resist the attempts to displace them.

Those involved understand better than anyone that it is all about the economy – or rather, their privileged access to it – through political connections. They only pretend it is about 'race' because this is the tried and tested way to ensure that voters keep their benefactor in power and themselves in their gondolas. Once they are strapped in, they can (without adding value through effort, skill, price or product improvement) use their connections to protect risk-free accumulation by preventing a competitive economy from providing better-quality goods and services more affordably. Better still, if they can insert themselves as a middleman in a transaction (for example, to meet the requirement of race quotas), they can score a good cut without having to contribute any value at all. This is called 'rent-seeking'. And when this form of corruption is exposed, the default is to blame 'white capitalists'.

After the Nene debacle, the *Mail & Guardian* provided a classic example of the default to race. 'Some ANC leaders,' the front page reported in its final 2015 issue, 'believe bosses manipulated global markets in order to topple the president and say he is under siege by capitalists who are colluding with anti-Zuma campaigners inside the party.'

Lindiwe Zulu, who emerged as the spokesperson for these 'ANC leaders', analysed the market's collapse as a function of the ANC's internal succession battle. Had the business community rallied around Zuma, 'as they were obliged to do' after his appointment of the unknown back-bencher, Des Van Rooyen, as finance minister, all would have been well, argued Zulu. But instead, the market 'took sides' with Zuma's opponents. That, she said, was the cause of the rand's precipitous decline.

The fact that markets were reacting to political cronyism and corruption (because these destroy the foundation of a successful economy) seems to have eluded Ms Zulu, our minister of small business development.

Was this the dominant perception in the Zuma cabinet, I asked myself. If it was, how would the reappointed finance minister Pravin Gordhan fulfil his stewardship of the economy? And how could he reboot our economy if his cabinet colleague, the minister of small business development no less, believed that growing the economy merely involved adding new spokes and gondolas to the ANC's Ferris wheel, and requiring markets to support the incumbent's patronage network?

The NDP answers this question. Apart from a capable state, another precondition for success is competent leadership in all spheres of government and civil society, who understand their roles and functions.

It is impossible to build a capable state without competent leaders. What's more, in a democracy, voters choose their leaders. That's why they get the government they deserve.

So if we want to fix the economy, we're back to politics, stupid.

Human beings are – or so we like to believe – the pinnacle of creation. We are capable of rational and abstract thought, and of linking cause and effect. We can learn from experience, and adapt to new circumstances. Why, then, is it so difficult for us to use these faculties to learn from the experience of the few countries that have succeeded in building prosperous, inclusive, stable, peaceful societies that limit huge disparities in wealth?

The country analogy often used to epitomise what is possible is stable and secure Denmark, where people have opportunities in a strong economy and where disparities are contained. The question is: why is it so difficult to 'get to Denmark'?

This is the question Francis Fukuyama tackles in his two-volume masterpiece, *The Origins of Political Order* and *Political Order and Political Decay*.

Drawing on an extensive analysis from evolutionary biology (the politics of our primate ancestors), anthropology, economic history and political science, in different societies over millennia, he draws a profound conclusion. There are, he says, only three necessary conditions for societies to undertake the journey to the destination symbolised by the mythical 'Denmark'. These are the combination of a capable state, the rule of law and a culture of accountability, including accountable government.

Neither the development nor the convergence of these three pivotal institutions can be assumed. On the contrary, their fortuitous confluence has been the rare historical exception; a combination over centuries of conflict, conquest, compromise and coincidence, as well as the individual agency of great leaders making bold choices at critical times.

Why these three specific things? And why in combination?

The answer is best illustrated by Fukuyama's compelling analysis of what happens in their absence. This provides the foil for us to understand why the rule of (just) law is essential to provide a fair and predictable framework which regulates human interaction and prevents arbitrary actions that undermine other people's rights and freedoms.

Accountability ensures mechanisms to prevent the powerful from becoming corrupt and abusing their power to extract unearned wealth, or undermine the rights and opportunities of others. A culture of accountability in a society includes the concept of individual responsibility, in which (for example) parents are held accountable for fulfilling their basic obligations towards their children.

The capable, professional state creates the institutions that make the rule of law and accountability a reality in people's lives, while providing goods, services and infrastructure that market mechanisms are unable to provide affordably for everyone who needs them. This is the context which, in a free society, creates opportunities for individuals, families, organisations and communities to improve their lives through effort and hard work.

If the combination of a capable state, the rule of law and accountability does indeed comprise the 'holy trinity' of conditions that are necessary to begin the journey to the most ideal society of which fallible humans are capable – and I believe it does – how can we apply this formula to our circumstances?

Unfortunately, there is no step-by-step DIY kit. On the contrary, says Fukuyama, the fact that there are countries capable of achieving these three prerequisites is 'the miracle of modern politics'. It is enough of a miracle that it has happened in more or less homogenous societies (such as Denmark). It has never happened before in a country as ethnically diverse, and as historically divided, as South Africa. That, in short, summarises our challenge.

When we adopted our negotiated constitution in 1996, we thought we had wrapped up at least two of the essential components for success: the rule of law and accountable government. We completely underestimated what it would take to turn form into substance and fill the mould we had cast. Accountable government, for example, is meaningless if voters fail to hold corrupt leaders to account through the ballot box; and the rule of law is a hollow concept if powerful politicians flout it with impunity, for example by firing independent prosecutors who dare to lay charges against them (or against others in their network). Playing the race card gives corrupt leaders a free pass to abuse their power and undermine the institutions we need to build a prosperous society that can significantly reduce poverty.

We did not sufficiently appreciate that the failure to build a capable state, based on strong professional institutions, functioning independently of party politics, would destroy both the rule of law and accountable government – the key preconditions, in a democracy, for growth and jobs.

But above all, we had absolutely no idea of how difficult it would be to build a capable, professional state that does its job efficiently while also defending its independence from encroachment by political leaders and other vested interests. Indeed, even in countries without the rule of law and accountable government, a capable state has succeeded in lifting hundreds of millions of people out of poverty, as Fukuyama's detailed analysis of China demonstrates.

Sir Michael Barber, whose expertise in building state capacity is recognised worldwide following his game-changing work with Tony Blair's Labour government, said something to me in a meeting once that struck me like a blow to the solar plexus: 'Building a capable state,' he said, 'is the great moral issue of our time.'

The more I think about it, the more I agree.

The South African government has cast racial transformation as the great moral issue of our time. And, given the history of our country, this too is essential. We have to find ways of ensuring that these are complementary – not contradictory – imperatives. We must start by asking ourselves why, if a capable state is essential for progress in all societies, it is so difficult to achieve.

Fukuyama begins his explanation with a fascinating account of attempts to implant modern political institutions into traditional societies by using the example of the transition to independence of Papua New Guinea (from Australia) and the Solomon Islands (from Britain). The established assumption of democracies, on which the new institutions were based, was that the people would make electoral choices between political parties on the basis of competing policies and programmes; that government, once elected, would serve all the people; and that independent state institutions would curb political patronage and power abuse.

The result of these assumptions, he says, was chaos, because 'most voters in Melanesia do not vote for political programs; rather, they support their Big Man and their wantok'.*

The concept of the 'wantok' is fascinating and explains a lot, not just in Melanesia. It derives from the pidgin adaptation of the English 'one talk', referring to people who share a common language and culture, and to whom members of the group owe their primary allegiance. On the island of Papua New Guinea, explains Fukuyama, with a population of just over eleven million people, there are more than 900 mutually incomprehensible languages, each of which forms its own 'wantok' and is led by a Big Man who earns his position by distributing resources to his followers. They protect him if he looks after them. 'Without resources to distribute he loses his status as leader.'†

It is hardly surprising, therefore, that when Big Men got elected to the institutions of parliament, they devoted their time and energy trying to funnel resources to their own wantok.

'From the standpoint of many foreigners, the behaviour of Melanesian politicians looks like political corruption. But from the standpoint of the islands' traditional tribal social system, the Big Men are simply doing what Big Men have always done, which is to distribute resources to their kinsmen. Except that now they have access not just to pigs and shell money but also to revenues from mining and logging concessions.' Sounds familiar.

'It takes only a couple of hours to fly from Port Moresby, Papua New Guinea's capital, to Cairns or Brisbane in Australia,' notes Fukuyama, 'but in that flight one is in some sense traversing several thousand years of political development'‡ – although he concedes that patronage remains rampant in many political systems worldwide, including the US Congress.

In South Africa, we are trying to span millennia within the confines of a single country in the space of a few decades. Should we even be trying? Is it patronising (or even racist) to think that a constitutional democracy based on a capable state, the rule of law and accountability, and in which everyone's rights are protected, is preferable to tribal systems, in which the 'Big Man' (or several 'big men') distribute resources to their kinsmen and those who find their favour?

If our answer to the first question is no (because the answer to the second question is yes), what is the alternative? A return to escalating civil war? An attempt to carve up South Africa into separate pieces, enabling each tribe (including the 'white one') to have its own territory, in which their chosen big man (or woman)

---

* Francis Fukuyama, Preface to *The Origins of Political Order: From Prehuman Times to the French Revolution* (Profile Books, 2011), p. xiv
† Ibid., p. xiii
‡ Ibid.

could distribute patronage and regulate access to land? South Africa has been dragged down this road before, with disastrous consequences.

One choice that the ANC cannot make, however, is to turn itself into a super-tribe in one country to dispense patronage to the connected few. This will make the two moral issues of our time – a capable state and racial transformation – impossible to reconcile. And it will be a recipe for permanent conflict, cronyism, corruption and decline, which can only end in a criminal (rather than capable) state.

Apartheid has also been attempted, with calamitous consequences too numerous to list. Southern Africa cannot and should not try to recreate the history of the warring tribes of Europe, who fought ongoing battles to determine the extent of their territories, culminating in the disaster of the Second World War.

The vast majority of South Africans, however, have rejected this option, for very sound reasons, economic, political, social and ethical. So we have no option but to press on and achieve democracy's holy trinity in one country. Unless we do, our complex, plural society cannot establish the foundation necessary for a decent, peaceful life in the modern world, based on economic progress and social inclusion.

And who knows, when eventually enough countries around the world are sufficiently far along this road, we may develop the capacity to transcend national entities (which are actually just larger, more complex wantoks) and we could find ourselves moving to the next phase of human evolution and organisation on this blue planet.

Nation states (and nationalism) could then recede into history. But that is another battle for another day. For now, it's enough of a challenge to get South Africa to work according to the 'trinity' formula, which, incidentally, we devised ourselves.

This is an important point to emphasise. No one forced this formula down our throats. It was not imposed on us by a retreating colonial power. Our constitution is not a colonial imposition. We made this conscious choice ourselves when we reached agreement on our new constitution, which creates the three conditions necessary for progress. We understood it in theory then. Our problem is translating it into practice, now.

We are in the fortunate position of being able to learn from the success and failures of other countries that have traversed the path from kinship, through tribalism, to a modern prosperous democracy. If we learn the right lessons, we don't have to go through thousands of years of conflict first.

Or do we?

I have come to the conclusion that we can't leapfrog over the hard knocks entirely.

Institutions and belief systems, says Fukuyama, are durable (or sticky) because people imbue them with intrinsic value and meaning, and because so many vested interests attach to them.

And, indeed, I believe there are institutions and practices from tribal society that we want to retain. In South Africa, the most celebrated is the notion of Ubuntu. *Umntu ngumntu ngabantu*, as the Nguni saying goes: a person is a person through other people. In its primordial form, it epitomises 'wantokism' – people of the same small band or tribe looking out for each other's interests, which all too often degenerates into a form of 'us vs them'. Can we apply it in an inclusive context?

In fact, I believe it will be impossible to rise above our racial or ethnic wantoks unless we trust each other and genuinely believe that people from outside our own kinship or ethnic group can, and do, have our well-being and interests at heart. This is the form of Ubuntu we need to nurture in our modern institutions. But we must ensure that it does not degenerate into yet another warm, fuzzy cover behind which to promote group patronage, protect privilege, oppose professionalism and undermine independent institutions.

If these essential checks and balances fail, the conditions for becoming a successful inclusive society perish with them. If we allow patrimonialism to engulf our institutions, our transition will fail before we begin, as has happened to so many other countries who have attempted the perilous passage to 'Denmark'.

Ubuntu cannot be a substitute for modern institutions, but it can infuse them with a spirit of service and commitment that supports, rather than undermines, professionalism.

Shortly after my re-election as premier of the Western Cape in 2014, I gave a presentation on the provincial government's new five-year strategic plan to an audience drawn from a range of different sectors. At question time, someone asked: 'It all sounds very efficient and organised, but where is the heart?'

My reply was: 'The efficiency and organisation *is* the heart. Caring for others is not a warm, fuzzy feeling. A caring state requires exceptional professionalism, strong systems and accountability. This is Ubuntu in action, and it is very difficult to achieve. It requires hard-working, skilled people, and strong performance-management systems, which many people find uncomfortable. We must never allow Ubuntu to degenerate into a convenient excuse for patronage, poor performance, shoddy systems and lack of effort.'

So, I believe, traditional values can improve the institutions and attributes that will get us to 'Denmark', but should never be used as an excuse to replace and undermine them.

In fact, I would take the argument even further than Fukuyama. 'Getting to Denmark' requires not only changing our ingrained cultures and belief systems; it requires actually inverting the primordial instincts that enabled human beings to survive and evolve in the first place.

All human beings are social animals who have the capacity to understand and respect hierarchies. This formed the basis of the original kinship groups that developed into tribes, led by alpha males to facilitate reproduction, internal co-operation and protection from external danger. Individual interests were subordinate to the tribe, from which our ancestors derived their identity and secured their survival. Serving and protecting the tribe, and its leader, was each individual's priority, in return for protection from hunger and danger. Tribal competition was a zero-sum game: my tribe's gain was your tribe's loss, and vice versa.

A successful democracy requires us to invert this pyramid of assumptions. The leader is accountable to the people, not the other way around. The core unit of social value is the individual, with inalienable rights and freedoms that the group cannot supersede. Progress is not regarded as a zero-sum conflict over a static resource base, but as a positive-sum cycle of growth, distribution and inclusion (involving both market and state mechanisms) that extend opportunities and defend individual rights.

Of course, humans remain social animals whose existence has meaning through associating with others, in groups with which they identify and feel comfortable, but the difference in a democracy is that individuals choose their group affiliations. Identity is not ascribed by birth, or imposed by others. Indeed, each individual can choose a variety of group identities, much like 'do-it-yourself' toppings on a pizza. So, someone might define herself as a vegetarian, atheist, lesbian, music-loving, chess-playing Tswana-speaker – and identify with a range of different groups to meet the social needs of these multiple components of her identity. No individual is 'owned' by any group, whether racial, religious, linguistic or cultural. Individuals make their own choices. The protection role, previously played by the homogenous group into which an individual was born and to which he owed allegiance, is replaced by strong, professional, independent institutions of state, created under a constitution and laws, specifically designed to protect each person's rights and freedoms, and extend their opportunities, to chart their own course in life.

In this system, a right cannot be imposed on a person. People choose to exercise their rights. And they cannot be arbitrarily taken away.

'Freedom' is the word we use to describe this condition. In successful democracies, individuals are able to use their freedom to live lives they value. This rarely happens without individual effort, discipline and hard work. And it never happens in the absence of a facilitative institutional context, exemplified by a capable state.

In a democracy, individual leaders come and go. Their role is to leave the institutions stronger, more professional, independent and intact so that progress towards freedom and prosperity can continue.

This requires an enormous mind shift, not only for leaders, but for their followers as well. It is hardly surprising that such a profound transition takes a long time. But those countries that have made the most progress in this direction have enabled their citizens to improve their life circumstances, often dramatically.

Even those parts of the world that think they have made good progress towards this ideal are now facing the fundamental shock of cross-cultural global migration and a rapidly integrating international economy. They are often at a loss as to how to deal with the impact of these forces.

South Africa is already a cauldron of the conflictual dynamics that many other, more homogenous, parts of the world have only recently begun to experience. If, in our plural, multicultural South African society, we can find a way to 'achieve Denmark' – 'a law-abiding, peaceful, stable, democratic, inclusive, prosperous and well-governed country with very low levels of corruption', as Fukuyama describes it – we can be an example to the world.*

Without inflating our importance, this is how I frame the Democratic Alliance's (and my own) responsibility. It is this purpose that propels me out of bed every morning; it is something I believe is worth fighting for.

And let me be clear. It won't happen without a fight.

It never has, anywhere.

As Fukuyama says: 'The struggle to create modern political institutions was so long and so painful that people living in industrialised countries now suffer from an historical amnesia regarding how their societies came to that point in the first place.'†

I have never felt any desire to sidestep this responsibility by leaving for a more Denmark-like country. If I did, I would lose my sense of purpose and, with it, my happiness.

But I am also relieved that, in today's world, we can avoid the fights that involve armies, weapons of war, and bloodshed. Our constitution, as it stands, provides a sufficient framework within which we can fight this battle through contesting ideas, through the courts, through elections, through the media (including social media), and through winning power legitimately wherever possible so that we can play our part in achieving the secular holy grail of a capable state, the rule of just law, and accountability.

This is the reason I chose to leave the opposition benches in parliament to take up the position of mayor of Cape Town in 2006. Despite the slim chances of holding together a fragile coalition of seemingly incompatible parties, with a wafer-thin majority, it offered the DA a real opportunity to try to establish the basis of a capable state, albeit only at local level, initially. I think we succeeded

---

* Francis Fukuyama, *The Origins of Political Order*, p. 431
† Ibid., p. 14

sufficiently in Cape Town within three years to persuade a majority of voters to give us the same chance in the Western Cape Province, in 2009.

We believe it will be possible, over the short span of a generation, for South Africans to see and experience the difference in outcomes between places governed by a capable, professional state, and those provinces and towns regressing into patrimonialism and predation. If this assumption is correct, citizens of different backgrounds will increasingly make free choices on the basis of contesting policies and ideas, and not because they owe their allegiance to their wantok, or its party-political equivalent.

And if this happens, perhaps we can truncate the millennia that lie between being owned by, and beholden to, your group, on the one hand, and being an autonomous individual, making free choices and living a life that has intrinsic meaning and purpose, on the other.

That, in a nutshell, describes why I do what I do. And will keep on doing.

Acknowledgements

WRITING A BOOK has been different from all my previous writing experiences, and has required the support and help of family, friends and colleagues.

The excavation of my family's story was a challenging and sometimes painful but rewarding experience. I wish to thank my second cousins Gay Bamberger and her brother Michael, in New York, my cousin Jacqui Zille Logan in Cape Town, and her brother Glen Zille in Sydney, for their committed and generous help in putting together the pieces of the puzzle of the Marcus/Zille family. Philip Krawitz, a Cape Town businessman, put exceptional energy into helping me uncover the fate of some of our relatives who perished in Nazi Germany. He introduced me to Searle Brajtman and Yad Vashem, which contains the world's most comprehensive holocaust memorial archive. In addition, Gwynne Robins introduced me to Paul Cheifitz, a historical researcher, who helped me establish the fate of some of my relatives, and track down others I did not know I had, in unlikely places across the globe.

In Cape Town, Trace Venter used her exceptional research skills to find any information I was unable to track down for myself.

Many friends and colleagues rallied behind this project, as they always do when I need them. I mention them alphabetically, so as not to create a hierarchy: Lenie Agulhas, Ragel Beukes, Edwena Booysen, Jerome Booysen, Jenny Cargill, Lorika Elliott, Sandra Francisco, Anna Friesley, Brent Gerber, Caroline Knott, Dewald Kuhn, Janet Lodewyk, Zita Lugalo, Robert MacDonald, Hajirah Mahomed, Ntsikelelo Makatesi, Wandisile Maneli, Sidney Mayman, Michael Mpofu, Marcus Naidoo, Sandra Rhoda, Lenell Ruiters, Janine Schouw, Donnae Strydom, Malibongwe Tafani, Penny Tainton, Arthur Thomas, Jamie Turkington, Carin Viljoen, Grace Voyiya and Lizzie Xoseka. They helped me in every imaginable way, from clipping newspapers to internet research and document extraction, and endless cups of tea – not to mention driving me around so that I could spend many hours writing in the back seat. Above all, it was very important to be able to compare my recollections of important incidents and events with theirs.

Thank you to the speaker of the City of Cape Town, Dirk Smit, for enabling me to retrieve relevant documents from the City's archives; and to Brent Gerber and Lucas Buter for facilitating the same access in the province. I am grateful to

James Selfe and Elsabe Oosthuysen for giving me easy access to the DA's records; and Johan van der Berg and Greg Krumbock for sharing key findings drawn from their rich research data. Liana van Wyk always managed to find the DA statistics I needed. Thank you to Advocate J.C. Gerber for his advice on how to retrieve archival records from the SAPS.

Rose Rau, who was the Western Cape Metro regional director of the DA during the seven-year battle for the soul of the party, was of invaluable assistance in helping me reconstruct a timeline of the period in history we would far rather have put behind us. In addition, Liz Brunette, Owen Kinahan, Ian Neilson, Demetri Qually, Denise Robinson, Debbie Schafer and Belinda Walker helped me reconstruct details of that difficult time.

Hubertus von Welck and Barbara Groeblinghoff of the Friedrich Naumann Stiftung, as well as their predecessors and their colleagues, played a crucial role in supporting our cause at the most precarious and difficult moments.

Martin Plaut, a long-standing friend, political analyst and retired BBC World Service News's Africa editor, offered to read chapters for me and returned them with insightful comments in record time. His expert editing advice proved invaluable and helped me improve initial drafts. Michael Cardo, Gavin Davis, Tim Harris, Geordin Hill-Lewis, James Selfe and Trace Venter did the same for several key chapters that required an expert eye and incisive analysis. Caroline Knott and Donnae Strydom proved to be expert proofreaders. Of course, any residual errors are my own.

This book has been a valuable catalyst for me and my siblings, Carla and Paul, to discuss difficult issues and memories from our childhood. They really cared about, and contributed to, this project as they have towards everything else I have ever done.

My husband, Johann, was there as a sounding board, and we spent many happy, humorous hours discussing various aspects of the book and comparing our recollections.

One of these discussions led to the title for this book. We were watching our favourite television series *Borgen* (about the political and domestic struggles of a woman politician, after being elected, unexpectedly, as Danish prime minister).

In that particular episode, a colleague said something like this to her: 'It's unlike you to give up without a fight.'

Johann turned to me and said, 'That's something I could have said to you. In fact, how about that for the title of your book – *Not Without a Fight*?

I knew we had it.

I nevertheless want to thank the twitterati who made #NameZillesMemoirs trend on 29 July 2015 shortly after Penguin Random House announced they would publish my book. There were some excellent suggestions, such as *To Helen Back*, *Twar and Peace*, *From Godzille to Vuvuzille*, and *Zille: No Vanilla*. If Johann's suggestion hadn't been the best, I would have taken one of yours.

Johann's meticulously filed records were also a great help. Our sons, Paul and Thomas, provided the gentle ribbing and provocative commentary that has always been there, in the background, since their earliest years.

One of the reasons I chose Penguin Random House as the publisher was that they offered me Alison Lowry as an editor. I had heard a lot about her and wanted to work with her. I have learnt an enormous amount from her sensitive, straightforward and unsentimental expertise, her artistry with words, and her dry humour. She surpassed my inflated expectations, as did Marlene Fryer, my ultra-efficient publisher, and Robert Plummer, who added his own deft and detailed touch. Ryan Africa's cover design, based on a photo of me by Eric Miller, captures the story in a single picture.

HELEN ZILLE
AUGUST 2016

Abbreviations

ACDP: African Christian Democratic Party
AMP: Africa Muslim Party
ANC: African National Congress
ANCYL: African National Congress Youth League
BBBEE: broad-based black economic empowerment
BBC: British Broadcasting Corporation
BEE: black economic empowerment
CBD: central business district
CNA: Central News Agency
CODETA: Convention of Democratic Taxi Associations
COPE: Congress of the People
COSATU: Congress of South African Trade Unions
CP: Conservative Party
DA: Democratic Alliance
DP: Democratic Party
ECC: End Conscription Campaign
EEA: Employment Equity Act
EFF: Economic Freedom Fighters
Fedex: Federal Executive
FF+: Freedom Front Plus
GF&A: George Fivaz & Associates
HNP: Herstigte Nasionale Party
ICD: Independent Complaints Directorate
ICOSA: Independent Civic Organisation of South Africa
ID: Independent Democrats
IDASA: Institute for Democracy in Africa
IEC: Independent Electoral Commission
KDF: Khayelitsha Development Forum
LI: Liberal International
MEC: member of the executive council
MK: Umkhonto we Sizwe
MP: member of parliament
MPL: member of the provincial legislature
NCOP: National Council of Provinces

NDP: National Development Plan
NIA: National Intelligence Agency
NNP: New National Party
NP: National Party
NPA: National Prosecuting Authority
NPP: National People's Party
NUSAS: National Union of South African Students
PAC: Pan Africanist Congress
PADLAC: People's Anti-Drug and Liquor Action Committee
PAGAD: People against Gangsterism and Drugs
PFP: Progressive Federal Party
PRAAG: Pro-Afrikaans Action Group
SABC: South African Broadcasting Corporation
SACP: South African Communist Party
SADTU: South African Democratic Teachers Union
SANCO: South African National Civic Organisation
SAPS: South African Police Service
SPCA: Society for the Prevention of Cruelty to Animals
SONA: State of the Nation Address
SOPA: State of the Province Address
SRC: student representative council
TRC: Truth and Reconciliation Commission
UCT: University of Cape Town
UDF: United Democratic Front
UDM: United Democratic Movement
UIF: United Independent Front
UOFS: University of the Orange Free State
UP: United Party
WC: Western Cape
WCC: World Council of Churches
Webta: Western Cape Black Taxi Association
Wits: University of the Witwatersrand
ZCC: Zion Christian Church
ZIPRA: Zimbabwe People's Revolutionary Army

Index

2010 World Cup 250, 251–252, 299, 327–328

academic freedom 81
accountability 189, 502–509
ACDP 144–145, 226, 227, 237, 253, 494
Adams, Claudine 486
affirmative action 189, 377
Africa Hinterland Safaris 109
Africa Muslim Party *see* AMP
African Christian Democratic Party *see* ACDP
African National Congress *see* ANC
Afrikaans, as medium of instruction 492
Agang 373–374, 410–419, 422–431
Agulhas, Lenie 405
AIDS *see* HIV and AIDS
Aimes, Frances 123
Allen, Reagan 408
AMP 226, 227, 233, 236, 249–253
ANC
    affirmative action 189, 386
    as banned organisation 46, 97
    BBBEE 378
    DA and 189–220, 463, 493
    elections 142–146, 160, 221–234, 312–313, 338–339, 448
    'floor-crossing' 162–167, 263, 268, 273–276, 278–279
    GF&A investigation 288–289
    Grove case 129, 138
    negotiated settlement 99–101, 116–117
    Operation Vula 106–110
    'state capture' 342–343, 500–501
    'taxi wars' 111–114
    Western Cape local government 238–239, 242–243, 305
    Youth League 319–320, 374
Annett, Captain 196–197
anorexia 36–39, 85, 482
Anthony, Brother 33
apartheid 45–46, 69–70
Aranes, Joe 328–329

Arendse, Cameron 405
Arendse, Sheval 233–234
Asmal, Louise 115
Association for Rural Advancement 69
Avis 93–94
Avivi, Doron 5

Baillie, Dr 87
Ballenden, Wendy 60
Barber, Sir Michael 503
Barkhuizen, Superintendent 216
Barnard, Niel 147, 149–151, 166
Baron, Geoff 218
Baron, Judy 90
bathroom, construction of private 237–238
Bax, Doug 95
BBBEE 377–378
BBBEE Amendment Bill 378–385, 394–396
Beau Soleil Music School 124–125
Bedford, Tommy 75
BEE 377, 485
Beeka, Cyril 266, 299
Beeld 73, 75, 398
Bekker, Koos 125
Beneke, Senior Superintendent 214–215
Berlin Wall, fall of 99, 100–101
Bermuda conference 99–100
Bernstein, Ann 39
Bester, Hennie 142, 147, 166, 202
Beukes, Ragel 409
'big-man' politics 147–150, 156–160, 504
Biko, Steve 40, 46–52, 57–58, 292, 421
Bisho massacre 117
black economic empowerment *see* BEE
#BlackLivesMatter 481
Black Sash 34, 35, 92, 94, 96–98
black trade union movement 81–83
'Black Twitter' 491–492
Blair, Tony 341–342
Bloom, Jack 337–338
Bluen, Kelly-Jo 497

Blumenthal, Ella 1, 4
Bock, Derrick 251
Boipatong massacre 116–117
'Bols' story 52–53
Booi, Nyami 93
Bosman, Frouwien 384–385
Botha, Pik 55–57
Botha, P.W. 55, 56, 99, 147
Botha, Sandra 317
Botha, Superintendent 243
Botha, Theuns 158–159, 163–164, 168, 170–175, 185–186, 227, 256–259, 263, 269, 273, 278, 281, 287, 293
Boughey, Paul 316, 468
Bout, Busi 124
Bowler, William 34
bowls 26
Braunsberg, Herman 4
Brindley, David 33
Britain 15–17
broad-based black economic empowerment *see* BBBEE
Broad-Based Black Economic Empowerment Amendment Bill *see* BBBEE Amendment Bill
Brown, Lynne 306
Bruce, Peter 420–421
Brynard, Carin 320–321
Brynard, Kobus 158–159, 169–170, 186, 259, 275, 278
Budlender, Geoff 80
'bugging' *see* surveillance
Burger, Die 171–174, 256, 294
Burger, Inspector 215
Burwana, Andile 206
Business Day 288, 356, 388–389, 400, 420–421, 452, 484, 489, 497
Buso, Bongi 219
Buthelezi, Mangosuthu 118

cabinet lekgotla 324–327
cadre deployment 148–149, 189
Calland, Richard 471
candidate-selection process, DA 158–160, 177–178, 314–317
capable state 502–509
Cape Argus 285, 318, 328–329
Cape Times 278, 285
Cape Town 486–487
Cape Town City Council 110–113

Cape Town City Improvement District 251
Cape Town Cycle Tour 434
Cape Town fire and disaster management service 223
Cape Town Press Club 363
Cape Town stadium 251–252
Cardo, Michael 490
Carlisle, Robin 174
Carnation Revolution 41
Carnegie Inquiry, Second 121
Carolus, Cheryl 377
Carte Blanche 426–427
Carville, James 497
Chaaban, Badih 249–253, 263–274, 276–278, 283–284, 288, 297, 299, 309–310
Chaaban, Diana 249
Cheifitz, Paul 4
China 492–494
Chinese South Africans 380–381
Christian Institute 78, 80
Churchill, Winston 341, 429
Cilliers, Koos 276
Citizens Movement for Social Change 361–362
Citizen, The 54
City Improvement District 251
City Press 418–419
Clarion 70–71
Clark, Maureen and Bradbury 16
Clarke, Dick 99
Clarks (store) 25
'Clause 14' 158–159, 165
Clegg, Nick 363
coalition government 142, 144–146, 222–223, 225–239
CODETA 115
Coetsee, Kobie 98
Coetzee, Ryan 143, 151, 155, 183, 226–227, 232, 245, 254, 260, 305, 316–317, 335–336, 344, 362–364, 456
Commonwealth Conference, Lusaka 42
concentration and internment camps 1, 4, 14, 16
Congress of the People *see* COPE
Conservative Party 99–100, 115
constitutionalism 365
Constitutionally Speaking (blog) 250
Convention of Democratic Taxi Associations *see* CODETA
COPE 309, 311–314, 316–318, 333–334, 339, 374, 445, 494
Cornelissen, Captain 206–207, 209

INDEX

Cosmann, Agnes 15
Cosmann, Carl Maximilian 9–18
Cosmann, Emilie (Mila) 9–18
Cosmann, Felix 15
Cosmann, Leopold 11
Cosmann, Otta 15, 18
Cosmann, Ulrich 15
Coto, Mike 94
critical race theory 480–493
crony appointments 148–149, 189
Crossroads 201–205, 210–211
crybullies 480
Crystal, Russell 240–244, 246
'cultural appropriation' 491
Cupido, Pauline 227

DA
    Agang and 410–419, 422–431
    BEE 377–400
    candidate selection 158–160, 177–178, 314–317
    communications network 354–355
    diversity in 320, 333–337, 342–344
    elections 177–187, 221–240, 305, 309, 311–315, 317–318, 329, 337–340, 374–375, 419–420, 431–432, 438–443, 447–449, 477, 494
    Erasmus Commission 301
    FLC 170–171
    'floor-crossing' 267, 278
    formation of 153–188
    GF&A investigation 287–291
    growth of 84, 189–220, 313
    ID and 184, 298, 333–334
    internal conflict 171–174, 237, 239–240, 243–247
    'Know Your DA' campaign 387, 399
    lawfare programme 330–331
    racism 487–488
    send-off party for Helen Zille 471–476
    Some Day group 182–185, 187, 246, 254
    'spy tapes' 321–322, 329–330
    succession battle 449–464, 466–471
    Western Cape local government 508–509
    Young Leaders programme 336
    Youth 320
dagga 62
Dakar conference 99
Dana, Simphiwe 358
Dandala, Mvume 312
Daniels, Aimee 445
Davidson, Ian 39, 253–254, 260, 337, 352, 359

Davies, Rob 380
Davis, Dennis 313
Davis, Gavin 301, 303, 316, 349–350, 384, 389, 391, 423, 455–457, 467
Day, Chris 53
deafness 2, 21–24
De Beer, A.J. 293
De Beer, Zach 116, 120
decolonisation 480, 489, 492
Defence and Aid Fund 115
De Klerk, Elita 84
De Klerk, Frits 316, 405
De Klerk, F.W. 84, 100–102, 105, 107, 115–117, 120, 162
De la Cruz, Danny 169–170, 185
De Lange, Deon 281
De Lange, Johnny 95
De Lille, Patricia 184, 226, 233, 252–253, 267–269, 273, 274, 284, 291, 298, 311, 333–334, 338, 340, 413–415, 417, 419, 422–426
Delport, Tertius 170, 260
Delta camp 63
Democratic Alliance *see* DA
'democratic centralism' 189
Democratic Party *see* DP
Denmark 501
Department of Economic and Social Development 250–251
depression 7, 23–24, 32, 67, 75–76, 87–88, 90–91, 137, 376
Derby-Lewis, Clive 117
Desai Commission 166, 168, 292
Destiny magazine 479
De Villiers, Rene 39–41
De Villiers, Wim 492
De Vos, Pierre 250, 301–302, 305–306
Diwali 493
Dlamini, Jacob 358
Dlamini, Mcebo 491
dogs 61, 191, 412, 434–438, 444, 465
Doman, Willem 256
Dosi, Inspector 208
DP 116, 119, 120, 137–139, 141–146, 151–169, 175, 187
Dreyer, Anchen 246, 333, 463–464
Drinking Man's Diet, The 36
drugs 62, 277
Dugard, Jackie 115
Dugmore, Cameron 97–98
Dugmore, Gillian 97

519

Dummett, Michael 81
Du Plessis, Barend 52–53
Du Plessis, 'Doepie' 433
Du Preez, Pierre 170
Du Toit, Inspector 214–215
Du Toit, Philip 269, 270–271, 284–287, 293–295
Du Toit, Pieter 469
Dyantyi, Richard 239, 243, 268, 297

Earl, David 28
Earl, Geoffrey 28
Ebrahim, Achmat 251
ECC 88, 94–95, 98–99, 101
economic freedom 497–500
Economic Freedom Fighters *see* EFF
EEA Amendment Bill *see* Employment Equity Amendment Bill
EFF 316, 374, 475, 477, 494, 498
Eglin, Colin 55–57, 183, 400–401
Ehrenreich, Tony 318
elections
    1948 general 17–18
    1987 general 95–96
    1994 general 119
    1999 general 160
    2000 local government 153, 160
    2004 general 177–181
    2006 local government 181–187, 221–234
    2009 general 312–313, 333
    2011 local government 337–340
    2014 general 342, 419–420, 438–443, 447–449
    2016 local government 420, 477, 494
electricity blackouts 223–224
Elese, Depoutch 201–202, 205
Eliot, T.S. 8
Elliott, Lorika 404
Ellis, Mike 138
emigration 96, 508
Employment Equity Amendment Bill 378–379, 381–383, 386–394, 396–400, 455–456
enclave state, concept of 200–201
End Conscription Campaign *see* ECC
enemies, in politics 249
English, as medium of instruction 492
Erasmus, Nathan 201, 295, 300–301, 305
Erasmus Commission 295–306
Erleigh, David 157
Erwin, Alec 223–224
exchange rate 497

Facebook 357–358, 480
Fair Lady 88
Faleni, Tutu 444
Fanaroff, Bernie 41–42
farmworkers' strike 367
Federal Alliance 153
Federal Legal Commission *see* FLC
#FeesMustFall 478–482
feminism 31, 36, 41–42
FF+ 226, 227, 231, 447
Fienies, Martin 233
FIFA World Cup (2010) 250, 251–252, 299, 327–328
Figlan, Mzuvukile 'Archie' 211–213, 216
Fihla, Mr 210–211
financial aid for university students 121–123, 485
Financial Times 490
Finweek 245–246
fire and disaster management service, Cape Town 223
First, Ruth 489
First World War 2
FLC 170–171
'floor-crossing' 162–167, 175, 183, 263–278, 312, 474
Forde, Fiona 357
Fortuin, Mrs 204
Foxcroft, John 289–290
Fraenkel, Max 5
Franjola, Matt 59–68
Frank, Irvin 486
Fransman, Marius 393
Fraser-Moleketi, Geraldine 150
freedom 507–508
Freedom Front Plus *see* FF+
Freedom Under Law 331
Frere, Paulo 82
Freudian psychology 38
Friedman, Steven 39
Friedrich Naumann Foundation 234, 317, 464
Friend, The 76, 78
Friesley, Anna 409
Froneman, Sampie 79
Fukuyama, Francis 315, 501–508
Fuller Hall 35–36
F.W. de Klerk Foundation 331

Galgut, Oscar 50–51
Gana, Makashule 462
Gasnolar, Andrew 419, 427
Gaunt, Eleanor 124

INDEX

Gaunt, Trevor 124
Gazi, Lungiswa 190–192, 198, 200
gender roles 31, 36, 41–42
General Workers' Union 82
George Fivaz & Associates *see* GF&A
Gerber, Brent 234–236, 238, 247, 254–255, 300, 324
Germany 2–6, 9–17
GF&A 265–266, 269, 284, 287–289, 294
Giffard, Chris 99
Gill, Gwen 406
Gladwell, Malcolm 379
Gluckman, Jonathan 47
Godsell, Bobby 39, 337
Goettert, Liesl 258
Gold Fields 377–378
Goldschmidt, Theo 15
Goldstone Commission 115
'gonzo' journalism 54–55
Good Hope FM 301
Gophe, Xolile 200
Gordhan, Pravin 294, 501
'gotcha' journalism 55–56
Gqozo, Oupa 117
Graaff, Sir De Villiers 79
Gramsci, Antonio 116
GrandWest Casino 271–272
Grant, Margaret 4
Green Point stadium 251–252
Grindrod, Simon 226, 252–253, 266, 268, 272, 333
Groote Schuur Minute 105
Grove case 129–132, 137–138, 141
Grove Primary School 124, 129–132, 137–138, 141
Gubangca, Koliwe 191–192
Gugulethu police station 208
Gugushe, Mr 200
Gupta family 499–500
Gutman, Theodore 9
Gwangxu, Xolile 212
Gwayi, Melford 202, 203

Hain, Peter 74–75
Hall, Gillian 39
Hani, Chris 117–118
HARDtalk 262
Harksen, Jürgen 166
Harms, Louis 308
Harris, Brian 66
Harris, Tim 385–386
Hassiem, Wasfie 236, 251–252

Hathorn, Paula 99
Hattingh, Chris 180
Hawking, Stephen 178
hearing loss 2, 21–24
Heine, Heinrich 466
Helen Suzman: Bright Star in a Dark Chamber 420–421
Helen Suzman Foundation 183, 331
hemp 123
Hendricks, Ishmael 409
Herbst, Hein 180
Herenigde Nasionale Party (HNP) 18
Hersch, Colin 48–49
Herstigte Nasionale Party (HNP) 78–79
Hertzog, Charl 79
Herzfeld, Julius 15
Herzveld, Bobby 328
Herzveld, Erna 328
Hewu, Mzwandile 129–132
Hill, Pat 261
Hill-Lewis, Geordin 316, 348, 352–354, 359, 379–381, 386, 389–390, 423, 446, 448, 467
Hitler, Adolf 12–13
HIV/AIDS 307, 323, 488
Hlatshwayo, Will 139–140
HNP *see* Herenigde Nasionale Party; Herstigte Nasionale Party
Hogan, Barbara 98
Holderness, Nicky 180
Holliday, Tony 43–44
Holocaust 1, 4–6, 9–15, 23
Holomisa, Bantu 311
Homberger, Herbert 4
Homberger, Paul 3
Horwood, Owen 56
housing allocations 201–205, 211–212
Human, J.J. 79
human rights 507
Humphrey, Hazel 28–29
Hunter, Peter 124

ICD 204–205, 211
ICOSA 259
ID 184, 226–227, 231–234, 237, 252–253, 259, 263, 266–267, 273, 274–276, 298, 311, 317–318, 333–334, 340
IDASA 145
Idesis, Harold 93
IEC *see* Independent Electoral Commission
IFP *see* Inkatha Freedom Party

Independent Civic Organisation of South Africa *see* ICOSA
Independent Complaints Directorate *see* ICD
Independent Democrats *see* ID
Independent Electoral Commission 225, 236, 274
Independent Newspapers Group 57, 250, 290–291
Independent Online 281
Independent Party 116
Information Scandal 53–54, 56–57
infrastructure 498–499
Inkatha Freedom Party 118, 313
Inside Mail 56, 59
Institute for Democracy in Africa *see* IDASA
International Shanghai Food and Wine Festival 492–493
interracial relationships 11, 488–489
investment 498–499
Ipser, Claude 180
Isaacs, Anwar 274, 295–296, 299

Jacobs-Croucamp, Tatiana 298–300, 303–304
Jacobs, Fanie 180
Jacobs, Peter 243
James, Wilmot 333, 362, 367–370, 379–385, 388, 399, 410–412, 419, 427–431, 458, 467
Jansen, Jonathan 483
Januarie, Officer 210
Jenkin, Tim 106, 110
Jesse, Dieter 19
Jewish cemetery, Pinelands 1
Johnson, Bill 183–185, 255, 293, 347
Johnson, Inspector 214–215
Joko, Bennet 228–229, 231, 233
Jonas, Senior Superintendent 210
Jones, Peter 47
Jordaan, Josie 290, 296
Jordaan, Willem 173
Joubert, Jan-Jan 450, 458–460, 462, 471

Kalako, Lerumo 94
Kalako, Shaun 206, 209–210
Kantey, Mike 224
Kaschula, Nat 142
Kasrils, Ronnie 280
Katzen, Kitt 53
Katzenstein, Bertha 14–15
KDF 212
Kebble, Brett 308
Kelly Girl 39
Kenny, Andrew 70

Kenny family 6–7
Kentridge, Sydney 50–51
Keurbooms River, holidays at 21, 89, 246–247, 357
Khayelitsha 110–112, 211–219, 221
Khayelitsha Development Forum *see* KDF
Khoza, Irvin 323
kintsukuroi 22–23
Kirsh, Natie 429
Kissinger, Henry 327–328, 447
Kitshoff, Rene 260
Kivedo, Basil 101–102
Klaasens, Nellie 409
Knott, Caroline 404–405
Kohler Barnard, Dianne 333
Kok, Benedictus 76–77, 79–80
Kokwe, Noma-Afrika 295
Koornhof, Piet 43
Krige, Steyn 33–34
Kristallnacht 4, 13–15
Kruger, J.T. 46, 50–51
Kuhn, Melanie 405
Kula, Sakhele 206
Kunene, Thandeka 121–123
Kuper, Jos 371, 374
Kupiso, Michael 114
Kwana, Agrenett 201

Labour Party (Britain) 341–342
Lagunya (taxi association) 111–112, 114
Land Bill 439, 442–443
Landingwe, Danile 199
Langa 190–201
Lange, Jan 78
Langenhoven, Hanna 171–174
Lang, Ivor 48–49
Lategan, Ken 170
'Lebs' (Lebanese motorbike gang) 30
Ledergerber, Emar 309
Ledwaba, Aubrey 330
Lee, Basil 179
Leeuwenhof 328, 409, 433–434, 437, 443
Legal Resources Centre 204–205
Lekganyane, Bishop 446–447
Lekota, Mosiuoa 'Terror' 309, 311, 334
Lengisi, Reginah 193–194, 198–200
Leon, Tony
  background 39, 57, 120
  BBBEE 378
  elections 177–178

formation of DA 153–155, 161–162, 164–165, 174
growth of DA 190, 198, 203, 216, 313
Helen Zille and 137–138, 183–187, 232, 245, 471–475
leadership election, 2007 255–257, 260–261
'muscular liberalism' 143
NNP and 399
'Save Democracy in Cape Town' march 241–242
Trollip Commission 244
Le Roux, Ingrid and Pieter 89, 99
Leshilo, Thabo 418
Lewis, Bobby 136
Liberal International (LI) 490
Liesbeeck Gardens (university residence) 121
Lifman, Mark 299
Lilliesleaf Farm museum 109
Lincoln, Abraham 118
Lingelethu West Town Council, Khayelitsha 110–111
Lipschitz, Bella 27
load-shedding 223–224
Local Road Transportation Board 113
Lodewyk, Janet 405
Loubser, Andrew 180
Loubser, J.D. 47
Lowenherz, Alixe 124, 434
Luckett, Sid 355, 361–362
Ludidi, Thobile 211–212, 218–219
Lund, Troye 245
Lupini Brothers 82
Luyt, Louis 153
Luyt, Sir Richard 80

MacDonald, Robert 245, 262, 291, 405
Madikizela, Bonginkosi 219, 221–223, 235, 320
Madikizela-Mandela, Winnie 96, 221
Madisha, Willie 312
Maduna, Timothy 200
Magele, Malusi 90
magistrate's courts 43
Magubane, Peter 45–46
Maharaj, Mac 106–110
Maharaj, Zarina 106
Mahomed, Hajirah 409
Mail & Guardian 500–501
Maimane, Daniel 475
Maimane, Kgalaletso 475
Maimane, Mmusi 171, 337–338, 356, 413, 428, 431, 450, 461–463, 475–477, 488

Maimane, Natalie 475, 488
Majola, Richard 464
Majozi, Mfundo 250
Makeleni, Mambhele 192–198
Maker, Armien 277
Makgotsi, Jakob 79
Makhosana, Phumzile 130
Maki, Eliot 211
Makoba, Ntomboxolo 405
Malada, Brutus 362, 367
Malala, Justice 361
Malan, D.F. 18
Malan, Wynand 116
Malangabi, Victor 206, 209–210
Malema, Julius 353, 366, 374, 431, 446, 477
Manci, Senior Superintendent 210
Mandela, Nelson 83, 98, 100–101, 107, 117–118, 120, 266, 311, 401
Mangcu, Xolela 484–486
Mantashe, Gwede 320
Manye, Christopher 'Bricks' 109
Manyi, Mzwanele Jimmy 386, 400
Maphatsoe, Kebby 319–320
Mapongwana, Michael 112–114
Mapongwana, Nomsa 112
Mapunguza, Nongejile 205
Maqungwana, Bongani 241
Marais, Erik 259
Marais, Kobus 259
Marais, Peter 161–162, 165, 172, 174, 192
Marcus family 2–5
Marcus, Helene [grandmother] 1–8, 25
Maree, Gretl [daughter-in-law] 21, 433–434, 438, 443, 471
Maree, Isabel [sister-in-law] 22, 260, 466
Maree, Jacques 358
Maree, Johann [husband]
 background of 67, 73–84, 93–94, 99–100
 father of 67, 68–69, 75
 meets and marries Helen Zille 65–71, 85, 369, 407–409, 433
 children of 85–92, 126, 443
 Grove case 127–129
 political career of Helen Zille 114, 137, 229–232, 246, 254–255, 259–261, 279–281, 293, 295, 319, 339, 364, 371–372, 468, 471–472
 home invasions 133–135
 dogs 436–437
Maree, Michiel (Mike) [brother-in-law] 75

Maree, Paul [son]
  birth 86
  youth 89–90, 92, 94–95, 99, 102, 114, 124–126, 133–137, 142, 180, 182, 434–435
  at university 230, 292, 437
  wedding 433–434, 438, 443
  send-off party 471
Maree, Thomas [son] 86, 91, 99, 124–126, 133–137, 142, 230–231, 237, 262, 292, 328, 437, 443, 471
Marhwanqana, Themba 203
Marrs, Dave 288
Mashaba, Herman 494
Mashele, Prince 362, 367–369, 373–374
Mashobane, Shadow 303
Matiwane, Mzwandile 205–210
Max, Lennit 187, 293
Maxwele, Chumani 477–478
Maynier, David 174, 198, 348–349, 353, 355–357, 430, 467
Mazibuko, Lindiwe 344–360, 362–363, 366, 373, 375, 384, 387–388, 393–398, 411–413, 419–420, 425, 428–432, 449–462, 467
Mazwembe, Storey 82–83
Mbeki, Moeletsi 362, 369, 372–374
Mbeki, Thabo 100, 233, 249, 296, 307–308, 326–327
Mbembe, Achille 485
Mbete, Baleka 305, 377
Mbhele, Zakhele 405
Mbuqe, Herbert 409
McCarthy, Leonard 321–322
McHenry, Don 55–56
Mchunu, Sizwe 365
Mehlomakhulu, Zora 82
membership fraud 156–157, 186
Memela, Tootsie 109
Memoirs of a Born Free 483
Merkel, Angela 160, 328
Mervis, Joel 141
Meyer, Ivan 333, 474
Meyer, Roelf 311–312
Mfaco, Bulelani 103–104, 471
Mfaco, Dorothy 97, 103–104
Mfeketo, NomaIndia 184, 233
Mfengwana, Mzuvukile Rasta 187, 201
Mgoqi, Wallace 230, 234, 236
Minnie, Warren 133
Minnie, Wendy 133–134
Mitchells Plain 277–278

MK 94, 98, 101, 106–110, 122
Mkalipi, Thembinkosi 400
Mkhatshwa, Nompendulo 479
Mkhize, Nomalanga 489
MK Military Veterans Association 319–320
Mnqasela, Masizole 211–213, 216–219, 221, 228–229, 349
Moakes, Jonathan 316, 354, 362, 413, 427–428
Modisane, Cameron 451
Moffitt, Shaun 407
Mohamed, Mansoor 251, 272
Mokgalapa, Stevens 490
Moni, Telelo 219
Moosa, Essa 201
Moria (Limpopo) 443–447
Morkel, Gerald 142, 149–151, 162–165, 167–170, 179
Morkel, Kent 168, 183–187, 227, 232–233, 259, 263, 267–269, 271, 274–276, 278, 284, 287, 295–296
Moroccans (gang) 266
Morris, Michael 233
Motau, Sej 352, 398
Motlanthe, Kgalema 500
Mouneimne, Michael 250
Mouneimne, Omar 250
Mpi, Phakamthe 206
Mpofu, Michael 405
Mpongo, Kululwa 194, 196–199
Mpshe, Mokotedi 321–322, 330
Mputing, Abel 102, 136–137
Mputing, Chulumanco 102, 140, 443
Mputing, Grace 102, 136, 140, 279, 409, 435–438, 444
Mputing, NgoweNceba 102, 437–438, 443
Msimanga, Solly 494
Mufamadi, Sydney 243
Mulder, Connie 54, 56
Mumbai 493
Municipal Structures Act 239
Murphy, Caryle 59, 67
Musi, Mr 198
#MustFall movement 478–482, 491–492
Myburgh, James 389
Myeni, Dudu 499

Napo, Joey 433
Nathan, Wendy 32
National Democratic Movement 116
National Department of Public Works 360

National Development Plan *see* NDP
National Energy Regulator 224
National Intelligence Agency *see* NIA
National Party *see* NP
National People's Party *see* NPP
National Press Union 50
National Prosecuting Authority *see* NPA
National Union of South African Students *see* NUSAS
Naudé, Beyers 77–78
Naudé, Fanie 77–78
Nazism 9–15, 20
Ndaba, Charles 110
Ndayi, Mr 205
Ndongeni, Michael 113
NDP 499, 501
Ndungane, Njongonkulu 145
necklacing 96
negotiated settlement 83–84, 98–102, 107–108, 115–119
Neilson, Elmarie 200, 206–207, 209
Neilson, Ian 227, 251
Nel, Louis 53
Nelson Mandela Bay metro 338–339, 448–449, 494
Nemuramba, Enocent 406, 408
Nene, Nhlanhla 497–500
New Age, The 57
New National Party *see* NNP
New Rest 210–211
Ngcokoto, Lizo 93–94
Ngcono, Miriam 235
Ngcuka, Bulelani 321–322
Ngonyama, Smuts 312
Ngxekana, Hitler 203
NIA 202–203, 224–225, 250, 269, 279–281, 373
Nicholson, Chris 300, 305–307
Nimbe, Mr 215
Njonga, Eric 'Kabila' 203
Nkandla scandal 363, 365–366
Nkomokazi, Valencia 157, 192–194, 200
NNP 142, 144–145, 151–188, 217, 474
non-racialism 104, 488
  see also racism
Nortje, Johan 285, 293, 295
NP 43, 52–57, 79, 99–100, 111, 115, 143, 315
NPA 306, 321, 329
NPP 266, 274, 283, 309
Ntandane, Captain 208–209
Ntsekhe, Refiloe 474

Ntsinde, Inspector 213–214
nuclear power 223–225, 499
NUSAS 39, 40, 82, 97
Nyanda, Siphiwe 106, 108, 110
Nyoka, Nolitha 219
Nzimande, Blade 320

Obama, Barack 371
Odendaal, Lynda 312
Old Testament, story from 280–281
Omar, Abdullah 266
One City initiative 111
Oosthuysen, Elsabe 317, 462
Operation Vula 106–110
opposition parties, new 311–316
Origins of Political Order, The 501–508
ototoxic medication 24
Outliers 379
Ozinsky, Max 101–102

PAC 226, 228
PADLAC 277–278
PAGAD 277
Palazzolo, Vito 266
Pan Africanist Congress *see* PAC
Papua New Guinea 503–504
'particularism' 489
Paton, Carol 400
patronage selection 148–149, 189
Paulse, Gavin 164, 231
Peace Committee 113
Peach, Mark 419
Pearce, Yasir 274
People Against Gangsterism and Drugs *see* PAGAD
People's Anti-Drug and Liquor Action Committee *see* PADLAC
Petros, Mzwandile 285, 286, 288 289, 291
pets 61, 412, 434–438, 465
Phaswana, Arthur 122–123
Phaswana, Fred 123
Philippi 205–210
Phillip, Steven 406–407
Pielsticker, Emilie (Mila) *see* Cosmann, Emilie (Mila)
Pielsticker, Jochen 19
Pierce, Nigel 301
Plato, Dan 180, 313, 338
Pokwana, Vukile 329
police 192–200, 202–206, 270–271, 286, 291–293

Political Order and Political Decay 501–508
Politicsweb 389
Pollak, Joel 261
Ponzi scams 5
Portugal, Carnation Revolution 41
post-holocaust trauma 23
post-partum depression 7, 87–88, 90–91
PRAAG 256
'present game' 21–22
Press, Ronnie 106
Press Council 50–51
Prevention and Combatting of Corrupt Activities Act 274, 287
Price, Byron 30–32
Price, George 30–31
Pringle, Stuart 200, 278
Prins, Marthinus 51
Pro-Afrikaans Action Group *see* PRAAG
professionalism 506
Progressive Federal Party 79, 95, 116, 346
Progressive Party 39–41, 54, 84, 116, 158, 400
Purchase, Felicity 180

Qabaka, Vuyisa 360

Rabie, Pierre 260
racism 11, 129–131, 144, 477–498
   see also non-racialism
Radeen Fashions 407
Ramatlakane, Leonard 243
Ramphele, Mamphela 90, 121, 131, 133, 136–137, 334–337, 340–344, 355–357, 361–364, 366–374, 410–419, 422–431
Rand Daily Mail 32–33, 39–46, 49–57, 59
'rape culture' 42
Rasool, Ebrahim 144, 250, 279, 284–286, 288–291, 293, 295–298, 304–305, 328–329
Rau, Rose 276
Raymond, Frank 199–201, 216, 218–219, 278
Reagan, Ronald 441
Rees, Mervyn 53
referendum of 1992 115–116
Reid, Stan 27
'rent-seeking' 500
Renwick, Robin 420–421
Rhoda, Sandra 409
Rhodes, Cecil John 478
Rhodesia 62–64
#RhodesMustFall movement 478–482
Rhoodie, Eschel 54

Rhymes, Edward 307
Richardson, Mike 288
Rivonia 18, 27, 30
Roberts, Mary 190
Rogers, Owen 297
Rohde, Martina 20
Roodt, Dan 256–259, 278
Roosevelt, Theodore 473
Rosebank House College 93
Rothgiesser, Walter 18
Roux, Sergeant 29
Roux, Sophie 29
rugby tour to England (1969/70) 74–75
rule of law 502–509
Russia 499
Rutstein, Theo 39

SAA *see* South African Airways
Sabdia, Gulam 236
Sackur, Stephen 262
SACP 189
SADTU 129–132
Saldanha Bay, Special Economic Zone 392–393
Sambata, Linda 218
Samuels, Gawa 167
SANCO 192–201
SAPS *see* police
Sasman, David 272
SA Today 329, 389–390, 396–398
Saunderson-Meyer, William 302–303
Saunders, Stuart 121
'Save Democracy in Cape Town' march 239–243
scapegoating 487
Schmidt, David 103
Schmidt, Hendrik 390
schools 26–27, 360–361
Schouw, Janine 359, 406–409, 438–440, 471
Schreiner, Jenny 97–98
Score supermarket 211–212
Scorpions 321
Second Carnegie Inquiry into Poverty and Development 121
Second World War 7, 16–17
segregated facilities 45–46, 69–70
Selfe, James
   BBBEE Amendment Bill 395
   candidate-selection system 170
   coalition government 174, 227–228
   'floor-crossing' 266, 269, 287
   lawfare programme 331

leadership of DA 185, 255–257, 468
Lindiwe Mazibuko and 348, 449–450, 462, 467
meetings with Mamphela Ramphele 362, 372, 413
meets Helen Zille 137
value to DA 171, 317
separation of party and state 207, 235, 268, 288, 290, 305–306, 393
Seremane, Wetshotsile 'Joe' 255, 261, 333
Serritslev, Anthea 233
sexual harassment 36, 41–42, 92
Shandler, David 101, 103, 110, 120
Shilowa, Mbhazima 309, 311–312
Shivuri, Station Commander 216
Sicetsha, Nontombana 205
Sigonya, Koliswa 205
Simon, Rawdon 34
Simon, Robyn 34
Sipayile, Ms 206
Skwatsha, Mcebisi 93–94, 273, 275
Slabbert, Frederik van Zyl 57
Slabbert, Jan 78
Slabbert, Martin 405
sleep, lack of 23
Smit, Dirk 231, 237, 252, 264–266, 268–272
Smith, Ashley 328
Smith, Jerome 409
Smith, J.P. 265
Smith, Mervyn 331
Smuts, Dene 151, 350
Soal, Peter 39
social grants 498
social media 357–358, 360–361, 477, 480, 486–487, 490–492
Sogayise, Zamayedwa B. 212
Soko, Mills 369–370, 410
Solomon Islands 503–504
Some Day group 182–185, 187, 246, 254
South African Airways 499
South African Associated Newspapers 39, 54
South African Communist Party *see* SACP
South African Congress of Trade Unions 81
South African Democratic Teachers Union *see* SADTU
South African National Civic Organisation *see* SANCO
South African Schools Act 124, 129
Soviet Union 99, 100–101
Soweto uprising 52
Sparks, Allister 32–33, 44, 46–51, 57, 65, 472

Sparrow, Penny 480
SPCA 436–437
Special Economic Zone, Saldanha Bay 392–393
Speed, Ken 291–292
'Spinachgate' case 486
Springbok Legion 7
Springbok rugby tour to England (1969/70) 74–75
'spy tapes' 321–322, 329–330
Star 39–40
'state capture' 331, 342, 500–501
St David's Catholic school 33
Steenhuisen, John 253, 260, 464, 468, 477
Stellenbosch University *see* University of Stellenbosch
Sternberg, Renato 5
Sternberg, Susanna 5
Stewart, Fiona 289–292, 296–298, 300, 493
Steytler, Jan 475
St Mary's School for Girls 30
stockpiling of weapons 210–211
Streek, Barry 65
street renaming 161–162
Strydom, Donnae 320, 404–407
St Stithians College 33
Study of History, A 83–84
Sunday Express 53–54, 79
Sunday Independent 375, 483
Sunday Times 236–237, 449–450, 459–461
Sunday Tribune 375
Supreme Court of Appeal 387
surveillance 279–281, 321
'survivor's guilt' 6, 14
Suzman, Helen 39–40, 79, 84, 145, 312, 420–421, 429, 472
Swain, Kevin 300, 305–306
Swart, Marius 260

Tagg, Fay 124
Tavares, Olli 299
taxes 498
'taxi wars' 101, 111–115
Taylor, Catherine 79
Teljoy 39
tender system 238, 253, 329
Ten Per Cent, Mr 238–239, 249
Terblanche, Koos 79
Thamm, Marianne 357
Thiyiwe, Nomboniso 213–216
Thompson, Hunter S. 54, 61

527

Thompson, Theresa 230
Thulo, Keabetswe 338, 465
Thulo, Lydia Puleng 338, 465
Times, The 74, 358
Tiyesi, Mr 205
Tom, Nomahobe 203–205
Topo, Makazi 205
Toynbee, Arnold 83
TRC 111, 116
Trent, Eddie 260
Treurnicht, Andries 52–53
Trollip, Angela 350–352
Trollip, Athol 244, 247, 255–256, 261, 317, 345–352, 358–359, 418, 458, 461, 467, 494
Trout, Trevor 266–267, 269
Truth and Reconciliation Commission *see* TRC
Tshabalala, Mbuso 110
Tshwane 448–449, 494
Tucker, Benjamin 48–49, 57–58
Turkington, Jamie 405
Tutu, Desmond 113
Twala, Mzukisi 296
Twala, Zithulele 296
Twitter 357–358, 360–361, 490–492, 494

Ubuntu 506
UCT 34–37, 70–71, 80, 120–121, 477–478, 484–485
UDM 226, 227, 231, 238–241, 311, 374, 494
Ufundo 122–123
UIF 226, 228
Ujima 122
Ulianitski, Irina 265
Ulianitski, Yulia 265
Ulianitski, Yuri 'the Russian' 265–266, 270, 299
Umkhonto we Sizwe *see* MK
Umyezo Wama Apile school 360–361
United Democratic Front 92
United Democratic Movement *see* UDM
United Independent Front *see* UIF
United Nations 300
United Party (UP) 40, 79
United Women's Organisation 97, 103
Universal Party (UP) 226, 233
University of Cape Town *see* UCT
University of Fort Hare 79
University of Stellenbosch 121, 492
University of the Orange Free State 76–81
University of the Witwatersrand 39, 68–69, 485
UP *see* United Party; Universal Party

urbanisation 300
Uys, Juan Duval 271–272, 283

Van Damme, Phumzile 379
Van der Berg, Johan 415, 448
Van der Berg, John 295
Van der Velde, Frank 113
Van der Walt, Desiree 474
Van der Westhuizen, Andricus 398
Van Harmelen, Miss 27
Van Heerden, Advocate 78, 80
Van Heerden, Niel 269, 287
Van Olst, Marc 344
Van Onselen, Gareth 349, 355, 398–399, 420, 431, 451–458, 461–462, 471
Van Rensburg, Leon 179, 231, 258
Van Riet, Roelof 295
Van Rooyen, Des 497–498, 500
Van Schalkwyk, Marthinus 153, 155, 161–163, 172, 175, 242, 315, 399, 474
Vearey, Jeremy 243
Veltman, Willem 264
Venezuela 490
Venter, Trace 405
Verbaan, Aly 265
verligtes and *verkramptes* 43, 52–54
victimhood 6, 104
Viljoen, Carin 235, 403–404
Viljoen, Constand 118
Viljoen, Piet 291–292, 294
Vlok, Adriaan 111
Vlotman, Bahia 274
Vogelsang, Franz 14
Volksblad, Die 75, 78
Vorster, John 50, 51, 53–54, 56
Vorster, Stephanus Johannes 242–243, 278
Voyiya, Eunice 89–90, 92, 102
Voyiya, Grace 102, 136, 140, 279, 409, 435–438, 444
Voyiya, Nomawethu 92

Wa Azania, Malaika 483–484
Walker, Belinda 161
Waluś, Janusz 117
Washington Star 54
Waters, Mike 151
Watkyns, Brian 169–171
Watson, Watty 359, 390, 396
WCC 74
Webta 111–113

INDEX

weight loss 36–39, 85, 482
Weil, Simone 8
Wentzel, Jill 96
Western Cape Black Taxi Association *see* Webta
Western Cape General Workers' Union 82
Western Cape Workers' Advice Bureau 82
West Wing, The 174
'whiteness' 480–493
Wiehahn Commission 83
Wildlife and Environment Society 224
Williams, Abe 167–168
Williams, Captain 215
Williams, Charlotte 253
Wilson, Francis 80
Wilson, Lindy 92
Wilson, S.J. 204
Windhuk (ship) 2
Wits *see* University of the Witwatersrand
Woodmead School 33–34
Worrall, Denis 116
World Council of Churches *see* WCC
World Trade Centre, storming of 118
World War I 2
World War II 7, 16–17
Wrottesley, Steve 60

Xaba, Wanelisa 482–483
Ximbi, Dumisani 231, 238

Yach, Theodore 251
Yad Vashem archive 4
Yengeni, Tony 98, 101
Yes, Minister (TV series) 146
Yom Hashoah Holocaust memorial service 1
Young, Ernle 78

Zibi, Songezo 452
Ziegelaar, Les 270–271, 295–296
Zihlangu, Dorothy 'Shoes' 97, 104
Zille, Carla [sister] 1–2, 19, 21–24, 27–29, 31–32, 88, 232, 260–261, 412, 464–466
Zille, Heinrich [ancestor] 19–20
Zille, Heinrich [uncle] 2–3, 6–7, 19
Zille, Helen
 family 1–20, 21–28
 youth 1–2, 5, 8–9, 18–19, 26–35
 on smoking 30, 62
 university studies 34–37, 39, 70–71
 anorexia 35–39, 482
 early career 39–41
 as journalist 32–33, 39, 41–57, 59
 and Matt Franjola 59–68
 marriage to Johann Maree 65–71, 433
 children 85–92, 94–95, 99, 124–126, 132–133, 180, 433–434, 438
 Bermuda conference 99–100
 as freelance consultant 101–104, 110–117
 as director of public affairs and development, UCT 120–123, 131–133, 136–140
 Grove case 124, 126–132, 137–138, 141
 home invasions 133–137
 political career 39–41, 43–44, 92–102, 137–139, 141–247, 249–254, 263–281, 283–331, 333–401, 410–464, 466–468
 health 180–181
 as DA leader 57, 245–247, 253–262
 on support staff 264, 403–410
 surveillance 279–281, 321
 awards 308–309, 464
 at Leeuwenhof 328, 409, 433–434, 437, 443
 on social media 357–358, 360–361
 Zion Christian Church pilgrimage 443–447
 steps down as DA leader 468–476
 on racism 477–498
 on economic freedom 497–509
Zille, Helene [grandmother] *see* Marcus, Helene
Zille, Johann Gottlob [ancestor] 20
Zille, Mila [mother] 7, 9, 12, 14–19, 23–35, 37–38, 43, 67–68, 87, 105–109, 138–139, 228, 232, 260–261, 294–295, 303, 338, 376, 406, 412, 438, 444, 464–466
Zille, Paul [brother] 32, 33, 105–108, 225, 465–466
Zille, Walter [grandfather] 2–3, 7
Zille, Wolfgang [father] 1–2, 4–9, 17–19, 23–26, 31–32, 37–38, 67, 87, 105–109, 182, 443–444
Zimbabwe 62–64
Zion Christian Church 443–447
Zizar, Tony 303
Zulu, Lindiwe 501
Zuma, Jacob 256–258, 296, 306–307, 312–313, 318–319, 321–327, 342, 365, 393, 479, 497–501

529

Do you have any comments, suggestions or feedback about this book or any other Penguin titles? Contact us at **talkback@penguinrandomhouse.co.za**

*

Visit **www.penguinrandomhouse.co.za** and subscribe to our newsletter for monthly updates and news